ENGLISH EPISCOPAL ACTA

VII

HEREFORD 1079–1234

ENGLISH EPISCOPAL ACTA

ENGLISH EPISCOPAL ACTA
VII

HEREFORD 1079–1234

EDITED BY
JULIA BARROW

Published for THE BRITISH ACADEMY
by OXFORD UNIVERSITY PRESS

Oxford University Press, Walton Street, Oxford OX2 6DP

Oxford   New York   Toronto
Delhi   Bombay   Calcutta   Madras   Karachi
Kuala Lumpur   Singapore   Hong Kong   Tokyo
Nairobi   Dar es Salaam   Cape Town
Melbourne   Auckland   Madrid
and associated companies in
Berlin   Ibadan

Published in the United States
by Oxford University Press Inc., New York

British Library Cataloguing in Publication Data
English Episcopal Acta. — Vol. 7: Hereford,
1079–1234
I. Barrow, Julia
262.3
ISBN 0–19–726109–4

Typeset by Saxon Graphics Ltd., Derby, England
Printed in Great Britain
on acid-free paper by
The Cromwell Press Limited
Melksham, Wiltshire

FOR ALL MY TEACHERS
ESPECIALLY
PIERRE CHAPLAIS
WITH GRATITUDE

CONTENTS

LIST OF PLATES
(between page cxii *and page* cxiii)

ACKNOWLEDGEMENTS

The present work, an extended and much altered version of my Oxford University D.Phil. thesis, 'The Bishops of Hereford and their Acta' (1983), was read and commented on in earlier stages of its compilation by Dr Pierre Chaplais, my doctoral supervisor, and by Dr Henry Mayr-Harting and Professor C. N. L. Brooke, my examiners; more recently it has been read in its entirety by Dr David Smith and Professor C. N. L. Brooke. I owe deep thanks to all of them for many helpful corrections and much useful advice. I have also received help and information on many subjects, including the whereabouts of particular charters, from Dr John Blair, the late Professor C.R.Cheney, Dr Mary Cheney, Dr David Crouch, Dr Diana Greenway, Dr Christopher Harper-Bill, Dr Brian Kemp, Dr Una Rees and Dr Nicholas Vincent. On the subject of the early history of the diocese of Hereford I have benefited from discussion with Mr S. R. Bassett and Dr Alan Thacker; Professor John Beverley Smith gave me advice on the treaty between Llywelyn and Philip Augustus; Dr Charles Duggan gave me assistance with papal decretals addressed to Bishops Robert de Melun and Robert Foliot; Dr Teresa Webber commented on the handwriting and Dr Malcolm Parkes on the punctuation of the 1085 landgrant of Bishop Robert of Lotharingia; Dr Rodney Thomson commented on the handwriting of original charters of the years 1131-1163 at or connected with Hereford; Dr Richard Sharpe answered many queries on Latin vocabulary; Dr Alison Pearn (now Bennett) permitted me to refer to her Ph. D. thesis, and Mr Bruce Coplestone-Crowe read through all the charters to identify hitherto unidentified Herefordshire placenames. I am very grateful to all the above and to all my other friends who have assisted me in this edition. Responsibility for errors is mine.

I should like to express my thanks for permission to publish unpublished material to the following: the Dean and Chapter of Canterbury Cathedral, the Dean and Chapter of Gloucester Cathedral, the Dean and Chapter of Hereford Cathedral, the Dean and Chapter of Wells Cathedral and the Dean and Chapter of Westminster Abbey; the Bodleian Library, Oxford; the British

Library; the Keeper of the Public Record Office; the Warden and Fellows of All Souls College, Oxford; the Master and Fellows of Balliol College, Oxford; the Bishop of Hereford; the Archives-Départementales of Eure, Orne and of Maine-et-Loire; the County Record Offices of Shropshire and Wiltshire; the County Record Office of Herefordshire and Diocesan Record Office of Hereford; Lady Labouchere; Shrewsbury Local Studies Library; the Bibliothèque Nationale, Paris; Madame la Marquise de Mathan, Sémilly, Manche; Lambeth Palace Library; Keele University Library, and the University of London Library. I am also grateful to the Dean and Chapter of Hereford, the County Record Offices of Shropshire and Wiltshire, Keele University Library, the British Library and the Public Record Office for permission to reproduce photographs of charters and seals.

It is a great pleasure to be able to thank all the librarians and archivists, both at the institutions mentioned above and also at the National Library of Wales and at Worcester Cathedral, for all the help which they have given me; among them I would like to give particular thanks to Miss Marion Halford of Shropshire County Record Office, to Canon David Welander of Gloucester Cathedral, to Miss Joan Williams of Hereford Cathedral Library and above all to the late Miss Penelope Morgan of Hereford Cathedral Library.

Financial support for my doctoral thesis was provided by the Scottish Education Department, and additional help with travelling expenses was given by Corpus Christi College, Oxford. I am very grateful to both, and also to the Alexander von Humboldt-Stiftung, Bonn, and the British Academy for awarding me post-doctoral fellowships, which, although they were largely used to pursue research on other topics, did much to assist the completion of this book. The Episcopal Acta Committee of the British Academy provided financial assistance for the acquisition of photographs. My deepest thanks go to my parents for their loving support and warm encouragement over many years.

MANUSCRIPT SOURCES CITED

Aberystwyth, NLW: 7851: *49-53, 112, 174, 231-5, 282, 306, 364-5.*

Alençon, A-D Orne: H937: *134.*

Angers, A-D Maine-et-Loire: H3710, no. 3: *45;* H3710, no. 4: *47;* H3710, no.8: *106A*; H3711: *45, 47, 106, 106A.;* H3713: *45, 47, 106, 106A.*

Cambridge, Trinity College: 0. 2. 1: *66-68;* R. 4. 11: *64.*

—University Library: Ely Diocesan Records, Liber M: *67-8;* Dd. ix 38: *308.*

Canterbury, D. & C. Archives and Library: Ch. Ant. A49: *64;* Ch. Ant. A51: *64;* Ch. Ant. C110 no. 1: *297;* Ch. Ant. C115 no.5: *3;* Ch. Ant. C115 no.7: *6;* Ch. Ant. C115 no.15: *9;* Ch. Ant. C115 no.24: *59;* Ch. Ant. C115 no.38: *118;* Ch. Ant. C115 no. 46: *178;* Ch. Ant. C115 no. 65: *243;* Ch. Ant. C115 no. 72: *243;* Ch. Ant. C115 no. 100: *129;* Ch. Ant. C115 no.84: *292;* Ch. Ant. C117 no.9: *3*; Ch. Ant. C117 no. 14: *6;* Ch. Ant. C117 no. 27: *9;* Ch. Ant. C134: *14;* Ch. Ant. C136-7: *14;* Ch. Ant. D107-8: *14;* Christ Church Letter II 239: *247;* Eastry Correspondence Group iii no. 91: *248;* Register A: *1, 3, 6, 9, 13, 59, 118, 129, 178, 292.*

Ely, D. & C. MS (Liber Eliensis): *66-68.*

Evreux, A-D Eure: H251: *142, 187, 322;* H590: *34, 162, 164, 218-9, 304-5, 354;* II F2463: *141.*

Gloucester, D. & C. Muniments: Seals and Deeds, vol. VIII, no. 1: *4, 77, 330-1, 333;* St Peter's Register A: *20, 119, 136, 189;* St Peter's Register B: *18, 76-7, 79-80, 328-9.*

Hereford, Cathedral Library: 0. 6. xii: *159.*

—D. & C. Muniments: 159: *App. I;* 486-7: *App. I*; 724: *App. I;* 741: *150,*

202, 258; 754: *317;* 959: *App. I;* 1082: *322;* 1099: *369;* 1111: *338;* 1165: *340;* 1319: *366;* 1358: *289;* 1359: *202;* 1360: *107;* 1361: *337;* 1362: *197;* 1363: *239;* 1364: *254;* 1365: *160;* 1379: *151;* 1380: *256;* 1381: *173;* 1382: *168;* 1383: *149;* 1384: *255;* 1385: *85;* 1386: *199;* 1387: *186;* 1388: *344;* 1389: *342;* 1390: *367;* 1525: *145;* 1808: *342;* 2045: *196;* 2098: *343;* 2175: *348;* 2178: *154;* 2181: *192;* 2182: *143;* 2775: *App. I;* 2776: *201;* 2777: *84, 336;* 2778: *341;* 2866: *286.*

—Diocesan Registry: see Herefordshire County Record Office.

—Herefordshire County Record Office: Episcopal Estates and Revenues Muniments, Box no. 16: *369;* Registers of Bothe, Foxe and Boner: *244, 257;* Registrum Ade de Orleton: *299, 347;* Registrum Ricardi de Swinfield: *28, 75, 84, 236, 285, 295, 336, 341-2, 348, 370;* Registrum Thome de Cantilupo: *77, 331, 368.*

Keele, University Library, Raymond Richards Collection, Miscellaneous Historical Materials 53/4: *147.*

London, BL: Additional Ch. 7013: *App. II;* Additional Ch. 13285: *293A;* Additional Ch. 19585: *138;* Additional Ch. 19587: *110;* Additional MS 15668: *188, 250, App. II;* Additional MS 18461: *188, 250, App. II;* Additional MS 47677: *161, 266;* Additional MS 49996: *191;* Additional MS 50121: *217;* Arundel MS 19: *237, 283-4, 312, 315;* Cotton Ch. XI 60: *12;* Cotton Ch. XIII 6: *29;* Cotton MS Cleopatra E i: *1, 6, 9, 13, 59, 118;* Cotton MS Domitian A iii: *11, 30-3, 94-100, 111, 137, 169, 210-6, 267-70, 279, 300-3, 308-10, 349-53;*

Cotton MS Domitian A v: *3;* Cotton MS Otho B xiv: *220, 271-3, 314, 316;* Cotton MS Titus A i: *66-68;* Cotton MS Vespasian B xix: *64;* Cotton MS Vespasian B xxiv: *69, App. II*; Cotton MS Vespasian E xxv: *108, 170, 308, 362;* Cotton MS Vitellius E xv: *229;* Egerton MS 3031: *11, 30, 95-7, 99-100, 108-11, 169-70, 210-1, 215, 308-10;* Harleian MS 391: *238;* Harleian MS 3586: *361;* Harleian MS 1708: *108, 308;* Harleian MS 5804: *324-5;* Stowe MS 425: *363.*
—Lambeth Palace: MS 415: *183;* MS 2214: *363.*
PRO. C53/19: *319;* C66/169: *348;* C66/225: *360;* C66/226: *226-8, 277, 358-9;* C115 G31/4095: *2;* C115 K1/6679: *35-41, 43, 103-5, 121, 166, 276, 355;* C115 K1/6681: *App. II;* C115 K2/6683: *10, 13A, 35-44, 57, 102-5, 121-2, 166, 172, 223, 225, 276, 280, 355, 357;* C115 L1/6689: *35, 43, 122, 355;* C150/1: *4, 21, 71-4, 77-8, 194, 275, 296, 327, 330-3;* E40/2383: *230;* E164/22: *113-5*; E210/380: *App. II;* E210/2086: *46;* E315/61: *128, App. II;* E326/10846: *179;* E326/11837: *326;* E326/12983: *184;* E327/52: *319;* E327/399: *46;* E329/370: *295;* JUST1/615: *348;* SCl 6/19: *307;* SC7 19/12: *190;* SC7 35/8: *190.*
—St Paul's Cathedral: MS W.D. 1: *263.*
—University of London Library: Fuller Collection, 19/30: *287.*
—Westminster Abbey Muniments, no. 2857: *167;* no. 22492: *App. II;* Book 10: *167.*
Oxford
—Balliol College, MS 271: *7, 15-17, l9, 21-7, 55, 86, 86A-B, 88-92, 125-6,*
152-7, 203-9, 260-2, 313, 345-6, 371, App. I.
—Bodl.: Deposited Deeds, All Souls College, c1, Alberbury 110: *316A;* MS Carte 108: *61-3, 136, 208, 245, 293;* MS Dep. C392: *139-40, 185;* MS Dep. 393: *139-40, 185;* MS Dugdale 11: *56, 101, 127;* MS E Musaeo 249: *21, 60, 65, 82, 87, 93;* MS Gough Shropshire 4: *287;* MS Jones 23: *311;* MS Laudian Misc. 647: *66-8;* MS Lyell 15: *129A;* MS Rawlinson B328: *App. I, App. II;* MS Rawlinson B329: *83-5, 116, 123, 135, 150, 163, 182, 198-200, 202, 221, 255-9, 278, 281, 288-9, 311, 317-8, 323, 336-7, 339, 341-3, 348, 354, App. I, App. II;* MS Tanner 127: *14;* MS Top. Salop. c. 1: *147;* MS Wood Empt . 10: *171.*
—Christ Church D. & C.: MS 341: *70;* MS 343: *229.*
Paris: BN: Collection Moreau MS 276: *162, 218;* nouv. acq. lat. 1930: *106A.*
Semilly, Manche: manuscripts of Mme la Marquise de Mathan: Dom Lenoir MSS, vol. xxiii: *34, 101, 162, 218.*
Shrewsbury, Local Studies Library: Deed 77: *231;* Deed 372: *233;* Deed 376: *235;* Haughmond cartulary: *81, 146-8, 195, 252-3, 298, 334-5.*
—Shropshire County Record Office: 259/1: *294;* 2922 Additional: *146, 195, 252, 298, 335;* 4220/2: *147, 252.*
Trowbridge, Wiltshire County Record Office: 9/15/2: *180;* 9/15/4: *244.*
Wells, Cathedral, D. & C. Muniments: Liber Albus vol . I: *264-5.*
Worcester, Cathedral Library: MS A 4: *58, 117, 177, 241-2, 290-1.*

PRINTED BOOKS AND ARTICLES
CITED, WITH ABBREVIATED REFERENCES

Abingdon cartularies — *Two cartularies of Abingdon abbey,* edd. C.F. Slade and G. Lambrick (Oxford Historical Society n.s. 32, 1990).

Acta Stephani Langton Cantuariensis archiepiscopi a.d. 1207-1228, ed. K.Major (CYS 50, 1950).

Adam of Eynsham, *Magna vita Sancti Hugonis,* ed. D.Douie and D.H.Farmer, 2 vols. (London and Edinburgh 1961-2).

N.Adams, see *Canterbury cases*

Ancient charters, ed. J.H.Round (PRS 10, 1888).

A.O. and M.O.Anderson, edd. *The chronicle of Melrose* (London 1936).

Anglia Sacra – ed. H.Wharton, 2 vols. (London 1691)

Ann. Mon. – *Annales Monastici,* ed. H.R.Luard, 5 vols. (RS 1864-9).

App. – *Appendix concilii lateranensis,* in *Sacrorum conciliorum nova et amplissima collectio,* 31 vols. (Florence etc. 1759-98), xx.248-453

D.Baker, ed. *The church in town and countryside (Studies in church history* 16, 1979).

A.T.Bannister, *The cathedral church of Hereford* (London 1924).

A.T.Bannister, ed. *A descriptive catalogue of the manuscripts in the Hereford cathedral library* (with introduction by M.R.James) (Hereford 1927).

F.Barlow, *The English church 1000-1066,* 2nd edn (London 1979).

G.W.S.Barrow, *The Anglo-Norman era in Scottish history* (Oxford 1980).

J.Barrow, 'Cathedrals, provosts and prebends: a comparison of twelfth-century German and English practice', *Journal of Ecclesiastical History,* xxxvii (1986), 536-564.

J.Barrow, 'Hereford bishops and married clergy', *Historical Research,* lx (1987), 1-8.

J.Barrow, 'A twelfth-century bishop and literary patron: William de Vere', *Viator,* xviii (1987), 175-189.

J.Barrow, 'Vicars choral and chaplains in northern European cathedrals 1100-1250', in *The ministry: clerical and lay,* ed. W.Sheils and D.Wood (*Studies in Church History* 26, Oxford 1989), 87-97.

S.E.Bartleet, 'History of the manor and advowson of Brockworth', *TBGAS,* vii (1882), 131-71.

R.Bartlett, *Gerald of Wales* (Oxford 1982).

S.R.Bassett, 'Churches in Worcester before and after the conversion of the Anglo-Saxons', *The Antiquaries Journal,* lxix (1989), 225-56.

S.R.Bassett, ed. *The origins of Anglo-Saxon kingdoms* (Leicester 1989).

D.Bethell, 'The making of a twelfth-century relic collection', in

G.J.Cuming and D.Baker, edd. *Popular belief and practice* (Studies in Church History 8, 1972), 61-72.

BIHR – *Bulletin of the Institute of Historical Research*

W.de G.Birch, ed. *Cartularium saxonicum*, 3 vols. and index (London 1885-99).

W.de G.Birch, 'The Great Seal of King Henry I', *The Journal of the British Archaeological Association*, xxix (1873), 233-62.

E.Bishop, *Liturgica historica* (Oxford 1918).

J.Blair, ed. *Minsters and parish churches* (Oxford 1988).

J.Blair, 'The twelfth-century bishop's palace at Hereford', *Medieval archaeology*, xxxi (1987), 59-72.

J.Blair and R.Sharpe, edd. *Pastoral care before the parish* (Leicester, 1992).

Bouquet, *Recueil des historiens* – M.Bouquet, *Recueil des historiens des Gaules et de la France*, 24 vols., with vols.14-24 being a continuation published by the Académie des Inscriptions et Belles Lettres (Paris 1738-1904).

H.Bradshaw and C.Wordsworth, *Lincoln cathedral statutes*, 3 vols. (Cambridge 1892-7).

Brecon cartulary – 'Cartularium prioratus S.Johannis Evangeliste de Brecon', ed. R.M.Banks, *Archaeologia Cambrensis*, 4th ser., xiii (1882), 215-308 and xiv (1883), 18-49, 137-168, 221-236, 274-311.

M.Brett, *The English church under Henry I* (Oxford 1975).

C.N.L.Brooke, *The English church and the Welsh border* (Woodbridge 1986).

C.N.L.Brooke, see also Z.N.Brooke and A.Morey

Z.N. and C.N.L.Brooke, 'Hereford cathedral dignitaries in the twelfth century', *Cambridge Historical Journal*, viii, no.1 (1944), 1-21, and supplement ibid., viii, no.3 (1946), 179-85.

E.St J.Brooks, ed. *Register of the Hospital of St John the Baptist without the North Gate, Dublin* (Irish Manuscripts Commission 1936).

Brut y Tywysogion, ed. T.Jones (Cardiff 1955).

Cal. Ch. Rolls – *Calendar of the charter rolls (1226-1516)*, 6 vols. (HMSO 1903-27).

Cal. papal reg. – *Calendar of entries in the papal registers relating to Great Britain and Ireland: papal letters (1198-1492)*, ed. W.H.Bliss and J.A.Twemlow, 14 vols. (London 1893-1960).

Cal. Pat. Rolls – *Calendar of the patent rolls preserved in the P.R.O. (1232-1509)*, 52 vols. (HMSO 1891-1916).

Canterbury cases – *Selected cases from the ecclesiastical courts of the province of Canterbury, c.1200-1301*, ed. N.Adams and C.Donahue Jr (Selden Society 95, 1981).

Canterbury professions – ed. M.Richter (CYS 67, 1973).

CDF – *Calendar of Documents preserved in France ... a.d. 918-1206*, ed. J.H.Round (HMSO 1899).

B.G.Charles and H. D. Emanuel, edd. *Calendar of the earlier Hereford cathedral muniments*, 3 vols., cyclostyled (Historical Manuscripts Commission, National Register of Archives, 1955).

C.R.Cheney, 'Cardinal John of Ferentino, papal legate in England in 1206', *EHR*, lxxvi (1961), 654-60.

C.R.Cheney, *English bishops' chanceries 1100-1250* (Manchester 1950).

C.R.Cheney, *From Becket to Langton: English church government 1170-1213* (Manchester 1956).

C.R.Cheney, *Hubert Walter* (London 1967).

C.R. and M.Cheney, see *Letters of Pope Innocent III*

M.G.Cheney, 'The compromise of Avranches and the spread of canon law in England', *EHR*, lvi (1941), 177-97.

M.G.Cheney, *Roger, bishop of Worcester, 1164-1179* (Oxford 1980).

Chichester acta – *The acta of the bishops of Chichester 1075-1207*, ed. H.Mayr-Harting (CYS 56, 1964).

Chodorow and Duggan see *Decretales ineditae*

Cirencester cartulary – *The cartulary of Cirencester abbey*, ed. C.D.Ross and M.Devine, 3 vols. (Oxford 1964-77).

Close rolls 1227-1231 – *Close rolls of the reign of Henry III (1227-72)*, 14 vols (HMSO 1902-38), vol. i.

H.M.Colvin, 'Holme Lacy: an episcopal manor and its tenants in the twelfth and thirteenth centuries', in *Medieval Studies presented to Rose Graham*, ed. V.Ruffer and A.J.Taylor (Oxford 1950), 15-40.

1 Comp. – *Compilatio prima* in *Quinque compilationes antiquae*, ed. E.Friedberg (Leipzig 1882).

B.Coplestone-Crow, 'The fief of Alfred of Marlborough in Herefordshire in 1086 and its descent in the Anglo-Norman period', *Transactions of the Woolhope Naturalists' Field Club*, xlv (1986), 376-414.

Councils and Synods I, II – *Councils and Synods with other documents relating to the English Church, I*, edd. D.Whitelock, M.Brett and C.N.L.Brooke, 2 vols. (Oxford 1981); *Councils and Synods with other documents relating to the English Church, II*, edd. F.M.Powicke and C.R.Cheney, 2 vols. (Oxford 1964).

F.G.Cowley, *The monastic order in South Wales, 1066-1349* (Cardiff 1977).

D.Cox, 'Two unpublished charters of King Stephen for Wenlock priory', *Transactions of the Shropshire Archaeological and Historical Society*, lxvi (1989), 56-59.

D.Crouch, *The Beaumont twins* (Cambridge 1986).

D.Crouch, ed. *Llandaff episcopal acta 1140-1287* (Publications of the South Wales Record Society 5, 1989 for 1988).

CRR – *Curia Regis Rolls ... preserved in the P.R.O.*, 15 vols. (HMSO London 1922-72).

CYS – Canterbury and York Society Publications

H.C.Darby and I.B.Terrett, *The Domesday geography of midland England,* 2nd edn. (Cambridge 1971).

R.R.Darlington, ed. *Vita Wulfstani* (Camden 3rd ser. 40, 1928).

W.Davies, *An early Welsh microcosm* – Royal Historical Society, Studies in History Series 9 (London 1978).

Davis, *Cartularies* – G.R.C.Davis, *Medieval Cartularies of Great Britain: a Short Catalogue* (London and New York 1958).

DB   *Domesday Book, seu Liber Censualis Willelmi Primi Regis Angliae*, edd. A.Farley et al., 4 vols. (Record Commission 1783-1816).

Decretales ineditae saeculi xii,   edd. S.Chodorow and C.Duggan, from the papers of W.Holtzmann (Monumenta Iuris Canonici, ser. B, Corpus collectionum 4, Vatican City 1982).

J.C.Dickinson and P.T.Ricketts, edd.   'The Anglo-Norman chronicle of Wigmore abbey', *Transactions of the Woolhope Naturalists' Field Club*, xxxix (1969), 413-45.

G.H.Doble,   'The Leominster relic-list', *Transactions of the Woolhope Naturalists' Field Club*, xxxi (1942), 58-65.

R.A.Donkin,   'Settlement and depopulation on Cistercian estates during the twelfth and thirteenth centuries, especially in Yorkshire', *BIHR*, xxxiii (1960), 141-65.

N.Drinkwater,   'Hereford cathedral: the bishop's chapel of St Katherine and St Mary Magdalene', *Archaeological Journal*, cxi (1954), 129-137.

André Du Chesne,   *Histoire de la maison de Béthune* (Paris 1639).

André Du Chesne, ed.   *Historiae Francorum scriptores...*, 5 vols. (Paris, 1636-49).

C.Duggan,   'Equity and compassion in papal marriage decretals to England', in W. van Hoecke and A.Welkenhuysen, edd. *Love and marriage in the twelfth century* (Leuven 1981), 59-87.

Eadmer, *Historia novorum* – ed. M.Rule, RS 1884.

Early charters of the cathedral church of St Paul, London,   ed. M.Gibbs (Camden 3rd ser. 58, 1939).

EEA   – *English episcopal acta i Lincoln 1067-1185* and *iv Lincoln 1186-1206*, ed. D.M.Smith (British Academy 1980-86); *ii Canterbury 1162-1190* and *iii Canterbury 1193-1205*, ed. C.R.Cheney with E.John and B.Jones (British Academy 1986); *v York 1070-1154*, ed. J.E.Burton (British Academy 1988); *vi Norwich 1070-1214*, ed. C.Harper-Bill (British Academy 1990).

J.G.Edwards, V.H.Galbraith and E.F.Jacob, edd.   *Historical essays presented to James Tait* (Manchester 1933).

EHR   – *English Historical Review*

Ekwall   – Eilert Ekwall, ed. *The concise Oxford dictionary of English place-names*, 4th edn (Oxford 1960).

Ep. Cant.   – *Epistolae Cantuarienses: Chronicles and Memorials of the Reign of Richard I*, vol. 2, ed. W.Stubbs (RS 1865).

Extra   – *Decretalium Gregorii papae IX compilatio*, ed. E.Friedberg (*Corpus iuris canonici*, vol. ii. Leipzig 1881).

J.G.Evans and J.Rhys, edd.The text of the Book of Llan Dâv (Oxford 1893).

EYC   – *Early Yorkshire Charters*, vols.i-iii ed. W.Farrer (1914-6) vols.iv-xii ed. C.T.Clay, and index to vols.i-iii by C.T. and Edith Clay (Yorkshire Archaeological Society, Records Series, extra series, 1935-65).

Eynsham cartulary   – *The cartulary of the abbey of Eynsham*, ed. H.E.Salter, 2 vols. (Oxford Historical Society 49, 51, 1907-8).

R.W.Eyton, *Antiquities* — R.W.Eyton, *Antiquities of Shropshire*, 12 vols. (London 1853-60).

R.W.Eyton, *The court, household and itinerary of King Henry II* (London 1878).

W.Farrer, *Honors and knights' fees* — 3 vols. (London and Manchester 1923-5).

W.Farrer, Itin. — W.Farrer, 'An outline itinerary of King Henry the first', *EHR* xxxiv (1919), pp.303-82; 505-79.

Fasti ecclesiae anglicanae 1066-1300, ed. D.E.Greenway, vols. i-iv (London 1968-91).

H.R.P.Finberg, *Early charters of the West Midlands* (Leicester 1961).

Flaxley cartulary — *Cartulary and historical notes of the Cistercian abbey of Flaxley*, ed. A.W.Crawley-Boevey (Exeter 1887).

Florence of Worcester, *Chronicon ex chronicis*, ed. B.Thorpe, 2 vols. (English Historical Society, London 1848-9)

Foliot, Gilbert — see *GFL* and A.Morey and C.N.L.Brooke

M.Franklin, 'The identification of minsters in the midlands', *Anglo-Norman Studies*, vii (1985), 69-88.

V.H.Galbraith, 'An episcopal landgrant', *EHR*, xliv (1929), 353-72.

V.H.Galbraith, 'Girard the chancellor', *EHR*, xlvi (1931), 77-9.

A.Gandilhon, *Catalogue des actes des archevêques de Bourges antérieurs à l'an 1200* (Bourges and Paris 1927).

R.Gem, 'The bishop's chapel at Hereford: the rôles of patron and craftsman', in S.Macready and F.H.Thompson, edd. *Art and patronage in the English Romanesque* (Society of Antiquaries Occasional Papers, n.s. 8, 1986), 59-72.

Gervas. Cant. — *Historical works of Gervase of Canterbury*, ed. W.Stubbs, 2 vols. (RS 1879-80).

Gesta regis Henrici II, ed. W.Stubbs, 2 vols. (RS 1867).

GFL — *Letters and charters of Gilbert Foliot*, ed. A.Morey and C.N.L.Brooke (Cambridge 1967)

M.Gibbs, ed. *Early charters of the cathedral church of St Paul, London* (Camden third series 58, 1939).

Giles — *Gilberti episcopi primum Herefordensis deinde Londoniensis epistolae*, ed. J.A.Giles, 2 vols. (Patres ecclesiae Anglicanae, London and Oxford 1846).

Giraldus, *Opera* — *Giraldus Cambrensis opera*, ed. J.S.Brewer, J.F.Dimock, and G.F.Warner, 8 vols. (RS 1861-91).

Gloucester cartulary — *Historia et cartularium monasterii Sancti Petri Gloucestriae,* ed. W.H.Hart, 3 vols. (RS 1863-7).

'Gloucester register' — 'Register Pertaining to the churches of the monastery of St Peter's Gloucester', ed. D.Walker, in *An Ecclesiastical Miscellany*, Publications of the Bristol and Gloucestershire Archaeological Society, Records Section, 11 (1976), 3-58.

M.Grabmann, *Geschichte der scholastischen Methode*, 2 vols. (Freiburg 1909-11).

C.S.Greaves and J.Lee-Warner, 'Charter of Cuthwulf bishop of Hereford', *Archaeological Journal*, xxx (1873), 174-80.

Diana Greenway, 'The false *Institutio* of St Osmund' in Diana Greenway, Christopher Holdsworth and Jane Sayers, edd. *Tradition*

and change: essays in honour of Marjorie Chibnall
(Cambridge 1985), 77-101.

Charles Guéry, *Histoire de l'abbaye de Lyre* (Evreux 1917).

Haddan and Stubbs – A.W.Haddan and W.Stubbs, edd. *Councils and ecclesiastical documents relating to Great Britain and Ireland*, 3 vols. (Oxford 1869-71).

Haughmond cartulary – *The cartulary of Haughmond abbey*, ed. U.Rees (Cardiff 1985).

Hereford charters – *Charters and records of Hereford cathedral*, ed. W.W.Capes (Cantilupe Society, Hereford 1908).

J.Hillaby, 'Hereford gold: Irish, Welsh and English land. Part 2', *Transactions of the Woolhope Naturalists' Field Club*, xlv (1985), 192-270.

J.Hillaby, *The book of Ledbury* (Buckingham 1982).

J.Hillaby, 'The origins of the diocese of Hereford', *Transactions of the Woolhope Naturalists' Field Club*, xlii (1976-8), 16-52.

Historians of the *The historians of the church of York and its*
Church of York – *archbishops*, ed. J.Raine, 3 vols. (RS 1879-94).

HMCR – *Reports of the Royal Commission on Historical Manuscripts* (London 1870+)

C.Hohler, 'St Osyth and Aylesbury', *Records of Buckinghamshire*, xviii, pt. i (1966), 61-72.

J.C.Holt, *The Northerners* (Oxford 1961).

W. Holtzmann see *PUE*

W.Holtzmann and *Papal decretals relating to the diocese of Lincoln*
E.W. Kemp, edd. (Lincoln Record Society 47, 1954).

U.Horst, *Die Trinitäts- und Gotteslehre des Robert von Melun* (Mainz 1964).

HRH – D.Knowles, C.N.L.Brooke and V.C.M.London, edd., *The Heads of religious houses: England and Wales 940-1216* (Cambridge 1972).

J.B.Hurry, *Reading Abbey* (London 1901).

JL – *Regesta pontificum romanorum ... ad annum 1198*, ed. P.Jaffé, 2nd ed. S.Loewenfeld et al., 2 vols (Leipzig 1885-8).

John of Salisbury – *The Letters of John of Salisbury*, ed. W.J.Millor, H.E.Butler and C.N.L.Brooke, 2 vols. (Edinburgh and London 1955 and Oxford 1979).

John of Salisbury, *Historia pontificalis*, ed. M.Chibnall (London and Edinburgh 1956).

John of Salisbury, *Metalogicon*, ed. C.C.J.Webb (Oxford 1929).

John of Worcester – *The Chronicle of John of Worcester*, ed. J.R.H.Weaver, Anecdota Oxoniensia, Medieval and Modern Series, part xiii (Oxford 1908).

A.Joris, 'Espagne et Lotharingie vers l'an mil. Aux origines des franchises urbaines', *Le Moyen Age*, xciv (1988), 5-19.

B.R.Kemp, 'The churches of Berkeley Hernesse', *TBGAS*, lxxxvii (1968), 96-110.

B.R.Kemp, 'Hereditary benefices in the medieval English church: a Herefordshire example', *BIHR*, xliii (1970), 1-15.

B.R.Kemp,   'The monastic dean of Leominster', *EHR*, lxxxiii (1968), 505-15.

N.R.Ker,   *English manuscripts in the century after the Norman Conquest* (London 1960).

D.Knowles,   *The episcopal colleagues of Archbishop Thomas Becket* (Cambridge 1951).

T. Lacomblet,   ed. *Urkundenbuch für die Geschichte des Niederrheins,* 4 vols. (Düsseldorf 1840-56).

L.Landon,   *The itinerary of King Richard I, with studies on certain matters of interest connected with his reign* (PRS, n.s. 13, 1935).

R.E.Latham,   ed. *Revised medieval Latin word-list from British and Irish sources* (British Academy 1965).

A.Lecoy de la Marche,   ed. *Oeuvres complètes de Suger* (Société de l'histoire de France 139, 1867).

B.A.Lees,   ed. *Records of the Templars in England in the twelfth century: the inquest of 1185* (British Academy Records of Social History 9, 1935).

W.A.L(eighton),   'Old Shropshire Deeds', *Transactions of the Shropshire Archaeological Society*, xi (1886), 171-192.

Leland's Itineraries   – ed. L.Toulmin Smith, 5 vols. (Oxford 1906-10).

J.Le Neve,   see *Fasti ecclesiae anglicanae*

E.Lesne,   'Les origines de la prébende', *Revue historique de droit français et étranger*, 4th ser. viii (1929), 242-90.

Letters of Pope Innocent III concerning England and Wales: a calendar, ed. C.R. and Mary Cheney (Oxford 1967).

J.E.Lloyd,   *A History of Wales,* 3rd edn, 2 vols. (London 1939).

M.Lobel,   ed. *Historic towns,* vol. i (London and Oxford 1969).

Luffield priory charters   – ed. G.R.Elvey, 2 vols. (Northamptonshire Record Society 22, 26, 1968-75).

D.E.Luscombe,   *The school of Peter Abelard* (Cambridge 1969).

P. Magdalino, ed.   *The perception of the past in twelfth-century Europe* (London, 1992).

Mainzer Urkundenbuch   ed. M.Stimming and P.Acht, 2 vols. in 3 parts (Darmstadt 1932-71).

W.Maleczek,   *Papst und Kardinalskolleg von 1191 bis 1216* (Vienna 1984).

A.Marchandisse,   'L'obituaire de la cathédrale Saint-Lambert à Liège. Notes pour une édition', *Le Moyen Age*, xcvi (1990), 411-20.

P.Marchegay,   'Les prieurés anglais de Saint-Florent près Saumur', *Bibliothèque de l'Ecole des Chartes*, xl (1879), pp.154-94.

R.M.Martin,   ed. *Les oeuvres de Robert de Melun*, 4 vols. (Spicilegium sacrum lovaniense 13, 18, 21, 25, 1932-52).

R.M.Martin,   'L'oeuvre théologique de Robert de Melun', *Revue d'histoire ecclésiastique*, xv (1920), 456-89.

E.Mason,   *St Wulfstan of Worcester* (Oxford 1990).

H.Mayr-Harting,   *The coming of Christianity to Anglo-Saxon England* (London 1972).

A.Mercati,   'La prima relazione del cardinale Nicolò de Romanis sulla sua legazione in Inghilterra (1213)', in

H.W.C.Davis, ed. *Essays in history presented to Reginald Lane Poole* (Oxford 1927), 274-89.

A.L.Moir, *Bromfield Priory and Church in Shropshire* (Chester 1947).

Mon. Ang. — W.Dugdale, *Monasticon Anglicanum*, ed. J.Caley, H.Ellis and B.Bandinel, 6 vols. in 8 (London 1817-30 and 1846).

Monastic Britain, South Sheet (Ordnance Survey 1954).

A.Morey, *Bartholomew of Exeter* (Cambridge 1937).

A.Morey and
C.N.L.Brooke, *Gilbert Foliot and his letters* (Cambridge 1965).

G.M(orris), 'Early deeds relating to Shropshire', *Collectanea topographica et genealogica*, v (1838), 175-181.

MTB — *Materials for the history of Thomas Becket*, ed. J.C.Robertson, 7 vols. (RS 1875-85).

J.Noonan, 'Gratian slept here: the changing identity of the father of the systematic study of canon law', *Traditio*, xxxv (1979), 145-72.

N.P.S. — New Palaeographical Society, 1st ser. (London 1903-12), 2nd ser. (London 1913-30).

OED — J.A.H.Murray et al. edd. *New English dictionary on historical principles* [= *Oxford English Dictionary*], 10 vols. in 20 (Oxford 1888-1928).

Oseney cartulary — *Cartulary of Oseney abbey*, ed. H.Salter, 6 vols. (Oxford Historical Society 89-91, 97-8, 101, 1929-36).

R.Page, 'Anglo-Saxon episcopal lists, part iii', *Nottingham Medieval Studies*, x (1966), 2-24.

S.Painter, *The reign of King John* (Baltimore 1949).

M.Parisse, 'Les chartes des évêques de Metz au XIIe siècle', *Archiv für Diplomatik*, xxii (1976), 272-316.

B.Parkinson, 'The Life of Robert de Bethune by William de Wycombe: translation with introduction and notes', unpd. Oxford B.Litt. thesis (1951).

E.Phillimore, 'The Annales Cambriae and the Old-Welsh Genealogies from Harleian MS 3859', *Y Cymmrodor*, ix (1886), 143-83.

PL — J.-P.Migne, ed. *Patrologiae latinae cursus completus* (Paris, 1844-64).

K.Potter and
R.H.C Davis edd. *Gesta Stephani* (Oxford 1976).

Potthast — A.Potthast, ed. *Regesta pontificum romanorum inde ab anno post Christum natum MCXCVIII ad annum MCCCIV*, 2 vols. (Berlin 1874-7).

PRS — Pipe Roll Society Publications

PRS n.s. — Pipe Roll Society, new series

PUE — *Papsturkunden in England*, ed. W.Holtzmann, 3 vols. (Abhandlungen der Gesellschaft der Wissenschaften zu Göttingen, phil.-hist. Kl., N.F. 25, 1930-1; 3. Folge 14-15, 1935-6; 3. Folge 33, 1952).

Ralph of Diss, *Opera historica*, ed. W.Stubbs, 2 vols. (RS 1876).

R.Rawlinson, *The History and Antiquities of the City and Cathedral*

Church of Hereford (London 1717).

Reading cartularies   – *Reading abbey cartularies*, ed. B.R.Kemp, 2 vols. (Camden 4th ser., 31 and 33, 1986-7).

The Red Book of the Exchequer,   ed. H.Hall, 3 vols. (RS 1896).

W.Rees,   *A history of the Order of St John of Jerusalem in Wales and on the Welsh border* (Cardiff 1947).

Reg. Bothe   – *Registrum Caroli Bothe, episcopi Herefordensis, AD MDXVI-MDXXXV*, ed. A.T.Bannister (CYS 28, 1921)

Reg. Cantilupe   – *The register of Thomas of Cantilupe, bishop of Hereford (A.D.1275-1282)*, transcr. R.G.Griffiths with introd. by W.W.Capes (CYS 2, 1907).

Reg. Orleton   – *Registrum Ade de Orleton episcopi Herefordensis AD MCCCXVII- MCCCXXVII*, ed. A.T.Bannister (CYS 8, 1908).

Reg. Swinfield   – *Registrum Ricardi de Swinfield, episcopi Herefordensis MCCLXXXIII-MCCCXVII*, ed. W.W.Capes (CYS 6, 1909).

C.Renardy,   'Les écoles liégeoises du IXe au XII siècle: grandes lignes de leur évolution', *Revue belge de philologie et d'histoire*, lvii (1979), 309-28.

H.G.Richardson,   'Letters of the legate Guala', *EHR*, xlviii (1933), 250-9.

M.Richter,   *Giraldus Cambrensis,* 2nd edn (Aberystwyth 1976).

Robert de Torigni,   *Chronicle* – *Chronicles of the reigns of Stephen, Henry II and Richard I*, ed. R.Howlett, 4 vols., (RS 1884-9), vol. iv.

J.Armitage Robinson,   *Somerset historical essays* (London 1921).

Roger of Howden,   *Chronica,* ed. W.Stubbs, 4 vols. (RS 1868-71).

Roger of Wendover,   – ed. H.O.Coxe, 4 vols. *(English Historical Society Flores historiarum 1841-4)*.

Rot. Ch.   – *Rotuli chartarum ... 1199-1216,* ed. T.D.Hardy (Record Commission 1837).

Rot. lit. claus.   – *Rotuli litterarum clausarum ... 1204-1227,* ed. T.D.Hardy, 2 vols. (Record Commission 1833-44).

Rot. lit. pat.   – *Rotuli litterarum patentium ... 1201-16,* ed. T.D.Hardy (Record Commission 1835).

J.H.Round,   *The commune of London and other studies* (London) 1889).

J.H. Round,   *Feudal England* (London 1895).

RRAN   – *Regesta regum anglo-normannorum, 1066-1154,* ed. H.W.C.Davis, C.Johnson, H.A.Cronne and R.H.C.Davis, 4 vols. (Oxford 1913-69).

RS   – Rolls Series: the chronicles and memorials of Great Britain and Ireland during the middle ages published under the direction of the Master of the Rolls (HMSO 1856-96).

M.Saché,   ed. *Inventaire sommaire des archives départementales antérieures à 1790. Maine-et-Loire. Archives ecclésiastiques. Série H, vol. II: H1833-H3768* (Angers 1926).

St Frideswide's Cartulary   – *The cartulary of the monastery of St Frideswide at*

	Oxford, ed. S.R.Wigram, 2 vols. (Oxford Historical Society 28, 31, 1895-6).
A.Saltman,	*Theobald, archbishop of Canterbury* (University of London Historical Studies 2, 1956).
I.J.Sanders,	*English baronies* (Oxford 1960).
Sandford Cartulary	– *(The)*, ed. A.M.Leys, 2 vols. (Oxfordshire Record Society 19, 22, 1938-41).
H.E.Savage,	ed. *The great register of Lichfield cathedral* (William Salt Archaeological Society Collections for 1924 [1926]).
Sawyer	– P.H.Sawyer, *Anglo-Saxon charters: an annotated list and bibliography* (London 1968).
P.H.Sawyer,	ed. *Domesday Book: a reassessment* (London 1985).
J.E.Sayers,	*Papal judges delegate in the province of Canterbury, 1198-1254: a study in ecclesiastical jurisdiction and administration* (London 1971).
W.W.Shirley,	*Royal and other historical letters illustrative of the reign of Henry III*, 2 vols. (RS 1862-6).
R.Shoesmith,	ed. *Hereford city excavations, Vol. I: Excavations at Castle Green* (Council for British Archaeology research report 36, 1980).
Shrewsbury Cartulary	– *(The)*, ed. U.Rees, 2 vols. (Aberystwyth 1975).
P.Sims-Williams,	*Religion and literature in western England, 600-800* (Cambridge 1990).
H.Singer,	*Neue Beiträge über die Dekretalensammlungen vor und nach Bernhard von Pavia*, Sitzungsberichte der kaiserlichen Akademie der Wissenschaften in Wien, 171, phil.-hist. Klasse, Abh. I (1913).
R.C.Smail,	'Latin Syria and the West, 1149-1187', *TRHS*, 5th ser., xix (1969), 1-20.
B.Smalley,	*The Becket controversy and the schools* (Oxford 1973).
B.Smalley,	'The school of Andrew of St Victor', *Recherches de théologie ancienne et médiévale*, xi (1939), 145-67.
B.Smalley,	*The study of the Bible in the middle ages*, 2nd edn (Oxford 1952).
R.W.Southern,	*Robert Grosseteste: The growth of an English mind in medieval Europe* (Oxford 1986).
D.Spear,	'Les archidiacres de Rouen au cours de la période ducale', *Annales de Normandie*, xxxiv (1984), 15-50.
F.M.Stenton,	*Anglo-Saxon England*, 3rd edn. (London 1971).
W.Stevenson,	'A contemporary description of the Domesday Survey', *EHR*, xx (1907), 72-84.
G.Stollberg,	*Die soziale Stellung der intellektuellen Oberschicht im England des 12. Jahrhunderts* (Lübeck 1973).
Symeon of Durham,	*Opera omnia*, ed. T.Arnold, 2 vols. (RS 1882-5).
TBGAS	– *Transactions of the Bristol and Gloucestershire Archaeological Society*
A.Thacker,	'Early ecclesiastical organisation in two Mercian burhs', *Northern History*, xviii (1982), 199-211.
A.Thacker,	'Kings, saints and monasteries in pre-Viking Mercia', *Midland History*, x (1985), 1-25.
H.Tillmann,	*Die päpstlichen Legaten in England bis zur Beendigung der*

	Legation Gualas (1218) (Bonn 1926).
R.H.Treharne,	*Simon de Montfort and baronial reform: thirteenth-century essays*, ed. E.B.Fryde (London 1986).
TRHS	– *Transactions of the Royal Historical Society*
VCH	– *The Victoria History of the Counties of England*, ed. H.A.Doubleday, W.Page, L.F.Salzman, R.P.Pugh and C.Elrington (London 1900- in progress)
Vetus Registrum Sarisberiense	– ed. W.H.R.Jones, 2 vols. (RS 1883-4).
A.-D. von den Brincken,	*Studien zur lateinischen Weltchronistik bis in das Zeitalter Ottos von Freising* (Düsseldorf 1957).
D.Walker, ed.	*Charters of the earldom of Hereford, 1095-1201*, Camden Miscellany, vol. xxii (Camden Society, 4th ser. 1, 1964).
D.Walker,	'Miles of Gloucester, earl of Hereford', *TBGAS*, lxxvii (1958), 66-84.
D.Walker,	'Some charters relating to St Peter's abbey, Gloucester', in *A medieval miscellany for D.M.Stenton*, ed. P.M.Barnes and C.F.Slade, (PRS n.s. 36, 1962 for 1960), 247-268.
Waltham charters	– *The early charters of Waltham abbey, 1062-1230*, ed. R.Ransford (Woodbridge 1989).
E.Warlop,	*De vlaamse adel voor 1300*, 3 vols. (Handzame 1966).
Welsh ep. acts	– *Episcopal acts relating to Welsh dioceses*, ed. J.Conway Davies, 2 vols. (Historical Society of the Church in Wales. 1946-8).
WH	– *Regesta decretalium saeculi xii*, ed. S.Kuttner and C.Duggan, from the papers of Walther Holtzmann, forthcoming.
D.Whitehead,	'St Ethelbert's Hospital, Hereford: its architecture and setting', *Transactions of the Woolhope Naturalists' Field Club*, xlv (1986), 415-25.
D.Whitelock, ed.	*Anglo-Saxon wills* (Cambridge 1930).
W.E.Wightman,	*The Lacy family in England and Normandy, 1066-1194* (Oxford 1966).
William of Malmesbury,	*Gesta pontificum*, ed. N.E.S.A.Hamilton, R.S. (1870).
Winchcombe cartulary	– *Landboc sive registrum monasterii beatae Mariae virginis et sancti Cenhelmi de Winchelcumba*, ed. D.Royce, 2 vols. (Exeter 1892).
Worcester cartulary	– *The Cartulary of Worcester cathedral priory (Register I)*, ed. R.R.Darlington (PRS n.s. 38, 1968).

OTHER ABBREVIATIONS

A–D	Archives départementales
Add. MS	Additional MS
archbp	archbishop
archdn	archdeacon
BL	British Library, London (formerly British Museum)
BN	Bibliothèque Nationale, Paris
Bodl.	Bodleian Library, Oxford
bp	bishop
cal.	calendared
Ch.	Charter
Ch. Ant	Charta Antiqua
D. & C.	Dean and Chapter
NLW	National Library of Wales, Aberystwyth
n.s.	new series
om	omitted
pd	printed
PRO	Public Record Office, London
s.-ex	late-century
s.-in	early-century
s.-med	middle-century
s.½	first half of century

INTRODUCTION

THE DIOCESE

Although the history of the diocese of Hereford goes back to the foundation of a see for the Magonsaete in the late seventh century, documentation is sparse until the late eleventh century. Three succession lists preserve the names of the bishops from the foundation, and give Putta as the first bishop. Although he has sometimes been assumed to have been identical with Putta, bishop of Rochester, who resigned from his see in 676, it is likely that he was a quite separate person.[1] The earliest documentation of the name Hereford occurs only in the eighth century, and the earliest evidence which appears to suggest that the see was fixed at Hereford is ambiguous: this is William of Malmesbury's recording of an epitaph, set up by Bishop Cuthbert between 736 and 740 to commemorate his three immediate predecessors, Tyrhtil, Torhthere, and Weahlstod, and the *regulus* Milfrith and his wife Quenburga. Although William enters the inscription under his account of Hereford, it is likely that he had not read it *in situ* as an inscription, but had found it elsewhere in a manuscript, and the poem itself makes no mention of any placename.[2] Hardly any episcopal acta written before 1079 survive: a charter of Bishop Tyrhtil of c.704-5, a charter of Bishop Cuthwulf of between 840 and 852 and four professions of obedience made to the archbish-

---

1 On the Magonsaete, see K.Pretty, 'Defining the Magonsaete', in S.R.Bassett, ed. *The origins of Anglo-Saxon kingdoms*, 171-83; on Putta, see P.Sims-Williams, *Religion and literature in western England, 600-800*, 87-8. Two placenames near Hereford, Putson and Putley, contain an element which is probably the personal name Putta, but as the name was a common one these cannot be assumed to have any connection with the bishop.

2 On the episcopal lists see R.Page, 'Anglo-Saxon episcopal lists, part iii', 2-24, esp. 6, 10 and 15; discussed by J.Hillaby, 'The origins of the diocese of Hereford', 16-52. For Bishop Cuthbert's poem, recorded by William of Malmesbury, see idem, *Gesta pontificum*, 298, and discussion by P.Sims-Williams, *Religion and literature in western England, 600-800*, 339-43. The earliest documented references to Hereford are in *Annales Cambriae* (E.Phillimore, 'The Annales Cambriae and the Old-Welsh Genealogies from Harleian MS 3859'), s.a. 760, and W. de G.Birch, *Cartularium Saxonicum*, no.298 of 799 x 801. The latter provides the first reference to a bishop bearing the title 'of Hereford'.

ops of Canterbury in the ninth century.[3] Narrative sources produced
by monastic houses within the diocese are practically unknown, save
the chronicle of the abbey of Wigmore of the thirteenth century,[4]
though chronicles produced at Worcester and Gloucester are infor-
mative about the see of Hereford,[5] and William of Wycombe, prior of
Llanthony, wrote a Life of one of the bishops of Hereford, Robert de
Béthune, a former prior of his house.[6] A short history of the foundation of Llanthony also contains useful material.[7] Hereford cathedral
produced no historian of the see, unlike Durham, York, or Canterbury. The shortage of historical writings is in large part the result of
the fact that there were few religious houses in the diocese. Those that
did exist were small, Abbey Dore being perhaps the largest. To some
extent, too, it is because Hereford cathedral was always a foundation
of secular clerks or canons, for, though there are notable exceptions,
such as Hugh the Chanter at York Minster, secular canons rarely felt
so inspired as monks, or perhaps could rarely be so easily impelled as
monks, to write the history of their own communities. However,
Gerald of Wales, a canon of Hereford, produced a Life of one of the
cathedral's two patrons, St Ethelbert.[8]

The date of foundation of the diocese has been generally accepted
to lie just before 680, at the time when Archbishop Theodore of
Canterbury (as has also usually been supposed) decided to split up
the large diocese of the Mercians and provide sees for the Mercian
subkingdoms of the Hwicce and the Magonsaete, the latter being
bestowed on Putta.[9] Two recent theories have been advanced to place
the original site of the see elsewhere, at Leominster in one instance

3 For Tyrhtil's charter see M.Gibbs, *Early charters of St Paul's cathedral*, 3-4 (Sawyer,
no.1785); for Cuthwulf's charter (Sawyer, no.1270) see C.S.Greaves and J.Lee-Warner,
'Charter of Cuthwulf Bishop of Hereford', 174, with facsimile between 174 and 175, and also
Hereford charters, 1-2; for the professions of obedience made by Bishops Wulfheard (801),
Eadwulf (probably the bishop of Hereford consecrated between 825 and 832), Deorlaf
(consecrated 857 x 866), and an unnamed bishop of Hereford, perhaps Mucel (consecrated 857
x 866), see *Canterbury professions*, nos. 4, 16, 24, 25.
4 J.C.Dickinson and P.T.Ricketts, edd. 'The Anglo-Norman Chronicle of Wigmore Abbey'.
5 Florence of Worcester, *Chronicon ex chronicis*; John of Worcester, *Chronicle*; *Gloucester
Cartulary*, vol. i.
6 William of Wycombe's Life of Bishop Robert was edited by H.Wharton, *Anglia Sacra*,
ii.293-321, and by B.Parkinson, 'The Life of Robert de Bethune by William de Wycombe:
translation with introduction and notes', unpd. Oxford B.Litt. thesis (1951).
7 BL Cotton Julius D x, fos.31-53v, partly printed in *Mon. Ang.* vi.128-34.
8 On Gerald of Wales' *Vita Ethelberti* see R.Bartlett, *Gerald of Wales*, 217.
9 Cf. F.M.Stenton, *Anglo-Saxon England*, 134, but H.Mayr-Harting, *The coming of
Christianity to Anglo-Saxon England*, 131-2 is more cautious.

and at Lydbury North (or perhaps Ledbury) in the other,[10] but neither is conclusive. But the foundation of an Anglo-Saxon diocese at Hereford c.680 would not be at all incompatible with early churches at Leominster and other sites, if we extend the recent findings of S.R.Bassett on the see of Worcester westwards; he has shown that there was a major church, though not necessarily of episcopal status, in Worcester before Theodore founded the new see, and that it is unwise to assume that between the 650s and the 680s the regions of the Hwicce and the Westerna (later called the Magonsaete) formed part of the diocese of the Mercians.[11]

The extent of ecclesiastical organisation in these regions before Anglo-Saxon immigration is still a barely-touched subject, and will never be fully knowable, but it is likely that some network of churches existed. For an area immediately adjacent to the territory of the Magonsaete, Ergyng, later absorbed into the diocese of Hereford, we have evidence from the Book of Llandaff for a very dense network of churches, several of which were within a ten-mile radius of Hereford. Already in the late sixth century there was a monastic community at Llandinabo, and monasteries at Ballingham, Dewchurch and Moccas are mentioned in the early seventh century.[12] For Hereford itself, the position is less clear: it has been suggested by R.Shoesmith and D.Whitehead that a church of possibly the seventh century existed on the site later occupied by the Anglo-Saxon collegiate church of St Guthlac in Hereford, but the evidence which they adduce is too weak to prove their case, though it is likely that a cemetery lay on the site by the eighth century.[13] Leominster, where a royal monastery is said in a tradition reported by Leland to have been founded by Merewalh, a prince of the Magonsaete, after the middle of the seventh century, and in addition Much Wenlock, Lydbury and Ledbury might possibly have had early churches.[14] It is highly unlikely that any of these

10 J.Hillaby, 'The origins of the diocese of Hereford', 16-52; P. Sims-Williams, *Religion and literature in western England, 600–800,* 91.

11 S.R.Bassett, 'Churches in Worcester before and after the conversion of the Anglo-Saxons', 225-56; idem, 'Church and diocese in the West Midlands: the transition from British to Anglo-Saxon control' in J. Blair and R. Sharpe, edd. *Pastoral care before the parish,* 13–40.

12 W.Davies, *An early Welsh microcosm,* 134-5.

13 R.Shoesmith, ed. *Hereford city excavations, vol. I: excavations at Castle Green,* 52. I am grateful to S.R.Bassett for comment.

14 On Leominster, see B.Kemp, 'The monastic dean of Leominster', 505-6; on Much Wenlock: H.P.R.Finberg, *The early charters of the West Midlands,* 197-9. On Lydbury (or Ledbury), see n.15 below.

churches controlled a large diocese on the Anglo-Saxon model: rather, as S.R. Bassett has argued for Worcester, each church probably served an area equivalent in size to that of an early Anglo-Saxon minster parish or between ten and twenty modern parishes. Merewalh's foundation at Leominster, if it was a nunnery or a mixed community, is unlikely to have been the see of a bishop, but could well have been one of a group of important churches more or less independent of each other existing in the area in the seventh century. A twelfth century tradition at *Lidebiri* (either Ledbury, or Lydbury North), reported in a letter of Gilbert Foliot, records that it was formerly a see-church and the burial place of several bishops,[15] but this tradition, even if true, would not necessarily have to refer to the bishops of the Anglo-Saxon diocese of the Magonsaete, but might perhaps concern a seventh-century community at *Lidebiri*, or else be an extravagant claim based on the fact that Lydbury North and Ledbury were episcopal manors.

Although the western boundary of the diocese, owing to the shifts in the political frontier between the Anglo-Saxons and the Welsh, did not become fixed until the twelfth century and even later, the other borders – to the north the River Severn, to the east the pre-1974 county boundary between Herefordshire and Worcestershire, to the south the Severn estuary – were probably the original late seventh-century ones. Later, the areas of Archenfield (Ergyng) and Straddle (Ystradwr) were absorbed into the diocese. In the case of Ergyng this was probably as late as the mid-eleventh century, since it formed the main sphere of influence of Bishop Herewald, the predecessor of the line of bishops who later fixed their see at Llandaff. C.N.L. Brooke has suggested that the fall of Gruffydd ap Llywelyn, king of Deheubarth, in 1063, may have led Herewald to concentrate his episcopal activities on the areas to the southwest of Ergyng.[16] Domesday shows that much of Archenfield was in English royal lordship, but that it had not been under direct English control for long, as it had not been hidated.[17] By the late eleventh century, therefore, the diocese of

15 For the twelfth century claim that *Lidebiri* was the original see of the diocese, see *GFL*, no.227, and discussion by P. Sims-Williams, *Religion and literature in western England, 600-800*, 91. Sims-Williams' argument that on etymological grounds Lydbury North is more likely than Ledbury to be the *Lidebiri* of *GFL* no.227 should be modified to take account of the fact that Gilbert Foliot's predecessor as bishop of Hereford, Robert de Béthune (1131-48), had given the church of Lydbury North to the canons of Shobdon (*Mon. Ang.*, vi.345), but no mention of Shobdon is made in Gilbert's letter.
16 C.N.L. Brooke, *The church and the Welsh Border*, 10-11, 35-6, 92-4.
17 DB i, fo. 181a-b.

Hereford thus contained the Forest of Dean (Gloucestershire west of the Severn), a few parishes in Worcestershire, in particular Tenbury Wells, Shropshire south of the Severn (but excluding the area surrounding Condover and Cound to the south of the river, and including Little Wenlock to the north),[18] a few parishes in Radnorshire and Montgomeryshire, all of Herefordshire except the area around Longtown, which formed part of the rural deanery of Ewias in the diocese of St David's, and the town of Monmouth and a few surrounding parishes.[19] Archenfield and Straddle were claimed by the diocese of Llandaff in the 1120s and 1130s and Bishop Bernard of St David's, in claiming metropolitan status for his see in the 1140s, held that the bishop of Hereford should be one of his suffragans, but these claims were successfully fought off under Robert de Béthune.[20] A century later, however, Bishop Ralph de Maidstone of Hereford petitioned the pope to settle further disputes over boundaries between the bishops of Hereford, St David's, Llandaff and St Asaph.[21]

As a diocese Hereford was remarkably poor in monastic houses. The most ancient churches in the area were a group of sixth- and seventh-century foundations in Ergyng for which evidence survives in the Book of Llandaff, and the churches of Leominster and Much Wenlock, royal foundations of the seventh century. Alan Thacker has suggested that St Guthlac's in Hereford may well have been founded in the eighth century, probably as a royal Mercian establishment to rival the cathedral.[22] St Guthlac's was probably always a collegiate foundation, while Leominster and Much Wenlock were probably both joint houses of men and women in origin. By the eleventh century Much Wenlock was a community of secular clerks and Leominster a nunnery. All three were refounded as Benedictine priories for men between 1080 and 1143, Much Wenlock becoming a

18 For a possible reason why Condover and Cound formed part of the diocese of Lichfield, see S.R.Bassett, 'Church and diocese in the West Midlands', in J. Blair and R. Sharpe, edd. *Pastoral care before the parish*, 35–8.
19 Monastic Britain, South Sheet.
20 *Councils and synods* I ii.757; p.xl below.
21 *Cal. papal reg.*, i (1198-1304), 151.
22 A.Thacker, 'Kings, saints and monasteries in pre-Viking Mercia', 5. If St Guthlac's was eighth century in origin, the original dedication was probably to a different saint (Guthlac died in 715); however, the church might well have been associated with devotion to St Guthlac from the start, since one of Guthlac's most devoted supporters was Aethelbald, king of Mercia 716-757. I am grateful to A.T.Thacker for his comments.

daughter house of the Cluniac abbey La Charité sur Loire.[23] The *monasterium* of Bromyard is mentioned in the charter of Bishop Cuthwulf and in a tenth-century will; by 1086 it formed part of a large episcopal manor of thirty hides, one hide of which was held by two priests, presumably the successors of the original community, and one hide and three virgates by a chaplain who could well have been one of the bishop's own community at Hereford.[24] Bromfield minster had twenty hides and a community of twelve canons in the time of King Edward; in addition, Lydbury North, Morville, one of the churches at Chirbury, Alberbury, Stottesdon, Stanford Lacy, Burford, Avenbury, Stoke Edith, Fownhope, Llanwarne, Marcle and Ledbury all bear signs, recorded in Domesday or in subsequent evidence, of having been minster churches.[25]

The post-Conquest period effected great changes in the nature and status of these churches. Morville was added to the endowments of Shrewsbury abbey and became a dependent priory; Chirbury became an Augustinian priory;[26] Leominster, a royal nunnery and manor, was bestowed by Henry I on Reading in 1123, and became a priory over which Reading tried to maintain tight control.[27] Gloucester abbey was supremely efficient in taking over old minster churches, picking up St Guthlac's in Hereford, Bromfield, and also a recent late eleventh-century collegiate foundation, St Peter's in Hereford.[28] From the mid-twelfth century, the pattern of monastic life in the diocese was, therefore, essentially one of small Benedictine and Augustinian priories, the former mostly dependent on bigger Benedictine houses outside the diocese. A further Augustinian house was founded *de novo* at Shobdon in the 1130s by a local knight, Oliver de Merlimond, who had been deeply impressed by St Victor in Paris; it was later moved to Wigmore.[29] The diocese's only two Cistercian houses, Abbey Dore

23 For Leominster see B.Kemp, 'The monastic dean of Leominster'; for Much Wenlock see *VCH Shropshire*, ii.38-9.

24 For Cuthwulf's charter see n.3 above; D.Whitelock, *Anglo-Saxon Wills*, 54-5, 165; DB i, fo.182c.

25 J.Blair, 'Secular minster churches in Domesday Book', in P.H.Sawyer, ed. *Domesday Book: a reassessment*, 108; on Marcle see no.34 below; on Ledbury and Llanwarne see *Reg. Cantilupe*, 27, 141-2, 185, and *Reg. Swinfield*, 464, 538; on Morville, Alberbury and Chirbury see *VCH Shropshire*, ii.29, 48, 59.

26 On Morville and Chirbury see ibid., 29, 59 and nos.51, 52, 184, 295, 319 below.

27 B.Kemp, 'The monastic dean of Leominster', 505-7 and nos.11, 110, 300 and 352 below.

28 On St Guthlac's see no.21 below; on Bromfield see J. Blair, 'Secular minster churches', 128-9; on St Peter's, Hereford, see Gloucester cartulary, i.84-5.

29 B.Smalley, 'The school of Andrew of St Victor', 146-51.

and Flaxley, were founded about ten to fifteen years later. Nunneries were few, especially before the thirteenth century. The nunnery at Leominster, badly affected by a scandal in the mid-eleventh century, had presumably been suppressed long before Henry I granted it to Reading; the foundation of Aconbury occurred late in the period covered by this edition, and no episcopal acta of the period survive for the house. Hereford acquired a Franciscan house in the 1220s but it too leaves no trace in the episcopal records of the period up to 1234. In the 1220s a Grandmontine house was founded at Craswall, and shortly afterwards another at Alberbury.[30]

THE BISHOPS

Between the years 1079 and 1234 the see of Hereford was occupied by fourteen bishops, one of whom, Roger, died before he could be consecrated. There is no space for a detailed study of each, but brief biographical sketches are given to place the individual bishops in context, by providing notes on their origins, previous careers and the main features of their diocesan administration. This is all the more necessary since only a few of them have been examined in detail hitherto.[31] The series of sketches begins not in 1079, however, but 1061, a year which marks a decisive break with the past. It was in this year that the diocese received its first non-indigenous bishop, Walter, who set a trend for the appointment to the see of clerks from the royal household which was to last until the 1120s. Both Walter (1061-79) and his successor, Robert (1079-95), were Lotharingians, and owed their promotion to the favour shown to Lotharingian clerks by Edward the Confessor; even though Robert was only made bishop long after the Conquest his career in England had probably begun before 1066.[32] The educational standards and the esprit de corps of English secular cathedral chapters in the first half of the eleventh century were

30 J.Hillaby, 'Hereford gold: Irish, Welsh and English, part 2, The clients of the Jewish community at Hereford 1179-1253: four case studies', 197, for Craswall; on Alberbury, see *VCH Shropshire*, ii.47-50 and no. 316A below.
31 On Robert de Béthune see n.4 above; on Gilbert Foliot see A.Morey and C.N.L.Brooke, *Gilbert Foliot and his Letters*; on Robert de Melun chiefly B.Smalley, *The Becket Controversy and the Schools*, and also n.100 below; on William de Vere, J.Barrow, 'A twelfth-century bishop and literary patron: William de Vere'.
32 F.Barlow, *The English church 1000-1066*, 81-4, 156-8. His identification of Robert of Lotharingia with Robert the monk of Stow (Lincs) (ibid., 157) is, however, unlikely.

weak;[33] this was not a problem where appointments to the episcopate were concerned, since monks could be made bishops, and were, in large numbers, but it did cause problems in filling positions in the royal household, for these posts had to be occupied by men of some education who were prepared to be mobile. The best source of educated manpower was the north-western area of the Empire, particularly the area around Liège; Liège's cathedral school was one of the best in northern Europe in the eleventh century.[34] Remunerating such men in England was easy: they could be made canons in minster churches, for these already by the tenth century were dividing up their lands among their inmates in what was in fact, though not in name, a fore-runner of the system of individual territorial prebends which becomes clearly visible in most secular English cathedral and collegiate foundations after the Conquest.[35] The Lotharingian Reginbald the chancellor and Albert of Lorraine amassed large numbers of canonries and the properties associated with them in the mid-eleventh century.[36] We may assume that Walter and Robert of Lotharingia were also rewarded in this way, though our only definite evidence for their sources of income apart from the bishopric of Hereford concerns some prebends which Robert acquired at Bampton in Oxfordshire and in St Paul's Cathedral after the conquest and probably – in the latter case almost certainly – after he became bishop.[37]

WALTER

Walter's exact origins are unknown. He became chaplain to Edith, Edward the Confessor's queen, was appointed bishop late in 1060, and was consecrated by Pope Nicholas II in 1061.[38] He swore obedi-

---

33 Barlow's survey of the English dioceses (ibid., 208-31) shows that the only cathedral communities with a strong interest in learning were Canterbury and Worcester.

34 C.Renardy, 'Les écoles liégeoises du IXe au XIIe siècle: grandes lignes de leur évolution', 309-28.

35 M.Franklin, 'The identification of minsters in the Midlands', 69-88.

36 On Reginbald and Albert see F.Barlow, *The English church 1000-1066*, 156-7; J.H.Round, 'Regenbald the chancellor', in idem, *Feudal England*, 421-30; J.Campbell, 'The Church in Anglo-Saxon Towns', in D.Baker, ed. *The church in town and countryside*, 130-1; J.H.Round, 'Ingelric the Priest and Albert of Lotharingia', in idem, *The Commune of London and other Studies*, 28-38.

37 DB i, fo. 155a; *Fasti*, i.42. J.Blair, 'Secular minster churches in Domesday Book', in P.H.Sawyer, ed. *Domesday Book: a reassessment*, 126-7, points out that Robert's acquisitions at Bampton and also at Writtle in Essex were probably intended to provide money for his clerks and chaplains.

38 Florence of Worcester, *Chronicon ex chronicis*, i.218; Symeon of Durham, ii.173-4.

ence to William I before Christmas 1066, but rarely attended court thereafter.[39] According to the returns for the estates of the church of Hereford in Domesday, Walter allowed the episcopal holdings in Hereford to depreciate and granted some episcopal land just outside the city walls to William fitz Osbern, who promptly used it for a new market place, and who gave Walter less valuable property in exchange.[40] He died, according to William of Malmesbury, in an odour of infamy.[41] No charter issued by him survives.

ROBERT OF LOTHARINGIA

Robert presents a strong contrast. Almost certainly educated in Liège,[42] he made the most of the opportunities offered by the schools there, developing a strong interest in mathematics and chronology. He did not lose contact with intellectual circles in the Empire, for after he became bishop he had a copy of the chronicle of Marianus Scotus brought to England, and in or just after the year of the compilation of Domesday Book he wrote a short commentary on the introduction to Marianus' chronicle.[43] He probably became a clerk of Edward the Confessor, perhaps as early as c.1050, and also a friend of Bishop Wulfstan of Worcester.[44] This friendship, and doubtless also the fact that Robert was a foreigner, helped to ensure his appointment to the see of Hereford in 1079.[45] Like Walter, he was not frequent in attendance at the royal court, but unlike Walter he vigorously set himself to restore the episcopal estates to productivity. He combined this with putting the cathedral community on a firmer economic and institutional footing; from Domesday we can see that he gave each canon, and his three episcopal chaplains, individual holdings on the episcopal

39 Florence of Worcester, i.228. Walter occurs in the witness lists of *RRAN*, i, nos.64 and 148 (the latter is spurious).
40 DB i, fo.181c.
41 William of Malmesbury, *Gesta pontificum*, 300.
42 A.Joris, 'Espagne et Lotharingie vers l'an mil. Aux origines des franchises urbaines', 13, n.29 refers to the inclusion of Robert's name in Liège cathedral obit book. The obit book of St-Lambert is apparently no longer in existence, but was copied before it disappeared: see A.Marchandisse, 'L'obituaire de la cathédrale Saint-Lambert à Liège', 411-20.
43 W.Stevenson, 'A contemporary description of the Domesday Survey', 72-84; on Marianus see A.-D. von den Brincken, *Studien zur lateinischen Weltchronistik bis in das Zeitalter Ottos von Freising*, 166-173.
44 William of Malmesbury, *Gesta pontificum*, 300; *Vita Wulfstani*, ed. R.R.Darlington, 62; F.Barlow, *The English church 1000-1066*, 157. E.Mason, *St Wulfstan of Worcester*, 120, thinks Robert and Wulfstan only met after Robert's consecration.
45 Symeon of Durham, ii.208.

estates.[46] He built an imposing two-storeyed episcopal chapel.[47] He may well have appointed the first archdeacon of Hereford, Heinfrid, who first occurs in 1085, and also the first dean, Gerard, probably to be identified with his brother Gerard, who also occurs in 1085. Both occur as witnesses in an original land-grant issued by Robert. The only other surviving charter issued by Robert is his profession of obedience.[48]

GERARD

The next five bishops, most of whom had rather short pontificates, were all curial clerks; Gerard (9 June 1096-1100) was the nephew of Bishop Walkelin of Winchester and of Abbot Simeon of Ely, and made his early career in Rouen cathedral, where he was cantor and perhaps also, by 1091, archdeacon.[49] He is also said by Hugh the Chanter to have held the office of chancellor to William I and later to William Rufus; V.H.Galbraith found evidence to corroborate this in two royal writs, one of either William I or William II witnessed by 'G. cancell'' and the other of William II witnessed by 'Gir' cancell''.[50] Although both writs survive only in cartulary copies and the scribes of the cartularies might have confused 'cant'' (i.e. *cantore*) with 'cancell'' or 'cancellario', the fact that no name of a church is given makes it more likely that a royal chancellor, rather than the cantor of a cathedral, is being intended. Gerard was clearly highly regarded by William Rufus, for he sent him to Rome to negotiate with Pope Urban in 1095 on the question of William's recognition of Urban, together with the problem of how Anselm should receive the pallium. Gerard was rewarded in 1096 with the see of Hereford[51] and was not long afterwards translated to the see of York.[52] No genuine charters issued by him as bishop of Hereford survive. One highly important innovation at Hereford which can probably be attributed to him is the

46 DB i, fos.181c-182d.
47 R.Gem, 'The bishop's chapel at Hereford: the roles of patron and craftsman', in S.Macready and F.H.Thompson, edd. *Art and patronage in the English Romanesque*, 87-96.
48 Nos. 2 and 1 below.
49 V.H.Galbraith, 'Girard the chancellor', 77-9; for Gerard the archdeacon see D.Spear, 'Les archidiacres de Rouen au cours de la période ducale', 22, 43. It was possible and indeed common to combine holding a dignity and an archdeaconry in northern France (and elsewhere in northern Europe) in this period.
50 V.H.Galbraith, 'Girard the chancellor' (as note 49).
51 Eadmer, *Historia novorum*, 68, 74.
52 *EEA* v, p.xxiv.

introduction of the rite of Rouen cathedral, which, as Edmund Bishop showed, formed the basis of the Use of Hereford cathedral until the Reformation. Gerard, who as cantor of Rouen cathedral would have been responsible for much of the organisation of the services, is the man likeliest to have brought knowledge of the Rouen Rite to Hereford.[53] On Gerard's translation, custody of the see was given by Henry I to his chaplain, Bernard, almost certainly the Bernard, priest of the church of Hereford and chaplain or chancellor of the queen who became bishop of St David's in 1115. He occurs in 1101 or 1102 validating a grant of William son of Baderon to Monmouth Priory by breaking a knife 'under his foot, because he could not break it with his hands'.[54] As successor to Gerard, however, Henry I nominated his larderer, Roger, at Michaelmas 1102,[55] but he died in early October, too soon to be consecrated.[56]

REINHELM

The origins of the next bishop, Reinhelm, are unknown. He had become chancellor to Queen Matilda, Henry I's first wife, before 3 September 1101; he was invested with the see of Hereford probably after Christmas 1102[57] and Henry I ordered his consecration in 1103, at the hands of Archbishop Gerard of York. Under pressure from Anselm, Reinhelm repented of his behaviour and surrendered his ring and staff.[58] He was consecrated by Anselm on 11 August 1107.[59] As bishop, he assisted at the consecration of Llanthony Priory in 1108, and settled a dispute with Gloucester Abbey concerning Hereford's burial monopoly according to the terms of which Hereford's monopoly was confirmed in return for Gloucester having complete control over the church of St Peter in the new market place in Hereford.[60]

53 Edmund Bishop, *Liturgica historica*, 276-300. On the strength of a Llanthony manuscript Edmund Bishop suggested Robert de Béthune as the man likeliest to have introduced the Rouen rite to Hereford, but Robert had no known ties with Rouen and it is therefore probable that Llanthony obtained knowledge of the rite through Robert after he became bishop.

54 CDF, no.1138.

55 Symeon of Durham, ii.235; Eadmer, *Historia novorum*, 141; *Councils and synods, I*, ii.673.

56 William of Malmesbury, *Gesta pontificum*, 303; Florence of Worcester, *Chronicon ex chronicis*, ii.5.

57 *RRAN*, ii, p.xi; William of Malmesbury, *Gesta pontificum*, 303; Florence of Worcester, ii.51; *Councils and synods, I*, ii.657.

58 Ibid., and Eadmer, *Historia novorum*, 144.

59 Ibid., 187; Florence of Worcester, ii.56; *Symeon of Durham*, ii.239.

60 F.G. Cowley, *The monastic order in South Wales*, 30; M.Brett, *The English church under Henry I*, 98.

Since Hereford cathedral's obit book refers to Reinhelm as 'fundatoris ecclesie' it is likely that he was responsible for commencing the rebuilding of the cathedral, on a new site almost certainly to the north of the old Anglo-Saxon one and blocking the middle of Hereford's original east-west axis, which had probably connected Castle Street and King Street. He died on 27 October 1115.[61] No document issued by him survives except his profession of obedience, though a Gloucester forgery composed in about 1200 is attributed to him.[62]

GEOFFREY DE CLIVE

He was succeeded, not long after his death, by a chaplain of Henry I, Geoffrey de Clive, who was consecrated on 26 December 1115.[63] Geoffrey's chief characteristic, according to William of Malmesbury, was stinginess, and this is perhaps borne out by his attempt to reclaim for the episcopal demesne land which had been granted out as prebends since the time of Robert of Lotharingia.[64] Geoffrey died on 2 February 1119[65] and the see remained vacant until 7 January 1121, when Henry I arranged the election of his keeper of the seal, Richard de Capella.[66]

RICHARD DE CAPELLA

Richard's activities are not well attested, though slightly more charters survive from his episcopate than from those of Reinhelm or Geoffrey. By the spring of 1127 Richard was having to defend his diocese in the legatine council of May against the territorial claims of Urban, bishop of Llandaff, who was demanding Ergyng (Archenfield) and Ystradwr (Golden Valley),[67] but Richard died not long afterwards, on 15 August,[68] and in the long vacancy which followed

---

61 On the alignment of the cathedral, see J.Blair, 'The twelfth-century Bishop's palace at Hereford', 71; the date of Reinhelm's death is given as 27 October by Florence of Worcester, ii.68, and as 28 October by Bodl. MS Rawlinson B328, fo.43.

62 No.7 below.

63 Florence of Worcester, ii.68.

64 William of Malmesbury, *Gesta pontificum*, 304; *RRAN*, ii, no.1101.

65 Symeon of Durham, ii.254; however John of Worcester, 14, gives the date as 3 February and Bodl. MS Rawlinson B328, fo.4v, as 4 February.

66 John of Worcester, 15-16; Eadmer, *Historia novorum*, ii.290-1; Florence of Worcester, ii.75; however, Symeon of Durham, ii.259, gives the date as just before Candlemas 1121 at Windsor.

67 John of Worcester, 23-5; Florence of Worcester, ii.86; *Councils and synods, I*, ii.744; M.Brett, *The English church under Henry I*, 81.

68 John of Worcester, 25; Bodl. MS Rawlinson B328, fo.31v says 16 August.

Urban was free to pursue his case at the papal curia untroubled by opposition.

ROBERT DE BETHUNE

Urban was finally thwarted by one of his own flock, Robert de Béthune, the prior of Llanthony, who eventually succeeded Richard. Robert de Béthune is the first bishop of the see for whom a large enough body of charters (about forty) survives to analyse. In addition we have a Life of Robert written by his friend and admirer William of Wycombe, a canon, and for some years the prior, of Llanthony. William's Life is too apt to side with Robert to be wholly reliable, but it does present a vivid picture of Robert's activities as diocesan, in particular of the difficulties which he faced in travelling around his diocese.[69] Robert's origins have never before been elucidated: Robert de Torigni refers to him as a Fleming,[70] but this has to be reconciled with the statement of William of Wycombe that he and Robert came from the same *patria* and that their places of birth were next to each other, and presumably, therefore, in Buckinghamshire. Moreover, Robert as a young man was on close enough terms with Abbot Richard of St Albans (1097-1119) to ask him for advice about his religious vocation,[71] and it is unlikely that he would have known Richard well had he lived near Béthune. Apart from the toponym, there is no evidence that Bishop Robert was connected with the Flemish de Béthunes, one of the most prominent families of Flanders, which held the advocacy of the abbey of St Vaast, Arras.[72] The head of this family was granted land in England by Henry II just before 1160,[73] but there is nothing to suggest that they had had connections with England before this point. The question can be easily solved by assuming that

69 Robert's biography by William of Wycombe was edited by H.Wharton, *Anglia Sacra*, ii.293-321, but omitting the miracle stories and making full use of only one of the two manuscripts in which the work survives, Lambeth Palace MS 475, the other being BL Cotton Julius D x. A fuller edition is to be found in B.J.Parkinson, 'The Life of Robert de Bethune'. William of Wycombe's view of Dean Ralph of Hereford seems to be blinded by prejudice.

70 Robert de Torigni, *Chronicle*, ed. R.Howlett, *Chronicles of the Reigns of Stephen, Henry II and Richard I*, iv.121.

71 *Anglia sacra*, ii.295-6. Abbot Richard of St Albans is only referred to in the Cotton manuscript (fo.5): see B.J.Parkinson, 'The Life of Robert de Bethune', pp.115-16.

72 B.J.Parkinson, 'The Life of Robert de Bethune', p.254, quoting A.Duchesne, *Histoire de la maison de Béthune*, 570, says there is no evidence to connect Bishop Robert with the family of the advocates of Arras.

73 E.Warlop, *De vlaamse adel voor 1300*, ii.65ff. and see H.Hall, ed. *The Red Book of the Exchequer*, i.24 and ii.692, 697.

Robert's parents, who are described by William of Wycombe as being of knightly rank ('ex illustri satis ordine militari')[74] and thus of rather lower status than the advocates of Arras, were Flemings who had settled in Buckinghamshire at the time of the Norman Conquest. Since Robert's eldest brother was called Gunfrid and since the village of Chocques is close to Béthune it is possible that Robert's parents were clients of the tenant in chief Gunfrid de Chocques;[75] if this were the case Robert might conceivably have been the son or grandson or nephew of Wibald, the tenant of Gunfrid's only Buckinghamshire manor, Wingrave.[76] Robert's parents set him to learn his letters; on their deaths, when Robert was still quite young, he was brought up by his eldest brother, Gunfrid, a schoolmaster. Robert became a schoolmaster himself, teaching the trivium. He then went to France to study *divina pagina* under William of Champeaux and Anselm of Laon. He returned to teaching but was already eager to enter the religious life, and when he had freed himself of various family commitments he became an Augustinian canon at Llanthony,[77] which had only shortly before been founded as a priory, though it had existed as a hermitage since the late eleventh century.[78] Robert's verve won him the respect of his fellow-canons, who made him prior at some point before the mid 1120s, and also the admiration of the local landowners, two of whom, Payn fitz John and Miles the Constable, recommended him to Henry I as a candidate for the see of Hereford.[79] In spite of pressure from Bishop Urban and self-doubts about his suitability for the episcopate, Robert was compelled to give way by Innocent II in 1131.[80] Once in office, Robert immediately put up a strong and successful defence of Hereford's claims to Ergyng and Ystradwr against Urban.[81] Later, in 1145, he was one of several Canterbury suffragans to protest against the claim by Bishop Bernard of St

74 *Anglia sacra*, ii.299.

75 DB, i, fo.152c; W.Farrer, *Honors and knights' fees*, i.20, 29; G.W.S.Barrow, *The Anglo-Norman era in Scottish history*, 22n, 45n; *Anglia sacra*, ii.299.

76 DB i, fo.152c.

77 *Anglia sacra*, ii.299-301.

78 Cowley, *The monastic order in South Wales*, 30.

79 *HRH*, 172; *Anglia sacra*, ii.304; D.Walker, 'Miles of Gloucester, earl of Hereford', 70.

80 J.G.Evans and J.Rhys edd., *The text of the Book of Llan Dâv*, 57-8; *Welsh episcopal acts*, ii.630.

81 *Councils and synods, I*, ii.757; M.G.Cheney, 'The compromise of Avranches and the spread of canon law in England', 179n.

David's that St David's was a metropolitan see. Hereford was one of the dioceses claimed by Bernard for his province.[82]

Robert was the first of a series of four Hereford bishops who were to make their careers entirely outside the royal household. Three of the four, however, had acquired administrative experience before becoming bishop – Robert de Béthune and Gilbert Foliot by having been heads of religious houses, and Robert Foliot by having been an episcopal clerk and an archdeacon. Diocesan administration at Hereford in the 1130s and 1140s was complicated by sporadic, but often bitter, warfare. Llanthony was attacked in a Welsh raid in 1135 and the canons fled to take refuge with Robert, who together with Miles of Gloucester found a new site for them on land granted by Miles just outside Gloucester (Lanthony by Gloucester); Robert helped to restore the endowments of the community with some of the prebends of Hereford cathedral.[83] In 1139 relations between Robert and Miles broke down when Miles decided to support Matilda. Robert accompanied Stephen while he was campaigning in the area;[84] meanwhile the cathedral was taken over by Geoffrey Talbot as a fortress from which to besiege Stephen's troops in the castle.[85] In 1141 Robert went over to Matilda's side and briefly he and Miles, now earl of Hereford, were once more on good terms, and collaborated in the creation of St Guthlac's Priory, Hereford, as a union of the churches of St Guthlac and St Peter, in 1143.[86] Shortly afterwards the two men fell out again and Miles died in excommunication at the end of the year.[87] Robert spent some time in the northern part of his diocese during these years, but he was far from idle: his presence in Shropshire gave him plenty of scope for one of his most important tasks as diocesan, the consecration of new churches to serve outlying communities. The impetus for the creation of new churches came from local landowners, but Robert assisted them, not least by using the political disturbances as an excuse for consecrating graveyards, ostensibly as refuges.[88] The foundation of graveyards possibly more than that of churches helped to break down the powers of the old minster parish churches, because they

82 No.14 below.
83 F.G.Cowley, *The monastic order of South Wales, 1066-1349*, 31; nos.35-7 below.
84 D.Cox, 'Two unpublished charters of King Stephen for Wenlock priory', 56-9.
85 John of Worcester, 58; K.Potter and R.H.C. Davis edd.. *Gesta Stephani*, 108-10.
86 No.21 below.
87 D.Walker, 'Miles of Gloucester, earl of Hereford', 77.
88 Nos.29-31 and 48, 50, 51 and 56 below.

entailed a direct attack on the older churches' burial monopolies, one of their main financial assets.[89] Many of Robert's charters shed light on this side of his activity, especially those which he issued for Shrewsbury abbey and Leominster priory, and his policy was continued energetically by his successor.[90]

Robert died at Rheims just after the end of the 1148 council, on 16 April; by a curious coincidence his three immediate successors in the see had also attended,[91] and the first of these, Gilbert Foliot, may well have owed his appointment to his having been in Rheims on Robert's death, though it is likely that he would have been elevated to the episcopate sooner or later.

GILBERT FOLIOT

Gilbert was probably the son of the steward of the earl of Huntingdon, a Lincolnshire knight called Robert Foliot. His mother was the sister of Bishop Robert Chesney of Lincoln.[92] In his early or mid-twenties he entered Cluny, and was soon made prior of Abbeville.[93] On the death of Abbot Walter of Gloucester in 1139, Gilbert was suggested as a possible successor by Miles of Gloucester and was nominated by Stephen. He was consecrated by Robert de Béthune on Whitsunday 1139.[94] Gilbert supported Matilda but was also diplomatic enough to keep on good terms with the other side, particularly where the interests of his abbey were at stake.[95] He also found time to write and to travel, accompanying Archbishop Theobald on two missions to Eugenius III.[96] It was on the second of these that he visited Rheims. Theobald won Eugenius III's approval for Gilbert's appointment to the see of Hereford and consecrated him at St Omer on 5 September 1148.[97] As bishop Gilbert had to remedy certain problems inherited from his predecessor – he had to try to restore the chapter's revenues, somewhat depleted through Robert's generosity to Llanthony, and to

89 A.T.Thacker,'Early Ecclesiastical Organisation in Two Mercian Burhs', 205, and J.Blair, 'Introduction: from minster to parish church', in idem, ed. *Minsters and parish churches*, 13.
90 *GFL*, nos.290, 301, 335-7.
91 Gilbert Foliot and Robert Foliot were certainly both present, Robert de Melun probably (see below); for Robert de Béthune's death, see *Anglia Sacra*, ii.314-9.
92 A.Morey and C.N.L.Brooke, *Gilbert Foliot and his Letters*, 39, 33.
93 Ibid., 73, 147.
94 Ibid., 79.
95 Ibid., 88; *GFL*, no.26; but see also nos.10, 14, 27, 32, 69.
96 Ibid., nos.7 and 70n; Morey and Brooke, *Gilbert Foliot and his letters*, 156; *Councils and synods*, *I*, ii.818-9.
97 Morey and Brooke, *Gilbert Foliot and his letters*, 96-7.

win back two episcopal castles, which had been alienated.[98] His abili-
ties were generally recognised by his contemporaries, and although
translation to another diocese was uncommon in the twelfth century
Gilbert was obviously destined for a more important position than the
see of Hereford. After Thomas Becket had been made archbishop of
Canterbury, there was general agreement that Gilbert should become
bishop of London, and he was translated in March 1163.[99]

ROBERT DE MELUN

Apart from Gilbert, Robert de Melun is the only twelfth-century
bishop of Hereford who has received much attention from historians.[100] His origins are completely obscure, though we know that he
was English by birth. He studied in Paris under Abelard and Hugh
of St Victor, and succeeded Abelard as a teacher on the Mont-Ste-
Geneviève in 1137, later moving to Melun in 1142 to teach theology.[101]
He returned to Paris in 1147 to help mount an attack on Gilbert de la
Porrée; it is almost certain that he attended the Council of Rheims in
this connection.[102] Very probably he spent the next fifteen years or so
in Paris; this was the period when he wrote at least two of his surviving
works, the *Questiones de Epistolis Sancti Pauli* and the *Sentences*.
Robert's theology is cautious and subtle rather than innovative.[103]
After Gilbert had been translated to London, Thomas Becket seems
to have invited Robert to England to be made bishop of Hereford; it
is possible that the original suggestion came from Alexander III.[104]
Thomas consecrated Robert on 22 December 1163 at Canterbury.[105]

98 *GFL*, nos.80, 327, and D.Crouch, *The Beaumont twins* (Cambridge 1986), 40n.

99 Morey and Brooke, *Gilbert Foliot and his letters*, 99.

100 M.Grabmann, *Geschichte der scholastischen Methode*, ii.323-58; the works of Robert de Melun were edited by R.M.Martin, *Les oeuvres de Robert de Melun*; R.M.Martin, 'L'oeuvre théologique de Robert de Melun', 466-8; B.Smalley, *The study of the Bible in the middle ages*, 73-4, 215-6, 217, 219, 228-30; eadem, *The Becket conflict and the schools*, 51-8; U.Horst, *Die Trinitäts- und Gotteslehre des Robert von Melun*; D.E.Luscombe, *The school of Peter Abelard*, 281-98; David Knowles, *The episcopal colleagues of Archbishop Thomas Becket*, 9, 28-9, 77, 87-8, 97, 104.

101 U.Horst, *Die Trinitäts- und Gotteslehre*, op. cit., 329; D.E.Luscombe, *The school of Peter Abelard*, 283; John of Salisbury, *Metalogicon*, ed. C.C.J.Webb, 78-9; *Les oeuvres de Robert de Melun*, ed. R.M.Martin, i, p.viii.

102 John of Salisbury, *Historia pontificalis*, ed. M.Chibnall, 161; D.E.Luscombe, *The school of Peter Abelard*, 281; U.Horst, *Die Trinitäts- und Gotteslehre*, 6-7.

103 For the dating of Robert's writings see U.Horst, *Die Trinitäts- und Gotteslehre*, 13-23, but cf. also, on the dating of Gratian's *Decretum*, one of the works which influenced Robert, J.T.Noonan, 'Gratian slept here: the changing identity of the father of the systematic study of canon law', 160-1.

104 *MTB*, iii.24 and v.344-5; Mary Cheney, *Roger, bishop of Worcester*, 14.

105 Gervas. Cant., i.176; in *Ann. Mon.*, i.49 and iv.381, however, the date is given as 1164.

Robert's time as bishop was troubled by the Becket dispute; though he was ideologically on Becket's side he did not feel that he could give him strong support. In July 1165 Gilbert Foliot and Robert were requested by Alexander III to mend relations between Henry II and Becket; they had no success.[106] Robert then acted closely with Gilbert for over a year, but when Thomas and his supporters remonstrated with him in the summer of 1166,[107] Robert determined to go to France to join them. In late January 1167 he travelled to Southampton, but was turned back by a papal envoy and died on 26 February 1167.[108]

ROBERT FOLIOT

A long vacancy followed Robert's death. It was not until 1174 that Thomas' successor was consecrated, and his consecration was swiftly followed by those of several of his suffragans. The appointment of Robert Foliot as bishop of Hereford was a compromise: he was a moderate supporter of Thomas Becket who was also a cousin of Gilbert Foliot. Robert's immediate family cannot be identified, though it is possible that they lived in Oxfordshire.[109] He evidently received a good education, but there is no evidence as to where he studied. Bishop Alexander of Lincoln made him a canon of Lincoln before 1142,[110] and on Alexander's death he attended the council of Rheims to obtain Eugenius III's advice about the election of a successor.[111] When Chesney was made bishop of Lincoln, Robert became one of his clerks and then, before January 1152, archdeacon of Oxford.[112] When Becket became archbishop Robert became one of his circle of *eruditi*, but this did not prevent him from maintaining good relations with his cousin Gilbert, who used him as an intermediary.[113] Later, Gilbert repaid Robert by urging his election to the see of Hereford.[114] Robert was elected after Easter 1173 and consecrated on

106 *MTB*, i.58 and iv.355; D.Knowles, *The episcopal colleagues*, 104-5.

107 *MTB*, v.451-8.

108 Ibid., iii.87, and vi.150-4.

109 A.Morey and C.N.L.Brooke, *Gilbert Foliot and his letters*, 44. Robert's exact kinship with Gilbert is unknown. It is however possible that Robert was related to Richard Foliot of Warpsgrove in Oxfordshire: see no.171 below.

110 *EEA* i, no.20; *Fasti ecclesiae anglicanae 1066-1300*, ed. D.E.Greenway, iii.74.

111 *GFL*, no.75.

112 *EEA* i, pp.xliv-xlv and nos.83-4; *Fasti*, iii.35.

113 *GFL*, no.204; *MTB*, vi.607-610.

114 *GFL*, no.224.

6 October 1174.[115] As bishop he spent little time at the royal court and was most active in hearing ecclesiastical cases. We know of at least 23 papal mandates delegating cases to him and another 13 letters of advice on interpreting canon law;[116] in addition he was one of only four English bishops to attend the Third Lateran Council.[117] Robert was, after Roger of Worcester, Gilbert Foliot, Bartholomew of Exeter and Baldwin of Ford, one of the most active English papal judges-delegate of the period. He often drew abuses or problems to Alexander III's attention, and sought papal approval in the form of decretals to tackle the difficult question of clerical marriage. This was widespread in Robert's diocese, and very probably everywhere in England, but there were no means of removing all married clergy at once, nor, if they had been removed, would there have been enough men to replace them.[118] Other problems frequently arising in the diocese, which occur several times in Robert's acta, were arguments over parish boundaries and burial rights; some of these arose because of the activity of his two predecessors in founding new churches, but one was caused by the activities of a recently-founded house of Hospitallers near Hereford, which buried laymen not attached to the house, even during interdicts.[119] Robert was generous to the cathedral chapter but also made use of it to provide archdeaconries and prebends for his own kinsmen, thus strengthening the position of the Foliot family at Hereford.[120] He died on 9 May 1186.[121]

WILLIAM DE VERE

William de Vere was one of the nine children of Aubrey de Vere, the king's chamberlain, and his wife Alice de Clare. Born about 1120, he was brought up at the court of Henry I and Henry's second wife, Alice. He was promised the chancellorship by Matilda in 1141 when he must still have been quite young, but nothing came of this, and he

---

115 R.W.Eyton, *Court, household, and itinerary of Henry II*, 175 and n.1; Ralph of Diss, *Opera historica*, i.392.
116 JL 13953-5, 13952; M.G.Cheney, *Roger, bishop of Worcester*, App. I, nos.42, 57 and App. II, nos.51, 68, 126; nos.164 and 124, 130-3, 141, 161, 167, 170 below; W.Holtzmann and E.W.Kemp, ed. *Papal Decretals relating to the diocese of Lincoln*, 28, no.xii; JL 14311, 14196; BL Add. Ch.7013; H.Singer, *Neue Beiträge über die Dekretalensammlungen vor und nach Bernhard von Pavia*, 283-4.
117 Roger of Howden, *Chronica*, ii.171.
118 J.Barrow, 'Hereford bishops and married clergy, *c.*1130-1240', 1-8.
119 Nos.127, 128, 132, 137, 138, 157 below.
120 Nos.149-51 below.
121 *Ann. Mon.*, i.53 and iv.385; Bodl. MS Rawlinson B328, fo.17v.

became a clerk in the household of Archbishop Theobald of Canterbury.[122] Between 1161 and 1162 he obtained a prebend at St Paul's, but shortly after this resigned it to become an Augustinian canon at the small priory of St Osyth's at Chich in Essex, perhaps out of devotion to his mother, who had spent her widowhood there as a corrodian, and who had only recently died. William wrote a Life of St Osyth, which survives only in a summarised form.[123] In 1177 Henry II refounded the secular minster of Waltham as an Augustinian house and canons were drawn from three priories to serve it, four of them from Chich. One of these was William, who is mentioned as one of the two clerks of works responsible for work on Waltham in all the Pipe Rolls between 1177 and 1182 except 1178.[124] It is possible that he accompanied his nephew William de Mandeville, earl of Essex, to the Holy Land on a diplomatic mission for Henry II in the autumn of 1177; the prologue in one of the two manuscripts of the earliest Anglo-Norman verse version of the Epistle of Prester John states that a William de Vere visited the Holy Land.[125] William's activities between 1182 and 1185 are uncertain, but in 1185 and 1186 he was sent on eyre, on two long circuits. On 25 May 1186 William was elected bishop of Hereford, and his consecration followed on 10 August. From this point he was less actively involved in royal service, though he was sent on eyre four times in the 1190s, and at least once acted as host during negotiations between Henry II's envoys and the Welsh. Most of his energies went into his work as diocesan.[126] He tried to protect the rights of vicars when parish churches were appropriated and was the first bishop of Hereford to make effective use of the charter of inspeximus, a type of document especially useful for protecting the rights of distant abbeys anxious not to lose valuable original charters while prosecuting lawsuits.[127] Literary and scientific activity in and around the cathedral chapter was encouraged, and

122 J. Barrow, 'A twelfth-century bishop', 175-6.
123 Ibid., 176-7; for the Life see *Leland's itineraries*, v.171; C.Hohler, 'St Osyth and Aylesbury', 63-4.
124 J.Barrow, 'A twelfth-century bishop', 178-9.
125 Ibid., 179-82.
126 Ibid., 182-3. According to Gerald of Wales, Bishop Peter of St David's had hoped to be translated to the see of Hereford: *Welsh episcopal acts*, i.295.
127 pp.xcv–xcvi.

William gave positions in his household to young *magistri*, including, most notably, the young Robert Grosseteste.[128]

GILES DE BRAOSE

Following William's death on Christmas Eve 1198 the cathedral chapter wished to elect Walter Map as his successor and sent proctors to Richard I in France to ask for permission to do this. While they were still travelling, Richard died.[129] John had other plans for the bishopric, which he used to reward one of his close followers, William de Braose, by giving it to William's son Giles. William had extensive lordships in southern England and France, but his most important territories were in the Welsh Marches, in Brecon and Upper Gwent. Since Brecon was adjacent to the see of Hereford this gave the family an absolute pre-eminence in the southern Welsh Marches.[130] Giles' age, education and career prior to his election are completely unknown, but since he was one of the eldest of William's children, and since William married before 1170,[131] it is likely that he was about thirty on his election (the minimum canonical age for consecration as bishop). The only two mentions of Giles before he became bishop give no hint of his activities or status. Giles was elected early in 1200 and consecrated on 24 September in that year, in St Catherine's chapel, Westminster, to the disapproval of the monks of Canterbury, who appealed unsuccessfully against this and finally had to be satisfied by writing a separate profession of obedience in addition to the one presumably written at Westminster.[132] The early years of his pontificate were relatively untroubled and busy. Giles was often mandated to act as papal judge-delegate.[133]

By the latter months of 1206 John had lost his trust in Giles' father, and ordered his justiciar in Ireland, Meiler fitz Henry, to attack the Braose lands in Limerick.[134] By March 1208 William de Braose's

---

128 J.Barrow, 'A twelfth-century bishop', 184-7; my reluctance definitely to identify the Robert Grosseteste in William de Vere's household with Robert Grosseteste the future bishop of Lincoln should be corrected: see R.W.Southern, *Robert Grosseteste*, 65-6.
129 Adam of Eynsham, *Magna Vita Sancti Hugonis*, ii.131-2.
130 S.Painter, *The reign of King John*, 43-4.
131 F.M.Powicke, 'Loretta, countess of Leicester', in *Historical essays presented to James Tait*, ed.J.G.Edwards, V.H.Galbraith and E.F.Jacob, 248, 271-2.
132 No.243 below.
133 *The letters of Pope Innocent III: a calendar*, ed. C.R. and M.G.Cheney, nos.340, 546, 551, 559, 560, 778.
134 S.Painter, *The reign of King John*, 123, 221, 240-1.

Herefordshire lands were also under threat; Giles had to accompany John, perhaps as surety for his father. John ordered the sheriff of Herefordshire to take over the episcopal estates, and though he briefly allowed them to be returned to Giles they were commanded to be taken back into royal control again on 23 May.[135] Giles then fled to France. His flight, which took place later than that of the bishops of London, Ely, and Worcester, was clearly a response not to John's ecclesiastical policies but to his antagonism towards the Braose family;[136] once Giles was in France, however, he associated himself with Stephen Langton, who presided at the funeral of Giles' father, who died in France in 1211. Giles' mother and eldest brother had meanwhile been handed over to John, imprisoned and starved to death.[137] During these years it is possible that Giles helped Llywelyn of Gwynedd to make his treaty with Philip Augustus in 1212, for the Braoses were allies of the princes of North Wales.[138] This alliance was to figure strongly during the remaining years of Giles' life. After his return from exile in 1213 he kept the peace for over a year, but when John gave his Gloucestershire lands to Brian fitz Count, Giles joined the opposition and raised support in the Welsh Marches.[139] Only the visit of the papal legate, Nicholas of Tusculum, whom Giles accompanied on a tour of the Marches,[140] helped to restore peace. In May 1215 Giles rebelled again, in alliance with Llywelyn, and regained control of his father's castles, but in October he was ready to make peace with John,[141] and while the arrangements were being made to hand back his estates he died, at Worcester, on 17 November.[142]

HUGH DE MAPENORE

On Giles' death Hereford cathedral chapter elected their dean, Master Hugh de Mapenore, against the express wishes of John, who had sent them a list of suitable nominees to choose from. John appealed to the papacy on the grounds that the chapter had still been excommunicate

---

135 *Rot. chart.*, 177-8; *Rot. litt. claus.*, i.112-13; *Rot. Litt. Pat.* 83.

136 *CRR*, v.152; cf. also *Ann. Mon.*, iv.396.

137 F.M.Powicke, 'Loretta' (as n.131), 260-1; Roger of Wendover, *Chronicle*, ii.48-9.

138 R.F.Treharne, 'The Franco-Welsh treaty of alliance', in idem, *Simon de Montfort and baronial reform: thirteenth-century essays*, 345-60.

139 *Rot. chart.*, 195; *Rot. litt. claus.*, i.200, of 15 May 1214; *Mon Angl.*, vi, pt. i, 350.

140 Ibid., vi.350 (though Nicholas is called Guala, in error). See also no.248 below.

141 J.C.Holt, *The Northerners*, 35; J.E.Lloyd, *A History of Wales*, ii.644-5; *Brut y Tywysogion*, ed. Thomas Jones, 204-5.

142 Bodl. MS Rawlinson B328, fo.46.

when they held the election, but Honorius III was not disposed to be hostile to the chapter and the case was settled in their favour after John's death in October 1216.[143] Hugh was the son of Robert de Mapenore and his wife Matilda, minor gentry from the village of Hampton near Leominster in Herefordshire.[144] His first occurrence is as a clerk in the household of William de Braose between 1189 and 1196; he was already styled *Magister*.[145] On Giles' election to the see of Hereford, he became one of Giles' clerks, and very soon afterwards was made dean of the cathedral, probably late in 1201.[146] Although the chapter now played a much smaller part in the episcopal administration than in the previous century, it was more vigorous and self-assertive in Hereford itself, and many of the surviving Hereford charters of the period, whose numbers increase hugely from about 1190 onwards, were produced by scribes associated with the cathedral and were often witnessed by members of the chapter.[147] Dean Hugh and several of his colleagues were often instructed to act as papal judges-delegate.[148] As dean, Hugh also had to defend the chapter's rights in an advowson case and in a case which threatened the cathedral's burial monopoly.[149] In 1208 Hugh briefly visited Ireland, where he is to be found witnessing charters of William de Braose,[150] but it is likely that he spent most of the remainder of the period of Giles' exile in Hereford. As bishop he attended Henry III's forces at the battle of Lincoln in 1217 and was present at Worcester in 1218 when Llywelyn made peace with Henry; soon afterwards, Hugh had the duty of escorting the South Welsh to do homage to Henry.[151] Many of Hugh's surviving charters are simply confirmations of ones issued by his predecessors; however, he went beyond their confirmations in allowing Reading abbey to strengthen its hold over its subordinate priory of Leominster, by giving it the right to appoint and depose priors at will. In imitation of a grant by William de Vere to Cormeilles abbey,

143 *Cal. papal reg.*, i.40; *Ann. mon.*, iv.406 and i.62.
144 No.301 below.
145 *CDF*, 461.
146 See Appendix I.
147 Hereford D. & C Muniments, nos.159, 595, 1115, 972-3.
148 *Letters of Innocent III: a Calendar*, ed. C.R. and M.Cheney, nos.546, 559-60, 629, 896, 903, 1164.
149 *CRR* iv.23, 42, 230, 302 and v.38; for the burial case, see *Hereford Charters*, 44.
150 E.St.J.Brooks, ed. *Register of the Hospital of St John the Baptist without the New Gate, Dublin*, nos.433 and 463.
151 A.O. and M.O.Anderson, edd. *The chronicle of Melrose*, 68; *Rot. claus.*, i.378-9; *Cal. pat. rolls*, 1216-1225, 149-50.

he gave Lire abbey the right to turn its churches in the diocese into a prebend of the cathedral.[152] Hugh may perhaps have had problems in restoring the finances of the episcopal estates, which must have suffered greatly between 1208 and 1215, for his household was much smaller than those of his predecessor and his successor.[153] However, his years in office coincided with continuing prosperity in the city of Hereford and a growing sense of frustration on the part of the merchants and particularly the Jewish community at the restrictions imposed on them by the bishop. A large part of the town lay in the bishop's jurisdiction, with the result that its inhabitants were largely free from prosecution for debt or delinquency by royal or municipal officers, and Hereford's annual fair belonged to the bishop, who tried to prevent other commercial activity while it was taking place. Hugh may possibly have tried to recoup the financial losses suffered by the bishopric by making demands on Hereford's Jews, for in June 1218 the sheriff was ordered to prevent Hugh from molesting them.[154] Hugh died suddenly on 16 April 1219.[155]

HUGH FOLIOT

Hugh's successor was another member of the cathedral chapter, Hugh Foliot, who for many years had been archdeacon of Shropshire. He was the uncle of a William Foliot of Horton in Northamptonshire, who was almost certainly the son of another William Foliot and the grandson of the Roger Foliot who held three fees of Walter de Wahull; it is likely therefore that Hugh and his brother Thomas were younger sons of Roger and Roger's wife Roheise.[156] Very probably Hugh was also a cousin of Gilbert and Robert Foliot, and it was to Robert that he owed his early promotion. He occurs for the first time in Robert's entourage, as yet without office or dignity, probably before 1180 (certainly before 1183).[157] Robert made him archdeacon of Shropshire and in this capacity he witnesses at least five of Robert's acta.[158] Although references to Hugh over the next thirty-five years are

---

152 Nos.308-10 and 305 below.
153 Pp.lx-lxi below, on household.
154 *Cal. pat. rolls*, i.157; in general on prosperity see M.Lobel, 'Hereford', in eadem, ed. *Historic towns*, vol. i, not consecutively paginated.
155 See note to no.296 below: the date of Hugh's death is given in Bodl. MS Rawlinson B328, fo.14.
156 On Hugh's nephew see W.Farrer, *Honors and knights' fees*, i.83.
157 For Hugh's first appearance see no.168 below.
158 Nos.135, 156, 166, 171 and 173 below.

plentiful, they shed little light on his activities, since, with the exception of two documents which he helped to issue as papal judge-delegate, they are mostly merely mentions of his name in witness lists.[159] He was well thought of, however, for John urged Giles de Braose to recommend him to the chapter of St David's as a candidate for the see in 1215, and he seems to have been rich enough to exercise patronage on a small scale: Sir Richard Southern has shown how it was probably Hugh who gave help to Robert Grosseteste in his years of difficulty following William de Vere's death.[160] In addition, Hugh took an interest in the career of his much younger brother Master Thomas Foliot, who became a canon of Lichfield by the early years of the thirteenth century. Thomas also acquired the rectory of Launton in Oxfordshire which he then relinquished, probably to take up the rectory of Ashwell in Hertfordshire, which he is to be found holding in 1215.[161] After Hugh became bishop he made Thomas precentor of Hereford cathedral and then treasurer; the treasury was theoretically an inferior dignity to the precentorship, but it was much better endowed and therefore the move was an advancement.[162]

After Hugh de Mapenore died, Hugh Foliot was one of three proctors sent by Hereford chapter to Henry III to beg for a congé d'élire, and was elected bishop shortly after, in June 1219, and consecrated in October.[163] As bishop, Hugh Foliot appointed the diocese's first bishop's official, thus bringing Hereford into line with other English sees, in some of which officials had existed since the late twelfth century.[164] During his episcopate Canon Elias of Bristol founded a hospital in Hereford for the elderly and infirm, which he placed under the control of the cathedral chapter. Hugh, in evident emulation, founded a hospital at Ledbury in about 1230, which he also placed under the chapter's supervision.[165] He encouraged the independence of the chapter by readjusting the endowments of certain prebends to ensure that the chapter no longer had to worry about episcopal interference (the prebends in question had previously been

159 *Letters of Innocent III: a Calendar*, no.964; *Worcester cartulary*, 72-3, quoted by R.W.Southern, *Robert Grosseteste*, 67.
160 *Rot. litt. claus.*, i.203; R.W.Southern, *Robert Grosseteste*, 67-8.
161 J.E.Sayers, *English papal judges delegate*, 117.
162 See Appendix I.
163 *Cal. pat. rolls 1216-25*, 191; *Ann. mon.*, iv.410 and i.64.
164 No.334 below; on the introduction of bishops' officials into English dioceses, see C.R.Cheney, *English bishops' chanceries*, 20-1.
165 *Hereford charters*, 57-61; nos.342, 344, 348 below.

endowed, perhaps only on a temporary basis, with property belonging to the episcopal estates). Hugh also enhanced the value of the cathedral's dignities by granting their holders the privilege of the year of grace, which meant that their executors could use the revenues from the dignities for a year after their deaths to pay their debts and for pious bequests.[166] Charters relating to the episcopal estates – landgrants, for example – only start to survive in large numbers from Hugh Foliot's time, and their remarkably uniform wording suggests that the lordship was well administered. In 1225, after the reissue of the Forest Charter, Hugh assisted with the deforestation of areas ordered to be taken out of the royal forest, by holding a series of inquests into the royal forest in Gloucestershire.[167] He died on 7 August 1234 and was succeeded as bishop by the then dean of Hereford, Ralph of Maidstone.[168]

THE EPISCOPAL FAMILIA

It cannot be determined whether the pre-conquest bishops had any ecclesiastical household separate from the community of clergy serving the cathedral, though this seems to be unlikely. Evidence for episcopal chaplains at Hereford begins in the pontificate of Robert of Lotharingia, and is to be found in the Domesday entry for the church of Hereford. In this entry are many references to clerks holding of the bishop; some of them are described more specifically as clerks of the bishop, one as a chaplain, and three as chaplains of the bishop, one of them holding a hide at Bishop's Frome and the other two some unhidated land around the town of Hereford.[1] (There are in addition several references to priests, but these are almost certainly priests serving churches on the manors of the church of Hereford).[2] The coincidence between the total number of clerks and chaplains and the

166 Nos.336-43 for Hereford cathedral chapter.
167 Nos.357, 363, 366-70 and 328-9.
168 *Ann. Mon.*, i.93; iv.80, 426; Bodl.MS Rawlinson B328, fo.30.

1 Clerks, often in pairs, occur holding land on the estates of the church of Hereford at Lulham, Preston, *Bertune* (untraced, in the hundred of Dinedor), Woolhope, Preston Wynne, Withington, Donnington (1 episcopal clerk), Bishops Frome (1 episcopal chaplain), Canon Pyon (3 episcopal clerks), Huntington, Moreton on Lugg, Bromyard (1 chaplain), the Moor in Straddle Hundred, unhidated land around Hereford (2 episcopal chaplains) (Domesday Book i, fos.181c-182d).
2 At Bromyard the two priests who occur holding a hide are probably the remnants of the old minster community at Bromyard which was mentioned for the first time in the ninth century; the chaplain who holds another hide was probably one of the members of the bishop's community of clerks (Domesday Book, i, fo.182c).

later number of cathedral prebends at Hereford is striking, and suggests that Bishop Robert of Lotharingia (1079-95) had carefully organised the episcopal and cathedral estates as a single unit which was at the same time capable of providing for the individual needs of the cathedral clergy.[3] The fact that the episcopal chaplains are mentioned separately from the rest of the clergy may perhaps mean that Robert had envisaged a separate foundation of chaplains to serve his episcopal chapel, built on a Lotharingian plan,[4] and two-storeyed, forming a chapel dedicated to St Mary Magdalen and one dedicated to St Catherine, but the chapel, although it later acquired its own distinct endowments, was always under the shadow of the cathedral chapter; later, Bishop William de Vere granted the chapel of St Mary Magdalen to the chapter and in 1233 Bishop Hugh Foliot followed suit with the chapel of St Catherine.[5] In Robert of Lotharingia's sole surviving charter[6] we find among the witnesses a list of eight followers of the bishop who are clearly clerics, since the bishop's men who follow them are referred to as laymen; three of the clerks at least (Gerard, Heinfrid and Leuuin, i.e. Leofwine) were members of the cathedral community, since Heinfrid is known to have been archdeacon and Gerard and 'Liwin' occur, both titled dean, in the cathedral obit book, and very probably the others were too, though their exact status is not known.[7] Since it is likely that the total number of Robert's charters was small the main function of his chaplains must have been to say mass.

We know nothing of the households of Robert's immediate successors and it is not until the episcopate of Bishop Robert de Béthune (1131-1148) that we have any evidence for the episcopal following. The witness lists of Robert's charters show that Robert preferred

3 J.Barrow, 'Cathedrals, provosts and prebends', *Journal of Ecclesiastical History*, xxxvii (1986), 557-8.
4 R.Gem, 'The bishop's chapel at Hereford: the roles of patron and craftsman', in S.Macready and F.H.Thompson, edd. *Art and patronage in the English Romanesque*, Society of Antiquaries Occasional Papers, n.s., viii (1986), 87-96.
5 Nos.198 and 343 below. The dedication to St Mary Magdalen, though it would be a very early one in England, could well be original: see J. Barrow, 'A Lotharingian in Hereford' (forthcoming).
6 No.2.
7 On Heinfrid, see Z.N. and C.N.L.Brooke, 'Hereford cathedral dignitaries', *Cambridge Historical Journal*, viii (1944-6), 14, 183; on Gerard and Liwin (Leofwine) see Appendix i below.

where possible to issue charters during synods where various parish priests, rural deans and members of local religious houses, as well as members of the cathedral chapter, could testify.[8] Several members of the cathedral community, especially the dignitaries, Master Hugh de Clifford, Master Eustace and Master Ranulf fitz Erchemar, appear so often that they probably formed a circle of episcopal advisers, and to this circle we may add William of Wycombe, prior of Llanthony, and another Llanthony canon called Hugh.[9] In addition to these, Robert had one chaplain, called William, who occurs early in the 1130s,[10] and two chaplains (in no.28 referred to as clerks), David and Walter.[11] A charter issued by Abbot William of Lire probably in 1148 and witnessed by Robert de Béthune is also witnessed by two clerks, Walter and Roger, who were doubtless in Robert's following.[12] There are no means of identifying any of these with any of the drafters of Robert's acta, several of which were in any case, as we shall see, drafted by the beneficiaries. While it is not impossible that either William de Wycombe or Canon Hugh of Llanthony might have had a hand in drafting any of the numerous acta which Robert issued for Llanthony, this group of charters as a whole has no shared features and each document could easily have been drafted by a different clerk.

The arrival of Gilbert Foliot brought a marked increase in the size of the episcopal household.[13] The influence of Llanthony Priory disappeared overnight. David the chaplain may have become a canon; he may conceivably be identifiable with the Canon David de Aqua

8 Nos.30, 33, 55, and *Shrewsbury cartulary*, no.338 all mention synods held by Robert de Béthune; no.49 (see *Shrewsbury cartulary*, no.350b) notifies a confirmation made in a chapter held by the bishop at Stanton in southern Shropshire (it is not certain which Stanton) and attended by clergy; three formal settlements (nos.17, 34 and 53) were made in the chapter of Hereford cathedral; no.27, a confirmation, was issued in the cloister of St Guthlac's priory in the presence of members of the cathedral chapter, a rural dean and several priests.

9 Nos.15, 16, 18, 21, 23, 27, 28, 47 and 51.

10 PRO C115 K2/6683 (Llanthony cartulary A1), fo.218r, section x, no.1, possibly of 1134, and cf. ibid., fo.288r. Robert de Béthune's steward, Nicholas, also occurs ibid., in section x, no.1 on fo.218.

11 Nos.51, 52 (David and Walter as chaplains) and no.28 (David and Walter as clerks).

12 PRO C115 K2/6683 (Llanthony cartulary, A1), fo.26r, section i, no.61. This is probably a charter of Abbot William II of Lire, whose predecessor Hildier died on 25 or 26 December 1147 (C.Guéry, *Histoire de l'abbaye de Lyre* [Evreux, 1917], 29), and William might have met Robert de Béthune while the latter was on his journey to Rheims in the spring of 1148 or perhaps at Rheims. According to Guéry (ibid., 29) Abbot William I of Lire died in or before 1130.

13 A.Morey and C.N.L.Brooke, *Gilbert Foliot and his letters* (Cambridge 1965), 268-9.

who occurs under Gilbert and Robert de Melun.[14] It is just possible that Robert's chaplain Walter might be identifiable with the Walter of Clun who occurs as Gilbert's chaplain. Otherwise the appointments were all new. Gilbert had two chaplains, Gilbert and Walter of Clun, who appear fairly often and over the same period, though never in the same document. Gilbert may have begun his career in Gilbert Foliot's service as a clerk (he is referred to as such in one charter).[15] In addition Gilbert had several clerks, Hugh, Geoffrey (probably Master Geoffrey de Clifford, who became a canon of Hereford before the end of Gilbert's episcopate), Roger, Ivo, Ralph, who attests as *scriptor* in *GFL* no.326 (no.93 below), and Ambrose, identified by A.Morey and C.N.L.Brooke as Master Ambrose the Roman lawyer.[16] Although the number of clerks employed by Gilbert Foliot as bishop of Hereford was far smaller than the number he employed as bishop of London, it is large in proportion to the number of acta which he issued and it is likely, even though Hereford at this period must have lacked the educational advantages of London, that Morey and Brooke's comment about the nature of Gilbert's episcopal household in London holds good for Hereford: 'It is clear, in fact, that his household was more than an administration in being: it was also a school in which the young Foliots and others who had attracted the bishop's attention and won his patronage were brought up, and served an apprenticeship in the career of ecclesiastical law and administration'.[17]

Even though hardly any charters survive from the episcopate of Robert de Melun the main figures in his administration are identifiable. Robert had a steward called Alfred (see no. 122) who is almost certainly identifiable with his clerk Alfred whom he sent on a mission to Henry II in Caen in 1166,[18] who again can probably be identified with Robert Foliot's chaplain Alfred. Employing clerics as stewards was not unknown: Bishop Hugh Foliot did so too in the 1230s.[19]

14 On Canon David de Aqua see ibid., p.268, and J.Barrow, 'The bishops of Hereford and their *acta*', unpd. Oxford D.Phil. thesis, 1983, p.515.
15 *GFL*, no. 230.
16 A.Morey and C.N.L.Brooke, *Gilbert Foliot and his letters* (Cambridge 1965), 288-9.
17 Ibid., 215.
18 *MTB*, vi. 74.
19 See below. The employment of clerks as stewards was not uncommon, even in the households

Robert is known to have had at least one chaplain, Osbert (see no. 122).

Evidence is much fuller for the episcopate of Robert Foliot: it is clear that the episcopal household was now a much larger and more developed organisation than it had previously been at Hereford. It was not, however, completely separate from the chapter; some men were attached to both. Master Eustace, a canon, attests Robert's acta fairly frequently.[20] William de Stokes, William Foliot (the brother of the archdeacon Ralph Foliot) and Walter of Colwall began their careers under Robert as clerks, evidently influential ones, and Robert made William de Stokes a canon.[21] He made William Foliot a canon as well (no. 142). William Foliot and Walter of Colwall acted for Robert in an agreement between Robert and Llanthony Priory (no.172). Since Walter the steward of Bishop Robert sometimes occurs next to William Foliot in witness lists and never occurs simultaneously with Walter of Colwall, it seems probable that the two are identical; Walter would therefore be another cleric acting as a steward. It is likely that Walter of Colwall was the Walter appearing in Robert Foliot's entourage at Winchcombe in 1177,[22] and he might also have been the Walter *scriptor* who attests no. 125. Master Eustace, the two Williams and Walter evidently stood at the top of Robert's household; next came his chaplains. Robert employed four chaplains during his episcopate: John the canon, John the priest, Reginald and Alfred. John the canon and John the priest occur together in one charter issued during the first five years of Robert's episcopate (no. 145); thereafter John the priest is no longer mentioned, though he may have continued to serve Robert, as the references to John the chaplain after 1179 do not always specify that he was a canon.[23] Reginald occurs as episcopal chaplain on three occasions between 1174 and 1183, one of these being the composition between Bishop Robert and Hugh Parvus

of lay magnates, after *c.*1150 (personal communication from Dr David Crouch).

20 Nos.145, 147, 149, 152, 163, and Mary Cheney, *Roger, bishop of Worcester, 1164-1179* (Oxford 1980), Appendix I, no.28a, and BL Add. Ch. 7013, a composition of 1177 in which Robert Foliot acted as judge.

21 On these men see nos.125, 142, 145, 150, 153, 154, 156, 160, 171, 172, 173 below. William de Stokes was still a clerk when no.125 was issued but had become a canon by 1183: see no.153.

22 BL Add. Ch. 7013 and Mary Cheney, *Roger, bishop of Worcester, 1164-1179* (Oxford 1980), App. I, no.28a.

23 Nos.150, 152, 171, 173 below.

made in 1176.[24] From the early 1180s Reginald no longer appears in Robert's entourage, but he still occurs as a chaplain.[25] He was evidently the chaplain of the chapel of St Mary Magdalen, part of Robert of Lotharingia's two-storey chapel, which he resigned during the episcopate of Bishop William de Vere (see no.198); subsequently he became a cathedral canon, and on his death left a glossed psalter to the chapter. If, as seems quite likely, this was Hereford Cathedral Library MS O. 6. xii, which contains either the original or a very early copy of the 1177 agreement between Robert Foliot and Hugh de Lacy (no.159), Reginald may well have been the scribe of the agreement. John the canon and Alfred occur together in seven charters,[26] five of which can be dated to the second half of the episcopate, and very probably the other two, nos.150 and 152, for which no closer determining dates can be found than 1174 × 1186, are also later than 1179.

Lower down the hierarchy a fluctuating group of clerks attests Robert's acta up to about 1180, some of them occurring only once (Nicholas of Lewknor, Robert de Landa, Master Osbert, and Geoffrey Folet).[27] Already by 1176, however, Robert had engaged Theobald, who occurs then as his clerk and in two other charters, one of them definitely later than 1179, as his almoner.[28] A William who occurs as almoner in no.152 may well be William Foliot. Robert's other clerks, Bartholomew of Eynsham, Osbert of Ledbury, Ernald of Stokes, Reginald of Upton, probably identifiable with Reginald *emptor* and Reginald the clerk, Ranulf of Salwarpe, Bertram, Hervey, Henry, and Richard *scriptor* appear in charters dating, either certainly or probably, from after c.1179.[29] Bertram, Hervey, Henry and Richard occur only once and Ernald of Stokes only twice, but the others attest frequently. Osbert of Ledbury had connections with Hereford

---

24 Mary Cheney, *Roger*, App. I, nos.28 and 28a (= Hereford D & C Muniments 2771). See also nos.147, 149 below.
25 Hereford D & C Muniments, no.727, witnessed by Bishop Robert (Foliot) and Dean Jordan, and therefore 31 December 1180 x 9 May 1186.
26 Nos.142, 150, 152, 154, 156, 171, 173.
27 It is not certain if Robert de Landa and Geoffrey Folet were clerks. Nicholas of Lewknor is probably the Master Nicholas of Lewknor, incumbent of the chapel of Cassington, Oxfordshire, who occurs c.1192 x March 1195, *EEA*, iv, no.61.
28 Mary Cheney, *Roger*, App. I, nos.28, 28a; nos.152 and 163 below.
29 Nos.142, 150, 152, 156, 160, 163, 171, 173 below; the dating of nos.150 and 152 cannot be more closely determined than the limits of the episcopate.

cathedral before Robert became bishop;[30] but Bartholomew of Eynsham, to judge from his surname, might have encountered Robert while the latter was archdeacon of Oxford.

William de Vere's household is not only quite different in its personal composition from Robert Foliot's; it is also larger and contains a significant number of clerks with the *magister* title. In one of William's earliest charters, no.195, datable 1186 × 1187, we find (Master) Richard Brito, whom William had perhaps met in London, two chaplains, Reginald (presumably Reginald chaplain of St Mary Magdalen's), Richard, Master Osbert and Geoffrey of St Osyth's, evidently a contact William had made when he was a canon there. Master Richard Brito, together with William Foliot, also attests no.203 of 1186 × 1187/8, issued just before Bishop William made them dean and precentor respectively. In no.203 we find two clerks who were to be very active in William's household appearing for the first time, Master William of Calne and (Master) John of Colchester.[31] Master William of Calne attests charters datable 1186 × 1193 (no.210), 1191 (no.229), and 1191 × 1198 (no.206). At some point before 1190 Bishop William instituted William into the church of Stottesdon on the presentation of the abbot and monks of Shrewsbury (perhaps on William's recommendation) (nos.231, 232) William was also the parson of an unidentified church, referred to as *Eys* in a papal document, of which he was deprived by the diocesan in the late 1190s.[32] This church could have been Eastnor, which was in the bishop of Hereford's gift, but is perhaps more likely to have been the parish church of Ewias Harold in the diocese of St David's.[33] It is possible that a rift had occurred between William de Vere and William de Calne after the latter had entered the service of Archbishop Hubert Walter,[34] probably in or soon after 1193. Master John of Colchester occurs in charters datable 1186 × -1190 (nos.231, 232), 1186 ×

30 *Hereford charters*, 16-17 (Hereford D & C Muniments no.2768) datable c.1158 x 1163; cf. also Hereford D & C Muniments no.155 and Bodl. MS Rawlinson B329, fo.17v.

31 Master John of Colchester's toponymic is given here and in nos.204 and 211 as Gloucester, but this seems to be in error: nos.203 and 204 survive only in the 14th-century cartulary of St Guthlac's priory, Hereford, which is full of scribal errors.

32 *The letters of Pope Innocent III concerning England: a calendar*, ed. C.R. and M.Cheney (Oxford 1967), nos. 92, 93.

33 Ibid. and no.190 below.

34 Cf. *EEA*, ii, p.xxxi.

November 1191,[35] 1186 × 1193 (nos.210, 211) and 1186 × 1198 (nos.187 and 199). No.187, in which Master John is referred to as canon of Hereford, is also attested by Richard *scriptor*, perhaps the Richard the chaplain of no.195.

In about 1190 William's household was enlarged by the arrival of three new *magistri*, Master Robert Folet, Master Nicholas of Hampton or Wolverhampton and Master John Clementis. Master Robert Folet was a canon of St Paul's until at least *c*.1192, when he attests Ralph of Diss's Statute of residence;[36] his first clearly datable appearance at Hereford is in 1191 (No.229), and he, Nicholas and John, always in this order, attest charters of 1190 × 1198 (no.205), 1186+ × mid 1190s (no.196), 1195 (no.200, excluding John), and 1195/6 × 1198 (no.209). By April 1195 × 1198, when they attest a charter together (no.201), they were all canons of Hereford. Although they also occur as clerks in charters which cannot be dated more closely than the limits of the episcopate,[37] it is probably safe to put the date of their entry into William's service at about 1190 because they do not attest the charters which can definitely be dated to the early years of the episcopate. In the early thirteenth century Robert and John were both appointed as papal judges-delegate, Robert in a case of 1205 concerning Gloucester Abbey,[38] and John in a case of 1212 concerning Brecon.[39] Nicholas became archdeacon of Shropshire in 1219; it seems safe to assume that William de Vere had appointed all three for their legal expertise.

Beneath Masters Robert, Nicholas and John in William's household in the middle years of his episcopate came the chaplains Master Osbert and William, who most often occur together;[40] Master Osbert had probably been in William's household from the start.[41] In a charter of 1195/6 × 1198 Master Osbert attests as chaplain with John the chaplain (no.209), the latter perhaps being identifiable with the

---

35 *Waltham charters*, no.210 (1186 x November 1191).
36 *Fasti ecclesiae anglicanae, 1066-1300, i, St Paul's*, ed. D.E.Greenway (London 1968), 86.
37 Nos.226, 227, 228, 236 below.
38 *The letters of Pope Innocent III concerning England: a calendar*, ed. C.R. and M.Cheney (Oxford 1967), no.629.
39 *Brecon cartulary*, xiv.234.
40 Nos.179, 180, 196, 204, 205, 206, 207, 208, 226, 227, 228, 236; William on his own occurs in nos.201, 229 and 235, Osbert on his own in nos.195 and 200.
41 No.195; also *Waltham charters*, no.210 of 1186 x November 1191.

John the deacon who attests no.200 of 1195. Following them came the clerks who lacked the *magister* title, Reginald Foliot,[42] Ralph, variously described as almoner, deacon or clerk, Geoffrey, described as deacon or clerk,[43] and Roger de Vere, who may have been a layman.[44] Reginald Foliot was a nephew of Bishop Peter de Leia of St David's (1176-1198), who made him a canon there; he was a rival of Gerald of Wales for the bishopric of St David's when it fell vacant in 1198. Gerald (who therefore naturally loathed him) said that Reginald's name was put forward by the chapter of St David's twice not because of any merit on his part but because he was not Welsh, and the chapter feared that a list consisting only of Welsh names would anger King John. Gerald describes Reginald as having been William's *notarius*.[45]

Gerald recommended to William de Vere the last, and best known, clerk to enter his service, Master Robert Grosseteste. Since Gerald probably made Robert's acquaintance while he was visiting Lincoln between the autumn of 1194 and 1195, it is likely that Robert did not enter William's household until 1195.[46] Robert Grosseteste attests nos.207, 208, and 209 and is probably identifiable with the Master Robert who occurs together with Master Robert Folet in no.228. As his most recent biographer, Sir Richard Southern, remarks: 'he might reasonably have looked forward to early promotion. But then the calamity befell him which was most to be feared by a rising young man: on Christmas Eve 1198 the bishop, his patron, died before he had provided Grosseteste with a benefice'.[47]

Most of William's surviving acta are witnessed by at least some of his household clergy and often by at least one or two members of the cathedral chapter as well. Lay servants, sometimes William's own and sometimes those of members of the chapter, attest on occasion, and the senior lay members of his household, especially the steward (three men occupied this post during William's episcopate) and the cham-

---

42 Nos.196, 200, 206, 226, 227, 228, 235, 236; wrongly as Reginald Folet in no.205 and as Roger Foliot in no.209.
43 Nos. 204, 205, 206, 226, 236, 237; possibly identifiable with the Geoffrey of St Osyth's who witnesses no.195.
44 Nos.204, 209, 226, 228.
45 Giraldus, *Opera*, i.95, iii.298.
46 R.W.Southern, *Robert Grosseteste* (Oxford 1986), 65, quoting Giraldus, *Opera*, i.249.
47 R.W.Southern, *Robert Grosseteste*, 66.

berlain, quite often.[48] All the senior lay members of William's household attest no.196, issued for Hereford cathedral chapter. Documents
for Haughmond Abbey and Shrewsbury Abbey may well have been
issued in Shropshire, since they are attested by a few prominent
Shropshire laymen.[49] The tenants of the bishop attest relatively rarely,
occurring only in the charters notifying the grant of land at Easton to
William's steward (nos.179, 180), the admission of a parson on the
presentation of Robert de Bockleton, one of William's tenants
(no.182), one of the charters for Hereford cathedral (no.196), and the
charter notifying the settlement between two of William's tenants,
William de Burghill and William the chamberlain (no.239).

Bishop Giles de Braose brought an entirely new group of clerks to
Hereford with him. A few of William de Vere's household, for example Master Nicholas of Wolverhampton and Master Osbert, can be
found witnessing two of Giles' charters (nos.252, 287), but they were
by now canons and so not strictly dependent on Giles' favour. The
senior clerks in Giles' household at the start of his episcopate were
Master Philip of Lindsey, Master Theobald of *Len'*, and Master
Hugh de Mapenore,[50] and within about a year of Giles' consecration
Master Philip had become a canon and Master Hugh, who had
previously been a clerk of Giles' father,[51] had been made dean, his first
dated occurrence in this office being at Michaelmas 1202. In addition
Giles' household in 1200-1 contained his kinsman Hugh de Braose (it
is not certain whether he was of lay or clerical status) (nos.244, 289),
Master Philip Map, the nephew of Walter Map (No.244), two chaplains, William and Simon (no.244), and perhaps also Master Albinus,
who later became chancellor of the cathedral, though it is possible that
he was attached to the cathedral chapter rather than to Giles' *familia*.[52]

After 1201 Master Theobald remained the most important clerk in
the household until Giles' death, his final occurrence in Giles' service
being 1214 × 1215 (no.262).[53] During the remaining fourteen years

---

48 Nos.196, 199, 207, 221, 223, 227.
49 Nos.195, 231, 232, 235.
50 Nos.244, 252, 260, 287, 289.
51 *CDF*, 461 of 1189 x 1196.
52 No.289 and also no.277 of 1200 x 1208.
53 See also nos.245, 253, 256, 257, 259, 277, 282, 283, 284, 288 and *Hereford charters*, 39. The
last mentioned (Hereford D. & C. Muniments no.1090) was witnessed by Richard de Seignes

of Giles' episcopate the composition of the household and the order in which the clerks attest charters remained unusually constant, in spite of the fact that Giles spent the period between 1208 and 1213 in exile, mostly in France. Next to Theobald in rank came Master Geoffrey of Ludlow,[54] though on two occasions we find Master Richard Rufus instead (nos.257, 283); following them came Master Philip Map.[55] The chaplains followed, usually Richard and Ranulf,[56] though Richard and David are the chaplains attesting no.282 and Richard and Ranulf are joined by another Richard in no.256. Simon, who had been the chaplain in 1200/1, occurs as chaplain again 1201 × 1203,[57] but thereafter testifies as a mere clerk, usually in the company of William,[58] who is perhaps to be identified with the William Parvus who occurs as clerk in 1201 × 1203.[59] A Nicholas clerk testifies with William the clerk in no.257. This consistency of witnesses makes a closer dating of many of Giles' charters very difficult, particularly since members of the cathedral chapter now attest far fewer episcopal acta than had been the case in the twelfth century, and when they do so, attest in markedly smaller numbers. The charters which Giles issued as feudal landlord tend to have almost exclusively lay witnesses; Giles' household clergy witnessed the acta arising out of diocesan business, for example, confirmations to religious houses of their possessions and licences of appropriation. The fact that members of the chapter attest much less often suggests that many acta were issued while Giles was outside Hereford, whether on visitations or while staying at one of his manors.

The episcopal household shrank under Hugh de Mapenore (1216-1219). Almost certainly the episcopal revenues had suffered both while Giles was in exile and after his return, since he spent much of the last two years of his life trying to recover the Braose family estates, and Hugh may well have faced financial problems; perhaps, however,

---

as sheriff of Herefordshire and therefore cannot be later than 1203: see B.G.Charles and H.D.Emanuel, edd. *Calendar of the earlier Hereford cathedral muniments*, i.146.
54 Nos.245, 253, 256, 259, 262, 277, 282, 284, 288 and *Hereford charters*, 39.
55 Nos.245, 256, 257, 282.
56 Nos.245, 259, 262, 277, 284.
57 No.244 of 1200 x 1201; *Hereford charters*, 39.
58 Nos.245, 256, 259, 262, 277, 282.
59 *Hereford charters*, 39.

the fact that Hugh had been dean made it seem an obvious choice to him to rely on his ex-colleagues in the chapter for advice. In his earliest datable charter, of 1216 × 1217/8, Master Albinus, Master Theobald and Master Geoffrey, Giles' ex-clerks, all occur as canons (no.298), and in addition we find two clerks, Gregory and Robert. These two occur in subsequent charters as chaplains,[60] and following them come Nicholas (of Abergavenny) and Theoderic as clerks.[61] Since Gregory, Nicholas and Theoderic do not occur in charters which can be definitely attributed to Hugh Foliot, it seems likely that nos.293, 311, and 295, which cannot otherwise absolutely certainly be attributed to Hugh de Mapenore, were in fact issued by him. The only *magistri* apart from those in the cathedral chapter who took any active part in Hugh's household were Master S., clerk of the bishop (no.311), who is probably identifiable with Master Stephen of Thornbury who became canon of Hereford during this period (nos.295, 293), Master Walter of Garsington, parson of Rudford,[62] and Master Elias of Buckehill'.[63] Elias and Canon Stephen also occur in a charter issued by either Hugh de Mapenore or Hugh Foliot which cannot be dated more closely than 1216 × 1221 (no.315).

Elias was the only member of Hugh de Mapenore's household who was also employed by Hugh Foliot, occurring in the early and late 1220s and perhaps as late as 1234.[64] During the earlier years of the episcopate the other senior clerks attesting were mainly cathedral canons: Hugh Foliot's brother Master Thomas,[65] Master Peter of Abergavenny (nos.317, 336), Master Simon de Freine (nos.318, 346), Master W(alter) de Mouncy,[66] Master John of Worcester (no.339, 358), Master Richard Rufus (no.339), and Elias of Evesham, who on one occasion attests as episcopal chaplain.[67] Hugh's brother Thomas continued to play an active role in the episcopal familia, attesting

60 Nos.293, 295, 308, and 309; also no. 299, where Robert occurs as almoner, and 311 in which Gregory occurs on his own.
61 Nos.295, 308, 309; Nicholas occurs on his own in no.293.
62 Nos.293, 295 and cf. 296.
63 Nos.293, 295, 311.
64 Nos.319, 339, 358, 359; the Master G. de Bukehull' who witnesses no.337 should probably be Master E. de Bukehull'.
65 Nos.317, 318, 323, 337.
66 Nos.318, 337, 339.
67 Nos.319, 323, 336.

many of the latter's charters up to 1234.[68] In addition Hugh employed Master William Platun who occurs as a member of his familia throughout his episcopate.[69] During the earlier 1220s Hugh also employed Master Robert Haket (nos.345, 371), Walter of Banbury, probably a layman, who for a period was episcopal steward (nos.337, 339), Robert the chaplain (no.319), Adam of Shrewsbury (nos.371, 345) and Godfrey and Roger the clerks (nos.323, 319). Walter of Banbury, Adam of Shrewsbury and Godfrey remained in Hugh's service till his death;[70] Adam was briefly Hugh's steward c.1230 and shortly after this, after Master Thomas Foliot had become treasurer (in 1230 or just after), Adam was collated to a prebend in the cathedral (no.341). Other clerks who helped to manage the temporalities were John of Ross who was Hugh's bailiff there (nos.341, 370) and Adam of Ledbury[71] who for a time was steward of the episcopal hospital in Ledbury (no.363) and finally became parson of Staunton on Arrow (no.355). To provide advice in more strictly ecclesiastical matters Hugh acquired two new *magistri* in the middle years of his episcopate, Master Peter of Northampton (nos.357, 359) and the first ever episcopal official in the diocese, Master Richard of Hereford (nos.357, 334), and at a rather lower level a new chaplain, Roger, and a new clerk, William of Diddlebury, who both appear to have been appointed after 1230 (nos.335, 360).

DIPLOMATIC OF THE ACTA

I: INTERNAL FEATURES

The Hereford acta of the period 1079-1234 can be broken into three separate groups chronologically: those of 1079-1127, a period for which very few charters survive, those of 1131-1167, a period during

---

68 Nos.334, 335, 341, 355, 357, 360, 367, 370.
69 Nos.322, 323, 335, 341, 345, 355, 359, 360, 371.
70 Nos.335, 355, 359, 360, 363, 366, 367 and probably no.341 if Godfrey is identifiable with Godfrey of Marcle (on which see pp. cviii-cix below).
71 Nos. 322, 341, 359.

which there was no real attempt at standardization and when, although most episcopal acta were probably drafted by episcopal clerks,
a significant proportion of acta were composed by beneficiaries, and
finally those of 1174-1234, in which we see a clearly evolving episcopal
writing office.

1079-1127

Acta survive from all the five pontificates between 1079 and 1127, but
only in tiny numbers. There are professions of obedience made by
Robert of Lotharingia, Gerard, Reinhelm and Geoffrey de Clive
(nos.1, 3, 6, and 9): all of these are beyond doubt Canterbury products.[1] In addition there survive Robert of Lotharingia's charter of
1085 enfeoffing Roger de Lacy with the manor of Holme Lacy (no.2),
two spurious charters, one forged by Gloucester Abbey and purporting to be issued by Gerard (no.4) and the other probably forged by
Gloucester Abbey and purporting to be issued by Reinhelm (no.7),
two charters of Richard de Capella, one of which may have been
reworked (nos.10 and 11), and finally references to three charters now
missing issued by Gerard, Reinhelm and Richard (nos.5, 8 and 12).
Robert of Lotharingia's 1085 charter, which survives in the original,
is a chirograph written in a book hand, and lacks any trace of sealing
arrangements. The surviving half of the chirograph is presumably the
part that was kept by Roger de Lacy, since it survived in the archives
of the Scudamores, who were lords of Holme Lacy in early modern
times. It has a twelfth-century endorsement which states that the
other half of the chirograph was kept by Gloucester Abbey; perhaps
they acquired it when St Peter's, Hereford, acquired the church of
Holme Lacy.[2] The fact that Robert of Lotharingia and his successors
seem not to have tried to keep one half for themselves is puzzling and
suggests that they felt no interest in keeping an archive. If we discount

---

1 Canterbury professions, p.lxxv. The 'original' of Gerard's profession is a copy made at
Canterbury c.1200 (ibid., 35, quoting N.R.Ker, *English manuscripts in the century after the
Norman conquest* [Oxford 1960], 18) but early copies survive as well: see ibid., 17, and list of
fontes to no.3.
2 Cf. no.7; the charter is spurious, but Holme Lacy church was in the control of St Guthlac's
priory, the successor to St Peter's, by the time of Robert de Béthune. V.H.Galbraith, however,
thought that the Scudamore exemplar of no.2 had originally been in the possession of the bishops
of Hereford and that the de Lacy family had put their exemplar in the charge of Gloucester
abbey for safe keeping ('An episcopal landgrant', 353).

certain early charters which originally belonged to Gloucester but which were transferred to Hereford in the eighteenth century, the earliest surviving document in the Hereford Dean and Chapter Muniments is no.1095, a charter issued by the chapter in 1132. The bishops of Hereford themselves did not start to keep an archive until later: first under Gilbert Foliot, though this seems to have been more in the nature of a personal archive, which he took with him to London when he was translated,[3] and then not until the following century.[4] Robert of Lotharingia's charter is written in the third person and is not in the form of a letter, but begins, after a pictorial invocation, with the words 'Hoc privilegium Rotbertus Herefordensis aecclesiae episcopus ... notari precepit'. There follow the descriptions of two agreements, each concerning a separate piece of land, with a separate witness list for each; the first witness list is preceded by the date. Among the witnesses are eight members of Hereford cathedral community and four clerks of Roger de Lacy, but there is no way of knowing who was responsible for drafting and writing the charter.

The charter for Gloucester purporting to have been issued by Gerard (no.4) is a licence of appropriation dated 1100. Every feature of this document is suspect. Not only are licences of appropriation an anachronism for the turn of the eleventh and twelfth centuries, but one of the churches mentioned in the charter is known not to have been granted to Gloucester until upward of thirty years later. The text of Gerard's charter survives only in a cartulary copy of an inspeximus issued by Bishop Hugh Foliot, who states that the original of Gerard's charter had been burnt in 1122 and that what he was inspecting was a copy sealed by Bishop Simon of Worcester (1125-1150), but in fact the internal features of the charter, especially the use of the first person plural and the placing of the address before the name and title, suggest that the charter could not be earlier than the second half of the twelfth century. The form of the greeting is practically the same as that used by Hugh Foliot himself in his inspeximus, no.330. The address contains the phrase 'hanc nostram cartam inspecturis vel audituris' which is not found elsewhere in Hereford acta in the period up to 1234

---

3 *GFL*, 8.

4 Giles de Braose's charter for Walter of Goosebrook (no.285) survives in the muniments of the episcopal estates, but may have been acquired by the bishops later. Otherwise there is no evidence of an archive until the first episcopal register for Hereford, that of Thomas de Cantilupe: see D.M.Smith, *Guide to bishops' registers of England and Wales* (London 1981), 95.

(the preferred phrase at Hereford in the early thirteenth century was 'to whom this present writing [or charter] may come'). We may presume that this charter was composed at Gloucester, which had been actively engaged in forgery in the middle of the twelfth century,[5] and which had perhaps not lost its knack or initiative.

Another likely product of Gloucester Abbey forgers is the charter purporting to have been issued by Bishop Reinhelm (1107-1115) for Gloucester Abbey and the prior of Hereford (no.7). This charter confirms grants of churches by Hugh de Lacy to Gloucester Abbey and in addition gives the monks the right to appoint and remove the vicars of these churches at will. This clause, almost certainly an anachronism in the 1110s,[6] was probably the main aim of making the forgery. The charter, in the form of a letter, is likely to be a forgery because of its consistent use of the first person plural. Its greeting 'salutem et benedictionem', and the words 'Inde est quod' opening the notification show papal influence, and would accord better with a mid-twelfth century date of composition.

One of Richard de Capella's two surviving charters is a confirmation of the extent of the parish of Leominster issued in 1123 for Reading (no.11). Though not written in the form of a letter, it is in the first person, in a mixture of the first person singular and plural, and opens with the dispositive clause: 'Ego dei gratia Herford' episcopus Ricardus manu propria mea concessi et confirmavi ...'. It ends with a statement that the extent of the parish had been attested by aged and trustworthy men, and then an additional clause of confirmation by the bishop, this time in the first person plural, and then the date. The charter is similar in form, and almost identical in its opening words, to one issued by Archbishop William of Canterbury for Reading between 1123 and 1130,[7] which is also in the first person singular with a switch to the plural at the end, and the two were presumably drafted by the beneficiaries. The other surviving charter of Richard is written in letter form and is consistently in the first person plural (no.10). This makes it probable that this charter, which notifies that Richard has dedicated the church of St Owen's, Gloucester, and

5 C.N.L.Brooke, 'St Peter of Gloucester and St Cadoc of Llancarfan' in idem, *The church and the Welsh border in the central middle ages* (Woodbridge 1986), 59-65; A.Morey and C.N.L.Brooke, *Gilbert Foliot and his letters* (Cambridge 1965), 124-146.
6 See note to no.7.
7 Printed by A.Saltman, *Theobald, archbishop of Canterbury* (London 1956), 438-9, and cal. in *Reading cartularies*, i.144, no.174.

which has at least a genuine basis,[8] was rewritten a little later in the twelfth century. One feature of the original, however, may well have been left unaltered: the anathema, rare in Hereford acta of a later date.

1131-1167

The distinguishing feature of Hereford episcopal diplomatic in this period (as in other dioceses) is its extreme variety of phraseology. Furthermore, the proportion of charters composed by beneficiaries, though these form only a minority of the output, is much higher than in the late twelfth century, and it would be useful to analyse these before we turn to the question of stylistic developments among the bishops' own clerks.

Working out how many of Robert de Béthune's charters were drafted by beneficiaries should on the face of things be easy to determine, since Robert issued relatively large groups of charters for relatively few individual houses: five for Gloucester abbey, together with seven for Gloucester's dependency, the priory in Hereford, four for Leominster priory, ten for Llanthony priory, five for Shrewsbury abbey and three for Monmouth priory, as well as scattered acta for Worcester, Tintern and other places. In fact, the wide variety of vocabulary and terminology used makes the task impossible in most cases, especially given that there are only four surviving originals, even though three of these are for one single beneficiary (Monmouth priory). Evidence of composition on the part of the beneficiary is, however, clear for Gloucester abbey and Monmouth priory. At least three of the Gloucester charters (nos.16, 18, and 20) and very probably four of the St Guthlac's charters (nos.21, 22, 25, and 27) seem to have been drafted by one person not otherwise involved in the writing of Robert's acta. One of his distinguishing features is the use of the phrase 'per manum meam' in charters confirming the grant of churches (nos.16, 20, 25, 27). Martin Brett has pointed out that the use of this formula derives from advice from Paschal II to Anselm of Canterbury in 1102 to the effect that abbots should not receive parish churches directly from the hands of lay benefactors but from the hand of the bishop.[9] This formula is not to be found in Robert's confirma-

8 See note to no.10.
9 M.Brett, *The English church under Henry I* (Oxford 1975), 141-3.

tions of grants of churches to other religious houses (though no.46 for Monmouth has 'in manu mea'), but does occur in another episcopal charter for Gloucester, one issued by Bishop Simon of Worcester.[10] Other features of Simon's charter – the address and the corroboration – show that it was drafted by the same clerk, employed by Gloucester, who was responsible for Robert's acta. Another distinguishing feature of the Gloucester draftsman is his use of a corroboration – only twelve of Robert's charters have this (nos. 15-17, 22, 25-7, 36, 45, 47, 52 and 53) and all but five of them are for Gloucester or its dependency. Two of the Gloucester acta are addressed to Hereford's dean and chapter and one to the archdeacon, dean and ministers of the church of Hereford (nos.18, 20, 16); six of the others have addresses standard elsewhere in twelfth-century English episcopal acta but not otherwise found in Robert de Béthune's acta: 'omnibus (or universis) sancte matris ecclesie filiis' (nos.22, 23, 24, 25, 26, 27). Nos. 18 and 20 share the same greeting, not otherwise used by Robert: 'salutem et Dei ac (or et) suam benedictionem'.

Two out of Robert's three charters for Monmouth are in the same hand and were probably issued at the same time (nos.45, 47); no.46, also an original, is in a different hand. Both no.45 and no.47, unusually among Robert's acta, display a consistent use of the first person plural; both have arengae and corroborations, and both have anathemas with almost exactly similar wording. The only inconsistency between them is the use of the spelling *Monemuda* for Monmouth in no.47 and *Munemutha* in no.45. It is overwhelmingly likely that they were prepared by the beneficiary.

For the rest (apart from the letter to Eugenius III, presumably drafted by Canterbury personnel)[11] it is hard to tell whether Robert's *acta* were drafted by his own clerks, those of his beneficiaries, or clerks from other churches who merely happened to be present at the ecclesiastical gatherings at which so many of Robert's charters were issued.[12] He certainly had clerks of his own to cope with his personal correspondence and those acta dealing with individual parish churches such as Kyte Hardwick and Tenbury. These clerks cannot, however, have aimed at a consistent style. Somewhat surprisingly,

10 *Gloucester cartulary* i.247, quoted by M.Brett, *The English church under Henry I* (Oxford 1975), 43.
11 Cf. note to no.14.
12 See p.lii above.

given that several of Robert's clerks were canons of Llanthony, the many charters which he issued on Llanthony's behalf do not form a consistent group.

Gilbert Foliot's clerks were responsible for drafting the great majority of his acta, and we shall look at the distinguishing features of their style shortly. Just as Robert de Béthune's loyalty to Llanthony did not extend to allowing the priory to draft his charters, Gilbert, too, employed his own clerks in the charters which he issued for his old house. Stray charters for Lire (no.101 [*GFL* no.331]), Leominster (99 [*GFL* no.341]), Brecon (61 [*GFL* no.290]) and Monmouth (106 [*GFL* no.333]) are not in letter form – that is, they lack *intitulationes*, addresses and greetings – and might perhaps have been the work of the beneficiaries, or, particularly in the case of the Brecon charter, which is rather clumsily written, hastily put together by some local clerk. Drafting on the part of the beneficiary can be more clearly detected in a group of Gilbert's charters concerning Leominster (nos.95 [*GFL* no.335], 96 [*GFL* no.336], 100 [*GFL* no.334], and 108 [*GFL* no.338]). Unlike nos.94, 97 [*GFL* no.337], 110 [*GFL* no.339], 109 [*GFL* no.342], and 111 [*GFL* no.343], which also concern Leominster, or, in the case of 110, its mother house Reading, this group has addresses which do not contain the word 'dilectis' (much favoured by Gilbert's clerks), and are written in the first person singular.[13] Furthermore, nos.95, 96, 100, and 108 do not contain corroborations, although the overwhelming majority of Gilbert's acta do. In the case of no.111 (GFL no.343), Gilbert's scribes followed the wording of the disposition of a charter of Richard de Capella, to which, however, they added their own protocol and corroboration. We can also see this process in two charters of Robert de Melun, no.121 for Llanthony, which is based on several charters of Robert de Béthune and Gilbert Foliot,[14] and no.123 for Master Ranulf fitz Erchemar, based on a charter of Gilbert Foliot (no.107 [*GFL* no.311]).

Even by the 1130s the basic form of a document notifying a transaction or ordering subordinates to perform a duty was not fixed. The underlying trend was to compose episcopal charters in the form of a letter, with name of issuer, an address and a greeting. Sometimes this

---

13 The address of no.98 (*GFL* no.340) has been omitted by the copyist of the Leominster cartulary, but the charter is in the first person plural and so does not appear to be the work of the draftsman of nos.95, 96, 100 and 108.
14 Nos.35, 36, 37 and 103 (*GFL* no.328) and 104 (*GFL* no.329).

could lead to the production of charters which are not far removed from personal letters. When Robert de Béthune tried to win back the church of Henlow in the diocese of Lincoln for Llanthony priory, instead of issuing a confirmation of the original transaction in formal and legal terms he wrote a series of four letters to Bishop Alexander of Lincoln and his subordinates: stylistically these are clearly personal letters rather than charters.[15] On the other hand, several of Robert de Béthune's and Gilbert Foliot's charters are not written in the form of a letter, with an address and a greeting, but open simply with the notification.[16] Nor, in this period, is there consistency in the use of the first person singular or plural to denote the bishop, although under Gilbert Foliot there is a marked increase in the popularity of the latter. *Ego* occurs in over half Robert de Béthune's acta, *nos* in nine, and a mixture of *ego* and *nos* in eight, while two charters are entirely in the third person. About one quarter of Gilbert's acta use the first person singular, and only one (no.96 [GFL 336]) uses a mixture. Even as late as the episcopate of Robert de Melun the first person singular makes an appearance (no.123).

INTITULATIO

In the period 1131-1167 it was extremely uncommon for bishops' surnames (whether toponymics or patronymics) to be mentioned in their charters, and Robert de Béthune, Gilbert Foliot and Robert de Melun are always simply Robert, Gilbert, or R. or G., though with slight variations of spelling (Robert de Béthune is referred to once as Rogerus, but this is obviously a copyist's error). In originals Robert de Béthune is Rotbertus in nos.45 and 46 and Robertus in nos.14 and 47, while Gilbert is abbreviated to G. in nos.85 (*GFL* no.316), 107 (*GFL* no.311) and 110 (*GFL* no.339); nos.59 (*GFL* no.289) and 64 (*GFL* no.293), in which he occurs as Gilebertus and Gill', were definitely not the work of Gilbert's own clerks. No original of Robert de Melun survives. The three bishops styled themselves in a variety of ways, but the devotional formula was almost invariably *dei gratia*. This is often omitted under Gilbert Foliot,[17] but is always used by

15 Nos.39-42.
16 Nos.15, 19, 30, 75 (*GFL* no.303), 78 (*GFL* no.306), 81 (*GFL* no.310), 116 (*GFL* no.312), 91 (*GFL* no.317), 99 (*GFL* no.341), 101 (*GFL* no.331), 106 (*GFL* no.333) and 117 (*GFL* no.348). No.17 begins with the date.
17 Nos.60, 62, 64, 65, 66, 67, 70, 75, 76, 77, 82, 101, 105, 110, 113, 114.

Robert de Béthune and Robert de Melun. In one instance *divina miseratione* occurs in a charter of Gilbert,[18] but this is almost certainly a lapse on the part of the scribe of the Shrewsbury cartulary, who appears to have used the common formula of a later generation. The most popular style for all three bishops was *dei gratia Herefordensis episcopus*, which occurs, sometimes with slight variations in word order, twenty-eight times in Robert de Béthune's acta, thirty-six times under Gilbert and twice (out of four surviving acta) under Robert de Melun; forms with *dei gratia Herefordensis ecclesie episcopus* are much rarer. Styles containing terms such as *minister* or *minister humilis*, already common in letters in this period, but which were only to become the norm in episcopal charters by the end of the century, occur in ten of Robert de Béthune's acta, twelve of Gilbert's, and two of Robert de Melun's.[19] They seem not to have appeared in Robert de Béthune's acta before the 1140s, and then mostly in acta drafted outside Robert's own household.[20]

INSCRIPTIO

Here we see a very wide variation in form, with over sixty different addresses used, only twelve of them more than once. This is mainly due to the fact that charters such as confirmations which later in the century would have had a general address are much more likely to have a personal address. Robert de Béthune's charters of confirmation are sometimes addressed to a fellow bishop where the property or the beneficiary concerned is in a different diocese (nos.36, 39-42, 58); where the property is in the diocese of Hereford his charters are often addressed to his subordinates, an archdeacon or the dean and chapter of the cathedral in addition to the faithful.[21] Robert issued no charters for his cathedral chapter: the reason for addressing them was that if necessity required they would have to act as episcopal officials to uphold the terms of the grant. Occasionally he addressed the beneficiaries themselves.[22] Both Robert de Béthune and Gilbert addressed

18 No.112 (*GFL* no.344) and see note.
19 Cf. *EEA*, ii, p.liv on Thomas and Theobald's titles. It was Thomas' frequent use of *minister humilis* in charters which led to its general popularity in late twelfth century episcopal *acta*.
20 Nos.14, 22, 24, 34, 45, 46, 53 and 54; nos.56 and 58 cannot be dated more closely than the limits of the episcopate.
21 Nos.28, 37, 50, 51, 57, and three charters probably drafted by Gloucester clerks, nos.16, 18 and 20.
22 No.45, drafted by Monmouth; also no.52.

a few of their charters to their successors (nos.44, 47, 107) and Robert de Melun, relying on the texts of no.44 and no.107 to produce his own confirmations, copied them (nos.121, 123). Gilbert's addresses show nearly as much variation as Robert de Béthune's, but he tends to restrict the use of personal addresses to letters and mandates,[23] and adopts a more general address, either to all the faithful, or, very often, to the faithful of the diocese, for example 'dilectis sibi in Domino universis Herefordensis ecclesie parochianis et filiis' (no.83), or 'dilectis sibi in Cristo filiis clero et populo in episcopatu Herford' constitutis' (no.109). The practice of opening the address with the word *dilectis* seems to have been a hallmark of Gilbert's scribes, as we can see in twenty charters for a very wide variety of beneficiaries, and some degree of standardisation can be observed in the occurrence of 'Dilectis sibi in Domino universis sancte matris ecclesie filiis' in six charters.[24] Sometimes the address is more akin to that of a charter issued by a secular magnate 'omnibus hominibus suis tam clericis quam laicis' (no.104), or, even more markedly, in the case of a charter of Robert de Béthune, 'omnibus fidelibus de Herefordesira clericis et laicis, francis et anglicis' (no.55). Addresses of the type standard in episcopal acta of the late twelfth century, 'to all the faithful of Christ' or 'to all the sons of holy mother church', occur in about a quarter of Robert de Béthune's and Gilbert's acta, and in the case of Robert's acta, mostly in charters issued by beneficiaries, notably St Guthlac's priory.[25] Of Robert de Melun's four surviving acta, two have the address 'universis sancte matris ecclesie filiis' (nos.119 and 122).

Even where the address is truly a general one, and not limited to the bishop's flock or his clergy, it almost always follows the *intitulatio*. In only three of Robert de Béthune's acta does it precede the *intitulatio*, in his letter to Eugenius III (naturally enough) (no.14), in one (but only one) of his letters to Bishop Alexander of Lincoln (no.42), and in the charter notifying the union of the churches of St Peter's and St Guthlac's, Hereford (no.21), which, we may safely assume, was a Gloucester product. The address precedes the *intitulatio* in sixteen of Gilbert's charters, including a letter addressed to Eugenius III

---

23 E.g. no.115 (*GFL* no.347); but cf. no.105 (*GFL* no.330), a notification of a grant by a layman to Llanthony priory addressed to the bishop of Worcester, reminiscent of no.36.
24 Nos.60, 69, 71, 73, 79, 83, 86, 87, 93, 94, 97, 102, 109 and 111. *Dilectis sibi in Domino universis sancte matris ecclesie filiis* occurs in nos.67, 70, 82, 110, 113 and 114.
25 Nos.22-27, 34, 36, 46.

(no.66), the notification addressed to Bishop John of Worcester (no.105 [*GFL* no.330]), and all the charters with the address 'Dilectis sibi in Domino universis sancte matris ecclesie filiis'. The address follows the *intitulatio* in all four of the charters which were definitely issued by Robert de Melun, and in two of the four charters which cannot definitely be attributed to either Robert de Melun or Robert Foliot (nos.126 and 128).

SALUTATIO

Four of Robert de Béthune's charters[26] and ten of Gilbert Foliot's[27] lack a greeting. The most popular form of greeting in Robert de Béthune's acta was *salutem*, which occurs twenty-two times, in charters for a wide variety of recipients, though predominantly for Llanthony priory; this form was also fairly popular among Gilbert Foliot's scribes, occurring ten times. Gilbert's scribes, the scribes who drafted acta to be issued by Gilbert for Leominster, and the scribes at Gloucester abbey who drafted acta to be issued by Robert de Béthune had a preference for greetings reflecting papal influence, such as *salutem et benedictionem* (nos.16, 26, 27, 62, 89, 95, 96, 97, 100, 108; and see also 31, 46), *salutem et dei ac suam benedictionem* (nos.18, 20), salutem et gratiam (nos.88, 92), and *salutem, gratiam et benedictionem* (nos.25, 73, 79, 80, 83, 86, 87, 93, 94, 109, 111 and see also no.52). Papal influence is also faintly visible in the greeting used in one of Robert de Melun's charters for Llanthony (no.122); more strongly in the use of the term *imperpetuum* rather than a greeting in his settlement of the dispute between Gloucester and Brecon (no.119). Pious exhortations to follow Christ, rather than greetings in the strictest sense, occur in a few charters of Robert de Béthune and Gilbert: *vivendo monacum imitari et assequi Cristum* (no.45, drafted by Monmouth), *dominum exspectare soliciti et venientem gratulanter amplecti* (no.21, drafted by Gloucester), *a rege qui militant glorie assequi dominum* (no.113), and *introitum et exitum in Cristo felicem* (no.44).

ARENGA

The usual method of opening the main text of twelfth century English episcopal charters was a notification, unadorned by any pious phrase.

26 Nos.15, 17, and 19 for Gloucester abbey and no.30 for Leominster priory.
27 Nos.61, 78, 81, 91, 99, 101, 106, 116 and 117; there was originally a greeting in no.98 but it was omitted by the copyist.

Only at Canterbury was the use of the arenga fairly common, and even there it underwent a marked decline between the pontificates of Theobald and Hubert Walter. In their reluctance to employ arengae English episcopal acta show a divergence from the practice both of the papal curia and also of drafters of twelfth-century episcopal charters in the Empire, where episcopal acta were closely modelled on imperial diplomata and in most cases open with arengae.[28] Arengae occur in only nine of Robert de Béthune's acta, and at least four of these were not drafted by his scribes.[29] Three arengae touch on the fallibility of memory and the need for transactions to be committed to writing (nos.47, 53, 58), and the letter to Eugenius III defending Archbishop Theobald's primacy over Bishop Bernard of St David's says that the truth must always be defended especially where it is most in danger (no.14). In his letter to Abbot Suger Robert says that he is not capable of returning Suger's generosity in kind, but can only thank him (no.54). The other arengae are concerned with the duties enjoined on a bishop through his office: that just as he must punish persecutors of the church so he must also encourage benefactors with his blessing and prayer (no.45); that just as bishops must love religious most, so they must particularly ensure their profit (no.52); that since bishops rejoice in the prosperity and peace of religious they must prevent them from falling into poverty (no.36), and that, since it is a bishop's duty to promote the well-being of the church of God it is right for him to join fragmented parts into a solid whole so that divine

28 A cursory examination of those charters issued by the archbishops of Mainz published in *Mainzer Urkundenbuch*, ed. M.Stimming and P.Acht, 2 vols. in 3 parts (Darmstadt 1932-71) (the majority) shows that well over half the twelfth century archiepiscopal acta employ arengae; of the charters issued by twelfth century archbishops of Cologne published by T.Lacomblet, ed. *Urkundenbuch für die Geschichte des Niederrheins*, 4 vols. (Düsseldorf 1840-1856), vol. i, admittedly by no means a complete collection of Cologne archiepiscopal charters, the great majority throughout the period have arengae; M.Parisse, 'Les chartes des évêques de Metz au XIIe siècle', *Archiv für Diplomatik* 22 (1976), 286, states that most 12th century Metz episcopal charters have arengae. P.Johanek, *Die Frühzeit der Siegelurkunde im Bistum Würzburg*, Quellen und Forschungen zur Geschichte des Bistums und Hochstifts Würzburg, 20 (Würzburg 1969) does not give totals of arengae used at Würzburg in the twelfth century but points to an increase after the middle of the century (284-5), and gives many examples of arengae; in general on types of arengae see H.Fichtenau, *Arenga* (MIÖG, Ergänzungsband 18, Vienna 1957). By contrast to the favour shown to the arenga in the Empire, A.Gandilhon, *Catalogue des actes des archevêques de Bourges antérieurs à l'an 1200* (Bourges and Paris 1927), pp.cxviii, cxliii, clvi shows a steady decline in the use of the arenga during the twelfth century in the charters issued by archbishops of Bourges.

29 Nos.14, 21, 45 and 47 were not drafted by episcopal scribes; nos.21 and 47 show use of the cursus, planus and velox in no.21 and planus in no.47. Arengae also occur in nos.36, 52, 53, 54 and 58.

service can be increased (no.21). The last-mentioned, which occurs, suitably enough, in the charter uniting the churches of St Peter and St Guthlac in Hereford, is somewhat clumsily expressed in two separate clauses.

Arengae occur in a similar proportion of Gilbert's acta – about one fifth (twelve in all), but a conscious restriction of the use of arengae to particular types of document is visible. Most of the arengae in Gilbert's charters occur in notifications of settlements or notifications of grants in which there is some possible future danger of disruption, and thus the most common type of arenga is the one stressing the need to commit agreements or transactions to writing[30] or at least to memory (no.105 [GFL 330]); the arenga in one composition says that it is Gilbert's duty to ensure that the dispute is not reopened, and does not mention the need to write things down (no.93 [GFL 326]). By contrast, no.82 mentions seals as well as writing. In a similar vein, the arenga in no.90 (GFL 324), the notification of a grant to St Guthlac's, says that grants by the faithful must be preserved with the authority of witnesses and the protection of charters. A composition concerning Reading abbey says that it is the bishop's duty to settle disputes (no.109 [GFL 342]).[31] Somewhat more unusual is the arenga in the indulgence which Gilbert issued for Reading, which describes the great dignity accorded to the apostles before proceeding to more specific praise of St James as the brother of John the apostle (no.110 [GFL 339]). Eight of Gilbert's arengae display the use of the cursus, equally divided between the planus and the velox.[32]

Only one of Robert de Melun's charters contains an arenga: no.121, a general confirmation for Llanthony. It states that reflecting on the episcopal office warns him to confirm the acts of his predecessors: 'Officii nostri consideratio nos admonet ea que a decessoribus nostris utiliter statuta sunt intuitu caritatis et pacis roborare'.

---

30 Nos.65 (*GFL* no.294), 73 (*GFL* no.302), no.82 (*GFL* no.314), no.89 (*GFL* no.323), no.113 (*GFL* no.345), no.114 (*GFL* no.346) and no.64 (*GFL* no.293), though the last was issued jointly with other bishops and was probably not the work of Gilbert's clerks.

31 Cf. also the stress on episcopal duty in no.113 (*GFL* no.345).

32 The cursus planus occurs in nos.65 (*GFL* no.294), 73 (*GFL* no.302), 82 (*GFL* no.314), 110 (*GFL* no.339); the cursus velox occurs in nos.89 (*GFL* no.323), 93 (*GFL* no.326), 105 (*GFL* no.330) and the jointly issued no.64 (*GFL* no.293).

NARRATIO

Narrationes or specific preambles occur only rarely in the charters of Robert de Béthune and Gilbert, in about ten of Robert's and five of Gilbert's.[33] Although the usual literary purpose of a *narratio* is to act as a buffer between the arenga and the disposition by focusing the reader's attention (once it has been arrested by the arenga) on the specific circumstances of the case, few of Robert and Gilbert's *arengae* are followed by *narrationes* (nos.14, 21, 36, 52, 82, 90). Where this happens the *narrationes* often open with words favoured by papal clerks such as 'Quoniam', 'Unde', 'Inde est' and 'Eapropter'. Most of the *narrationes* are, however, free-standing, though in the case of no.32, in which Robert notifies that he has dedicated altars at Leominster and grants an indulgence to benefactors of the priory, the *narratio*, which takes the form of a statement that Robert has dedicated the altars, follows a prayer: 'precor vobis omnibus et in Domino Iesu Cristo exhortor, cuius sanguine redempti estis, ut diligatis ecclesiam beati Petri de Leom'...'. Robert de Melun's general confirmation for Llanthony (no.121) does not have a *narratio*, properly speaking, but introduces the disposition with the words 'Inde est quod'.

NOTIFICATIO

Notifications occur in all but twelve of Robert de Béthune's acta and all but thirteen of Gilbert Foliot's;[34] charters with arengae and/or *narrationes* tend not to have notifications as well, though there are exceptions.[35] Several acta have no protocol and begin simply with a notification.[36] Practically no form of notification is used more than once by any bishop, apart from 'Noverit dilectio vestra' (nos.22, 24, 34, 51, 70, 79, 86, 88), usually followed by oratio obliqua, 'Noverit itaque dilectio vestra' (nos.96, 114), 'Noverit universitatis vestre discretio' (nos.119, 123), 'Sciant presentes et futuri' (nos.96, 99), 'Sciatis' (nos.74, 85 and also 33), and, in three of the charters composed for Robert de Béthune by Gloucester abbey, 'Noverit sancta fraternitas vestra' (nos.16, 18, 20). Although the variation in form is considerable, it is accomplished within the limits of a narrow choice of

---

33 Nos.14, 21, 32, 36, 39, 40, 50, 52, 57 and nos.71 (*GFL* no.300), 76 (*GFL* no.304), 82 (*GFL* no.314), 87 (*GFL* no.321), and 90 (*GFL* no.324).
34 Nos.14, 17, 21, 32, 36, 39, 45, 47, 50, 52-4, 71, 73, 76, 82, 87, 89, 90, 94, 97, 110, 111, 113 and 115.
35 Nos.40, 47, 53, 58, 64, 65, 105, 109 and 114.
36 See p.lxxi, n.16 above.

vocabulary, and in the great majority of cases some part of the verb *nosco* is employed; *scire* and *significare* are much less common.

DISPOSITIO / INIUNCTIO

The dispositive clauses in Robert de Béthune's acta are usually expressed very simply; sometimes, where the charters confirm grants made by other people, there is no attempt to phrase the sentence so that the bishop is the subject of the verb in the indicative (nos.38, 30, 33, 49), and even where this is the case the charters are still mostly records of transactions (*Beweisurkunden*) rather than themselves having dispositive force (*Geschäftsurkunden*). The actual transaction was performed by means of a symbolic gesture, as we see specifically in, for example, no.27, where the donor places his hand on a book on an altar.[37] Exceptions to this rule are the grants of permission to Gloucester and St Guthlac's to move vicars into or out of parish churches at will (nos.16, 20, 26), and an indulgence issued to benefactors of Leominster priory: 'Ego quoque ... relaxo omnibus ... de iniuncta penitentia dies xx' (no.32). Often the disposition is not clearly differentiated from the *narratio*; this is particularly true of the letters written to Bishop Alexander of Lincoln in the Henlow case (nos.39-42). The only surviving institution (no.15) is expressed in a forward-looking form, rather than as a grant of a church, feudal-fashion, to a priest: 'ego Robertus ... suscepi Stephanum presbiterum in vicariam ... et eidem curam animarum ... commisi'. Injunctions are uncommon. One is tacked on to the disposition as a series of participles (no.37); two are almost in the form of a corroboration ('Hec autem donatio a me facta volo, confirmo, et precipio dei auctoritate et nostra ut firma et inconcussa ... permaneat'.[38] One injunction, in a charter issued for, and probably drafted by, the abbey of Lire in Normandy, is expressed in the form which was becoming standard in episcopal acta of the twelfth century: 'Quare volo et episcopali auctoritate precipio...' (no.34).

---

37 Cf. the somewhat similar process in no.46.
38 No.18 and cf. also no.58.

The great majority of Gilbert's acta, too, are *Beweisurkunden*, and again the bishop is not always the subject of the dispositive clause,[39] especially not in compositions, which usually run along the lines of 'controversiam, que ... diu agitata est, in presentia nostra hoc tandem fine conquievisse'.[40] No.78 (*GFL* no.306), a licence to Gloucester abbey to appropriate churches, contains a clause in which Gilbert allows the abbey to install and remove vicars at will and therefore is effectively a *Geschäftsurkunde*, as are Gilbert's three indulgences.[41] Gilbert issued only three institutions, nos.75-77 (*GFL*, nos.303-5), all for Gloucester abbey; all three charters are in effect licences to Gloucester to appropriate. No standard phrase is used for the act of institution; however, the verb *impersonare* occurs in nos.76 and 77. Injunctions occur in six of Gilbert's acta;[42] only one of these refers to episcopal authority (no.67 [*GFL*, no.296]).

The dispositions in Robert de Melun's acta make the bishop the subject, except no.119, which notifies the settlement of a dispute. No.121, for Llanthony, with its dispositive verbs in the present tense, is more or less a *Geschäftsurkunde*. None of the charters definitely ascribable to Robert de Melun contains an injunction, though two of the charters possibly ascribable to him do: 'Volumus etiam et firmiter precipimus' (no.126) and 'Quod vero ratum et stabile episcopali auctoritate imperpetuum esse precipimus' (no.128). The latter is clearly a cross between an injunction and a corroboration.

SANCTIO

Sanctions occur in only five of Robert de Béthune's acta (nos.21, 29, 35, 45, 47), two of which were drafted by Monmouth (nos.45, 47) and one by Gloucester (no.21) for the union of the churches of St Peter and St Guthlac in Hereford. This last is a *sanctio positiva* with an *apprecatio*, a single *Amen*. The *sanctio* in no.29 notifying the consecration of the cemetery at Kyte Hardwick is purely negative, and

---

39 Nos.69 (*GFL* no.298), 100 (*GFL* no.334), 103 (*GFL* no.328), 105 (*GFL* no.330) and 108 (*GFL* no.338).
40 No.79 (*GFL* no.307); cf. also nos.65 (*GFL* no.294), 70 (*GFL* no.299), 83 (*GFL* no.313), 88 (*GFL* no.322), 93 (*GFL* no.326), 99 (*GFL* no.341), 102 (*GFL* no.327) and 109 (*GFL* no.342).
41 Nos.69 (*GFL* no.298), 98 (*GFL* no.340) and 110 (*GFL* no.339). No.99 (*GFL* no.341) for Leominster, which says that in the future the priory may install and remove priests at will, is a *Beweisurkunde*.
42 Nos.67 (*GFL* no.296), 72 (*GFL* no.301), 75 (*GFL* no.303), 85 (*GFL* no.316), 110 (*GFL* no.339) and 115 (*GFL* no.347).

shows papal influence: 'Si quis ergo huic eius donationi et nostre confirmationi contraire presumpserit, nisi commonitus resipiscat, dei et nostram maledictionem incurrat'. The sanctions in nos.35, 45, and 47 are both negative and positive, and those in nos.45 and 47 have very similar wording, as follows:

no.45	no.47
Si quis autem hec violare quod absit *attentaverit, eum*	*Si quis autem* hanc nostram confirmationem cassare aut infringere *attentaverit, divino*
examini *iudicii divini* *relinquimus. Conservatores* autem et defensores huiuscemodi facti *dei et nostra* *benedictione* salutamus.	*iudicio eum relinquimus.* *Conservantibus* vero *benedictio dei* *et nostra* concedatur.

Sanctions are even rarer in the acta of Gilbert Foliot.[43] No.77 (*GFL*, no.305), a confirmation of a grant by Bernard of Neufmarché to Gloucester abbey, contains, built into the corroboration, a statement that the bishop has excommunicated all those who may in the future disrupt the terms of the grant. Only one of Robert de Melun's charters (no.122, for Llanthony) has a sanction, both positive and negative; this, like the sanction in no.106, follows the witness list.

CORROBORATIO

The corroboration is rare in Robert de Béthune's acta and occurs mostly in charters issued by the beneficiary, especially Gloucester abbey (nos.15-17, 22, 25-7) and Monmouth priory.[44] Five of the corroborations in charters for Gloucester and St Guthlac's end with the phrase 'sigilli mei impressione (*or* attestatione, *or* auctoritate) confirmo', showing the use of the cursus planus (nos.15, 16, 22, 25 and 27), and two of these corroborations have exactly identical wording (nos.25, 27). The *cursus* was also used in the corroboration in one of the Monmouth charters, here the *cursus tardus*: 'Hanc igitur nostram donationem et pretexati Rotberti cum libero assensu concessionem episcopali auctoritate firmantes, ratam haberi et inviolatam permanere decernimus'. One of the charters for Shrewsbury abbey has a

---

43 Nos.69 (*GFL* no.298) and 73 (*GFL* no.303); also 106 (*GFL* no.333) for Monmouth, following the witness list, and no.106A (*GFL* no.332), a confirmatory clause for Monmouth.
44 Nos.45 and 47; also in nos.36 for Leominster and 52 and 53 for Shrewsbury.

corroboration showing use of the *cursus velox* (no.52): '...et sigilli munimine fecimus roborari'; the other builds the entire witness list into the corroboration (no.53).

Corroborations occur in the overwhelming majority of Gilbert Foliot's acta, with the exception of the group of charters for Leominster discussed above, which were probably drafted by the beneficiary. Adrian Morey and C.N.L.Brooke have emphasized the care taken by Gilbert's clerks over the wording of corroborations.[45] Most of Gilbert's corroborations mention the bishop's seal, and a minority, though quite a sizeable minority (about a quarter), show the use of the *cursus*, almost always the *planus* or the *tardus*. The *velox* is used in no.72 (*GFL* no.301) and also no.112 (*GFL*, no.344): 'presenti scripto et sigilli nostri testimonio confirmamus'. Mostly, however, when Gilbert's clerks ended the corroboration with the verb *confirmamus*, as they often did, they made no effort to fit it into the rhythm of the *cursus*, perhaps because it can only be used in the *velox*, which they seem to have disliked. Three of Robert de Melun's acta have corroborations. All mention the bishop's seal, and one (no.119) his authority as papal judge delegate. No.121 ends with the *cursus velox* '...testium confirmamus' and no.122 with the *tardus* '...roborari precepimus'.

ESCHATOCOL

No attempt was made to establish a fixed form for the eschatocol in the charters of Robert de Béthune. Most charters contain, but do not invariably end with, a witness list; in no.21, for example, the witness list is in the middle of the charter, and it ends with an *apprecatio*. The witness list is usually introduced with 'Hiis testibus' or 'Testibus', though eleven charters have their own individual forms, such as 'coram testibus' (no.38). Six of the charters lacking witness lists end with a farewell. Ten charters contain neither witness lists nor farewells, though one of these ends with a date (no.36). Dates are more common in Robert's acta than they were to be in those of any of his successors up to the episcopate of Hugh Foliot. There is no consistency in the position of the date in the charter (no.17 actually opens with the date), and not much in the form of dating. The date in no.36 is according to regnal year, the date in nos.17, 27, 33, 47 and 55 is according to the Incarnation, with the day also being supplied in

45 *GFL*, 25.

no.27, and the transaction in no.30 is simply described as 'Acta sunt hec in synodo Herford'. Specific references to synods, both in the dating or in the witness list, occur in three of Robert's charters, all of which were issued in the first years of the episcopate (nos.30, 33, 55); the witness lists of later charters make it clear that Robert had a preference for issuing documents in large ecclesiastical gatherings, but these usually seem from the names of those attending to have been convened on an *ad hoc* basis.[46]

Just over a third of Gilbert's charters have witness lists, most commonly introduced with 'H(i)is testibus', though there is a wide variety of forms, for example 'Teste tota sancta sinodo mea' (no.75 [*GFL*, no.303]), or 'Huius etiam donationis sunt testes' (no.106 [*GFL*, no.333]). Another twelve charters end with farewells, usually *Valete*. Gilbert's letter to Eugenius (no.66 [*GFL*, no.295]) contains a more elaborate farewell: 'Incolumitatem vestram ecclesie sue diu profuturam in longa tempora conservet omnipotens Deus'. Many of Gilbert's charters have no real eschatocol and end simply with the corroboration, though in several of these cases the ending has presumably been omitted by the scribe of a cartulary; the scribes of the cartularies of Leominster priory and Gloucester abbey were particularly prone to do this. Of Robert de Melun's charters, no.119 has no witness list and ends with the date according to the Incarnation and year of his episcopate, nos.121 and 123 end with witness lists, and no.122 has a witness list followed by a *sanctio*.

1174-1234

After the long vacancy which followed the death of Robert de Melun, several changes took place in the form of Hereford episcopal acta. Some of these had already begun to take shape under Gilbert Foliot and Robert de Melun, but the accession of Robert Foliot marks a definitive change, a move towards a more consistent style and the development of a variety of fixed formulae, especially in the disposition, which eventually allowed the development of different types of document.

Only one forgery is discernible in this period, no.155, purportedly issued by Robert Foliot, an attempt by St Guthlac's priory, Hereford,

---

46 See p.lii, n.8 above.

to re-establish control over its ancient Saxon parish. Only one of the charters shows clear signs of having been drafted by the beneficiary, a charter of Robert Foliot for Llanthony notifying a composition between Llanthony and a member of Robert's household (no.172). The composition was made in the chapter at Llanthony in Robert's absence, and the form of the address, the placing of it after the intitulatio, and the form of the notification all differ from those normally preferred by Robert's clerks; it may, however, have been drafted by a scribe called in for the occasion. There are some examples of beneficiaries, Llanthony and Leominster in particular, presenting charters issued by previous bishops to form the basis of new ones (nos.166, 168, 225, 269, 276, 303). In the case of Llanthony this may have been because some of the grants being confirmed had originally been made by Robert de Béthune from the episcopal estates, which possibly made the Llanthony canons anxious to have these properties confirmed to them by each succeeding bishop. Leominster needed mandates with which to threaten its parishioners and vicars in case of failure to pay tithes, and these had to be issued by the current bishop. Otherwise, the practice of using old charters to form the basis of the wording of new ones was beginning to be superseded by the charter of inspeximus, the verbatim quotation of an old charter within a new one. This was already being experimented with by Robert Foliot and William de Vere and it became common under Giles de Braose. The need for beneficiaries to prepare charters had vanished since the bishops would now ensure, when they were moving round the diocese, that at least one of the clerks in their entourage was capable of drafting documents: a group of three charters issued for Shrewsbury abbey concerning the grant of a parish church and an institution were all evidently drafted by the same clerk (nos.233-235), possibly either Master Robert Folet or Reginald Foliot, both of whom occur in the witness list to no.235.[47]

Naturally, this did not mean that all charters issued in the name of the Hereford bishops in this period were the products of their own writing office. Certain charters of William and Giles (nos.185, 223, 280) differ from the rest in opening with the notification ('Sciant... quod ego'), a feature common in charters issued by laymen. Two of

---

47 The witness list of no.235 suggests a small mobile group of clerks, not a big gathering in Hereford. Nos.233 and 235 survive in the original and were written by the same scribe, possibly a local Shrewsbury one; see p.cvi.

the charters are grants to tenants (nos.223, 280) and the third is a notification by William that he has dedicated a chapel in the diocese of Worcester (no.185): all three could well have been drafted by clerks not in the bishop's employment pressed temporarily into service. Charters issued jointly with other bishops, the mandate issued by Roger of Worcester and Robert Foliot to Bermondsey (no.134), and the letter of safe conduct issued by Seffrid of Chichester and William de Vere for the monks of Christ Church Canterbury (no.183), and two letters written by English bishops to Innocent III in 1205 (no.263) and 1206 (no.264), were almost certainly not drafted by Hereford clerks. The same is also true of the settlement issued by Robert Foliot and Abbot Adam of Evesham in the case concerning Luffield priory, a dependency of Westminster abbey, which ended up being heard in the royal court, quite possibly at Westminster (no.167). The wording of the address '... ad quos iste littere pervenerint' is different from the forms preferred by Robert Foliot's clerks. Most probably the drafting was carried out by a clerk of Henry II or of Westminster abbey. All the professions of obedience made by bishops of Hereford in this period followed the form of wording laid down by Christ Church Canterbury, and most of them are Canterbury products, though it is possible that William de Vere's is a holograph.[48] Two exemplars survive of Giles de Braose's, because he was consecrated at Westminster, to the great annoyance of the monks of Canterbury: one of the exemplars was probably written by a Westminster scribe (no.243). No profession of obedience seems to have been made by Hugh Foliot.

Apart from the forgery, thirty-seven charters of Robert Foliot survive, though the total is probably thirty-eight, since no.125 should probably be attributed to him. Eleven of these survive in the original (including the profession of obedience); in addition there are references to a further eight now lost. Fifty-four charters, fourteen of them in the original, and his profession of obedience, also in the original, survive for William, with mentions of a further nine. Of the original acta, one survives in two exemplars (no.187), and another two originals, which concern the grant of land to William's steward (nos.179, 180), have almost exactly the same wording in the disposition and differ only in minor particulars such as the choice of address, *intitulatio*, greeting and corroboration. The two were probably drafted by

48 No.178; see note thereto.

the same clerk, who seems to have been consciously experimenting with a terser style, more reminiscent of a charter issued by a lay magnate, in 179 – it is even written in the first person singular, rather unusually – and a more 'ecclesiastical' style in no.180. Rather fewer charters survive from Giles' episcopate, because he spent several years in exile: forty-one charters, eleven of them in the original, including the profession of obedience, with mentions of a further seven. Nineteen charters survive from Hugh de Mapenore's episcopate, four of them originals, including the profession of obedience. Two others now lost survive in mentions. Forty-nine of Hugh Foliot's charters survive, twelve of them in the original, and there are references to a further seven. Of the charters which cannot be definitely be ascribed to Hugh Foliot or Hugh de Mapenore, two (nos.314, 316) only survive in mentions. No.313, to judge from its address, is a charter of Hugh Foliot, while no.315 is perhaps a charter of Hugh de Mapenore.

INSCRIPTIO

Several changes are noticeable in the address. There is now a clear distinction between the specific and the general address, the latter encompassing all believers and not just all the inhabitants of the diocese. The general address is now placed at the opening of the charter. This rule, though broken by a few of Robert Foliot's charters,[49] is usually strictly adhered to. There is less variation in the form of the general address, certain forms being used again and again. The two preferred ways of addressing all Christian believers in late twelfth and thirteenth century English episcopal acta were 'To all sons of holy mother church' and 'To all Christ's faithful', and at Hereford the former was by far the more popular until the episcopate of Hugh Foliot (1219-1234). 'Universis sancte matris ecclesie filiis' occurs in seventeen of Robert Foliot's acta, and in no.125, probably issued by Robert Foliot, in seven of William de Vere's acta, and three of Giles de Braose's. William and Giles's clerks preferred to open the address with 'Omnibus', and to expand the phrase a little. 'Omnibus sancte matris ecclesie filiis' occurs six times in the acta of each, 'omnibus sancte matris ecclesie filiis ad quos presens scriptum pervenerit' occurs fifteen times in William's acta and fourteen times in Giles'. Occasionally 'carta' or 'littere' takes the place of 'scriptum', and one

---

49 Nos.157, 168 (imitating charters of Gilbert Foliot and Robert de Melun) and 169-72.

of Giles' acta has '... ad quos tenor presentium pervenerit' (no.262). Another of Giles' acta has 'Universis Cristi fidelibus presens scriptum visuris vel audituris' (no.274), and '... presens scriptum visuris (*or* inspecturis)' was to become quite common under Hugh de Mapenore (nos.293, 294, 295, 308-10) and Hugh Foliot (nos.318, 346, 348, 357, 359-361). No particular form of address predominates under Hugh de Mapenore; Hugh Foliot's clerks use 'Universis Cristi fidelibus ad quos presens scriptum pervenerit' twelve times, and 'Universis sancte matris ecclesie filiis ad quos presens scriptum pervenerit' six times. Specific addresses in charters issued by all five bishops show little imaginative variation. Subordinates are sometimes described as *dilectis* (nos.134, 151, 183 [not drafted by William's clerks], 229, 302), though not always (nos.212, 344), while superiors, and, out of courtesy, abbots, are described as *venerabilibus* (nos.186, 234, 248, 297); Hugh de Mapenore addresses Ralph de Neville, dean of Lichfield, as 'Viro venerabili et amico in Cristo karissimo', and places Ralph's name before his own as a mark of respect (no.307), probably because Ralph was acting as the royal chancellor.

INTITULATIO

Giles and Hugh de Mapenore are never referred to by their surnames in their charters, but Robert Foliot and William de Vere sometimes are and Hugh Foliot frequently, probably to make sure that his acta were not confused with Hugh de Mapenore's. All the surviving original acta of Hugh Foliot, with the exception of no.369, which may possibly in any case been issued by Hugh de Mapenore, give his surname; five originals of William de Vere (nos.179, 180, 199, 202 and 231), one original, and one early copy of a charter of Robert Foliot (174, 150) use surnames.

On the whole there was little variation in the titles used by the bishops in the years 1174-1234, and one single form 'Dei gratia Herefordensis episcopus' was overwhelmingly preferred by the scribes of Robert, William, and Hugh Foliot. It is used 20 times by Robert, 24 times by William, six times by Giles, seven by Hugh de Mapenore, and no fewer than twenty-nine times by Hugh Foliot. *Dei gratia Herefordensis ecclesie minister humilis*, however, was also quite popular among Robert and William's clerks, who used it 11 and 12, or possibly 13, times respectively. Some experimentation occurred during this period: William de Vere's clerks tried out 'dei permissione' and 'dei miseratione' (nos.215, 228, 189, 205, 227, 241, 194, 225), and also 'divina miseratione' (nos.198, 280), simultaneously being experimented with by the clerks of Archbishop Baldwin of Canterbury,[50] which with 'divina permissione' was to be the fashionable expression in the early thirteenth century.[51] 'Divina permissione Herefordensis ecclesie minister' was the most common devotional formula used by Giles de Braose, occurring 17 times.

In the whole collection there is only one charter issued by a bishopelect, no.169, issued by Robert Foliot for Reading, in which he is termed 'dei gratia Her(e)f' ecclesie electus'.

SALUTATIO

Robert Foliot's clerks had no single favourite form of greeting but varied between *salutem* (nos.134, 135, 139, 146, 167-8, 170-1) and *perpetuam/eternam in Domino/Cristo salutem* (nos.129A, 137, 138, 141-2, 147-50, 152, 154, 156, 160-1, 163, 166, 172, 174, 177). Sometimes a more complicated form of words was chosen to lay more emphasis on salvation: 'salutem in eo qui est salus eterna credentium' (nos.136, 153), 'salutem in auctore salutis' (no.151), or 'salutem quam a domino speramus'.[52] William de Vere, Giles de Braose, and Hugh de Mapenore all had a clear preference for 'eternam in domino salutem', which is found 21 times in William's acta, 20 in Giles', and 10 in Hugh's, and Hugh Foliot's clerks favoured the shorter 'salutem in domino', which occurs 23 times. It also appears ten times in William's acta. In letters to superiors, greeting would be combined with reverence, and, in one particularly oily letter of excuse written by Giles to Stephen Langton, subjection as well (nos.247, 297, and especially 248). Although on the whole salutations in this period are standardised some real inventiveness was shown by Giles's clerks in charters for favoured beneficiaries, mostly Hereford cathedral chapter: 'utriusque vite salutem in domino' (no.254), 'in illam feliciter introire

---

50 *EEA*, ii, p.lv. Their contemporaries at Lincoln were more conservative: cf. *EEA*, iv, pp.xxx-xxxi. Devotional formulae of this type had been used by French bishops since the early twelfth century: see A. Gandilhon, *Catalogue des actes des archevêques de Bourges antérieurs à l'an 1200* (Bourges and Paris 1927), pp.cxix-cxx.

51 Cf. esp. nos.293-5, 297-8, 306, 307, 310-11 of Hugh de Mapenore and nos.318, 331, 335-6, 347-8 and 361 of Hugh Foliot.

52 No.162, very like 'salutem que nunc est et quam speramus a domino' in no.129 which is probably an act of Robert Foliot. However an examination of the two charters suggests that they were not drafted by the same clerk.

beatitudinem quam preparavit deus diligentibus se' (no.259), 'presentis vite felicitatem <et> eternam beatitudinem' (no.283 for Tintern), and 'presentis vite prosperitatem et salutis eterne beatitudinem' (no.257). An examination of the wording of nos.257 and 283 shows that they were almost certainly drafted by the same clerk.

ARENGA AND NARRATIO

In the late twelfth century the usual means of introducing the disposition was the notification. Arengae and *narrationes*, singly or together, had always been exceptional at Hereford, and were destined to remain so, in marked contrast to Canterbury, where they had been used in a substantial minority of documents until the middle of the twelfth century and had then undergone a decline.[53] They occur in only five of Robert Foliot's acta, six of Giles', five of Hugh de Mapenore's and eight or perhaps nine of Hugh Foliot's. William's clerks, however, showed more fondness for them, and about a third of his charters contain them. Arengae had never had any function save ornament, but a certain refinement in their use can be seen at Hereford in the late twelfth century. In addition to being used in charters for especially favoured beneficiaries,[54] they commonly occur in licences of appropriation, where they almost always express the bishop's duty to be generous to religious who themselves have to provide for the poor. Presumably the point of this was to emphasize that monastic houses could not count automatically on taking over parochial revenues.[55] This type of arenga is sometimes found in licences of appropriation issued by bishops of other dioceses,[56] but much less frequently; indeed, other bishops often used arengae stressing the need to commit transactions to writing in licences of appropriation.[57] Clerks used arengae carefully; certain types of acta, most notably grants to lay tenants, never have them.[58]

---

53 *EEA*, ii, p.lxii.
54 Or perhaps for beneficiaries who paid more, as suggested in *EEA*, ii, p.lxii.
55 See p.xcv.
56 *EEA*, ii, nos.82, 91 and iii, nos.402, 446 and 565. The last-mentioned is an inspeximus by Archbishop Hubert Walter of a charter of Bishop Henry of Worcester; the arenga occurs in Henry's charter.
57 *EEA*, ii, nos.40, 289 and iii, nos.335, 346, 581, 587, 641 and also no.567, in a charter issued by Bishop Henry of Worcester contained in an inspeximus by Archbishop Hubert Walter.
58 But cf. no.159, a composition with a lay tenant.

The main sources of ideas for wording were the documents of other bishops and more particularly of popes, but the influence was usually exercised indirectly. Openings such as 'Iustitie ac rationis' (no.198) and 'Quoniam iustis postulantium desideriis' (no.293) are taken from papal documents of the first half of the twelfth century and later.[59] 'Iustis postulantium desideriis' is a variant of the phrase 'iustis petentium desideriis', one of the most frequent openings of papal arengae.[60] However, papal arengae were not usually quoted in their entirety at Hereford. Indeed, direct copying of a papal formula occurs only once, in an indulgence of Hugh Foliot (no.344) which follows the form to be used by episcopal indulgences laid down by Innocent III at the Fourth Lateran Council (c.62). Direct borrowing from Canterbury draftsmanship is observable in a charter of Robert Foliot:

Robert Foliot:	Archbishop Richard of Canterbury:
no.159, dated June 1177:	*EEA* ii, no.198, 1174 x 1175:
Ne lites semel terminate *iterum*	*Ne semel* sopite *lites iterum*
ex malignitate alicuius seu	*suscitentur* et bonum pacis
oblivio *resuscitentur*, earum	contentio rediviva perturbet,
finem scripto *commendare* est	cause legitimo *fine* decise
necessarium.	dispositione provida literis
	commendantur.

The arenga in Archbishop Richard's charter has even closer similarities with one in another charter of Richard, a composition in favour of Hereford cathedral, issued at Westminster in March 1177,[61] and both Richard's charters are witnessed by Peter of Blois, who may, just possibly, have been responsible for drafting the arengae.[62] Reginald the chaplain, the Hereford clerk most likely to have drafted no.159,[63] accompanied Robert Foliot to Westminster in March 1177 and witnessed a notification of the settlement issued by Bishop Roger of Worcester.[64] Possibly Peter, or another Canterbury clerk, had

---

59 *JL* nos.5880, 7596, 7618, 7720, 8030, 8050, 8446, 8587, 8740, 8991, 9841, 9856, 10132, 10864 for the former and *PUE*, i, no.99, dated 1163 for the latter.
60 For a list of the papal documents issued before 1198 in which this phrase occurs see *JL*, ii.795-6.
61 *EEA*, ii, no.136.
62 *EEA*, ii, p.lxiv.
63 See note to no.159.
64 M.G.Cheney, Roger, Bishop of Worcester 1164-79 (Oxford 1980), 260-1, Appendix I, no.28.

brought along a collection of formulae and Reginald made notes from it.

Another source of wording was Scripture; the arengae in nos.201, 254, 344 and 348 all contain biblical quotations, no.348 from several different books. Often the influences were closer to home. In his general confirmation for Conches abbey, William de Vere copied the arenga used by Robert Foliot in his general confirmation for Conches verbatim (nos.142, 187), and Hugh de Mapenore copied an arenga used by William in a confirmation for Leominster (nos.215-6, 301).

Certain similarities can be observed in pairs of William's own acta, which suggest that one clerk was responsible for each pair, though of course direct influence from one clerk on another cannot be ruled out:

no.205 for St Guthlac's
Quoniam ea que nobis
presentibus *legitime acta*
sunt nostre auctoritatis
munimine desiderant
roborari volumus *et cupimus*
perpetue stabilitatis robor
optinere.

no.214 for Leominster
Quoniam ea que legitime acta
sunt nostreque auctoritatis
munimine desiderant roborari
perpetue stabilitatis robur
cupimus *et* optamus *optinere*

no.215 for Leominster
Quoniam religiosorum
loca pio semper et *benigno*
favore sunt promovenda,
illorum propensius *religiosorum*
necessitatibus relevandis
quodam favoris privilegio
tenemur assistere, qui
indigentium onera et
advenientium sarcinas
misericorditer et benigne
noscuntur sustinere

no.227 for Much Wenlock
Cum religionis studia *benigno sint*
persequenda *favore illis* tamen
religiosorum necessitatibus
relevandis quodam favoris
privilegio tenemur assistere, quas
pro participandis *indigentium*
oneribus benevolentia karitatis
ipsos *novimus* religiosis *sustinere*

The sentiments expressed in arengae vary little. References to the duties of episcopal office occur in many of them,[65] often in phrases loosely modelled on a common opening of papal arengae 'Ex iniuncto

---

65 Nos.142, 156, 162, 187-8, 191, 207, 217, 225, 236, 257, 348.

nobis officio'. It was an episcopal duty to protect the property of religious (no.142, 187, 207, 225, 236, 255), and to beautify God's house (no.257); more generally it was right to protect pious benefactions and the deeds of one's predecessors (no.331, 340, 342). Two of Hugh Foliot's charters stress the necessity of good works for salvation (nos.344, 348). The need to commit transactions to writing, or at any rate to preserve them (nos.250, 259), is the burden of about a third of the Hereford arengae (nos.156, 159, 166, 198, 205, 208, 214, 236, 250, 259, 276, 313, 346), and this form is common in confirmations and compositions, though nos.236 and 259 are licences of appropriation. About half the arengae of this period stress the duty to be generous to religious, or, in the case of charters for Hereford cathedral chapter, those who serve the Lord, and eleven licences of appropriation contain arengae of this type (nos.162, 188, 201, 204, 215, 216, 217, 227, 228, 301, 309, 360); so too does one notification of a grant of advowson, no. 293.

In this period most arengae are immediately followed by *narrationes*.[66] Nos 189, 209, 210, 226, 247, 282, 296 and 308 have *narrationes* only. Two of the charters with arengae have no *narratio* properly speaking but open the *dispositio* with 'Inde est quod' (no.225) and 'Eapropter' (no.236). While the usual practice was to keep the arenga and *narratio* separate, with general principles being expressed in the former and the specific circumstances of the case being rehearsed in the latter, some of the episcopal clerks gave themselves more freedom and made the division between the two less clear-cut. When William, moved by loyalty to his ancestors, was faced with the need to grant a licence of appropriation to his mother's family's foundation of Tintern, against the rules of the Cistercian order, the circumstances of the case were so specific as to warrant an introduction which opens with the subordinate clause: 'Licet ex consuetudinibus ecclesie Anglicane non sit permissio monachis Cisterciensis ordinis ecclesias parochiales in usus suos convertere ...', while the duty of being generous was expressed in personal, specific terms and effectively formed the narratio (no.237). Often, the language of the *narratio* could be as flowery as that of an arenga. One of William's clerks composed a discourse comparing the dependence of St Guthlac's on the cathe-

---

66 Nos.142, 156, 159, 162, 166, 187, 188, 191, 198, 201, 204, 207, 215-7, 227-8, 237, 254, 257, 259, 276, 301, 309, 341, 344, 348 and 360.

dral with a daughter being suckled by her mother (no.209); here the *narratio* is tucked into part of the *dispositio*, and there is no arenga. Giles' and Hugh Foliot's clerks occasionally use biblical quotations in *narrationes*, comparing the canons of Hereford cathedral with the unmuzzled ox treading out the corn (no.254), or expatiating on the rewards which Abraham and Lot received for their hospitality (no.348).

The *narratio* in this period almost never forms a sentence on its own (no.254 is an exception), but is usually a participial phrase, or, more rarely, a subordinate clause (nos.209, 257, 340, 344). The opening words, usually sonorous, follow papal practice: *Cum itaque, Cum igitur, Hinc est quod, Inde est quod, Attendentes.*

NOTIFICATIO

Since where there are *narrationes* these usually lead directly into the disposition it is very unusual to find Hereford episcopal charters, at any rate in the period before Hugh Foliot, which have a notification in addition to an arenga and a *narratio*. It is also unusual to find notifications in mandates. Even so, they occur in the great majority of charters issued by Robert Foliot, Giles, and Hugh Foliot, and about two thirds of the charters issued by William and Hugh de Mapenore. The favourite forms of notification among Robert Foliot's clerks were 'Noverit universitas vestra' (ten times), 'Universitati vestre notum facimus' (six times) and 'Notum vobis facimus' (five times), but other forms were sometimes tried, as for example 'Universitatem vestram scire volumus et memoriter tenere' (no.171), and 'Ad universorum notitiam pervenire volumus' (no.141). William's clerks had no preferred form, though 'Noverit universitas vestra' occurs five times; on the whole they liked to begin with 'Universitati vestre' and vary the verb – 'innotescimus', 'significamus', 'presenti pagina significandum duximus' and the like (see nos. 200, 209, 196, 199, 202-3, 208, 221, 242). Hugh de Mapenore's clerks, too, had no fixed choices. Giles' clerks had a definite preference for 'Noverit universitas vestra' (seventeen times), and Hugh Foliot's clerks were equally divided between this phrase and 'Noveritis' (fourteen times each). 'Ad universitatis vestre notitiam volumus pervenire' and variants occur from William's time onwards, but are never very common (nos.231, 281, 196, 214, 252, 260, 310, 362, 351). The use of the verb 'scire' is rare throughout this period and only three charters omit address, intitulatio and greeting and open 'Sciant ... quod ego' (no.185, 223, 280).

DISPOSITIO

This period saw the development of particular formulae in the dispositive clauses for specific purposes which allowed a growing differentiation in types of document – the inspeximus, the composition, the institution, the indulgence and the mandate, for example. The terminology applied to distinguish them is modern, but the emergence of separate genres was clearly understood and deliberately advanced at the time. Though a significant number of episcopal charters in this period are, or appear to be, dispositive, notably some of the grants and the indulgences and many of the licences of appropriation, most of the charters were still evidentiary in character. Institutions invariably were, and so, too, were compositions, where the verbs are always in the perfect and the bishops themselves are not the subjects of the dispositive clause, save once, where Robert Foliot states that he heard the agreement (no.140). The dispute being settled was usually referred to as *controversia* (nos.125, 141, 145, 153, 159, 174, 208, 214, 275, 287) or *causa* (nos.129A, 139, 161, 167, 169, 170, 206, 239), less often as *lis* (nos.129A, 136, 291, 296, 312, 365) and also in one case as *questio* (no.296); this noun usually forms the subject and the verb is often *conquievit* (nos.129, 153, 206, 214, 275, 291, 296, 365). References to papal authority, where the cases had been delegated to the bishops, are expressed in terms which doubtless quote the wording of the original papal mandate, as for example in the following:

no.139 (for Cirencester):
causam ... cognitioni nostre
a sede apostolica delegatam
fuisse remota appellatione
terminandam

no.141 (for Conches)
controversia ..... a sede
apostolica appellatione remota
cognoscenda et terminanda
commissa fuisset

and the even closer examples:
no.161 (for Kenilworth):
quod, cum causa ... nobis ab
apostolica sede, appellatione
remota, cognoscenda et
terminanda commissa fuisset,

no.174 (for Shrewsbury):
quod, cum controversia ... nobis a
sede apostolica cognoscenda et
terminanda, appellatione remota,
commissa fuisset, eadem

eadem causa,partibus in presentia nostra constitutis, hoc fine quievit.

controversia in presentia nostra et multorum et magnorum virorum hoc fine quievit.

Most surviving compositions of the period 1174-1234 were issued by Robert Foliot, including the four just quoted. The small number of compositions issued by his successors makes generalisations for the years after 1186 harder, but they seem to have preferred simpler wording and to have wanted to stress the amicable nature of compositions (nos.275, 296, 312, 365). The range of vocabulary is always restricted.

Three types of charter were specifically ecclesiastical in character and could only be issued by bishops, the institution, the licence of appropriation and the indulgence. Only two indulgences issued by Hereford bishops over this period survive; though separated by forty years, their wording is almost identical:

no.238 for Waltham: nos ... de iniuncta sibi penitentia quadraginta dies relaxamus

no.344 for St Ethelbert's hospital: nos ... de iniuncta sibi penitencia ... viginti dies relaxamus

Institutions and licences of appropriation, however, are much more plentiful, and show some evolution towards a common form. Institutions are always expressed in the perfect tense (nos.135, 152, 182, 194, 195, 203, 209, 221, 231, 232, 235, 245, 256, 279, 284, 313, 317, 318, 333, 334, 335, 359 and 360). Institutions of religious houses as rectors are sometimes worded in feudal terminology: 'we have granted to the church of Haughmond the church of Stokesay to hold with all its appurtenances by perpetual right, and we have invested the abbot himself, brother Richard, with the said church of Stokesay in the place of his church' (no.195). Two institutions of religious houses in parish churches stress the induction: 'nos ... ecclesiam ... dictis abbati et conventui inperpetuum possidendam concessimus, et eosdem in corporalem possessionem eiusdem ecclesie induci fecimus' (nos.335 and cf. no.209). For institutions of individual clerics as rectors and vicars the emphasis lay on receiving (*recepimus, suscepimus*) the intended incumbent, on the presentation of the patron, and instituting him (*instituimus, constituimus*). Survival of feudal terms is visible only

once, in no.152, issued by Robert Foliot, and even here canonical
expressions creep in as well, although the grammar (*recepisse ...
Stephano*) is somewhat strained as a result:
no.152:
nos ad presentationem prioris et conventus monasterii Sancti Guthlaci Heref' recepisse et concessisse Magistro Stephano, notario domini regis, ecclesiam suam de Bertwaldestreu tenendam in perpetuam
elemosinam libere et quiete ab omni prestatione census ipsumque
exinde personam canonice instituisse.

As early as Robert's episcopate we find the form which was to be
adhered to thereafter, with only minor changes:
no.135:
nos ad presentationem Ricardi de Boclinton' recepimus Robertum
clericum ad ecclesiam de Boclinton, ipsumque R. in eadem ecclesia
... personam canonice et absque omni reclamatione instituimus.

There is no surviving institution of a vicar from Robert Foliot's
episcopate, but William de Vere and his successors are careful to stress
that vicars are perpetual (203, 221, 235, 245, 256, 279, 284), though
no.313, issued by either Hugh de Mapenore or Hugh Foliot, curiously
fails to do so. The relative scarcity of vicars until the 1180s was largely
because the trend for monastic houses to appropriate parish churches
did not really take hold in the diocese until after 1186 (Robert Foliot
issued only two licences of appropriation to William de Vere's eight).[67]
In any case, some of the monastic houses in the diocese, in particular
Leominster and Much Wenlock, were the successors of powerful
Saxon minsters with large parishes, and were careful to maintain
burial rights when small local churches were set up within the large
parish, and to insist, where possible, that the priests serving them
were termed, simply, chaplains.[68] The phraseology for licences of
appropriation is less fixed than for institutions, but the term 'in
proprios/ suos usus' occurs almost invariably, sometimes with the
verb *appropriare* as well. The verb for giving permission is usually
concedere, often in the present tense (*concedimus*), and Robert and
William stressed the sense of licence by using the noun *licentia*

---

67 Nos.148, 150, 188, 210, 216, 227-8, 236-7, 250, 253, 259, 277, 301, 306, 309, 346, 358 and
360.
68 Nos.215-6, 228 and see also no.148 for Haughmond. On Leominster see B.Kemp, 'Some
aspects of the *parochia* of Leominster in the 12th century' and J.Croom, 'The fragmentation of
the minster *parochiae* of south-east Shropshire', both in J.Blair, ed. *Minsters and parish churches;
the local church in transition, 950-1200* (Oxford 1988), especially 75-7 and 90-1.

(no.148) or part of the verb *licet* (nos.105, 188, 227), or else the adjective *licitum* (nos.215, 216, 228, 237). In one charter William uses *indulsimus* instead (no.210).

A more amorphous group of dispositive clauses is to be found in confirmations, recognitions and grants which form the bulk of surviving acta. The verbs used in confirmations are in most cases *concedere* and *confirmare* together, often with *ratum habere* as well. In over half the cases the verbs are in the present tense (*concedimus et confirmamus*), the rest usually in the perfect infinitive. Very often the bishop remarks that he has 'inspected' the charters of his predecessors (these are sometimes qualified as 'authentic'), but summarises their contents without quoting them verbatim.[69] The present tense should not be viewed as automatically dispositive, especially not in confirmations, but the wording of one of Giles' charters for Hereford chapter suggests dispositive intent:

no.254:

'ecclesiam ... in manu nostra ... resignatam concedimus et conferimus, sicut ante ex ... predecessoris nostri ... donatione eisdem est concessa'.

Occasionally much simpler statements are to be found: 'quod ego ... dedicavi' (no.185) or 'quod ego emi' (no.197) in two charters of William de Vere. Recognitions will sometimes use a verb such as *cognovimus* or *testificamur* (nos.232 and 282), but more often a third party is the subject of the dispositive clause, and the bishop's presence at the transaction is referred to in phrases such as 'coram nobis' or 'in presentia nostra'. Grants of land by the bishops to members of their familia are always explicitly evidentiary in form, being invariably in the perfect, usually the perfect infinitive. Robert Foliot preferred 'concessisse et dedisse/reddidisse' (160, 168, 172) but his clerks had no fixed order for terms such as 'libere et quiete' or 'iure hereditario', and there is no mention of term days. His successors slowly refined the wording to make it run 'dedisse et concessisse et hac nostra carta confirmasse ... pro homagio et servitio suo' (no.179, in the first person singular, and 180, 285, 299, in the first person plural) and stated the term days. Under William de Vere the term days on the episcopal estates were Christmas, Lady Day, St John the Baptist's Day and Michaelmas (nos.179 and 180), but from Giles' time onwards Christmas was replaced by the feast of St Andrew (nos.280, 299, 337, 357,

---

69 As opposed to true charters of inspeximus, on which see pp.xcv-xcvi.

363, 366, 367). From no.278 it appears that Hereford cathedral chapter had two term days in the early thirteenth century, Michaelmas and Lady Day. Hugh Foliot's clerks used one form, with only tiny variations, for feudal grants:

no.370 (and see 357, 363, 366, 367 and 368)

nos dedisse et concessisse X pro homagio et servitio suo ... tenendam et habendam sibi et heredibus suis de nobis et successoribus nostris in feodo et hereditate, libere et quiete et integre ...

The practice of guaranteeing grants only began under Hugh Foliot (nos.339, 341, 357, 363, 366 and 367) and two of his grants lack warranties (nos.368 and 370). The wording of grants to religious houses was usually simpler than that of grants to laymen but less consistent. The term 'in perpetual (or free) alms', though sometimes used in confirmations issued by Robert Foliot, for example nos. 154 and 166, occurred only once in an episcopal grant, one of William de Vere for Worcester (no.241), before the episcopate of Hugh Foliot, under whom a fixed formula, 'in puram et perpetuam elemosinam' (nos.337, 339 and 358), evolved.

INSPEXIMUS

The 1170s saw the introduction of the charter of inspeximus, the verbatim quotation of one charter within another, in the sees of Worcester, London, Bath, and York,[70] and the earliest inspeximus issued by a bishop of Hereford may well be contemporary, though it cannot be more closely dated than 1174 × 1186: it is a charter of Robert Foliot quoting and confirming a charter of Abbot Joseph of Reading concerning the vicarage of Brimfield (no.137). Since this type of document was new to Robert's clerks the clause introducing Joseph's charter does not adopt the practice, which was to become standard in charters of inspeximus, of using a verb such as *vidimus* or *inspeximus*, but runs 'Super concessionem ... talis ... litterarum forma nobis transmissa est'. William de Vere issued three charters of inspeximus. One of them (no.211) quotes a charter of Abbot Hugh of Reading making arrangements for the vicarage of Leominster (it would appear that Reading played an important role in establishing the inspeximus at Hereford: seven charters of inspeximus were issued for Reading and Leominster by Hereford bishops between 1174 and

70 *EEA*, ii, p.lxvii.

1234). Abbot Hugh's text is introduced with the words 'nos instrumentum ... in hec verba inspexisse'. The second confirms and quotes
a charter of Robert Foliot for Lire Abbey (no.218), and the third
quotes an indignant letter written by the abbot of Gloucester, a party
in a case which had been delegated to William and two other judges
(no.186), and here the letter is introduced with the words 'Litteras ...
in hec verba suscepimus' – a wording which was probably reserved
for the quotation of documents involved in legal processes, since Giles
de Braose quotes a mandate of Innocent III with 'Mandatum domini
pape suscepimus in hec verba' (no.264). After 1200 the number of
charters of inspeximus rose; Giles issued seven, Hugh de Mapenore
two and Hugh Foliot ten (nos.252, 258, 260, 266, 268, 288, 290, 300,
311, 316A, 322, 330, 336, 347, 351, 353, 359, 361 and 362). The
introductory clauses are usually expressed in *oratio obliqua*, after the
notification; with the exception of no.266, the verb of inspection is
always *inspexisse* (or *inspeximus*). The contents of the documents being
quoted are referred to with the words 'in hec verba' or 'sub hac forma'
or some variant such as 'sub huius continentie forma' (no.260).

INIUNCTIO

Surviving mandates are rare, and of the eleven surviving from this
period, six were issued for Leominster priory. Four of these are
mandates issued by each successive bishop from William's time onwards, ordering archdeacons and other officials to ensure that
Leominster's property was not molested, and Leominster evidently
brought William's mandate back to each new bishop for a restatement.
The wording of the injunction, 'Auctoritate qua fungimur vobis in vi
obedientie precipimus, quatinus ... ' is repeated each time (nos.212,
269, 303 and 349). The other mandates are not dissimilar; indeed,
Hugh Foliot used exactly the same wording in a mandate issued on
behalf of Shrewsbury Abbey. The verb is variable, however – *mandamus* (nos.134, 191 and 302), *precipimus* (no.151), or *iniungimus*
(nos.213 and 344).

CORROBORATIO

Corroborations are to be found in practically all documents, the major
exceptions being mandates, for which they were unnecessary, and
indulgences. In charters of inspeximus a single sentence will act as
dispositive clause and corroboration.[71] The choice of vocabulary in all

corroborations of Hereford bishops in this period is extremely restricted, and closely resembles the vocabulary used by their contemporaries. The opening words are often a monosyllable followed by a disyllable, for example *Quod quia*, *Ut ergo*, *Ne ergo* or *Ut autem*. The bishop will then express his wish that the transaction will be preserved: 'Quod quia firmum et stabile manere volumus' (no.147) or 'Et ut hec conventio rata decetero permaneat et inconcussa' (no.208), or that it will not be called into doubt by the passing of time: 'Quod ne tractu temporis in dubium revocetur' (no.214 and cf. 211) or by the working of human cunning: 'Quod ne de cetero cuiuslicet calliditate in ambiguitatem vel alterationem possit revocari' (no.212). The 'strengthening' phrases come in the main clause, sometimes with a single verb such as *confirmamus*, and more often, especially from William de Vere's episcopate onwards, with a phrase such as *confirmare curavimus*, *corroborare curavimus*, or *communire curavimus*. The switch to this double verb ending seems to be mainly to allow the use of the *cursus*, the *tardus* in this case, though sometimes *testimonio communimus*, with a *velox* ending, is preferred. William's clerks seem to have been more keen to use the *cursus* than were those of his successors. Use of phrases with 'duximus', as in 'duximus roborandum', are rare at Hereford, except under Hugh de Mapenore (nos.293, 301 and 306), in contrast to Lincoln where they were favoured.[72] The main clause almost invariably refers to the document (mainly presenti scripto or carta) and to the apposition of the seal or seals. Only nos.146, 226, 231, 258, and 287 fail to mention the seal. In nos.211 and 204, both issued by William de Vere, the writing of the document is described as 'presentis pagine inscriptione', and other similarities in these two charters make it possible that the two were drafted by the same clerk. Otherwise the choice of language in corroborations, here as in other English dioceses, is so standardised that it is unsafe to attempt any identification.

SANCTIO

The *sanctio* is almost unknown in Hereford acta of this period, but does occur twice in charters of Giles de Braose. In one of these

---

71 Cf. *EEA*, ii, p.lxxi; these are, as C.R.Cheney points out, not strictly corroborations at all.
72 *EEA*, iv, pp.xxxvi-xxxvii.

charters, a confirmation for the Norman abbey of Cormeilles, the sanctio is built into the middle of the corroboration:

Ut hec autem concessio firma sit et stabilis perseveret, omnes illos qui ei contradicere presumpserint auctoritate a domino nobis data a communione fidelium sequestramus, ita quod in die districti examinis summi iudicis indignationem sentiant et cum iniquis accipiant portionem, *necnon presens scriptum et caractere sigilli nostri et capituli roboravimus* (no.250).

Both the two clauses in this *sanctio* show the use of the *cursus velox.* The other *sanctio*, in an original charter for Hereford cathedral chapter (no.255), comes at the end of the charter, which has neither a witness list nor a valediction. It follows the wording favoured by the papal curia, somewhat adapted for local use:

districtius inhibentes, ne cuiquam nostre iurisdictioni supposito liceat hanc nostri beneficii confirmationem infringere, vel ei ausu temerario contraire. Si quis vero hoc attemptare presumpserit, indignationem Dei omnipotentis necnon et beate Marie et beati Ethelberti et nostram se noverit incursurum.

DATE

Dates are rare in Hereford acta before the very end of Hugh Foliot's episcopate; they occur four times in Robert Foliot's charters, three times in William's, once each in charters of Giles and Hugh de Mapenore and six times in charters of Hugh Foliot. In most of these cases the date comes at the very end or just before the witness list; in other words, it is intended to be part of the eschatocol, but on three occasions it comes before the corroboration (161, 275 and 332) and in one charter, a composition issued by Hugh de Mapenore, it is part of the *narratio* (no.296). It was too rare an item for the clerks to have a clear idea of where it belonged. Only one of the charters with dates has a farewell (no.238) and only six have witness lists (nos.129A, 170, 188, 200, 342 and 341). Eventually, the dating clause would edge out the witness list, in imitation of French practice. There had never been a period when French episcopal acta completely ceased to bear dates, but the use of dates became practically invariable, and witness lists increasingly disappeared, during the last two decades of the twelfth century; at Bourges witness lists were hardly used after 1191.[73] This

---

73 A.Gandilhon, *Catalogue des actes des archevêques de Bourges* (Bourges and Paris 1927), p.clxvi.

process occurred in England about four decades later. Two of the dated Hereford acta of this period were drawn up for a transaction involving a French house, a prebendal arrangement made in 1195 between Hereford cathedral and the Norman abbey of Cormeilles (nos.188 and 200). Otherwise, dates were used only in compositions (and only a few of these: nos.159, 161, 170, 275, 266 and 365) or in indulgences (nos.238 and 344) until the 1230s (nos.332, 342 and 343).

The date usually begins 'Facta est hec transactio/ concessio/ compositio' (or other noun). The term 'datum' is never used, but two of Hugh Foliot's acta begin the date with 'Actum est' (nos.332 and 344) and two, issued on the same occasion, with identical dating formulae: 'Et hoc fecimus sollempniter convocato clero et populo in maiori ecclesia Hereford" (nos.342 and 343). Then the year is given, invariably the year of the Incarnation until the pontificate of Hugh Foliot, three of whose acta are dated by the year of grace (nos.332, 342 and 343), and two (nos.344 and 365) by the Incarnation. The pontifical year is never given, nor is the regnal year,[74] although William de Vere's indulgence for Waltham, issued at the dedication of the chapel of St Thomas the Martyr, after giving the year of the Incarnation (1188), states that the dedication took place in the year when Henry II took the cross. William's indulgence, issued on 13 March, is the only Hereford actum of this period which allows us to see which starting point the clerk has chosen for the year; in this case the clerk has used a Nativity dating, for Henry II took the cross on 21 January 1188. Place-dates occur in six acta (nos.129A, 170, 293, 332, 342 and 343); five acta give the day according to the ecclesiastical calendar (nos.170, 238, 332, 342, 343) and four according to the Roman one (nos.129A, 159, 293 and 296).

ESCHATOCOL

By far the most frequent eschatocol is a witness list. In most cases this is introduced with the words *Hi(i)s testibus*, or, much less frequently, *Testibus*, but occasionally Robert Foliot's clerks put the lists into the nominative and headed them with a phrase such as 'Huius recognitionis testes sunt' (no.163 and see nos.153 and 136), or used the genitive, introduced 'sub presentia istorum testium' (no.166, and see

---

74 This marks a contrast with the experimentation in Canterbury *acta* and with the paractice of Hugh of Wells at Lincoln: see *EEA*, ii, p.lxxv and *EEA*, iv, p.xxxviii.

141). Certain cartularies, those of Leominster priory and Gloucester abbey in particular, are prone to cropping witness lists down to 'His testibus etc' – the cartulary of Worcester cathedral priory, only marginally more helpful, includes only the first name in each list. It is quite possible, therefore, that some of the charters lacking any eschatocol originally had one (nos.137, 138, 196, 215, 313 and 330 may well have had witness lists), and two have certainly been mutilated (nos.184 and 266), but there survive three originals, two compositions and a confirmation, with neither a witness list nor a farewell (nos.167, 197 and 294).

Although the rules for the use of the farewell were not absolutely clear-cut, there is a definite preference for not using it with a witness list (no.141 is the only exception), and its use is generally restricted to letters and mandates. Sometimes it was, however, used in confirmations or compositions (nos.141, 232 and 346). The most common form of the farewell is *Valete*, especially in mandates. More complicated forms were used for addressing superiors – 'Valeat semper in domino sanctitas vestra' to Archbishop Hubert Walter and to Guala (nos.247, 297) and 'Valeat cara nobis paternitas vestra semper in domino' to Archbishop Stephen Langton (no.248). To show respect to Ralph Neville, even though he was of lower ecclesiastical rank, Hugh de Mapenore used the plural – Valete semper (no.307).

II: PALAEOGRAPHY

1079-1127

From the period 1079-1127 four originals only survive, three of which are professions of obedience (the professions made by Gerard, Reinhelm and Geoffrey) written by Canterbury scribes; the 'original' of Gerard's profession is, however, a copy made about 1200.[1] The only original charter, Robert of Lotharingia's land-grant (no.2), was probably produced locally, though it cannot be associated with any particular scriptorium. It was written in a text hand, by a scribe probably of continental origin or who had trained on the continent, and who

---

1 *Canterbury professions*, p.xxix; N. R. Ker, *English manuscripts in the first century after the Norman conquest* (Oxford 1960), 18.

employed the old Irish punctuation of *positura*, a triangle formed of a comma and two dots.[2]

1131-1167

Relatively few of the charters issued by Robert de Béthune and Gilbert Foliot (as bishop of Hereford) survive in the original, four of Robert's and five (one of them in two exemplars) of Gilbert's. In addition no.106A, a charter of Earl Roger of Hereford with a corroborative clause issued by Gilbert, survives in the original. Of Robert de Melun's acta only his profession of obedience, a Canterbury product, survives in the original. It is likely that none of Robert de Béthune's surviving originals was written by a clerk belonging to the episcopal familia, and only one of Gilbert's, no.110, seems to have been written by one of his clerks. Of the four issued by Robert, no.14, a letter to Eugenius III, is written in a cursive hand with a certain amount of juncture. The hand is well-formed, regular and compact; the scribe uses the sign ÷ for *est* three times and dots íí and óó (cóóperator). In slant and general appearance the hand resembles that of a companion letter, with the same text, written by Nigel, bishop of Ely, but slight divergences in spelling and in the form of abbreviations and of minuscule 'g' leave positive identification in doubt. Theobald almost certainly circulated the text of the letter to his suffragans and five of the six who wrote to Eugenius III used the same text; quite possibly Theobald sent fair copies written by his scribes to be sealed by the bishops.

Robert's other three originals, nos.45-47, in text hands, were all issued for Monmouth priory. The scribe of no.46 wrote a regularly formed text hand, the letters very round and somewhat wide in comparison to their height. Ascending strokes have small serifs. The sedilla is used consistently for æ; *et* is always represented by an ampersand, the upper lobe of which is joined to the slanting stroke.

---

2 Personal communication from Dr Tessa Webber; on the punctuation, see M.Parkes, 'The contribution of Insular scribes of the 7th and 8th centuries to the "grammar of legibility"', in *Graphia ed interpunzione del latino nel Medio evo*, September 1984 (1985).

Scribe I: the scribe of nos.45, 47, and 106A (a corroborative clause by Gilbert Foliot in a charter of Earl Roger of Hereford), all issued for Monmouth priory, also wrote an even text hand, similar in general appearance to that of no.46, though the uprights are slightly shorter and the lobes slightly narrower. Majuscule and minuscule G are formed differently from those in no.46 and the upper lobe of the ampersand does not join the slanting stroke. Monmouth was a dependent house of St Florent near Saumur, but the mother house had no influence over the choice of scribes for these charters, for both Scribe I and the scribe of no.46 were trained in English schools.[3] Scribe I might possibly have been connected with Hereford cathedral, since his hand bears a resemblance to that of Hereford Dean and Chapter Muniments no.1095, a charter of 1132 recording a grant by the canons of Hereford to Peter of Hereford.[4] The script of Hereford Dean and Chapter Muniments no.1095 has similarities with the hand of Hereford Cathedral MS O. 5. xi: -*orum* abbreviation, saucer-shaped *n/m* abbreviations, *or* juncture, majuscule *E*, and minuscule *g*. However, there are certain divergences in the ampersand, in the height of tall letters and the form of the sedilla.

Of Gilbert's originals, his profession of obedience, no.59, was perhaps written by a scribe temporarily employed by Theobald in northern France, and no.64, which survives in two exemplars, is a letter issued by a group of several bishops acting as judges-delegate. It is unlikely that Gilbert's clerks were in any way responsible for either.[5] No.110 (*GFL* no.339), an indulgence issued by Gilbert Foliot for Reading, unlike the other surviving originals issued by Gilbert as bishop of Hereford, is in an experienced and well-formed cursive hand which is almost certainly identifiable with Hand I of Bodleian MS E Musaeo 249, although the form of minuscule *g* is somewhat different.[6] No.107 (*GFL* no.311), issued by Gilbert Foliot for a canon of Hereford, is in text hand, similar in type to the hands of Scribe I and the hand of no.46, but less assured and regular.

---

3 I am grateful to Dr R.M.Thomson for his advice on nos.45, 47 and 106A.
4 Hereford D. & C. Muniments no.1095 is partially illustrated by N.R.Ker, *English manuscripts in the century after the Norman Conquest* (Oxford 1960), pl.16a.
5 On no.59 see *Canterbury professions*, p.xxx; on no.64 see *GFL*, 27, n.2.
6 Hand I of Bodl. E Musaeo 249 is illustrated in *GFL*, plates II and III, though no.110 below (*GFL* no.339) is not identified as the work of this scribe in *GFL*.

By the middle of the twelfth century Hereford cathedral was trying to build up its library and it is almost certain that it was running a scriptorium to produce some of the manuscripts; O. 5. xi, O. 6. xii, O. 5. iv, O. 2. i, O. 4. v, and O. 8. viii may well have been products of this scriptorium, but this does not pretend to be a complete list.[7] The scribe of O. 5. xi and perhaps some of his colleagues may well have have been employed to write charters for the bishops and for the cathedral chapter. Furthermore, the scribe of the largest part (the second scribe) of the Herefordshire Domesday, ordered to be made by Henry II at some point between 1160 and 1170, may well have been connected with the cathedral, for his hand is almost certainly identical with that of Hereford Dean and Chapter Muniments no.1088, issued by Dean Ralph, who died between 1158 and 1163, and he may possibly also have written no.85 (GFL no.316), for minuscule p, q, and g, and majuscule V are alike, though the *pre* abbreviation is different. The editors of the Herefordshire Domesday describe the hand of the second scribe as curial in character, but they also note his local knowledge of place names;[8] in any case it would not be impossible for a Hereford scribe to have acquired experience at the royal court.

1174-1234

During this period the vast majority of surviving originals appear to have been the products of scribes in the episcopal household, or, if freelance scribes, ones who often found employment in episcopal service, for the same hands often occur in charters for different beneficiaries. Several wrote charters for more than one bishop and also for the cathedral chapter. Originals not the work of Hereford scribes mostly fall into two groups, professions of obedience and letters jointly issued with other ecclesiastics; of the former, William de Vere's, may possibly be a holograph,[9] and one of the exemplars of Giles de Braose's may perhaps have been written by a scribe available

7 A full study of this question must await the appearance of the new catalogue of the cathedral library by R.M.Thomson, in continuation of the work of the late Sir Roger Mynors.
8 *Herefordshire Domesday*, ed. V.H.Galbraith and James Tait, PRS n.s. 25 (1950), p.xvi.
9 See note to 178.

for employment at Westminster, where Giles was consecrated.[10] The other exemplar is a Canterbury product, as are probably, though not certainly, the professions of Robert Foliot and Hugh de Mapenore.[11] Where bishops of Hereford acted as judges delegate in the company of other ecclesiastical authorities, especially if the hearing did not take place in Hereford, they did not necessarily employ their own scribes. No.134, a mandate issued jointly by Bishops Roger of Worcester and Robert Foliot, is written in a cursive hand which bears no resemblance to any identifiable Hereford hand, and may well have been the work of one of Roger's scribes, while no.167, a composition issued by Bishop Robert Foliot and Abbot Adam of Evesham, is written in a cursive hand bearing no resemblance to that of any identifiable Hereford scribe. It was possibly a Westminster product.

The remainder of the surviving originals issued by Robert Foliot were written by at least four scribes, two of whom also worked for the cathedral chapter and for Robert's successor, William. No.142, a confirmation for Conches abbey, is in a text hand, written with a thick quill which gives the writing a heavy appearance. It was written by an English, not a Norman, scribe, because the name *Edithestoc'* is written with an *aeth*; the scribe may possibly be identifiable with the scribe of no.159, an agreement copied into the back of Hereford Cathedral MS O. 6. xii in a hand somewhat later than the one responsible for the rest of the manuscript. Tironian *et*, majuscule *M*, *it* and *ti* ligatures and minuscule *g* are similar, but there are divergences in the ampersand and the majuscule *W*. The scribe of no.159 is perhaps identifiable with Reginald, Robert Foliot's chaplain.

Scribe II – Richard: One scribe was largely responsible for writing episcopal acta under Robert Foliot, and also worked for Hereford cathedral chapter and William de Vere, writing nos.138, 147, 149, 160, 168, 173, 187, and also Hereford D. & C. Muniments no. 155. He testifies as Richard *scriptor* in nos.160 and 187. Almost certainly he won Robert's favour by being able to write not only a legible and attractive cursive hand but also a more formal variant of this script, almost but not quite a text hand, which was suitable for those occa-

---

10 See note to no.243.
11 *Canterbury professions*, pp.xxxii, xxxiv.

sions when beneficiaries requested a grander-looking document (nos.147, 187). Both Scribe II and the scribe of no.145 wrote without much juncture; no.145 is in a cursive hand which bears similarities (minuscule *g*, majuscule *T* and *N*) to the hand of Scribe II, but there are slight differences in the writing of abbreviations which make definite attribution impossible. Scribe II favoured a broad quill and gave letters plenty of space, especially for descenders in *s*, *r*, *n*, and *g*, which sweep away to the left, compensating for a slight backward slant to be found in the cursive variant of the script (the writing in the more formally written charters is upright). Other characteristics are majuscule *N* with a horizontal middle stroke and two forms of Tironian *et*, both unbarred, one with a long slanting downward stroke to the left, and the other, shorter, ending with a slight tick to the right. Minuscule *m* usually consists of a horse-shoe shaped left-hand arch from the shoulder of which springs the right-hand arch, the end of which is drawn down leftwards well below the line. A similar *Æ* diphthong is used in nos.149 and 187. The script bears a general resemblance to those of two early scribes of Henry II,[12] one of whom also wrote charters for two archbishops of Canterbury, Thomas and Richard.[13]

Scribe III: Scribe III's hand bears a general resemblance to Richard's, but is more compact and displays several late twelfth-century features used only rarely or not at all by Scribe II, such as doubled strokes in majuscule letters, and ascenders with split tops or streamers, especially in the more formally written examples, such as no.180. Tironian *et* is broad and short, minuscule *g* has a long horizontal tail, many of the final 's's look like reversed 'Z's, and majuscule *D* is triangular in shape. Scribe III was employed by Robert Foliot and Dean Jordan in the 1180s, writing nos.151 and Hereford D. & C. Muniments no.2863, but found fuller use of his skills under William de Vere, for whom he wrote 179, 180, 184, 186, 199 and 231. The *e* of *Ver* (William's surname) is topped with a stroke like an acute accent in nos.179, 180 and 231. As far as the surviving evidence allows us to judge, scribe III was the scribe most frequently employed by William, and may have been a full-time member of the episcopal familia. In all,

---

12 Compare with T.A.M.Bishop, *Scriptores regis* (Oxford 1961), scribes nos.xxv and xxvii.
13 T.A.M.Bishop's scribe xxvii also wrote charters for Archbishops Thomas and Richard of Canterbury: *EEA*, ii, p.xliii.

if we disregard William's profession of obedience, his surviving originals were written by six scribes.

Scribe IV: Scribe IV wrote only two charters for William, both for the same beneficiary, Shrewsbury Abbey (nos.233, 235), and it is possible that he lived in Shropshire, for his hand does not occur in any of the Hereford D. & C. Muniments. Nos. 233 and 235 were however probably both drafted by a clerk or clerks in William's household;[14] doubtless they were dictated. Scribe IV has idiosyncratic spelling, sometimes inconsistent: *Robertus* is always spelled as *Robbertus*, but Shrewsbury is rendered as *Salopesb'* and *Salobesb'*. Descenders in *s* and *p* end with a slight kink and the bottom stroke of *g* forms a diamond-shaped lobe. The hand is fussy and inelegant.

Scribe V: Scribe V worked for William de Vere and Giles de Braose, and wrote nos.196, 287, and 289. Two of these, 196 and 289, are written with a thin quill in a cursive hand with a backward slant. The main feature in common is majuscule *H*, a bold letter with a serif on the ascender and one (in 196) or two (289) horizontal strokes across the arch. Majuscule *N* and *W* are also similar, and majuscule *O* in 191 is like majuscule *Q* in 289. The Tironian *et* has a wavy top; it is barred in 289 but not 196. Minuscule *g* is similar in both, though in 289 it has an additional thin stroke projecting to the left. No. 287 is a more formal, stiffer variant, upright rather than slanting, but with the same majuscule *H* and a wavy-topped Tironian *et*. Minuscule *g*, though the bottom stroke is drawn out in a straight line to the left, has the same additional thin stroke as no.289. Majuscule *S*, as in no.196, is very short and wide.

Scribe VI also worked for William and Giles, writing nos.201, 202 and 247; in addition he produced Hereford D. & C. Muniments no.659, issued by Dean Richard de Brito. The main features of this script are the juncture – *n, t, u, r, c* and *i* are often joined to each other at top and bottom, giving the writing a boxy appearance – and the majuscule *R*, with its very tall lobe. The Tironian *et* is barred and upright, usually taller than it is wide. Final strokes of *m, n,* and *s* are drawn down in a curve to the left.

---

14 Save for the placing of the *intitulatio* before the *inscriptio*, their internal features do not vary from those of other charters issued by William; see diplomatic section above.

Scribe VII was employed by William and Giles and wrote a charter issued by a tenant of the cathedral chapter called Richard Pirun. Four of his charters survive, nos. 239, 244, and 252, and Hereford D. & C. Muniments no.1. He frequently makes use of the *titulus*. The most distinctive characteristic of the hand is the tall pointed lobes in majuscule *P* and *R*; the *P* is often adorned with a serif, and has a foot projecting to the right. Two types of Tironian *et* are used, both barred, a tall upright one in 239 and Hereford D. & C. Muniments no.1 and a shorter slanting one in 244, 252 and Hereford D. & C. Muniments no.1. The two charters written for Giles display serifs on *H* and *L*, and the tops of *s* and *f* are formed by separate transverse strokes written with the full width of the quill above which the much finer ends of the ascenders project.

The scribe of no.255, a confirmation for Hereford cathedral, does not seem to have written any other surviving Hereford episcopal acta, though the hand has a strong resemblance to that of Scribe VI, being boxy-looking and having a similar suprascript *a*. Ascenders are, however, more generously decorated, with loops, in 255, and the Tironian *et* is shorter and wider.

Scribe VIII: Scribe VIII worked for Giles, Hugh de Mapenore, Hugh Foliot and Hereford cathedral chapter. He wrote nos.248, 254, 256, 295, 297 and 336 and Hereford D. & C. Muniments nos.1280 and 1285. The loops under minuscule *g* and *s* are the main identifying features; the long sweeping Tironian *et* (unbarred in no.256, otherwise barred) is another. Majuscule *S*, *R*, *H* and *N* are heavily Gothicized, and there are two types of majuscule *M*, also Gothicized. The *titulus* is used frequently. Unfortunately several of these charters lack witness lists, but Richard the chaplain testifies in no.256 and in Hereford D. & C. Muniments no.1285, and was possibly the scribe. The scribe of no.307 wrote a very vigorous hand similar to those of VIII and XII, especially with respect to minuscule *x* and *g* and majuscule *D*. Final *-us* abbreviations and suprascript *a*, and the Tironian *et*, are, however, different.

Scribe IX: Scribe IX began by working for Giles de Braose and Hereford cathedral chapter and very probably worked some thirty years later for Hugh Foliot. At the turn of the twelfth and thirteenth centuries he wrote Hereford D. & C. Muniments no.274 for Dean Richard Brito and shortly afterwards no.258 for Giles; much later he wrote no.344 for Hugh Foliot and Hereford D. & C. Muniments no.2175 for Dean Thomas of Bosbury. The main characteristic of this hand is its use of very tall upright ascenders with loops; the double *s* with loops on the second shaft occurs in all four documents. By contrast, descending strokes are short and unemphasized. Elongated majuscule *M*, triangular majuscule *A*, majuscule *U* in the form of a square-looking *Y*, and, in the two later documents, the practice of inserting tiny circles into majuscule *N* and the Tironian *et*, are also distinguishing marks.

Scribe X: Scribe X worked for Hugh Foliot and for Hereford cathedral chapter, and wrote no.340, probably also no.369, and Hereford Dean and Chapter Muniments nos.1273, 1275, 2071, and 2118. He usually used a fluent cursive script, highly Gothicized, whose distinguishing features are a Tironian *et* with a tiny loop at the left end, lower loops in minuscule *g*, minuscule *x* with its left lower stroke brought sharply back to the right, and minuscule *m* with the final stroke pulled down to the left and then to the right. No.369 appears to be a more formal variant; the majuscule *H* is similar and there are some looped Tironian *et* signs, but the minuscule *g* is written stiffly, with no lower loop.

Scribe XI (?): The scribe of no.366 may also have written Hereford D. & C. Muniments no.1390. Feathered ascenders, *-us* abbreviation, and minuscule *g* are all similar. The script of HDCM 1390, however, is elongated and decorative, while that in no.366 is more compact and less cursive and a much thicker quill has been used, so certain identification is not possible.

Scribe XII (Godfrey of Marcle): There are general similarities between this hand and that of Scribe X, but the latter is more regular and differs from XII in the writing of Tironian *et* and minuscule *g*. Scribe XII wrote three charters, nos.322, 326, and Hereford D. & C. Muniments no.1082, in formal and decorative scripts, and nos.319, 341, 342, and 343, in a simpler, more cursive manner. No.322 and Hereford D. & C. Muniments 1082 both concern the abbey of Conches, no.322 being a charter of inspeximus issued by Hugh Foliot for Conches and HDCM no.1082 being the confirmation by Abbot Renaud of Conches of an annual payment by the abbey to Hereford cathedral. It is dated 1232 and it seems very likely that the two charters were issued together, in Hereford, at the same time. While both are fine pieces of writing they are surpassed by no.326 for Dore, the abbreviations in whose protocol are decorated with tiny fleur-de-lys.

The distinctive characteristics of this hand are the lower loops of minuscule *g* (Scribe XII used two forms, as can be seen most clearly in Abbot Renaud's charter where they occur side by side), the lower loops of final *s*, majuscule *A*, *S* and *M*, and suprascript *a*. No.322 and Abbot Renaud's charter show the same *con-* abbreviation and decorative loops under majuscule *H*. Nos.319, 341, 342, and 343 all show use of the ÷ sign for *est*. The final witness in no.319 is Godfrey the clerk, and since Godfrey the clerk also witnesses no.322 and Godfrey of Marcle, clerk, witnesses no.341, it seems possible that he was the scribe.

Discounting professions of obedience and several compositions issued by Hereford bishops as papal judges delegate away from Hereford, there was a clear tendency on the part of Hereford bishops after the middle of the twelfth century to rely on scribes living in Hereford, particularly those who also found freelance employment at the hands of the cathedral chapter. Hereford evidently attracted well-trained scribes and doubtless these trained others: the scribe of Hereford D. & C. Muniments nos.576 and 1086 had clearly been influenced by Scribe II (Richard). It is possible that some of them were not permanent members of the episcopal household; clearly, however, bishops liked to have on their staffs at least one first-class scribe at any time. Richard, Godfrey and Scribes VII and VIII all produced fine work. It was thus unnecessary for bishops, even on the occasions when they had left Hereford (as in the case of no.147 for Haughmond, which to judge from the witness lists was probably issued in Shropshire), to have their charters prepared for them by the beneficiaries, and even when a local scribe was employed, as was probably the case for nos.233 and 235, the drafting was apparently the work of a member of the episcopal household. A comparison of the internal features within each scribe's group of charters suggests that it was common, but not invariable, for drafting and writing to be carried out by a single individual.[15] Among Scribe II's charters, nos.138, 147 and 173 show similarities of wording, and the corroborations of nos.149 and 160 are like each other, while no.187 has a rather different phraseology and might have been composed by the clerk responsible for no.142, which

---

15 It is of course possible that pairs of clerks, a *dictator* and a scribe, might have worked together.

is in a different hand. No.168 simply copies charters issued by previous bishops. Differences of subject matter of the acta written by Scribes III, VI, IX and X make comparisons difficult, though nos.180 and 199, the work of Scribe III, were probably drafted by a single clerk, who also very probably composed no.179 as the pair to no.180, trying to achieve a terser, less ecclesiastical style. Among Scribe VII's charters, nos.239, 244 and Hereford Dean and Chapter Muniments no.1 have similar corroborations, while the wording of no.252 is close to that of a charter written by Scribe VIII, no.254. Of Scribe VIII's charters, nos.248, 254, 256 and 297 show some similarities with each other, but not nos.295 and 336. All of Scribe XII's charters save no.326 were probably drafted by one clerk.

The largest group of surviving originals is that in Hereford Dean and Chapter Muniments, but the episcopal acta in this collection were not produced by the beneficiaries: the scribes who wrote them also wrote episcopal acta issued for private individuals and for other religious institutions. Moreover the episcopal acta in the Hereford Dean and Chapter Muniments all appear to have been drafted by episcopal clerks, while charters in the same hands issued by other benefactors are few and, with the exception of Dean and Chapter Muniments no.1, show great differences in drafting, being more simply expressed. Very probably the majority of the scribes who wrote charters for the bishops in the period 1174-1234 found most of their employment in the episcopal service, but when episcopal business was slack they could easily write charters on behalf of the dean and chapter.

III: SEALS AND SEALING ARRANGEMENTS

There are no indications as to whether any of the bishops of Hereford before Robert de Béthune possessed a seal. It is likely that Robert of Lotharingia did not, for his charter for Roger de Lacy (no.2) is authenticated simply by being a chirograph, and shows no traces of having been sealed. Genuine episcopal charters from the period 1100-1127 do not mention seals, but they are far too few, however, for us to say conclusively that the bishops who issued them had none. Several of Robert de Béthune's charters refer to the use of a seal, in one case that of Gloucester abbey (no.17) but more usually Robert's own, and of the four surviving originals three show signs of sealing arrangements (nos.14, 46, 47) and one of these three bears the only surviving impression of Robert's seal (no.46). No.14, a letter, was sealed on a tongue, and then fastened with a wrapping tie; traces of tongue and tie survive. No.46 was sealed on a tag, which was passed through a slit cut near the bottom of the charter, which had not been folded to make a turnup, and the seal was then attached the wrong way round. No.47 was probably sealed in the same way as no.46, since there is a semi-circular tear at the foot of the charter. No.45, the fourth surviving original, has no trace of sealing arrangements and was probably never sealed. The impression attached to no.46 is a fragment measuring 45 × 35 mm, with no part of the legend surviving and no reverse or counterseal. It seems to have depicted a bishop standing holding a staff in his left hand.

Two impressions of Gilbert Foliot's seal as bishop of Hereford survive (nos.64, 110 [*GFL*, nos.293, 339]); one is attached on a tongue (no.110, an indulgence) and the other on silk cords (no.64, a letter jointly issued by several bishops). Both are apparently from one matrix, a pointed oval about 80 × 60 mm depicting a bishop in full pontificals, his mitre with the horns to the sides, holding a staff in his left hand and raising his right hand in blessing. W. de Gray Birch recorded the legend of the impression attached to no.110 as ....TVS. DEI. GRA. HEREFORDEN............ ,[1] and so the original legend probably ran GILEBERTVS DEI GRA' HEREFORDENSIS EPISCOPVS. No reverse or counterseal was used.

No impression of Robert de Melun's seal survives; the only original document issued by him to have come down to us is his profession of obedience, which was unsealed, in accordance with convention. He certainly had a seal, however, for most of his charters refer to one.

Four impressions of Robert Foliot's seal survive (nos.138, 147, 167, 168), all taken from one matrix. This was a pointed oval, 80 × 49 mm (to judge from the most complete impression, no.167), and showed a bishop standing, dressed in full pontificals (again, as on Gilbert's seal, the horns of the mitre are to the sides), raising his right hand in blessing and holding his staff in his left. The head of the crosier turns

---

1 *GFL*, 26; see also W. de Gray Birch, *Catalogue of seals in the department of manuscripts in the British Museum*, 6 vols. (London 1887-1900) i, nos.1599, 1901.

inward. None of the impressions gives us the legend complete, but by putting them together we obtain + ROB..TVS. DEI. GRATIA. ....ORDENSIS EPISCOPVS. IIII. (Robert was the fourth Bishop Robert of Hereford). Three of the impressions bear a counterseal, in all cases an oval antique gem, 25 × 20 mm, with the legend + SIGILLUM ROBERTI. The design depicts two animals; in the nineteenth century W. de Grey Birch described it as a lion chasing a stag under a tree to the right.[2] Robert's seals were mostly attached on the tag, though three charters, two of which are mandates, show signs of having been sealed on a tongue (nos.134, 145, 151).

Only two impressions of William's seal survive (nos.180, 202), both in fairly good condition, and in addition there are casts of his seal and *secretum* in the British Library.[3] The seal impressions are from the same matrix, a pointed oval about 78 × 47 mm, depicting the bishop standing, in full pontificals, with staff in left hand and the right hand raised in blessing. The crosier head turns inward and the horns of the mitre are to the sides. The legend does not survive well on the two surviving impressions; that on the cast reads + SIGILLVM: WIL-LELMI. DEI GR.... ..REFORDENSIS. EPISCOPI. William's *secretum*, to be found on the reverse of the impressions on both nos.180 and 202, was, like Robert Foliot's, an antique gem. William's depicted two sows suckling their young (the second sow is only clearly visible on the British Library cast). The gem is round, about 30 mm in diameter, and bears the epigrammatic legend: + WILL'I. DE. VER CELO SECRETVM ('I conceal the secret of William de Vere'). At least two and perhaps four of William's surviving original charters were sealed on the tongue (nos.186, 197 and perhaps 184 and 199), but the more normal method was sealing on the tag.

Four impressions of Giles de Braose's seal survive, one of which is broken in two, and in addition there are casts of his seal and counter-seal in the British Library.[4] Again, one single matrix was used during the pontificate, a pointed oval about 75 × 42 mm. The seal depicts a

---

2 Ibid., i.236, no.1600.

3 BL Seal casts xliii, 54, 55. See also the description in W. de Gray Birch, *Catalogue of seals*, i.236-7, no.1601.

4 Impressions on nos.252, 256, and 258, and in addition on Westminster Abbey D. & C. Muniments no.22492, a composition of a dispute in which Giles acted as judge (see C.R. and M.Cheney, edd. *Letters of Innocent III concerning England* [Oxford 1967], no.551). The casts are BL Seal casts lv.62 and 63. See also, for a description, W. de Gray Birch, *Catalogue of seals*, i.237, no.1602.

SCRIBE II–RICHARD

ACTA OF BISHOP ROBERT FOLIOT

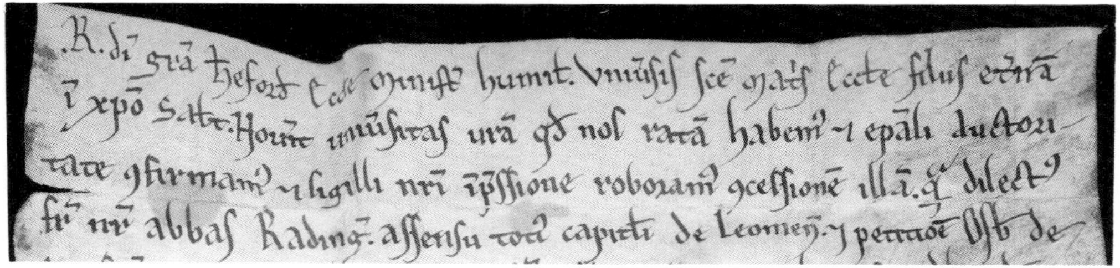

British Library

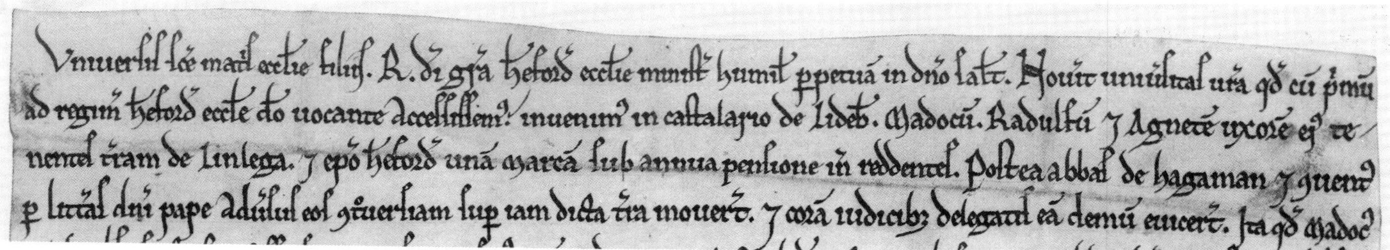

No. 138

Keele University Library

No. 147

Dean and Chapter of Hereford

No. 149

PLATE I

SCRIBE III

ACTA OF BISHOP WILLIAM DE VERE

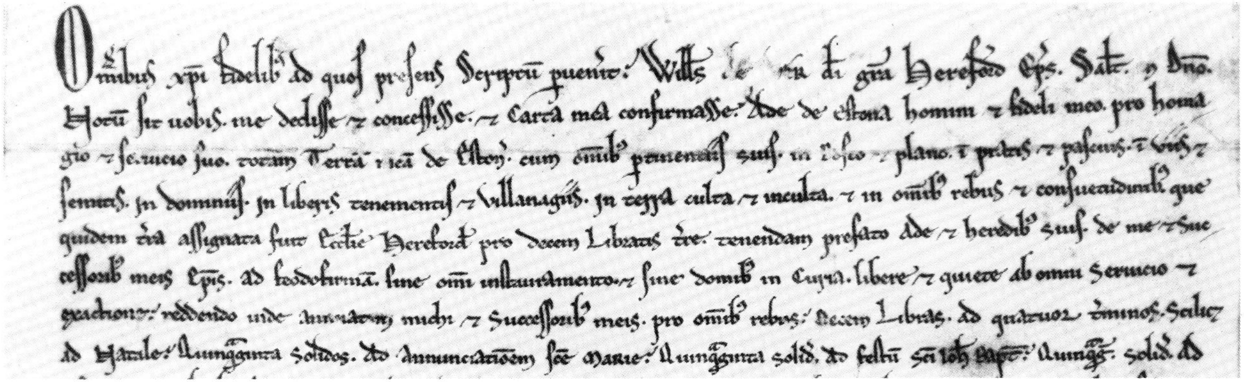

Public Record Office

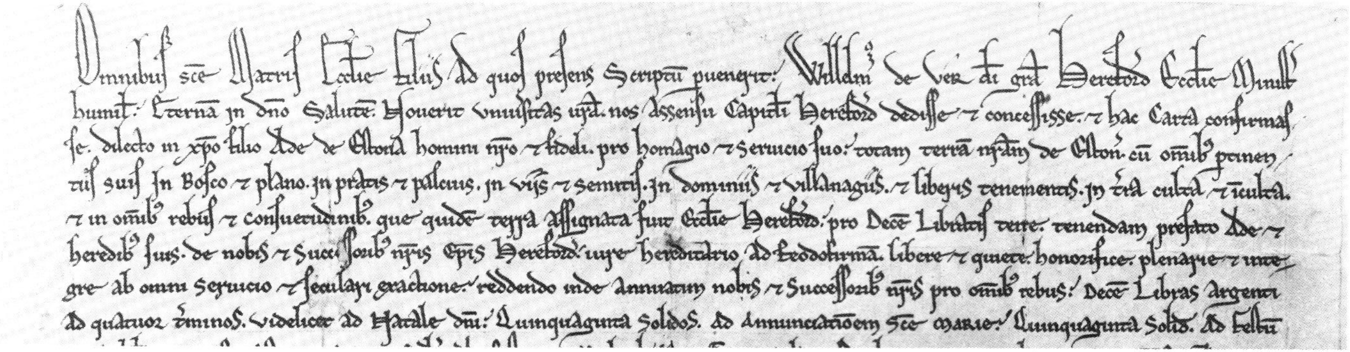

No. 179

Wiltshire County Record Office

No. 180

PLATE II

SCRIBE VII

ACTUM OF BISHOP WILLIAM DE VERE

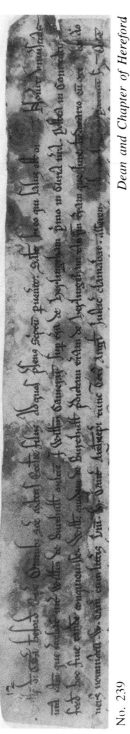

No. 239

Dean and Chapter of Hereford

ACTA OF BISHOP GILES DE BRAOSE

No. 244

Wiltshire County Record Office

No. 252

Shropshire County Record Office

PLATE III

SEAL AND SECRETUM OF BISHOP HUGH FOLIOT

No. 340   *Dean and Chapter of Hereford*

COUNTERSEAL OF BISHOP HUGH FOLIOT

No. 366   *Dean and Chapter*
                    of Hereford

PLATE IV

bishop standing, holding a staff in his left hand (head turning inward) and raising his right hand in blessing; the bishop's tunicle is decorated with delicate criss-cross embroidery, visible on nos.256 and 258. The horn of the mitre is at the front. By collating the legends we obtain + SIGILLV. E(G)IDII. DEI GRA..A. HEREFORDENSIS EPIS-COPI. For his counterseal Giles used a small pointed oval matrix about 43 × 27 mm, showing a cleric, with a tonsured head, standing on a small pedestal and holding a closed book. The legend reads + SECRETVM EGIDII DE BRAOSE. Most of Giles' surviving original charters were sealed on the tag, except no.258, sealed on fine plaited silk cords, and nos.247 and 248, both of which were letters and were probably sealed on the tongue.

One seal impression survives which can probably be ascribed to Hugh de Mapenore, that attached to no.294, a charter for Buildwas abbey. Both the seal and counterseal (a seal *ad causas*) of this impression are different from the seal, the *secretum* and the seal *ad causas* known definitely to have been used by Hugh Foliot, and though it is possible that Hugh Foliot in the course of his episcopate used two episcopal seals and two seals *ad causas* it more likely that the impression on no.294 represents the seal of Hugh de Mapenore. This impression is a fragment only, about 43 × 43 mm, showing a figure in ecclesiastical vestments holding a staff in his left hand, and standing against a plain background. The right hand and head are broken off. The only part of the legend which can be read runs ..(G)ONIS, evidently part of + SIGILLVM HUGONIS.... with the name in the genitive. The counterseal is a pointed oval, 43 × 32 mm; it depicts a bishop kneeling to the right beneath a tripartite pointed arch above which the Virgin is enthroned with the Child on her knee. The legend reads (A)VE MARIA: GRACIA (P).... DOMINVS TECVM. The impression is attached with a tag; Hugh's two other surviving originals, both letters, show traces of having been sealed on the tongue.

Six impressions of Hugh Foliot's seal survive, and there are casts of his seal and his seal *ad causas* in the British Library.[5] The impressions were made from a pointed oval matrix measuring about 74 × 46 mm, showing a bishop in full pontificals, standing with a staff (head turned inwards) in his left hand and raising his right hand in blessing.

5 Nos.316A, 340-1, 343-4, 366; BL Seal casts lv.64 and 65; see also W. de Gray Birch, *Catalogue of seals*, i.237, no.1603 (with a description of the seal *ad causas* depicting St Ethelbert).

The horn of the mitre faces forward. The matrix was a fine piece of craftsmanship; the drapery is sinuous and graceful. To the left of the bishop are two crescent moons, and, according to the British Library cast, groups of small pea-like objects, probably stars, lying between the moons. The legend is fairly complete on the impression attached to no.340, where it runs + HUGO. FOLIOT. DEI GRATI(A) (H)EREFORDENSIS EPISCOPVS. The seal of no.340 is the only one to preserve Hugh's *secretum*, an antique gem 31 × 27 mm, depicting two figures, perhaps Hercules, to the right, and a larger figure, evidently a giant, to the left; the legend runs + SIGLLV' (sic) HUGONIS FOLIOT. The other five impressions of Hugh's seal bear his seal *ad causas* on the reverse. This was a pointed oval, about 55 × 35 mm, showing a king standing on a corbel, bearing a sceptre fleur-de-lizé in his right hand, and with two crescent moons on each side. The surviving impressions may be rather worn, since the cast in the British Library shows three crescent moons and three pointed stars on each side of the figure. The legend, fairly complete in each case, ran + SANCTVS ATHILBERTVS REX ET MARTIR. Most of Hugh Foliot's surviving originals were sealed on the tag, with the exception of nos.341 and 344, which were sealed on plaited silk cords.

EDITORIAL METHOD

The aim of the English Episcopal Acta series is to publish in extenso all original charters issued by English bishops, whether previously published or not, and all previously unpublished charters surviving in copies.[1] Previously published charters are printed only if the existing editions are not easily accessible or are unreliable: otherwise they are all calendared. This volume adheres to this scheme, but with one major modification: the charters issued by Gilbert Foliot, which were edited, together with his letters, by the late Adrian Morey and by C.N.L.Brooke,[2] are here simply calendared, whether or not they survive in the original. One charter of Gilbert Foliot which escaped the notice of Adrian Morey and C.N.L.Brooke is here published in full from a text supplied by C.N.L.Brooke.[3] Gilbert's letters are not

1 For fuller details about the principles of selection and edition adopted by the series, see *EEA* i, pp. lxi-lxiv.
2 *GFL.*
3 No. 94 below.

included in this edition, even in a calendared form, but those issued
by the other Hereford bishops are, because, with one exception, a
letter of Robert de Béthune to Abbot Suger of St-Denis requesting
the gift of some relics, they concern aspects of canon law and episcopal
administration, and therefore usefully supplement the picture of
diocesan activity provided by the charters. Where charters are calendared their witness lists are reproduced in full.

The arrangement of the charters is firstly according to episcopate,
but since hardly any of the charters issued before the 1230s bear dates,
a purely chronological organisation is impossible, and within each
episcopate the charters are grouped alphabetically by recipient. However, the reader's attention is drawn to the fact that in certain cases
involving mother abbeys and dependent priories, chiefly Reading
abbey and its priory of Leominster and also Gloucester abbey and its
priory of St Guthlac's in Hereford, it has not always been possible to
establish whether a charter should be listed under the mother or the
daughter house. Under each recipient, charters are given in chronological order in so far as this can be ascertained. Charters which
cannot be securely assigned to either Robert de Melun or Robert
Foliot are placed in a separate section after the charters of Robert de
Melun; charters which cannot be securely assigned to either Hugh de
Mapenore or Hugh Foliot are placed in a separate section after the
charters of Hugh de Mapenore. Lost charters are denoted by an
asterisk placed immediately before the series number. Where there is
evidence of an episcopal transaction, but no specific evidence that this
was consigned to writing, no separate series number is given but the
transaction is included in the main sequence and is given the number
of the preceding actum, with a letter appended (e.g. *13A); a similar
number plus letter system is used for corroborative statements appended by Gilbert Foliot to charters issued by other people. Forged
charters are denoted by a cross preceding the series number.

After the caption to each charter follow the date, if known, or
limiting dates enclosed in square brackets, and thereafter the list of
manuscript sources, distinguished by sigla. A is invariably used for
originals (A^{1}and A^2 in those cases where two exemplars survive); BCD
etc. are used for copies, listed in chronological order as far as this is
known, B being the earliest. Unless otherwise stated, B serves as the
basis of the edition for those charters for which no originals survive.
Post-medieval copies are not as a rule referred to, save where no

medieval copies survive. Where the original survives, brief descriptions of its dimensions (greatest width and greatest depth, plus depth of turnup, where applicable), its sealing arrangements and its medieval endorsements are provided. Modern endorsements are only given when they give information about the history of the charter. In the case of cartulary copies, a brief account of the date and of any former pagination is given; rubrics are only mentioned if they shed light on the contents of the charter or reveal archival arrangements. Following the list of manuscript sources a list of previous editions is given, where applicable. Where appropriate, textual notes follow the text of the charter, and historical notes come at the end.

The spelling of originals has been retained, but 'i' is treated as the equivalent of 'i' and 'j' and 'u' is used as a vowel, 'v' as a consonant. The rules concerning 'i', 'u' and 'v' also apply to copies, and here in addition 'c' has been changed to 't' in cases where classical Latin would demand it – 'confirmatio', 'servitium'. The name 'Christus' is spelled 'Cristus' throughout (cf. Pierre Chaplais, 'The spelling of Christ's name in medieval Anglo-Latin', *Journal of the Society of Archivists*, viii (1987), 261–80). Abbreviated Christian names are extended where the full form of the name is clear, but names indicated by initials only are not extended. Modern usage has been adopted in respect of capital letters in both originals and copies. Conjectural readings are placed within pointed brackets, readings supplied from other manuscripts are placed within square brackets and insertions and interlineations are denoted by the marks \ /. The punctuation of originals has been retained, but modern punctuation has been applied to copies. Ampersands and tironian symbols are not reproduced. Manuscripts are collated, but where the originals survive the variant spellings of copies are only rarely included.

Where charters bear dates these are stated after the caption without parentheses. Otherwise, limiting dates are given, separated by multiplication signs, in square brackets (e.g. [1186 × 1198]). Modern dating practice in starting the year on 1 January is followed. In providing limiting dates, extensive use has been made of the following works, which are not usually cited and to which the reader is invited to refer: Diana Greenway's new edition of John Le Neve's *Fasti Ecclesiae Anglicanae 1066-1300* to provide dates for dignitaries and canons of the cathedrals of St Paul's and Lincoln and archdeacons attached to dioceses with monastic cathedrals, *Handbook of British*

Chronology to provide dates for bishops and earls, and, for the personnel and foundation dates of religious houses, *Heads of Religious Houses*, and *Medieval Religious Houses: England and Wales*. Some closing dates are determined by the periods of office of certain canons and dignitaries of Hereford, and a full explanation of the careers of the men in question is provided in Appendix I below.

ROBERT OF LOTHARINGIA

1. Profession of obedience

Profession of obedience made to Lanfranc, archbishop of Canterbury.

[29 December 1079]

   B = BL, Cotton MS Cleop. E i, fo.28va-b. s.xii in. C = Canterbury D. & C. Register A, fo.232v. s.xiv med

   Pd, *Canterbury Professions*, 31, no.41.

2. Roger de Lacy

Grant to Roger de Lacy of the manor of Holme Lacy for the service of two knights.

1085

   A = PRO, C115 G31/4095 (Chancery Masters Exhibits, Duchess of Norfolk, Scudamore Deeds). Endorsed: Altera pars habetur Gloucestre in ecclesia beati Petri apostoli (s.xii[1]); Cyrographum de hamma (s.xii med); De servicio duorum militum apud Homme Lacy (s.xiv). 349 × 210 mm. Polled chirograph; no sealing arrangements.

   Pd, V.H.Galbraith, 'An Episcopal Landgrant', *EHR*, xliv (1929), 371-2, with facsimile opposite 353.

+ Hoc privilegium Rotbertus Herefordensis æcclesiae episcopus inter illum et Rogerum filium Waltheri notari precepit de terra quadam nomine Hammæ et quæ ad illam pertinent. quæ est æcclesiae sanctae Marie genitricis Dei. et Sancti Adelberti martiris. quam terram predictus episcopus in proprio dominio ad victum ecclesiæ et sui tenebat. Hanc predictus miles videlicet Rogerus. ab episcopo per amicos. et per pecuniam requisivit. Episcopus vero consilio suorum concessit illi eandem terram. ea conventione ut duobus militibus serviet sibi. sicuti pater eius fecit ubicumque necesse fuerit. necnon et ea conventione. ut homines episcopi de Hamtuna atque de Hereforda et qui ad eam pertinent. de silva accipiant ligna. solummodo ad opus episcopi quantum sibi necesse erit ad comburendum. et ad mansiones restaurandas. et porci de eisdem maneriis ex eadem silva pascantur. illi scilicet qui proprii fuerint episcopi. et eo insuper adhuc tenore. si Rogerus monachus efficiatur. vel moriatur. quod neque mater. neque uxor. neque filii. neque fratres. neque aliquis parentum suorum de hac terra supradicta se intromittant. sed episcopus quicumque tunc erit ad proficuum sanctæ æcclesie et sui absque ulla contradictione qualis tunc fuerit recipiat. Hoc actum est anno dominice incarnationis millesimo. lxxx.vo. indictione. viiia. Huius rei testes sunt. comes Rogerus. et filius eius Hugo. et alter filius Everardus. et comitissa. et vicecomes Warinus. Osbertus filius Ricardi. Drogo filius Pontii. Gerardus de Tornai. Willelmus Malbedan. Gislbertus*a* cognistabilis Rogeri comitis. De hominibus episcopi. Gerardus*b* frater eius. Hainfridus archidiaconus. Ansfridus presbiter. Willelmus. Leuuinus. Alfuuardus. Saulfus. Aluuinus; laici. Udo. Athalardus. Franco. Arnulfus. Tedbaldus. Rotbertus. Gozo. Osbertus. Petrus. Ricardus pincerna. De hominibus Rogeri. clerici. Raulfus. Gosfridus. Odo. Geroldus.; laici. Walterus. Heribertus de Furcis. Ricardus de Stantuna. Herimannus de Dreuuis. Rotbertus de Baschevilla. Ricardus de Eschetot. Willelmus de Ebroia. Raulfus de Salcet. Nicolaus. Gotmundus.; Predictus Rogerus tenet adhuc aliam terram de victu proprio episcopi scilicet Onieberie tali conditione. quamdiu vixerit unoquoque anno in festivitate Sancti Martini. xx. solidos dabit. et post obitum suum vel etiam si monachus efficiatur. qualiscumque tunc terra illa fuerit. ad episcopum absque ulla contradictione redibit. Huius rei testes sunt. Ansfridus de Cormelis. Edricus. de Uuendloc. Alter Edricus. dapifer. et omnes supradicti excepto Rogero comite et familia sua

CYROGRAPHUM*c*

*a*sic.   *b*G of Gerardus *corr. fr.* L.   *c Top half of letters visible.*

For the de Lacy family and their connection with Holme Lacy, see (in addition to Galbraith, *art. cit.*), Domesday Book, i, fo.181d, W.E.Wightman, *The Lacy Family in England and Normandy, 1066-1194* (Oxford, 1966), 128-9, 153, and H.M.Colvin, 'Holme Lacy' in *Medieval Studies Presented to Rose Graham*, ed. V.Ruffer and A.J.Taylor (Oxford, 1950), 15-40. The de Lacy family denied in the 1170s that they owed any more than the service of one knight and this led to a dispute between them and Bishop Robert Foliot which was settled in no.159

below. Gerard, brother of Robert of Lotharingia, whose name occurs at the head of the bishop's clergy, suggesting that he was the leader of the cathedral clergy, is probably identifiable with the otherwise unidentifiable Dean Gerard whose obituary is recorded on 6 December in the cathedral obit book (Bodl. MS Rawlinson B328, fo.49v). The Leuuinus mentioned among the bishop's clergy is probably to be identified with the Dean Liwin whose obituary is recorded on 13 November (ibid., fo.45); presumably Liwin succeeded Gerard at some point between 1085 and the appointment of Erchemar as dean in the early twelfth century. The William who occurs among the episcopal clerks was identified by Galbraith (*art. cit.*, 360) with William, clerk of the bishop, who held half the church of Lydbury in 1086 (Domesday Book, i, fo.252b).

GERARD

3. Profession of obedience

Profession of obedience to Anselm, archbishop of Canterbury.

[15 June 1096]

> A = Canterbury, D. & C. Ch. Ant. C115, no. 5. No medieval endorsements. 210 × 52 mm.
>
> B = Ibid., Ch. Ant. C117, no. 9. s.xii med. C = Ibid., Register A, fo.232v. s.xiv med. D = BL, Cotton MS Dom. A v, fo.14v.
>
> Pd from A, *Canterbury Professions*, 35, no.53, and from D, *Historians of the Church of York*, iii.15.

Ego Gerardus Herefordensis ecclesie electus. et a te reverende pater Anselme sancte Cantuariensis ecclesie archiepiscope et tocius Britannie primas antistes consecrandus. tibi et omnibus successoribus tuis canonicam obedientiam me per omnia servaturum promitto. et signo sancte crucis confirmo. +[a]

[a] *autograph cross, A. BC omit* et signo ... confirmo.+

A was written c.1200: N.R.Ker, *English manuscripts in the century after the Norman conquest* (Oxford 1960), 18.

†4. Gloucester abbey (spurious)

Licence to Gloucester abbey to appropriate the churches of Churcham (with the chapel of Bulley) and Preston and to take an annual pension from the church of Taynton. Dated 15 July 1100

> B = Gloucester Cathedral, Seals and Deeds, vol. VIII, no.1, contained in an inspeximus of Hugh Foliot (no.330 below) contained in an inspeximus of Bps Robert of Bath and William of Llandaff datable 1275 × 1287. C = PRO C150/1 (Gloucester abbey cartulary), fos.48r-v, no.177. s.xiv ex. Contained in an inspeximus of Hugh Foliot, as above.
>
> Pd from C, *Gloucester cartulary*, i.250-1, no.177.

Omnibus sancte matris ecclesie filiis hanc cartam nostram inspecturis vel audituris Gerardus dei gratia Hereforden' episcopus salutem in eo qui est vera salus animarum. Universitati vestre notum facimus per presentes quod[a] nos anno gratie millesimo centesimo idibus Iulii una cum venerabilibus fratribus nostris[b] dominis Sampsone Wygorn', Gundulfo Roffen', et Herveo Bangoren' coepiscopis dedicationi et consecrationi ecclesie beatorum apostolorum Petri et Pauli quam reverendus abbas Serlo in villa Glavorn'[c] construxerat nostram presentiam simul et ministerium cum omni qua potuimus exhibuisse devotione. Et quia loci prefati conventus quamplures defectus ut in ornamentis ecclesie et aliis sibi necessariis patiebatur, nos divine caritatis intuitu predicti conventus necessitatibus compatientes de consensu totius capituli nostri Hereforden' concessimus predictis abbati et conventui Glavorn' cenobii et successoribus eorum has[d] subscriptas ecclesias perpetuis temporibus habendas et in proprios usus convertendas ad suam et ecclesie sue perpetuam sustentationem, videlicet ecclesiam de Chircham[e] cum capella de Bolleya[f] et decimis et aliis pertinentiis suis, ecclesiam de Preston' cum omnibus pertinentiis suis, salva honestis capellanis qui in dictis ecclesiis ministrabunt rationabili sustentatione. Concessimus etiam[g] eisdem religiosis duas marcas annue pensionis de ecclesia sancti Laurentii de Teynton' et etiam perceptionem decimarum omnium terrarum suarum quas propriis laboribus vel sumptibus suis excoluerint in diocesi nostra, videlicet maneriorum suorum de Hyneham et Chircham,[h] de Preston' et de Brumpton',[i] [j] de Leden', et etiam duas garbas totius decime hominum suorum de Leden',[j] de Hyda, salvis rectori ecclesie de Yarkulle[k] annuatim duobus solidis et una summa frumenti, de Rodelei,[l] salva rectori ecclesie de Westbury tertia garba decime provenientis de dominicis[m] terris de Rodele.[n] Concessimus etiam eisdem omnes decimas de omnibus dominicis terris domini de Ewyas sitis in parochia de sancta Keyna et decimam cuiusdam culture[o] in Poston. Preterea omnes ecclesias, decimas, terras et possessiones quas hactenus in nostra dyocesi sunt adepti eis auctoritate episcopali et unanimi capituli nostri consensu confirmamus perpetuis temporibus possidendas, et, ut ea que premissa sunt futuris temporibus inconcussa permaneant, presentem cartam nostram tam sigilli nostri quam sigilli capituli nostri Hereforden' appositione duximus roborandum. Teste tota synodo nostra.

^{a}fo.48v C. ^{b}nostris *om.*, B. ^{c}'Glouc' C. ^{d}haas C. ^{e}Chirchehamme C. ^{f}Bulleya C.
^{g}etiam *om.*, B. ^{h}Hynehamm', de Chirchehamm' C. ^{i}Brompton' C.
$^{j-j}$*inserted after* dominicis terris de Rodele C. ^{k}Harehull' C. ^{l}Rodlee C. ^{m}proventus
C.
^{n}Rodleye C. ^{o}*B adds* terre.

Hugh Foliot's charter of inspeximus (no.330) states that the original of Gerard's
charter was burnt in 1122 and that what he inspected was a copy sealed by Bp
Simon of Worcester (1125-1150). The form of Gerard's charter shows that it was
written at the earliest in the last quarter of the twelfth century (note the use of the
first person plural and the form of the general address, the notification and the
corroboration), and possibly later. At least some of the content, too, is spurious:
Gloucester abbey did not acquire Taynton church until the 1130s (see no.18
below), and the arrangement by which it obtained the tithe of Monkhide, agreeing
to pay the rector of Yarkhill two shillings and a measure of wheat a year, dates
from c.1158 × 1163 (*GFL* no.307). Preston church still had only the status of a
chapel as late as 1131 × 1148 (see no.48 below). Very probably the rest of the
content is also spurious.

*5. Sutton parish

Adjudgement of land to Sutton parish.
                                [15 June 1096 × December 1100]

Mention only, in charters of Bp Robert de Béthune and Hereford cathedral
chapter, dated 1132, recording the composition of a dispute between Nicholas of
Sutton and Godric of Marden. Gerard's grant is said to have been witnessed. See
no.55 below.

REINHELM

6. Profession of obedience

Profession of obedience to Anselm, archbishop of Canterbury

[11 August 1107]

A = Canterbury D. & C. Ch. Ant., C115, no.7. No medieval endorsements. 170 mm wide; 40 mm deep at left edge, 35 at right. Remains of a tongue; no seal survives.

B = Ibid., Ch. Ant., C117, no. 14. s.xii med. C = BL, Cotton MS Cleop. E i (Register of the see of Canterbury), fo. 30v. s.xii med. D = Canterbury D. & C. Register A (The Prior's Register), fo.232v. s.xiv med.

Pd from A, *Canterbury professions*, 36, no.57.

Ego Reinelmus Herefordensis ecclesie electus. et a te reverende pater Anselme sancte Cantuariensis ecclesie archiepiscope et totius Britannie primas antistes consecrandus. tibi et omnibus successoribus tuis[a] canonicam obedientiam me per omnia servaturum promitto.

[a]tibi canonice succedentibus *interlineated in a later hand, A.*

†7. Gloucester abbey (spurious)

Confirmation to the monks of Gloucester and to the prior of Hereford of the churches granted to them by Hugh de Lacy, St Peter's, Hereford, St Owen's, Hereford, Holme Lacy, Castle Frome and Stoke Lacy.

[11 August 1107 × 27/28 October 1115]

B = Oxford, Balliol College, MS 271 (cartulary of St Guthlac's Hereford), fo.102v, no.455. s.xiv in.

Rein(elmus) dei gratia Heref' episcopus archid',[a] decanis, universisque fidelibus et filiis Heref' episcopatus salutem et benedictionem. Qui domino devotius obsequitur digne ab ipsius fidelibus inpetrantibus iustis exauditur.[b] Inde est quod universitati vestre presenti scripto notificamus nos dilectis fratribus monachis Glouc' et nomi-

natim priori de Heref' et ipsius loci conventionis ecclesias et ecclesiastica beneficia concessisse que sibi ab Hugone de Lacy concessa sunt
et donata et ipsius carta quam inspeximus confirmata, scilicet ecclesiam Sancti Petri de Heref', cum omnibus prebendis et pertinentiis
suis, et ecclesiam Sancti Audoeni in eadem civitate, ecclesiam de
Hamme, et ecclesiam de Froma, et ecclesiam de Stok' in Herefordsira,
et quicquid ad eas pertinet in capellis, terris, et decimis, videlicet de
porcis et agnis, de lano et caseis, de vitulis, de pullanis equorum, de
pasnagio, de feno, et lacte et lino. Has iamdictas ecclesias cum omnibus ad ipsas pertinentibus iamdictis fratribus concedimus et episcopali auctoritate confirmamus, ut in predictis ecclesiis pro voluntate
sua vicarios intrent^c et ammoveant si eis fideliter non servierint, salvo
iure et dignitate episcopali. Valete.

^{a}*uncertain whether singular or plural.* ^{b}*exaudiuntur B.* ^{c}*intrarant B.*

A charter of Hugh de Lacy (ibid., fo.93v), notifying the grant of churches by the
hand of Bp Reinhelm, is described as 'a suspect source' by Martin Brett, *The
English Church under Henry I* (Oxford 1975), 142n. The language of Reinhelm's
charter, with its use of the first person plural and papal features such as the
salutation and the opening of the notification, suggests that it was forged in the
mid-twelfth century or later. The references to (rural) deans in the address and to
vicars in the disposition are unusually early. Vicars and (rural) deans are mentioned in the so-called 1092 Worcester synodal document (*Councils and Synods I*,
ii.635-9) and in the decrees of the 1108 London primatial council (*ibid*, ii.702). The
Worcester synodal document is probably a forgery of the middle of the twelfth
century: see J.Barrow, 'How the twelfth-century monks of Worcester perceived
their past', in P.Magdalino, ed. *The perception of the past in twelfth-century Europe*
(London 1992), 60–9. The terms dean (to mean a rural dean) and vicar (to mean
the substitute for a parson) are not met with frequently in the early twelfth century.
Vicars and a vicarage are mentioned in two episcopal acta apparently of roughly
the same date as no.7, one of Bishop Ralph Luffa of Chichester (1091-23) *(Chichester acta*, no.5, 1107 x 1123) and the other of Archbishop Th., either Thomas II
(1109-1114) or Thurstan (1114-1140), of York (*EYC*, vi, no.11, and *EEA*, v, no.29),
but Ralph's charter reads as though the sentences referring to vicars were added
subsequently to a pre-existing charter, while Archbishop Th.'s charter, which
survives in the original, is written in a hand of the second half of the twelfth
century, since several of its majuscule letters have doubled strokes, and therefore
must be a forgery.

*8. Sutton parish

Confirmation of Bishop Gerard's adjudgement of land to Sutton parish.
[11 August 1107 × 27/28 October 1115]

Mention only, in charters of Bishop Robert de Béthune and Hereford cathedral chapter dated 1132 (see no.55 below) recording the composition of a dispute between Nicholas of Sutton and Godric of Marden.

GEOFFREY DE CLIVE

9. Profession of obedience

Profession of obedience to Ralph, archbishop of Canterbury.

[26 December 1115]

A = Canterbury, D. & C., Ch. Ant. C115, no.15. No medieval endorsements. Irregular shape. 152 × 128 mm. Possibly originally sealed on a tongue; tongue and seal do not survive.

B = Ibid., Ch. Ant. C117, no.27. s.xii med. C = BL, Cotton MS Cleop. E i (register of the see of Canterbury), fo.31v. s.xii med. D = Canterbury, D. & C. Register A (The Prior's Register), fo.232v, s.xiv med.

Pd from A, *Canterbury professions*, 38, no.66.

Ego GOSFRIDUS ad regimen ecclesie Herefordensis electus. et a te reverende pater Radulfe sancte Cantuariensis archiepiscope et totius Britannie primas antistes consecrandus: tibi et omnibus successoribus tuis canonicam obedientiam me per omnia exhibiturum profiteor.

RICHARD DE CAPELLA

(†) 10. St Owen's church, Gloucester (possibly spurious)

Dedication of the church of St Owen's (St Audoenus), Gloucester, at the request of Walter of Gloucester. [20 October 1123 × 29 March 1125]

> B = PRO, C115 K2/6683 (Llanthony cartulary, A1), fo.25r, section i, no.52. s.xiv med. Rubric: Carta Roberti Heref' episcopi de dedicatione ecclesie Sancti Audoeni Glouc' et cimiterii et parochii (*sic*) eiusdem et de confirmatione prebende et capellarum, decimarum, terrarum et elemosinarum quas Walterus de Glouc' eidem ecclesie dedit et carta sua confirmavit.

R. dei gratia Hereford' episcopus omnibus filiis et fidelibus sancte Wygorn' ecclesie salutem. Notum sit vobis omnibus quod ex debito nobis iniuncto officio et petitione Walteri de Gloec' dedicavimus ecclesiam Sancti Audoeni de Glouc' et cimiterium ibi fecimus et parochiam attitulavimus, et canonica institutione et episcopali auctoritate confirmavimus in prebendam libere et quiete et absque omni controversia et calumpnia omnes capellas et decimas et terras et elemosinas quas ibi predictus Walterus in presentia nostra donavit, et per cartam suam assignavit. Statuimus etiam et decrevimus quod quemadmodum ecclesia sancti Audoeni ex conquestu Anglie tenuerat sua *ª* ecclesiastica beneficia principaliter*ª* de antecessoribus ipsius Walteri qui eam fundaverant et postea de ipso Waltero sicut in futuro teneat in capite omnes possessiones suas que coram nobis ei concesse sunt, et per nos confirmate, de ipso Waltero et heredibus eius in perpetuum, quicumque terras illas habeat unde decime hic sunt attitulate. Quisquis autem huius ecclesie bona diripuerit et iniuste abstulerit, aut potestate tyrannica detinuerit, anathema sit.

ª-ª over erasure, B.

The form of this document, with its use of the first person plural, suggests that the wording of the charter might have been altered in the second half of the twelfth century. However, it was probably based on a genuine charter of Bp Richard, since a forger would have thought it more natural to write a confirmation issued by a bishop of Worcester. Walter of Gloucester's grant to St Owen's, Gloucester, is printed by D.Walker, *Charters of the Earldom of Hereford, 1095-1201*, Camden

Miscellany, vol.22, Camden Society, 4th ser., i (1964), 37-38. Walker dates Walter's grant and this charter to 1095, after the death of Wulfstan, bp of Worcester, and before the death of Robert of Lotharingia, partly because of the rubric to this document in the Llanthony Cartulary (see above) and partly because Walter is not referred to as constable, a title which he acquired later. But the Bp R. must be Richard de Capella (16 January 1121 – 15 August 1127), because Walter's grant is witnessed by an archdn Thurstan, evidently Thurstan, one of the archdns of the diocese of Worcester, whose first dated occurrence is 24 September 1122 and who died or resigned after 1140/1. Walter of Gloucester died in 1126. Bp Richard could have issued his confirmation if (as seems likely) he was acting as vicar of the see of Worcester during the Worcester vacancy between 20 October 1123 and 29 March 1125.

11. Reading abbey

Confirmation to Reading abbey of its possession of Leominster church and its associated parish, listing the constituent settlements, which were testified to by old and authoritative men as belonging to Leominster parish: Broadward, Knoakes (Court), Monkland, both Dilwyns, Luntley, Kinnersley, Woonton, both Sarnesfields, Titley, Hope-under-Dinmore, Wharton, Newton, Gattertop, Stoke Prior, both Hatfields, Risbury, Humber, Edvin Ralph, Butterley, Broadfield, both Hamptons, Ford, Hennor, Eyton, Hampton Wafer, Stockton, Ashton, Brimfield, Upton, Middleton, Drayton, Hamnish, Whyle, Pudleston, Brockmanton, Ford Abbey, Luston, Eye and Croft; these men also said that much else had belonged to the parish of Leominster, but that they would say nothing of this because it was too long ago.   1123 [after 15 April]

> B = BL, Egerton MS 3031 (Reading abbey cartulary), fos.54v-55r. s.xii ex. C = BL, Cotton MS Domitian A iii (Leominster priory cartulary), fo.59v. s.xiii med. D = Ibid., fos.64v-65r, in an inspeximus of Giles de Braose. An inspeximus by Bishop Hugh de Mapenore, ibid., fos.66-v, has been copied out by the scribe with the omission of the text of Richard's charter.
>
> Pd, *Mon. Ang.*, iv.56, and, from B, C, D, *Reading cartularies*, i.287-8, no.354.

Actum[a] est anno Verbi Incarnati mcxxiii regnante Henrico rege feliciter[b].

[a] etc' *add.; text ends here,* D.
[b] regante *add. after* feliciter B; regnante... feliciter *om.,* C.

For the date, see *Reading cartularies, loc. cit.*; for a summary of the early history of Leominster church, which had alternated between being a foundation for nuns and a secular minster, see B.R.Kemp, 'The monastic dean of Leominster', *EHR*, lxxxiii (1968), 505-6. In the mid-eleventh century the church and the lordship of Leominster, a small ancient shire which also formed the church's *parochia*, were granted to Edith, wife of Edward the Confessor, and when she died they passed to the crown. Henry I used them as part of the original endowments of Reading Abbey, which he had founded in 1121, and his grant of Leominster was mentioned in Calixtus II's confirmation of 19 June 1123 (*PUE*, iii, no.9, and cf. *Reading cartularies*, i.15-16). For later confirmations by bishops of Hereford see *GFL*, no.343 (no.111 below), and also below, nos.300 and 352. Giles' inspeximus is no. 268.

*12. Walter of Gloucester

Grant to Walter of Gloucester and his heirs of Little Hereford and of Ullingswick in Herefordshire in return for the service of two knights.

[7 January 1121 × April 1121]

Mention only, in a confirmation of Henry I, issued at Cheddar, probably *c*.April 10, 1121: BL, Cotton Ch. XI, 60, pd W. de Grey Birch, 'The Great Seals of King Henry I', *The Journal of the British Archaeological Association*, xxix (1873), 258; cal. *RRAN*, ii, no.1268; see also Farrer, *Itin.*, 251, and note by J.H.Round in *Ancient Charters*, (PRS, 10, 1888), 19. Henry confirms the grant made by a Bp R. of Hereford, whom Round takes to be Reinhelm and the editors of *RRAN* take to be Richard. Round showed that the grant must be prior to the marriage of Miles of Gloucester in the summer of 1121 (on the marriage see D.Walker, 'Miles of Gloucester, earl of Hereford', *TBGAS*, lxxvii [1958], 68). Richard de Capella was elected and received the temporalities of his see on 7 January 1121 and was consecrated on 16 January, and it is quite possible that the deed was his. Ullingswick was held by an unnamed knight from the bishop at Domesday, and at Little Hereford, which had seven hides, half a hide was held by a priest and half by a radman (*Domesday Book*, i, fos. 181d, 182d).

ROBERT DE BETHUNE

13. Profession of obedience

Profession of obedience to William, archbishop of Canterbury.

[28 June 1131]

B = BL, Cotton MS Cleop. E i (register of the see of Canterbury), fo.35va. s.xii med. C = Canterbury, D. & C. Register A (The Prior's Register), fo.232v. s.xiv med.

Pd from B, C, *Canterbury professions*, 41, no.78.

*13A. The sick poor of Dudston

Confirmation of a grant by Miles of Gloucester of half the manor of Barrington to the sick poor of Dudston near Gloucester.

[28 June 1131 × 16 April 1148, possibly 1136]

Mention only, in a confirmation of Miles' grant issued by Bp Simon of Worcester (PRO C115 K2/6683, fo.64v), who says that Robert confirmed Miles' grant while he was dedicating the chapel of the community of Dudston; Robert dedicated the chapel in Simon's absence, perhaps therefore in 1136, when Simon was abroad (see no.35). Simon does not specify whether Robert's confirmation was in writing or not. On the Dudston community, see E. Kealey, *Medieval Medicus* (Baltimore 1981), 112.

14. Eugenius III

Letter to Pope Eugenius III supporting Archbishop Theobald of Canterbury in his case against Bishop Bernard of St David's concerning the primacy of the see of St David's.

[18 February 1145 × 12 October 1146]

A = Canterbury, D. & C. Ch. Ant. D 108. Medieval endorsement: Testimonium Roberti Hereford' contra Bernardum Menevensem qui resilire voluit a subiectione Cantuar' archiepiscopi. 196 mm wide, 141 mm deep at left, 109 mm deep

at right. Remains of tongue and wrapping tie. Seal does not survive.
B = Bodl., Tanner MS 127, p.340. s.xvii.
Cal., *PUE*, ii.14; *Welsh ep. acts*, i.264; M.Richter, *Giraldus Cambrensis*, 2nd
edn. (Aberystwyth 1976), 131; *HMCR*, v.453. A letter of Bp Robert of Bath with
exactly the same text is printed by Haddan and Stubbs, i.353.

Reverentissimo domino ac patri .E. dei gratia summo pontifici sanc-
titatis sue servus. Robertus eadem gratia Heref'. ecclesie dev(ot)us*a*
minister. salutem. cum debita obedientia. Cum in omnibus veritati
standum sit. ibi precipue veritatis testimonio innitendum est ubi ipsa
maxime periclitatur. Unde cum nunc de periculo et diminutione
matris nostre Cantuariensis ecclesie agi audiamus. cui frater noster et
coepiscopus. B. de Sancto David. debitam ex professione subiectionis
obedientiam subtrahere velle dicitur *?* non sine periculo nostro veritatem tacere posse videmur. Confidenter igitur et secure in conspectu
maiestatis vestre attestamur. quod retroactis temporibus inconvulsum stetisse audivimus et nostris deinceps illibatum stetisse cognovimus. Predicta itaque metropolis nostra cum in multis et magnis
dignitatibus pre*b* ceteris regni nostri ecclesiis. a temporibus beati
Augustini Anglorum apostoli multipliciter effloruit. a nobis ante hac*c*
auditum non est quin predicti .B. predecessores prefate metropolitane
sedis archiepiscopis. suffraganei. obedientes. extiterint. et ab eis
denique consecrati et illi scripto professionis obligati fuerint. Ut
autem et ad tempora moderna et ad hunc ipsum .B. redeamus. ipse
per impositionem manus*d* .Rad'. Cant' archiepiscopi. promotus
fuisse. et scripta professione que adhuc in eadem ecclesia permanere
dicitur. obligatus teneri dinoscitur. Postmodum vero post nostram
scilicet promotionem. istum ad vocationes bone memorie Willelmi
Cant' archiepiscopi frequenter venire. et eius canonicis iussionibus
tanquam unum ex ceteris suffraganeis suis obedienter et sine contradictione obtemperare meminimus et vidimus. Iste denique est qui a
venerabili*e* domino. Alb'. Hostiensi episcopo. tunc apostolice sedis
legato. ad patris nostri. Teob'. qui nunc ord' Cant' ecclesie deo
auctore presidet consecrationem*f* evocatus tanquam suffraganeus. et
minister. atque cóóperator nobiscum astitit. Eapropter cum eodem et
pro eodem archiepiscopo nostro. sanctitati vestre supplicantes exoramus. ne suggestioni sepedicti .B. que ex fabulosa antiquitate sive ex
antiqua fabulositate. fundamentum et initium sumit *?* aurem accom-
modetis. sed pretaxatam matrem nostram in dignitatum suarum statu

incolumem servetis. Bene valeat paternitas vestra in Cristo domine pater.

ᵃpartly illegible A. *ᵇtear obscures bottom stroke of* p *A.*
ᶜsic A (also in Canterbury D. & C. Ch. Ant. C136 and C137: cf. note below). *ᵈ* n *of*
manus *illegible A.ᵉvene- illegible A; supplied from Ch. Ant. C136 and C137. ᶠ-sec- illegible A; supplied from Ch. Ant. C136, C137.*

Five other bps, Henry of Winchester, Robert of Bath, Nigel of Ely, Robert of Exeter, and Everard, ex-bp of Norwich, wrote to Eugenius III at the same time. Apart from Everard's letter, which survives only in a copy (Oxford, Bodl. MS Tanner 127, p.339), the originals of their letters survive as Canterbury D. & C. Ch. Ant. C134, C136, D107 and C137 respectively. All the bps except Henry of Winchester used the same text, and Robert of Bath and Nigel of Ely employed the same scribe. There are some similarities of script between Robert de Béthune's letter and Nigel's, but it is not certain if they were written by the same man. According to *Welsh ep. acts*, 197-8: 'These letters from the suffragans of Canterbury seem to have been of the nature of a round robin, and were probably solicited by archbp Theobald from all his suffragans, but only the six which have been mentioned here survived'. For the dating, see *PUE, loc. cit.* and *Councils and Synods I*, ii.813-4. Pope Eugenius III was consecrated 18 February 1145, but if Robert's letter was written at the same time as Everard's it must be later than April/early May 1145, since Everard was still bp at this point (ibid., ii.811). Everard died 12 October, probably 1146.

15. Gloucester abbey

Institution of Stephen, priest, as vicar of Holme Lacy on presentation by Walter, abbot of Gloucester. [1131 × 1137, poss. 1134]

B = Oxford, Balliol College MS 271 (cartulary of St Guthlac's, Hereford), fo. 56v. s.xiv in.

Notum*ᵃ* sit omnibus tam presentibus quam futuris quod, vacanti post decessum Iohannis presbiteri ecclesia beati Cutberti de Hamma quam Hugo de Lacy aliquando prius concesserat deo et Sancto Petro et abbati et monachis Gloec', ego Robertus episcopus Hereforden' prebens auctoritatem et assensum eidem concessioni ad presentationem et petitionem Walteri abbatis Gloec' suscepi Stephanum presbiterum in vicariam ipsius ecclesie de Hamma et eidem curam animarum sub hoc tenore commisi, ut michi quidem et ministris*ᵇ* meis de episcopalibus respondeat abbati vero et monachis de annuo censu quem eis debet de ipsa ecclesia et omnibus ad eam pertinentibus per omnia fidelis existat. Hoc autem quia firmum esse volo scripti presentis et sigilli mei auctoritate confirmo. Hiis testibus. Roberto

cantore, Briennio thesaurario, Gilberto de Eborac', magistro Eustachio, magistro Ranul', Pagano filio Iohannis, Milone constabulario[c],
Helia de Sey, Roberto Brien, Hugone Brien et aliis.

[a]N *of* notum *omitted for rubricator, B.* [b]minstris, B. [c]constabilario, B.

Payn fitz John died in 1137. Martin Brett, 'The Organization of the English
Secular Church in the Reign of Henry I' (unpublished Oxford D.Phil. thesis,
1968), p.278, points out that the witness list of this document is similar to that of
the 1134 agreement (no.17) and that the two were probably issued at the same
time.

16. Gloucester abbey

*Confirmation to Abbot Walter and the community of St Peter's, Glouces-
ter, of the parsonage of St Cuthbert's, Holme Lacy, granted by Payn fitz
John with the assent of his wife Sybil.* [1134 × 1139]

B = Oxford, Balliol College, MS 271 (cartulary of St Guthlac's, Hereford), fo.55v,
no.220. s.xiv in.

Rogerus[a] dei gratia Hereford' episcopus archid(iacono)[b], decano[c], et
omnibus ministris Hereford' ecclesie ceterisque sancte ecclesie fidelibus salutem et benedictionem. Noverit sancta fraternitas vestra
quod ego episcopali auctoritate concessi Waltero abbati et conventui
Sancti Petri Glouc' plenum personatum in ecclesia Sancti Cutberti
de Homme ultra Waiam cum terris et decimis \et/ omnibus pertinentiis suis quam Paganus filius Iohannis pro anima sua et pro animabus
antecessorum suorum, annuente hoc Sibilla, coniuge sua, per manum
meam in perpetuam[d] elemosinam eis donavit. Concedo etiam predicto abbati et monachis ut in predicta ecclesia pro voluntate sua
vicarios mittant et amoveant[e] si legitime non servierint. Hoc quia
ratum et inconvulsum manere volo sigilli mei inpressione confirmo.
Hiis testibus, Petro archidiacono, Radulfo decano, Gilberto de Ebor',
Ranulfo filio Erchrem', Ingulfo presbitero, Willelmo decano de Baysham, Gozo[f] presbitero de Sancto Martino, Stephano presbitero de
Hamma, Simone[g] presbitero de Kylpek, Hugone clerico de Sancto
Petro, etc.

[a]*sic B.* [b]*Probably singular; see no.33n.* [c]*or* decanis B. [d]imperpetuam B.
[e]ammoveant B.
[f]*sic for* Gozone B. [g]Sioms B.

Archdn Peter is presumably Archdn Peter of Hereford, not Archdn Peter le Kauf who was made archdn of Shropshire probably only shortly before 1148. Abbot Walter of Gloucester died in 1139. Ralph was probably not made dean of Hereford Cathedral until 1134.

17. Gloucester abbey

Composition between St Peter's abbey, Gloucester, and Hereford cathedral over St Peter's, Hereford.   **1134**

B = Oxford, Balliol College, MS 271 (cartulary of St Guthlac's, Hereford), fo.97v, no.431. s.xiv in.

Anno ab incarnatione domini mcxxxiiii, in presentia secundi Roberti Heref' episcopi, apud Heref', in capitulo eiusdem ecclesie, facta est firma pax et bona de querela et de calumpnia illa quam de introitu ecclesie Sancti Petri de Hereford' adversus abbates et monachos Glouc' episcopi et canonici Heref' ecclesie transactis temporibus habuerant, et quicquid calumpnie vel querele de introitu predicte ecclesie abbatibus et monachis Glouc' fuerat obiectum. Totum hoc prefatus episcopus anno tertio sue prelationis Waltero abbati et monachis Glouc', dei gratia et sua, necnon et consilio Innocentii Romane ecclesie summi pontificis, Willelmi Cantuar' archipresulis, quieti servorum dei et paci sancte ecclesie fidelius consulentium, canonicorum etiam conventu, Pagano[a] Iohannis filio, illius ecclesie patrono,[b] hoc ipsum approbantibus et concedentibus, iuste et canonice condonavit et pacificavit. Et ut illa pax absque omni querela et calumpnia inperpetuum stabilis permaneat, de ecclesia Sancti Petri de Heref' et omnibus beneficiis eiusdem ecclesie pertinentibus domnum abbatem Walterum in presentia canonicorum absque contradictione et calumpnia saisivit atque[c] introitum illius in eandem ecclesiam totam atque[c] huius concordiam auctoritate et benedictione sua et hoc sigillo ecclesie sue diligenter confirmavit. Hiis t(estibus), Godfrido abbate Glouc',[d] Pagano filio Iohannis, Milone constabulario, Helya de Say, Brione thesaurario, Gilberto de Eboraco, etc'.

[a]paganorum B.   [b]corr. from Pagano B.   [c]quia *sic* B.   [d]*sic* B.

The Godfrey mentioned in the witness list is probably Godfrey, abbot of Winchcombe 1122-1137.

18. Gloucester abbey

Notification addressed to the dean and chapter of Hereford cathedral of his grant of St Lawrence's church, Taynton, Gloucestershire, to Gloucester abbey, at the request of Matilda de Watteville, the lady of Taynton.
[1134 × 16 April 1148]

> B = Gloucester Cathedral, D. & C. Muniments, St Peter's Register B, p.21, no.53. s.xiv ex.

Robertus dei gratia Herefordensis episcopus decano totique capitulo eiusdem ecclesie ceterisque sancte ecclesie fidelibus salutem et dei ac suam benedictionem. Noverit sancta fraternitas vestra quod ego episcopali auctoritate donavi abbati et conventui Sancti Petri Glouc' ecclesiam Sancti Laurentii de Teintona cum omnibus pertinentiis suis simulque in territorio eiusdem ville capellam heremitorii cum una virgata terre, et hoc feci petitione et concessione Matildis eiusdem ville domine. Hec autem donatio a me canonice facta volo, confirmo, et precipio dei auctoritate et nostra ut firma et inconcussa in perpetuum predicte abbatie permaneat. Testibus, Henrico eiusdem ecclesie presbitero, Hugone canonico Lanton', et aliis multis.

> For Matilda, see *GFL* no.304 (no. 76 below), where Bp Gilbert Foliot grants Gloucester abbey licence to appropriate St Lawrence's, and institutes Samson the sacrist of Gloucester in the church. Robert's charter is probably not earlier than 1134, as there seems to have been no dean of Hereford in the years 1131-1134.

19. Gloucester abbey

Grant to Abbot Gilbert Foliot and the monks of Gloucester of part of his land at Eign to build a new monastic church dedicated to Sts Peter and Paul, in exchange for some land near the city ditch.
[11 June 1139 × 22 August 1140]

> B = Oxford, Balliol College, MS 271 (cartulary of St Guthlac's, Hereford), fo.104v, no.464. s.xiv in.

Notum sit omnibus presentibus et futuris quod ego Robertus dei gratia Heref' episcopus concessi Gilberto abbati Glouc' et fratribus eiusdem loci consensu capituli mei de Heref' partem terre que est

iuxta Igene habentem in quantitate octo acras, ut in eodem loco
edificatur ecclesia ad honorem dei et sanctorum apostolorum Petri et
Pauli et propter amorem monastice religionis secundum institutionem Sancti Benedicti, et ego accepi ab eis aliam terram secundum
eandem quantitatem que est iuxta fossatum civitatis a boreali^a parte
ne^b ecclesia Heref' aliquid detrimentum patiatur proprie^c possessionis. Hec autem omnia facta sunt coram Galfrido Talabot qui est
dominus et advocatus eiusdem loci in cuius feudum transiit terra
quam dedi eis sicud illa in meum quam accepi ab eis.

^aab oriali B.   ^bnec B.   ^chard to read B.

Geoffrey Talbot, a supporter of the Empress Matilda, died 22 August 1140 of
wounds received in battle (John of Worcester, 49f., 58n). Gilbert Foliot became
abbot of Gloucester in 1139. The churches of St Peter's and St Guthlac's were
united in 1143 and moved to a site just to the north of the city defences, probably
the land at Eign given to them by Robert de Béthune in this charter; the name
Eign refers to land outside the walled town to the west, but also to the area to the
north-east of the walls, as here.

20. Gloucester abbey

*Confirmation to Gloucester abbey of a grant by Harald of Ewyas of the
parsonage of St Foy of Foy.*   [11 June 1139 × 16 April 1148]

B = Gloucester Cathedral, D. & C. Muniments, St Peter's Register A, fo.159r,
no.256. s.xiv ex.
Cal., 'Gloucester register', 18, no.24.

Robertus dei gratia Hereford' episcopus decano totique capitulo eiusdem ecclesie ceterisque sancte ecclesie fidelibus salutem et dei ac
suam benedictionem. Noverit sancta fraternitas vestra quod ego episcopali auctoritate concessi abbati et conventui Sancti Petri Gloucestrie plenum personatum in ecclesia Sancte Fidis de Eton' cum terris
et decimis et omnibus pertinentiis suis, quam Haraldus de Ewias per
manum meam in perpetuam^a elemosinam eis donavit. Concedo etiam
abbati et monachis ut in predicta ecclesia pro voluntate sua vicarios
intrent^b et amoveant, si eis fideliter non servierint. Testibus, Aluredo,
quem ex presentatione venerabilis Gilberti abbatis Glouc' vicarium
in eadem ecclesia suscepi, et aliis.

^aimperpetuam B.   ^bint'ant B.

Gilbert Foliot became abbot of Gloucester in 1139. The St Foy venerated at Foy was not St Faith of Conques but a Britonic saint, Moi or Mwy (Ekwall, 186): the earliest version of the name of the church, in a ninth-century document in the Book of Llandaff, is Lann Timoi (W.Davies, *An Early Welsh Microcosm*, 136).

21. Gloucester abbey

Notification that the churches of St Guthlac's in the castle and St Peter's in the market have been united and that a new church has been built to house the community outside the city walls of Hereford. [1143]

B = Bodl. E Musaeo 249 (letter collection of Gilbert Foliot), fo.38r-v. s.xii 2/2. C = Oxford, Balliol College, MS 271 (cartulary of St Guthlac's, Hereford), fos.104r-v, no.462. s.xiv in. D = PRO, C150/1 (Gloucester abbey cartulary), fos.335r and 336r (new foliation), no.980. MS s.xiv ex, but this charter in a 15th century hand. Fo.336 is badly wormed. The text here is taken from C.

Pd, from B, Giles, no.123 and PL 190:834-5; from *D*, *Gloucester cartulary*, 236-7.

Dilectis sibi[a] in Cristo fratribus, universis sancte[b] matris[c] ecclesie filiis, R. dei gratia Heref'[d] episcopus dominum exspectare[e] sollicite[f] et venientem gratulanter amplecti. Quia ecclesiam dei regendam et aliqua sui portione administrandam, domino permittente, suscepimus, eius commoditati quoad possumus consulere ac[g] providere, credita nobis dispensatione, debemus. Quod ita recte fieri arbitramur si, confracta solidando et que dissipata sunt in corpus unum redigendo, tam incolumitati eius quam ampliando divino cultui studuerimus deservire. Quoniam igitur omnibus pie credentibus manifestum habetur, nec[h] forum religioni convenire nec castellum, quod[i] tumultus et sanguinum locus est, servientium domino paci congruere, ecclesiam beati Petri in foro Heref'[j] sitam et ecclesiam Sancti Guthlaci[k] intra ambitum castelli ipsius[l] importune positam et omnes possessiones et parochias et dignitates[m] earum in unius ecclesie corpus redegimus,[n] et eam ecclesiam[o] apostolorum Petri et Pauli et Sancti Guthlaci, quam extra civitatem ipsam, in loco religioni aptissimo, edificari fecimus, ad serviendum domino in perpetuum episcopali auctoritate sancivimus,[p] et ne auctoritate nostra gravare quempiam aut iuri cuiuspiam preiudicare videamur, tam hiis qui sunt quam filiis qui [fo.38v *B*] nascentur et exsurgent[q] post nos, presenti scripto notum facimus Rogerum de Port, qui ecclesiam Sancti Guthlaci diu iniuste, utpote laicus, tenuerat, et possessiones eius indigne distribuerat,^{r} peccatum hoc^s grande humiliter cognovisse et in presentia mea et fratris Radulfi decani nostri, et canonicorum nostrorum ^{t}magistri Hugonis de Cliffort, et magistri Hugonis de Norhamptona^u et domini Hugonis de Calco,^{t} et aliorum tam clericorum quam laicorum quamplurium, ecclesiam^v ipsam ut divinis officiis plenius assignaretur in manu nostra penitus refutasse. Ipso itaque Rogero devote supplicante,^{w} venerabili etiam fratre nostro Gilberto^x abbate Glouc'^{y} et conventu^z ipsius benigne annuente, predictas ecclesias in unam coniunximus, et hanc, illarum possessionibus, dignitatibus, et pertinentiis omnibus fundatam et dotatam, perpetue apostolorum Petri et Pauli et Sancti Guthlaci venerationi designavimus. Et^{aa} quia conventum fratrum ibidem^{bb} deo servientium et ibidem regulariter viventium [104v C] per manum^{cc} predicti abbatis Glouc', deo disponente, suscepturi sumus, hanc ipsam^{dd} apostolorum et Sancti Guthlaci ecclesiam prefati abbatis, omniumque successorum eius, obedientie, et ecclesie beati Petri Glouc' custodie et subiectioni, capitulo^{ee} ecclesie nostre in hiis omnibus unanimiter assentiente commisimus. Quicumque ergo hoc pietatis opus pie attenderint manumque auxiliatricem ad hoc confirmandum cum fideli devotione porrexerint perpetuam que inibi agentur oracionum communionem episcopalem a me qualicumque ecclesie ministro benedictionem, a summo^{ff} autem pontifice Cristo eternam consequantur retributionem. Amen.

^{a}om. BD. ^{b}sancti D. ^{c}om. D. ^{d}Herefordensis dei gratia BD.
^{e}expectare BD. ^{f}solicite C. ^{g}et B. ^{h}ne C.
^{i}conveniret castellum qui B; convenire nec castellum qui C.
^{j}Hereford' B; Herfordie D. ^{k}Gutlaci BD (BD use this spelling throughout).
^{l}illius B. ^{m}augmentationes C. ^{n}redigimus C.
^{o}ea ecclesia BC; ea ecclesiis D.
^{p}sanctivimus BD; sanctimus C. ^{q}exurgent B. ^{r}corr. ex tribuerat C.
^{s}hoc peccatum ergo corr. ex peccatum ergo C. $^{t-t}$Hug' de Clifford B.
^{u}Norhamtona D. ^{v}start of fo.336 D.
^{w}supplicante C. ^{x}om. B; Gilleberto D.
^{y}Gloecestrie B (B uses this spelling throughout).
^{z}conventui C. ^{aa}om. C. ^{bb}ibidem fratrum B;fratrem ibidem C.
^{cc}per m- illegible (lacuna) C. ^{dd}ips- illegible (lacuna) C.
^{ee}-ulo illegible C. ^{ff}C reads affirmo for a summo.

Roger de Port's charter granting the church of St Guthlac and its prebends to Gloucester abbey (*Gloucester cartulary*, iii.257-58) is dated 1163, a mistake by the cartulary copyist for 1143 (C.N.L.Brooke, *The church and the Welsh border*, 55, n.19) and this charter was doubtless issued at the same time or shortly afterwards. Earlier he had resigned the church into the hands of Robert de Béthune, and this transaction had been witnessed by Bp Bernard of St David's (*Mon. Ang.*, iii.623). Roger had validated it with a knife, a method used by Bernard himself some years earlier (see introduction, p.xxxv).

22. St Guthlac's priory, Hereford

Confirmation to St Guthlac's priory of the churches and tithes of St Peter's, Hereford, Holme Lacy, St Owen's, Hereford, Ocle Pychard, Mordiford with the chapel of Bartestree, and Sutton St Michael, and tithes from Staunton on Wye, Risbury, Wheathill, Humber, Butterley, Street, Weobley, Burghope, Bodenham, Maund, Stoke Lacy, Weston Beggard, Kempley, Gattertop, Oxenhall and Lugwardine.

[1143 × 16 April 1148]

B = Oxford, Balliol College, MS 271 (cartulary of St Guthlac's, Hereford), fo.105r, no.466. s.xiv in.

Robertus dei gratia Herefordensis ecclesie minister humilis universis sancte matris ecclesie filiis salutem. Noverit dilectio vestra me episc<opali auctoritate>*a* et hoc presenti scripto concessisse et confirmasse ecclesie apostolorum Petri et <Pauli et>*a* Sancti Guthlaci et monachis Hereford' ecclesiam Sancti Petri que est in <foro Hereford'>*a* cum prebendis, terris et decimis et omnibus ad eam pertinentibus, ecclesiam <Sancti Cutberti>*a* de Hamma cum terris et decimis et omnibus ad eam pertinentibus et e<cclesiam>*a* Sancti Audoeni de Hereford' cum*b* omnibus ad eam pertinentibus et ecclesiam de Acla, <et ecclesiam>*a* de Mordeford et capellam de Bertwaldestreu, et ecclesiam de maiori <Suttona>*a* cum omnibus pertinentiis suis, duas partes etiam totius decime dominii de <Stantona>*a*, et de Russebur', et de Wethull', et Humbra, et Buterleia, et de Streta, et <de Web>bleia*a* et de Burhopa et de Bodeham, et de Maghena et de Stoka, et de <Westo>na*a* et de Kempleia et totam decimam de Godredeshopa et de Oxenh<ale et>*a* tertiam etiam partem decimarum vilanagii de Lugwardin. Que omnia pre<fate ?>*a* ecclesie, et fratribus ibidem deo servientibus in elemosinam perpetuam iure possidenda <pre>senti*a* carta et sigilli mei attestatione confirmo.

a lacuna B.   *b et* B.

The churches of St Peter and St Guthlac were united in 1143 (see no.21). Lacunæ are filled from no.204 below

23. St Guthlac's priory, Hereford

Confirmation to St Guthlac's Priory of the chapels of Ocle Pychard, Lugwardine, Mordiford and Bartestree and the tithe of the vill of Bartestree.   [1143 × 16 April 1148]

> B = Oxford, Balliol College, MS 271 (cartulary of St Guthlac's, Hereford), fo.99v, no.436. s.xiv in.

(R)od'[a] dei gratia Herefordensis episcopus universis sancte matris ecclesie filiis salutem. Noverit vestra dilectio me episcopali auctoritate et hoc presenti scripto confirmasse petitionem domine M. imperatricis monachis ecclesie sancti Petri et sancti Guthlaci Hereford' has capellas perpetuo iure possidendas, scilicet capellam de Acle Walteri Maltravers, et capellam de Lugwardin, et capellam de Mordeford'. Confirmo eis etiam capellam de Bertwaldestre et decimam eiusdem ville quod fecerunt Rodbertus Corbet et Walterus frater, successor eius. Testibus, Willelmo de Wycumbe et Gilberto cantore Heref', et aliis.

[a] *Initial omitted (to be supplied by rubricator) B.*

Terminus a quo as for no.22. Empress Matilda finally left England early in 1148. Gilbert's first dated occurrence as cantor was in 1144. The omission of William de Wycombe's title (he became prior of Llanthony in 1137, and only ceased to be prior after 1148) is somewhat surprising.

24. St Guthlac's priory, Hereford

Confirmation to St Guthlac's Priory of grants made by Earl Miles of Hereford, Roger son of Picard, Robert Corbet and Walter son of Hingar.
[1143 × 16 April 1148]

> B = Oxford, Balliol College, MS 271 (cartulary of St Guthlac's, Hereford), fo.106r, no.470. s.xiv in.

Robertus dei gratia Herefordensis ecclesie minister humilis universis sancte matris ecclesie filiis salutem. Noverit dilectio vestra me episcopali auctoritate et hoc presenti scripto confirmasse concess<um>[a] capelle de Lugguardina quod fecit Milo comes Hereford' et concessum capelle <de>[a] Acle quod fecit Rogerus filius Picardi, et concessum capelle de Bristoldestro quod f<ecit>[a] Robertus Corbet et concessum decime eiusdem quod Walterus Corbet fecit, frater et successor eius, et concessum ecclesie de Mordeford' quod Walterus filius Hingar<>[a] fecit deo et ecclesie beati Petri et sancti Guthlaci et monachis Heref' ibidem deo servient<ibus>[a] perpetuo iure in elemosina possidenda.

[a] *lacuna B.*

For the *terminus a quo* see no.22.

25. St Guthlac's priory, Hereford

Notification that Walter de Turri has granted the church of Sutton St Michael to St Guthlac's Priory, provided that Robert Albus may hold the church as long as he lives.

[1143 × 16 April 1148]

B = Oxford, Balliol College, MS 271 (cartulary of St Guthlac's, Hereford), fo.89r, no.391. s.xiv in.

Robertus dei gratia Herefordensis episcopus omnibus sancte matris ecclesie filiis salutem, gratiam et benedictionem. Universitati vestre notum facio quod Walterus de Turri per manum meam dedit ecclesiam Sancti Michaelis \de/ Suttona monachis ecclesie sanctorum apostolorum Petri et Pauli et sancti Guthlaci Heref' cum omnibus pertinentiis suis libere et quiete in perpetuam elemosinam possidendam, salvo iure et consuetudine episcopali; concessi etiam assensu utrorumque, scilicet Walteri et monachorum, quod Robertus Albus eandem ecclesiam de prefatis monachis teneat quamdiu vixerit et in habitu seculari manserit. Idem vero Robertus super sanctum evangelium coram me in audientia multorum iuravit quod predicte ecclesie monachis fidelis erit, quod artem nec ingenium exquiret quo monachi aliquod impedimentum vel detrimentum huius possessionis incurrant. Huic rei quod ita processerit testimonium perhibeo et testimonium meum sigilli mei impressione confirmo.

For the *terminus a quo* see no.22. On Sutton see note to no.55.

26. St Guthlac's priory, Hereford

Grant to Abbot Gilbert Foliot and the monks of Gloucester and the monks of St Guthlac's, Hereford, of the church of St Michael of Sutton, with tithes and lands, at the request of Walter de Turri.

[1143+ × 16 April 1148]

B = Oxford, Balliol College, MS 271 (cartulary of St Guthlac's, Hereford), fo.88v, no.389. s.xiv in.

Robertus dei gratia Herefordensis episcopus universis sancte matris ecclesie filiis salutem et benedictionem. Noverit universitas vestra me concessisse Gilberto abbati Gloc' et monachis beatorum apostolorum Petri et Pauli et Sancti Guthlaci Hereford' ecclesiam Sancti Michaelis de Suttona cum terris et decimis cunctisque beneficiis eidemque ecclesie pertinentibus, salvo iure episcopali, annuente et petente Waltero de Turri eiusdem ecclesie de Suttona patrono*[a]* videlicet et advocato. Concessi et abbati et monachis canonice eiusdem ecclesie introitum et ut in predicta ecclesia pro voluntate sua vicarios mittant, et si legitime non servierint sub conscientia episcopi amoveant.*[b]* Hanc autem conventionem a me canonice factam volo et episcopali auctoritate precipio ut predicte ecclesie firma et inconvulsa imperpetuo permaneat. Hiis testibus, Radulfo decano, Petro archidiacono Heref', Gilberto cantore, Hamel' subpriore et Patricio cellerario Hereford', Radulfo decano de Weston', Hugone purc' sacerdote, Waltero de Bromyard, Ada clerico, et aliis.

[a]om. B.   *[b]ammoveant B.*

This charter was presumably issued after the death or resignation of Robert Albus, the parson (see no.25). See also note to no.55.

27. St Guthlac's priory, Hereford

Notification that Thomas de Freine has granted the church of Presteigne to St Guthlac's priory, provided that Walter de Freine may hold the church from the monks for the rest of his life.

Monday 9 April 1145

B = Oxford, Balliol College, MS 271 (cartulary of St Guthlac's, Hereford), fo.76v, no.324. s.xiv in.

(R)odbertus^a dei gratia Herefordensis episcopus omnibus sancte matris ecclesie^b filiis salutem et benedictionem. Universitati vestre notum fieri volo quod Thomas de Fraxino per manum meam reddidit ecclesiam de Presthamede monachis ecclesie apostolorum Petri et Pauli et sancti Guthlaci que est sita iuxta villam Heref', cum capellis, terris, et decimis, et omnibus pertinentiis suis, sicut^c de iure ecclesie Sancti Guthlaci, et manu propria per quendam librum super altare sanctorum apostolorum et sancti Guthlaci posuit.^d Concessi etiam assensu utrorumque, scilicet Thome et monachorum, quod Walterus de Fraxino eandem ecclesiam de prefatis monachis teneat quamdiu vixerit et in habitu seculari manserit. Idem vero Walterus coram me in audientia multorum in verbo veritatis promisit quod de predicta ecclesia monachis fidelis existet et quod artem nec ingenium exquiret quod predicti monachi aliquod impedimentum vel detrimentum huius possessionis per tenuram suam incurrant. Huius conventionis recognitione reddidit decimam de parva Coura et absque omni reclamatione liberam et quietam concessit. Huic rei quod ita processerit testimonium perhibeo et testimonium meum sigilli mei inpressione confirmo. Acta sunt hec anno ab incarnatione domini mcxlv, feria ii post dominicam in Ramis Palmarum, in claustro monachorum apud Hereford. Hiis testibus, Radulfo decano, Petro archidiacono, Gilberto de Eboraco, Ranulfo filio Erchem', Hugone de Cliff' presbitero, Radulfo de Bromiard, Nicholao decano de Frome, Stephano presbitero de Ham', Hugone presbitero, Aug(ustino) presbitero, Roberto de Candos, Waltero de Mocr' et multis aliis.

^a*Initial letter omitted (for rubricator ?) B.*
^b*om. B.*   ^c*sicud B.*
^dquamdiu vixerit et in habitu manserit *added but then cancelled B.*

The de Freine family, originally subtenants of the de Port family, lived at Freen's Court, Sutton, near Hereford. Walter and a later de Freine, Simon, possibly Thomas' son, were canons of Hereford.

28. John, the bishop's nephew

Grant in fee farm to his nephew John of land at Litley bought from Roger earl of Hereford (as tenant-in-chief) and from William Brito (as subtenant), which John is to hold for one gold mancus a year from the bishop, and also grant of land at Wetbetha *in Bromyard.*   [1144 × 1148]

B = Hereford, Herefordshire County Record Office, Registrum Ricardi de Swin-field (formerly Hereford Diocesan Registry), fo.109v old fol., fo.107v new fol.; 1283 × 1317, here April 1295. Heading: Munimenta terre de Luteleya.

Pd, *Hereford charters*, 10.

Robertus dei gratia Heref' episcopus capitulo Heref' et omnibus sancte ecclesie filiis salutem. Notum sit vobis me adquisivisse ecclesie Heref' et precibus et pecunia et amore a Rogero comite Hereford', tanquam a capitali domino, et a Willelmo Britone, tanquam a tenente hereditario iure, terram de Lutteleya, et hoc testatur scriptura eorum que in ecclesia nostra reposuimus. Hanc eandem terram dedi Iohanni nepoti meo libere in feodo et hereditate et ei et heredibus suis, tenendam de me et successoribus meis, ita ut de recognitione det singulis annis episcopo Hereford' unum mancum^a auri pro omni servitio. Preter hoc dedi Iohanni libere et in feudo terram de Wete-betha, scilicet terciam partem unius hyde pro libero servitio secundum morem episcopatus. Harum donacioni testes sunt: Radulfus decanus Heref', Gilbertus cantor, Odo archidiaconus Salopsir' et canonicus^b Hereford', Magister Willelmus canonicus Heref', Willel-mus priore Lanthon', Radulfus decanus Bromyard, Eylwyn decanus, David et Walterus clerici episcopi, Edulphus presbiter Bosebur', Willelmus presbiter Estenovere, Reginaldus canonicus Bromyard, Rogerus sacerdos, Theodulphus de Bromyard et Arnaldus filius eius, Reginaldus nepos episcopi, Ricardus de Huntiland', Arnaldus de Monewyta^c et Arnaldus filius eius, Willelmo de Claira, Robertus de Dunitona, Willelmus filius Ger', Godefridus de Colewall', Radulfus Perer, Godefridus pincerna episcopi.

^{a}unam mancam B. ^{b}canonici B. ^{c}? *sic for* Monemuta B.

For dating, see Z.N. and C.N.L.Brooke, 'Hereford Cathedral Dignitaries in the Twelfth Century', *Cambridge Historical Journal*, viii (1944), 19. This charter is not printed or even mentioned by Capes in his edition of Swinfield's register (*Reg. Swinfield*).

29. Kyte Hardwick

Notification that he has just consecrated a cemetery at Kyte Hardwick, in the parish of Tysoe, Warwickshire, at the request of Roger Gifford, with the assent of Prior Ralph of Stone.   [probably 1139 × 1140]

B = BL Cotton Ch. XIII, 6 (23) (Charter roll relating to Kenilworth Priory and Stone Priory). s.xii 2/2.

Robertus dei gratia Hereford' episcopus universis ecclesie fidelibus salutem. Noverint omnes tam posteri quam presentes quod ego benedixi cimiterium apud Herdewic, villam Rogeri Giffard, petitione ipsius, et assensu Radulfi prioris, in cuius parrochia de Thiesho predicta Herdewic esse dinoscitur. Dedit autem \ipse/ Rogerus, eiusdem fundi dominus, matri ecclesie de Thiesho in perpetuam elemosinam, partim pro servitio capelle, partim pro dampnis que predicto priori et ecclesie sue fecerat, l. acras ex una parte ville, et totidem ex altera, et vi. acras ad Croftam cum prato adiacente, sicut ab eo divisum est, eo tenore quod hec omnia ad opus prefate ecclesie warantizabit et omnimodo adquietabit. Si quis ergo huic eius donationi et nostre confirmationi contraire presumpserit, nisi commonitus resipiscat, dei et nostram maledictionem incurrat. Valete.

Tysoe is in the diocese of Worcester, and Robert may have been acting as vicar of the diocese of Worcester in the absence of his friend Bp Simon, at Rome with Archbp Theobald in 1139, as suggested by B.J.Parkinson, 'The Life of Robert de Bethune by William de Wycombe', unpublished Oxford B.Litt. thesis (1951), p.65. Stone Priory was founded about 1135, and Ralph was almost certainly its first prior.

30. Leominster priory

Composition between the monks of Leominster and Miles the Constable over the parish of Broadfield, Herefordshire, issued by Robert de Béthune in the synod of Hereford with abbots Walter of Gloucester, Godfrey of Winchcombe and Herbert of Shrewsbury; the monks of Leominster are to have scrifcorn *and* romescot *(Peter's pence) as previously and in August one acre each of wheat and oats from the demesne, and the church of Bodenham is to have burial rights and other benefits.*

[28 June 1131 × 6 March 1137]

B = BL, Egerton MS 3031 (Reading abbey cartulary), fo.56v. s.xii ex. C = BL, Cotton MS Dom. A iii (Leominster priory cartulary), fo.60r. s.xiii med.

Pd, *Reading cartularies*, i.262-3, no.326

Godfrey, abbot of Winchcombe, died on 6 March, almost certainly in 1137; Abbot Herbert of Shrewsbury died in 1138. *Scrifcorn*, described by B.R.Kemp (*Reading cartularies*, i.290n) as a due peculiar to Leominster, where it seems to have replaced churchscot, was probably a payment in corn to the priest for absolution at Easter, by analogy with the word shriftsilver.

31. Leominster priory

Notification to the faithful of the diocese that he has consecrated the graveyard in Hatfield.   [28 June 1131 × 16 April 1148]

> B = BL, Cotton MS Dom. A iii (Leominster priory cartulary), fos.60r-v new fol., fos.58r-v old fol. s.xiii med. Rubric: De conditione consecrationis cimiterii in Hethfeld'. Idem[1].

R. dei gratia Hereford' episcopus omnibus fidelibus parochie sue salutem et benedictionem. Notum vobis esse volumus quod ego consecravi cimiterium in Hethfelda tanquam augmentum quoddam cimiterii de Leom', hac conditione, ut quicquid oblationis ad sepulturam cuiuslicet defuncti ibidem evenerit, vel quod ipsemet defunctus adhuc vivens pro se dandum sue matri ecclesie de Leom' divisit, totum sit proprie monachorum de Leom', tanquam si corpus ipsum defuncti in principali [fo.60v] cimiterio Leom' sepeliretur, hoc proviso, ut clericus quicumque in illa capella ministravit securitatem faciat prefatis monachis quod hoc ius ipsorum fideliter eis, quantum in ipso est, observaverit. Capella autem ipsa, in hiis que ad servitium episcopi pertinent, non sicut iure ecclesia, sed sicut capella habeatur.

[1] Reference to Robert de Béthune, who issued the immediately preceding charters in the cartulary.

32. Leominster priory

Notification of his institution of a feast of relics annually on 10 October within the parish of Leominster, of his dedication of an altar of the Holy Cross and an altar of St Mary Magdalen, St Margaret and St Catherine in Leominster priory church and of a grant of indulgences to the priory's benefactors.   [28 June 1131 × 16 April 1148]

B = BL, Cotton MS Dom. A iii (Leominster priory cartulary), fo.74r (new fol.), fo.72r (old fol.). s.xiii med. Rubric: Rob' Hereford'.

Pd, *Mon. Ang.* iv.56.

R. dei gratia Heref' episcopus omnibus Cristianis salutem. Precor vos omnes et in domino I(esu) Cristo exhortor, cuius sanguine redempti estis, ut diligatis ecclesiam beati Petri de Leom' et fratribus ibi deo servientibus pacem et honorem pro posse vestro conservetis, et auxiliis et elemosinis et beneficiis eos sustentare in caritate Cristi studeatis. Novimus vero*a* et certis experimentis didicimus prefatam ecclesiam a deo diligi et in ea sanctorum reliquias contineri maiore et preciosiore multitudine quam verbis explicare possimus. Statuimus igitur et manere in perpetuum decrevimus in eadem ecclesia et per eius parochiam vi id' Octobris festivum diem sollempniter celebrari in honore omnium sanctorum quorum reliquie ibi continentur, quatinus deus pater omnipotens et dominus noster I(esus) Cristus, cooperante sancto spiritu, omnibus hac die ad ecclesiam venientibus, et de elemosinis suis debita obsequia fratribus exhibentibus, pacem tribuat in hac vita, et salutem in perpetua. Ego quoque, confisus de misericordia dei, et meritis sanctorum, et orationibus fratrum, tam ibi quam apud Rading' deo servientibus, relaxo omnibus qui devote corde confessi fuerint et elemosinas ad prefatam ecclesiam detulerint de iniuncta penitentia dies xx. Dedicavimus quoque in eadem ecclesia altare sancte Crucis in cuius festivitatibus singulis vii dierum penitentiam relaxamus, et aliud quoddam altare ibidem sacravimus in honore Sancte Marie Magdal', Sancte Margarete, Sancte Katerine, in quarum trium festivitatibus singulis dies tres indulgemus.

*a*u (?) B.

The mixed use of the first person singular and plural suggests that this is a charter of Robert de Béthune. A Bp G. of Hereford, almost certainly Gilbert Foliot, issued a similar charter (*GFL*, no.340 and no.98 below). A list of the relics owned by the church of Leominster was drawn up in 1296 and inserted into the register of Bp Richard de Swinfield (*Reg. Swinfield*, 124-5; it is commented on by G.H.Doble, 'The Leominster relic-list', *Transactions of the Woolhope Naturalists' Field Club*, xxxi [1942], 58-65, and by D.Bethell, 'The making of a twelfth-century relic collection', in *Popular Belief and Practice*, edd. G.J.Cuming and D.Baker [Studies in Church History 8, 1972], 65-6). The list mentions relics of St Margaret and of the Cross but not of St Catherine or of St Mary Magdalen. It is conceivable, though no more than a speculation, that Bp R. suggested their inclusion in the dedication because they were the patron saints of the episcopal chapel at Hereford. A vicarage was subsequently established at the altar of the Cross in Leominster: see nos.211, 215-6, 270, 279 and 353.

33. Leominster priory

Notification to the archdeacon and clergy of the diocese of Hereford that the abbot of Conches is to give twelve pence a year to the church of Leominster for the third part of the tithe of Monkland.   1137

> B = BL, Cotton MS Dom. A iii (Leominster priory cartulary), fo.60r (fo.58r old fol.). s.xiii med.

Robertus dei gratia Heref' episcopus archid(iacono) et omni clero Hereford' ecclesie salutem. Sciatis quod abbas de Castaillions reddit singulis annis ad festum Sancti Michaelis xii denarios ecclesie Leomen' pro tertia parte decime de Monekesleona, unde habent corpora. Hoc autem statutum est coram me in synodo Heref', presente ipso abbate de Cast', anno domini mcxxxvii.

> Monkland formed part of the property of the Norman abbey of Conches (diocese of Evreux, department of Eure); see below, nos.142, 187 and 322. It is not certain when Hereford diocese acquired its second archdeaconry; see A.Morey and C.N.L.Brooke, *Gilbert Foliot and his Letters* (Cambridge 1965), 199, 268.

34. Lire abbey

Notification that he has adjudged the churches of Fownhope and Marcle to the abbey of Lire, in Normandy, the former of which the abbot of Lire had been disputing with the abbess of Elstow, and confirmation to Lire of the churches of Tenbury, Eardisland, Lydney, Tidenham, Linton and Wilton.   [1142 × 1147]

> B = Dom Lenoir MSS (in possession of Mme la Marquise de Mathan, Semilly, Manche), vol. xxiii, fo.37. s.xviii. Consulted from a microfilm in the Borthwick Institute of Historical Research, York.
>
> Summary, Evreux, A-D Eure, H590, fos.324v-5r, no.xiii. s.xviii.

R. dei gratia Herefordensis ecclesie minister humilis omnibus sancte ecclesie fidelibus salutem. Noverit dilectio vestra quod H., abbas de Lira, in presentia mea et capituli Herefordensis ecclesiam de Hopa versus abbatissam de Alnestou canonice dirationavit, quam prefati abbatis ecclesia antiquitus per plures annos, quiete et in pace, donatione Herefordensis episcopi[a] Gerardi et cum libero assensu et concessione Aitropi, tunc temporis illius ecclesie advocati, possidebat,[b] quod idem abbas per multos legales testes hoc idem coniuramento affirmantes probavit. Quare volo et episcopali auctoritate precipio ut illam ecclesiam, prout antiquitus tenuerat, in pace et quiete habeat et teneat. Similiter, ecclesiam de Merkeleia, ecclesie de Lira antiquitus subiectam, illi concedo, in qua meo tempore inveni duos sacerdotes, unum concubinarium, alium vero concubinarium et symoniacum, quod in presentia mea et capituli mei cognitum et probatum fuit. Hiis autem concubinariis ecclesiastico iudicio ab ecclesia de Merchelai eiectis, illam liberam et quietam ecclesie de Lira noscitur, et eo amplius ut domnus[c] abbas illos monachos poneret. Alias vero ecclesias quas in mea parrochia ecclesia de Lira habet, ecclesiam videlicet de Tameteberia, et illam de Lena, ecclesiam de Lideneia, ecclesiam de Tedeham, cum rebus ad illas pertinentibus volo et episcopali auctoritate precipio ut quiete et in pace eas habeat et teneat; similiter ecclesiam de Lintun', et ecclesiam Sancte Brigidis.

[a]episcopi *om. B.*   [b]possida't *B.*   [c]donnus *B.*

The abbot of Lire in question is Hildier II (1142-1147); cf. C.Guéry, *Histoire de l'abbaye de Lyre* (Evreux 1917), 657. The church of St Bridget is the church of Wilton which was at Bridstow. Both Marcle and Fownhope (see Domesday Book, i, fo.187b) were small minster churches with more than one priest; the church of Marcle is recorded in Domesday Book (i, fo.179d) as belonging to St Mary of Cormeilles, but perhaps the Domesday clerks confused Cormeilles with St Mary of Lire.

35. Llanthony Priory

Notification to Bishop Simon of Worcester that he has granted the churches in Prestbury to Llanthony priory.

[22 December 1135 × 21 December 1136, probably 1136]

B = PRO, C115 K1/6679 (Llanthony cartulary, A9), fo.114v. s.xiii med. C = Ibid., fos.114v-115r. D = PRO, C115 K2/6683 (Llanthony cartulary, A1), fo.122v, section vi, no.24. s.xiv med. E = Ibid., fo.122v, no.25. F = Ibid., fo. 45r, section i, no.140, in an inspeximus issued by Prior Richard and the monks of Worcester cathedral priory, 20 February 1277. G = Ibid., fo. 42r, section i, no.134, in an inspeximus dated 18 September 1308 issued by Prior John and the monks of Worcester cathedral priory of several charters including Prior Richard's inspeximus. H = PRO, C115 L1/6689 (Llanthony cartulary, A4), fo.126r, section ci. s.xv.

Rotbertus dei gratia Hereford' ecclesie episcopus Symoni eadem gratia Wygorn' episcopo omnibusque[a] sancte ecclesie fidelibus tam presentibus quam futuris salutem. Sicut amore religionis religiosarum ecclesiarum prosperitati ac paci congaudere debemus, sic[b] earum indigentie misericorditer concurrere, tranquillitati tam in presens quam in posterum providere debitum est opus caritatis. Propterea quia novimus possessiones Lanthoniensis ecclesie per bellicam cladem plus satis imminutas, dedi priori et conventui eiusdem ecclesie duas ecclesias in Presteburia, unam sub montibus, alteram super montes, cum decimis aliisque elemosinis omnibus eisdem ecclesiis pertinentibus aut contingentibus, exceptis duabus portionibus decime de dominio meo, [c]quas habent decanus et cantor Hereford, de blado scilicet tantum et de leguminibus, sicut consuetudinem inveni. De parco autem, et de hiis que seminañtur vel colliguntur infra designatum ambitum parchi, decima remanet ecclesie, quia terra fuit[d] villanorum. Hanc igitur elemosine nostre donationem[c] vobis presenti scripto decrevimus notam fieri, et eis ratam futuris temporibus confirmari. Datam anno primo regni Stephani regis Anglorum.

[a]omnibus quoque H. [b]corr. from sicut B.
[c-c]omitted and replaced with quam elemosinam CE. [d]fuit terra FG.

Robert made this grant to Llanthony after the canons had had to leave their priory and take refuge with him in 1136 owing to the disturbances in the Welsh Marches following the death of Henry I. Simon bishop of Worcester was absent in Louvain when Robert made this grant and so Robert had to notify him formally (B.J.Parkinson, 'The Life of Robert de Bethune by William of Wycombe', unpublished Oxford B.Litt. thesis, 1951, pp.31-32, and cf. *Ann. Mon.* ii.219). This charter and nos.36 and 37 represent the grant of four Hereford cathedral prebends which Gilbert Foliot tried unsuccessfully to have returned to the cathedral after he had succeeded Robert as bishop in 1148 (*GFL*, nos.80, 327). Hereford cathedral was granted an annual pension of 60s and half a hide in Barton under the terms of the 1148 agreement.

36. Llanthony priory

Grant to Llanthony Priory of the church of Prestbury, with a chapel, the church of Bishop's Frome, land called The Moor, and the mansio *held by Ernald the priest.* [1136 × 16 April 1148, possibly 1146]

B = PRO, C115 K1/6679 (Llanthony cartulary, A9), fo.114r. s.xiii med. C = Ibid., C115 K2/6683 (Llanthony cartulary, A1), fo.122r, section vi, no.21. s.xiv med.

R. dei gratia episcopus Hereford' omnibus fidelibus sancte ecclesie salutem. Notum sit omnibus vobis quod ego, prenoscens paupertatem canonicorum Lanthon', dedi eis in perpetuam elemosinam, ad augmentum subsidii, ecclesiam de Prestebur' cum capella pertinente,[a] ecclesiam de Froma cum suis pertinentiis omnibus, et terram que Mora vocatur, et mansionem quam Ernaldus presbiter tenuerat cum xi acris terre. Gratia et pax a deo nostro omnibus conservantibus hanc elemosinam; perturbantibus autem iudicium dei super eos.

[a]pertinenti BC.

In his Life of Robert de Béthune William de Wycombe says that Robert granted land called *Mora* to Llanthony between 1136 and 1148 to support an influx of twenty canons who had been driven away from their foundation owing to the barrenness of the ground (*Anglia Sacra*, ii.314). This might conceivably be a reference to the canons of Shobdon, who had been driven out by Hugh de Mortimer, and who appear to have sought refuge at Llanthony (*Mon. Ang.* vi.345) in about 1146 before peace was made between them and Hugh in 1147.

37. Llanthony priory

Notification to the dean and chapter of Hereford of his grant to Llanthony priory of three assarts in Prestbury, which had been held by Leofric Figulus, Leofwyn Rufus and Ernwy for 9d. a year, to hold for 12d. a year.   [1136+ × 16 April 1148]

B = PRO, C115 K1/6679 (Llanthony cartulary, A9), fo.113v. s.xiii med. C = PRO, C115 K2/6683 (Llanthony cartulary, A1), fo.122r, section vi, no.17. s.xiv.

R. dei gratia Hereford' episcopus Radulfo eiusdem ecclesie decano, totique capitulo et universis sancte ecclesie filiis salutem. Noverit sancta dilectio vestra quod tria exarta in Presteburia, que Leuricus Figulus et Lefwyn Rufus et Erni per ix denariorum redditum per annum tenuerunt, priori de Lanthon' eiusdemque loci[a] fratribus per xii denariorum redditum per annum tenenda et ad ecclesiam de Presteburia pertinenda in perpetuam elemosinam concesserim et dederim, monens, obsecrans et episcopali auctoritate precipiens ut bene et in pace, remota omni vexatione, teneant. Testibus, canonicis de Hereford, magistris Willelmo et Odone, Radulfo decano de Bromyard.[b]

[a]B *adds* conventui, *expunged*.   [b]Brommard BC.

According to William de Wycombe Robert granted the vill of Prestbury to the canons of Llanthony some time after he granted them the two churches of Prestbury (*Anglia Sacra*, ii.313). By a curious coincidence, the three thegns who held the vill of Thornbury (Herefordshire) in the time of King Edward were named Leofric, Lifing and Ernwy (Domesday Book, i, fo.186b), and it seems possible that these are identifiable with the three tenants in this charter, who had, in any case, presumably died before Robert issued it. At Domesday three free men had seven ploughs and their own men on the vill of Sevenhampton, held by Durand of Gloucester from the Church of Hereford as part of its large manor of Prestbury (ibid., i, fo.165a), and it is conceivable that these might have been Leofric, Leofwine, and Ernwy.

38. Llanthony priory

Notification of an agreement between Robert de Chandos and Prior William de Wycombe of Llanthony concerning the rights of Robert's mother Margaret to land at Kenchester.   [1137 × 16 April 1148]

B = PRO, C115 K1/6679 (Llanthony cartulary, A9), fo.93v. s.xiii med. C = PRO, C115 K2/6683 (Llanthony cartulary A1), fo.159r (sect. ix, no.20). s.xiv.

Cal., S.E.Bartleet, 'History of the Manor and Advowson of Brockworth', *TBGAS*, vii (1882), 141.

R. dei gratia*a* episcopus Hereford' omnibus fidelibus sancte ecclesie salutem. Notam*b* vobis facimus conventionem que coram me facta fuit inter Robertum de Chandos et \Willelmum/ priorem Lanth'. Roth-bertus*c* de Candos*d* cum amicis suis requisivit dominum priorem pro domina Margareta matre sua, ut ei permitteret tenere Kenecestram in suos usus pro debito subsidii sui quod exigebat ab eo. Prior vero, licet non recognosceret nec intelligeret*e* debitum quod exigebat, se-cundum quod erga illam egerat, pro amore tamen pacis, et consilio amicorum suorum, permisit prefate Margarete ut teneret Ken' in suos usus, sicut petebat de ecclesia et priore Lanth', quamdiu*f* ipsa viveret vel donec meliori consilio redderet eam ecclesie. Rothbertus igitur, secundum quod definitum fuit, fecit securitatem ecclesie Lanthon' et priori quod pro illa permissione quam prior faciebat Kenec' nunquam alienaretur ab ecclesia Lanthon', nec ipse, nec aliquis quem ipse cohibere posset, faceret inde violentiam vel perquireret ingenium aliquid vel occasionem ad dampnum Lanthon' ecclesie. Hoc affidavit Rotbertus de Chandos in manu mea, excluso omni malo ingenio, coram testibus me ipso, Rotberto episcopo^g Heref', Sampsone, Hugone Cliffort, et aliis.

^{a}gratia *om. B.* ^{b}*corr. from* Notum, *C.* ^{c}c *added and expunged, B.* ^{d}Chandos *C.*
^{e}intelligent *C.* ^{f}quandiu *B, C.* ^{g}*Text in C ends here.*

William de Wycombe became prior in 1137.

39. Llanthony priory

Notification to Bishop Alexander of Lincoln that Nigel fitz Erfast granted the church of Henlow to Llanthony priory in Robert's presence.
[24 September 1143 × 17 December 1146]

> B = PRO, C115 K1/6679 (Llanthony cartulary, A9), fo.157r-v. s.xiii med. C = Ibid., C115 K2/6683 (Llanthony cartulary, A1), fo.226r, section x, no.69. s.xiv med.

Robertus dei gratia episcopus Hereford' Alexandro eadem gratia^a episcopo Linc', fratri et amico suo in Cristo, et successoribus eius, ministris quoque eorum, archidiaconis et decanis salutem et orationes. [fo.157v *B*] Ad precavendam iniuriam aliquorum, quales agnovimus, qualesque credimus non defuturos, qui elemosinas suas et antecessorum suorum moliuntur tollere hiis quibus date erant et in suos usus revocare, voluerunt fratres Lanthon' ecclesie et rogaverunt me, postquam ad episcopatum^b assumptus sum, ut \ius/ quod haberent in ecclesia de Henlawe scripto episcopalis testimonii eis apud nos testificarer. Noveritis igitur tam vos quam successores vestri quod Nigellus filius Erfasti, me presente et audiente, recognovit et concessit prefatis fratribus de Lanthon' donationem quam eis fecerat de ecclesia de Henl', scilicet eam advocaturam et iurisdictionem quam in ea habebat, sicut advocatus eius et feodi in quo sita erat, quod eis dederat in elemosinam. Rogamus igitur fraternitatem vestram in caritate dei quatinus ius prefate ecclesie manu teneatis, si aliquis de heredibus Nigelli eos inde vexare voluerit. Valete.

^{a}gratia *om. B.* ^{b}episcopatam *C.*

Innocent II confirmed Llanthony's possessions, including Nigel fitz Erfast's grant, in 1131 (*PUE*, i.240), but in a subsequent confirmation, dated 30 April 1142, he omitted it (ibid., i.251-253). Innocent died on 24 September 1143, and Robert's letter was written between his death and the issuing of Eugenius III's bull for Llanthony of 17 December 1146, which confirms Nigel's grant. It was probably written before nos.40 and 41 below. Bp Alexander of Lincoln issued two notifications, one of Nigel's grant of land at Henlow, the other of his grant of the church, to Archdn Nicholas of Bedford (who first occurs as archdn in 1145) which were prompted by Robert de Béthune (*EEA* i, nos. 45, 46). See also M.Brett, *The English Church under Henry I* (Oxford 1975), 147-148.

40. Llanthony priory

Letter to Bishop Alexander of Lincoln complaining that his diocesan officers are not doing justice to Llanthony in the case of Henlow church in Bedfordshire. [24 September 1143 × 17 December 1146]

B = PRO, C115 K1/6679 (Llanthony cartulary, A9), fo.158r-v. s.xiii med. C = PRO, C115 K2/6683 (Llanthony cartulary, A1), fo.226v, section x, no.71. s.xiv med.

A. dei gratia episcopo Lincoln' amico et confratri suo Robertus eadem gratia*[a]* Heref' episcopus salutem. Significatum est nobis quosdam ex vestris qui in officiis agunt episcopalibus dissimulare se scire quid iuris habeant canonici in ecclesia de Heneslawe*[b]* cuius donationem nec viderint, ut dicunt, nec audierint. Meo quoque super hac \re/ testimonio veritatis increduli sunt et detractant, seu*[c]* forte donationem prefate ecclesie nobis fieri non viderunt, seu*[c]* forte testimonium meum de concessione et recognitione Nigelli necdum audierunt. Audiant igitur vel nunc et nolint esse increduli sed fideles; audiant quod dico, quod episcopali scripto perhibeo, quia Nigellus filius Erfasti, sicut dedit canonicis et ecclesie de Lanth' terram quam habebat in Hanelawe,*[d]* ita concessit eisdem quicquid iuris in ecclesia de Han' sicut advocatus eius habebat. Sed, quia aliqui malivoli iactaverant vel voluerant quod Nigellus eam concessionem non recognoscebat, ideo postquam episcopus ordinatus sum, idem Nigellus, coram me positus et interrogatus, liquido recognovit eandem concessionem et coram testibus legitimis*[e]* confirmavit. Sicut igitur veritas hec sibi constat immobilis, sic ubi necesse fuerit eius ero testis immutabilis. Huius vero rei testimonium meum vos <ex verbis> prefatorum ministrorum vestrorum †episcopus dominus† et Magister David*[f]* in abbatia Glouc' ex ore meo audistis et absque scrupulo incredulitatis, sicut decebat, accepistis, ipsamque ecclesiam ad testificationem et intercessionem meam episcopali auctoritate et scripto ecclesie Lanth' confirmastis. Nec vos solus sed et papa Romanus sancte memorie

Innocentius, testimonio nostro bene credulus, et intercessioni pro fratribus Lanthon' auditor propitius, omnes possessiones eorum, et, inter ceteras, quicquid Nigellus nobis dederat ecclesie Lanthon', apostolica auctoritate, sub anathematis sententia, confirmavit, eosque cum suis omnibus in beati Petri suaque protectione susceptos legati sui tutele sua vice commendavit. Viderint igitur qua ratione, quo exitu fratres nostros inquietent prefati increduli, supra episcopum, supra dominum papam diligentiam suam,^{g} ne aliter dixerim, extendentes. Non enim est discipulus super magistrum, neque servus maior domino suo.^{h1} Quoad^i illud quod obtendere dicuntur, ut noceant audisse se potius, quod Nigellus, postquam a Lanthon' rediit, prefatam ecclesiam filiabus suis [fo.158v *B*] dederit et filiis eius post eum, patet ratio quam frivola sit immo quam nulla donatio cuiusquam in rem alienam quamque sacrilegio proximum sit, ut homo qui sibi suisque omnibus renuntiat et sub pastoris obedientia ligatur, eo nesciente potestatem sibi contra fidem ecclesie sue usurpetur, quod, si temptare presumpserit, perniciosum sit episcopo presidenti tolerare. Valete.

^{a}eadem gratia *repeated B*. ^{b}Henesl' *C*. ^{c}sed *BC*. ^{d}Henl' *C*. ^{e}legittimis *BC*.
^{f}Dudum *BC* . ^{g}suam *repeated B*. ^{h}ser. ma. d'. suo *BC*. ^{i}Nam *BC*.
^{1} Matth.10^{24}.

The text of *B* (from which *C* was copied) is corrupt, and the sentence 'Huius vero rei .... ecclesie Lanth' confirmastis' is uncertain. 'Ex verbis' has been added as an editorial emendation; 'episcopus dominus' is certainly wrong as it stands. This letter and no.41 were probably written shortly after no.39. Master David is possibly identifiable with the David who became archdn of Buckingham before September 1142, and the meeting at Gloucester presumably occurred before this date.

41. Llanthony priory

Notification to Bishop Alexander of Lincoln that Nigel fitz Erfast granted land at Henlow to Llanthony priory with the consent of his lord, Henry d'Aubigni, and that Richard, Nigel's heir, refused to do service for it, although he was bound to render this according to the terms of the grant.   [24 September 1143 × 17 December 1146]

B = PRO, C115 K1/6679 (Llanthony cartulary, A9), fos. 157v-8r. s.xiii med. C = PRO, C115 K2/6683 (Llanthony cartulary, A1), fo.226v, section x, no.70. s.xiv med.

Robertus dei gratia episcopus Hereford' dilecto domino et confratri suo A. Linc' episcopo et successoribus eius omnibus fidelibus ecclesie sancte salutem. Testimonium perhibeo veritati quam certius agnovi, quod, scilicet, Nigellus filius Erfasti dedit ecclesie et canonicis Lanthon' de terra sua in elemosinam totum scilicet tenementum quod tenebat de domino suo Henrico de Albing' in Henneslawa,[a] et hanc elemosinam dedit[b] liberam ab omni servitio et consuetudinibus que ad ipsum vel heredes suos exigere vel facere pertinebat, preter commune geldum regis, tali definitione ut servitium quod de illo tenemento fieri solebat prefato domino suo Henrico suppleret de alia terra sua, quam de eo tenebat in Merst'. Hoc concessit prefatus Henricus de Alb'; hoc confirmavit rex Henricus. Cum autem, defunctis patribus, Robertus, heres Henrici, servitium suum requireret a Ricardo filio Nigelli, Ricardus, violato pacto patris sui, requisivit illud et gravius accepit de elemosina patris sui. Hanc igitur indignam angariam, me intercedente et operam dante pro fratribus meis Lanthon', redemerunt erga Robertum xx marcis argenti et uno palefrido, ea pactione definita inter Robertum et Ricardum et ab utraque \parte/ concessa, ut prefatum servitium nec Robertus nec heredes eius ultra requireret a Ricardo vel herede suo, nec Ricardus nec heres[c] eius a canonicis Lanthon'. Hanc libertatem confirmavit Robertus fratribus et ecclesie Lanthon' coram me, tam scripto quam testibus subnotatis, Nigello fratre Roberti, Sicilia[d] [fo. 158r B] matre eius, Radulfo priore de Coteis, Symone monacho de Wardon' et aliis.[e]

[a]Heneslawe C. [b]BC add in. [c]Henr' C. [d]scilicet C. [e]Ward' corr. fr. War'; et aliis om. C.

This charter was issued at the same time as no.40. Ralph prior of *Coteis* was prior of Cotes in Northamptonshire (see *HRH*, 228, where, however, he is dated to 1163 × 1186, on the assumption that this charter must have been issued by either Robert de Melun or Robert Foliot).

42. Llanthony priory

Notification to Bishop Alexander of Lincoln, Nicholas archdeacon of Bedford, Robert d'Aubigni and Richard fitz Nigel, testifying to Nigel fitz Erfast's grant to Llanthony priory made while Robert was prior.

[24 September 1143 × 17 December 1146]

B = PRO, C115 K2/6683 (Llanthony cartulary, A1), fos.229v-230r, section x, no.88. s.xiv med.

R. dei gratia episcopus Heref' A. eadem gratia Linc' episcopo et Nicholao archidiacono eius de Bedef', et Roberto de Albign', et aliis baronibus de Bedefordsyra, et Ricardo filio Nigelli salutem. Dudum scripsi et misi ad cognitionem vestram et publicam audientiam testimonium meum de ecclesia de Henl', quam Nigellus filius Erfasti dedit in elemosinam ecclesie nostre de Lanth', tempore quo ego eram prior, et quod eandem donationem postea recognovit [fo.230r] coram me, cum episcopus essem, et coram aliis testibus et concessit et confirmavit, sed quia nuper cum*a* in Bedef'syram venissem sensi quod prefatus Ricardus et, ex amicis eius, aliqui non investigantes veritatem sed querentes occasionem dicebant quod fratres nostri de Lanthon' de prefata ecclesia non habebant aliud munimentum nisi solum testimonium meum; iccirco ostendendam duximus vobis, et illis qui hoc dicunt, cartam Nigelli sigillatam de prefata donatione et recognitione quam ego pro veritate paratus sum ubicumque debeo legitime*b* testificari. Valete.

*a*eum B. *b*legittime B.

This charter (to judge from its language) was issued after nos.39, 40 and 41. Nicholas' first datable occurrence as archdn was in 1145/6 and his predecessor last occurred after 1141. The *terminus ad quem* for this charter is probably the same as that of nos.39 and 40.

43. Llanthony priory

Notification of the grant of a virgate in Prestbury to Llanthony priory made by Ernald the knight when he became a canon there.   [? 1144]

B = PRO, C115 K1/6679 (Llanthony cartulary, A9), fo.111r. s.xiii med. C = PRO, C115 K2/6683 (Llanthony cartulary, A1), fo.120v, section vi, no.4. s.xiv med.
D = PRO, C115 L1/6689 (Llanthony Cartulary A4), fo.126v, sect. ci. s.xv.

Rotbertus*a* dei gratia Hereford' ecclesie episcopus omnibus sancte ecclesie fidelibus salutem. Notum vobis facio quod ego conniventia capituli mei concessi et confirmavi canonicis Lanth' donationem unius virgate terre in Presteburia quam Ernaldus dedit ecclesie Lanthon' quando vitam suam in ea mutavit. Hanc donationem concessit

Radulfus filius Ernaldi. Et, ne occasione illius virgate servitium episcopi minueretur in aliquo, conventionem habuit Radulfus quod idem
servitium integre faceret episcopo Hereford' quod pater eius facere
debuerat, et virgata illa quam pater eius dabat libera permaneret
ecclesie; de hoc vero feodum eius quod retinebat esset[b] pro obside.
Testibus capitulo Heref' et halimoto Presteb'.

[a]Robertus CD.   [b]esse BD.

This charter was probably issued at the same time as another confirmation of
Ernald's grant, issued by Dean Ralph and Hereford cathedral chapter at a meeting
in the chapter in 1144 at which Ernald and his son both agreed to the terms,
Ernald's son also agreeing to provide for his mother and sisters (PRO C115
K1/6679, fo.111, C115 K2/6683, fo.120v, section vi, no.5, and C115 L1/6689,
fo.126v, sect. ci). See also nos.103 and 104 below.

44. Llanthony priory

*Confirmation of a grant to Llanthony priory by Walter son of Earl Miles
of Hereford of land at Alvington and notification that he has dedicated
a chapel and cemetery set up by the Llanthony canons.*

[shortly after 16 July 1147]

B = PRO C115 K2/6683 (Llanthony cartulary, A1), fo.91r, section iv, no.102.
s.xiv med.

R. dei gratia episcopus Heref' omnibus successoribus suis in episcopatu Heref' ecclesie introitum et exitum in Cristo felicem. Testimonium meum huic scripto commemorandum reliqui super facto quod
agnovi, videlicet quod Walterus filius comitis Heref' dedit canonicis
Lanthon' terram quam habebat in Elventon' in perpetuam elemosinam cum omnibus pertinentiis eius in mora et in bosco, cuius rogatu
confirmavi prefatis fratribus illius elemosine donationem, quia in meo
episcopatu continebatur. Porrectis insuper ab eodem Waltero precibus meo interventu ad dominum Papam Eugenium impetravit ut
ab eo confirmaretur. Quoniam vero frequentibus hostilitatis incur-
sibus prefata[a] terra vastata erat et habitatores dispersi, providimus
quo modo spe pacis aliqua et ecclesiastice protectionis fiducia coloni
revocarentur et haberent ibi ac facerent quod Cristiani deberent, unde
benediximus ibi cimiterium et capellam quam fratres ibi noviter
construxerant. Et, quia inceptum[b] opus pietatis non gravandum erat,

sed levitate fovendum, postulantibus fratribus concessimus et constituimus ut capella illa non sicut ecclesia, sed sicut capella serviret episcopo Heref', et clericus eorum quem ibi haberent liber foret ab omnibus exactionibus, sex tantum denarios annuatim reddens episcopo.

*a*nostra *add. and exp. B.*   *b*ceptum *B.*

Walter's grant was not mentioned in Eugenius III's confirmation of 17 December 1146 but was confirmed in his bull of 16 July 1147 (*PUE*, i.273-4): B.J.Parkinson, 'The Life of Robert de Bethune by William of Wycombe', unpublished Oxford B.Litt. thesis, 1951, p.15.

45. Monmouth priory

Confirmation to Prior G(eoffrey) of Monmouth of the grant by Robert fitz Baderon of the church of St Roald of Treget (Llanrothal) to Monmouth priory.   [28 June 1131 × 1144]

   A = A-D Maine-et-Loire (Angers), H3710, no.3. 12th-century endorsement, not in hand of charter: de Munemutha. de ecclesia beati Rualdi. 223 mm wide at top; 233 mm wide at base; 141 mm deep at left and 135 mm at right. No trace of any sealing arrangements.
   B = Ibid., H3711 (charter roll of St-Florent, Saumur), item 8. s.xii. End of document missing. C = Ibid., H3713 (Livre blanc of St-Florent, Saumur), fos.125v-126r. s.xii.

   Pd, P.Marchegay, 'Les prieurés anglais de Saint-Florent près Saumur', *Bibliothèque de l'Ecole des Chartes*, xl (1879), 181-2, no.20.
   Cal., *CDF*, 409, no.1141.

Rotbertus dei gratia Hereford' ecclesie minister humilis. G. priori de Munemutha. vivendo monacum imitari et assequi Cristum. Sicut nostri ordinis est ecclesie persecutores digna animadversione coercere et repellere ; ita ecclesiam honore debito venerantes et de suis substanciis substentantes. nostra sunt qua possumus benedictione digni et oratione fulciendi. Eapropter frater venerande*a* Rotbertum Baderonis filium domino deo attente commendamus et pro*b* sua salute fideliter exoramus. Cuius assensu et concessu nos quoque concedimus et donamus ecclesie beate Marie de Munemutha tuo prioratui commisse ecclesiam beati Rualdi de TREGET. eique inperpetuum subiectam subservire precipimus. episcopali dignitate omnino intemerata manente. Hanc igitur nostram donationem et pretaxati Rotberti cum libero assensu concessionem episcopali auctoritate firmantes. ratam haberi et inviolatam per manere*c* decernimus. Si quis autem hec violare quod absit attentaverit.' eum examini iudicii divini relinquimus. Conservatores autem et defensores huiuscemodi facti.' dei et nostra benedictione salutamus. Vale*d*

*a*frater venerande *over erasure A.*   *b*text ends here B.   *c*as two words A.
*d*Vale *possibly written in another hand A.*

This charter is apparently in the same hand as no.47, which is dated 1144, and it was probably issued either at the same time or else earlier, as the latter confirms the grant of Treget church to Monmouth. Monmouth priory was a dependent priory of the abbey of St-Florent, Saumur.

46. Monmouth priory

Confirmation to Monmouth priory of grant by Richard de Cormeilles and his brothers of the church of Tarrington, Herefordshire.

[1134 × 1144]

A = PRO, E210/2086. 13th-century endorsement: Confirmatio domini episcopi Hereford' de ecclesia de Thadintun'. 153 × 100 mm. Pricking at right side for ruling. No turnup, but sealed on a tag; seal attached facing the wrong way round. Seal: natural wax, fragment only, 45 mm long × 35 mm wide. No reverse or counterseal. No legend visible; of the design only part of the bishop's body with his left arm and some of his staff visible.

Rotbertus dei gratia Herefordensis ecclesie humilis minister.' omnibus sancte ecclesie filiis tam presentibus quam futuris. salutem et benedictionem. Omnes*a* certissime sciant fideles. quod Ricardus de Cormelles. et fratres sui. divina admoniti inspiratione. pro parentum suorum. et pro suis etiam animabus. deo et sancte Marie. et sancto Florencio. monachisque apud Monemutam commorantibus.' ecclesiam de Tadintona cum rebus que ad eam pertinent omnes libere dederunt. et semper absque calumpnia habendam concesserunt. hoc autem donum in capitulo Herefordie presente canonicorum conventu. predictus Ricardus. in manu mea qui episcopus eram. cum textu e\u/uangeliorum humili devotione donavit.' quod ego ipse quoque ibidem in manu Gofredi prioris cum eodem textu tradidi et pontificali auctoritate confirmavi. Hoc revera totum viderunt. et diligenter annuerunt .' Radulfus decanus. Gislebertus de Ewroic.

Briencius thesaurarius. ceterique eiusdem ecclesie canonici. et plures alii ;

*[superscript a]*O *of* omnes *projects into left margin A.*

*[a]*O *of* omnes *projects into left margin A.*

Richard of Cormeilles' grant, issued with the consent of his brothers Robert and Alexander and witnessed by Baderon (lord of Monmouth) and his wife Rose, survives as PRO E327/399 (printed by P.Marchegay [cited above, no.45], 180, no.18). It is in a different hand from Robert de Béthune's charter. Robert's charter can probably be dated after 1134, since Ralph became dean of Hereford only after this date, and before 1144 (cf. no.47), and is probably from towards the end of that period – Baderon, who presumably witnessed Richard's charter in his capacity as lord of Monmouth, succeeded before 1144. Tarrington in Herefordshire is listed in Domesday Book (i, fo.186b) as a manor of Ansfrid of Cormeilles. No.46 was not written by the same scribe as nos.45 and 47.

47. Monmouth priory

Confirmation of a grant by Guienoc and of grants by Guienoc's nephew, William fitz Baderon, to Monmouth priory, listing the churches given: Dixton, Goodrich, Welsh Bicknor, Hope Mansell, Longhope, Tibberton, Stretton Grandison, Ashperton, Little Lydney (now St Briavels), Staunton, Huntley, Tarrington (the gift of Richard de Cormeilles) and Llanrothal. 1144

A = A-D Maine-et-Loire (Angers), H3710, no.4. 12th-century endorsement: de monemuda. 15th-century endorsement: in anglia terra. 280 × 383 mm. No turnup, tongue, or tie, but there is a semicircular hole at the bottom edge of the document which suggests that a slit for a tag may originally have been cut there.

B = Ibid., H3711 (charter roll of St-Florent, Saumur), item 8 (dating clause of this charter only, attached to the beginning of the text of no.45 above). s.xii. C = Ibid., H3713 (Livre blanc of St-Florent, Saumur), fos.123va-124va. s.xii.

Pd., P.Marchegay, 'Les prieurés anglais de Saint-Florent près de Saumur', *Bibliothèque de l'Ecole des Chartes*, xl (1879), 182-3, no.21.
Cal., *CDF*, 409-410, no.1142.

Robertus dei gratia Herefordensis episcopus succe[ssorib]us^a suis. et universis sancte dei ecclesie filiis, perpetuam in domino salutem. Quoniam processu temporis a memoria hominum multa elabi. et antiquari videntur.[,] tam futuris quam presentibus notum fieri dignum duximus quod Guienocus dominus de Monemuda. pro salute anime sue et parentum suorum. eterna sibi sine dubio sperans inde adquirere premia .[,] omnes ecclesias de terra sua cum ipsarum pertinentiis. hoc est cum decimis suis omnibus et ceteris beneficiis ad ipsas omnino pertinentibus deo. et monachis obedientie sancte Marie de Monemuda que obedientia beati Florencii de Salmuro iuris esse dignoscitur. in elemosinam perpetualiter concessit et donavit *?* et legitimis testibus confirmavit quorum nomina hec sunt. Rado monacus frater supradicti Guienoci. David monacus cognomento Taxius. Dodomandus. et Herveus sacerdotes. Normandus filius Gosberti. Hugo de Clocestria.*ᵇ* Reinaldus grossus. Willelmus autem Guienoci nepos ei in honorem succedens. easdem ecclesias. et cetera beneficia ad honorem dei. et sancte Marie concessit. diligenter conservavit. et protexit. Quod Badero huius Willelmi filius. et Rohesia eius uxor. qui nunc temporis eundem honorem habent. et honorifice gubernant. Ita esse factum congratulantur. et confirmant et beneficiis ad augent*ᶜ* ecclesiam videlicet Sancti Tedioci. ecclesiam Sancti Egidii de Castello Godrici. ecclesiam Sancti Custenin de Biconovria. ecclesiam de Hopa Pagani filii Baderonis. ecclesiam de Haillilda Hopa. ecclesiam de Tibristonia. ecclesiam de Stratonia. ecclesiam de Aspretona. ecclesiam de Lindeneia. ecclesiam Sancti Nicholai de Stantonia. capellam de Honteleia. ecclesiam vero Sancti Petri de Tatintonia quam Ricardus de Cormeliis pro sue et sui patris anime. et matris remedio. nichil omnino in eadem ecclesia neque in decimis neque in ceteris beneficiis ad ipsam pertinentibus sibi retinens. deo. et supradictis monachis nostro tempore largitus est *?* supranominatis ecclesiis adiungi non incongruum nobis videtur. ecclesiam quoque Sancti Roaldi de Treket cum apendiciis*ᵈ* ipsius. et decimis omnibus de eodem Treket que nuper monitu nostro et voluntate a Roberto Baderonis sepe dicte obedientie inperpetuum concessa est *?* pretaxatis ecclesiis adhiberi volumus. Eas itaque episcopali auctoritate Herefordensi capitulo attestante et adprobante. pontificali dignitate intemerata permanente. in honorem dei. et Sancti Florentii sigillo nostro corroboramus et communimus et ut predictus Guienocus et heredes ipsius eas donaverunt. libere inperpetuum concedimus. Predicti autem capituli inrefragabiles personas in testimonium adduci sanum videtur. que in presenti cartula contineri videntur. Radulfus decanus. Briencius tesaurarius. Gillebertus cantor. Rannulfus Archimeri. magister Reinaldus. Hugo de Clifordia. Ordgarus. Galterus. Hosbertus. Magister Eustachius. Hugo partes. Hec autem eapropter et auctoritate nostra et testibus prenominatis ita stabilimus ne future posteritati aliqua dubitatio inde suboriri videatur. Si quis autem hanc nostram confir-

mationem cassare aut infringere attentaverit divino iudicio eum relinquimus. conservantibus vero benedictio dei et nostra^e concedatur.
Anno ab incarnatione domini nostri Iesu Cristi. Millesimo. centesimo. quadragesimo. quarto. facta est ista confirmatio. Donatio vero
ipsarum ecclesiarum facta est in tempore Willelmi regis qui Angliam
devicit. et sibi nobiliter subiugavit. excepta ecclesia Tatintonie. et
ecclesia de Treket que nostro tempore et nostro monitu donate
fuerunt ;

^{a}*lacuna a; supplied from C.* ^{b}*? sic for* Glocestria *AC.* ^{c}*as two words A.*
^{d}*sic A;* appendiciis *C.* ^{e}*text of B starts here.*

William fitz Baderon's grants are printed by Marchegay, *art. cit.*, 175-6, 177-9,
nos.12, 13, 15, 16. For a confirmation of Richard de Cormeilles' grant of Tarrington church see no.46.

*48. Preston chapel

*Confirmation of the status of Preston chapel and cemetery in Botloe
hundred, Gloucestershire, as subject to their mother church (perhaps a
confirmation issued on the dedication of the chapel and cemetery).*
[28 June 1131 × 16 April 1148]

Mention only, in a confirmation issued by Bp Gilbert Foliot after he had dedicated
the cemetery at Upleadon, Gloucestershire, *GFL*, no.301 and no.72 below, and
Gloucester cartulary, i.375-6. The name of the mother church of Preston is not
given.

49. Shrewsbury abbey

*Notification of a confirmation by Elias de Say, lord of Clun, of the grant
of the vill of Brompton made to Shrewsbury abbey by his brother Henry.*
[28 June 1131 × 16 April 1148]

B = NLW, MS 7851 D (Shrewsbury Cartulary), p.308, no.350b. s.xiv.

Pd., *Shrewsbury cartulary*, ii.315.

Brompton is in Berrington in Shropshire.

50. Shrewsbury abbey

Mandate to Dean Ralph and Hereford Cathedral Chapter to recognise grants of churches and tithes made by the faithful to Shrewsbury abbey and notification of the chapels and cemeteries recently consecrated by Robert. The chapels, at Oldbury, Billingsley, Aston Eyre, Aldenham, Underton, Tugford and Baucott (the two last being counted as one chapel) are to remain subject to their mother church, Morville, and a rural dean, Aelfric (Elvericus), recognises that the chapel of Abdon is also subject to its mother church.   [early 1138+]

B = NLW, MS 7851 D (Shrewsbury Cartulary), pp.297-9, no.333. s.xiv.

Pd, *Shrewsbury cartulary*, ii.302-3.

Robert states that he found it necessary to consecrate the cemeteries in the wake of recent disturbances, which Una Rees (*Shrewsbury cartulary*, loc. cit.) suggests are those that occurred early in 1138.

51. Shrewsbury abbey

Notification to Dean Ralph and Hereford cathedral chapter that he has dedicated a chapel and cemetery at Astley in Shropshire, which is to remain a chapel subject to Morville church, and that the lord of Astley has endowed Astley chapel with half a virgate, an assart worth four shillings, and a house in the vill.   [on or after 14 October, *c*.1138+]

B = NLW, MS 7851 D (Shrewsbury Cartulary), pp.306-7, no.348. s.xiv.
Pd, *Shrewsbury cartulary*, ii.313.

Hiis testibus, Rainaldo priore de Wenel', Petro archidiacono, Hugone, canonico Lanton', Ricardo et Elurico decanis, David et Waltero capellanis meis.

Robert states that he dedicated the chapel on St Calixtus' Day (14 October). Una Rees suggests (*Shrewsbury cartulary*, loc. cit.) that as Astley chapel is not one of the chapels mentioned in no.50 above as having been recently consecrated, this charter must have been issued after *c*.1138, but not long after, because it has the same witness list as a charter of Robert fitz Aer granting land at the dedication of Aston Eyre cemetery; the cemetery at Aston is not referred to in no.50, although the lands granted by Robert to the chapel are. It is possible that Robert fitz Aer's charter (*Shrewsbury cartulary*, ii.312) may have been issued some time after the actual grant.

52. Shrewsbury abbey

Confirmation to Shrewsbury abbey of its possession of Morville church, the pensions from its chapels and various tithes.

[*c.*1138 × 16 April 1148]

B = NLW, MS 7851 D (Shrewsbury Cartulary), pp.299-300, no.334. s.xiv.
Pd, *Shrewsbury cartulary*, ii.303.

Hiis testibus, Reinaldo priore de Wonlok, Petro archidiacono, Hugone canonico, Ricardo decano, David capellano, et pluribus aliis.

In *Shrewsbury cartulary* it is suggested that this charter was issued after no.50 because it mentions the recently consecrated chapels of Astley, Billingsley, and Oldbury, but possibly before no.53 whereby Billingsley manor (no mention is made of the chapel as such) was awarded to Sées abbey in a composition datable 1144 × 1148. The witness list of this charter is very like those of no.51 and of Robert fitz Aer's grant to Aston Eyre chapel (*op. cit.*, ii.312) and all three charters may possibly have been issued at the same time.

53. Shrewsbury abbey

Notification of a composition between Abbot John of Sées and Abbot Ranulf of Shrewsbury concerning the church of Diddlebury and the manor of Billingsley, by which the church was awarded to Shrewsbury and the manor to Sées.   [March 1144 × 16 April 1148]

B = NLW, MS 7851 D (Shrewsbury Cartulary), p.301, no.337. s.xiv.
Pd, *Shrewsbury cartulary*, ii.306.

Hanc autem conventionem in presentia nostra et capituli nostri Hereford' ecclesie et venerabilis fratris nostri Gilberti Gloecestrie abbatis, priorum etiam Reginaldi de Weneloc et Edmundi de Liministria, archidiaconorum vero Willelmi Lond' et Godefridi Wigorn' factam episcopali auctoritate sanctimus et sigilli nostri impressione communimus.

Godfrey was appointed archdn of Worcester in or soon after March 1144.

54. Abbot Suger of St-Denis

Letter requesting Suger to send him some relics, particularly ones of St Denis.   [28 June 1131 × 16 April 1148]

> No manuscript source for this letter can be traced. Lecoy de la Marche (see below) refers to a copy in a manuscript belonging to the Dupuy brothers, but this letter does not apparently occur in the manuscripts in the Dupuy collection in the Bibliothèque Nationale.
> Pd, André Du Chesne, ed. *Historiae Francorum Scriptores*, 5 vols. (Paris 1636-49) iv.500; Bouquet, *Recueil des historiens*, xv.498; *PL*, clxxxvi.1359-60; A.Lecoy de la Marche, ed. *Oeuvres complètes de Suger* (Société de l'histoire de France, Paris [1867]), 420-1, and cal. ibid., 295.

> Lecoy de la Marche dated this letter to the final months of Robert's life, presumably on the assumption that Robert wrote to Suger while he was attending the 1148 Rheims council. This is probable, but an earlier date cannot be ruled out, since Robert might possibly have encountered Suger in the first decade or so of the twelfth century when he was studying in France.

55. Sutton parish church

Notification of the settlement between Nicholas (incumbent?) of Sutton and Godric (incumbent?) of Marden concerning the parochial sequela *of a virgate held by Stephen the portreeve on the fee of Humphrey the sheriff and a virgate held by Reinerius the carpenter at Sutton and land held by him on the fee of Roger de Chandos at Wisteston; the case was heard in the second synod held by Robert at Hereford and judgement was given to Nicholas.*   1132, before 27 June

> B = Oxford, Balliol College, MS 271 (cartulary of St Guthlac's, Hereford), fo.88v, no.388. s.xiv in.

R.[a] dei gratia Herefordensis episcopus omnibus fidelibus de Herefordesira clericis et laicis, francis et anglicis salutem. Notum sit presentibus et posteris anno ab incarnatione domini mcxxxii,[b] primo autem anno episcopatus eiusdem Roberti, sinodo vero secunda, inter Nicholaum de Suttona et Godricum de Maurdin causam actam esse et terminatam de terra Nigelli ostiarii et hominum eiusdem, scilicet de una virgata quam tenuit Stephanus portareva de feodo Unfridi vic(ecomitis) et alia virgata quam tenuit Reinerus carpentarius apud Suttona et de terra quam tenet de feodo Rogeri de Candos apud

Wistanestunam quam pretaxatus Godricus acclamabat in parochia ecclesie de Maurdin, et Nicholaus ecclesie de Suttona. Adiudicavit autem illam ecclesie de Suttona in parochiam sancta sinodus Herefordensis perpetuo possidendam canonico iudicio, tum propter triennalem possessionem atque etiam ampliorem quietam et inconcussam quam predictus Godricus pertemptavit infringere, nec potuit, quia eam sibi ecclesia Suttunensis legitimis et irrefragabilibus[c] testibus vendicabat, tum etiam propter donationem eiusdem terre quam Gerardus venerabilis Hereford' episcopus ei fecerat, quam et testibus approbabat, tum propter confirmationem predicte donationis quam fecerat Reinelmus episcopus successor Gerardi. Huic iudicio sinodali interfuerunt Godfridus abbas Wynchelcumbensis, et Bernardus prior de Clenildepurda, et Osbertus prior de Brunfelda, et Willelmus subdecanus Salesburie, et Brientius thesaurarius, et Petrus archidiaconus, et Gilbertus Eborac', et Hugo et Renulfus,[d] attestante Roberto cantore cum capitulo Hereford et tota sinodo.

[a]*omitted (for rubricator) B.*   [b]mcii *sic, B.*   [c]*irrefragalibus B.*   [d]*sic for* Rannulfus B.

The text of this charter is repeated almost word for word in a document issued by Hereford cathedral chapter, *ibid.*, fo.88, no.387, from which it is possible to correct *mcii* to *mcxxxii. Clenildepurda* is the scribe's misreading of *Kenildepurða* or Kenilworth. By the 1140s there were parishes of Sutton St Michael and Sutton St Nicholas; Sutton St Michael, to which Wisteston, later a chapelry, was attached, belonged to St Guthlac's priory, to which it was granted by Walter de Turri 1143 × 1148 (cf. nos. 25 and 26 above). It was later awarded to the Hospitallers to hold from St Guthlac's. Sutton St Nicholas passed into the possession of St Guthlac's in the mid-12th century. See below, nos.87, 92, 126, 156 and 157.

56. Tenbury church

Notification that he has dedicated cemeteries at the chapels of Rochford and Kyre Wiard and confirmation to Tenbury church of its rights as a mother church over them.   [28 June 1131 × 16 April 1148]

B = Oxford, Bodl. MS Dugdale 11, fo.67r. s.xvii.

Pd, *Mon. Ang.* vi, pt ii, 1093, no.xiv.

R. dei gratia Herefordensis ecclesie humilis minister archidiaconis etc' salutem. Notum vobis fieri volumus quod capelle[a] de Rachefordia et de Cura sunt pertinentes ad ecclesiam de Temeteberia et[b] episcopalia iura reddentes sicut capelle matri ecclesie. Apud capellas vero,[c] ad pauperum refugium, constringente[d] necessitate, a me facta sunt cimiteria concessu predicte matris ecclesie de Themetberia, salva tam dignitate sua quam possessione. Corpora que voluerit apud se habebit; que vero iusserit, remanebunt. Capella iterum de Rachafordia, pro quadam terra quam eadem[e] mater ecclesia libere tenebat, et pro concessu cimiterii, singulis annis in die sancti Michaelis matri ecclesie tres solidos persolveret. Capella de Cura eidem matri ecclesie pro concessu cimiterii singulis annis tertia die ante Nativitatem Sancte Marie xii denarios persolvet.

[a]capella B.   [b]in B.   [c]n° capellas *for* capellas vero B.   [d]constringere B.   [e]idem B.

Tenbury Wells church, in Worcestershire but in the diocese of Hereford, was one of the English properties of Lire abbey. In spite of the occurrence of the phrase 'minister humilis' (owing to a lapse of concentration by the copyist ?), this is almost certainly an *actum* of Robert de Béthune because of its mixed use of first person singular and plural, and because Robert de Béthune's episcopate saw the largest number of dedications of chapels and cemeteries. Many of the latter were required to provide sanctuary during the disturbances of the Anarchy, and this charter was probably issued in the early 1140s. A feature of many charters notifying such dedications is the confirmation of the rights of the *matrix ecclesia*, especially burial dues; see also nos. 29, 31, 44, 46, 48, 50, 51, and *GFL* no.301. The mother church of Tenbury is being allowed the right to choose which bodies it wants to bury so that it can have the richest deceased with the biggest soulscots (mortuary gifts).

57. Tintern abbey

Notification that Tintern abbey has, with the consent of Archbishop Theobald of Canterbury, removed the parish of Woolaston together with a virgate in Elfredestona *to Alvington so that the peace of Tintern's* mansio *at Woolaston is not disturbed.*   [16 July 1146 × 16 April 1148]

B = PRO, C115 K2/6683 (Llanthony cartulary, A1), fo.91v, section iv, no.104. s.xiv med.

Rotbertus dei gratia episcopus Heref' capitulo Herefordensis ecclesie et omnibus fidelibus salutem. Notum sit omnibus tam modernis quam futuris quod cum Henricus abbas Tynternie consilium et assensum obtinuisset domini Cantuariensis archiepiscopi Teobaldi, ut propter necessarias causas mansionem suam demutaret apud Wlavestonam, cumque meipsum rogasset prefatus archiepiscopus noster ut huic facto preberem assensum meum et expedimentum, quod possim, assensi libens, ut igitur apud Wlaveston' liberius et quietius hospitari possent, secundum consuetudinem ordinis sui, voluntate et petitione prefati abbatis demutavi parochiam de Wlvest' apud Alwuynton' cum una virgata terre que est in Elfredestona et cum ceteris pertinentiis eius, ita ut deinceps pastorem haberent in Aluynton', et inde requirerent ibique facerent parochialia iura sua, sicut eatenus facere debuerant in Wlavest'. Teste,[a] conventu Tynt' et conventu Lanth'.

[a] *sic B.*

This charter must be slightly later than no.44 above. Abbot Henry of Tintern's predecessor occurs in about 1139 and died before 1148, and Henry became abbot of Waverley between 1154 and 1161. Tintern eventually appropriated the church of Woolaston; see below, no.237. Evidently they wished to have their grange at Woolaston undisturbed by nearby settlement; it was quite common for Cistercians to drive out local inhabitants (R.A.Donkin, 'Settlement and depopulation on Cistercian estates during the twelfth and thirteenth centuries, especially in Yorkshire', *BIHR*, xxxiii [1960], 141-65). *Eldfredestona, Alvredestone* in Domesday Book, was in Woolaston.

58. Worcester cathedral priory

Grant of the parsonage of Lindridge to David prior of Worcester and all his successors. [1143 × 1145]

B = Worcester, Cathedral Library, MS A4 (Worcester cathedral Register), fo.27r, no.200. s.xiii med.
Pd, *Worcester cartulary*, no.200.

Huius autem donationis testes sunt Gilebertus abbas Gloecestr', etc.

David was prior of Worcester between 1143 and 1145.

GILBERT FOLIOT

59. Profession of obedience

Profession of obedience to Archbishop Theobald of Canterbury.
[5 September 1148]

A = Canterbury, D. & C. Archives, Ch. Ant. C115, 24.

B = BL Cotton MS Cleop. E i (register of the see of Canterbury), fos. 36v-37r. s.xii med. C = Canterbury, D. & C. Archives, Reg. A (The Prior's Register), fo.233r. s.xv.

Pd, *GFL*, 353, no.289; *Canterbury professions*, 45, no.91.

60. Benedict

Notification that a certain Benedict, forced by judgement of Bishop Robert de Béthune's court to swear his innocence of his brother's death or complicity therein with the support of seven priests, has done so with an oath sworn by twelve priests. [soon after 5 September 1148]

B = Bodl. MS E Musaeo 249 (letter collection of Gilbert Foliot), fo.21r. s.xii ¾.
Pd, Giles, no.89; *GFL*, 396-7, no.349.

61. Brecon priory

Notification that he has established four cemeteries at the request of Nicholas of Maund and of the prior and monks of Brecon, at Maund, Rowberry, The Vern in Bodenham, and Broadfield, and that he has laid down the terms on which services are to be held at the chapels of Maund, Rowberry and The Vern, saving the dignity of the mother church of St Mary's of Bodenham; Nicholas of Maund has granted land at Maund and Risbury to the mother church. [5 September 1148 × 1154(?)]

B = BL Harleian MS 6976, fos.15r-16r. C = Bodl. MS Carte 108, fo.266r. s.xviii.

Pd, *Brecon cartulary*, xiv.20-21, and *GFL*, 353-4, no.290.
See also no.73.

62. Brecon priory

Confirmation of the grant by Roger, earl of Hereford, of mills at and above Burghill, to settle a dispute which had arisen between the monks of Brecon and the canons of Llanthony.   [5 September 1148 × 1154]

B = Bodl. MS Carte 108, fo.266v. s.xviii.
Pd, *Brecon cartulary*, xiv.21, and *GFL*, 355, no.292.

The dispute had arisen because Roger's father, Miles of Gloucester, had given the church of Burghill, previously granted by his father-in-law Bernard of Neufmarché to Brecon, to his own foundation of Llanthony Secunda near Gloucester.

63. Brecon priory

Confirmation of the grant by Walter del Mans and his wife Agnes of the church of Humber to Brecon priory.   [5 September 1148 × 1155]

B = Bodl. MS Carte 108, fo.266r. s.xviii.
Pd, *Brecon cartulary*, xiv.21, and *GFL*, 355, no.291.
See also no.245 below.

64. St Augustine's abbey, Canterbury

Notification by Bishops Richard of London, Rotrou of Evreux, Robert of Bath, William of Norwich, Hilary of Chichester, Gilbert of Hereford, and Robert of Lincoln, papal judges-delegate, that Silvester, abbot of St Augustine's, has made his profession to Archbishop Theobald.

17 July 1157

A[1] = Canterbury, Dean and Chapter Archives, Ch. Ant. A 51.
A[2] = Ibid., Ch. Ant. A 49.
B = BL Cotton MS Vesp. B 19 (Gervase of Canterbury), fo.62r-v. s.xiii 2/3. C = Cambridge, Trinity College, MS R. 4. 11 (Gervase of Canterbury), fo.103r-v. s.xiv.

Pd., Gervas. Cant., i.164-5; *Chichester acta*, no.21; *GFL*, 356-7, no.293.

65. Crediton church, Devon

Settlement, as papal judge-delegate, of the case between John, a clerk, and Reginald of Pagham, concerning the church of Crediton; each is to have half the church. [1161 × March 1163]

> B = Bodl. MS E Musaeo 249 (letter collection of Gilbert Foliot), fo.141v. s.xii ¾.
>
> Pd, Giles, no.129, and *GFL*, 357, no.294.

66. Ely cathedral priory

Letter to Eugenius III informing him of the current position of the case between Henry the clerk and the monks of Ely concerning the manor of Stetchworth. [December 1152]

> B = Ely, Dean and Chapter, MS (Liber Eliensis), fos.166v-169r. s.xii/xiii. C = Cambridge, Trinity College, MS O.2.1, fos.159v-161r. s.xii ex. D = Bodl. MS Laud. Misc. 647, fos.96r-97r. s.xiv in. E = BL Cotton MS Titus A 1, fos.44r-46v. s.xii/xiii.
>
> Pd, *PUE*, ii, no.74; *Liber Eliensis*, 355-6; *GFL*, 358-61, no.295.

67. Ely cathedral priory

Execution of the decision by Anastasius III upon the case between Henry the clerk and the monks of Ely concerning the manor of Stetchworth, in favour of the monks. [Late 1154]

> B = Ely, Dean and Chapter, MS (Liber Eliensis), fo.170v. s.xii/xiii. C = Cambridge, Trinity College, MS O.2.1., fo.162v. s.xii ex. D = Bodl. MS Laud Misc. 647, fos.97v-98r. s.xiv in. E = BL Cotton MS Titus, A1, fo.47v. s.xii/xiii. F = Cambridge, University Library, Ely Diocesan Records, Liber M, fo.87r. s.xiii/xiv.
>
> Pd, *Liber Eliensis*, 361, and *GFL*, 361-2, no.296.

68. Ely cathedral priory

Mandate to Henry the clerk and others who had invaded the manor of Stetchworth, ordering them to leave it on pain of anathema.

[after September 1154]

B = Ely, Dean and Chapter, MS (Liber Eliensis), fos.170v-171r. s.xii/xiii. C = Cambridge, Trinity College, MS O.2.1, fo.162v. s.xii ex. D = Bodl. MS Laud. Misc. 647, fo.98r. s.xiv in. E = BL Cotton MS Titus A i, fo.47v. s.xii/xiii. F = Cambridge, University Library, Ely Diocesan Records, Liber M, fo.87r-87v. s.xiii/xiv.

Pd, *Liber Eliensis*, 361-2 and *GFL*, 362, no.297.

69. Evesham abbey

Confirmation of grants by Hugh, son of Roger, and his wife Margaret of a cell dedicated to St John the Baptist at Southstone Rock (in Stanford-on-Teme, Worcs.) to Evesham, and by Payn de Noyers of the island of Serpeham to the same cell, together with an indulgence of fifteen days to benefactors of the cell.

[5 September 1148 × March 1163]

B = BL Cotton MS Vesp. B xxiv, fo.17v. s.xii/xiii. C = BL Harleian MS 3763, fo.87v. s.xii/xiii.

Pd, *GFL*, 363, no.298.

70. Eynsham abbey

Settlement as papal judge-delegate of the case between the abbot of Eynsham and Alan clerk of Slaughter (Glos.), concerning the demesne tithes of Naunton (Glos.) belonging to the fief of Roger de Oili: Alan recognises that the tithes belong to Eynsham and is permitted to farm them for an annual pension of 3s.

[5 September 1148 × 18 April 1161]

B = Oxford, Christ Church Dean and Chapter MS 341 (Eynsham abbey cartulary), fo.22v.

Pd, *Eynsham cartulary*, i, no.45, and *GFL*, 363-4, no.299.

His testibus: Radulfo de Saucei, Willelmo de Sceldeslega, Reginaldo de Cudinton', Rogero de Cornwelle, Eilrico presbitero de Rollendrith, Hugone Crollebacun, Waltero de Hard(e)pirer', Hugone clerico et multis aliis.

71. Gloucester abbey

Notification that when he was abbot of Gloucester, Roger son of Hugh Parvus settled a dispute with Gloucester abbey concerning a virgate at Quedgeley, by granting the abbey a virgate in Brookthorpe manor in return for seven marks and the right to hold the virgate at Quedgeley directly from the earl of Hereford.   [soon after 5 September 1148]

B = PRO C150/1 (Gloucester abbey cartulary), fo.10v. s.xiv ex.

Pd, *Gloucester cartulary*, i.176-7 and *GFL*, 364-6, no.300.

72. Gloucester abbey

Notification that he has made a cemetery at Upleadon as a refuge for the poor; Upleadon chapel is to remain a chapel to its mother church.
     [1148 × 1163, ? c.1148]

B = PRO C150/1 (Gloucester abbey cartulary), fo.104r. s.xiv ex.

Pd, *Gloucester cartulary*, i.375-6, and *GFL*, 366, no.301.

73. Gloucester abbey

Confirmation to Gloucester abbey at the request of Roger, earl of Hereford, and of Hugh, lord of Kilpeck, of Kilpeck priory and its endowments: the church of St David, Kilpeck, with its chapel of St Mary, and Hugh's demesne chapels and tithes, that is tithes on the lands of The Vern and Venn's Green in Bodenham, Broadward in Leominster, Hopton Sollers, Taynton, and Bledisloe, together with pensions from the churches of Baysham and St Nicholas, Hereford.   [5 September 1148 × 1155]

B = Gloucester, Cathedral Library, Register A, fo.72v-73v. s.xiv ex.

Pd, *GFL*, 366-8, no.302.

Hiis testibus Baderone de Monem', Roberto de Watteuyll', Mauricio vicecomite, Radulpho Avenel, Willelmo de Miner', Oliver' de la Mare [fo.73v], Rogero de Burchull', Waltero Walensi, Waltero de Fraxino, Hugone de Scudimor', Alano fratre predicti Hugonis de Kylpec, et aliis.

See also no.61.

74. Gloucester abbey

Grant to Gloucester abbey of a neif, William, son of Robert, Gilbert's vine-dresser in Ledbury.   [5 September 1148 × March 1163]

> B = PRO C150/1 (Gloucester abbey cartulary), fo.112r. s.xiv ex.
> Pd, *Gloucester cartulary*, ii.4 and *GFL*, 372, no.309.

75. Gloucester abbey

Institution of Robert de Haseley, monk of Gloucester, as parson and prior of the church of Bromfield, Shropshire; Bromfield is to retain its freedoms as a royal chapel by the command of Henry II.   [c.1155]

> B = Hereford, County Record Office, formerly Hereford, Diocesan Registry, Registrum Ricardi de Swinfield, fo.152r. 1282 × 1317.
> Pd, *Reg. Swinfield*, 426, and *GFL*, 368, no.303. Tr., A.L.Moir, *Bromfield Priory and Church in Shropshire* (Chester 1947), 44-5.

Teste tota sancta sinodo mea.

76. Gloucester abbey

Institution of Samson, sacrist of Gloucester, as parson in the church of St Lawrence, Taynton, at the request of Matilda de Wattevile, lady of Taynton, who had persuaded Alfred the previous parson to resign the church into Gilbert's hands; Alfred is to continue to hold the church for a pension of 10 marks a year.   [c.1158]

B = Gloucester, Cathedral Library, Register B, p.20. s.xiv ex.
Pd, *GFL*, 368-9, no.304.

Teste capitulo nostro.

See no.4 above.

77. Gloucester abbey

Confirmation of grant by Bernard de Neufmarché to Gloucester abbey of Much Cowarne church, and licence to appropriate the church to the sacrist's department, together with confirmations of various tithe arrangements in other parishes. [c.1158]

B = Gloucester, Cathedral Library, Seals and Deeds, viii, I (1275 x 1287). C = Hereford, County Record Office, formerly Hereford, Diocesan Registry, Registrum Thome de Cantilupo, on verso of inserted slip after fo.17. 1275 × 1282. D = Gloucester, Cathedral Library, Register B, p.57. s.xiv ex. E = PRO C150/1 (Gloucester abbey cartulary), fo. 49-v. s.xv?. F = Ibid., fo.248r-v, no.917. s.xv.

Pd, *Gloucester cartulary*, i.252-3 and iii.6; *Reg. Cantilupe*, 49-50, and *GFL*, 369-70, no.305.

...teste tota nostra synodo Herfordensi.

78. Gloucester abbey

Appropriation to Gloucester abbey of the churches of Much Cowarne and Taynton. [c.1158 × March 1163]

B = PRO C150/1 (Gloucester abbey cartulary), fo.248r, no.916. s.xv?.
Pd, *Gloucester cartulary*, iii.5, and *GFL*, 370, no.306.

79. Gloucester abbey

Settlement of the dispute between Hugh, clerk of Yarkhill, and Patrick, sacrist of Gloucester, concerning the tithe of Monkhide in Yarkhill. [c.1158 × March 1163]

B = Gloucester, Cathedral Library, Register B, p.55. s.xiv ex.
Pd, *GFL*, 370-1, no.307.

Hiis testibus: Waltero archidiacono, magistro Waltero, Gileberto m(onach)o, Rogero clerico, Hugone clerico, Lodewico.

80.   Gloucester abbey

General confirmation to Gloucester abbey of the pensions and tithes granted for lights and ornaments to the church (to the sacrist's depart-ment) in nos.17-20 above.   [c.1158 × March 1163]

B = Gloucester, Cathedral Library, Register B, p.75. s.xiv ex.
Pd, *GFL*, 371, no.308.

81.   Grenta son of Leofwin

Grant to Grenta son of Leofwin with the consent of Adam, son of Roger, of the land which Grenta's uncle Roger held in Linley, Shropshire, to hold free for the first two years, for ½ mark in the third year and for one mark per year thereafter; Grenta is also to provide the service of one serjeant for castleguard for 40 days per year in the episcopal castle at Lydbury.
[c.1150 × March 1163]

B = Shrewsbury Local Studies Library, Haughmand abbey cartulary, fo.136r.
Pd, Eyton, *Antiquities*, xi.208 (abbrev.); *GFL*, 372, no.310; *Haughmond cartulary*, 145-6, no.700.

Hiis testibus: Petro archidiacono, Ricardo filio cancellarii, Waltero archidiacono.

See nos.147 and 252.

82.   Hereford cathedral

Settlement of the dispute between Herbert canon of Hereford and William chaplain of Archbishop Theobald concerning the church of Inkber-

row (Worcs.): the church of Inkberrow and its chapel of St Lawrence are recognised to belong to Herbert's prebend and Herbert has allowed William a perpetual vicarage in them for a pension of 30s per year.

[1148 × 1163]

B = Bodl. MS E Musaeo 249 (letter collection of Gilbert Foliot), fo.37v. s.xii¾.
Pd, Giles, no.122; *GFL*, 375, no.314.

The scribe omits the witnesses' names.

83. Hereford cathedral

Settlement of the dispute between Hereford cathedral and the Chandos family concerning land at Wariduna *(near Moreton on Lugg): Robert de Chandos has surrendered* Wariduna *to the cathedral to enlarge the prebend held by David the priest.* [*c.*1155 × 1158]

B = Bodl. MS Rawlinson B329 (Hereford cathedral cartulary), fo.160r. s.xiii-xiv.
C = Ibid., fo.11r. s.xv.
Pd., *GFL*, 374, no.313.

Hiis testibus: Radulfo decano Hereford', Reginaldo cantore, Petro archidiacono, Ivone thesaurario, magistro Rannulfo, magistro Willelmo de Salesbur', magistro David, Waltero capellano, et Hereberto clerico Roberti de Candos; Rogero et Symone de Candos, Hugone forestario, Willelmo filii Willelmi et Rogero fratre eius, Rogero de Lurneye, Ricardo Talebot, Philippo Alis et de halimot de Walint' Rein(aldo) et Stephano, Hugone et altero*ᵃ* Rein(aldo), Roberto et Nicholao et aliis.

*ᵃ*alteri *B.*

On David the priest (Canon David de Aqua) see below, no.149.

84. Hereford cathedral

Notification that Robert de Chandos has granted the church of St Margaret, Wellington, to Hereford cathedral as a prebend.

[1158 × 1163]

B = Hereford D. & C. Muniments, no.2777, in a charter of inspeximus issued by Hugh Foliot (no.336 below). C = Bodl. MS Rawlinson B329 (Hereford cathedral cartulary), fo.160v. s.xiii-xiv. D = Hereford, Diocesan Registry, now County Record Office, Registrum Ricardi de Swinfield, fo.21v (17v). s.xiii ex. E = Bodl. MS Rawlinson B329, fo.10v. s.xv.

Pd, *Hereford charters*, 17; *Reg. Swinfield*, 55 and 55-6; *GFL*, 375-6, no.315.

Hiis testibus: Nicholao episcopo de Landaf', Gaufrido decano Hereford', archidiaconis Petro et Waltero Foliot, Reginaldo cantore, Ivone thesaurario, cum toto Herefordensi capitulo.

85. Hereford cathedral

Mandate to Robert de Chandos that he should allow the parson of the church of Wellington to have common pasture for horses and oxen with Robert's and fuel and fencing material from Robert's wood.   [*c*.1163]

A = Hereford D. & C. Muniments, no.1385. B = Bodl. MS Rawlinson B329 (Hereford cathedral cartulary), fo.14r. s.xv.

Pd, *Hereford charters*, 18; *GFL*, 376, no.316.

*85A. Hereford, chapel of St Mary Magdalen

Grant to, not necessarily in documentary form.   [1148 × 1163]

Mention only, no.198 below.

86. St Guthlac's priory, Hereford

Notification that Robert son of Jordan has resigned two acres and one virgate which he had held for 4s from the monks: Prior Robert paid 32s for the agreement.   [1148 × 1155 or 1159 × 1160]

B = Oxford, Balliol College, MS 271 (cartulary of St Guthlac's, Hereford), fo.103v. s.xiv in.

Pd, *GFL*, 381, no.325.

Hiis testibus: Mauricio vicecomite Heref', Willelmo presbitero, magistro Galfrido et Rogero clericis episcopi.

86A. St Guthlac's priory, Hereford

Confirmatory clause by Gilbert to Ralph de Baskerville's confirmation of the grant made by his father Roger de Baskerville to Gloucester abbey of land held by Ralph Balee and others.   [1148 × 1155]

> B = Oxford, Balliol College, MS 271 (cartulary of St Guthlac's, Hereford), fo.101r. s.xiv in.
>
> Pd, *GFL*, 377, no.318.

86B. St Guthlac's priory, Hereford

Confirmatory clause by Gilbert to the grant by Aubrey de Loges, widow and nun, of half her land at Upper Lyde.   [1148 × c.1155]

> B = Oxford, Balliol College, MS 271 (cartulary of St Guthlac's, Hereford), fo.65r. s.xiv in.
>
> Pd, *GFL*, 377, no.319.

87. St Guthlac's priory, Hereford

Confirmation of Robert de Béthune's foundation of St Guthlac's priory and of its possessions, the churches of Holme Lacy and Edvin Loach, Avenbury, Ocle, and Mordiford, the chapels of Larport, Bartestree, the church of St Owen's, Hereford, and the chapels of Felton, Little Cowarne, Dormington, Load in Somerset, Sutton St Nicholas ('parva Suttona'), Maund, and the church of Marden.

[1148 × 1163, probably after 1150]

> B = Bodl. MS E Musaeo 249 (letter collection of Gilbert Foliot), fo.388r. sxii ¾.
> C = Oxford, Balliol College, MS 271 (cartulary of St Guthlac's, Hereford), fo.103r. s.xiv in.
>
> Pd, Giles, no.125; *GFL*, 378-9, no.321.

See nos.21 and 22 above. This charter was probably issued after or at the same time as no.92 below.

88. St Guthlac's priory, Hereford

Settlement of the case between St Guthlac's and Ernisius concerning the church of Edvin: Ernisius renounces his right to the church in return for three marks payable over a two-year period. [1148 × 1163]

B = Oxford, Balliol College, MS 271 (cartulary of St Guthlac's, Hereford), fo.53r. s.xiv in.

Pd, *GFL*, 379, no.322.

See no.125 below.

89. St Guthlac's priory, Hereford

Confirmation to St Guthlac's of a grant by John of Marden of two-thirds of his demesne tithes at Larport. [1148 × 1163]

B = Oxford, Balliol College, MS 271 (cartulary of St Guthlac's, Hereford), fo.69r. s.xiv in.

Pd, *GFL*, 379-80, no.323.

90. St Guthlac's priory, Hereford

Notification that Adam de Port has granted all his land in Rushock with the consent of the abbot and convent of Vaucelles to St Guthlac's. [1148 × 1163]

B = Oxford, Balliol College, MS 271 (cartulary of St Guthlac's, Hereford), fo.82v. s.xiv in.

Pd, *GFL*, 380, no.324.

91. St Guthlac's priory, Hereford

Grant to St Guthlac's of the meadow which belonged to the prebend of Walter of Bromyard and of land which had belonged to Walter next to the meadow to hold for an annual pension of one mark. [c.1150 × 1155]

B = Oxford, Balliol College, MS 271 (cartulary of St Guthlac's), fo.97r. s.xiv in.
C = Ibid., fo.103v. D = Ibid., fo.104v.

Pd, *GFL*, 376-7, no.317.

His testibus: Rogero comite, Radulfo decano, Gilberto cantore, Petro archidiacono Hereford', Waltero archidiacono Salop', Waltero de Bromgzart, Gaufrido de Cliff', Ambrosio, Rogero clerico, et multis aliis.

92. St Guthlac's priory, Hereford

Confirmation to St Guthlac's of Philip Alis' grant of the advowson of the church of Sutton.   [*c*.1150 × ?*c*.1155]

B = Oxford, Balliol College, MS 271 (cartulary of St Guthlac's, Hereford), fo.88v. s.xiv in.

Pd, *GFL*, 378, no.320.

...testibus: Waltero archidiacono, Hugone de Clifford', magistro Randulfo, canonicis Hereford', Galfrido, Gilberto, Ivone, Rogero clericis episcopi; Willelmo Folet, Willelmo Pouher, Gerin de Loges, et aliis multis.

See note to no.55. The charter does not state whether this was the church of Sutton St Nicholas ('little Sutton') or Sutton St Michael ('great Sutton'). The former is more probable, since Sutton St Michael had been granted to St Guthlac's by Walter de Turri in the 1140s (nos.25 and 26 above), but it is possible that Philip Alis might also have had some claim to Sutton St Michael.

93. ?Holdgate church

Settlement of the case between Master Godfrey and Ernald his paternal uncle concerning the church of Castellum: *Ernald recognises that Godfrey is the rector and Godfrey receives Ernald as vicar on payment of an annual pension of half a mark.*   [*c*.1155 × *c*.1158]

B = Bodl. MS E Musaeo 249 (letter collection of Gilbert Foliot), fo.183r. s.xii ³⁄₄.

Pd, Giles, no.186; *GFL*, 381-2, no.326.

His testibus: Radulfo decano, Petro archidiacono, Galtero archidiacono, magistro Rannulfo, Henrico fratre comitis, Ivone thesaurario, Radulfo de Ledeb', magistro Galfrido de Cliford', magistro Galtero de Ardep', Rogero de Burkell', Rogero filio Mauricii, Radulfo scriptore.

94. Leominster priory

Confirmation that the graveyard at Hatfield consecrated by Robert de Béthune for the benefit of Leominster should be considered as an augmentation of the graveyard of Leominster; and that all offerings made for burial should belong to Leominster and the clerk who serves the chapel is to recognise the monks' right to these. [1148 × 1161]

B = BL Cotton MS Dom. A iii (Leominster priory cartulary), fo.61r. s.xiii med.

G. dei gratia Heref' episcopus dilectis sibi in domino universis sancte Hereford' ecclesie filiis salutem, gratiam et benedictionem. Predecessoris nostri pie recordationis Roberti Heref' quondam episcopi vestigia sequentes, quod ab eo in consecratione cimiterii de Hethfeld' utilitati ecclesie de Leom' provisum est concessa nobis a domino potestate confirmamus, scilicet ut consecratum ab eo cimiterium in Hethfeld' tanquam augmentum quoddam habeatur cimiterii de Leom', hac conditione, ut quicquid oblationis ad sepulturam cuiuslibet defuncti ibidem evenerit totum sit proprie monachorum de Leom', tanquam si corpus ipsum defuncti in principali cimiterio Leom' sepeliretur. Hoc proviso ut clericus quicumque in illa capella ministraverit securitatem faciat prefatis monachis quod hoc ius ipsorum fideliter eis, quantum in ipso est, conservabit. Capella autem ipsa in hiis que ad servitium episcopi pertinent non sicut mater ecclesia set sicut capella habeatur.

This charter was confirmed by archbishop Theobald of Canterbury (ob. 1161): A.Saltman, *Theobald, archbishop of Canterbury* (London 1956), 440-1, no.217. For Robert de Béthune's dedication see no.31 above.

95. Leominster priory

Notification of the consecration of a cemetery at Hampton Wafer at the request of Robert de Hampton as a sanctuary for his men; furthermore Robert gave the tithes from the demesne and the villeins of Hampton and thirty acres of arable to Leominster and promised to pay half a mark annually which he had unjustly detained.

[1148 × 1163, perhaps before 1154]

B = BL Egerton MS 3031 (Reading abbey cartulary), fo.55r. s.xii ex. C = BL Cotton MS Dom. A iii (Leominster priory cartulary), fo.62r. s.xiii med.

Pd, *GFL*, 387-8, no.335; cal., *Reading cartularies*, i.281-2, no.346.

Presentibus et audientibus his testibus: Waltero Foliot archidiacono de Salopesb', Waltero de Clune capellano episcopi, Hugone nepote episcopi, et multis aliis.

See also no.214.

96. Leominster priory

Notification of the consecration of a cemetery at Risbury as a sanctuary for the men of Leominster priory and the men of Nicholas of Maund, and of a grant by Nicholas of Maund of the tithe of the land of his men, an acre from each virgate and twelve acres from the demesne, half the demesne tithe in his lifetime and the whole tithe after his death.

[1148 × 1163, perhaps before 1154]

B = BL Egerton MS 3031 (Reading abbey cartulary), fo.55v. s.xii ex. C = BL Cotton MS Dom. A iii (Leominster priory cartulary), fo.61r. s.xiii med.

Pd, *GFL*, 388, no.336; cal., *Reading cartularies*, i.298-9, no.368.

Huius rei testes sunt Walterus Foliot archidiaconus Salopesb', Hugo nepos episcopi, et multi alii.

97. Leominster priory

Notification that at the demand of the abbot of Reading he has consecrated a cemetery at Hampton 'Mapnors' and that Peter of Mapenore has granted the chapel in the cemetery, forty acres and the tithe from his demesne and his men's land to the mother church of Leominster.

[1148 × 1163]

B = BL Egerton MS 3031 (Reading abbey cartulary), fo.55v. s.xii ex. C = BL Cotton MS Dom. A iii (Leominster priory cartulary), fo.62r. s.xiii med.

Pd, *GFL*, 388-9, no.337; cal., *Reading cartularies*, i.279, no.342.

98. Leominster priory

Indulgence to those who visit Leominster priory on the feast of Sts Peter and Paul and make benefactions, releasing them from forty days' penance.

[1148 × 1163]

B = BL Cotton MS Dom. A iii (Leominster priory cartulary), fo.74r. s.xiii med.

Pd, *GFL*, 390, no.340.

99. Leominster priory

Notification of the settlement in Gilbert's presence of the dispute between Leominster priory and Serlo, priest of Kinnersley over the chapel and tithes of Eywood: Serlo recognises that the chapel does not belong by right to Kinnersley church and in return is permitted to have the care of it for his life for an annual pension of 5s.

[1148 × 1163]

B = BL Egerton MS 3031 (Reading abbey cartulary), fo.56r. s.xii ex. C = BL Cotton MS Dom. A iii (Leominster priory cartulary), fo.61v. s.xiii med.

Pd, *GFL*, 391, no.341; cal., *Reading cartularies*, i.277, no.339.

The witnesses' names are omitted in both copies.

100. Leominster priory

Notification that Walter del Mans and his wife Agnes have granted to Leominster priory the virgate and meadow at Priddleton in Humber which William son of Symer holds for 4s annually and 12d from the rent of a mill, and that Gilbert has consecrated a cemetery at their chapel of

Humber, provided that only one body is buried there, the rest being buried at Leominster as before.

[*c.*1150 × 1154]

B = BL Egerton MS 3031 (Reading abbey cartulary), fo.56r. s.xii ex. C = BL Cotton MS Dom. A iii (Leominster priory cartulary), fo.61v. s.xiii med.

Pd, *GFL*, 386-7, no.334; cal., *Reading cartularies*, i.283, no.348.

Huius rei testes sunt ex parte monachorum: Walterus Foliot archidiaconus Salopesb', Hugo nepos episcopi, W(alterus) de Clun capellanus episcopi, Adam de Eya decanus Leom', G. capellanus de Humbre, Ailbricth vicarius eius, P(etrus) de Mapp', R. fratre eius, Herew' filius Alwardi, Hugo de Leomin', Walclinus dapifer; ex parte Walterii: Matheus filius eius, W. nepos eius, et multi alii.

101. Lire abbey

Confirmation to Lire abbey of all its churches in the diocese of Hereford: Much Marcle, Linton, Wilton, Dewsall, Tenbury, Fownhope, Eardisland, Lydney, and Tidenham, and testification that Tidenham church was adjudged to Lire in the bishop's court against the men of Earl Gilbert (de Clare) and that the chapel of Albrighton was adjudged to them in the general synod against the monks of Monmouth priory.

[1148 × 1149]

B = Dom Lenoir MSS (Mme la Marquise de Mathan, Sémilly, Manche), vol.xxiii, no.83, p.484. s.xviii. C = Bodl. MS Dugdale 11, fo.66v. s.xvii.

Pd, *Mon. Ang.* vi.1093; *GFL*, 384-5, no.331.

His testibus: Magistro Hugone de Clifford', et Waltero de Bromyeard, et Hugone Foliot, et Haro(l)do et Ture, Bernardo de Hopa et Wimund de Linton', et Willelmo de Merchelay, et Adam decano de Roos et Adam de Wiltona, et Gilberto de Suttum', et tota generali sinodo.

See also nos.162, 218, 305 and 354.

102. Llanthony priory

Settlement of the dispute between Hereford cathedral and Llanthony priory: Llanthony is to retain the possessions granted to it by Bishop Robert de Béthune save for half a hide at Barton and must pay an annual pension of 60s. [*c.*1148]

> B = PRO C115 K2/6683 (Llanthony cartulary, A1), fo.125r, sect. vi, no.39. s.xiv med.
>
> Pd, *GFL*, 382, no.327.

> See nos.35-7 above.

103. Llanthony priory

Confirmation of the grant by Ralph son of Ernald of ten acres in Prestbury to Llanthony priory. [1148 × 1163]

> B = PRO C115 K1/6679 (Llanthony cartulary, A9), fo.113r. s.xiii med. C = PRO C115 K2/6683 (Llanthony cartulary, A1), fo.121v, sect. vi, no.15. s.xiv med.
>
> Pd, *GFL*, 383, no.328.

104. Llanthony priory

Confirmation of an agreement between Ralph son of Ernald and Llanthony priory: Ralph has granted half a virgate and an arm of land to Llanthony for which he will continue to perform service for the bishop and church of Hereford, and in return the canons will provide Ralph's mother with clothes and food in her lifetime. [*c.*1150 × 1163]

> B = PRO C115 K1/6679 (Llanthony cartulary, A9), fo.113r. s.xiii med. C = PRO C115, K2/6683 (Llanthony cartulary, A1), fos.121v-2r, sect. vi, no.16. s.xiv med.
>
> Pd, *GFL*, 383, no.329.

Testibus: Waltero archidiacono Solopesir', Radulfo de Wycherch', et aliis.

105. Llanthony priory

Notification addressed to John, bishop of Worcester that when Gilbert visited Oakley (in Gloucestershire, now lost) to dedicate the church there, Ralph the Butler freed assarted land there which he had previously given to Llanthony from all service.   [1151 × 1157]

> B = PRO C115 K1/6679 (Llanthony cartulary, A9), fo.113v. s.xiii med. C = PRO
> C115 K2/6683 (Llanthony cartulary, A1), fo.122r, sect. vi, no.18. s.xiv med.
> Pd, *GFL*, 383-4, no.330.

106. Monmouth priory

Confirmation of the grant by Roger earl of Hereford of the church of St Andrew of Awre and grant of the parsonage of the church after the death of Hugh the priest.   [1148 × 1155]

> B = Angers, A-D Maine-et-Loire, H3713 (Livre blanc of St Florent, Saumur),
> fo.125v. s.xii. C = Ibid., H3711 (charter roll of St Florent, Saumur), no.11.
> s.xii.
> Pd, Marchegay, *BEC*, 40 (1879), 185; *GFL*, 386, no.333; cal., *CDF*, no.1144, and
> *Inventaire sommaire......: Maine et Loire..., Série H*, ii, ed. M.Sache, 473, cf.
> 474.

Huius etiam donationis sunt testes: Radulfus Herefordensis ecclesie decanus, et Petrus archidiaconus, et Ernulfus prior sancti Gud<l>aci, et Robertus prior supradicte Monemue, et Ricardus de Vestbiria, Galfridus de Cliffordia, et Walterus de Cluna, et Hugo de Caples, Gilebertus de Valford, et Walterus de Fredne.

106A. Monmouth priory

Corroborative clause appended by Gilbert to a charter of Roger earl of Hereford granting the church of St Andrew of Awre and land of Haiward to Monmouth priory.   [1148 × 1155]

> A = Angers, A-D Maine-et-Loire, H3170, no.8.
> B = Ibid., H3713 (Livre blanc of St Florent, Saumur), fo.126r-v. s.xii. C = Ibid.,
> H3711 (charter roll of St Florent, Saumur), no.10. s.xii. D = BN, nouv. acq.
> lat. 1930, fos.140v-141r.

Pd, Marchegay, *BEC*, 40 (1879), 183-5; *GFL*, 385, no.332; cal., *CDF*, no.1143, and *Inventaire sommaire....: Maine et Loire..., Série H*, ii, ed. M.Sache, 473, cf. 474, 502.

107. Master Ranulf fitz Erchemar

Confirmation to Master Ranulf of the land which his father Erchemar had held in Hereford on which he had had his house, and its appurtenances, a field at Cocedeh' *and a garden at Barton.*

[*c.*1150 × 1163, probably early]

A = Hereford D. & C. Muniments, no.1360.

Pd, *Hereford charters*, 11-12; *GFL*, 372-3, no.311.

His testibus: Waltero archidiacono, magistro Hugone de Clifort, Gisleberto capellano.

See also nos.123, 168 and 199 below.

108. Reading abbey

*Notification that Roger earl of Hereford has granted to Reading abbey the hamlet (*villula*) of Broadward which he received from Hugh de Kilpeck in exchange for Kingstone.*   [1148 × 1155]

B = BL Egerton MS 3031 (Reading abbey cartulary), fo.55r. C = BL Cotton MS Vesp. E xxv (Reading abbey cartulary), fo.66v. D = BL Harl. MS 1708 (Reading abbey cartulary), fo.120v.

Pd, *GFL*, 389, no.338; cal., *Reading cartularies*, i.265, no.330.

Huius donationis isti sunt testes: ego G. episcopus Herefordensis cum toto capitulo nostro, Baderun de Munemue, Walterus de Clifford, et multi alii.

109. Reading abbey

Settlement of the case between Reading abbey and Gilbert of Hampton concerning the tithes of Hampton, which belonged by long-standing right to Leominster but which Gilbert had detained during the time of war.

[1154 × 1163]

B = BL Egerton MS 3031 (Reading abbey cartulary), fo.56r. s.xii ex.
Pd, *GFL*, 391-2, no.342; cal., *Reading cartularies*, i.279, no.343.
Cf. below no.267.

110. Reading abbey

Grant of an indulgence to Reading abbey.
[1155 × 1163, probably 1163]

A = BL Add. Charter 19587.
B = BL Egerton MS 3031 (Reading abbey cartulary), fo.58r-v. s.xii ex.
Pd, *GFL*, 389-90, no.339; cal., J.B.Hurry, *Reading Abbey* (London 1901), 163, and *Reading cartularies*, i.149, no.185.

111. Reading Abbey

Confirmation to Reading abbey of the charter issued by Bishop Richard of Hereford to the abbot of Reading confirming the grant of the parish of Leominster to Reading.   [1158 × 1161]

B = BL Egerton MS 3031 (Reading abbey cartulary), fo.55r. s.xii ex. C = BL Cotton MS Dom. A iii (Leominster priory cartulary), fo.60v. s.xiii med.
Pd, *GFL*, 392-3, no.343; cal., *Reading cartularies*, i.288-9, no.356.

For Richard's confirmation see no.11 above. See also nos.268, 300, and 352.

112. Shrewsbury abbey

Confirmation to Shrewsbury abbey of tithes at Cold Weston, Henley, Stottesdon, Walkerslow, Newton, Sibton Carwood and Yockleton, granted to assist the building of the abbey church.   [? c.1150 × c.1158]

B = NLW, MS 7851D (Shrewsbury abbey cartulary), pp.296-7. s.xiv. C = ibid., p.297, in inspeximus issued by Dean Ralph and the chapter of Hereford cathedral.
Pd, *GFL*, 393, no.344; *Shrewsbury cartulary*, ii.301-2, no.331.

Hiis testibus: Waltero archidiacono, David de Aqua, magistro Nicholao, magistro Edwardo, magistro Galfrido canonicis Hereford', et aliis quampluribus.

113. St Mary's, Warwick

Decision as papal judge-delegate with Godfrey archdeacon of Worcester in the case between the canons of the collegiate church of St Mary's and the canons of the priory of St Sepulchre's, Warwick, concerning parochial rights, in favour of St Mary's. [1161 × 1162]

B = PRO E164/22, fo.18r. s.xv.
Pd, *GFL*, 394-5, no.345.

114. St Mary's, Warwick

Notification that when the decision in no.113 was made, the canons of St Mary's allowed the prior of St Sepulchre's to hold a portion of the disputed parish for an annual pension of ten shillings in his lifetime, as long as he remains prior. [*c*.1162]

B = PRO E164/22, fo.19v. s.xv.
Pd, *GFL*, 395, no.346.

115. St Mary's, Warwick

Mandate to Godfrey archdeacon of Worcester to instruct the rural dean to ensure that the terms of nos.113-14 are fulfilled. [1162 × 1163]

B = PRO E164/22, fo.20r. s.xv.
Pd, *GFL*, 396, no.347.

116. William Folet

Grant in fee to William Folet of the land which Gilbert had bought in Hereford from Robert de Chandos, in return for suit of court and for acting as the bishop's cup bearer at great feasts.
[*c*.1155 × 1163, probably early]

B = Bodl., MS Rawlinson B329 (Hereford cathedral cartulary), fo.121r. s.xiii-xiv.
Pd, *GFL*, 373-4, no.312.

Hiis testibus: Petro archidiacono Heref', Waltero archidiacono Salop', Reginaldo cantore, Ivone thesaurario, Hugone Foliot, Radulfo de Ledeb', magistro Gaufrido de Clifford, Ricardo Foliot et Rogero canonicis Herefordensibus, Gileberto capellano et Hugone clerico episcopi, Willelmo presbitero de Estenovera, Aluredo presbitero de Longaduna, Radulfo presbitero de Bosebur', Aluredo et Roberto vicariis de Ledebur'; militibus autem Willelmo de Chesney, Henrico fratre comitis, Radulfo de Verdun, Roberto Foliot et Rogero fratre eius, Rogero Foliot et Serlone fratre eius, et Radulfo Foliot nepote episcopi, Roberto de Abbatot et Osberto nepote eius, Willelmo Puher et Rogero de Mortuna, Willelmo de Mefflituna, Willelmo de Alkrug', Baldewino de Dunintona, Ranulfo Britone de Mortuna; mancipiis episcopi Roberto de Breyles, Roberto dispensatore, Roberto pincerna, Reginaldo camerario; pueris autem Radulfo Foliot, Willelmo Foliot, Willelmo Banast(re) et Rogero fratre eius.

117. Worcester cathedral priory

Confirmation of Bishop Robert de Béthune's grant of the rectory of Lindridge in Worcestershire. [1148 × 1163, possibly early]

B = Worcester Cathedral, D. & C., Reg. A4, fo.xxvii. s.xiii med.

Pd, *GFL*, 396, no.348; *Worcester cartulary*, 108, no.202.

See nos.177, 241, 242, and 290 below.

ROBERT DE MELUN

118. Profession of obedience

Profession of obedience to Archbishop Thomas Becket.

[22 December 1163]

A = Canterbury D. & C. Ch. Ant. C115, no.38. No ancient endorsements. 195 × 80 mm.

B = BL, Cotton MS Cleopatra E i (register of the see of Canterbury), fo.38r. C = Canterbury D. & C. Register A (The Prior's Register), fo.233v. s.xiv med.

Facsimile of A, N.R.Ker, *English manuscripts in the century after the Norman Conquest* (London 1960), pl.18c.

Facsimile of B, *N.P.S.*, ii, pl.62.

Pd, from A, *Canterbury professions*, 50, no.103.

Ego Robertus ad regimen Herfordensis^a ecclesie electus. et more antecessorum meorum a^b te venerande pater THOMA sancte Cantuariensis ecclesie archiepiscope. antistes ex more consecrandus.ʔ sancte Cantuariensi ecclesie. et tibi tuisque successoribus canonice substituendis – subiectionem canonicam et obedientiam^c me per omnia exhibiturum esse promitto. et per manum propriam signo crucis confirmo. +^{d}

^{a}Herefordensis *BC.* ^{b}*accent on a A.* ^{c}obe *B.* ^{d}*autograph cross A.*

Dashes as punctuation marks came in in the reign of Stephen, or at least after 1100, N.R.Ker, *op. cit.*, 47-8.

119. Gloucester abbey

Settlement, as papal judge-delegate, between Gloucester abbey and John the priest of Llanvaes about the tithes of the demesne of Brecon beyond the Usk.

1165

B = Gloucester Cathedral, Register A, fos.101v-102r, no.148. s.xiv ex.

Cal., 'Gloucester register', 23, no.44.

Rodbertus dei gratia Hereford' ecclesie minister humilis universis sancte matris ecclesie filiis imperpetuum. Noverit universitatis vestre discretio controversiam quandam inter monachos beati Petri de Glouc' et Iohannem presbiterum de Lameys diutius extitisse super duabus partibus decime dominii de Brechennio ultra Uscam in Lameis, scilicet pecorum, caseorum et omnium aliarum rerum, de quibus decime dari debent, ipsamque a domino papa nobis delegatam subscripte compositionis fine ad ultimum quievisse. Convenientibus hinc inde partibus in [fo.102r] presentia nostra, prefatus Iohannes petitioni abbatis et monachorum Glouc' cessit seseque eis in annua pensione xii d. infra octo dies natalis domini, apud Glasburiam dum vixerit solvendorum, pro supradicta decima obligavit. Hanc compositionem nos, ratam habentes, concedimus ipsamque auctoritate delegati iudicis et sigilli nostri impressione confirmamus. Actum anno verbi incarnati m°clx°v^{to}, episcopatus nostri secundo.

See also no.136.

*120. Hereford, chapel of St Mary Magdalen

Grant or confirmation to the episcopal chapel of St Mary Magdalen, Hereford, of the oblations made on solemn days by the episcopal household when the bishop is in Hereford, and of the tithe of the market in Hereford.
[1163 × 1167]

Mention only, in a confirmation of by Bp William de Vere of grants by Bps Gilbert Foliot, Robert de Melun, and Robert Foliot (below, no.198). It is not possible to make out from William's confirmation which bishop made which donation, except that a reference to Gilbert Foliot suggests that he gave the chapel tithes from land which he was assarting in the Forest of Dean. It is therefore possible that these two other grants were made by Robert de Melun. See also note to no.343 below.

121. Llanthony priory

Confirmation to Llanthony priory of grants by his predecessors Bishops Robert de Béthune and Gilbert Foliot.
[1163 × 1167]

B = PRO, C115 K1/6679 (Llanthony cartulary, A9), fos.115r-116r. s.xiii med.
Rubric: Confirm' Rob' Melun episcopi Hereford' de omnibus possessionibus

quas de ecclesia Hereford' habemus. C = PRO, C115 K2/6683 (Llanthony cartulary, A1), fo.123r, sect. vi, no.28. s.xiv med.

Robertus dei gratia Hereford' ecclesie minister omnibus successoribus suis[a] salutem. Officii nostri consideratio nos admonet ea que a decessoribus nostris utiliter statuta sunt intuitu caritatis et pacis roborare. Inde est quod predecessoris mei bone memorie Roberti Herefordensis episcopi donationes quas dedit canonicis regularibus de Lanthon' ratas habemus, et ecclesie de Lanthon' perpetuo possidendas presenti scripto confirmamus. Quod etiam venerabilem fratrem nostrum Gilbertum qui nos in hac sede precessit [fo.115v B], qui et postmodum factus est London' episcopus, et conventum fratrum nostrorum de Hereford', sicut eorundem tam viva voce quam scripto cognovimus, fecisse manifestum est. Nunc itaque quia iustitie et rationis ordo suadet ut qui a successoribus desiderat mandata servari decessorum suorum proculdubio voluntatem et statuta custodiat, predicti predecessoris[b] mei pie recordationis Roberti donationes sicut in cartis ipsius legimus[c] expressius et confirmavimus, videlicet terram extra burgum Hereford', que Mora vocatur, liberam et quietam ab omni servitio et consuetudine, excepto quod una hyda terre de Holemera regis geldum[d] persolvit, mansionem etiam quam Ernaldus presbiter tenuerat extra burgum Hereford' cum x acris terre, liberam et quietam ab omni servitio et consuetudine, et similiter etiam[e] acram unam mansioni prefate contiguam de terra Fulconis, ecclesiam quoque de Froma cum omnibus pertinentiis suis, et duas ecclesias in Presteb', unam sub montibus, alteram super montes, scilicet ecclesiam de Sevenhamton' cum terris et decimis, aliisque elemosinis omnibus eisdem ecclesiis pertinentibus aut contingentibus, exceptis duabus portionibus decimarum de dominio meo quas habent decanus et cantor Hereford', de blado scilicet tantum et de leguminibus; de parco autem de Prestebur' et de hiis que seminantur vel colliguntur intra designatum ambitum parchi decima remanet ecclesie de Prestebur' quia terra fuit villanorum; tria quoque exsarta in Prestebur' que Leuricus Figulus et Lefwynus Rufus et Erni per ix denariorum redditum per annum tenuerunt, que prefatus episcopus R. per xii denariorum redditum per annum tenenda et ad ecclesiam de Prestebur' pertinenda in perpetuam elemosinam concessit et dedit. Unam etiam virgatam terre in eadem villa quam Ernaldus miles dedit eidem ecclesie quando vitam suam in ea mutavit, liberam et quietam ab omni servitio et consuetudine, ita ut heredes eius idem servitium quod pro hac terra episcopo debent de reliquo feodo suo persolvant; preterea dimidiam virgatam terre in eadem villa, cum brachia quadam que eidem appendere solet, quam concedente Gilberto episcopo Radulfus, predicti Ernaldi filius, cum matre sua, quando eam in sororem susceperunt, in perpetuam elemosinam [fo.116r *B*] dedit, liberam et quietam ab omni servitio et consuetudine, ita ut ipse et heredes sui idem servitium quod pro hac terra episcopo debent de reliquo feodo suo persolvant; ex eiusdem quoque Radulfi donatione x acras terre, quas dedit in perpetuam elemosinam, liberas et quietas ab omni servitio et consuetudine. Hec omnia, sicut singula in singulis cartis predecessorum nostrorum[f] episcopi Roberti et episcopi Gilleberti confirmata legimus, unum in scriptum redigentes, nostri quoque sigilli inpressione in presentia subscriptorum testium confirmamus, Gaufridi decani, Magistri Rannulfi, Magistri Roberti de Clara, Magistri Willelmi de Saresberia et aliorum.

[a] *sic BC.* [b] predecessores *BC.* [c] *C adds* designare. [d] *corr. from* geldis *C.* [e] et *BC.* [f] vestrorum *C.*

Much of the text of this charter is taken word for word from three charters of Robert de Béthune (above, nos. 35-37), though the number of acres attached to Ernaldus' *mansio* has shrunk from eleven to ten; Robert de Melun here also confirms two charters of Gilbert Foliot to Llanthony (*GFL*, nos.328, 329 [nos.103-4 above]). The awkward use of third person, first person singular and first person plural to describe the issuer suggests that the drafting might conceivably have been the work of the beneficiaries. Certainly Llanthony brought back this charter to Robert de Melun's successors for reconfirmation and this text was used again and again (see below, nos.166, 225, and 276).

122. Llanthony priory

Grant of the lesser tithes of the demesne of Prestbury to Llanthony Priory.
[23 August 1164 × 27 February 1167]

B = PRO C115 K2/6683 (Llanthony cartulary A1), fo.122v, sect. VI, no.xxvii. s.xiv med. Rubric: Carta Roberti Heref' episcopi ecclesie Lanth' facta. de minutis decimis in manerio suo de Presteburi xxvii. C = PRO C115 L1/6689 (Llanthony cartulary A4), fos.127r-v, s.xv med. (AD 1449).
The text is here taken from C.

Robertus[a] dei[b] gratia Hereford' episcopus universis sancte matris ecclesie filiis[c] salutem et benedictionem a domino. Notum sit omnium vestrum caritati nos intuitu pietatis concessisse et in perpetuam elemosinam dedisse ecclesie de Lanthon', in manerio nostro de Presteb', tam in valle quam in montanis, totam minutam decimam de dominico nostro^d in agnis et porcis, in lana et caseis. Hanc autem elemosinam perpetuam stabilitatem habere volentes, eam in scripto redigi et sigilli nostri impressione roborari precepimus. Hiis testibus,^{e} Domino Rogero Wig'^{f} episcopo, Henrico Exon' archidiacono, Alured' senescallo nostro,^{g} Magistro Simone Luwel', Willelmo priore Sancti Aug(ustini) de Brist', Gilleberto et Sampsone clericis domini Wig' episcopi, Osberto capellano nostro, et Guidone canonico^g et sigillo nostro. Prohibemus autem sub anathematis interminatione ne quis contra huius elemosine assignationem ullo umquam^h in tempore venire vel eam infringere attemptet; eidem vero assensum suum una nobiscum prebentibus sit gratia et pax a domino nostro Iesu Cristo.

^{a}Rotbertus B. ^{b}de C. ^{c}filiis *om.* C. ^{d}nostro *om.* B. ^{e}T. *for* Hiis testibus B.
^{f}Wygorn' B. $^{g-g}$ *om.* B. ^{h}unquam B.

This charter must have been issued after Roger became bp of Worcester in 1164 and before Master Simon Lovel became archdn of Worcester in 1167. Henry became archdn of Exeter *c.* 1161 (A.Morey, *Bartholomew of Exeter* [Cambridge 1937], 119). No canon Guy occurs in Hereford cathedral in this period, and the one appearing here was probably a canon of St Augustine's, Bristol, or of Lanthony by Gloucester. Robert de Melun's seneschal Alured is almost certainly to be identified with his clerk of the same name who was sent by Robert to Henry II in Caen in 1166 (*MTB*, vi.74), and may possibly also be identifiable with Robert Foliot's chaplain Alured. A curious feature of this charter is the mention of Robert's seal at the end of the witness list, especially since it has already been mentioned in the corroboration; it is likely that the charter was drafted or interpolated by the beneficiaries.

123. Master Ranulf fitz Erchemar

Grant to Master Ranulf, a canon of Hereford cathedral, of land which had been held by Ranulf's father Erchemar.
                    [22 December 1163 × 27 February 1167]

B = Bodl., MS Rawlinson B329 (Hereford cathedral cartulary), fo.149v. s.xiii-xiv.
   15th century marginalia: Carta donationis orti apud le Berton.

R. dei gratia Herefordensis episcopus omnibus episcopis in ecclesie Herefordensi canonice substituendis ceterisque eiusdem ecclesie tam prelatis quam subditis in Cristo salutem. Noverit universitatis vestre

discretio me concessisse et reddidisse in feudo et iure hereditario
Magistro Rannulfo canonico meo terram quam pater suus Er-
chemerus Hereford' tenuit, in qua diu domicilium habuit et ipse
Rannulfus post eum a tempore venerabilis Ricardi huius ecclesie
episcopi, cum pertinentiis suis, videlicet agro qui est apud Cocedeh',
et orto quodam qui est apud Berthon'. Pro predictis hominium eius
recepi; pro servitio autem debet ter in anno convenienter submonitus
placitis meis interesse Hereford' et successorum meorum. Preterea
concessi ei et reddidi mansuram quandam*a* quam predecessor meus,
episcopus G., eidem in augmentum dederat prope predictum domicilium, de me et successoribus meis simili modo et prefato servitio
tenendam. Hiis testibus, Gaufrido Hereford' decano, David et
Radulfo de Ledebur' canonicis.

*a*quamdam *B*.

The text of this charter is based on no.107 (*GFL* no.311), though it uses the
unusual term *hominium* instead of *hominagium*. The appearance of Ralph of
Ledbury in the witness list suggests that this is a charter of Robert de Melun rather
than of Bishop Robert Foliot (see J.Barrow, 'The Bishops of Hereford and their
Acta, 1163-1219', unpublished Oxford D.Phil. thesis, 1983, p.522). Robert Foliot
made a grant of the same land to Master Ranulf's son, who was also called Ranulf
(see below, no.168), and William de Vere bought the land from young Ranulf in
the 1190s so that he could donate it to the cathedral chapter (see below, no.199).

BISHOP ROBERT

(UNCERTAIN WHETHER ROBERT DE MELUN OR ROBERT FOLIOT)

*124. Pope Alexander III

Letter to Pope Alexander III requesting advice about proceeding against clerks with concubines in the diocese of Hereford.
[22 December 1163 × 27 February 1167 or 6 October 1174 ×
spring 1181]

Mention only, in Alexander III's reply, undated, addressed to *Rodberto Herefordensi episcopo*: *WH*, no.332a; printed *Decretales ineditae saeculi xii*, edd. S.Chodorow and C.Duggan,104-5, no.60.

125. St Guthlac's priory, Hereford

Composition of a dispute between St Guthlac's priory and Osbern, a priest, about the chapel of Edvin (Loach); St Guthlac's is to allow Osbern to hold the chapel for an annual pension of two shillings, while they retain the tithes of Upper Lyde, and Osbern is to pay the episcopalia and an annual sum of three shillings to the mother church at Clifton on Teme.
[22 December 1163 × 27 February 1167 or 6 October 1174 × 13
August 1178]

B = Oxford, Balliol College MS 271 (cartulary of St Guthlac's, Hereford), fo.53r, no.206. s.xiv in. C = Ibid., fos.97v-98r, no.432.

Universis sancte matris ecclesie fidelibus Robertus dei gratia Herefordensis ecclesie minister salutem^a que nunc est et quam speramus in domino^a. Caritati vestre notum fieri volumus quod controversia que vertebatur inter priorem et monachos Hereford' et Osbernum presbiterum super capella de Yedevenna^b in hunc modum inperpetuum conquievit. Prior quidem et monachi,^{c} retentis sibi decimis de Ludes, concesserunt iamdicto Osberno prefatam capellam, cum pertinentiis suis, pro duabus solidis annuatim in festo beatorum apostolorum Petri et Pauli apud Heref' solvendis. Osbernus vero episcopalia solvet, et ecclesie de Clifftona^d de tribus solidis nomine capelle annuatim reddendis tanquam matrici ecclesie respondebit. De hac autem conventione legitime tenenda et fideliter abbati Glouc' et priori et monachis Hereford' et ecclesie sue inposterum servanda sepedictus^e Osbernus super textum evangeliorum^f coram nobis in capitulo nostro iuramentum prestitit.^{g} Quod ut ratum et inconcussum permaneat presenti scripto confirmamus ^{h}et sigillis nostri et ecclesie nostre appositione communimus.^{h} Hiis testibus Gaufrido decano Hereford', Waltero archidiacono Salop', Reginaldo cantore, Magistro Ranulfo,^{i} Magistro Simone, Magistro David, Waltero scriptore^j canonicis Hereford', Magistro Aldredo^k capellano decani, Willelmo de Stokes.

$^{a-a}$*om. C.* ^{b}*Zedevenna B; Gedevenna C.* ^{c}*monachis C.* ^{d}*ecclesia de Cliftona C.*
^{e}*lacuna C.* ^{f}*ewangelorum B; ewangliorum C.* ^{g}*-um prestitit missing because of a lacuna*
C. ^{h}*om. C.* ^{i}*Rannulfo C.* ^{j}*text of C ends here with* etc'. ^{k}*Aldreo B.*

Archdn Walter died on 13 August, almost certainly in 1178. The date of the death of Reginald the cantor is unknown, though his earliest known successor was not appointed until after William de Vere had become bishop; Reginald's last dated appearance is 2 October 1172 (Ibid., fos.15v, 108r). The attestations of Master Aldred and of William de Stokes make it likely that this is a charter of Robert Foliot. Gilbert Foliot had settled a dispute between St Guthlac's and a priest called Ernisius over this church during his pontificate (*GFL*, no.322 [no.88 above]).

126. St Guthlac's priory, Hereford

Confirmation to St Guthlac's priory, Hereford, of the grant made to them by Walter de Turri which had been confirmed by Bishops Robert de Béthune and Gilbert Foliot.
[22 December 1163 × 27 February 1167 or 6 October 1174 × 9 May 1186]

B = Oxford, Balliol College, MS 271 (cartulary of St Guthlac's, Hereford), fo.89r, no.394. s.xiv in. 15th century marginalia: De ecclesia de Sutton.

Robertus dei gratia Heref' ecclesie minister humilis universis sancte matris ecclesie filiis perpetuam in domino salutem. Notum sit vobis omnibus quod concedimus et episcopali auctoritate confirmamus donationem quam fecit Walterus de Turri deo et ecclesie beatorum ap(ostolorum) Petri et Pauli et Sancti Guthlaci Hereford' monachis ecclesiam Sancti Michaelis de Sutton, cum terris et decimis et omnibus pertinentiis suis, libere et honorifice, salva dignitate et consuetudine episcopali. Volumus etiam et firmiter precipimus ut quod Robertus bone memorie et venerabilis Gilbertus predecessores nostri confirmaverunt ratum et stabile in omnibus habeatur. Valete.

For the earlier confirmations by Robert de Béthune of the grant by Walter de Turri see above, nos.25, 26, and note to no.55; *GFL*, no.320 (above, no.92) is a confirmation of a grant of the church of Sutton (it is not specified whether this refers to Sutton St Michael or to Sutton St Nicholas) by Philip Alis. It is not possible to state whether this is a charter of Bp Robert de Melun or of Bp Robert Foliot, though diplomatic features such as the placing of the *intitulatio* before the address suggest the former. At some point before 1185 possession of the church of Sutton St Michael had passed to the Hospitallers of Dinmore, though St Guthlac's was able to claim a pension: see no.156 below.

127. Lire abbey

Notification of a composition between the church of Ross and the church of Wilton, belonging to Lire abbey in Normandy, concerning the burial of corpses from Cleeve.
[22 December 1163 × 27 February 1167 or 6 October 1174 × 9 May 1186]

B = Bodl., MS Dugdale 11, fo.67r. s.xvii.
Pd, *Mon. Angl.* vi. pt. ii, 1094.

Universis etc.,[a] Robertus dei gratia Herefordensis episcopus eternam in Cristo salutem. Noverit etc.,[a] quod, cum in presentia nostra mota fuisset questio inter ecclesiam de Ros, et ecclesiam monachorum de Lira, de Wilton, de corporibus de Cliva sepeliendis, tandem inter ipsas, partibus assentientibus, convenit imperpetuum unum predictorum corporum in cimiterio de Wilton, et aliud[b] in cimiterio de Ros, sine contradictione sepeliantur, omnibus obventionibus atque legatis exinde provenientibus inter predictas ecclesias equis portionibus dividendis, quicunque pro defuncto sepeliendo missam celebraverit, hoc tamen ordine servato, ubi celebraturi fuerint, prius celebret sacerdos ecclesie apud quam sepelietur, et demum alius. Nos igitur huic conventioni assensum prebuimus, etc.[a]

^a*sic B.*   ^balium *B.*

The use of the first person plural suggests that this charter was issued by either Bp Robert de Melun or Bp Robert Foliot, and not by Bp Robert de Béthune. MS Dugdale 11 is a volume of various extracts, including a set of charters copied from an old register of Lire abbey. The inventory of Lire Abbey cartulary (A-D Eure H590) does not give a summary of this agreement between the churches of Wilton and Ross.

128. Pershore abbey

Settlement of a tithe dispute between Pershore abbey and Alfred, priest of Mathon.
   [22 December 1163 × 27 February 1167 or 6 October 1174 × 9 May 1186]

B = PRO E315/61 (Pershore Cartulary), fo.109r. s.xiii-xiv.

R. dei gratia Herefordensis episcopus omnibus sancte dei ecclesie fidelibus salutem et benedictionem. Notum sit universitati vestre nos ecclesiam de Mathm' dedicasse et in ipsa dedicatione inter fratres Persor' et Alfred presbiterum de decimis eiusdem ville quandam controversiam audisse, et auditam sic discussisse, ut ecclesia Persor' duas partes omnium decimarum integre haberet et ipsa ecclesia de Mathm' tertiam. Sic quidem ab hominibus illius ville antiquitus fuisse didicimus, et ut sic perpetualiter permaneret in presentia nostra super altare dextris illorum illud confirmare fecimus. Quod vero ratum et stabile episcopali auctoritate imperpetuum esse precipimus. Valete.

The use of the first person plural suggests that the charter was not issued by Bp Robert de Béthune or any of his predecessors. The church of Mathon, a village on the border between Herefordshire and Worcestershire, had been appropriated by Pershore abbey by 1193 × 1195; the appropriation was confirmed by Bp Henry of Worcester, 1193-1195, and also by Archbp Hubert Walter at a point between April and October 1195 (*EEA iii.* 219-20, no. 565). *Therefore this charter must have been issued by either Robert de Melun or Robert Foliot. The reason for the involvement of a bp of Hereford in the dedication of a church in the neighbouring diocese of Worcester is unclear. One possible explanation is that he was acting as a vicar sede vacante,* in which case this charter must have been issued by Robert Foliot, either 9 August 1179 × 10 August 1180 or December 1184 × May 1186. Another possibility is that the uncertainty prevailing as to whether Mathon lay within Worcestershire or Herefordshire might have affected ecclesiastical boundaries.

Mathon was only definitely placed within the county boundary of Herefordshire in the nineteenth century; before that it had been divided between Herefordshire and Worcestershire (see H.C.Darby and I.B.Terrett, *The Domesday Geography of Midland England*, 2nd edn. [Cambridge 1971], p.59).

ROBERT FOLIOT

129. Profession of obedience

Profession of obedience made to Richard, Archbishop of Canterbury.
[6 October 1174]

A = Canterbury, D. & C. Ch. Ant. C115/100. No endorsements. 165 x 59 mm; not sealed.

B = Canterbury, D.& C. Register A (The Prior's Register), fo.233r. s.xiv med.

Pd from A, *Canterbury professions*, 51, no.108.

Ego Robertus ad regimen Herefordensis ecclesie electus et more antecessorum meorum a te venerande pater Richarde sancte Cantuariensis ecclesie archiepiscope. et totius Britannie primas. atque apostolice sedis legate consecrandus antistes sancte Cantuariensi ecclesie et tibi tuisque successoribus canonice substituendis. subiectionem canonicam et obedientiam me per omnia exhibiturum promitto et per manum propriam signo crucis confirmo. +[a]

[a]*autograph cross.*

129A. Abingdon abbey

Notification by Robert Foliot, bishop of Hereford, Baldwin, bishop of Worcester, and Roger, prior of Llanthony, acting as papal judges-delegate, that the dispute between Roger, abbot of Abingdon, William, incumbent of Shellingford, and Jordan de Turri, parson of Stanford-in-the-Vale, has been settled as follows: Shellingford is recognised to be a chapel of the mother church of Stanford-in-the-Vale and William must render 60s. annually to Jordan and his successors, but the residue of the chapel is recognised to belong to the abbey of Abingdon, whose abbot has the right of presentation on William's death and thereafter. St Paul's, London, 11 October 1184

B = Bodl., MS Lyell 15, fo.55r-v. s.xiv med. - xv med., here s.xiv med.

Pd, *Abingdon cartularies*, i.97-9.

The notification was witnessed but the names of the witnesses have been omitted by the copyist. Before the judges made their decision they received a letter from Bishop Joscelin of Salisbury saying that from authentic documents relating to transactions carried out fifty years earlier in the time of Bishop Roger, he had recognised Shellingford as a mother church whose advowson belonged to Abingdon; ibid., i.96-7.

*130. Pope Alexander III

Letter to Pope Alexander III asking for advice concerning (a) priests who take the religious habit and revert to their former state, (b) the times for conferring holy orders, (c) the times for conferring minor orders, (d) the entry of a married man into a monastery, (e) the possession of a benefice causa rei servande, *and (f) the possession of churches and wives by clerks in minor orders.*   [6 October 1174 × June/July 1181]

Mention only, in a decretal of Alexander III addressed to *Roberto Folioth Herefordensi episcopo, WH*, no.1017. Because the response touched on so many different topics it was split up into separate sections, each treated as a separate decretal, in the decretal collections:
(a) Super eo quod quesitum
(b) Sane super eo quod
(c) De eo autem quod quesisti
(d) Querenti etiam tibi/ Preterea utrum laicus
(e) Ad hec cum contingat
(f) Sane de clericis
(a), (d), and (f) are calendared in *JL* 13946: (b) and (c) ibid., 13948 and (e) ibid. 13949, and all six in *WH*, no.1017; they are printed in *App.* 21.2, 26.24-25, 5.4, 3.1, 18.5, and in *Extra*, 3.31.9, 1.11.2-3, 3.32.1, 2.14.1, and 3.3.2. For discussion of (d) and (f), see C.Duggan, 'Equity and compassion in papal marriage decretals to England', in W.van Hoecke and A.Welkenhuysen, edd. *Love and marriage in the twelfth century* (Leuven 1981), 84, 65-66. No.131 below may well have formed the opening section of this decretal (information supplied by Dr Charles Duggan). Robert's letter is unlikely to have been written later than early July 1181, since Alexander III died on 30 August.

*131. Pope Alexander III

Letter to Pope Alexander III asking for advice as to how to proceed in cases where papal letters have been obtained through falsehood or suppression of the truth.   [probably 6 October 1174 × June/July 1181]

Mention only, in a decretal of Alexander III addressed to *R. Herefordensi episcopo*: *Intelleximus ex parte tue fraternitatis/ ex tue fraternitatis relatu*, calendared *WH*, no.585, and *JL* 13950, and printed *App.* 7.13 and *Extra*, 1.21.11. For the dating, see note to no.130 above.

*132. Pope Alexander III

Letter to Alexander III complaining about the behaviour of the Hospitallers in the diocese of Hereford; they had buried corpses of excommunicates in ecclesiastical graveyards and, contrary to their licence, had opened churches lying under an interdict more than once a year.

[probably 6 October 1174 × June/July 1181]

Mention only, in a mandate of Alexander III addressed to *fratribus Hiersolimitani hospitalis*, on the complaint of the bp, warning them not to exceed the privileges granted to them by the apostolic see: *Pervenit ad nos ex transmissa*, calendared *WH*, no.707 and *JL* 13962, and printed *App.* 44.9 and *1 Comp.* 5.28.7. The letter of complaint is likely to have been written by Robert Foliot rather than by Gilbert Foliot or by Robert de Béthune, since the earliest foundation of the Hospitallers in the diocese of Hereford, Dinmore, was established in the latter years of the reign of Henry II: see no.157 below. For the *terminus ad quem* see no.130.

*133. Pope Alexander III

Letter to Pope Alexander III asking for advice in the case of A. who married the mother of the girl to whom he had been betrothed when she was an infant (in cunabulis*).*

[late 1176 or early 1177, before 6 March]

Mention only, in decretal of Alexander III, dated 6 March 1177, at Vestae (Litteras tue fraternitatis/ Litteras fraternitatis tue/ Fraternitatis tue litteras), addressed to *Herefordensi episcopo*: *WH*, no.631; *JL* 13947, and printed *App.* 12.2 and *Extra* 4.2.4. The decretal is discussed by C.Duggan, 'Equity and compassion in papal marriage decretals to England', in W.van Hoecke and A.Welkenhuysen, edd. *Love and marriage in the twelfth century* (Leuven 1981), 80-81.

134. Bermondsey priory

Mandate patent of Bishops Robert of Hereford and Roger of Worcester to R., prior, and the monks of Bermondsey telling Prior R. to come to

Cricklade on the second Monday after the feast of St Hilary, when the case brought by the abbey of St-Evroult against them over the church of Widford will be heard.   [Early January 1175]

A = Alençon, A-D Orne, H937. 13th-century endorsements: . Rob' Hereford'. et .R. Wigonie (the initial letter might be a Gothic V rather than a W) episcoporum de quadam monitione. Triangular chest mark. 155 mm wide × 60 mm deep at left side. Originally sealed on the tongue, and probably had a wrapping tie. There may have been two tongues, as there would have been two seals. The tongues and the tie have been torn off and do not survive.

Pd, M.G.Cheney, *Roger, Bishop of Worcester, 1164-1179* (Oxford, 1980), Appendix I, no.57, pp.288-290.
Cal., *CDF*, no.644.

Rob' Hereford' et Rogerus Wigorn' dei gratia dicti episcopi. dilectis in domino fratribus. R' priori et fratribus de Beremundesheia*ᵃ* salutem. Dilectioni vestre auctoritate apostolica mandamus quatinus illustrem virum comitem Legecest' monasterio Sancti Ebrulfi super \ecclesia/ de Wideford' satisfacere moneatis et modis omnibus inducere studeatis. et nisi eidem monasterio satisfecerit vobis prescripta auctoritate precipimus ut secundo die lune post festum Sancti Hilarii sufficienter instructi presentiam vestram nobis aput Criccheladam *ᵇ*exhibeatis procuratori illius monasterii super iamdicta ecclesia*ᵇ* secundum formam mandati apostolici quod vobis satis innotuit responsuri. Si autem evidenti causa prepediti die statuto ad nos accedere forte non poteritis sufficientem responsalem cum literis patentibus et rati cautionem pretendentibus pro vobis dirigere curetis hunc namque diem vobis peremptorium prefigimus. Valete.

ᵃ-eia *written so closely that* i *not clearly legible.*
ᵇ⁻ᵇwritten over erasure in same hand.

For the dating, see M.G.Cheney, *loc. cit.*

135. Bockleton church

Admission of Robert the clerk to the church of Bockleton on presentation by Richard de Bockleton.   [December 1183 × 9 May 1186]

B = Bodl., MS Rawlinson B329 (Hereford cathedral cartulary), fos.53v-54r. s.xv.

Universis sancte matris ecclesie filiis Robertus dei gratia Heref' episcopus salutem. Notum vobis facimus quod nos ad presentationem
Ricardi de Boclinton' recipimus Robertum clericum ad ecclesiam de
Boclinton, ipsumque R. [fo.54r] in eadem ecclesia cum omnibus
pertinentiis suis in bosco et plano, in pratis et pascuis, in terris,
decimis et obventionibus personam canonice et absque omni reclamatione instituimus. Quod ne imposterum deduci possit in irritum
presenti carta et sigilli nostri impressione confirmamus, salva in
omnibus tam nostra quam nostrorum successorum episcoporum
Heref' canonica iustitia. Hiis t(estibus), Waltero Lyncoln' ecclesie
cancellario, Hugone archidiacono Salopes', W. Folyot et aliis.

The wording of this document is almost exactly the same as that of no.182 below,
Bp William de Vere's institution of a clerk called William in Bockleton church,
and it is possible that one or both documents is a fake. On the other hand, the
witnesses to each charter, while perfectly possible chronologically, are too unusual
to have been the obvious choice for a forger. Walter Map probably became
chancellor of Lincoln Cathedral between December 1183 and December 1184.

136. Brecon priory

*Composition as papal judge-delegate of the dispute between Brecon Pri-
ory and Gloucester Abbey concerning the tithes of Talgarth.*

[1179 × 1181]

B = Gloucester Cathedral Library, Register A, fo.109r, no.163. s.xiv ex. C = Bodl.
   MS Carte 108, fo.265v. s.xviii.
Pd from C, *Brecon cartulary*, xiv.19.
Cal. from B, 'Gloucester register', 26, no.59.

Universis sancte matris ecclesie filiis Robertus dei gratia Hereford'
ecclesie minister humilis salutem in eo qui est salus eterna credentium. Notum sit vobis quod cum super decimis de dominio*a* de
Brechonia,*b* auctoritate domini pape coram nobis lis mota fuisset,
priori de Brechon' et conventui ab abbate et monachis Glouc'*c* tandem
de nostra licentia, transactione interveniente,*d* pax inter eos formata
est et tota controversia que eadem auctoritate suscita erat penitus
extincta, ita quidem quod fratres de Brechonia*b* de voluntate abbatis
de Bello,*e* appellatione quam fecerant coram nobis renunciata, tertiam
partem decimarum de dominio de Talgar que ad eos ante spectabant,

scilicet de lana, caseis, agnis, vitulis que ex vaccis et ovibus*f* proveniunt, abbati Glouc'*c* penitus resignaverunt. Predictus vero abbas
Glouc'*c* similiter decimas vitulorum et caseorum qui ex vaccis de
foresta de Brechen' proveniunt perpetuo possidendas, retentis sibi
decimis totius venationis et totius occisionis ante Natale apud Brechen', integre predictis fratribus de Brechen' concessit. Decime vero*g*
de Lameis in transactionem istam non veniunt. Et nos auctoritate
domini pape qua fungimur in hac causa*h* transactionem istam confirmamus. Huius rei testes sunt Gaufridus decanus, Radulfus archidiaconus, Ivo thesaurarius, *i*Magister Nicholaus, Willelmus de Stoc,
canonici Hereford, Magister Gilebertus de <>,*j* Ricardus, presbiter
de Bodeham, Henricus de Kilpec et Walterus frater eius, Milo de
Michecr', Osbertus clericus archidiaconi et plures alii.*i*

*a*dominico *C.* *b*Brechen' *C.* *c*Gloec' *C.* *d*interventi *C.* *e*corr. from abbatis de Bello
abbatis *C.* *f*omnibus *B.* *g*om. *C.* *h*corr. from carta *C.* *i-i*Hereford' et multi alii *B.*
*j*word omitted *C.*

The dating of this document to 1163 × 1167, as suggested by David Walker,
'Gloucester register', is not possible, for Ralph Foliot did not become archdn of
Hereford until 1179. Dean Geoffrey died on 31 December 1180 × 1183. Miles de
Mucegros, lord of Monnington on Wye, was sheriff of Herefordshire 1181-3 and
the fact that he is referred to without his title might mean that this charter was
issued before 1181. The tithes of Llanvaes (*Lameis*) were the subject of an earlier
dispute between Gloucester Abbey and John, priest of Llanvaes, settled by Robert
de Melun in 1165; see above, no.119. The Master Gilbert mentioned in the witness
list is evidently Master Gilbert de Cricklade, and almost all the witnesses to this
document reappear in no.153 below, which suggests that the two charters were
issued at the same time.

137. Brimfield church

*Confirmation (and quotation) of the concession made by J(oseph), abbot
of Reading, with the consent of Osbert vicar of Eye parish church, to
Master A. and the parishioners of Brimfield, allowing the bodies of the
poorer Brimfield parishioners to be buried at Brimfield, while the better-
off must continue to be buried at Eye.* [6 October 1174 × 9 May 1186]

B = BL Cotton MS Domitian A iii (Leominster cartulary), fo.60v. s.xiii med.

Pd, B.R.Kemp, 'Hereditary benefices in the medieval English church: a Herefordshire example', *BIHR*, xliii (1970), Appendix no.2, p.12.

The Leominster cartulary often omits corroboration clauses and witness lists; it
is not possible to say whether this document originally had these or not. This

charter contains a full quotation (apart from the eschatocol, if it originally existed) of a charter of Abbot Joseph of Reading; this is an interesting development on the way towards the inspeximus. Robert's charter does not use the verb *inspeximus*, but introduces the quotation with the words '...talis ... litterarum forma nobis transmissa est'. The word *forma* usually means a draft, but here probably means a copy. No.138 below was almost certainly issued at the same time.

138. Brimfield church

Confirmation of the concession made by the abbot of Reading, with the consent of the monks of Leominster, and at the request of Osbert (vicar) of Eye, that the poor parishioners of Brimfield should be allowed to be buried there rather than at Eye.   [6 October 1174 × 9 May 1186]

> A = BL Add. Ch. 19585. 14th-century endorsement: De pauperibus hominibus sepeliendis apud Brumfeld. 143 × 88 mm. Sealed on the tag; seal now detached from the document; natural wax; none of the legend on the face visible. Figure of bishop with arms raised. Secretum: gem, design no longer visible. Legend; (SIG)ILLUM ROBER........

.R. dei gratia Hereford' ecclesie minister humilis. Universis sancte matris ecclesie filiis eternam in Cristo salutem. Noverit universitas vestra quod nos ratam habemus et episcopali auctoritate confirmamus et sigilli nostri impressione roboramus concessionem illam quam dilectus frater noster abbas Rading' assensu totius capituli de Leomen'. et petitione Osberti de Eia fecit magistro .A. clerico de Brimf'. et eiusdem ville parrochianis. videlicet quod corpora pauperum parochianorum non deferantur ad cimiterium de Eia. set apud Brimf' sepulture tradantur. servata ubique indempnitate monasterii de Leomen'. et ecclesie de Eia ad quam capellam de Brimfeld spectare dinoscitur cetera vero corpora in dispositione sint Osberti de Eia et successorum eius : sicut in carta prefati abbatis continetur.

> See note to no.137.

139. Cirencester abbey

Settlement, as papal judge delegate, of the case between the canons of Cirencester and Reginald fitz Lambert, the priest, concerning the vicarage of Cheltenham; Reginald is to hold the vicarage, paying an annual pension of twenty shillings to Cirencester at three terms (Michaelmas,

Lady Day and St John the Baptist's Day), and he recognises that the land which had been held by his father, and which he said was part of his vicarage, is held in lay fee from the canons for an annual census of ten shillings. [6 October 1174 × 9 May 1186, late]

B = Bodl., MS Dep. C392 (Cirencester cartulary A, formerly Vestey Manuscripts, Stowell Park), fo.122r, no.422. s.xiii med. C = Bodl., MS Dep. C393 (Cirencester cartulary B, formerly Vestey Manuscripts, Stowell Park), fos.111v-112r. s.xiv ex.

Pd from BC, *Cirencester cartulary*, ii.379, no.422/453.

The dispute between Cirencester and Reginald probably blew up after an earlier dispute concerning the vicarage of Cheltenham, between Randulf the priest and Reginald the chaplain of Cheltenham, had been settled. In the settlement, datable 1174 × 26 April 1180 (*Cirencester cartulary*, ii.380-1, no.423/454), Randulf agreed to withdraw his claim.

*140. Cirencester abbey

Indulgence (jointly issued by the bishops of Worcester, Hereford, Exeter and Bath at a dedication of Cirencester Abbey). [17 October 1176]

Mention only, in an indult of Innocent III dated 28 April 1199 (*Cirencester cartulary*, i.162-3, no.164/96), discussed by M.G.Cheney, *Roger, Bishop of Worcester* (Oxford 1980), 61, n.9.

141. Conches abbey

Notification of agreement to the settlement of a dispute between the abbey of Conches and Roger of Tanworth about half of the church of Wootton in Warwickshire; Robert Foliot and Abbot Baldwin of Ford had been delegated as judges by the pope, but Robert had been unable to attend the hearing. [Shortly after 25 April 1178]

B = Evreux, A-D Eure, II F2463 (cartulary of Wootton Wawen), fo.30r. s.xv med.

Universis fidelibus R. dei gratia Hereford ecclesie minister humilis perpetuam in domino salutem. Ad universorum notitiam pervenire volumus quod, cum controversia que vertebatur inter abbatem et conventum Sancti Petri Castellionis et Rogerum Camewrda*[a]* super medietate ecclesie de Wotton', et dampnis sibi, ut asserebat, illatis, nobis et venerabili viro B., abbati de Forda, a sede apostolica appellatione remota cognoscenda et terminanda commissa fuisset, nos, quia multitudine negotiorum districti^b decisioni predicte cause interesse non potuimus, vices nostras memorato coniudici nostro delegavimus eapropter nos assensum prebentes transactioni que in presentia prenominati abbatis et honestorum et discretorum virorum super prescripta causa et dampnis datis facta est. Ipsam transactionem, secundum quod in autentico^c scripto sepedicti abbatis continetur, una cum eodem coniudice^d nostro in quantum ad nos pertinet auctoritate nobis commissa confirmamus et sigilli nostri testimonio communimus sub presentia istorum testium, Valteri^e archidiaconi, Radulfi Folioth, Roberti decani de Nene, Magistri^f Hernaldi de Buchinheham et Willelmi^g de Monkele. Benedictionem et valete in domino.

^{a}*Possibly a scribal error for* de Tanewrda, *i.e. of Tanworth (near Wootton).* ^{b}distriti *B.*
^{c}auctentiquo *B.* ^{d}comiudice *B.* ^{e}*sic B.* ^{f}Magistro *B.* ^{g}Willelmo *B.*

Abbot Baldwin's notification of the settlement (ibid., fos.29r-30r) is dated 25 April 1178 at Winchcombe. The abbot of Conches, with the agreement of certain monks, consented to pay Roger of *Camewrda* thirty shillings a year from his chamber, and in return Roger renounced his claim to half the church and agreed to drop his claim for damages.

142. Conches abbey

Confirmation to the abbey of Conches of the manor of Monkland, the church of that vill, and various parcels of tithe at Chadnor, Westhide, Bromsberrow, Stoke Edith, Showle Court in Yarkhill, Ashperton, Abberley, Berrow in Astley, Worsley in Rock, and Linden in Rock granted by Ralph de Toeny.   [1179 × 1186]

A = Evreux, A-D Eure H251. Badly damaged; top right corner eaten away. The document has been stitched together and also stitched to a backing, made out of a letter (not legible). It is thus not possible to read the endorsements on the document itself. Notes made on the backing (18th century hand): Cotte 4 Angleterre C de Robert de Hereford Evesq' Confirmat' des biens de Langleterre fol 113R 3e liasse armoire 30e. 217 mm wide at top; 265 mm wide at base; 188 mm deep. Originally sealed on the tag but tag and seal missing.

B = Ibid., H251. Inspeximus of Robert's charter by Bp Hugh Foliot (see below, no.322). C = Ibid., H251. Vidimus of Hugh Foliot's charter of inspeximus issued by Dean Ralph de Maidstone.

Universis sancte matris ecclesie filiis Robertus dei gratia Hereford'
ecclesie minister. eternam in Cristo salutem. Ex officio iniuncte
[nobis administrati]onis^a tenemur viris religiosis eatenus providere ?
ut beneficia a filiis sancte dei ecclesie in elemosinam perpetuam [sibi
collata pacifice et]^a absque omnium vexatione possidere valeant. Inde
est quod dilectis fratribus nostri abbati sancti Petri Castellionis et
mon[achis ibidem deo ser]vientibus^a paterna pietate prospicere cupientes. concedimus eis. et episcopali auctoritate confirmamus manerium de Munekeslen' [et ecclesiam]^a eiusdem ville cum universis
decimationibus et ceteris obventionibus et omnibus ad eam de iure
spectantibus salva honesta sustentatione vicarii. Confirmamus etiam
eis omnes decimas de dominio de Cabbenour'. cum uno hospite. et
decimam illius terre quam idem hospes de eis tenet [et de]cimam^a de
Hide in omnibus. Confirmamus etiam eis duas partes decimarum de
dominio de Bromesberga tam in magnis [quam]^a in minutis
d[ecimis]^a in omnibus et confirmamus eis duas partes decimarum de
dominio de Edidestoc. in omnibus cum uno hospite. et duas partes
decimarum de d[ominio]^a de la Hide. et duas partes decimarum de
dominio Willelmi de Scolle. et duas partes decimarum Hereberti de
Espretun' [et]^a unum burgagium in villa Hereford'. et duas partes
decimarum de dominio de Alboldelega. et in eadem villa duos hospites et duas partes decimarum de dominio del Bur. et duas partes
decimarum de dominio de Worvesleg'. et terra et mansura que fuit
Caure. et duas partes decimarum de feodo Osberti filii Rualdi. et duas
partes decimarum de dominio de Linde cum uno hospite. Has
elemosinas habent predicti monachi ex donatione Radulfi senioris de
Toenio. quas et alia si qua in episcopatu Hereford' habent beneficia
canonice [adepta] ? ^{a} eis confirmamus. salva dignitate Hereford' ecclesie et successorum nostrorum canonica iusticia. quod ne de cetero
deduci possit in irritum ? presenti carta et sigilli nostri testimonio
communimus. His testibus Willelmo de Stoc'. Willelmo Foliot.
Wa[ltero de]^a Colewell' Magistro Nicholao Divino. Iohanne canonico. Eluredo capellano. Bartholomeo de Eignesham. Osberto de
Ledeb'.

^{a}*lacuna A; supplied from B.*

William Foliot became a canon of Hereford after 1179. On Conches see also nos.
187 and 322.

*143. Master Germanus

*Grant to Master Germanus of a burgage next to the house of Robert de Homme in New Street (*in novo vico*) in Ledbury.*

[6 October 1174 × 9 May 1186]

Mention only, in a charter of Hugh the clerk, son of Master Germanus, granting the said burgage to Robert de Staning according to the terms of Robert's original grant and of its confirmation by Bp William de Vere (Hereford D. & C. Muniments, no. 2182).

*144. Gloucester abbey

Admission of Adam as vicar to the church of Much Cowarne on presentation by Abbot Hamelin of Gloucester; Adam is to pay a pension of five marks a year to Gloucester.   [6 October 1174 × 10 March 1179]

Mention only, in the notification by Dean Hugh de Mapenore and Hereford cathedral chapter of Gloucester Abbey's claims to the church of Much Cowarne, *Gloucester cartulary*, i.253, and also in the document setting a date for the hearing of the dispute between Richard and Elena Pancefot, Jordan and Eva de Wike on one side and Gloucester Abbey on the other, *CRR*, vii.216-7, Trinity Term 16 John. Abbot Hamelin was abbot of Gloucester from 1148 to 1179, and although the admission could be attributed to Bp Robert de Melun, it is more likely that it is a document of Robert Foliot, in view of the fact that Adam, the last vicar to be admitted before 1214, presumably died in 1213 or 1214.

145. Gloucester abbey

Settlement of a dispute between Hamelin, Abbot of Gloucester and S. de Fraxino concerning the mill at Ocle Pychard.

[6 October 1174 × 10 March 1179]

A = Hereford D. & C. Muniments, no.1525; chirograph with wavy indentation, the letters CIROGRAPH' running upside down at the top edge of the document with only the tops of the letters visible. No ancient endorsements. 172 mm wide; 88 mm deep at left, 62 mm deep at right. Document originally sealed on the tongue; tongue torn off and no trace of wrapping tie.

Pd, David Walker, 'Some Charters Relating to St Peter's Abbey, Gloucester', in *A medieval miscellany for D.M.Stenton*, ed. P.M.Barnes and C.F.Slade, P.R.S., new ser. xxxvi (1962), 261-2, no.7.

.R. dei gratia Hereford' episcopus omnibus fidelibus ad quos littere iste pervenerint ⸴ eternam salutem. Noverit universitas vestra. conventionem inter abbatem Gloecest' .H. et .S. de Fraxino militem habitam super molendino de Acle de quo multo tempore inter eos controversia extiterat ⸴ utraque parte in presentia nostra constituta ex eorum relatione _____^{a} audivimus. Quod etiam se perpetuo et fideliter observaturum ⸴ predictus miles tactis sacrosanctis ewangliis^b nobis inspicientibus iuravit. Ne ergo in posterum aliquo modo possit in irritum devocari ⸴ eamdem conventionem confirmamus. et presenti scripto et sigilli nostri appositione communimus. statuentes ut ita inter eos de cetero observetur quemadmodum in cyrographo inter eos descripto continetur. quod inspeximus et legimus. T. Iohanne can(onico) et Iohanne presbitero capellanis meis. Nicholao de Leueken'. Willelmo de Stoches. Magistro Eustachio. Roberto de la Landa. Theodbaldo;

^{a}*erasure covered with a line to fill up the space.* ^{b}*sic B.*

Abbot Hamelin died on 10 March 1179. S. de Fraxino was probably a relative of Simon de Fraxino or Simund de Freine, a canon of Hereford and the author of two Anglo-Norman poems (see J.Barrow, 'A twelfth-century bishop and literary patron', *Viator*, xviii [1987], 186-7). The de Freines lived at Sutton near Hereford.

146. Haughmond abbey

Notification that Hugh de Say has in his presence granted the church of Stokesay to Haughmond abbey.   [6 October 1174 × ?1177]

B = Shrewsbury Local Studies Library, Haughmond abbey cartulary, fo.206r. s.xv ex. C = Shrewsbury, Shropshire County Record Office, 2922 Additional (Dudmaston MS), fo.17r.

Pd, *Haughmond cartulary*, 212, no.1144.

Hugh de Say held Stokesay from 1172 to 1194 (R.W.Eyton, *Antiquities*, ix.260-1). Hugh de Say's grant (*Haughmond cartulary*, 212, no.1141, though misattributed by the scribe to Hugh de Lacy) was probably made between October 1174 and 1177, because it was also confirmed by Hugh de Lacy (ibid., 212, no.1142), who returned to Ireland after May 1177 and remained there almost continuously until he was murdered in 1186 (W.E.Wightman, *The Lacy family in England and Normandy, 1066-1194* [Oxford 1966], 191-4). It is possible that Robert Foliot's confirmation was issued shortly after Hugh de Say's grant, and that it is therefore datable 1174 × 1177.

147. Haughmond abbey

Restoration of Linley in More to Haughmond abbey on its renunciation by Madoc, Ralph, and Agnes, Ralph's wife, before papal judges-delegate.
[1179 × 31 December 1183]

A = Keele University Library, Raymond Richards Collection, Miscellaneous Historical Materials 53/4 (originally Phillipps MS 33757). Endorsements: De Linlega (12th century); A deede purporting a recovery had before the deligate (*sic*) of the pope of the landes of Linley by the abot (*sic*) & convent of Hagman against Madoc and Raphe and Agnes his wife and a resignation of their right into the handes of the Bishop of Hereford and his investing of the sayd abot (*sic*) and convent into the same land etc without date (16th century). 243 × 146 mm; sealed on a tag in green wax. Top of seal missing; remainder 50 mm long and 47 wide (originally slightly wider). Face: figure of a bishop in full pontificals raising his right hand in blessing; traces of a staff. Legend: ....DEI GRA.............. ; Secretum: 25 mm long × 21 mm wide, oval. Impossible to make out design in centre, which is presumably an antique gem. Legend: + SIGILLUM ROBERTI.

B = Shrewsbury, Shropshire County Record Office, 4220/2 (no. 252 below) in an inspeximus issued by Giles de Braose. C = Shrewsbury, Local Studies Library, Haughmond cartulary, fo.136v. s.xv ex. D = Bodl., MS Top. Salop. c. 1, p.5 of the paginated section of the MS; watercolour facsimile of A by Duke. s.xix med.

Pd from C, R.W.Eyton, *Antiquities*, xi.208-209; pd from B and C (no mention of A), *Haughmond cartulary*, 146-7, no.705.

Universis sancte matris ecclesie filiis .R. dei gratia Hereford' ecclesie minister humilis perpetuam in domino salutem. Noverit universitas vestra quod cum primum ad regimen Hereford' ecclesie deo vocante accessissemus ꞏ invenimus in castalario de Lideb'. Madocum. Radul-fum. et Agnetem uxor𝖍 eius tenentes terram de Linlega. et episcopo Hereford' unam marcam sub annua pensione inde reddentes. Postea abbas de Hagaman et conventus per litteras domini pape adversus eos controversiam super iam dicta terra moverunt. et coram iudicibus delegatis eam demum evicerunt. Ita quod Madocus et Radulfus consensu et assensu Agnetis uxoris eius coram .G. decano. et .R. archidiacono. et Ivone thesaurario. et Waltero senescallo. et multis aliis. terram illam sine omni reclamatione in manum nostram resig-naverunt. et nos abbatem et conventum de Hagman de eadem terra cum omnibus pertinentiis suis in bosco et plano in pratis. et aquis et pascuis et omnibus aliis locis ꞏ investivimus. tenendam de nobis et successoribus nostris \ in perpetuum sub annua pensione .xx. solidorum. solvendorum in duobus terminis. medietatem in Pente-

Hem

cost'. et alteram in festo beati Martini. Preterea. omni anno quo werra fuerit ad summonitionem nostram et baillivi nostri invenient in castello de Lideb' unum servientem per .xv. tantum dies per expensas suas. Et si forte dominus episcopus aliquando a liberis illius feudi hominibus auxilium exigere opus habuerit *:* tunc facient sicuti terra illa antiquitus facere consuevit. secundum recordationem curie nostre de Lideb'. Quod quia firmum et stabile manere volumus *:* presenti carta et sigilli nostri attestatione premunimus et confirmamus. His testibus .G. decano. Radulfo archidiacono. Ivone thesaurario. Reginaldo constabulario. Magistro Eustachio. Reginaldo capellano. Willelmo camerario. Willelmo decano de Bruge. Hugone decano de Iarchul'. Waltero decano de Humbre. Magistro Osberto. et multis aliis.

Ralph Foliot became archdn of Hereford after March 1179; Dean Geoffrey died on 31 December 1180 × 1183, probably earlier rather than later. This charter appears to have been issued in a diocesan synod, as it is witnessed by three rural deans; the archdnry of Shropshire was presumably vacant at this point, following the death of Walter Foliot, which probably occurred in 1178 (see appendix I). Hugh Foliot, his successor, witnessed several of Robert Foliot's acta, but all of these are certainly or probably post *c.*1180. See also nos.81 and 252.

148. Haughmond abbey

Licence to Haughmond abbey to appropriate the tithes of the vill of Stitt and to set up a church in the vill, which up to this time had only had an oratory.   [1179 × 31 December 1183]

B = Shrewsbury Local Studies Library, Haughmond abbey cartulary, fo.210v. s.xv ex.

Pd, *Haughmond cartulary*, 217, no.1181.

Testibus Willelmo Stokel, Radulfo archidiacono etc'.

The appropriation of Stitt church was confirmed by Dean Geoffrey (see note to no.147) and the chapter of Hereford cathedral (*Haughmond cartulary*, 147, no.707; the original is Shropshire County Record Office 4220/3). Geoffrey died in or after 1180. The *terminus post quem* is the appointment of Ralph Foliot as archdn of Hereford. It is highly unusual to find an archdn preceded in a witness list by a mere canon, even a prominent one like William de Stokes; it is possible that the scribe transposed the names.

149. Hereford cathedral chapter

Notification that Canon David de Aqua has granted the tithes from the land which he bought from Robert de Chandos to improve his prebend, to buy simnels for Hereford cathedral chapter once a year on St Milburga's day.   [6 October 1174 × 31 December 1183]

> A = Hereford D. & C. Muniments, no.1383. No ancient endorsements. 184 × 109 mm. Evidence of having been sealed on a tag.
>
> Pd, *Hereford charters*, 24.

Universis sancte matris ecclesie fidelibus Robertus dei gratia Hereford' ecclesie minister humilis. perpetuam in Cristo salutem. Notum vobis facimus quod dilectus frater noster et canonicus David de Aqua. assensu nostro dedit et concessit in perpetuam elemosinam ecclesie Sancte Marie et beati Æthelberti de Heref'. totam decimam cuiusdam terre. quam a^a bone memorie Rob(erto) de Chandos in augmentum prebende sue emit. ita quod singulis annis in festo beate Milburge virginis de eadem decima fiant siminelli. canonicis et vicariis memorate ecclesie necnon et cunctis sacerdotibus in villa Heref'. parochias regentibus distribuendi. Ut autem huius decime concessio rata in perpetuum et inconcussa permaneat.' nos eandem episcopali auctoritate et presenti scripto et sigilli nostri appositione confirmamus. His testibus. G. dec(ano). I. thesaurario. Magistro Iordano. Magistro Nicholao presbitero. Magistro Simone. Magistro Nicholao divino. Reginaldo capellano. Magistro Eustachio. Galfrido Folet. et multis aliis.

> ^{a}ā *sic.*

> Dean Geoffrey died on 31 December, 1180 × 1183. St Milburga, whose feast day was 23 February, was the patron saint of Much Wenlock. Simnels in the middle ages were usually buns or biscuits baked out of fine wheat flour (*A New English Dictionary*, ed. J.A.H.Murray, 10 vols. and supplement [Oxford, 1888-1933], ix, pt. i, 61). Canon David de Aqua was the prebendary of Moreton Parva (J.Barrow, 'The bishops of Hereford and their *acta*, 1163-1219', unpd. Oxford D.Phil. thesis, 1983, p.515).

150. Hereford cathedral chapter

Grant to Hereford cathedral chapter of the church of the episcopal manor of Upton Bishop to augment their commons.
                        [6 October 1174 × 9 May 1186, probably late]

B = Hereford D. & C. Muniments, no.741. Inspeximus by Bp Giles de Braose of Robert's grant and of William de Vere's confirmation of it. See below, no.258.

C = Bodl., MS Rawlinson B329 (Hereford cathedral cartulary), fo.171r. s.xiii-xiv.

Pd from B, *Hereford charters*, 40-42.

Universis sancte matris ecclesie filiis Robertus Foliot dei gratia Herefordensis ecclesie minister humilis perpetuam in domino salutem. Universitati vestre notum facimus quod nos, considerantes paucitatem bonorum ad communam dilectorum filiorum nostrorum canonicorum Hereforden' pertinentium Deo et Beate Marie et Sancto Adelberto[a] ibidem assidue et devote servientium, concessimus et dedimus eis ecclesiam manerii nostri de Hupton,[b] in augmentum communie[c] sue, libere et quiete et honorifice in perpetuum habendam, cum terris, decimis et obventionibus, et omnibus rebus et libertatibus ad eandem ecclesiam pertinentibus, sicut unquam eam aliquis melius, liberius, et quietius tenuit. Volumus etiam et statuimus ut post decessum Reginaldi clerici de Glouc',[d] quem ad presentationem eorundem canonicorum nostrorum perpetuum in eadem ecclesia constituimus vicarium, liceat eis ad libitum suum de eadem ecclesia de Hupton'[b] libere disponere, ita videlicet ut eam in proprios usus retineant, vel alii sub certa pensione pro sua voluntate committant, salva in omnibus episcopali dignitate. Ut autem hec nostra donatio in perpetuum rata et illibata permaneat, ipsam presenti scripto et sigilli nostri testimonio confirmamus. His t':[e] Henrico thesaurario London', Iohanne et Alur(edo) capellanis nostris, Magistro Edmundo, Waltero de Colewell,[f] Ernaldo de Stok,[g] Ranulfo de Salewarp', Bartholomeo de Eignesham', Osberto de Ledeb',[h] Bertramo et Herveio clericis nostris, Willelmo camerario, Petro de parco, Germano coco, Sampsone pistore, Henrico marescallo.[i]

[a]Beato Ethelberto C. [b]Uptuna C. [c]commune C. [d]Gloucestria C. [e]Hiis testibus C. [f]Colevile C. [g]Scot C. [h]Ledebur' C. [i]C adds et aliis.

Henry Banastre was treasurer of St Paul's, London, and a kinsman of the Foliot family (*Fasti Ecclesiae Anglicanae, 1066-1300, i, St Paul's*, ed. D.E.Greenway [London 1968], 21, and A.Morey and C.N.L.Brooke, *Gilbert Foliot and his Letters* [Cambridge 1965], 275). John and Alured appear to have been Robert Foliot's chaplains in the latter part of his episcopate. See also no.202.

151. Hereford cathedral chapter

Mandate to Dean Jordan and the cathedral chapter to remove a house which had been built on the burial ground of the cathedral.

[31 December 1180 × 9 May 1186]

A = Hereford D. & C. Muniments, no.1379. No ancient endorsements. 157 × 64 mm; originally sealed on the tongue, but this torn off.

Pd, *Hereford charters*, 22-23.

R. dei gratia Hereford' ecclesie minister humilis. Dilectis suis. Iordano decano et toti eiusdem ecclesie capitulo. salutem in auctore salutis. Meminisse potestis nos sepenumero vobis precipiendo iniunxisse. ut locus ille in quo constructa est domus que fuit Petri quondam archidiaconi. videlicet quantum ad ecclesiam et cimiterium Sancti Adelberti pertinet.' ab edificio illo vacuaretur et liberaretur. Et quoniam huic mandato nostro usque nunc supersedere non timuistis.' vestre discretioni in mandatis adhuc damus et in vi obedientie precipimus. quatinus procuretis modis omnibus quod illa pars atrii sancti in sepulturam fidelium a nostris predecessoribus benedicta et consecrata. et postmodum a viris indiscretis et quantum ad hoc sancte ecclesie honorem postponentibus. alienata.' ad cimiterium unde subtracta fuit. libere redeat. Si quis vero vobis hoc facere volentibus restiterit.' vos ipsi de eo sine personarum acceptione nostra subnixi auctoritate ecclesiasticam non differatis facere iustitiam. Bene valete.

Jordan became dean just after 1180; Archdn Peter of Hereford died on 15 March, probably in 1179. The cathedral was surrounded on three sides by a large graveyard and claimed a monopoly over burials in the city of Hereford from at least the early twelfth century (cf. the case of the burial of Ralph fitz Ansketill, 1108, in *Gloucester cartulary*, i.13, commented on by M.Brett, *The English church under Henry I* [Oxford 1975], 98) until modern times (A.T.Bannister, *The cathedral church of Hereford* [London 1924], 76-7). The origins of the monopoly, and of the graveyard, are uncertain: excavation of the area surrounding the cathedral would help to elucidate the problem. In Anglo-Saxon Hereford there had been an extensive graveyard surrounding the church of St Guthlac's, and archaeological evidence shows that it continued in use until the twelfth century, perhaps until the siege of the castle in 1140 (R.Shoesmith, ed. *Hereford city excavations vol. I: excavations at Castle Green* [Council for British Archaeology Research Report 36, 1980], 3, 48-54), or more probably until the removal of St Guthlac's to a new site outside the town in 1143 (see no.21 above). The cathedral evidently did not completely eliminate St Guthlac's as a rival: A.M.Pearn shows that in the fourteenth century St Guthlac's priory was believed to possess the right to bury its own tenants living in the city, and that in the same period the parish of St Peter's, controlled by St Guthlac's priory, successfully proved the right to mortuaries, though bodies were still to be buried at the cathedral ('Origin and development of Urban Churches and Parishes: a comparative study of Hereford, Shrewsbury and Chester', unpubl. Ph.D. thesis, Cambridge University, 1988, pp.175, 163-5).

152. St Guthlac's priory, Hereford

Admission to the church of Bartestree of Stephen the king's notary on presentation by the priory of St Guthlac's; Stephen has also been granted one third of the villeins' tithes at Lugwardine.

[6 October 1174 × 9 May 1186, probably late]

B = Oxford, Balliol College, MS 271 (cartulary of St Guthlac's, Hereford), fo.105r, no.467. s.xiv in.

Omnibus sancte matris ecclesie filiis R. dei gratia Herefordensis episcopus eternam in d(omino)^a salutem. Noverit universitas vestra nos ad presentationem prioris et conventus mon(asterii)^a Sancti Guthlaci Heref' recepisse et concessisse Magistro Stephano, notario domini Regis, ( )^b ecclesiam suam de Bertwaldestreu tenendam in perpetuam^c elemosinam libere et quiete^b ab omni prestatione census^d ipsumque exinde personam canonice instituisse. Pretere(a)^a idem Stephanus recepit de manu prioris, assensu iamdicti prioris, tertiam partem decimationis rusticorum de Lugwardin tenendam tota vita sua de eisdem monachis sub annuo canone quinque solidorum. Idem vero monachi exceperunt in donationem predicte ecclesie de Bertwaldestreu totam decimam dominii eiusdem ville, et duas partes decime rusticorum et omnia corpora defunctorum, et ad opus suum omnia ea tanquam de antiquo iure et monasterio suo prius^e percepta retinuerunt.^{f} Hiis testibus: Waltero senescallo, Magistro Eustacio, Iohanne et Aluredo, capellanis, Theobaldo elemosinario, Willelmo elemosinario, Reginaldo emptore etc.

^{a}*lacuna B.* ^{b}*short lacuna? B.* ^{c}*inperpetuam B.* ^{d}*scensus B.* ^{e}*pius B.* ^{f}*retinuerint B.*

It is probable that Walter became Robert's steward and that John and Alured became Robert's chaplains during the latter part of his episcopate.

153. St Guthlac's priory, Hereford

Composition of a dispute between the priors of St Guthlac's, Hereford, and Brecon over the burial rights over half a hide of land at Dudales Hope in Bodenham.   [1179 × 31 December 1183]

> B = Oxford, Balliol College, MS 271 (cartulary of St Guthlac's, Hereford), fo.59r, no.235. s.xiv in.

Universis[a] sancte matris ecclesie filiis Robertus dei gratia Herefordensis ecclesie minister humilis salutem in eo qui est salus eterna credentium. Cum esset in presentia nostra diu litigatum inter priorem de Hereforde et priorem de Brech' super sepultura et sequela parochiali de dimidia hida de Hopa quam Odo et eius filius Dyonisius tenuerunt, tota controversia hoc fine conquievit. Decime annone integre persolventur pretaxato[b] priori de Hereford' et sepultura colonorum terram tenentium virorum ac mulierum cum eorum divisa sequela parochiali et sepultura familiarum ibi servientium et etiam puerorum et omnes alii proventus ad ecclesiam de Bodeham spectabunt perpetuo. Eadem etiam ecclesia omnia spiritualia predictis colonis et familiis ministrabit. Hii sunt testes, Gaufridus decanus, Radulfus archidiaconus, Yvo thesaurarius, Magister Willelmus de Stok canonicus Hereford et Magister Gilbertus[c] de Cricall', Henricus de Kylpec et Walterus frater eius, Milo de Much', Ricardus presbiter de Bodeham, Osbertus clericus archidiaconi, et plures alii.

> [a]*Initial letter omitted for rubricator to fill in.*   [b]pretexato *B.*
> [c]Magistro Willelmo de Stok canonico Hereford et Magistro Gilberto *B.*

See note to no.136 above.

154. St Guthlac's priory, Hereford

Confirmation to St Guthlac's of the grant made to them by Henry II of the chapel of St Martin in Hereford Castle.   [1179 × 9 May 1186]

> B = Oxford, Balliol College MS 271 (cartulary of St Guthlac's, Hereford), fo.102r, no.450. s.xiv in.

Universis sancte matris ecclesie filiis Robertus dei gratia Heref' episcopus eter(nam in)[a] Domino salutem. Universitati vestre notum facimus quod dominus noster rex H. (s)^a nobis ei assidentibus apud Hereford' concessit et dedit capellam Sancti Mar(tini)^a que est in castello Heref' liberam et quietam cum omnibus pertinentiis suis a(bbati)^a Glouc' et priori Sancti Petri et Sancti Guthlaci Heref' in perpetuam elemosinam. N(os)^a igitur hanc donationem domini regis ratam habentes ipsam episcopali a(uctoritate)^a confirmamus^b et tam presentis^c scripti quam sigilli nostri testimonio communimus, salva in omnibus Heref' ecclesie dignitate et diocesani episcopi canonica obedientia. Hiis testibus: Radulfo priore Sancti Oswaldi, Iohanne canonico et Aluredo capellanis, Willelmo de Stock', Symone et Willelmo fratribus.

^{a}*lacuna B.* ^{b}confirmans *B.* ^{c}presenti *B.*

Henry II's grant, datable *c.*1179 × 1182 because it was issued at Hereford and witnessed by Archdn Ralph Foliot and by Ranulf le Poer, can be found in ibid., fo.93r, no.410; the original, Hereford D. & C. Muniments no.2178, is printed in *Hereford charters*, 22. A spurious version of Robert's confirmation can be found below, no.155. Ralph became prior of St Oswald's, Gloucester, in or after 1177.

†155. St Guthlac's priory, Hereford (spurious)

Confirmation to St Guthlac's of the grant made by Henry II of the chapel of St Martin in Hereford Castle, with its appurtenances, the church of Mansell Gamage and two parts of the demesne tithes of Yazor, Yarkhill, Howton in Kenderchurch, Arkstone in Kingstone, Wormington (lost) in Much Dewchurch, and all the tithe of the garden of Hugh de Lacy across the Wye and all the offerings from Hereford Castle, and also confirmation of the parish church of St Guthlac's within the castle bailey which is a mother church, with all its appurtenances, deaneries, prebends, dignities and parishes, that is the prebend of Dudales Hope in Bodenham, the chapel of Felton, the prebend of Ocle within the parish of Ocle Pychard, the prebend of Thinghill in Withington, and the prebend of Upper Lyde, which all, except the prebend of Ocle, are of the deaneries of the church of St Guthlac's.   [1179 × 9 May 1186]

B = Oxford, Balliol College MS 271 (cartulary of St Guthlac's, Hereford), fo.112v, no.499. The manuscript is s.xiv in., but this deed has been written in a 15th-century hand on a bifolium attached to the rest of the MS after the original binding.

Universis sancte matris ecclesie filiis R. Hereford' dei gratia episcopus eternam in domino salutem. Universitati vestre notum facimus
quod dominus noster rex Henricus secundus nobis assidentibus ei
apud Hereford' concessit et dedit capellam Sancti Martini que est in
castello Hereford' liberam et quietam cum omnibus pertinentiis suis
abbati Gloecestr' et priori et monachis in ecclesia beatorum apostolorum Petri et Pauli et Sancti Guthlaci Hereford deo regulariter
servientibus in perpetuam elemosinam. Nos igitur hanc donationem
capelle Sancti Martini cum omnibus suis pertinentiis scilicet ecclesia
de Maneshulle cum terris et decimis ad eam pertinentibus et cum
duabus partibus decime dominii de Iareshore et duabus partibus
decime dominii de Yarchulle et de Huggeton' et de Arcleston' et de
Wriminton et tota decima gardini Hugonis de Laci ultra Waiam et
omnibus obventionibus castelli Hereford' ac ipsam parochialem ecclesiam Sancti Guthlaci infra ambitum castelli Hereford que matrix
est aliorum cum omnibus suis pertinentiis, decaniis, prebendis, dignitatibus et parochiis, scilicet prebenda de Hope iuxta Magane,
capella de Felton', prebenda de Acle infra parochiam de Acle Pich-
ardi, prebenda de Yynghulle presbiterorum et parva Yynghull' que
sunt de parochia ipsius ecclesie Sancti Guthlaci – a fundatione cui-
usque parochiarum immediate pertinet^a ad priorem ipsius ecclesie
Sancti Guthlaci – et prebenda de Ludeloged^b infra parochiam de Pipa
que omnia sunt de decaniis ipsius ecclesie Sancti Gudlaci, prebenda
de Acle dumtaxat excepta, auctoritate episcopali confirmand' tam
presenti scripto quam sigilli nostri testimonio communimus. Hiis
testibus Radulpho priore Sancti Oswaldi et(c)'

^{a}cuiusque...pertinet *sic B.* ^{b}*recte* Ludeloges.

The prebends belonging to St Guthlac's are mentioned in a charter of Stephen
(*RRAN*, iii, no.398, datable 1136 × 1137), and *Ludeloges* is Lyde Prior, now Upper
Lyde, where land was granted to St Guthlac's by Albereda de Loges between 1148
and *c.*1155 (*GFL*, no.319). Thinghill 'of the priests' is now Thinghill Court and
Thinghill *parva* is now Thinghill Grange. The prebend at Ocle Pychard, which
was at Monkton, had originally formed part of the endowment of St Peter's,
Hereford, not of the collegiate church of St Guthlac's (Domesday Book, i,
fo.184a). St Guthlac's had been, before the Conquest, an important and well-en-
dowed church (R.Shoesmith, *Hereford city excavations, vol. i: excavations at Castle
Green* [Council for British Archaeology Research Report 36, 1980], 1-5), though
the extent of its pre-Conquest parish is uncertain. This charter represents a clumsy
attempt by the monks of St Guthlac's to claim the extensive parochial rights of a
head minster. It is clearly spurious, because there is no dispositive clause: the list
of properties being confirmed runs awkwardly into the corroboration. Moreover
there is no attempt to distinguish what has been granted by Henry II (the chapel

of St Martin) from the property which has belonged to St Guthlac's all along; this is doubtless because the forger began by copying no.154 and then added a separate list, presumably a pre-existing schedule, of properties.

156. St Guthlac's priory, Hereford

Confirmation of the composition made by his authority between Thomas, abbot of Gloucester, and Garnier of Nâblus, then prior of the Hospitallers in England, about the church of St Michael of Sutton, the chapel of Wistaston in Marden and tithes from Edvin Loach and Freen Court.

[1185 × 9 May 1186]

B = Oxford, Balliol College, MS 271 (cartulary of St Guthlac's, Hereford), fos.90r-v, no.397. s.xiv in.

Universis sancte matris ecclesie filiis ad quos presens scriptum pervenerit Robertus dei gratia Heref' episcopus eternam in domino salutem. Ad officium nostre sollicitudini commissum*ᵃ* pertinere arbitramur ea que canonice et rationabiliter coram nobis gesta sunt scripto*ᵇ* commendare ne quo forte modo neglecta oblivionis fuco obliterata depereant sed diligenter scripti memorie inserta inperpetuum reserventur inconcussa et permaneant illibata. Inde est quod venerabilium et dilectorum in Cristo fratrum, videlicet Thome dei gratia abbatis et totius conventus Glouc' et fratris Garini de Neapol' tunc prioris de Hospitali Ierosolimitano per Angliam, inspecta carta, in qua plenius continetur ad quem transactionis finem eidem fratres tandem devoverunt de ecclesia Sancti Michaelis de Sutton' unde diu litigabant, eidem transactioni auctoritatis nostre robur accommodavimus*ᶜ* que videlicet in hunc modum facta est: fratres prefati hospitalis tenebunt inperpetuum prescriptam ecclesiam Sancti Michaelis de Sutton' cum capella de Wystanestowe, et decimis Eaddefoni,*ᵈ* et decimis unius virgate terre in Magen', et cum terra et prato et decimis et obventionibus omnibus tam ecclesie quam capelle pertinentibus de abbate et conventu Glouc' et priore et monachis Hereford' sub pensione quatuordecim solidorum solvenda annuatim pro ea priori pro tempore et monachis Hereford duobus terminis, videlicet vii s' in annunciatione beate Marie et vii solidorum in festo Sancti Michaelis, celebranda hac solutione apud Heref' in domo monachorum Sancti Petri et Sancti Guthlaci per manum fratris pro tempore qui redditus hospitalis in Heref' [fo.90v] comitatu procurabit. Quod si domus hospitalis huic transactioni non steterit, postquam hoc priori domus hospitalis per Angliam denunciatum fuerit et solutionis cessatio demonstrata et non infra xl dies post denunciationem factam satisfactum, transactis xl diebus licitum erit prefatis monachis prenotatam ecclesiam de Sutton' nostra auctoritate tanquam suam de iure ingredi et sibi retinere. Fratres autem hospitalis de eadem ecclesia episcopalia solvent nichil quocumque iure sibi vendicabunt in parochia Sancti Nich(olai) de minori Sutton. Et quia transactionem hanc ratam et inconcussam in perpetuum permanere desideramus, eam nostra episcopali auctoritate et presentis carte patrocinio confirmamus et sigilli nostri appositione roboramus.[e] Hiis testibus: Waltero Linc' ecclesie cancellario, Hugone archidiacono Salopesir', Willelmo fratre Radulfi archidiaconi, Waltero de Colwell, Iohanne canonico <et>[f] Eluredo, capellanis nostris, Bartholomeo, Reginaldo,[g] Rannulfo, Osberto clericis nostris, Willelmo camerario et aliis.

[a]commissit. [b]scriptu. [c]accomodavimus. [d]sic, presumably for Yeddevenne, i.e. Edvin. [e]roboravimus. [f]om. [g]Reiqm', sic, presumably for Regin'.

Balliol College MS 271, fo.89v, no.395 is a copy of the composition between Garnier of Nâblus, Abbot Thomas of Gloucester and William, prior of St Guthlac's, about the church of St Michael of Sutton, dated 1185, which is contained in an inspeximus issued by Roger de Molendino, custos of the Hospital of Jerusalem, while he was on a visit to London with the Patriarch Heraclius of Jerusalem (for the date of Heraclius' visit to England, January to April 1185, see R.C.Smail, 'Latin Syria and the West, 1149-1187', TRHS, 5th ser. xix (1969), 18-19. Roger's inspeximus is dated 19 March 1185 (he must presumably have reckoned the start of the year from Christmas Day). The priory of the Hospitallers at Dinmore in Sutton was apparently founded in the latter years of the reign of Henry II: W.Rees, A history of the Order of St John of Jerusalem in Wales and on the Welsh border (Cardiff 1947), 39-40, and see also nos.132, 157. 'Magen' referred to above is probably the 'Mage' of Domesday Book, i, fo.183, which is at Freen's Court, Sutton.

157. St Guthlac's priory, Hereford

Notification of the composition between the Hospitallers of Dinmore (in Sutton) and the prior of St Guthlac's, Hereford, concerning the burials at Sutton St Michael.   [?1185 × 9 May 1186]

B = Oxford, Balliol College, MS 271 (cartulary of St Guthlac's, Hereford), fo.89r, no.393. s.xiv in.

Robertus dei gratia Herefordensis episcopus universis sancte matris ecclesie filiis salutem et benedictionem. Noverit universitas vestra hanc conventionem factam esse inter Alanum hospitalarium de Sutton' et fratres eiusdem loci et inter*a* priorem Hereford. Alanus et fratres predicti in presentia nostra promiserunt se nullos homines recepturos sepeliendos*b* in cimiterio suo quod apud Sutton habent, in parochia ecclesie de Sutton' que ibidem est, preter suos professos, eos videlicet qui in vita sua castitatem voverint, propriis renunciaverint*c* et habitum illorum susceperint, servientes de mensa sua, non uxoratos, non habentes mansiones extra curiam hospitalariorum et peregrinos ibidem decubantes. Preterea Alanus et fratres promiserunt quod conventionem istam sigillo prioris sui de Anglia et capitulo corroboraverint;*d* concesserunt etiam quod si a conventione ista recesserint dominus Heref' qui ibi pro tempore fuerit in capella sua de Suttu' divina celebrare prohibeat. Quod in posterum ratum et inconcussum permaneat nos sigilli nostri auctoritate confirmavimus.

*a*sic B. *b*sepiliendos. *c*renunciaverunt. *d*coroboraverunt.

This agreement may have been made after no.156 above. The composition between Alan and the prior of St Guthlac's can be found ibid., fo.89r, no.392. As early as ?1174 × 1181 Alexander III, at the request of the bp of Hereford, probably Robert Foliot, not Gilbert Foliot or Robert de Melun, had ordered the Hospitallers not to go beyond the terms of their privileges where burial was concerned: see above, no.132. By 1189 Alan appears to have become prior of Holy Cross, Winchester; he had been succeeded as prior of Dinmore by William (*Hereford charters*, 34).

*158. Chapel of St Mary Magdalen, Hereford

Grant or confirmation of a grant to St Mary Magdalen's chapel (the episcopal chapel, Hereford), of oblations on solemn days from the episcopal household and of the tithe from Hereford market.

[6 October 1174 × 9 May 1186]

Mention only, in no.198 below. Bps Gilbert Foliot and Robert de Melun also made grants to the chapel and it is not possible to distinguish who made which donation. The chapel of St Mary Magdalen was part of the episcopal chapel (see note to no.343).

159. Hugh de Lacy

Composition between the bishop and Hugh de Lacy, concerning the knight service due from the latter to the bishop for Holme Lacy.

3 June 1177

A? =Hereford Cathedral Library MS O. 6. xii, fo.193v. s.xii med. The agreement is written on the verso of the last leaf in a hand later than that of the rest of the manuscript, s.xii 2/2.

Pd, *A descriptive catalogue of the manuscripts in the Hereford cathedral library*, ed. A.T.Bannister (Hereford, 1927), 71-2, and by H.M.Colvin, 'Holme Lacy: An episcopal manor and its tenants in the twelfth and thirteenth centuries', in V.Ruffer and A.J.Taylor, edd., *Medieval studies presented to Rose Graham* (Oxford 1950), Appendix I, 36-37.

Ne lites semel terminate iterum ex malignitate alicuius seu oblivione resuscitentur ⸵ earum finem scripto commendare est necessarium. Cum itaque inter. Robertum Foliot Hereford' episcopum. et Hugonem de Laci fuisset controversia super servitio et hundredfe de terra que dicitur Hamma episcopo exigente plenum servitium duorum militum et hundredfe Hugone autem dicente se debere plenum servitium unius militis. et alterius tantum ad monstrationem et hundredfe omnino nichil ⸵ ipsa tandem hoc modo sopita est. Predictus Hugo recognovit in magna audientia se debere plenum servitium duorum militum de predicta terra Hereford' episcopo. et hundredfe quantum debetur de .vi. hudis guldandis que dicuntur esse in Hamma. Et hoc se absque contradictione plene soluturum in manu episcopi fideliter reddidit. Relevium quoque duorum militum quod retro fuit reddidit. Relevium unius militis reddendo una manu in unam manum episcopi. et relevium alterius militis altera manu in alteràm manum episcopi. et de hundredfe quod retro fuit ⸵ prefato R. episcopo solvendo satis fecit in capitulo Herefordensi ubi hec pax et recognitio facta fuit. Preterea convenit ut prefatus Hugo annuatim ad festum beati Martini solvat prebende quam Will' de Stoca habet in Herefordensi ecclesia .xx. solidos. pro terra que Oniberia dicitur. de quibus solidis dissensio erat an ab ipso Hugone. an a Willelmo milite solvi deberent. Hec pax facta fuit anno ab incarnatione domini nostri Iesu Cristi. m'. c. lxxvii. iii. Non'. Iunii.[a]

[a]*Underneath in a smaller hand someone else has copied out* Ne lites .... est necessarium.

On the disputed fiefs see no.2 above. Reginald, Bp Robert Foliot's chaplain until *c.* 1180 and thereafter probably chaplain of St Mary Magdalen's chapel, left a glossed psalter to Hereford cathedral chapter (Hereford cathedral obituary book, Bodl. MS Rawlinson B328, fo.2r); if this psalter was Hereford Cathedral Library MS O. 6. xii (a glossed psalter) he may possibly have been the scribe of this agreement. It is conceivable that this is the original; certainly it is contemporary.

160. Jordan of *Tanton*'

Grant to his serjeant Jordan of Tanton' *of a virgate at Warham in Breinton and of nine acres in Adamshill.*   [1179 × 9 May 1186]

A = Hereford D. & C. Muniments, no.1365. 15th century endorsement: litera Roberti episcopi de terra de Werham. 143 × 102 mm. Remains of tags for two seals, which do not survive.

Pd, *Hereford charters*, 21.

Universis sancte matris ecclesie filiis ⫶ Robertus dei gratia Herefordensis episcopus ⫶ eternam in domino salutem. Universitati vestre notum facimus nos concessisse et dedisse Iordano de Tanton', servienti nostro. pro servitio suo unam virgatam terre apud Warham. illam videlicet⫶ quam Ernulfus marescalcus tenuit⫶ libere et quiete ab omni servitio iure hereditario tenendam⫶ pro quatuor solidis. annuatim. Dedimus insuper eidem Iordano. pro servitio suo. novem acras super Adamishill'. libere et quiete pro decem et octo denariis. annuis ; iure hereditario possidendas. Ut autem héé donationes nostre perpetuam optineant firmitatem ; ipsas presenti scripto et sigilli nostri testimonio confirmamus. Hiis testibus. Radulfo Heref' archidiacono. Waltero senescallo. W. de Stoch'. W. fratre archidiaconi. W. camerario. Reginaldo filio Morini. Petro de Parco. Ernulfo pincerna. Mainardo de Burcota. et Radulfo filio eius. Henrico marescallo. Ricardo de Kent. Hugone de Fulch'. Ricardo scriptore. et multis aliis.

Ralph Foliot became archdn in 1179.

161. Kenilworth priory

Notification as papal judge-delegate of the composition of the case between Kenilworth Priory and Stoneleigh Abbey concerning the tithes of Stoneleigh church.   1180

B = BL Add. MS 47677 (Kenilworth Cartulary), fos.128v-129r. s.xvi, after 1514.

Universis sancte matris ecclesie filiis R. dei gratia Hereford' episcopus perpetuam in domino salutem. Universitati vestre notum facimus quod, cum causa que vertebatur inter canonicos de Kenell' et monachos de Stanley super decimis de Stanley nobis ab apostolica sede, appellatione remota, cognoscenda et terminanda commissa fuisset, eadem causa, partibus in presentia nostra constitutis, hoc fine quievit. [fo.129r] Ex parte siquidem monachorum de Stanley per manum N. abbatis et monachorum suorum in manu nostra fideliter promissum est, quod monasterium de Stanley solvet inperpetuum, pro memoratis decimis, v marcas argenti et dimidiam monasterio de Kenell', et dimittet eidem monasterio de Kenell' omnes terras et tenuras^a quas die transactionis tenebat, in pace et sine querela inperpetuum tenendas; adiectum quoque est ex parte monasterii de Stanley et in manu nostra fecerunt promissum quod si contigerit idem monasterium de Stanley terras aliquas infra parochiam de Stanley, vel alias parochias ecclesiarum de Kenell', terras aliquas quocumque modo acquirere, ex quibus emolumentum decimarum ecclesiis de Kenell' die transactionis pervenerit, monasterium de Stanley inde decimas sine contradictione persolvet. Quicquid autem retro temporibus de decimis ad ecclesiam de Stanley pertinentibus a monachis de Stanley detentum est: ad instanciam nostram, pro bono pacis, prior et canonici de Kenell' eis humiliter remiserunt. Et hanc transactionem se fideliter inperpetuum servaturos in manu nostra promiserunt. Facta est hec transactio anno ab incarnatione domini millesimo c^{o}lxxx^o super predictis decimis, memorata pecunia singulis annis de cetero ex integro ad festum Sancti Michaelis persolvenda. Quod quia ratum et inconcussum inposterum manere volumus, auctoritate domini Alexandri pape et nostra presentis etiam scripti sigilli quoque nostri testimonio confirmamus.

^{a}temmras *sic* B.

The case was originally delegated to Roger, bp of Worcester, who died in 1179, and to Robert Foliot, for John, prior of Trentham, wrote to them to give evidence about an earlier settlement by Bp Walter of Coventry (1149-1159). John's letter, *ibid.*, fo.128r-v, refers to Roger as 'A', but, as Mary Cheney points out, this must be a mistake (*Roger, Bishop of Worcester, 1164-1179* [Oxford 1980], 373). The Kenilworth cartulary contains another notification, described as a chirograph, of the settlement (BL Add. MS 47677, fo.129r-v), which is dated 1180, in the 20th year of Alexander III; as the 20th year of Alexander III ran from September 1178 to September 1179, it is conceivable that this might have been the date of the original mandate and that the clerk drafting the chirograph used it without thinking. Abbot N. of Stoneleigh was Nicholas, c.1178-88.

162. Lire abbey

Confirmation to the abbey of Lire in Normandy of its possessions in the diocese of Hereford: the churches of Tidenham, Lydney, Linton, Much Marcle, Fownhope, Dewsall, Eardisland, Tenbury Wells, and Wilton.
[6 October 1174 × 9 May 1186]

B = BN Collection Moreau, MS 276 (extracts from the cartulary of Lire abbey), fos.135r-6r. s.xviii (1764 × 1789). Contained in an inspeximus of Bp William de Vere, see below, no.218.

C = Dom Lenoir MSS, vol. xxiii (extracts from the cartulary of Lire abbey), collection of Mme la Marquise de Mathan, Sémilly, Manche, fo.33r, no.85. s.xviii. (Consulted from microfilm in the Borthwick Institute, York). Also contained in William de Vere's inspeximus.

Summarised, Evreux, A-D Eure H590, fo.325r, no. xiv. Summary only, of William's inspeximus. s.xviii.

Universis sancte matris ecclesie filiis Robertus dei gratia Hereford' ecclesie dictus episcopus salutem quam a domino speramus. Ex suscepte sollicitudinis [fo.135v B] officio viris religiosis provida dispensatione providere tenemur, ut tanto liberius contemplationi et orationi vacare debeant quanto in exterioribus victualium necessitatibus uberius habundant.[a] Eapropter Lirensis monasterii mediocritate considerata, cuius fundatio non in amplis terrarum possessionibus, sed in ecclesiis potius et decimationibus consistere noscitur, monachis in eodem monasterio divino mancipatis officio ad hospitum susceptionem et ad diffusioris[b] caritatis amplificationem, ecclesias cum capellis et omnibus pertinentiis suis quas in nostro habere noscuntur presulatu, videlicet ecclesiam de Tehedam,[c] ecclesiam de Lideneia, ecclesiam de Linton', ecclesiam de Merkelai, ecclesiam de Hopa, ecclesiam de Fonte-David, ecclesiam de Orleslen', ecclesiam de Thameteb'i,[d] ecclesiam de Wilton, votive pietatis studio concedimus et eis pontificali auctoritate roboramus. Verum ut vicariis[e] onus et curam regendarum animarum suscepturis honesta et sufficiens sustentatio ex prescriptis ecclesiis ministrentur, ipsis tertiam portionem omnium decimarum, oblationum et omnium obventionum ad iam dictas ecclesias sive [fo.136r *B*] ad altare aut cimiterium spectantium assignamus. Ne ergo posteritas evacuet quod equitate previa statuta esse cognoscitur, illud presentis scripti serie et sigilli nostri impressione duximus muniendum.

*a*habeant *B*.   *b*corr. from diffusionis *B*.   *c*sic for Tedeham *BC*.   *d*Gametheb'i *B*.
*e*Verum invicariis *B*.

For Lire's possessions in the diocese of Hereford see also nos.101, 218, 305 and 354.

163. Lire abbey

Recognition, at the dedication of the chapel of St Briavels, that it belongs to Lydney Church and that both belong to the Abbey of Lire.
[1179 × 9 May 1186]

B = Bodl., MS Rawlinson B329 (Hereford cathedral cartulary), fo.161v. s.xiii-xiv. C = *Ibid.*, fo.163v. D = *Ibid.*, fo.165v; contained in an inspeximus of Richard, Cardinal of Sant' Angelo.

Pd, *Mon. Ang.*, vi, pt. ii, 1094, no. xii, omitting the witness list. The text below is taken from *D*.

Universis sancte matris ecclesie filiis R. dei gratia Herefordensis ecclesie*a* episcopus eternam in Cristo salutem. Universitati vestre notum facimus coram nobis recognitum fuisse in dedicatione capelle de Sancto Briavello,*b* quam deo annuente fecimus, ipsam esse capellam pertinentem ad ecclesiam de Lyden' et utramque, videlicet ecclesiam de Lyden' et capellam de Sancto Braivello,*c* pertinere ad perpetuum ius Lyrensis monasterii*d* cum omnibus pertinentiis earum. Huius recognitionis testes sunt Radulfus archidiaconus Herefordensis, Magister Nicholaus,*e* Magister Eustachius,*f* Teobaldus elemosinarius, Willelmus frater Radulfi archidiaconi, Walterus de Ros, Alard de Dymmok et multi alii.

*a*ecclesie *om. C*.   *b*Brayvel *B;* Braivel *C*.   *c*Brayvello *B;* Braivel *C*.   *d*mon. *D*.
*e*Text of C ends here with the words *et multi alii*.
*f*Text of B ends here with the words *et alii multi*.

Ralph Foliot became archdn in 1179. See also no.221.

*164. Lire abbey

Letter of the bishops of Hereford and Worcester (Robert Foliot and Baldwin) to Lucius III requesting him to confirm to the abbey of Lire its possessions in their two dioceses.

[1 September 1181 × December 1184]

Mention only, in a summary of an inspeximus by Peter of Aigueblanche, bp of Hereford 1240-68, of various documents including a bull of Lucius III (Evreux, A-D Eure H590, fo.327r, no.xxviii). Lucius' bull mentions a letter in which the bishops asked him to confirm the possessions of Lire in the two dioceses concerned. Lucius was pope from 1181 to 1185; Baldwin was translated to Canterbury in December 1184 and his successor at Worcester was not elected until 1186.

*165. Llanthony priory

Confirmation to Llanthony priory of a grant by William Torel of the advowson of the church of Pencombe. [6 October 1174 × 9 May 1186]

Mention only, *CRR*, xi (1223-4), 232, no.1144.

166. Llanthony priory

Confirmation to Llanthony priory of grants made by his predecessors.

[13 August 1178 (prob. *c.*1180) × 9 May 1186]

B = PRO, C115 K1/6679 (Llanthony cartulary, A9), fos.116r-v. s.xiii med. C = PRO, C115 K2/6683 (Llanthony cartulary, A1), fos.123r-v, section vi, no.xxix. s.xiv med.

Universis sancte matris ecclesie filiis ad quos presens carta pervenerit Robertus Foliot dei gratia Hereford' ecclesie minister humilis eternam in domino salutem. Quoniam ecclesiastice possessiones a Cristi fidelibus in elemosinam viris religiosis collate exquisitis calumpniantium versutiis non numquam turbari solent, necesse est illas magnorum virorum et fide dignorum testimonio necnon et autenticorum scriptorum patrocinio communiri. Inde est quod, Lanthon' ecclesie et venerabilibus et deo dilectis canonicis regularibus ibidem deo servientibus paterna pietate et benignitate prospicere cupientes, inspectis cartis sanctorum patrum predecessorum nostrorum, quorum vestigiis inherere eorumque canonica statuta sequi optamus, omnia beneficia iam percepta seu in futurum canonice percipienda prefate ecclesie Lanthon' et canonicis nostra episcopali auctoritate et presentis scripti patrocinio confirmamus et sigilli nostri appositione roboramus. Confirmamus itaque eis terram extra burgum Hereford' que Mora vocatur liberam et quietam ab omni servitio et consuetudine, excepto quod una hyda terre de Holemera solummodo regis geldum persolvit, mansionem etiam^a quam Ernaldus presbiter tenuerat extra burgum Hereford' cum x acris terre liberam et quietam ab omni servitio et consuetudine, similiter et acram unam mansioni prefate contiguam de terra Fulconis, ecclesiam quoque de Froma cum omnibus pertinentiis suis,^{b} et duas ecclesias in Prestebur', unam sub montibus, alteram super montes, scilicet ecclesiam de Sevenhanton' cum terris et decimis aliisque elemosinis omnibus eisdem ecclesiis pertinentibus aut contingentibus, exceptis duabus portionibus decime de dominio meo quas habent decanus et cantor Hereford', de blado scilicet tantum et de leguminibus – de parco autem de [fo.116v B] Presteberia et de hiis que seminantur vel colliguntur intra designatum ambitum parchi decima remanet ecclesie de Presteb' quia terra fuit villanorum – tria quoque exarta in Presteberia^c que Leuricus Figulus et Lewynus^d Rufus et Erni per ix denariorum redditum per annum tenuerunt, que prefatus episcopus R. per xii denariorum redditum per annum tenenda et <ad>^{e} ecclesiam de Prestebur' pertinenda in perpetuam elemosinam concessit et dedit, unam etiam virgatam terre in eadem villa quam Ernaldus miles dedit eidem ecclesie quando vitam suam in ea mutavit, liberam et quietam ab omni servitio et consuetudine, ita ut heredes eius idem servitium quod pro ea facere debebant de reliquo feodo suo persolvant, preterea dimidiam virgatam terre in eadem villa, cum brachia quadam que eidem appendere solet, quam concedente Gilleberto^f Episcopo Radulfus predicti Ernaldi filius cum matre sua, quando eam in sororem susceperunt in perpetuam elemosinam dedit liberam et quietam ab omni servitio et consuetudine,^{g} ita ut ipse et heredes eius idem servitium quod pro hac terra episcopo debent de reliquo feodo suo persolvant; ex eiusdem quoque Radulfi donatione x acras^h terre quas dedit in perpetuam elemosinam, liberas et quietas ab omni servitio et consuetudine. Hec omnia sicut singula in singulis cartis predecessorum nostrorum episcopi Roberti et episcopi Gilberti, item Roberti confirmata legimus

unum in scriptum redigentes nostri quoque sigilli inpressione in
presentia subscriptorum testium confirmamus: Hugonis archidiaconi
Solopesir',[i] Magistri Mauricii medici, Iohannis canonici et aliorum.

[a]et *sic BC.*   [b]suis pertinentiis *C.*   [c]Prestebiria *C.*   [d]Lefwynus *C.*
[e]ad *omitted, but surely necessary for sense.*   [f]corr. from episcopo Gilleberto *C.*   [g]acris *C.*
[h]sic BC.   [i]sic BC.

Hugh became archdn of Shropshire *c.*1180; his predecessor died 13 August 1178.
For the charters of Robert de Béthune, Gilbert Foliot and Robert de Melun see
above nos.33-7, 103-4 and 121; see also nos.225 and 276.

167. Luffield priory

*Decision by Robert Foliot and Abbot Adam of Evesham, as papal
judges-delegate, in a case between Luffield priory and Hamo son of
Menfelin.*   [1177 × 1184]

A = Westminster Abbey Muniments, no.2857. 14th century endorsements: De
Ric' Herefordensis episcopi iur'. De ecclesia de Torneberge. xiii. 190 x 62 mm;
two seals, attached by tags. Left-hand seal: pointed oval, natural wax, 80 mm
long by 49 mm wide, partly damaged at base and top; bishop in full pontificals,
his right hand raised in benediction; legend: .... DEI
GRA...............ORDENSIS E?......... ; Secretum, 25 mm long by 20 mm wide,
gem of uncertain design; legend: + SIGILLUM ROBERTI. Right-hand seal:
pointed oval, natural wax, 70 mm long by 50 mm wide; figure of an abbot
holding a book in his left hand and carrying his staff in his right; legend:
S.GILL.............. (?ADE)............. (S)HAM.E........ ; no secretum.

B = Westminster Abbey Muniments, Book 10 (Luffield priory cartulary), fo.25r-
v.

Pd, C.R.Cheney, *From Becket to Langton* (Manchester 1956), 188-89, and *Luffield
priory charters*, i.45, no.39.

.R. dei gratia Herefordensis episcopus et .A. eadem gratia abbas
Evesham(en)sis omnibus ad quos litere iste pervenerint salutem.
Noverit universitas vestra quod causa que vertebatur inter priorem
de Luffeld. et Hamonem filium Menfelini nobis a domino papa
delegata[j] in presentia domini regis taliter terminata est. quod prior et
monachi petitionem quam habuerunt super cella predicti .H. de
Bradewella et monacho et eclesiis[a] de terra .H. eidem .H. et heredibus
suis omnino remiserunt et iuri quod se in eis habere asserebant in
perpetuum renuntiaverunt. Sepenominatus vero .H. assensu uxoris
sue et heredis sui prefatis priori et monachis et ecclesie de Luffeld.

decimam tocius panis sui de dominio lucro suo dedit et in perpetuum concessit. et ecclesiam preterea de Torneberga :ᵃ eis dedit liberam et quietam cum omnibus ad eandem ecclesiam pertinentiis.ᵇ Nos autem utriusque sigillo certificati hanc compositionem prescriptam sigillorum nostrorum munimine confirmamus.

ᵃ*sic.*   ᵇ*sic for* pertinentibus.

Elvey (*Luffield priory charters*) dates this charter *c.*1180 × 1184; Hamo son of Menfelin died in 1184, but there is no obvious explanation for Elvey's *terminus a quo.* However the charter is later than *Luffield priory charters,* no.36, which can be dated 1177 × 1182. Adam was abbot of Evesham from 1161 to 1189. Luffield priory's claim to Bradwell probably arose from the circumstance of its former prior, William, who died 12 December 1164, having been simultaneously prior of Bradwell (*HRH*, 30, 53).

168. Ranulf fitz Ranulf

Grant to Ranulf, son of Master Ranulf the canon, of the land on which his house stands and of a field and a garden, to hold as his father and grandfather held them.
                [10 August 1180 × 31 December 1183, ? probably early]

A = Hereford D. & C. Muniments, no.1382. 14th century endorsement: Carta R episcopi apud Berton. 160 × 92 mm. Sealed on a tag; seal 75 mm long × 48 mm wide; green wax, pointed oval, figure of a bishop raising his right hand in benediction and holding a staff in his left hand; legend: +ROB..TUS.DEI.GRATIA .... EPISCOPUS.IIII ; no reverse or counterseal.
Pd, *Hereford charters*, 24.

R. dei gratia Hereford' episcopus omnibus episcopis in ecclesia Hereford' canonice substituendis ceterisque eiusdem ecclesie tam prelatis quam subditis :ʲ salutem. Noverit universitas vestra nos concessisse et reddidisse in feudo et iure hereditario Rann(ulfo) filio Magistri Rann(ulfi) canonici nostri terram in qua domus eiusdem Magistri Rann(ulfi) canonici nostri sita est. cum omnibus pertinentiis suis. scilicet agro qui est apud Cocedehull'. et orto quodam qui est apud Berton'. tenendam sicut pater et avus suus eam tenuerunt concessione et donatione antecessorum nostrorum episcoporum et sicut eorum carte testantur. quas nos inspeximus. et pro eodem servitio faciendo quod in eisdem cartis predecessorum nostrorum continetur. Preterea concessimus ei et donavimus mansuram quandam que est prope predictam domum sicut antecessores nostri episcopi supradicto Magistro Rann(ulfo) concesserunt et per idem servitium quod in eorum cartis continetur. Hiis testibus. G. Hereford' decano. Ivone thesaurario. Ricardo Barre archidiacono Lexov(iensi). Magistro David. Magistro Symone. Willelmo de Stoches. Roberto de Landa. Hugone Foliot. Roberto de Hesel'. Toma Cruc. Waltero filio Helye. Roberto.

Richard Barre was instituted as a canon of Hereford by Bp Baldwin of Worcester, who was consecrated on 10 August 1180. Hugh Foliot became archdn of Shropshire in or shortly after 1180. Dean Geoffrey died on 31 December 1180 × 1183. For Master Ranulf and Ranulf his son, see above, no.123, and below, no.199.

169. Reading abbey

Notification (issued as bishop-elect) as papal judge-delegate of the settlement between Roger fitz Maurice on the one hand and Abbot Joseph and the monks of Reading on the other concerning the tithes of the demesne of Hampton Court near Leominster, which Roger claimed belonged to his church of Bacton: Reading Abbey allowed Roger to have the tithes in his lifetime on payment of a pension of a gold piece every year.

[April 1173 × 6 October 1174]

B = BL Egerton MS 3031 (Reading abbey cartulary), fo.55v. s.xii ex. C = *Ibid.*, fo.56v. D = BL Cotton MS Domitian A iii (Leominster priory cartulary), fos.59v-60r. s.xiii med.

Pd, *Reading cartularies*, i.279-80, no.344.

The dates are fixed by Robert Foliot's election and consecration. Roger fitz Maurice was a canon of Hereford, owned much property within the city of Hereford and was dean of the Vale of Evesham until his expulsion by the monks of Evesham in 1206 (*Chronicon abbatiae de Evesham*, ed. W.D.Macray, RS [1863], 196). The name Bacton is given as *Rokintun'* in B, *Bakint'* in C, and *Bachintun'* in D. See also no.267.

170. Reading abbey

Notification by Bishop Robert Foliot and Simon, abbot of St Albans, as papal judges-delegate, of the settlement of the dispute between Reading Abbey and St Augustine's Abbey, Bristol, concerning the churches of Berkeley: Bristol is to hold the churches in the name of the monks of

Reading for an annual payment of 20 marks, and both abbeys are to try to recover whatever has been detained by Gloucester Abbey or anyone else, which they will then divide in equal shares; Henry II has stated that he will ensure that as long as Henry, archdeacon of Exeter, lives, he (the archdeacon) will pay the 20 marks to Reading and whatever is due to the canons of Bristol. London, St. Luke's Day (18 October), 1175

B = BL Egerton MS 3031 (Reading abbey cartulary), fos.53v-4r. s.xii ex. C = BL Cotton MS Vespasian E xxv (Reading abbey cartulary), fo.119r. s.xiv in.

Pd, *Reading cartularies*, i.229-31, no.277.

Celebrata autem fuit hec transactio anno dominice incarnationis m°.c°.lxx°.v° die festo Sancti Luce evangeliste apud Londoniam. His t'[a] Henrico II rege Anglorum, Ricardo Cant' archiepiscopo, Gisleberto Lond' episcopo,[b] Ricardo episcopo Wint',[c] Roberto episcopo Heref', Bartholomeo episcopo Exon', Gaufrido episcopo Elyensi, Simone abbate Sancti Albani et ceteris.[d]

[a]*C reads* Teste *for* His t'. [b]G. episcopo London' C.
[c]*Text of B ends here with the words* Et multis aliis. [d]cetera C..

On the background to the case, see note in *Reading cartularies, loc. cit.*, and B.R.Kemp, 'The Churches of Berkeley Hernesse', *TBGAS*, lxxxvii (1968), 96-110. Henry archdeacon of Exeter was a son of Robert fitzHarding, lord of Berkeley, who granted the churches of Berkeley Hernesse, which he named as Berkeley, Wotton under Edge, Beverstone, Ashleworth, and Almondsbury, to his foundation of Bristol abbey soon after 1142; however Robert granted the churches to Henry to hold for his lifetime (Kemp, *art. cit.*, 101).

171. Richard Foliot

Grant of land (at Warpsgrove, Oxfordshire) to Richard Foliot; Ralph Foliot, the tenant, had resigned it in favour of his son Richard.
[1179, prob. *c.*1180 × 9 May 1186]

B = Bodl. MS Wood Empt. 10 (Sandford cartulary), fo.43v. s.xiii ex.

Pd, *Sandford cartulary*, i.122, no.170.

Hiis testibus, Hugone Salopschir' archidiacono, Willelmo fratre Radulfi archidiaconi, Waltero senescallo, Iohanne et Aluredo capellanis, Bartholomeo et Osberto clericis episcopi, Iohanne de Stanf',

Bernardo de Sapi, Roberto de Lacy, Willelmo camerario, Galfrido de camera et aliis.

Hugh Foliot probably became archdn of Shropshire c.1180, and Ralph Foliot became archdn of Hereford in 1179. This charter does not mention where the land in question was situated, but it must be the land at at Warpsgrove which Richard Foliot granted to the Templars in the 1220s: see *Sandford cartulary*, i.115-17.

172. Richard of Kent

Notification of a composition between Llanthony Priory and Robert's servant Richard of Kent concerning a piece of land at Prestbury.
[1179 × 9 May 1186]

B = PRO, C115 K2/6683, fo.125r (Llanthony cartulary A1). s.xiv med.

Robertus dei gratia Hereford' episcopus universis Cristi fidelibus salutem in domino. Universitatem vestram scire volumus et memoriter tenere dilectos nobis in Cristo R. priorem et conventum de Lanthon' petitione nostra concessisse Ricardo de Kent servienti nostro terram quandam apud Prestebur' quam Wulvericus tenuerat de eis, sub annuo censu trium solidorum et sex denariorum quamdiu^a in seculari habitu vixerit tenendam. Post mortem vero Ricardi prefata terra sine contradictione ad predictum conventum revertetur. Hec conventio facta fuit in capitulo de Lanthon' nobis petentibus, Willelmo fratre archid(iaconi) et Waltero de Colewell' vices nostras agentibus.

^{a}quam diu B.

The prior referred to is Roger of Norwich (-1174 – c.1189). Ralph Foliot became archdn 1179.

173. Richard of Kent

Grant of land at The Burcott in Holmer to his servant, Richard of Kent, who had nursed him when he was ill.
[1181 × 9 May 1186, probably late]

A = Hereford D. & C. Muniments, no.1381. No ancient endorsements. 217 × 140 mm, two tags, no seals remaining. Writing pale and in places ink coming away from the parchment.

Pd, *Hereford charters*, 25-6.

Universis sancte matris ecclesie filiis ad quos presens carta pervenerit? Robertus Foliot dei gratia Hereford' ecclesie minister humilis eternam in domino salutem. Noverit universitas vestra nos concessisse et dedisse servienti nostro Ricardo de Cantia qui nobis in nostra infirmitate nocte dieque sedulo ministravit. pro servitio suo terram de Burcot' extra burgum Hereford'. libere et quiete imperpetuum tenendam sibi et heredibus suis de nobis et nostris successoribus pro viginti solidis annuatim inde episcopo Hereford' pro omni servitio reddendis. quorum medietatem in annuntiatione beate Marie. et aliam medietatem in festo Sancti Michaelis Ricardus vel eius heres reddent.[a] Quod quia in perpetuum manere volumus ratum et firmum? presentis carte patrocinio confirmavimus. et sigilli nostri appositione roboravimus prohibentes nequis[b] super hoc tenemento inferat Ricardo et suis heredibus molestiam vel gravamen. His testibus Iordano decano Heref'. Hugone archidiacono Salopesir'. Ivone thesaurario. Willelmo Foliot. Rogero filio Mauricii. Magistro Willelmo medico? canonicis nostris. Iohanne et Aluredo capellanis nostris. Waltero de Colewell'. Ernaldo de S[t]oc'. Reginaldo de Uppet'. Rannulfo de Salewarp. O<sberto> et Henrico clericis nostris. Willelmo Folet. Roberto de la Hesel'. Hugone fratre eius. Iohanne de Stanford'. Willelmo laminario. Petro de parco. Henrico de Bath'. Germano. coco. Henrico marescallo. Samsone pistore. Reginaldo de la Mare. Henrico de Stanf'. Galfrido et Iohanne fratribus Iordani decani. Radulfo de Burcot'. Iordano de Tant'. Willelmo de Ipr'. Henrico Foliot. Alano de Alcrug'. Samuhel. Alano de la Dune. Alano de la Walle.

[a]*sic.* [b]*written as one word.*

Jordan became dean not before 1181 (his predecessor died 31 December 1180 × 1183). The mention of Robert Foliot's illness and the appearance of a doctor among the witnesses suggest that this charter may have been issued towards the end of Robert's life.

174. Shrewsbury abbey

Settlement, as papal judge-delegate, of a dispute between Shrewsbury Abbey and the sons of Fulk fitz Warin concerning the advowson of the church of Alberbury; Fulk gives Shrewsbury Abbey a virgate and a half at Tadlow, with tenants, free of all service except military service, which the monks or their lay tenants shall render to the tenant in chief.

[*c.*1180 × 9 May 1186]

B = NLW MS 7851 D (Shrewsbury abbey cartulary), pp.308-9, no.351. s.xiii ex. Pd, *Shrewsbury cartulary*, ii.316, no.351.

Hiis testibus, Radulfo, Ricardo, Warino filiis Fulconis, Magistro Roberto decano et aliis.

For the dating, see *Shrewsbury cartulary*, no.286.

*175. William the chamberlain

Grant to William the chamberlain of the land of Orlham in Ledbury.

[6 October 1174 × 9 May 1186]

Mention only, in a notification by Bishop William de Vere of the settlement of the case between William de Burchull and William the chamberlain concerning the land at Orlham, Hereford D. & C. Muniments, no.1363, pd., David Walker, 'Gloucester charters', in *A medieval miscellany for D.M.Stenton*, ed. P.M.Barnes and C.F.Slade, PRS, new ser., xxxvi (1962), 266, no.14, and below, no.239. William the chamberlain produced a charter of Robert Foliot granting him the land in support of his claim.

*176. William the janitor

Grant to William the janitor of lands in Prestbury.

[6 October 1174 × 9 May 1186]

Mention only, in a confirmation by Bp Giles de Braose of grants by Robert Foliot and Bp William de Vere, below, no.289.

177. Worcester Cathedral Priory

*Confirmation to Worcester Cathedral Priory of the parsonage of Lind-
ridge Church, granted and confirmed to Worcester by Bishops Robert de
Béthune and Gilbert Foliot.*   [6 October 1174 × 9 May 1186]

B = Worcester Cathedral Library, MS A4 (Worcester cathedral cartulary), fo.27r,
no.203. s.xiii med.

Pd, *Worcester cartulary*, 108, no.203.

Hiis testibus Willelmo de Stoc' etc'.

R.R.Darlington (*Worcester cartulary, loc. cit.*) attributes this charter to Bp Robert
de Melun, but since William de Stokes appears as the first witness (the original
witness list would have been much longer) it is probably a charter of Bp Robert
Foliot. William de Stokes probably became a canon of Hereford between 1174 and
1175: see Appendix I. See also nos.117, 241, 242, 290 and 291.

WILLIAM DE VERE

178.

Profession of obedience made to Baldwin, archbishop of Canterbury.
[10 August 1186]

A = Canterbury D. & C. Ch. Ant. C115/46. Possibly a holograph: see note. No ancient endorsements. 147 × 78 mm; not sealed.

B = Canterbury D. & C. Register A (The Prior's Register), fo.233r. s.xiv med.

Pd, *Canterbury professions*, 55, no.122.

+. Ego Willelmus Hereford'. ecclesie electus et a te reverende pater B. sancte Cant'. ecclesie archiepiscope. et totius Anglie primas consecrandus antistes. tibi et sancte Cant'. ecclesie et successoribus tuis canonice substituendis debitam et canonicam obedientiam et subiectionem me per omnia exhibiturum profiteor et promitto, et propria manu subscribendo confirmo. +

The crosses, presumably autograph, are written in the same colour of ink and probably with the same pen as the rest of the document.

179. Adam of Easton

Grant to his steward, Adam of Easton, of all his land of Easton for a rent of £10 a year.
[1196 × 24 December 1198]

A = PRO, E326/10846. 15th century endorsement: carta episcopi Willelmi de Ver de terra de Eston parva (?) Ade de Eston facta. The turnup and tag survive, but not the seal. 222 × 152 mm.

Pd from A, G.Stollberg, *Die soziale Stellung der intellektuellen Oberschicht im England des 12. Jahrhunderts* (Lübeck 1973), 168-169.

Omnibus Cristi fidelibus ad quos presens scriptum pervenerit *.* Willelmus de Ver dei gratia Hereford' episcopus. salutem in domino. Notum sit vobis me dedisse et concessisse. et hac carta mea confirmasse ? Ade de Estona homini et fideli meo. pro homagio et servicio suo. totam terram meam de Eston' cum omnibus pertinentiis suis. in bosco et plano. in pratis et pascuis. in viis et semitis. in dominiis. in liberis tenementis et villanagiis. in terra culta et inculta. et in omnibus rebus et consuetudinibus que quidem terra assignata fuit ecclesie Hereford' pro decem libratis terre. tenendam prefato Ade et heredibus suis. de me et successoribus meis episcopis. ad feodofirmam. sine omni instauramento. et sine domibus in curia. libere et quiete ab omni servicio et exactione ? reddendo inde annuatim michi et successoribus meis. pro omnibus rebus ? decem libras. ad quatuor terminos. scilicet ad Natale? quinquaginta solidos. ad annunciationem Sancte Marie ? quinquaginta solidos. ad festum Sancti Iohannis Baptiste? quinquaginta solidos. ad festum Sancti Michaelis? quinquaginta solidos. De hac vero terra homagium prenominati Ade in plena curia apud Herefordiam accepi. ipsamque terram cum omnibus pertinentiis suis? ego et successores mei debemus warantizare predicto Ade et heredibus suis? adversus omnes homines. Quod ut firmum et stabile perpetuo maneat? presenti carta et sigillo meo confirmavi. Hiis testibus. Ricardo decano Heref'. Radulfo eiusdem loci archidyacono. Hugone archidiacono de Salopesir' Waltero Map archidiacono Oxon'. Henrico de Mineriis. Willelmo de Saliceto. Iohanne de Kilpec. Gileberto Talebot. Magistro Nicholao de Hamton'. Magistro Osberto et Willelmo capellanis. Hugone de Hesela. Iohanne de Stanford'. et Henrico filio suo. Hugone de Dunr[a].*a* Hugone de Wauford'. Reginaldo Foliot. Alexandro de Estenor. Ricardo Britone. Mauricio de Cradelea. Gregorio de Everlea. et Willelmo. et Waltero et Thoma et Galfrido fratribus suis. Eustachio de Wttona et Iohanne de [Wika]*a* fratre suo. Petro Fulcherii et Ricardo fratre s[uo]*a* [Petro]*a* clerico de Linham. Et multis aliis.

*a*lacuna.

Walter Map became archdn of Oxford in 1196 or 1197. The witness list is very similar to that in Giles de Braose's confirmation (below, no.244), and is almost the same as that in no.180, another version of this grant, from which the lacunae in this charter have been supplied. *Estona* is Easton in Wiltshire (near Pewsey) (M.Jones, 'The Estates of the Cathedral Church of Hereford 1066-1317', unpubl. B.Litt. thesis, Oxford, 1958); Henry II had presided over a settlement between Robert Foliot and John, son of John the Marshall, over the manor of Inkberrow in Worcestershire, according to the terms of which Robert allowed John and his heirs to hold Inkberrow for the service of half a knight, and John quitclaimed ten librates in Easton (*Cal. Pat. Rolls, 1247-1258*, 259-60). The case was heard at Feckenham, probably in October 1175, since the settlement was witnessed by

Giles, bp of Evreux (ob.1180), who was escorting Henry's daughter Joan to Sicily in the autumn of 1176 when Henry visited Feckenham again (R.W.Eyton, *Court, Household and Itinerary of King Henry II* [London 1878], 206 for Giles escorting Princess Joan and 208 for Henry II's 1176 trip to Feckenham, in October). See also no.180.

180. Adam of Easton

Grant in feefarm of ten librates of land at Easton (another version of no.179).   [1196 × 24 December 1198]

A = Trowbridge, Wiltshire County Record Office 9/15/2 (Easton Priory Manuscripts); I am very grateful to Dr Brian Kemp for supplying me with this reference. Two early modern (16th c?) endorsements, in different hands: A graunt made by Will' Ver byshop of Herford to Adam of Eston of all the lande in Eston yeldding to the said byshop x li' by the yer etc'; to hand read the composition by Eredy (? Egidy) the bishop of Herrfurth <of> the land of Est<on>. 232 × 144 + 37 mm. Sealed with two seals on tags (left hand seal now detached). Left hand seal: pointed oval, in green wax, heavily varnished, depicting bishop in full pontificals, holding staff in left hand and raising the right in blessing. The impression is damaged at the base and sides and measures 70 × 43 mm. Legend: .SIG......................PI. Counterseal: Antique gem showing a sow and her young, surrounded by legend: + WILL'I DE VER CELO SECRETUM. The counterseal is about 30 mm in diameter.

Right hand seal: pointed oval, perhaps in green wax, but very heavily varnished, and very damaged and worn at base and sides, so that none of the legend remains; measurements: 73 × 45 mm. Depiction of Hereford cathedral. No counterseal.

Omnibus sancte matris ecclesie filiis ad quos presens scriptum pervenerit.' Willelmus de Ver dei gratia Hereford' ecclesie minister humilis.' Eternam in domino salutem. Noverit universitas vestra. nos assensu capituli Hereford' dedisse et concessisse. et hac carta confirmasse. dilecto in Cristo filio Ade de Estona homini nostro et fideli. pro homagio et servicio suo.' totam terram nostram de Eston'. cum omnibus pertinentiis suis in bosco et plano. in pratis et pascuis. in viis et semitis. in dominiis et villanagiis. et liberis tenementis. in terra culta et inculta. et in omnibus rebus et consuetudinibus. que quidem terra assignata fuit ecclesie Hereford'.' pro decem libratis terre. tenendam prefato Ade et heredibus suis. de nobis et successoribus nostris episcopis Hereford'.' iure hereditario ad feodofirmam. libere et quiete. honorifice. plenarie et integre ab omni servicio et seculari exactione.' reddendo inde annuatim nobis et successoribus nostris pro omnibus rebus.' Decem libras argenti ad quatuor terminos. videlicet ad Natale domini.' quinquaginta solidos. ad annuntiationem Sancte Marie.' quiquaginta solidos. ad festum Sancti Iohannis Baptyste.' quinquaginta solidos. ad festum Sancti Michaelis.' quinquaginta solidos. De hac vero terra. homagium prenominati Ade in plena curia nostra apud Hereford' accepimus. ipsamque terram cum omnibus pertinentiis suis.' debemus nos et successores nostri warantizare eidem Ade et heredibus suis adversus omnes homines. Quod ut firmum et stabile imperpetuum permaneat.' presenti carta et sigilli nostri apposicione confirmare et corroborare curavimus. Hiis testibus. Ricardo Hereford' decano. Radulfo eiusdem loci archidiacono. Hugone archidiacono Salopesir'. et capitulo Heref' hoc idem sigillo suo approbante. Waltero Map archidiacono Oxonie. Magistro Nicholao de Hamtona. Magistro Osberto et Willelmo capellanis. Reginaldo Foliot. Rogero de Ver. Alexa[nd]ro*a* de Estenor'. Ricardo Britone. Mauricio de Cradelea. Hugone de Hesela. Iohanne de Stanford' et Henrico filio suo. Hugone de Dunra. Hugone de Walford' ; Gregorio de Everleia et Willelmo. et Waltero. et Thoma et Galfrido fratribus suis. Eustachio de Wttona. et Iohanne de Wika fratre suo. Petro Fulchier'. et Ricardo fratre suo. Everardo de Everleia. Et multis aliis.

*a*nd *missing (hole in parchment)*.

Dating as no.179.

*181. Anselm de Mobray

Confirmation to Anselm de Mobray of a virgate in the manor of Prestbury.   [10 August 1186 × 24 December 1198]

> There is a mention of this charter in a confirmation by Bp Giles de Braose (1200-1215) of a grant of a virgate in the manor of Prestbury by Anselm de Mobray to Robert of London, son of Nicholas, acting on behalf of the heir of Hingelot; see below, no.281.

182. Bockleton church

Admission of William the clerk, on presentation by Robert de Bockleton, to the church of Bockleton.   [1187/8 × 24 December 1198]

B = Bodl. MS Rawlinson B329 (Hereford cathedral cartulary), fo.53v. s.xv.

Universis sancte matris ecclesie filiis W. dei gratia Heref' episcopus salutem. Notum facimus vobis quod nos ad presentationem Roberti de Boclinton' recipimus Willelmum clericum ad ecclesiam de Boclynton' ipsumque Willelmum in eadem ecclesia, cum omnibus pertinentiis suis in bosco et plano, in pratis et pascuis, in terris, decimis, et obventionibus, personam canonice et absque omni reclamatione instituimus. Quod ne imposterum deduci possit in irritum presenti[a] carta et sigilli nostri impressione confirmamus, salva in omnibus tam nostra quam nostrorum successorum episcoporum Heref' canonica iustitia. Hiis t' Hugone archidiacono Salopes', Willelmo precentore, Rogero filio Mauricii, Magistro Nicholao de Hampton, Willelmo Burchel', Milone Pichard', Waltero Haket, Alexandro constabulario, Roberto Warde et aliis.

[a]presentis B.

William Foliot became precentor 1187/8. See also note to no.135 above.

183. Christ Church, Canterbury

Safe conduct issued by Seffrid II, bishop of Chichester, William, bishop of Worcester, William, bishop of Hereford, Walter, abbot of Waltham, and Master Osbert de Camera for the monks of Christ Church Canterbury to go to and return from the king's court.　　　　[February 1188]

B = Lambeth MS 415 (Christ Church letter collection), fo.44v. s.xiii in.

Pd, *Ep. Cant.*, 168, and *Chichester acta*, 143, no.82.

For the background, see *Chichester acta, loc. cit.*, and J.Barrow, 'A twelfth-century bishop and literary patron: William de Vere', *Viator*, xviii (1987), 183.

184. Chirbury Priory

Confirmation to Chirbury priory of grants made by Robert de Bullers.
[c.1195 × 24 December 1198]

A = PRO E326/12983. The right half of this document is missing and some of the writing on the left half is illegible. There are no endorsements. It is impossible to be certain of the sealing arrangements, but it may have been sealed on the tongue. 115 mm deep; 121 mm wide at widest.

Universis sancte matris ecclesie filiis ad quos presens carta p(erven)erit W[   ]^a humilis. salutem gratiam dei et bene-dictionem. Quoniam e(x?) [   ]^a religiosis. deo iugiter famu-lantibus. diligenter fovere. et promovere et illibata custodii^b et ex [   ]^a sollicitudine tenemur.' ad instantem petitionem vener-abilis viri Roberti de Bulliers. inspecto ip(?) [   ]^a in Cristo filio. T. priori de Chiresb'i et canonicis regularibus in ecclesia Sancti Michaelis de Chir(es ?)[   ]^a Iohanni Ewangeliste. servien-tibus et in perpetuum servituris. prefatus Robertus indulsit.' nos auctoritate episc[   ]^a quas dictus Robertus prefatis canon-icis dedit et concessit. et carta sua confirmavit.' secundum quod in ec[   ]^a confirmamus. videlicet predictam ecclesiam de Chiresb'i. cum omnibus pertinentiis suis. et terram domin [   ]^a ad edificia eorum facienda. et totam terram et boscum in Snedo ad assartandum prout prefata [   ]^a dominium de Chirstoke. et una virgata terre quam Matheus tenet in Winesb'i et Landa[   ]^a assartare de bosco illo et assartum Gervasii fratris hospital'i^c et un[   ]^a dominium de Chira cum pis-caria. et un[   ]^a Chiresb'i quod b'[   ]^a id [   ]^d

^{a}lacuna. ^{b}last two letters uncertain. ^{c}sic, but uncertain.
^{d}last two or three lines of document completely illegible.

This charter is mentioned in a confirmation of Hugh (de Mapenore) for Chirbury; see below, no.295. The canons of Snead Priory moved to Chirbury c.1195. Prior T. is otherwise unknown and does not occur in *HRH*. See also no.319.

185. Cirencester abbey

Notification of the dedication of the chapel of Charlton at the request of Abbot Richard of Cirencester, saving the right of the mother church of Cheltenham.   [3 May 1190 × 24 December 1198]

B = Bodl. MS Dep. C392, (Cirencester Cartulary A, formerly Vestey Manu-scripts, Stowell Park), fo.120v, no.413. s.xiii ^{3}/4. C = Bodl. MS Dep. C393, (Cirencester Cartulary B, formerlyVestey Manuscripts, Stowell Park), fo.110r. s.xiv ex.

Pd from B, *Cirencester cartulary*, ii.372, no.413/444.

Cheltenham was in the diocese of Worcester, so that William de Vere could only have dedicated a chapel there during a Worcester vacancy, of which there were four during his episcopate: 3 May 1190 – July 1190; 27 June 1193 – 4 December 1193; 24/25 October 1195 – 15 January 1196, and from 24 September 1198 until after William's death, which occurred on 24 December 1198.

186. Abbot Richard of Cirencester and Prior Geoffrey of Llanthony

Letter to Abbot Richard of Cirencester and Prior Geoffrey of Llanthony quoting verbatim a complaint of Abbot Thomas Carbonel of Gloucester concerning a judgement which they had made.

[*c.*1189 × 24 December 1198, probably *c.*1189 × 1191]

A = Hereford D. & C. Muniments, no.1387. 15th century endorsement: Berkeleye. Sealed on the tongue; seal missing. Tongue attached by stitching. 189 × 85 mm.

Pd, David Walker, 'Gloucester charters', in *A medieval miscellany for D.M.Stenton*, ed. P.M.Barnes and C.F.Slade, PRS, new ser., xxxvi (1962), 265, no.13.

W. dei gratia Heref' episcopus. venerabilibus et dilectis in Cristo fratribus .R. eadem gratia abbati Cirenc'. et .G. priori Lanton'. salutem. Litteras domni abbatis Glouc'. in hec verba suscepimus. Venerabilibus dominis et amicis .W. dei gratia Heref' episcopo. et .R. eadem gratia abbati Cirenc' et .G. priori Lanton'. .T. eadem gratia abbas Glouc'. salutem. Mirari non sufficimus quod transactionem conditionaliter factam inter nos et abbatem et canonicos de Bristoll' super prebenda de Berkel' diocesano episcopo et nobis iuste contradicentibus.' sigillis vestris confirmastis. maxime cum vos domine episcope sigillum vestrum tali confirmationi appositum apud Glouc' habito consilio discretorum et honestorum virorum ad nostram conquestionem fregeritis. Unde siquid inde postea factum est.' per obreptionem factum esse dinoscitur. quia autem videmus causam nostram in h(oc) periclitari. et id fieri in preiudicium iuris nostri.' ne id locum optineat. vel ius nostrum ledere possit.' presentiam summi pontificis apellavimus.*a* rogantes si placet quatinus nobis et adversariis nostris diem certum prefigatis. ut quod forte perperam et minus provide factum esse. dinoscitur.' vestra discretione et communi consilio ad honorem vestrum et communis cause integritatem corrigatur. Honestius enim videtur quod factum vestrum revocetur provisione et discretione propria .' quam cohibitione et auctoritate summi pontificis. Valete in domino. ¶ Quia vero hec indiscreta precipitatio si doceri poterit. non solum nobis verum etiam utrique vestrum per apposita[b] nobisque ostensa prius sigilla. inputari debet. vobis mandamus et tam nobis quam fame nostre consulimus. quatinus in proximo ubi locum oportuniorem videritis. nos tres convenimus. communi consilio siquid in hac confirmatione precipitanter et altera parte reclamante attemptatum. est.' celeriter in irritum revocaturi. et utrique parti prout decet congrue satisfacturi. De die autem cum provideritis .' nobis significare curetis. Valete.

[a]*sic.*   [b]*The top of the second* a *is badly formed in the manuscript.*

Geoffrey of Henlawe became prior of Llanthony in about 1189. The settlement between the abbeys of Gloucester and Reading, recorded in a charter of Abbot John of Bristol (*Reading cartularies*, i.240-1, no.289), states that the case had been delegated to William and his colleagues by Clement III, and B.R.Kemp thinks it likely that the case was decided before or not long after Clement's death in March 1191 (ibid.). The churches of Berkeley Hernesse (the spiritual jurisdiction of Berkeley) had been bestowed by four separate benefactors on three different abbeys, Gloucester, Reading and Bristol in the 1140s; the prebend in question here was the last item to be adjudged. For the circumstances of the case see B.R.Kemp, 'The churches of Berkeley Hernesse', *TBGAS*, lxxxvii (1968), 96-110, esp. 108-9, and no.170 above. Abbot Thomas of Gloucester is here threatening the three judges with an appeal to the *curia*, but there is no evidence as to whether they were persuaded to change their minds or not.

187. Conches abbey

Confirmation for the abbey of St Peter's, Conches, of the manor and church of Monkland, of half the village of Dinedor, and of various tithes.
[10 August 1186 × 24 December 1198, possibly early]

A[1] = Evreux, A-D Eure H251. Endorsements: A Angleterre n 4 cotte 3 C de Guillaume Evesque de Herford sans datte – fol.112. v 3[c] Liasse armoire 30[c] (18th century). Confirmationes episcoporum (13th century) Heref' de decimis in Anglia in multis locis (15th century). 15th century notarial mark. The last line of the document is considerably damaged and the turnup is mostly missing; no surviving traces of sealing arrangements. Hole for filing in bottom left-hand corner. 277 × 168 + 9 mm.

A[2] = Ibid., H251. Endorsements: A Angleterre n 4. 3 C de Willaume Evesque de Herford' sans datte – fol 112v (18th century). Confirmacio de – Monquelune in Anglia in pluribus locis (late 14th or early 15th century). Most of the document's bottom right hand corner and bottom line are missing. Lines ruled for scribe. Hand same as that of A³. Originally presumably sealed on the tag, but no surviving traces of sealing arrangements. Hole for filing in bottom left hand corner. 245 × 166 mm.

Pd, not from the original but from a notarial instrument for Conches made by William Guerin, clerk and public notary in Evreux, dated Evreux, 22 August 1433, *Mon. Ang.* vi, pt.ii, 1026-7. William Guerin's copy noted that William's charter had been sealed with green wax.

Universis sancte matris ecclesie filiis Willelmus dei gratia Hereford' ecclesie minister etern[am]*a* in Cristo salutem. Ex officio iniuncte nobis administrationis tenemur viris religiosis eatenus providere *:* ut beneficia a filiis sancte dei ecclesie in elemosinam perpetuam sibi collata *:* pacifice et absque omnium vexatione possidere valeant. Inde est quod dilectis fratribus nostris abbati Sancti Petri Castellionis et monachis ibidem deo servientibus paterna pietate prospicere cupientes. concedimus eis et episcopali auctoritate confirmamus manerium de Munekeslen'. et ecclesiam eiusdem ville cum universis decimationibus et ceteris obventionibus et omnibus ad eam de iure spectantibus salva honesta sustentatione vicarii. medietatem quoque ville d[e Dun]ra*a* quam Hugo de Dunra tenet de eisdem monachis pro quinquaginta solidis annuatim reddendis in tribus terminis. videlicet tertia parte in purificatione Sancte Marie. et tertia in die Pentecostes. et tertia in festo Sancti Michaelis. Confirmamus etiam eis omnes decimas de dominio de Cabenour' cum uno hospite. et decimam illius terre quam idem hospes de eis tenet et de Hide in omnibus. Confirmamus etiam eis duas partes decimarum de dominio de Bromesberga. tam in magnis quam in minutis decimis in omnibus. et confirmamus eis duas partes decimarum de domino de Ediðestoc' in omnibus cum uno hospite. et duas partes decimarum de dominio de Hida. et duas partes decimarum de dominio Willelmi de Scholl'. et duas partes decimarum Hereberti de Æspertun'.*b* et unum burgagium in villa Hereford'. et duas partes decimarum de Alboldeleg. et in eadem villa duos hospites. et duas partes decimarum de dominio del Bur. et duas partes decimarum de dominio de Worvesleg'. et terram et mansuram que fuit Caure. et duas partes decimarum de feodo Osberti filii Rualdi et duas partes decimarum de Linda cum uno hospite. Has elemosinas habent predicti monachi ex donatione Radulfi senioris de Toeni[o]*a* quas et alia si qua in episcopatu Hereford' habent beneficia canonice adepta *:* eis confirmamus. salva dignitate Hereford' ecclesie. et successorum nostrorum canonica iusticia. quod ne de cetero ded[uci po]ssit*a* in irritum presenti carta et sigilli nostri tes[timoni]o*c* communimus. His testibus. Magistro Iohanne de Colec'. Willelmo de Stoc'. canonicis Hereford'. Magistro Stephano. et Magistro Osberto et R[icardo scripto]re*c* cleri[cis] n[ostris]*a* M[agistro Petro et Willelmo]*c* cl[erico]*c* de Len'. et [Rogero Turnel'. et Roberto de]*a* Offewrd'. Rogero de Livet.

> *a*lacuna *A*¹   *b*Aespertun *A*²   *c*lacuna *A*¹, *A*², supplied from Mon. Ang. .

> This was probably issued early in William's episcopate, because Master Osbert is not referred to as William's chaplain, an office which he obtained later in the pontificate. See also nos.142 and 322.

188. Cormeilles abbey

Grant to S., abbot, and the monks of Cormeilles, of a licence to appropriate the churches of Dymock, Newent and Kingsland, and the chapel of Pauntley, and notification that he has turned them into a prebend of Hereford Cathedral.   1195

> B = BL Add. MS 15668 (Newent priory cartulary), fo.50r. s.xiii med.
> C = BL Add. MS 18461 (Newent priory cartulary), fos.8v-9r. s.xiv in.

Willelmus dei gratia Hereford' episcopus omnibus sancte matris ecclesie filiis perpetuam in domino salutem. Quamvis ex iniuncto nostre sollicitudini officio teneamur parrochianorum nostrorum saluti in domino sollerter providere, propensius tamen virorum religiosorum utilitati invigilare debemus, qui pro erratis delinquentium ad deum intendunt, totamque etatem suam in dei laudibus expendunt. Hinc est quod nos, accepto ab omnibus bono odore integre fame Cormel' ecclesie, paterna pietate eidem prospicere cupientes et eiusdem facultates dilatare volentes, ecclesieque nostre honorem respicientes, concedimus prefate ecclesie Cormel' et eiusdem loci conventui et episcopali auctoritate, assensu capituli nostri, confirmamus quod liceat eis de cetero post decessum clericorum ecclesias quas in diocesi Hereford' habere noscuntur, videlicet de Dimmoch*a* et de Newent, de Kingeslen, capellam de Pantel', libere et sine aliqua contradictione sibi appropriare, et totum*b* emolumentum earum in usus proprios convertere, et pro arbitrio suo presbiteros idoneos in eisdem ecclesiis ministraturos constituere, salva dignitate ecclesie

Hereford'. Volumus etiam ad omnium notitiam devenire nos communi assensu Hereford' et Cormel' capitulorum de pretaxatis ecclesiis nostre diocesis in usus predictorum fratrum cum vacaverint plene convertendis prebendam unam in ecclesia Hereford' constituisse et eorundem assensu in capitulo nostro virum venerabilem amicum et fratrem nostrum in Cristo karissimum .S. abbatem Cormel' in canonicum Hereford' suscepisse, locum ei in capitulo et stallum in choro designantes, predictas ecclesias eidem in^c prebendam perpetuam et omnibus eius successoribus assignasse. Persona vero dicti abbatis humana forte ablata de medio, statuimus ut persona illa Cormel' monasterii, que potiorem post abbatem locum tenuerit, vacante abbatia Cormel' vices canonici in loco predicti abbatis in ecclesia interim optineat, donec abbas futurus substituatur et a nobis vel a successore nostro sine omni difficultate in prenominatam prebendam suam canonicus admittatur. Placuit etiam inter nos et memoratas ecclesias ut predictus abbas idoneum vicarium pro voluntate sua in ecclesia nostra statuat vice ipsius absentis ministrantem^d et assidue inibi residentiam facturum, qui cotidie panem et cervisiam^e canonico debitam vice abbatis dum ipse abbas absens fuerit ad victualium necessitatem percipiat. Predictus vero abbas, quamdiu in ecclesia nostra presens extiterit predictum panem et cervisiam iuxta consuetudinem ecclesie nostre ut canonicus habebit, et obventionibus dum in ecclesia presens steterit ad altare maius provenientibus plene ut canonicus communicabit. Preterea si contigerit abbatem Cormel' vel aliquem fratrem eiusdem loci diem ultimum claudere in^f nobis nuntiatum fuerit, nomina defunctorum in nostro ponentur martirologio^g ut in anniversariis diebus suis servitium defunctorum pro eis sicut pro canonicis nostris fiat. Et capitulum Hereford' cum inde fuerit requisitum in negotiis domini abbatis manum auxilii et consilii sumptibus domini abbatis porrigere tenetur, et ecclesie sue iura pro posse tueri et conservare. Et nos huic confirmationi nostre robur accommodantes^h eam presentis scripti patrocinio et sigilli nostri cum capituli Hereford' sigilli impressione communire curavimus. Hiis testibus: R. decano Hereford' et eiusdem loci capitulo, R. priore de Strigull', Ingerammo monacho, R. persona de Bekeford, Hamelino de Aquila, Willelmo Haket, Hugone pistore et multis aliis. Facta est autem hec concessio anno incarnationis dominice millesimo centesimo nonagesimo quinto.

^aDimok *C.*   ^b*om. C.*   ^c*C reads* designai *for* eidem in. *C.*   ^dministraturum *C.*
^eservisiam *C.*   ^fsic *BC.*   ^gmatrilogio *C.*   ^haccomodantes *B*; acomodantes *C.*

See also nos.200 and 250 below. William's confirmation for Cormeilles seems to have set a trend for Norman abbeys owning parish churches in England to turn them into cathedral prebends, so that the abbeys could rely on the cathedrals for some legal protection. Bp Seffrid II of Chichester granted a prebend in Chichester Cathedral to the abbot of Grestain between 1198 and 1204: see *Chichester acta,* 154-5, no.97 and note, and see also, for a list of references to similar arrangements elsewhere, J.Barrow, 'Vicars choral and chaplains in northern European cathedrals 1100-1250', in *The ministry: clerical and lay,* ed. W.Sheils and D.Wood, Studies in Church History xxvi (Oxford, 1989), 95-6.

189. Ewyas priory

Confirmation of charters of Harold, Robert and Robert son of Robert of Ewyas granting the churches of Kentchurch and Eton Foy to Gloucester abbey and the prior and monks of Ewyas.
[*c.*1187/8 × 24 December 1198]

B = Gloucester Cathedral Library, Register A, fo.155r, no.246. s.xiv ex.

Cal., 'Gloucester register', 23, no.44.

Omnibus sancte matris ecclesie filiis ad quos presens scriptum pervenerit. W. dei permissione Hereford' ecclesie minister eternam in domino salutem. Inspectis scriptis autenticis dilectorum in Cristo filiorum Haraldi de Ewias et Roberti filii sui et Roberti filii Roberti accepimus quod ad eorundem donationem et concessionem venerabilis frater noster Thomas dei gratia abbas Glouc' et prior et monachi Sancti Michaelis et Sancti Iacobi de Ewias ecclesias de Sancta Kama et de Sancta Foa de Eatton canonice adepti^{*a*} sunt. Nos vero, donationem et concessionem predictorum virorum ratam habentes, iamdictas ecclesias, videlicet de Sancta Kama et de Sancta Foa, priori et monachis de Ewias cum omnibus pertinentiis suis, sicut in instrumentis que de predictis viris habent expresse continetur, perpetuo possidendas concedimus et auctoritate episcopali confirmamus. Et ut hec nostra confirmatio rata et inconvulsa permaneat eam presentis^{*b*} pagine^{*c*} subscriptione et sigilli nostri appositione communire curavimus. Hiis testibus: Ricardo decano, Gilberto thesaurario et aliis.

^aadepta *B.*   ^bpresenti *B.*   ^c*corr. from* carte *B.*

Richard Brito became dean c.1187/8.

*190. *Eys* church

Admission of R. and S., clerks, as vicars in the church of Eys *(perhaps Eastnor, or possibly St Michael, Ewyas Harold).*
[10 August 1186 × 24 December 1198, probably after 1193]

Mentioned in two mandates of Innocent III, dated at the Lateran, 26 March 1199, to the abbots of Dore and Wigmore and to the prior of Leominster to see to the complaint of W. de Calne, parson of *Eys*, about R. and S., clerks, who had been instituted as vicars in the church of *Eys* by the diocesan (PRO, SC7 19/12 and SC7 35/8; pd, *Letters of Pope Innocent III concerning England and Wales: a Calendar*, ed. C.R. and Mary Cheney [Oxford, 1967], nos.92, 93). *Eys* certainly cannot be identified with Eye, which had another vicar at this point: see B.R.Kemp, 'Hereditary benefices in the medieval English church: a Herefordshire example', *BIHR*, xliii (1970), 10, n.1, and C.R. and Mary Cheney, 'The Letters of Pope Innocent III: additions and corrections', *BIHR*, xliv (1971), 106, nos.92-3. Eastnor, however, which was in the bp's gift (see *Reg. Swinfield*, 538) might be a possible identification. Another possibility is that the diocesan in question is not the bp of Hereford but the bp of St David's, presumably Peter de Leia, and that the church of *Eys* is the church of St Michael, Ewyas Harold, near which the knight Roald of Calne occurs holding the demesne of Hardwicke in March 1179 (*Gloucester register*, 48, where misdated to the late thirteenth century, though the document was issued by Dean G[eoffrey] of Hereford in the absence of Bp R[obert Foliot] at the Third Lateran Council). Ewyas priory owned the advowson of the church of St Michael (*Gloucester cartulary*, i.287). At some point before 1190 William de Vere instituted W(illiam) de Calne, who was one of his clerks, as rector in the church of Stottesdon, on presentation by the abbot of Shrewsbury (no.231 below).

191. Flaxley abbey

Mandate to the priests of the diocese of Hereford to excommunicate those molesting the monks of Flaxley abbey in the Forest of Dean.
[probably soon after 13 June 1192]

B = BL Add. MS 49996 (Charter Roll of Flaxley Abbey); dorse, 3rd membrane. s.xiii in. Rubric: Littere domini W. Hereford'. episcopi. universis episcopatus capellanis. sigillate.
Pd, *Flaxley cartulary*, 181, no.78.

W. dei gratia Hereford' ecclesie minister humilis, universis episcopatus Hereford' capellanis salutem et benedictionem. Ex debito potestatis nostre nobis incumbit religiosorum qui sub nobis sunt paci et tranquillitati providere, consulere, et congaudere. Quod sicud debemus ita et volumus, in hiis precipue in quibus magisteriam*a* habemus apostolice sedis auctoritatem; igitur pro dilectis filiis nostris monachis de Den' universitati vestre precipiendo mandamus quatenus, cum aliquis contra ipsorum monachorum privilegia eosdem gravare vel in eorum fratres vel res iniustam manum inicere presumpserit, eorundem monachorum voluntati adquiescatis super eisdem malefactoribus suis et excommunicationis sententia feriendis, cum [v]obis*b* innotuerit privilegiorum tenor et delinquentium culpa et monachorum gravamen, eosque non ex[p]ectato*b* archidiaconi vel decani concilio vel precepto presentium auctoritate litterarum excommunicare non differatis,

*a*magrãm (magisterialem ?) B.   *b*lacuna B.

William may be referring to a bull issued to Flaxley by Celestine III dated 13 June 1192 at Rome (*PUE*, i, no.444, and *Flaxley cartulary*, 178-80, no.77).

*192. Master Germanus

Confirmation to Master Germanus of a grant by Bishop Robert Foliot of a burgage in novo vico *in Ledbury.*
[10 August 1186 × 24 December 1198]

Mentioned in a grant by Hugh the clerk, son of Master Germanus, to Robert de Staning' of a burgage *in novo vico* in Ledbury. The grant is described as 'ab Willelmo successore suo confirmata pariter sum sigilli capituli Hereford' (Hereford D. & C. Muniments, no.2181).

*193. Gloucester abbey

Grant to Gloucester abbey of full parsonage in the church of Much Cowarne, with permission to the abbot of Gloucester to present a vicar to the church.   [10 August 1186 × 24 December 1198]

Mention only, *CRR*, vii.216-217, in a dispute between Richard and Elena Pancefot, Jordan and Eva de Wike on the one hand and Gloucester abbey on the other over the advowson of the church of Cowarne. Gloucester produced this charter of William's as part of their evidence. See also no.144 above and no.251 below.

194. Gloucester abbey

Admission of Master Ambrose to the parsonage of the church of Rudford on presentation by Abbot Thomas and the monks of Gloucester abbey.

[10 August 1186 × 24 December 1198]

B = PRO, C150/1 (Gloucester Cartulary), fo.165r new fol., fo.148r old fol., no.590. s.xiii ex.

Pd, *Gloucester cartulary*, ii.100-1, no.590.

195. Haughmond abbey

Grant to Haughmond Abbey of the church of Stokesay and investiture of Abbot Richard with it in the name of the abbey.

[10 August 1186 × August 1187, probably by June 1187]

B = Shrewsbury Local Studies Library, Haughmond abbey cartulary, fo.206r. s.xv ex. C = Shropshire County Record Office, 2922 additional (Dudmaston MS), fo.16r. s.xvi/xvii. D = Ibid., fo.3v, in inspeximus by Archbp Baldwin of Canterbury (the text of Baldwin's inspeximus in Shrewsbury Local Studies Library, Haughmond abbey cartulary, fo.206r, omits most of the wording of William's charter).

Pd from B, C, and D, *Haughmond cartulary*, 213, no.1147, and, from D, *EEA ii.* 238, no.278.

Testibus Ada abbate de Dore et Iordano decano, *a*Magistro Simone, Magistro Nicholao, domino Roberto de Haseleg, Magistro Galfrido de Winter, Magistro Willelmo Romano, Ricardo de Britone, Reginaldo capellano, Roberto de Cliff, Ricardo capellano, Radulfo de Arden, Philippo de Say, Magistro Osberto rictune,*a* *b*Galfrido de [Sancta] Ositha.*b*

*a-a*om. B., which reads merely etc'.   *b-b*om. BC.

For the dating, see *EEA* ii.238.

196. Hereford cathedral chapter

Confirmation of the grant by Archdeacon Ralph Foliot of Hereford of the tithe of the church of Cradley to Hereford cathedral chapter to make bread to distribute to the poor on the anniversary of Bishop Robert Foliot's death. [after 10 August 1186 × mid 1190s, probably early]

A = Hereford D. & C. Muniments, no.2045. 15th century endorsement: Litera episcopi W episcopi Folyot pro animabus distribu' pauperibus pro anima [Roberti ?] Folyot apud (?). 14th century endorsement: script'. 213 × 100 mm. Originally sealed on a tag; seal missing.

Pd, *Hereford charters*, 34.

Omnibus sancte matris ecclesie filiis ʔ Willelmus dei gratia Herefordens' episcopus ʔ salutem in domino ʔ Universitati vestre notum esse volumus. nos divine pietatis intuitu ʔ concessisse et presenti carta confirmasse capitulo Herefordensi decimam dominii ecclesie de Credeleiʔ concessione Radulfi Herefordensis archidiaconi ʔ tunc persone eiusdem ecclesie. ad inveniendos panes de septem ladis frumenti. distribuendos pauperibus die obitus Roberti Foliot Herefordens' episcopiʔ pro anima sua et aliorum episcoporum Herefordensium. et decimam terre de la Fineg'. quam predictus archidiaconus tempore huius concessionis in suo dominio tenebat. Predictum autem Herefordense capitulum nobis fideliter promisit ʔ quod in perpetuum quam diu predictam decimam habere potuerit ʔ prenominatos panes suis sumptibus factos ʔ inveniet. et distribui faciet. Et quia hanc nostram elemosinam in perpetuum ratam esse volumus. et firmiter observari ʔ eam presenti carta et sigilli nostri appositione corroboramus. Hiis testibus. Hugone Foliot archidiacono Salopes'. Magistro Roberto Folet. Iohanne Clem'. Magistro Nicholao de Wlfrunhamton'. Magistro Osberto et Willelmo capellanis. Reginaldo Folet. Radulfo elemosinario. Willelmo camerario. Alexandro senescallo. Ricardo marescallo. Willelmo dispensario. Henrico pincerna. Mauricio de Credel'. Ricardo le Bret. Radulfo de Chaurai. et multis aliis.

This charter was issued after Master Osbert became William de Vere's chaplain and before Adam of Easton became seneschal (see introduction, p.lvii).

197. Hereford cathedral chapter

Notification that his purchase of part of the land held by Walter of Donnington from Hereford cathedral chapter will not affect the service rendered by Walter and his heirs to the chapter.

[10 August 1186 × 24 December 1198]

A = Hereford D. & C. Muniments, no.1362. 14th century endorsement: terre de Donynton'. 150 × 61 mm. Probably originally sealed on a tongue; bottom left hand corner eaten away.

Universis sancte matris ecclesie filiis ad quos presens carta pervenerit. Willelmus dei gratia Hereford' episcopus. salutem. Notum vobis facio quod ego emi pro duabus marcis argenti a Waltero de Duniton' quandam partem tenementi quod idem Walterus tenet de capitulo Hereford' in villa de Duniton'. illam videlicet partem que inclusa est in parco meo. ex parte australi. ita tamen quod prefatus Walterus et heredes sui nichilominus facient integrum servicium capitulo Hereford' de residuo tenementi sicut fecerunt quando integrum fuit tenementum. Quod ne in posterum redundet in preiudicium capituli cuius assensu hec emptio prescripto meo facta est ⁊ presenti carta et sigilli mei testimonio testificari curavi.

198. Hereford cathedral chapter

Confirmation to the chapel of St Mary Magdalen, Hereford, of grants made by his predecessors, Bishops Gilbert Foliot, Robert de Melun and Robert Foliot, and grant of the chapel, on its resignation by Reginald the chaplain, to the dean and chapter of Hereford cathedral.

[1187/8 × February 1198]

B = Bodl. MS Rawlinson B329 (Hereford cathedral cartulary), fo.155r-v. s.xiii-xiv.

Universis sancte matris ecclesie filiis ad quos presens scriptum pervenerit Willemus de Ver divina miseratione Herefordensis ecclesie minister humilis eternam in domino salutem. Iustitie ac rationis ordo suadet ut ea que a predecessoribus nostris canonice sunt ordinata a nobis etiam robur et auctoritatem accipiant. Dignum est enim ut ea que rationabiliter gesta esse noscuntur nullius omnino in posterum refragatione turbentur. Hinc est quod nos, attendentes capellam Beate Marie Magdalen' de Hereford' a venerabilibus predecessoribus nostris Gileberto Foliot et Roberto Melud' et Roberto Foliot quibusdam elemosinis pia de-[fo. 155v]-votione fuisse dotatam, sicut ex eorundem scriptis autenticis oculata fide perpendimus, prefatas elemosinas eidem capelle episcopali auctoritate confirmavimus, videlicet oblationes solempnium dierum de domo episcopi cum episcopus fuerit Hereford' et totam decimam nundinarum Hereford', tam de seldagiis quam de theloneis et aliis earum exitibus, decimas etiam omnium assartorum que prescriptus G.Foliot episcopus in foresta de Dene fecit essartare, hiis insuper adiectis quod capellanus qui in predicta capella ministrabit, episcopo apud Hereford' moram faciente, ad mensam ipsius quasi unus ex clericis suis resideat; reliquo vero anni tempore ad victum suum de granario episcopi quinque ladas frumenti percipiat. Cum igitur, procedente tempore, prenominata capella, cum omnibus que predicta sunt ad eam pertinentibus, a dilecto filio nostro Reginaldo capellano in manu nostra libere et spontanea voluntate esset resignata,[a] nos eam cum prememoratis pertinentiis suis dilectis filiis nostris canonicis Beate Marie et Sancti Ethelberti de Hereford', ad quos, sicut ex fideli multorum assertione cognovimus,[b] antiquo iure spectabat, absque cuiusquam reclamatione restituimus et restituentes perpetuo habendam et possidendam concessimus et confirmavimus, adiungentes ut prefati canonici singulis annis tempore nundinarum quos voluerint procuratores constituant, qui servientibus nostris in nundinis et computationibus nostris singulis diebus assideant et portionem canonicis debitam, videlicet omnium obventionum et exituum earundem nundinarum decimam, ibidem incontinenti sine aliqua diminutione recipiant. Quia vero prefatas concessiones et confirmationes predecessorum nostrorum et nostras ratas et inviolatas volumus permanere, eas presentis pagine attestatione et sigilli nostri appositione communire curavimus. Hiis testibus, Ricardo decano et toto capitulo, Rogero et Ricardo capellanis decani et aliis.

[a]resingnata B.   [b]congnovimus B.

Richard Brito became dean in either 1187 or 1188. Archbp Hubert Walter issued a confirmation of three of William's grants to Hereford cathedral chapter between April 1195 and February 1198 (*EEA* iii.143-5). See also nos.158 and 343.

199. Hereford cathedral chapter

Grant to Hereford cathedral chapter of land bought from Ranulf son of Master Ranulf fitz Erchemar.

[10 August 1186 × February 1198, probably after 1190]

A = Hereford D. & C. Muniments, no. 1386. 14th century endorsement: Script'. 15th century endorsement: obitus W Veer. Possibly originally sealed on the tongue, but no trace of tongue or seal. 145 × 32 mm. B = Bodl. MS Rawlinson B329 (Hereford cathedral cartulary), fo.131v. s.xiii-xiv. C = Ibid., fo.41. s.xv. Pd from A, *Hereford charters*, 32.

Omnibus sancte matris ecclesie filiis ad quos presens scriptum pervenerit Willelmus de Ver. dei gratia Hereford' ecclesie minister humilis. salutem in domino. Universitati vestre notum fieri volumus. nos dedisse et concessisse deo et Beate Marie virgini. et capitulo Hereford' totam terram illam que est ante ianuam nostram apud Hereford'. que fuit Rannulfi filii Erkemari. et postea Rannulfi filii eiusdem. de quo predictam terram emimus. et ut emptionem nostram sine cuiusquam reclamatione in prenominatum capitulum contulimus liberam et quietem^a ab omni servitio. excepto ? quod canonici de Hereford' bis in anno mittent aliquem de suis ad halimotum nostrum? ad summonitionem nostram. Preterea. canonici fideliter promiserunt. quod diem nostrum anniversarium et dies anniversarios patris et matris nostre horis competentibus celebrabunt. et nos omnium orationum et benefitiorum que in predicta ecclesia Heref' fuerint? inperpetuum participes effecerunt Quod quia ratum et inconvulsum imperpetuum manere volumus? presenti scripto et sigilli nostri impressione confirmavimus. His testibus. Ada de Eston'. tunc senescallo. Magistro Nicholao de Hamton'. Magistro Iohanne Clementis.^{b} Magistro Osberto et Willelmo capellanis nostris. Reginaldo Foliot. Galfrido de Cicestr'. Radulfo diacono. et multis aliis.

^{a}*sic A.* ^{b}*Text of C ends here, with words* et aliis.

Reginald Foliot and Ralph the deacon entered William de Vere's household in the 1190s (see p.lviii). This was one of the grants to Hereford cathedral confirmed by Archbp Hubert Walter; the *terminus ad quem* is thus the same as for no.198.

200. Hereford cathedral chapter

Admission of Dean Richard of Hereford in the name of Hereford cathedral chapter to the church of Marden on presentation by the abbot and monks of Cormeilles. 1195

B = Bodl. MS Rawlinson B329 (Hereford cathedral cartulary), fo.151r-v. s.xiii-xiv.

Omnibus sancte matris ecclesie filiis ad quos presens scriptum pervenerit W. dei gratia Herefordensis ecclesie minister eternam in domino salutem. Universitati vestre innotescimus quod, accedens ad nos venerabilis frater noster abbas Cormel' cum literis conventus sui de abitione rati,[1] ecclesiam suam de Maurthyn, cum omnibus pertinentiis suis, capitulo Hereford' in augmentum commune sue, videlicet panis et cervisie, contulit, et dilectum in Cristo filium R. decanum nomine capituli in capitulo Hereford' in ecclesia illa instituendum presentavit, quem ad ipsius presentationem in eadem ecclesia instituimus et in corporalem possessionem eiusdem ecclesie per officiales nostros fecimus introduci. Quod quia [fo. 151v] perpetue stabilitatis robur optinere volumus presenti scripto et sigilli nostri munimine confirmare curavimus. Facta est autem hec concessio anno incarnationis domini m° centesimo nonagesimo quinto. Hiis testibus Magistro Roberto Folet, Magistro Nicholao, Magistro Osberto, Reginaldo Foliot, Iohanne diacono et multis aliis.

[1] *a letter* de ratihabitione *is a procuration.*

Cormeilles abbey's grant of Marden to Dean Richard Brito and Hereford Chapter is *ibid.*, fo.151r. It is also dated 1195 and has a similar, though longer, witness list. No.188 above was also issued at this time. This grant was also confirmed by Archbp Hubert Walter: see note to no.198 above.

201. Hereford cathedral chapter

Grant of the church of Madley to the canons of Hereford to augment their commons; Dean Richard will continue to hold a portion in the church for which he will pay the chapter an annual pension of ten shillings, and after his death the chapter may possess the church as freely as they possess the churches in their manors of Woolhope, Norton Canon, and Canon Pyon.
[April 1195 × 24 December 1198]

A = Hereford D. & C. Muniments, no.2776. 15th century endorsements: W de Ver super ecclesiis de Maddele'. 15th century notary's mark. Originally sealed on the tag, but no tag or seal surviving. 178 × 104 + 28 mm.

Pd, *Hereford charters*, 37.

Omnibus sancte matris ecclesie filiis W. dei gratia Herefordensis ecclesie minister humilis salutem in domino. Ex testimonio veritatis dicentis ad discipulos suos qui vos recipit me recipit.[1] intelligimus eterna remuneratione dignum. Cristo ministrantibus in necessitatibus suis subvenire. attendentes igitur devotionem dilectorum filiorum nostrorum canonicorum in ecclesia Herefordensi deo et sancte eius genitrici et Beato Ethelberto martiri ministrantium. et eis paterna benignitate in hiis in quibus usque ad tempora nostra gravem defectum passi sunt prospicere cupientes. ad supplementum communie sue que ante tempora nostra modica fuit et eis minus sufficiens. ecclesiam de Madel' caritatis intuitu ipsis contulimus assensu Ricardi decani. qui pro portione quam in eadem ecclesia habet tota vita sua dabit capitulo Herefordensi singulis*a* annis decem solidos nomine pensionis. Post cuius decessum concedimus predicto capitulo ut totam predictam ecclesiam cum omnibus pertinentiis suis possideant ita libere et quiete sicut possident ecclesias in Hopa et Nortuna et Pionia maneriis suis. Volentes igitur hanc nostram donationem predictis filiis nostris tam necessariam inviolabili stabilitate gaudere.' eam presenti scripto patrocinio et sigilli nostri testimonio confirmamus. His testibus. Ricardo decano. Willelmo precentore Herefordensi. Henrico cancellario Herefordensi. Magistro Symone. Willelmo Cumin. Magistro Nicolao de Hamptun'. R. Folet. Magistro Iohanne Clemente. canonicis. Willelmo capellano. Willelmo de Bromiard. Symone de Thardebigg'. Nicolao serviente precentoris. Roberto serviente Roberti Folet et multis aliis.

a space after singulis, *probably to allow for the centre fold, which must therefore precede the writing.*

[1] Matth. 10^{40}.

Henry de Vere became chancellor in the mid 1190s. This charter was not confirmed by Archbp Hubert Walter (see note to no.198 above) and so is almost certainly later than April 1195, the *terminus a quo* for Hubert's confirmation.

202. Hereford cathedral chapter

Confirmation of the grant by Bishop Robert Foliot [no.150] of the church of Upton Bishop to the chapter of Hereford cathedral.

[April 1195 × 24 December 1198]

A = Hereford D. & C. Muniments, no.1359. 15th century endorsement; Confirmacio. W. de Vere super collacione R. Foliot de ecclesia de Upton. 148 × 78 mm. Sealed on a tag; seal a pointed oval, natural wax, 78 × 47 mm. Legend of obverse: ....LLUM. WILLELM...............REFO(R).............. ; Counter-seal 29 mm in diameter; legend: .WILLI DE VER CEL. SECRETUM

B = *Ibid.*, no.741 (inspeximus by Bp Giles de Braose, datable 1201 × 1215). C = Bodl. MS Rawlinson B329 (Hereford cathedral cartulary), fo.171r-v. Bp Giles' inspeximus copied *ibid.*, fo.171v. s.xiii-xiv.

Pd from A, *Hereford charters*, 36-7.

Universis sancte matris ecclesie filiis Willelmus de Ver dei gratia Herefordensis ecclesie minister humilis eternam in domino salutem. Universitati vestre notum esse volumus nos ecclesiam manerii nostri de Uptona quam Robertus Foliot predecessor noster pie memorie capitulo Hereford' in aumentum communie sue contulit concessisse. et presenti carta nostra confirmasse predicto capitulo ut liceat ei omnes fructus predicte ecclesie. in proprios usus convertere vel cui voluerint pro certa concedere pensione. His testibus. Henrico de Ver cancellario. et magistro Willelmo Romano. et magistro Gileberto. et Symone de Langt'. et Reginaldo de Walteham. et Alexandro.

Dating as no.201.

203. St Guthlac's priory, Hereford

Admission of Geoffrey of Gloucester to the chapel of Dormington on presentation by Prior William and the monks of St Guthlac's, Hereford.
[10 August 1186 × 1187/8]

B = Oxford, Balliol College MS 271 (cartulary of St Guthlac's, Hereford), fos.49v-50r, no.181. s.xiv in.

[U]niversis*a* sancte matris ecclesie filiis ad quos presens carta pervenerit Willelmus dei gratia Heref' episcopus eternam in Cristo salutem. Universitati vestre notum fieri volumus nos, ad presentationem dilectorum in Cristo filiorum, videlicet Willelmi prioris et totius conventus Heref', suscepisse Galfridum clericum de Glouc' ad capellam de Dorminton', ipsumque in eadem capella absque omni reclamatione perpetuum [fo.50r] vicarium instituisse. Quod quia a nobis canonice et rationabiliter gestum est, ne inposterum alicuius malignitate*b* deduci possit in irritum, presentis carte serie et sigilli nostri appositione confirmare et corroborare curavimus. Hiis testibus, Willelmo de Stoc', Magistro Ricardo Britone, Willelmo Foliot, Iohanne de

Gloec', Magistro Willelmo de Caln', Magistro Radulfo de Toten', Magistro Michaele de Duket', Magistro Thoma de Lanton', Simone nepote prescripti prioris Willelmi de Kylpek et aliis.

*a*initial omitted to be supplied later by rubricator B.   *b*malignate B.

Richard Brito became dean and William Foliot precentor in either 1187 or 1188. William ceased to be prior of St Guthlac's before 1191.

204. St Guthlac's priory, Hereford

Confirmation to St Guthlac's, Hereford, of their possession of the churches of St Cuthbert of Holme Lacy, St Martin's in Hereford castle, St Owen's, Hereford, Ocle Pychard, Avenbury, Mordiford, Bartestree, Sutton St Michael, the chapel of Sutton St Nicholas, the churches of Monnington, and Moccas, and tithes from Staunton on Wye, Risbury, Wheathill, Humber, Butterley in Wacton, Street in Kingsland, Weobley, Burghope in Wellington, Bodenham, Rosemaund, Stoke Lacy, Weston Beggard, Kempley, Gattertop, Oxenhall and Lugwardine.

[10 August 1186 × 24 December 1198]

B = Oxford, Balliol College MS 271 (cartulary of St Guthlac's, Hereford), fo.98r-v, no.433. s.xiv in. C = *Ibid.*, fos. 99v-100r, no.437, in inspeximus by Giles de Braose, omitting the final part of William's text. D = *Ibid.*, fo.99r, no.435; inspeximus of Giles' deed by Stephen Langton.

Pd, as part of D, *Acta Stephani Langton*, ed. K.Major, CYS 1 (1950), 146-8.

Universis sancte matris ecclesie filiis ad quos presentes litere pervenerint, W. dei gratia Heref' episcopus eternam in domino salutem. Cum multiplici caritatis opere divina gratia animas fidelium salvandas mutaverat potissimum elemosinarum largitio et Cristi pauperum exhibitio recte credentibus expeditiorem*a* ad conspectum domini properant*b* accessum et in perhennitatis sue tabernaculum faciliorem ordinant*c* introitum, inde est quod nos, dilectorum nobis in Cristo filiorum videlicet monachorum in monasterio beatorum apostolorum Petri et Pauli et Sancti Guthlaci Hereford' domino devote famulantium honestam et regularem conversationem considerantes, et eorum possessiones et facultates secundum affectionis sue fervorem ad bonum hospitalitatis sustinendum et prescripta pietatis opera exequenda secundum ordinis sui institutionem non sufficere manifestius attendentes, possessionum et bonorum suorum quantitatem augere presertim ad perpetuam domus sue hospitalitatem ordinate sustinendam instinctu publice honestatis et communis utilitatis affectuose studuimus. Nos itaque ecclesiam Sancti Cudberti^d de Hamme ultra Wayam et capellam Sancti Martini intra ambitum castri Heref' constructam cum omnibus pertinentiis suis memoratis monachis sicud ex inspectione instrumentorum suorum ab antiquis temporibus eisdem canonice collatas indubitanter cognovimus, salva Heref' ecclesie dignitate et canonica obedientia nobis et successoribus nostris debita, episcopali auctoritate confirmamus, et decimas et obventiones earum in subscriptarum ecclesiarum, cum ipsas vacare contigerit, ad honestam, ut diximus,^{e} domus sue hospitalitatem iugiter conservandam, percipere in proprios usus et causis necessariis domus sue, liberam habendo inde dispositionem, convertere, salva conpetenti vicariorum sustentatione, pietatis et misericordie intuitu eisdem permisimus. Preterea nos vestigiis predecessorum nostrorum pietate nitentibus inherentes predicto monasterio et monachis ibidem deo servientibus possessiones, ecclesias et alia beneficia in liberam elemosinam concessa inperpetuum quiete possidenda confirmamus, ecclesiam^f scilicet Sancti Petri que est in foro Heref' cum prebendis, terris et decimis, et omnibus ad eam pertinentibus, ^{g}ecclesiam Sancti Audoeni de Heref', cum omnibus ad eam pertinentibus,^{g} et ecclesiam de Acla et ecclesiam de Agneburia, et ecclesiam de Mordford, et capellam de Britwaldest' et ecclesiam de maiori^h Suttona, cum omnibus pertinentiis suis, et capellam de minori Suttona, et ecclesiam de Moniton', cum omnibus pertinentiis suis, et ecclesiam de Mocres, cum pertinentiis suis, duas partes totius dominii de Stanton et de Russeburi [fo.98v B] [et Weth]ulla^i et^j Humbra et Buterleya, et de Strete et de Webbeleia^k et Burhopa, et [in Bodeh]am^i et^l Maghene et de^m Stoca et Weston' et de Kempeleia, et totam decimam de Godredeshopa et de Oxenhale, tertiam etiam partem decimarum villanagii^n de Lugwardin.^{o} Quod ne de cetero in dubium vel irritum revocari valeat, illud presentis pagine inscriptione et sigilli nostri appositione solempniter corroborari et confirmari curavimus. Hiis testibus Magistro Iohanne de Glouc', Magistro Osberto capellano nostro, Willelmo capellano, Magistro Eilmundo, Galfrido clerico, Rogero de Ver, Roberto de Laneham, Radulfo de Grafton', et aliis.

^{a}expeditorem *BCD.* ^{b}preparant *C;* preparavit *D.* ^{c}ordinavit, *repeated, D.*
^{d}Gudberti *B;* Gutberti *CD.* ^{e}duximus *BCD.* ^{f}ecclesia *B.* $^{g-g}$om. *C.*

ʰword erased after maiori *B.*   *ⁱlacuna B.*   *ʲCD add* de.   *ᵏ*Welbleia *C;* Webbleia *D.*
ˡC adds de.   *ᵐC om.* de; *D om.* et.   *ⁿ*vilinagii *B;* vilanagii *C.*
ºText of William's charter ends here in CD.

For Giles' inspeximus, see below, no.260.

205. St Guthlac's priory, Hereford

*Confirmation to St Guthlac's Priory of the pension of half a mark from
the church of Monnington on Wye, which Reginald Foliot will pay to St
Guthlac's after the death of Alfred the clerk.*

[*c.*1190 × 24 December 1198]

B = Oxford, Balliol College MS 271 (cartulary of St Guthlac's, Hereford), fo.71r,
no.295. s.xiv in.

Omnibus sancte matris ecclesie filiis W. dei permissione Heref' ecclesie minister eternam in domino salutem. Quoniam ea que nobis
presentibus legitime acta sunt nostre auctoritatis munimineᵃ desiderant roborari, volumus et cupimus perpetue stabilitatis robor optinere. Concedimus et confirmamus deo et Sancto Petro et Sancto
Guthlaco Hereford' dimidiam marcam quam Reginaldus Foliot clericus noster prioriᵇ Heref' nomine pensionis de ecclesia de Moniton'
post decessum Alfredi capellani reddere tenetur. Et si contigerit
Reginaldoᶜ Foliot premoriri, pensionem duorum solidorum quam
eidem R. prefatus A. nomine ecclesie de Moniton' reddere consuevit,
dicte priorie Hereford' quamdiu Dominus A. vixerit solvendam concedimus et presenti carta confirmamus. Hiis testibus. Roberto Folet,
Magistro Nicholao, Magistro I. Clementis, Magistro Osberto, Willelmo capellano, Reginaldo Folet, Radulfo dyacono, Galfrido clerico
et ceteris.

*ᵃ*muni/mine *B.*   *ᵇ*priore *B.*   *ᶜ*Rogerum *B.*

Reginald Foliot and Ralph the deacon entered William de Vere's household in the
1190s (see p.lviii).

206. St Guthlac's priory, Hereford

Notification of the settlement between John, prior of Hereford, and Matthew, clerk of Wheathill, about the demesne tithes of Wheathill.
[1191 × -1198, probably 1191 × 1193]

B = Oxford, Balliol College MS 271 (cartulary of St Guthlac's, Hereford), fo.90v, no.398. s.xiv in.

Omnibus sancte matris ecclesie filiis ad quos presens scriptum pervenerit, W. dei gratia Hereford' episcopus, eternam in domino salutem. Noveritis quod, cum causa que vertebatur inter dilectum in Cristo filium Iohannem, priorem Hereford', et Matheum,[a] clericum de Wethhull', super duabus partibus omnium decimationum dominii[b] de Wethull', quas dictus prior ad ecclesiam Sancti Guthlaci Hereford' de iure pertinere dicebat, coram nobis diutius agitaretur, tandem coram nobis et capitulo nostro Hereford' tali fine conquievit, videlicet quod dictus Matheus propria voluntate sua in iure confessus est quod iam dicte decime ad ecclesiam Sancti Guthlaci Hereford' de iure pertinebant, et, tactis evangeliis,[c] iuravit quod dictas decimas memorato priori et successoribus suis libere et quiete et absque contradictione et difficultate habere dimittet, et quod nunquam in vita sua eis gravamen vel molestiam inde inferret. Quod ne alicui in dubium veniat, presenti scripto et sigillo nostro confirmare curavimus. Hiis testibus, R. decano et capitulo Hereford', W. de Calna, Magistro Nicholao de Hampton', Magistro Osberto, W. capellano, Reginaldo Foliot, Radulfo et Galfrido diaconis, et aliis.

[a]Mathium *B*.   [b]domini *B*.   [c]ewangel' *B*.

John was almost certainly prior of St Guthlac's between Robert, who resigned in 1191, and Henry, who became prior before Bp William's death (see no.209 below). William de Calne seems either to have been a less active member of Bp William's household, or indeed perhaps to have left it, after Hubert Walter's translation to Canterbury in 1193.

207. St Guthlac's priory, Hereford

Grant to St Guthlac's of the mill in front of their gate.
[probably 1195 × 24 December 1198]

B = Oxford, Balliol College MS 271, fo.73v, no.311. s.xiv in.

Omnibus sancte matris ecclesie filiis ad quos presens scriptum pervenerit Willelmus dei gratia Heref' ecclesie minister humilis salutem
in domino. Cum ex officio nobis iniuncto singulorum necessitatibus
puro[a] conpati affectu et pleno pro possibilitate nostra subvenire
teneamur, effectum maxime viris religionis duximus concedendum
id in quo nullum ecclesie nostre vel nobis novimus imminere[b] pericu-
lum et eis pro certo scimus esse profuturum.[c] Hinc est quod, attendentes inopiam dilectorum filiorum nostrorum monachorum
Hereford', quam ex aque defectu sustinent, consilio et assensu capituli nostri, eis molendinum nostrum ante portam eorum positum[d]
quod tantum unam marcam argenti solvere consuevit pro duabus
marcis singulis annis nobis et successoribus nostris solvendis concessimus inperpetuum, videlicet unam marcam ad annuntiationem Beate
Marie et unam marcam ad festum Sancti Michaelis. Et ne imposterum super hoc emergat ambiguitas id presentis scripti et nostri
sigilli et sigilli capituli nostri confirmat et declarat auctoritas. Hiis
t(estibus), Ada de Eston, Magistro Nicholao de Hamptun, M(agistro)
Roberto Grossi Capitis, M(agistro) Osberto et Willelmo capellanis
nostris.

[a]puo B.   [b]invenire B.   [c]futurum B.   [d]positam B.

Gerald of Wales recommended Master Robert Grosseteste to William de Vere
probably after meeting him at Lincoln, doubtless the visit which he made between
autumn 1194 and the summer of 1195. There have been doubts as to whether this
Grosseteste can be identified with the future bp of Lincoln, but these are probably
groundless: see R.W.Southern, *Robert Grosseteste* (Oxford 1986), 65-6. This
charter is partly quoted in no.260 below.

208. St Guthlac's priory, Hereford

*Settlement of the case between St Guthlac's and Brecon priory concerning
the tithes of the demesne of Herbert de Furchis in Bodenham, with the
consent of the abbots of St Peter's, Gloucester, and St Martin's, Battle.*
[probably 1195 × 24 December 1198]

B = Oxford, Balliol College MS 271 (cartulary of St Guthlac's, Hereford), fo.21v,
no.29. s. xiv in. C = Bodl., MS Carte 108, fo.268r-v. s.xviii.
Pd from C, *Brecon cartulary*, xiv.25.

Universis sancte matris ecclesie filiis ad quos presens scriptum pervenerit Willelmus dei gratia Hereford'[a] ecclesie minister humilis eternam in domino salutem. Quoniam lites que transactionis beneficio finem sortiuntur[b] ad futurorum notitiam in scripturam rediguntur, universitati vestre presenti pagina significandum[c] duximus controversiam[d] que vertebatur inter monachos Hereford' et monachos de Brechen' super decimis de dominio Herberti de Furcis[e] in Bodeham assensu de Glouc' et Sancti Martini[f] de Bello abbatum hoc fine conquievisse: ita videlicet quod monachi Heref' percipient duas partes decimarum bladi totius dominii prenominati sive predictum dominium a domino vel villano vel quolibet alio cuiuscumque sit conditionis possideatur.[g] Et ideo de cetero percepturi sunt duas partes decimarum de tresdecim acris quas Willelmus Toch' et Willelmus filius molendinarii tenent et de tribus buttis et sex acris quas Radulfus de cimiterio tenet[h] et de [i] tribus acris quas tenet Adam presbiter[i] et de tribus acris quas tenet Hugo filius Agnetis et de novem acris quas Iordanus tenet, et de duabus acris quas Simon filius Ricardi tenet que omnia fuerunt de dominio. Et si forte dominus illius dominii vilanagium in dominium converterit, monachi Hereford' nichil de[j] decimis illis sub tali pretextu sibi poterunt vendicare, sed monachi de Brechen' illas decimas totas percipient. Preterea de partibus nemoris illius dominii que converse sunt vel de cetero convertentur in agriculturam a quocumque possideantur, monachi Hereford' medietatem percipient, monachi vero de Brechen'[k] alteram medietatem. Preterea monachi Hereford' percipient medietatem decimarum feni et de pisis et de fabis de supradicto dominio et monachi de Brechen'[k] alteram medietatem, et insuper iidem[l] monachi de Brechen'[k] percipient omnes minutas decimas ad altare provenientes.[m] Et ut hec conventio rata de cetero permaneat[n] et inconcussa, eam[o] fideliter observandam utraque pars in verbo veritatis in presentia nostra promisit et nos eam[o] sigilli nostri munimine et sigillis ecclesiarum utriusque partis, ne inposterum super hoc emergat ambiguitas, confirmare curavimus. Hiis testibus, Willelmo precentore Hereford', Magistro Simone, Magistro Nicholao de Hampton,[p] canonicis, magistro Roberto Grossi Capitis, Magistro Osberto et Willelmo capellanis, Willelmo[q] et Hugone de Bodeham, Willelmo de Kylpek et Nicholao capellanis, Helya[r] medico, Willelmo coco, Waltero de Esbeche, Roberto filio Ricardi, Ricardo decano de Brechen', Bernardo, Nicholao et Willelmo capellanis, Willelmo Deweas,[s] Aluredo Brun et multis aliis.

*a*Heford' *C.*   *b*sortuntur *B.*   *c*sigcandum *C.*   *d*controversia *C.*   *e*Euras *C.*
*f*Maram *C.*   *g*possideat *C.*   *h*B adds et de novem acris quas tenet.
*i-i*novem acris quas tenet Adam *C.*   *j*nil *C.*   *k*Brechon' *C.*   *l*idem *C.*
*m*pervenientes *C.*   *n*maneat *C.*   *o*ea *B.*   *p*Hamtun *C.*   *q*Milone *C.*
*r*corr. from Helea *B;* Helia *C.*   *s*de Ewias *C.*

Dating as for no.207.

209. St Guthlac's priory, Hereford

*Institution of Prior Henry of St Guthlac's, Hereford, in the church of
Holme Lacy.*   [probably 1195 × 24 December 1198]

B = Oxford, Balliol College MS 271, fo.97r-v, no. 430. s.xiv in. C = Ibid., fo.
106r-v, no.470. Inspeximus by Archbp Hubert Walter, datable 25 September
× 24 December 1198, of William's charter.

Pd from C with reference to B, *EEA iii* 145-7, no.491.

Omnibus sancte matris ecclesie filiis ad quos presens scriptum pervenerit, Willelmus dei gratia Herefordensis episcopus*a* salutem in
domino. Universitati vestre notificamus quod, cum Simon Foliot,
canonicus Heref', ecclesiam de Hamma in manus nostras sponte*b*
resignasset, et iuri, si quid in ea habeat, penitus renuntiasset, nos de
assensu et consilio capituli nostri dilectum in Cristo filium nostrum
Henricum, priorem ecclesie Sancti Guthlaci Hereford', in eadem
ecclesia instituimus, et*c* in possessionem eiusdem induci fecimus.
Tenuitati etenim facultatum predicte ecclesie Sancti Guthlaci et indigentie fratrum ibidem deo famulantium*d* compatientes, ut *e*uberius
habeant unde*f* pauperes reficiant, hospites admittant, et proprios
defectus aliquatenus suppleant,*g* prefatam*e* ecclesiam de Hamma in
usus prefatorum fratrum duximus esse convertendam, [fo.97v *B*]
[ne]*h* domus religiosa que lateri sedis episcopalis adheret, et quasi filia
ab uberibus ma[tris]*h* dependet, in urbe etiam, que*i* copiarum locus
est, constituta, inter sue matris habun[da]ntias*h* et vicinorum suorum
sufficientias graves facultatum patiatur angustias. Ut igitur pius circa
filiam matris probetur*j* affectus, concedimus ut prefatus H. prior et
eiusdem loci conventus pretaxatam ecclesiam de Hamma cum pertinentiis suis in usus suos plene convertant et omnia ad eam*k* spectantia
libere percipiant, et hanc concessionem nostram scripto presenti
confirmavimus*l* et sigillum nostrum una cum sigillo capituli nostri
huic confirmationi apposuimus. Hiis testibus, Roberto Folet, Mag-

istro Roberto Grossi Capitis, Magistro Nicholao de Hampton',[m] Magistro Iohanne Clementis, Rogero Foliot, Magistro Osberto et Iohanne capellanis nostris, [n]Radulfo tunc diacono[o] nostro, Rogero de Ver.[n]

[a]ecclesie minister humilis *C*.   [b]presentare *C*.   [c]*om. B*.   [d]deo famulantium *om. C*.
[e-e]*om. B*   [f]inde *C*.   [g]supleant *C*.   [h]*lacuna, B; supplied form C*.   [i]qui *C*.
[j]prohibetur *C*.   [k]ea *BC*.   [l]confirmamus *C*.   [m]Hamp[ ] *lacuna, C*.   [n-n]*om. B; B adds* etc'.
[o]deca[ ] *lacuna, C; probably a scribal error for* diacono.

For the dating, see no.207 above. William de Vere had a deacon called Ralph; see p.lviii.

210. Leominster priory

Grant of permission to the monks of Leominster to convert to their own uses the due known as scrifcorn, *consisting of twelve sheaves per virgate, traditionally paid by the parishioners of Leominster to their vicars, provided that the monks pay a sum of equivalent value to the vicar. The vicars had sometimes hindered the monks from collecting tithes from the parishioners, but the situation had come to the bishop's attention when the vicarage was vacant.*   [10 August 1186 × 1193]

B = BL Egerton MS 3031 (Reading abbey cartulary), fos.56v-7r. s.xii ex. C = BL Cotton MS Domitian A iii (Leominster priory cartulary), fo.62v. s.xiii med.

Pd, *Reading cartularies*, i.289-90, no.358.

His testibus,[a] Willelmo de Stok, vicearchidiacono, Magistro Iohanne de Colecestr', Martino clerico, et multis aliis.

[a]Hiis testibus etc' *C; text of C ends here*

For dating see *Reading cartularies, loc. cit.*; for *Scrifcorn* see note to no.30 above.

211. Leominster priory

Inspeximus of the instrument issued by Hugh, abbot of Reading, granting the perpetual vicarage of Leominster at the altar of the Holy Cross, with the chapel of Hope under Dinmore, to Walter of Stockton, clerk, and notifying the arrangement made between Gervase, dean of Leominster, and Walter concerning the duties and perquisites attached to the vicar-age: until Walter is ordained he is to have three chaplains who will say mass, receiving no more than one penny for each mass and bread and ale offered by the faithful, and on the principal feasts one penny only; Walter is to have payments for trentals and confession in Lent, and half a mark annually, paid by the dean of Leominster, in place of scrifcorn.

[10 August 1186 × 1193]

B = BL Egerton MS 3031 (Reading abbey cartulary), fo.57v. s.xii ex. C = BL Cotton MS Domitian A iii (Leominster priory cartulary), fo.63r. s.xiii med.

Pd, *Reading cartularies*, i.290-292, no.359.

His testibus,[a] Magistro Iohanne[b] de Gloec(estria), Magistro Iohanne de Calne.

[a]*Text of C ends here with* etc'. 　[b]Iohanne Magistro B, *marked for transposition.*

For dating and background see *Reading cartularies*. The vicarage 'ad crucem' was presumably attached to the altar dedicated to the Holy Cross by Bishop R(obert de Béthune) in no.32 above; see also nos.215-6, 270, 279 and 353. Walter the clerk came from Stockton in Kimbolton, Herefordshire. Master John of Calne is probably a scribal error for Master William of Calne.

212. Leominster priory

Mandate to the archdeacons, rural deans, and the priests in the diocese of Hereford to excommunicate those who molest the possessions of Leominster Priory.

[10 August 1186 × 24 December 1198]

B = BL Cotton MS Domitian A iii (Leominster priory cartulary), fo.64v. s.xiii med.

W. dei gratia Heref' episcopus archidiaconis, decanis et presbiteris in Heref' episcopatu constitutis salutem. Auctoritate qua fungimur vobis in vi obedientie precipimus quatinus statim ex quo querimonia monachorum de Leom' super rebus eorum ablatis, vel possessionibus suis turbatis, vel ob iniuriam sibi et hominibus suis illatam delata fuerit, nisi satisfacere voluerint auctoritate nostra omni occasione et dilatione postposita sollempniter omnes illos malefactores cum vobis nominati fuerint candelis accensis excommunicetis, et tanquam excommunicatos in quacumque parrochia fuerint ab omnibus usque ad condignam ablatorum satisfactionem cautius vitari precipiatis, et dum moram ibi fecerint divina celebrari ibidem prohibeatis. Valete.

See nos.269, 303 and 349.

213. Leominster priory

Mandate, on papal authority, to the chaplains and vicars under the jurisdiction of the church of Leominster to force their parishioners to pay their tithes.   [10 August 1186 × 24 December 1198]

> B = BL Cotton MS Domitian A iii (Leominster priory cartulary), fo.64r-v. s.xiii med.

W. dei gratia Heref' episcopus universis capellanis et vicariis ad ius Leom' ecclesie pertinentibus salutem. Mandatum domini pape suscepimus ut omnes parrochianos ecclesie Lem' [fo.64v] ecclesiastica censura et canonica pena coherceamus, ne de frugibus suis ne decimatis solidatas aut mercedes annuas servientibus suis assignent nec diurnas sed omnem integritatem cuiuslibet decime sive orti sive agri seu cuiuslibet lucri sine fraude et diminutione ecclesie Leom' fideliter persolvant. Huius itaque auctoritate mandati universitati vestre auctoritate apostolica et nostra in vi obedientie precipientes iniungimus ut formam prescriptam in decimis solvendis a cunctis parrochianis vestris teneri faciatis, ita ut qui aliter fecerint, eos sententie ecclesiastice subiciatis et a cetu fidelium tanquam infideles separetis et tanquam excommunicatos usque ad dignam satisfactionem a fidelibus vitari faciatis. Similiter et burgenses ad hoc compellatis quatinus secundum estimationem suam sicut volunt excommunicationis vitare sententiam de lucris suis decimas exsolvant.

214. Leominster priory

Notification of the settlement between the prior of Leominster and Simon le Wafre about the chapel of Hampton (Wafer).
[10 August 1186 × 24 December 1198]

B = BL Cotton MS Domitian A iii (Leominster priory cartulary), fo.64r. s.xiii med.

Omnibus sancte matris e(cclesie) f(iliis) W. Heref' episcopus salutem. Quoniam ea que legitime[a] acta sunt nostreque auctoritatis munimine desiderant roborari perpetue stabilitatis robur cupimus et optamus optinere, ad universitatis vestre notitiam volumus pervenire quod controversia que vertebatur inter priorem Lemen' et Symonem le Wafre super capella de Hent' tali fine conquievit. Videlicet quod quicumque pro loco et tempore in predicta capella fuerit vicarius perpetuus instituendus, communi assensu memorati prioris persone eiusdem capelle et domini fundi eiusdem capelle advocati domino episcopo presentabitur, reddendo inde annuatim predicto priori duos solidos nomine pensionis. Totum vero ius sepulture cum corporibus defunctorum ecclesie de Leom' in perpetuum remanebit. Eiusdem vero capelle vicarius de fidelitate ecclesie Lem' servanda et pensione fideliter solvenda sacramento corporaliter prestito se astringet et crisma de ecclesia Lem' recipiet. Quod ne tractu temporis in dubium revocetur, presenti scripto et sigillo nostro confirmare curavimus. T'.

[a]legittime B.

See also no.95.

215. Leominster priory

Licence to the monks of Leominster to appropriate the vicarage of the Holy Cross and the chapel of Hope, with the consent of Walter de Stockton.

[1187/8 × 24 December 1198, probably *c*.1193 × 1198]

B = BL Egerton MS 3031 (Reading abbey cartulary), fo.93v. s.xiii in. C = BL Cotton MS Domitian A iii (Leominster priory cartulary), fos.63v-64r. s.xiii med.

Pd, *Reading cartularies*, i.292-3, no.360.

Dating as for no.216. See also nos.32, 211, 270, 279 and 353.

216. Leominster priory

Licence to the monks of Leominster to appropriate the vicarage of the Holy Cross and the chapel of Hope, for the salvation of the souls of King Henry I and Queen Adeliza, of the souls of the bishops of Hereford and of Bishop William's parents and kinsmen.

[1187/8 × 24 December 1198, probably *c*.1193 × 1198]

B = BL Cotton MS Domitian A iii (Leominster priory cartulary), fo.63v. s.xiii med.

Omnibus sancte matris ecclesie filiis W. Heref' episcopus salutem. Quoniam religiosorum loca pio semper et benigno favore sunt promovenda, illorum propensius religiosorum necessitatibus relevandis quodam favoris privilegio tenemur assistere, qui indigentium onera et advenientium sarcinas misericorditer et benigne noscuntur sustinere. Attendentes igitur dilectorum in domino filiorum monachorum de Leom' hospitalitatis gratiam quam in relevandis pauperum indigentiis communicandis affluentium sarcinis supra vires facultatum suarum ipsos scimus et novimus impendisse, pro salute animarum regis H. et regine Alicie que me nutrierunt et multa beneficia michi contulerunt, et pro salute episcoporum Hereford' tam predecessorum quam successorum nostrorum, et pro salute anime mee et patris et matris mee, et omnium antecessorum et parentum meorum ad petitionem dilecti in Cristo filii H. abbatis Radig' et dilectorum filiorum R. decani et W. precentoris Heref' et Magistri Symonis Meludin' et Magistri Nicholai et aliorum canonicorum ecclesie nostre, volumus et auctoritate episcopali concedimus ut liberum sit et licitum predictis monachis vicariam que dicitur ad crucem Leom' et capellam de Hopa in usus hospitalitatis et pauperum convertere et omnia ad ipsam pertinentia percipere. Capellanos autem annuos qui populo divina celebrabunt quales noverint sibi ydoneos ad mensam suam habeant, qui nobis et successoribus nostris de spiritualibus respondeant, et predictis monachis de temporalibus satisfaciant. Et quia hanc concessionem nostram assensu et voluntate W. clerici de Stoctun' qui predictam vicariam tenuit et in manus nostras resignavit legitime*ᵃ* factam perpetuam et firmam volumus permanere, eam presenti scripto et sigilli nostri munimine confirmare curavimus. T' et c'.

*ᵃ*legittime *B*.

The wording of this document is the same as that of no.215 above, apart from the clause concerning the salvation of souls. Richard Brito became dean in 1187/8, but the document may well, as Dr Kemp suggests (*Reading cartularies*, i.293), be later than 1193, when the original section of Egerton MS 3031 was completed.

217. Lilleshall abbey

Confirmation to Lilleshall abbey of a pension of forty shillings a year paid by Philip de Stepelton. [shortly after 14 June 1188]

B = BL Add MS 50121 (Lilleshall abbey cartulary), fo.27r. s.xiii med.

Omnibus sancte matris ecclesie filiis ad quos presens carta pervenerit W. dei permissione Hereford' episcopus eternam in domino salutem. Ex officio karitatis ac paterne pietatis indulgentia illis precipue tenemur bene facere qui in relevando indigentium necessitatibus et communicandis affluentium sarcinis pia subventione semper intendunt. Attendentes igitur dilectorum in Cristo fratrum abbatis et conventus*a* de Lillesh' hospitalitatis gratiam quam in hospitum susceptione benigne semper inpendunt, pensionem xl s. quam de ecclesia de Wystan' iuxta compositionem inter dictos can(onicos) et Ph(ilippum) de Stepelton factam in curia domini regis sicut in cirographo inter eos concepto continetur recipere debent, nostra auctoritate duximus confirmanda et ne de cetero liceat alicui eam pensionem diminuere vel iniuste detinere et presenti scripto et sigillo nostro communire curavimus. Hiis t'.

*a*tam *sic* B, *instead of* conventus.

The case between William de Boterell, Isabel his wife and Philip de Stepelton their tenant on the one hand, and Lilleshall abbey on the other, was heard at Geddington 14 June 1188 (*ibid.*, fo.73r; R.W.Eyton, *Antiquities*, xi.359).

218. Lire abbey

Inspeximus of a charter of Robert Foliot confirming to the abbey of Lire its possessions in the diocese of Hereford, that is the churches of Tidenham,

Lydney, Linton, Much Marcle, Fownhope, Dewsall, Eardisland, Tenbury, and Wilton.
[10 August 1186 × 24 December 1198, possibly early]

B = BN Collection Moreau, MS 276, fos.135r-6r. (Paper MS, 1764 x 1789). C =
Dom Lenoir MSS (in possession of Mme la Marquise de Mathan, Sémilly,
Manche), vol. xxiii, fo.33r, no.85. s.xviii. Consulted from microfilm in the
Borthwick Institute of Historical Research, York.

Summarised, Evreux, A-D Eure H590, fo.325r, no.xv. s.xviii. Abstract of the
cartulary of Lire Abbey.

Willelmus dei gratia Hereford' ecclesie minister humilis universis
sancte matris ecclesie filiis eternam in Cristo salutem. Cartam venerabilis fratris nostri Roberti pie memorie quondam Hereford' episcopi
Lirensis monasterio super confirmatione beneficiorum ecclesiasticorum que idem monasterium et monachi loci illius in episcopatu
Hereford' habere dinoscitur indultam diligenter inspeximus, cuius
videlicet carte talis est forma: Universis sancte matris ecclesie filiis
Robertus dei gratia Hereford' ecclesie dictus episcopus salutem quam
a domino speramus. Ex suscepte sollicitudinis [fo.135v *B*] officio[a]
viris religiosis provida dispensatione providere tenemur, ut tanto
liberius contemplationi et orationi vacare debeant quanto in exterioribus victualium necessitatibus uberius habundant.[b] Eapropter
Lirensis monasterii mediocritate considerata, cuius fundatio non in
amplis terrarum possessionibus, sed in ecclesiis potius et decimationibus consistere noscitur, monachis in eodem monasterio divino
mancipatis officio ad hospitum susceptionem et ad diffusioris[c] caritatis amplificationem ecclesias cum capellis et omnibus pertinentiis
suis quas in nostro habere noscuntur presulatu, videlicet ecclesiam de
Tehedam,[d] ecclesiam de Lideneia, ecclesiam de Linton', ecclesiam de
Merkelai, ecclesiam de Hopa, ecclesiam de Fonte David, ecclesiam de
Orleslen', ecclesiam de Thametheb'i,[e] ecclesiam de Wilton, votive
pietatis studio concedimus et eis pontificali auctoritate roboramus.
Verum ut vicariis[f] onus et curam regendarum animarum suscepturis
honesta et sufficiens sustentatio ex prescriptis ecclesiis ministretur,
ipsis tertiam portionem omnium decimarum, oblationum et omnium
obventionum ad iam dictas ecclesias sive [fo.136r *B*] ad altare aut
cimiterium spectantium assignamus. Ne ergo posteritas evacuet quod
equitate previa statuta esse cognoscitur illud presentis scripti serie et
sigilli nostri impressione duximus muniendum. Nos itaque prescripti

predecessoris nostri Roberti[g] episcopi vestigiis firmiter inherentes prefato monasterio Lirensi et monachis ibidem deo famulantibus prescripta beneficia ecclesiastica in episcopatu Hereford' constituta episcopali auctoritate[h] confirmamus et presentis carte pagina et sigilli nostri attestatione roboramus. His testibus, Magistro Iohanne de Colec', Reginaldo capellano, priore de Neuwent, Osberto capellano de Lurton', Rannulfo de Tametheb'i,[i] Milone de Muchegros, Henrico de Miner',[j] Hugone de Walford, et multis aliis.

[a]nostro *om. BC.*   [b]habeant *B.*   [c]*corr. from* diffusionis *B.*   [d]*sic for* Tedeham *BC.*   [e]Gametheb'i *B.*   [f]ut vicariis: *B reads* invicariis.   [g]R. *B.*   [h]autoritate *C.*   [i]Thametheb'i *C.*   [j]Anner' *C.*

This document (a comparatively early inspeximus) may have been issued early in the period because Master John of Colchester (a canon of Hereford cathedral who occurs 1186 × 1190) does not occur in Hereford documents which can definitely be dated to the years after 1190.

*219. Lire abbey

Licence to the abbey of Lire to enjoy all the revenues of the church of Wilton, to compensate for losses during the time of war.

[10 August 1186 × 24 December 1198]

Abstract in an 18th century inventory of Lire cartulary, A-D Eure H590, fo.325r, no.xvi. There is no mention of whether the charter was dated or witnessed; it was apparently contained in a vidimus issued by Abbot H. of *Murival* (Henry, abbot of Merevale from 1195 to some point before 1222) and Abbot William of *Combes* (Abbot William II of Combe, 1192-*c*.1217), addressed to a Pope I. (Innocent III).

*220. Lire abbey

*Institution of an unnamed vicar in the chapel of Kyre Wyard (*Cura*) on presentation by the prior of Ocle (*Lyre Ocle*), a dependent priory of Lire Abbey, with the consent of the rector of Tenbury.*

[10 August 1186 × 24 December 1198]

Mention only, in BL Cotton MS Otho B xiv (inventory of Sheen priory), fo.14v. s.xv ex.

Lyre Ocle in Ocle Pychard in Herefordshire was a dependent priory of Lire abbey in Normandy, which also possessed the advowson of the church of Tenbury

(Worcestershire), of which Kyre Wyard was a dependent chapelry (see no.56 above).

221. Lire abbey

Admission of Gilbert fitz Payn, clerk, to the vicarage of the church of Lydney, on presentation by A., prior and general procurator for Lire abbey's possessions in England.

[10 August 1186 × 24 December 1198]

B = Bodl., MS Rawlinson B329 (Hereford cathedral cartulary), fo.166r-v. s.xiii-xiv. Contained in an inspeximus by Richard, cardinal deacon of Sant' Angelo, *ibid.*, fos.165v-166v.

W. dei gratia Herefordensis ecclesie minister humilis universis sancte matris ecclesie filiis ad quod presens scriptum pervenerit eternam in domino salutem. Universitati vestre notum facimus quod nos ad presentationem venerabilis et dilecti in Cristo filii A.*ª* prioris et generalis procuratoris bonorum Lyrensis monasterii in Anglia susce-pimus Gilebertum clericum filium Pagani ad ecclesiam de Lyden' ipsumque in eadem ecclesia perpetuum vicarium constituimus. Ita scilicet quod memoratus G. nomine vicarie tertiam partem omnium ad predictam ecclesiam pertinentium in capellis, terris, decimis, et obventionibus in integrum*ᵇ* possidebit et omnia onera ecclesie sustin-ebit. Duas vero partes ecclesie predicte de consensu predicti A. prioris sepedictus G. quamdiu vixerit possidebit, solvendo inde annuatim sexaginta solidos monachis Lyrensibus ad duos terminos, ad Pascha, ad festum Sancti Michaelis [fo.166v *B*] equaliter. Hanc vero solutio-nem faciendam et fidelitatem predicto monasterio observandam sac-ramento corporaliter prestito iuravit. Quodque perpetuum stabilitatis robur optinere volumus presenti scripto et sigillo nostro confirmavimus. Hiis testibus: Willelmo de Stok' vicearchidiacono, Roberto Folet, Magistro Iohanne, Magistro Osberto, Arnaldo de Stok', Pagano capellano, Ricardo camerario, Reginaldo Folioth, et multis aliis.

*ª*abbati *B*.   *ᵇ*inintegrum *written as one word B*.

The dating of this document is uncertain. The presence of Reginald Foliot would suggest a later date, the fact that Master Osbert is not referred to as chaplain an earlier one. See also no.162.

*222. Little Malvern priory

Grant to Little Malvern priory of the assarts of Deerfold.
[10 August 1186 × 24 December 1198]

Mention only, in a confirmation of Bp Giles de Braose (see below, no.274).

223. Llanthony priory

Grant to Llanthony priory of the land that belonged to Robert White in Prestbury sub montibus *for 31 pence a year.*
[10 August 1186 × 24 December 1198, probably early]

B = PRO, C115 K2/6683 (Llanthony Cartulary A1), fo.122r. s.xiv med.

Sciant presentes et futuri quod ego Willelmus dei gratia Heref' episcopus concessi canonicis Lanthon' ibidem deo et Beate Marie et Sancto Iohanni Baptiste servientibus terram que fuit Roberti le Wyte in Presteb' sub montibus pro xxxi d(enariis) inde annuatim reddendis ad terminos in quibus firma ville solet reddi. Quod ut ratum permaneat presenti scripto et sigillo meo confirmavi. T. Radulfo tunc sen(escallo), Roberto Folet, Magistro Iohanne Clementis et aliis.

Ralph had been succeeded by Adam of Easton as William de Vere's steward before the end of the episcopate: see nos.179 and 180.

*224. Llanthony priory

Confirmation of the grant of the advowson of the church of Pencombe to Llanthony.   [10 August 1186 × 24 December 1198]

Mention only, *CRR*, xi (1223-1224), 232, no.1144.

225. Llanthony priory

Confirmation to Llanthony priory of its possessions in the diocese of Hereford.   [1187/8 × 24 December 1198]

B = PRO, C115 K2/6683 (Llanthony Cartulary, A1), fo.126r. s.xiv med.

Universis sancte matris ecclesie filiis ad quos presens carta pervenerit
Willelmus de Ver divina permissione Hereford' ecclesie minister
humilis salutem, gratiam dei et benedictionem. Quamvis nos ex iniuncto nostre sollicitudini officio teneamur universorum Cristi fidelium indempnitati sollerter providere, faciliores tamen et
propensiores esse debemus circa virorum ecclesiasticorum possessiones*a* canonice adeptas in integritate conservandas easque ratione
comite ampliandas. Inde est quod dilectis in Cristo filiis nostris
canonicis de Lanthon' nostra episcopali auctoritate et presentis carte
patrocinio necnon et sigilli nostri testimonio confirmamus omnes
possessiones quas in episcopatu Hereford' in ecclesiis et capellis, in
terris, decimis et obventionibus, in bosco et plano, in pratis et pascuis,
in aquis et piscariis canonice adepti sunt, et quas a venerabilibus
predecessoribus nostris, quorum cartas super hoc eis indultas diligenter inspeximus, confirmatas et corroboratas esse scimus. Confirmamus itaque eis [fo.126v *B*] terram extra burgum Hereford' que Mora
vocatur liberam et quietam ab omni servitio et consuetudine, excepto
quod una hyda terre de Holemera solummodo regis geldum persolvit,
mansionem etiam quam Ernaldus presbiter tenuerat extra burgum
Hereford' cum x acris terre liberam et quietam ab omni servitio et
consuetudine, similiter et acram unam mansioni prefate contiguam
de terra Fulconis, ecclesiam quoque de Froma cum omnibus pertinentiis suis et duas ecclesias in Prestebur' unam sub montibus, alteram super montes, scilicet ecclesiam de Sevenhamton cum terris et
decimis aliisque elemosinis omnibus eiusdem ecclesiis pertinentibus
aut contingentibus, exceptis duabus portionibus decime de dominio
nostro quas habent decanus et cantor Hereford', de blado scilicet
tantum et de leguminibus; de parcho autem de Prestebur' et de his
qui seminantur vel colliguntur intra designatum ambitum parchi
decima remanet ecclesie de Prestebur', quia terra fuit villanorum; tria
quoque exarta in Prestebur' que Leuricus Figulus et Lefwynus Rufus
et Erni per ix denariorum redditum per annum tenuerunt, que predecessor noster R. episcopus per xii denariorum redditum per annum
tenenda et ad ecclesiam de Prestebur' pertinenda in perpetuam
elemosinam concessit et dedit, unam etiam virgatam terre in eadem
villa quam Ernaldus miles dedit eidem ecclesie quando vitam suam
in ea mutavit liberam et quietam ab omni servitio et consuetudine, ita

ut heredes eius idem servitium quod pro ea episcopo facere debebant de reliquo feudo suo persolvant; preterea dimidiam virgatam terre in eadem villa cum brachia quadam que eidem appendere solet, quam concedente Gilberto episcopo Radulfus predicti Ernaldi filius cum matre sua quando eam in sororem susceperunt in perpetuam elemosinam dedit liberam et quietam ab omni servitio et consuetudine ita ut ipse et heredes eius idem servitium quod pro hac terra debebant de reliquo feudo suo persolvant; ex eiusdem quoque Radulfi donatione x acras terre quas dedit in perpetuam elemosinam liberas et quietas ab omni servitio et consuetudine. T(estibus), Ricardo decano, Roberto de Heselega, Willelmo de Stokes, Rogero filio Mauricii, Waltero scriba et aliis.

*a*in inte *expunged and cancelled after* possessiones *B*.

Richard Brito became dean of Hereford in 1187/8. See also nos.35-7, 103-4, 121, 166 and 276.

226. Much Wenlock priory

Confirmation to Much Wenlock priory that the land of St Milburga is one parish subject to the mother church of Wenlock, as established by Richard (de Belmeis), bishop of London (1108-1128) and William, archdeacon of Hereford, judges delegate, in the presence of Reinhelm, bishop of Hereford (1107-1115), at an assembly at Wistanstow.
[10 August 1186 × 24 December 1198, probably late]

B = PRO, C66/226 (Patent Rolls), membrane 34, 1348, 22 Edward III, part iii, (in inspeximus of Edward III for Much Wenlock, dated 12 October, Westminster).
Cal., *Cal. Pat. Rolls 1348-1350*, 186.

W. dei gratia Hereford' episcopus omnibus ad quos presens scriptum pervenerit salutem in vero salutari. Ex auctentica inspectione veteris testamenti dilectorum fratrum nostrorum monasterii de Wenelok cognovimus terram scilicet Beate Milburge virginis totam esse unius parrochie et singulas capellas que in eadem terra constructe sunt ad matricem suam ecclesiam de Wenel' iure parochiali pertinere, sicut olim cognitum fuit et iudicio definitum per iudices delegatos, Ricardum videlicet pie memorie London' episcopum et Willelmum Hereford' archidiaconum presente et hoc ipsum attestante Reinelmo bone memorie Heref' episcopo et multis aliis viris prudentibus qui apud Wistanestow' ad hoc discutiendum et probandum convenerant. Ne igitur contingat vetus illud instrumentum, quod prefati iudices sigillorum suorum appositione roboraverunt,[a] quod et nos manu propria contrectavimus casu quolibet intercidere et deperire veritatis huius testimonium presenti scripto nostro renovamus et confirmamus. Hiis testibus, Roberto Folet, Magistro Nicholao de Hamt', Magistro Iohanne Clementis, Magistro Osberto, Willelmo capellano, Reginaldo Foliot, Rogero de Ver, Radulfo dyacono, Galfrido clerico, et multis aliis.

[a]roborarunt B.

There is a confirmation of William's charter *ibid.* by Bp Richard de Swinfield, dated at Tugford, 29 January 1284. Reginald Foliot and Ralph the deacon probably entered William de Vere's household in the 1190s. The 'vetus testamentum' here referred to is presumably a reference to the Testament of St Milburga (printed H.Finberg, *Early Charters of the West Midlands* [Leicester 1961], 201-4), a document of uncertain antecedents quoted by Goscelin of St Bertin in his Life of St Milburga. The use of the phrase 'judges delegate' to describe Bp Richard and Archdn William suggests that William de Vere's clerks were seeking a contemporary explanation for the fact that the judgement had not been given by the diocesan.

227. Much Wenlock priory

Licence to Much Wenlock priory to appropriate the churches of Holy Trinity, Wenlock, and Eaton under Heywood.
[10 August 1186 × 24 December 1198, probably late]

B = PRO C66/226 (Patent Rolls); membrane 34, 1348, 22 Edward III, part iii, in inspeximus by Edward III dated Westminster, 12 October.
Cal., *Cal. Pat. Rolls 1348-1350*, 186.

Omnibus sancte matris ecclesie filiis ad quos presens scriptum pervenerit W. dei permissione Hereford' ecclesie minister eternam in domino salutem. Cum religionis studia benigno sint persequenda favore illis tamen religiosorum necessitatibus relevandis quodam favoris privilegio tenemur assistere, quas pro participandis indigentium oneribus benevolentia[a] karitatis ipsos novimus religiosis sustinere. Attendentes igitur dilectorum in Cristo filiorum nostrorum fratrum Wenlocen' monasterii hospitalitatis gratiam quam hospitum aliorumque indigentium susceptionem ipsos supra vires facultatum suarum sepissime novimus impendisse facultatibus suis ad usus hospitum et indigentium destinatis dignum duximus et deo gratum in honore beate virginis Milb(u)rge episcopali auctoritate et pia provisione mediocriter adicere. Ad supplendas igitur predictorum fratrum insufficientias volumus et episcopali auctoritate concedimus ut liceat illis ecclesias Sancte Trinitatis de Wenlok et de Eatun' cum pertinentiis suis quietas et absolutas ab omni exactione et consuetudine episcoporum et officialium suorum in usus suos plene convertere, et tam decimas frugum quam aliarum rerum et obventiones omnes ad predictas ecclesias provenientes sine omni difficultate vel diminutione percipere et capellanos in eisdem ecclesiis ministrantes in mensa sua exhibere eisque pro sua voluntate in rationabilibus soldatis providere. Quod quia perpetue stabilitatis robur volumus optinere presenti scripto et sigilli nostri patrocinio confirmare curavimus. Hiis testibus, Magistro Roberto Folet, Magistro Iohanne Clemen(tis), Magistro Osberto, Willelmo capell',[b] Reginaldo Foliot, Radulfo et Galfrido clericis, Alexandro decano de Dudeleb', Willelmo de Lega, Ricardo Camr' et multis aliis.

[a]honeribus benivolentia B.   [b]*either* capellanis *or* capellano.

The presence of Reginald Foliot as a witness suggests a date after 1190 at least. There is a confirmation of this *ibid.* by Bp Giles de Braose; see below, no.277.

228. Much Wenlock priory

Licence of appropriation issued to Much Wenlock priory in respect of the church of Ditton Priors, to take effect after the death of Master Nicholas of Hampton, the then vicar.   [?1195 × 1198]

B = PRO, C66/226 (Patent Rolls) membrane 33, 1348, 22 Edward III, part iii, in an inspeximus by Edward III for Much Wenlock dated 12 October 1348, at Westminster. C = *Ibid.*, membrane 33, contained in an inspeximus of 1226 × 1234 issued by Hugh Foliot (below, no.359) after the death of Master Nicholas of Hampton; Hugh Foliot's inspeximus in turn is contained within Edward III's inspeximus of 1348 for Much Wenlock. D = *Ibid.*, membrane 33, contained in an inspeximus issued by Dean John and the chapter of Hereford, dated 1282; they also inspected Hugh Foliot's charter referred to in C above; these too are contained in Edward III's inspeximus.

Cal., *Cal. Pat. Rolls 1348-1350*, 189.

Omnibus sancte matris ecclesie filiis ad quos presens scriptum pervenerit W.[a] dei miseratione Hereford' ecclesie minister humilis eternam in domino salutem. Piarum mentium est viris religiosis in suis
necessitatibus tanto propensius[b] subvenire quanto ipsos obsequiis
divinis benignius invigilare et in relevandis indigentium necessitatibus propensius[c] credimus laborare. Attendentes igitur hospitalitatis
gratiam quam dilecti in Christo filii monachi Wenlocensis[d] monasterii
in communicandis advenientium sarcinis noscuntur impendisse, intuitu pietatis concedimus et presentium auctoritate confirmamus
predictis monachis ut licitum sit et liberum eis[e] ecclesiam de Dudinton'[f] cum omnibus pertinentiis suis post decessum Magistri Nicholai[g]
de Hamptun'[h] eiusdem ecclesie vicarii sibi appropriare et omnia inde
provenientia in usus suos convertere. Quod quia[i] perpetue stabilitatis
robur volumus optinere presenti scripto et sigillo nostro confirmare
curavimus. Hiis testibus, Roberto Folet,[j] Magistro Iohanne Clementis, Magistro Roberto, Magistro Osberto, Willelmo capell',[k] Reginaldo Foliot, Rogero[l] de Ver et multis aliis.

[a]Willelmus *D*. [b]propencius *BC*. [c]propencius *B*. [d]Wyloc' *D*. [e]om. *C*.
[f]Dudintun' *C;* Dodinton *D*. [g]Nicolai *B*. [h]Hamtun *B;* Hampton' *D*.
[i]*Text of C ends here with* et cetera. [j]Folyot *D*. [k]capellano *or* capellanis ?; capellano *in full, D*. [l]Fogerr' *B*.

The presence of Master Robert (Grosseteste ?) suggests that the document might
be later than 1195; see note to no.207 above. Hugh Foliot issued an inspeximus of
this charter after the death of Master Nicholas (no.359).

229. Osney abbey

*Confirmation of a grant by Hugh of Croft of the tithes of his demesne in
Wharton in Leominster to Osney abbey.*   [1191, before May]

B = BL Cotton MS Vitellius E xv (Osney cartulary), fo.163v. s.xiii in. C = Oxford,
    Christ Church D. & C. MS 343 (Osney cartulary), fo.204r. s.xiii ex.
Pd., *Oseney cartulary*, v.115.

Testibus Radulfo archidiacono Heref', Magistro Ricardo decano,
Magistro Roberto Folet,[a] Magistro Willelmo, Willelmo capellano et
multis aliis.

[a]Foliot *B;* Fol' *C*.

The Master William who appears as a witness is Master William de Calne; see *Oseney cartulary*, v.110-1. As Salter there points out, this deed was probably issued at the same time as Hugh de Croftes' (*ibid.*, v.110-1), which is dated 1191, as the witness lists are almost identical. William's charter refers to Pope Clement III without mentioning that he had just died, which means that the charter must be earlier than May 1191; Pope Clement III died in late March of that year.

*230. St Osyth's priory

Grant to St Osyth's priory, Essex, of land called Bunce *in the parish of St Peter the Less in London, which William had held as a tenant of the priory of Holy Trinity, Aldgate, London.*

[10 August 1186 × 1192, probably 1192]

Mentioned in a charter of Ralph, abbot of St Osyth's, dated 25 March 1192 (PRO, E40/2383), recounting the grant of the same land by S(tephen), prior of Holy Trinity, Aldgate (1170-1197). William de Vere is specifically referred to as Bp of Hereford. It is not stated whether his gift was formally expressed in writing. *Bunce* cannot be identified. Bosse Lane in the parish of St Peter the Less acquired its name much later: see M.D.Lobel, ed. *The British atlas of historic towns,* vol. iii (Oxford 1989), 67.

231. Shrewsbury abbey

Admission of Master William de Calne to the church of Stottesdon.

[10 August 1186 × 1190]

A = Shrewsbury Local Studies Library, Deed no. 77. 14th-century endorsement: Carta W. episcopi Hereford super pensione centum solid' ecclesie de Stottis-don'. 157 × 73 mm. Originally sealed on a tag; seal does not survive but tag bears traces of green wax.

B = NLW MS 7851 D (Shrewsbury cartulary), p.302, no.338b. s.xiii ex.

Pd from B, with reference to A, *Shrewsbury cartulary*, ii.308, no.338b.

Universis sancte matris ecclesie filiis Willelmus de Ver dei gratia Heref'. episcopus. salutem in domino. Ad universitatis vestre notitiam devenire volumus. nos ad presentationem dilectorum filiorum nostrorum abbatis et conventus Salopesb'. magistrum Willelmum de Calna in ecclesia de Stottesdun'. rectorem instituisse. ita quod singulis annis pro prefata ecclesia et capellis ad eam spectantibus prescriptis monachis centum sol(idos) nomine pensionis persolvet. Et quoniam memoratam pensionem salva honesta sustentatione vicarii in perpetuum posse persolvi cognovimus : iccirco ne in posterum cuiuslibet calliditate valeat imminui : episcopalis auctoritatis patrocinio et carte nostre testimonio sepedictis monachis pretaxatam pensionem in prescripta ecclesia confirmare curavimus. His testibus Willelmo filio Nicholai. Magistro Iohanne de Colec'. Philippo de Say. Iocelino de Boseham. Osberto de Kinlet.

For the dating, see no.232.

232. Shrewsbury abbey

Admission of Master William de Calne as rector to the church of Stottesdon, with all its chapels, Farlow, Wrickton, Aston Botterell and Wheathill, and appurtenances as his predecessor Gamel had held it, on presentation by Abbot Ralph and the monks of Shrewsbury; William is to pay Shrewsbury an annual pension of one hundred shillings at four terms.   [10 August 1186 × 1190]

B = NLW MS 7851 D (Shrewsbury cartulary), pp.309-310, no.351b. s.xiii ex.
Pd, *Shrewsbury Cartulary*, ii.317, no.351b.

Hiis t(estibus) Willelmo filio Nicholai, Magistro Iohanne de Colec', Philippo de Sai, et aliis.

Abbot Ralph died before 1190. William de Vere issued two letters of admission for Master William de Calne, this one and no.231 above, and the similarity of the witness lists suggests that they were issued at the same time. For Master William de Calne, see introduction, p.lvi.

233. Shrewsbury abbey

Notification that the right of presentation to the chapel of Aston Eyre belongs to Shrewsbury Abbey.   [c.1190 × Michaelmas 1198]

A = Shrewsbury Local Studies Library, Deed no.372. 13th-century endorsement: Carta episcopi ... de capella de Aston Aeri. 127 × 66 mm. Originally sealed on a tag but no tag or seal surviving.
B = NLW MS 7851 D (Shrewsbury cartulary), p.304, no.341. s.xiii ex.

Pd from A, G.M(orris), 'Early Deeds relating to Shropshire', *Collectanea Topographica et Genealogica*, v (1838), 177; W.A.L(eighton), 'Old Shropshire Deeds', *Transactions of the Shropshire Archaeological Society*, ix (1886), 173.

Pd from B, with reference to A, *Shrewsbury cartulary*, ii.310, no.341.

W. dei gratia Hereford' minister humilis. omnibus sancte matris ecclesie filiis ad quos presentes littere pervenerint. salutem in vero salutari. Universitati vestre significamus. quod Robbertus*a* filius Aer in presentia nostra constitutus coram multis clericis et laicis ore proprio et sponte sua confessus est ⁊ quod neminem ad capellam de Estun de iure potuit presentare. constanter asserens quod eadem capella iure advocationis ad abbatem et conventum de Salopesb' pertinebat et pertinet. Et ut nulla super hoc in posterum emergat ambiguitas ⁊ presenti scripto sigilli nostri testimonium imposuimus. Valete.

a sic A.

For the dating see no.235.

234. Shrewsbury abbey

Notification to the abbot and monks of Shrewsbury that Robert fitz Aer has renounced all claim to the advowson of the chapel of Aston Eyre, with the request that Shrewsbury accept as chaplain of Aston Peter of Hopton, whom Bishop William had instituted, in succession to William chaplain of Aston, who had resigned the chapel, on presentation by Robert.
[*c.*1190 × Michaelmas 1198]

B = NLW MS 7851 D (Shrewsbury cartulary), p.303, no.340. s.xiii ex.

Pd, *Shrewsbury cartulary* ii.309, no.340.

For the dating see no.235.

235. Shrewsbury abbey

Institution of Peter of Hopton, chaplain, as vicar of Aston Eyre, on presentation by Abbot H(ugh) of Shrewsbury, with the provision that demesne tithes and burials should belong to the mother church, Morville.
[*c.*1190 × Michaelmas 1198]

A = Shrewsbury Local Studies Library, Deed no.376. 14th-century endorsement: presentatio vicarie de Eston Aer. 144 × 98 mm. Originally sealed on the tag; seal does not survive.

B = NLW MS 7851 D (Shrewsbury cartulary), p. 304, no.342. s.xiii ex.

Pd, from A, G.M(orris), 'Early Deeds Relating to Shropshire', *Collectanea Topographica et Genealogica*, v (1838), 177; W.A.L(eighton) 'Old Shropshire Deeds', *Transactions of the Shropshire Archaeological Society*, ix (1886), 173.

Pd, from B, with reference to A, *Shrewsbury cartulary*, ii.310, no.342.

W. dei gratia Hereford' ecclesie minister humilis. omnibus sancte matris ecclesie filiis ad quos presentes littere pervenerint *:* eternam in domino salutem. Noverit universitas vestra nos ad presentationem karissimi fratris nostri H. dei gratia abbatis de Salopesb' et conventus eiusdem loci in capellam suam de Estona Petrum capellanum de Hoptun karitatis intuitu admisisse et eum in ipsa capella vicarium perpetuum canonice instituisse. ita scilicet quod idem Petrus dictam capellam cum omnibus pertinentiis suis sicut antecessores sui tenuerunt *:* tenebit. videlicet cum una virgata terre in villa de Estona et tertia parte decimarum segetum de tota terra consuetudinaria. Decime vero totius dominii que ad parrochialem ecclesiam spectant. et corpora defunctorum cum principalibus legatis. matrici ecclesie scilicet de Mamerfeld ad quam predicta capella pertinet *:* remanebunt. Memoratus autem Petrus singulis annis ad festum Sancti Michaelis octo solidos sub annua pensione matrici ecclesie de Mamerfeld persolvet. et nobis et officialibus nostris de omnibus consuetudinibus que ad ipsam capellam pertinent *:* respondebit. His testibus. Magistro Robberto^a Folet. Willelmo capellano. Reginaldo Foliot. Martino de Castello. Robberto^a de Hastinges.

^{a}*sic A.*

Hugh de Lacy was abbot of Shrewsbury from 1190 or shortly before 1190 until 1220/1221. This charter was probably issued at the same time as nos.233 and 234 above, before the death of Robert fitz Aer, who died before Michaelmas 1198; see *Shrewsbury cartulary*, 309.

236. The Templars

Licence to the Templars to appropriate Cardington Church.

[10 August 1186 × 24 December 1198, probably late]

B = Hereford, Herefordshire County Record Office, Registrum Ricardi de Swin-field (formerly Hereford, Diocesan Registry), fo.142r (old foliation), fo.141r (new foliation). 1283 × 1317, here s.xiv in. William's charter is contained in an inspeximus issued by the official of the archdeacon of London, dated 9 November 1303.

Pd, *Reg. Swinfield*, 396.

Omnibus sancte matris ecclesie[a] ad quos presens scriptum pervenerit, W. dei gratia Herefordensis ecclesie minister humilis eternam in domino salutem. Ius exigit et ratio comprobat ut que viris religiosis iuste collata sunt auctoritate episcopali muniantur; pietatis insuper suadet devotio ut beneficia collata et confirmata exigentibus meritis eorum usibus applicentur. Eapropter concedimus dilectis in Cristo filiis fratribus Militie Templi Iherusalem pro fide Cristi contra hostes fidei iugiter dimicantibus et non solum rebus et possessionibus verum nec corporibus propriis parcentibus ut liberum sit eis et licitum ecclesiam de Kerdintun' cum omnibus pertinentiis suis in usus suos convertere et omnia provenientia percipere, salvo iure Ernaldi capellani in vita sua, salvis etiam episcopalibus consuetudinibus et Herefordensis ecclesie dignitate. Quod quia perpetue stabilitatis robur volumus optinere presenti scripto et sigilli nostri munimine confirmare curavimus. Hiis test(ibus) Hugone archidiacono Salop', Magistro Roberto Folet, Magistro Nicholao de Hamptun', Magistro Iohanne Clementis, Magistro Osberto, Willelmo capell',[b] Reginaldo Foliot, Thoma Foliot, Radulfo diacono et multis aliis.

[a]filiis *om.* ?   [b]capellanis ?

The presence of Reginald Foliot among the witnesses suggests that this document was issued in the 1190s.

237. Tintern abbey

Licence to Tintern abbey to appropriate the church of Woolaston.
[*c.*1190 × 24 December 1198]

B = BL Arundel MS 19 (Tintern cartulary), fo.31r. s.xvi.

Partial translation of, F.G.Cowley, *The Monastic Order in South Wales, 1066-1349* (Cardiff 1977), 185.

Omnibus sancte matris ecclesie filiis ad quos presens scriptum pervenerit Willelmus dei gratia Hereford' episcopus eternam in domino salutem. Licet ex consuetudinibus ecclesie anglicane non sit permissio monachis Cisterc(iensis) ordinis ecclesias parochiales in usus suos convertere, nos tamen, quia ecclesiam Sancte Marie de Tinterne quam antecessores nostri fundaverunt quodam favoris privilegio^a diligimus, ut diligere tenemur, ad sustentationem fratrum deo ibidem servientium et relivandam ibidem confluentium necessitates aliquid facultatibus suis amplioris quadam dispensationis^b gratia ut commodius in exhibitione^c karitatis pauperibus possint adesse debemus adicere; concedimus igitur et karitative indulgemus ut liberum sit et licitum abbati et monachis de Tinterne ecclesiam de Wolanestun' et capellam de Alvintun' cum omnibus pertinentiis suis in usus suos convertere et omnes fructus et obventiones inde provenientes percipere, salva competenti sustentatione vicarii qui curam gerat animarum et nobis et officialibus nostris de spiritualibus respondeat. Quod ne tractu temporis in irritum revocetur presenti scripto et sigillo nostro confirmare curavimus. Hiis testibus, Willelmo archidiacono Hereford', Magistro Nicholao, Willelmo capellano, Magistro Iohanne Clim', Magistro Roberto, Galfrido de Lacy, Magistro Simone de Fraxino, Reginaldo Foliot, Radulfo diacono, et multis aliis.

^{a}dispensati sint gratia ut commodius in exhabitat' caritatis pauperibus possint *written between* privilegio *and* diligimus *and crossed out.* ^{b}dispensati sunt *sic B.* ^{c}exhibitatione *B.*

Archdn Ralph Foliot of Hereford died 20 December, either in 1198 or 1199. The William mentioned here is not his successor, but Canon William de Stokes, who was vice-archdn of Hereford at this time. Vice-archdns were sometimes referred to simply as archdns: J.Armitage Robinson, *Somerset Historical Essays* (London 1921), 88-90. The mention of Reginald Foliot suggests that this document is late in any case: see introduction, p.lviii. According to Cowley (*loc. cit.*) this is the earliest appropriation of a parish church by a Cistercian house in Wales.

238. Waltham abbey

Grant of forty days indulgence to all worshippers at, and benefactors of, the newly consecrated chapel of St Thomas at Waltham abbey.

13 March 1188

B = BL Harleian MS 391 (Waltham cartulary), fo.100r. s.xiii in.

Cal., *Waltham charters*, 186-7, no.277.

Universis sancte matris ecclesie filiis ad quos presens scriptum pervenerit Willelmus divina miseratione Herefordensis ecclesie minister humilis salutem in vero salutari. Ad universorum volumus devenisse notitiam quod nos inspectis diligenter privilegiis a sede Romana sacrosancte ecclesie Walthamensi indultis, quandam capellam infra eiusdem ecclesie septa constitutam, videlicet capellam infirmarie canonicorum regularium ibidem deo famulantium in honore dei et gloriose virginis Marie et beatissimi martiris atque pontificis Thome nomine debita cum sollemnitate*a* deo auctore consecravimus. In cuius dedicatione nos de dei misericordia que est super omnia opera eius plenius confisi omnibus eiusdem capelle veneratoribus et benefactoribus vere penitentibus et confessis de iniuncta sibi penitentia quadraginta dies relaxamus. Et singulis annis in die anniversario et tota illa septimana quindecim dierum relaxationem indulsimus omnibus illis qui eandem capellam visitare et elemosinarum largitione honorare cum omni devotione decreverint. Facta est autem hec dedicatio in crastino Beati Gregorii pape anno ab incarnatione domini millesimo centesimo octogesimo viii, anno videlicet quo illustris Anglorum rex Henricus secundus prescripte ecclesie advocatus signum dominice Crucis accepit. Valete.

*a*solennitate *B*.

William had before his elevation to the episcopate been a canon of Waltham and master of the king's works there. Henry II took the cross on 21 January 1188; for a note on the date see the introduction, p.xcix.

239. William de Burghill

Notification of a settlement between William de Burghill, knight, and William the chamberlain over land at Herlingeham *(Orlham in Ledbury).*

[*c*.25 December 1193 × 11 July 1198]

A = Hereford D. & C. Muniments, no.1363. 14th-century endorsement: scribit'. 203 × 112 mm. Originally sealed on a tag; seal and tag do not survive. The document is much damaged, with three holes and a great many stains.

Pd, David Walker, 'Gloucester charters', *A medieval miscellany for D.M.Stenton,* ed. P.M.Barnes and C.F.Slade, P.R.S., new ser., xxxvi (1962 for 1960), 266, no.14.

Willelmus dei gratia Hereford' episcopus omnibus sancte matris ecclesie filiis ad quos presens scriptum pervenerit. salutem in eo qui salus est omnium. Noverit universitas vestra causam que vertebatur inter Willelmum de Burchull' militem et Willelmum camerarium super terra de Herlingeham primo in curia nostra. postea in comitatu Hereford' hoc fine tandem conquievisse. Willelmus quidem de Burchull' predictam terram de Herlingeham tanquam terram que iure hereditario eum conti[nge]bat. adversus nominatum W. camerarium cum litteris domini H. Cant' archiepiscopi tunc totius Anglie iusticiario clamabat. asserens [Robertum Lambert] patruum suum eandem terram tota vita sua pacifice iure hereditario possedisse. Et in ea diem extremum vite sue nullo alio relicto herede preter ipsum ; clausisse. super hoc autem testes quamplures fide dignos hos ipsum probare offerentes ; producebat. Et ut sibi eiusdem terre restitutio fieret ; postulabat. Willelmus vero c[am'] e contrario asserebat se prenominatam terram ex dono predecessoris nostri Roberti Foliot bone memorie Hereford' episcopi tanquam vacantem post mortem predicti Roberti Lambert ass[e]cutum fuisse ; ipsumque eandem terram diutius quiete et pacifice nullo contradicente possedisse. Cumque causa hec diutius tam in nostra presentia quam in comitatu Hereford' [placi]tata fuisset amicis hinc inde intervenientibus hunc finem sortita est. Willelmus quidem cam(erarius) ius sepedicti Willelmi de Burchull' in eadem terra recognoscens eandem terram c[oram can]onic[is] Herefor[ ] militibus totius comitatus. sub presentia etiam Ade de Eston' tunc seneschalli nostri in hoc ex parte nostra assensum prebentis una cum carta predicti predecessoris resignavit et eam tactis sacrosanctis evangeliis pro se et heredibus suis in perpetuum ab–iuravit. Constitutis postmodo in presentia nostra tam W. de Burchull' quam .W. camerario factam [inter] eos conventionem plenius recognoscentes ut eam ratam haberemus. Et ut homagium et fidelitatem debitam de sepedicto W. de Burch' reciperemus ; instanter postulabant. Inspectis itaque cartis Gilleberti Fol(iot). Lond' episcopi et Roberti Foliot predecessorum nostrorum in quibus servicium annuatim predicte terre continebantur. in nullo ius nostrum vel successorum ledi attendentes prefatam conventionem ratam habuimus. et sepenominato W. de Burch' terram de Herlingeham cum omnibus pertinentiis suis sub annua sex solidorum pensione nobis successoribus nostris per[solvenda] perpetuo tenendam concessimus. salvo regali s[ervicio]. Pro hac nostra concessione dedit nobis predictus W. de Burch' unam marcam argenti. et Willelmo cam(erario) octo mar[cas argenti. Quod qu]ia firmum et stabile manere volumus presenti scripto et sigilli nostri attestatione confirmamus. Hiis testibus. Ada de Eston' tunc senescallo. Waltero de Travel' constabulario. Rogero le Poh'. Hugone de Dunre Hugone de Wlf'. Willelmo de Weldebof [ ]*a* de Stanf'. Roberto de Boclinton'. Reginaldo de Burch'. Ricardo de Maslo. Seer de Dimoc Rogero filio Mauricii. et multis aliis.

a lacuna, perhaps intentional; it should read Iohanne *(see no.179).*

The *terminus a quo* is the start of Hubert Walter's pontificate, and the *terminus ad quem* is the end of his justiciarship: see David Walker, *loc. cit.*. As Walker remarks, ibid., 257, n.1, *Herlingeham* is most probably to be identified with the farm of Orlham in Ledbury, since Ledbury was an episcopal manor.

*240. William the janitor

Confirmation to William the janitor of the lands and tenements in the manor of Prestbury which he had been granted by Bishop Robert Foliot.
[10 August 1186 × 24 December 1198]

Mentioned in a confirmation of 1200 × 1201 issued by Bp Giles de Braose (see below, no.289). Giles confirmed Robert and William's grant of lands and tenements with their easements in the manor of Prestbury. William the janitor was paying 14s a year for these according to the terms of Giles' deed.

241. Worcester cathedral priory

Notification that he has conceded to the monks of Worcester cathedral priory a pension of forty shillings from the vicarage of Lindridge.
· [10 August 1186 × 24 December 1198]

B = Worcester Cathedral Library, MS A4 (Worcester cathedral cartulary), fo.27v, no.205. s.xiii med.
Pd, *Worcester cartulary*, 109, no.205.

His testibus, Magistro Roberto Folet, etc'.

This charter might well have been issued after no.242 below, and could therefore be datable 1189 × 1198.

242. Worcester cathedral priory

Confirmation, to Prior Senatus and the monks of Worcester, of grants by William's predecessors of Lindridge Church to Worcester cathedral priory.   [1189 × 1196]

B = Worcester Cathedral Library MS A4 (Worcester cathedral cartulary), fo.27r-v, no.204. s.xiii med.

Pd., *Worcester cartulary*, 109, no.204.

Hiis testibus, Roberto de Heseleya, etc'.

Senatus was prior of Worcester from 1189 to 1196.

GILES DE BRAOSE

243. Profession of obedience

Profession of obedience made to Hubert Walter, archbishop of Canterbury.   [24 September 1200]

A¹ = Canterbury D. & C. Ch. Ant. C115, no.65. 13th-century endorsement: Anno gracie mcc facta est hec professio apud Westmon' in capella Sancte Katerine viii kl. octob'. contra apellationem (sic) a monachis Cant' super hoc factam. 115 × 36 mm, irregular shape; possibly remains of a wrapping tie.

A² = Ibid., Ch. Ant. C115, no.72. No ancient endorsements. 176 × 53 mm.

Pd, *Canterbury professions*, 60, no.142. Facsimiles of A¹ and A² ibid., plates IIIc and IIId respectively.

Ego Egidius Herefordensis electus profiteor sancte Dorobornensi ecclesie et tibi pater Huberte Archiepiscope tuisque successoribus canonice substituendis canonicam subiectionem. +ᵃ

ᵃ*autograph cross A¹; om. A².*

244. Adam of Easton

Confirmation to Adam of Easton of the land at Easton which Bishop William de Vere had given to him.
[24 September 1200 × 30 November 1201]

A = Trowbridge, Wiltshire County Record Office, 9/15/4 (Easton Priory MSS). (16th c?) endorsement: A confirmation made by Gylle byshop of Herford of lande gevyn to Adam of Eston to (sic) Wyll' Ver before that tyme byshop of Herford for the rent of x li' by the yer. 223 × 100 + 27 mm. Tags for two seals, a fragment of one of which (the right hand one) survives. This seal fragment, in varnished natural wax, 52 × 57 mm, depicting a church, is an impression of Hereford cathedral chapter seal; the legend has been largely broken off and the remaining part of the rim is worn. Counterseal: originally a pointed oval, 26 × 23 mm, it shows a seated figure; the head and shoulders are missing. It is probably taken from the same matrix as the counterseal to the chapter seal fastened to Hereford D. & C. Muniments no.659, a charter of Dean Richard Brito and the cathedral chapter of the very late twelfth century. Legend:

....LLV..........hERE ....
B = Hereford, Herefordshire County Record Office, Registers of Bothe, Foxe
and·Boner (formerly Hereford Diocesan Registry), fo.39r-v. s.xvi.
Pd, from B, *Reg. Bothe*, 60.

Omnibus sancte matris ecclesie filiis ad quos presens scriptum pervenerit Egidius dei gratia Hereford' ecclesie minister humilis eternam
in domino salutem. Noverit universitas vestra nos assensu capituli
Hereford' concessisse et hac carta nostra confirmasse dilecto in Cristo
filio Ade de Estona homini nostro et fideli totam terram de Estona
quam Willelmus de Ver episcopus predecessor noster bone memorie
prenominato Ade pro homagio et servitio suo dedit et concessit et sua
carta confirmavit. Hanc siquidem terram cum omnibus pertinentiis
suis predicto Ade concessimus in bosco in plano. in pratis. in pascuis.
in viis. in semitis. in dominiis. et villanagiis. et liberis [tenemen]tis.[a]
in terra culta et inculta. et in omnibus rebus et consuetudinibus
tenendam et habendam prefato Ade et heredibus suis de nobis et
successoribus nostris episcopis Hereford' iure hereditario ad
feodofirmam libere et quiete. honorifice. plenarie. et integre ab omni
servitio et seculari exactione. reddendo inde annuatim nobis et successoribus nostris pro omnibus rebus decem libras argenti. ad quatuor
terminos. videlicet ad Natale domini quinquaginta solidos. ad Annuntiationem beate Marie quinquaginta solidos. ad festum Sancti
Iohannis Baptiste quinquaginta solidos ad festum Sancti Michaelis
quinquaginta solidos. De hac vero terra hom[agium] prefati Ade in
plena curia nostra apud Bosebur' accepimus. ipsamque terram cum
omnibus pertinentiis suis debemus nos et successores nostri warantizare eidem Ade et heredibus suis adversus omnes homines. Quod ut
firmum et stabile in perpetuum permaneat ? presenti carta et sigilli
nostri appositione confirmare et corroborare curavimus. Hiis testibus. capitulo Hereford'. sigillo suo hoc idem approbante. Ricardo
decano Hereford'. Hugone archidiacono de Salopes'. Magistro
Philippo de Lindeseia. Magistro Theodbaldo de Len. Magistro Hugone de Mappenour'. Domino Hugone de Breus'. Magistro Philippo
Mapp'. capellanis episcopi Willelmo et Simone. Willelmo de Alde-
monneston'. Mauricio de Crad[eleg] ? Magistro Alexandro de Lide-
iard'. Alexandro de Estenour'. Gregorio de Everleia. et Waltero. et
Thoma. et Gaufrido fratribus suis. Eustachio de Wttun'. et Iohanne
de Wiche fratre eius. Petro Fulch'. et Ricardo fratre eius. [Henrico]
Sturmi. et multis aliis.

[a]surface of document worn A.

For William de Vere's original grant, see above, nos.179-80. Dean Richard died 30 November 1201.

245. Brecon priory

Collation of A(dam), chaplain, to the vicarage of Humber, as Brecon priory, which had the advowson, had delayed beyond the terms laid down by the (Third) Lateran Council without presenting a candidate.

[24 September 1200 × 9 April 1214]

B = Bodl. MS Carte 108 (Brecon cartulary), fo.267r. s.xviii.

Pd, *Brecon cartulary*, xiv.22.

Omnibus sancte matris ecclesie filiis ad quos presens scriptum pervenerit Egidius divina permissione Hereford' ecclesie minister eternam in domino salutem. Noverit universitas vestra quod cum contigisset[a] vicariam capelle de Humbr' ultra tempus in Laterano diffinitum concilio vacare, nos eiusdem auctoritate concilii, nec non et privilegiis nobis a domino papa super hoc indulti, eandem vicariam A. capellano contulimus et ipsum in eadem capella perpetuum vicarium cum omnibus ad eam de iure spectantibus canonice instituimus, salva pensione decem solidorum monachis de Brekon[b] annuatim de eadem capella persolvenda. Ut igitur hec nostra institutio rata permaneat et inconcussa, eam presenti scripto et sigilli nostri testimonio confirmavimus. Hiis testibus, Magistris Theobaldo, Galfrido de Ludel', Philippo Map', Ricardo et Ranulfo capellanis, Simone et Willelmo clericis et multis aliis.

[a]contingisset B.   [b]Brek.n B.

An Adam appears as (rural) dean of Humber in a case concerning the tithes of Humber, which was settled on 9 April 1214 (*The Letters of Pope Innocent III: a Calendar*, ed. C.R. and Mary Cheney [Oxford 1967], no.946). Because of the interdict the case may have arisen as early as 1207. A(dam), dean of Humber, also occurs below, no.302.

*246. Brecon priory

Institution of Nicholas as rector of the church of Byford, on presentation by Walter de Traveley in the name of Brecon priory, after the death of Miles, the rural dean, who had been the previous rector.

[24 September 1200 × 17 November 1215]

> Mention only, in a notification by Walter de Traveley that he had presented Nicholas for institution in the name of Brecon priory, and that he and his heirs recognised Brecon priory's right to the advowson (*Brecon cartulary*, xiv.223): see also below, no.293).

247. Hubert Walter, archbishop of Canterbury

Letter explaining why he had not allowed Juliana, a party in a matrimonial dispute, to appeal, and requesting guidance.

[24 September 1200 × 13 July 1205]

> A = Canterbury D. & C. Christ Church Letter II 239. No endorsements. 150 × 140 mm. Perhaps originally sealed on a tongue.
>
> Cal., *Canterbury Cases*, introduction, appendix i, 106, no.15.

Reverendo in Cristo patri et domino karissimo. H. dei gratia. Cant' archiepiscopo tocius Anglie primati E. divina permissione Hereford' ecclesie minister salutem et tam devote quam debite obedientie reverentiam. Vestra pater nobis litterarum vestrarum tenore significare decrevit dilectio quod appellationi a Iuliana muliere facte deferremus .' vel quare deferendum non esset vobis rescriberemus. Volentes igitur discretioni vestre tenorem negocii et veritatem rei evidentius intimare .' vobis significamus quod Matheus lator presentium coram nobis in iure comparens uxorem suam petiit Iulianam. asserens quod rebus suis asportatis ipsum corporis sui dominio spoliarat.[a] Facta siquidem per affirmationem et negationem litis contestatione predictus .M. ad sue intentionis assertionem testes induxit. Die vero secunde productioni assignata predicta Iuliana advocatorum munita consilio causam querens subterfugii .' in vocem appellationis prorupit. Verum ex parte adversa responsum est appellationem de iure non debere tenere. cum evidens esset et notorium quod iam per septennium in eadem domo. mensa et lecto tanquam vir et uxor commanserant et quod ipsum iuris ordine pretermisso corporis sui dominio spoliaverat. Facta igitur super huius rei evidentia in generali capitulo debita et diligenti inquisitione.ᵃ compertum est per famam vicinie quod res ita penitus se habuit sicut supradictus Math' in sue intentionis fundatione asseruit. siquidem cum peritorum in iure consilio pronuntiatum esset appellationem non tenere.ᵃ presente procuratore predicte Iul' et non reclamante. sepedictus .M. secunda usus est testium productione. Demum vero cum nil restaret nisi attestationum publicatio.ᵃ comparuit in iure Iul'. et iterum in vocem appellationis prorupit. Et cum requireretur ab eius advocato a quo gravamine vel qua ratione appellaret.ᵃ minus sane verba legis intelligens respondit. sufficit dicere appello.[1] Nos vero huic appellationi sicut nec priori non deferentes attestationes publicavimus. parati secundum iuris formam negocium diffinitive sententie calculo terminare. Interim vero ad vos sepedicta Iuliana accessit. et que bene recolitis ut credimus intimavit. Licet igitur certi sumus qualiter secundum ea que gesta sunt procedere debeamus.ᵃ vestrum tamen in hac parte postulamus consilium et consensum. volentes in omnibus discretionis vestre consilio non immerito instrui et informari. Valeat semper in domino sanctitas vestra.

ᵃ*sic for* spoliaverat.

[1]'Sufficit dicere "appello"' *(direct speech)*.

Hubert Walter died 13 July 1205. See also *EEA* iii, no.543.

248. Stephen Langton, archbishop of Canterbury

Litterae excusatoriae to explain Giles' absence from an episcopal consecration because he had to accompany the papal legate Nicholas of Tusculum on a journey in Wales.   [1214, before 5 October]

A = Canterbury D. & C. Eastry Correspondence, Group iii, leaf 21, no.91. Late 14th-century endorsements: Excusatio Deprecatio Hereford ut habeatur excusatus. eo quod non possit insistere consecrationi pro subscriptis causis. 170 × 53 mm; presumably originally sealed on the tongue, which does not survive.

Mentioned, *HMCR*, lv (*Var. Coll.* i), 251.

Venerabili in Cristo patri et domino karissimo. S. dei gratia Cant' archiepiscopo tocius Anglie primati et sancte Romane ecclesie cardinali E. divina permissione Hereford' ecclesie minister.ᵃ salutem. et tam devotam quam debitam cum omni humilitate reverentiam et subiectionem. Reverendo cetui \vestro/ et venerabilium fratrum et coepiscoporum nostrorum consecrationi die dominica proxima post festum Sancti Michaelis celebrande admodum affectaremus interesse.' nisi ad vos veniendi impotentia prone voluntati et affectuosis desideriis nostris se opponeret. Siquidem Dominus Legatus nuper ad partes declinavit Hereford.' cuius lateri secundum eius mandatum assistimus affectuosi et debiti. inter barbaras Walenses nationes ei ducatum exhibentes.' a quo tanquam a Domino dum in partibus nostris commoratur discedere nec possumus nec debemus. Supplicamus igitur paternitati vestre quatinus absentiam nostram benigne si placet habeatis excusatam. quam excusat evidens necessitas.' non affectata voluntas. Nos vero gratum habemus et acceptum quicquid in consecrandorum ordinatione una cum coepiscopis et fratribus nostris vestra prudentia disposuerit. Valeat cara nobis paternitas vestra semper in domino.

This is the oldest surviving original *litterae excusatoriae* at Canterbury. Nicholas of Tusculum visited the Welsh Marches in 1214, and the only consecration held by Stephen Langton at this season in Giles de Braose's lifetime was on 5 October 1214 (*HMCR, loc. cit.*), when Walter de Gray and Simon of Apulia were consecrated bps of Worcester and Exeter respectively. Giles had been one of the bps with whom Nicholas had negotiated near the beginning of his visit to England in the autumn of 1213; see A.Mercati, 'La prima relazione del cardinale Nicolò de Romanis sulla sua legazione in Inghilterra (1213)', in H.W.C.Davis, ed. *Essays in history presented to Reginald Lane Poole* (Oxford 1927), 274-89.

*249. Chirbury priory

Confirmation to Chirbury priory of its prebends and appurtenances.
[24 September 1200 × 17 November 1215]

Mention only, in a charter of Bp Hugh (de Mapenore ?) for Chirbury (see below, no.295).

250. Cormeilles abbey

Confirmation to the abbey of Cormeilles in Normandy of its churches in the diocese of Hereford, Dymock, Newent, and Kingsland, and the chapel of Pauntley, and of the prebend in Hereford Cathedral which had been given to the abbey by Bishop William de Vere.

[24 September 1200 × 17 November 1215]

B = BL Add. MS 15668 (Newent priory cartulary), fo.51r. s.xiii med. C = BL Add. MS 18461 (Newent priory cartulary), fo.10r-v. s.xiv in.

E. dei gratia Hereford' episcopus omnibus sancte matris ecclesie filiis salutem in domino. Quod ab^a antecessoribus fit^b divine pietatis intuitu non debet ab eorum successoribus extirpari. Eapropter universorum^c notitie volumus pervenire quod concessimus ecclesie Cormel' et eiusdem loci conventui quod liceat eis ecclesias quas habent in Hereford' diocesi, videlicet de Dimmoch, de Newent, de Kingeslen', et capellam de Pantele, libere et sine alicuius contradictione totumque earum proventum in propriis usibus possidere, et pro arbitrio suo presbiteros idoneos in eisdem ecclesiis ministraturos constituere, salva dignitate ecclesie Hereford', et preterea prebendam de supradictis ecclesiis et capella, ex assensu communi Willelmi episcopi et capituli in Hereford' ecclesia iure perpetuo stabilitam, ab abbate Cormel' et suis successoribus integre possidendam, atque in usus suos fratrumque suorum sine impedimento et difficultate imposterum optinendam, et locum in capitulo et stallum in choro a dictis episcopo et capitulo designatum, et ut habeat quisquis sit abbas Cormel' vicarium in ecclesia Hereford', qui pro se in dicta ecclesia Hereford' valeat ministrare panem et cervisiam sicut alii canonici recepturus. Ut hec autem concessio firma sit et stabilis perseveret, omnes illos qui ei contradicere presumpserint auctoritate a domino nobis data a communione fidelium sequestramus,^{d} ita quod in die districti examinis summi iudicis indignationem sentiant et cum iniquis accipiant portionem, necnon presens^e scriptum et caractere sigilli nostri et capituli roboravimus.

^{a}om. *BC*. ^{b}sit *B*. ^{c}universoris *BC*. ^{d}sequebamus *C*. ^{e}et presens *C*.

For William de Vere's charter, see above, no.188.

*251. Gloucester abbey

Letters patent confirming to Gloucester Abbey their possession of the parsonage of Much Cowarne for the past sixty years and more, and declaring that his predecessor Robert had admitted the last vicar on presentation by Abbot Hamelin of Gloucester.

[24 September 1200 × summer of 1214]

Mention only, *CRR*, vii.216-7, and *Gloucester cartulary*, i.253. Giles' charter was brought forward by Gloucester Abbey as proof against the claims of Richard and Elena Pancefot and Jordan and Eva de Wike to the advowson of the church in the summer of 1214. Elena and Eva were descendants of Hugh of Hazle, a mid-twelfth century tenant of the bps of Hereford: B.Coplestone-Crow, 'The fief of Alfred of Marlborough in Herefordshire in 1086 and its descent in the Norman period', *Transactions of the Woolhope Naturalists' Field Club*, xlv (1986), 403. Giles' charter was confirmed by Dean Hugh de Mapenore and the chapter of Hereford (*Gloucester cartulary, loc. cit.*).

252. Haughmond abbey

Inspeximus of a charter of Bishop Robert Foliot restoring Linley to Haughmond abbey.

[1200 × 1201/1202]

A = Shrewsbury, Shropshire County Record Office, no.4220/2 (originally Phillipps MS 27859). No ancient endorsements. 248 × 115 mm; sealed on a tag in green wax. Impression 75 mm long × 41 mm wide, pointed oval: right side slightly damaged but otherwise in good condition. Face: figure of a bishop in full pontificals, holding a staff in his left hand and raising his right hand in benediction. Legend: .SI(G)........................ HEREFORDENS.S EPIS.... ; Counterseal 43 mm × 27 mm, pointed oval; figure of an ecclesiastic holding a book in his hands. Legend: SECRETUM EGIDII DE BRAOSE.

B = Shrewsbury, Local Studies Library, Haughmond abbey cartulary, fo.137r. s.xv ex. C = Shrewsbury, Shropshire County Record Office, 2922 add., Dudmaston MS, fo.4r-v. s.xvi ex. – xvii in.

Pd from B with reference to A and C, *Haughmond cartulary*, 147, no.706.

Universis sancte matris ecclesie filiis tam presentibus quam futuris ad quos presens carta pervenerit ? Egidius dei gratia Heref' ecclesie minister humilis utriusque vite salutem in ipso domino salutari. Ad universitatis vestre notitiam volumus pervenire ? nos venerabilis domini Roberti predecessoris nostri Heref' episcopi cartam legisse. et diligenter inspexisse. que data est in hanc formam. Universis sancte matris ecclesie filiis Robertus dei gratia Heref' minister humilis perpetuam in domino salutem. Noverit universitas vestra quod cum primum*a* ad regimen Hereford' ecclesie deo vocante accessissemus ? invenimus in castalario de Lideb' Madocum. Radulfum. et Agnetem uxorem eius tenentes terram de Linleg'.*b* et episcopo Hereford' unam

marcam sub annua pensione inde reddentes. Postea abbas de Hagaman et conventus per litteras domini pape adversus eos controversiam
super iamdicta terra moverunt. et coram iudicibus delegatis eam
demum evicerunt. Ita quod Madocus et Radulfus consensu et assensu
Agnetis uxoris eius coram .G. decano et R. archidiacono. et Ivone
thesaurario. et Waltero senssesch'^{c} et multis aliis ; terram illam sine
omni reclamatione in manum nostram resignaverunt. et nos abbatem
et conventum de Hagaman de eadem terra cum omnibus pertinentiis
suis in bosco et plano. in pratis. et aquis. et pascuis. et omnibus aliis
locis ; investivimus. tenendam de nobis et successoribus nostris inperpetuum sub annua pensione viginti solidorum solvendorum in
duobus terminis. medietatem in Pentecost'. et alteram medietatem in
festo beati Martini. Preterea omni anno quo werra fuerit ; ad summonitionem nostram et ballivi nostri invenient in castello de Lideb'
unum servientem per quindecim tantum dies per expensas suas. Et si
forte dominus episcopus aliquando a liberis illius feudi hominibus
auxilium exigere opus habuerit ; tunc facient sicuti terra illa antiquitus
facere consuevit secundum recordationem curie nostre de Lideb'.
Quod quia firmum et stabile manere volumus ; presenti carta. et sigilli
nostri attestatione premunimus et confirmamus. Hiis testibus. G.
decano. Radulfo archidiacono. Ivone thesaurario. Reginaldo consta-
bil'.^{c} magistro Eustachio. Reginaldo capellano. Willelmo camerario.
Willelmo decano de Brugg'. Hugone decano de Herchull'. Waltero
decano de Humbre. magistro Osberto. et multis aliis. Nos igitur
relligionem^c abbatis et conventus de Hagaman per veridica multorum
testimonia comprobantes; [ipsis]^d eandem terram sicut eis secundum
tenorem carte felicis memorie. nominati predecessoris nostri. R.
Hereford' episcopi concessa est et confirmata ; littere vivacis
munimine sigillique nostri testimonio ; communivimus et con-
firma[vimus].^{d} Hiis testibus. magistro Philippo. magistro Hugone de
Mappenour'. Roberto de Furch'. magistro Nicholao de Wlfreneham-
ton'. magistro Osberto. magistro Gaufrido. Roberto Corbeth. Iohanne [E?]^e fratre eius. Bartholomeo de Mortun'. Gaufrido de Blie.
Waltero de Munetun'. Rogero Sprenghose. et multis aliis.

^{a}last three letters obscure, A. ^{b}terram de Linleg underlined, presumably by a modern hand,
A. ^{c}sic A. ^{d}lacuna, A; supplied from B. ^{e}lacuna, A; Ex B, for Extraneo. There should
be yet another name following.

Master Hugh de Mapenore became dean between 30 November 1201 and Michaelmas 1202. For Robert Foliot's charter, see above, no.147; see also no.81.

253. Haughmond abbey

Licence to Haughmond abbey to appropriate Stokesay Church, saving the right of Master Adam the vicar in his lifetime; after Master Adam's death the abbey is to assign a sufficient vicarage to the new vicar.
[30 November 1201 × c.1206]

B = Shrewsbury Local Studies Library, Haughmond abbey cartulary, fo.206r-v. s.xv ex.

Pd, omitting the corroboration, *Haughmond cartulary*, 213, no.1148.

Et ut hoc imposterum illesum et illibatum permaneat, presentis scripti attestatione et sigilli nostri appositione confirmare et corroborare curavimus. Hiis testibus, Magistro Theobaldo, Magistro Galfrido et Magistro Simone etc.

There is a confirmation of this deed datable 1201 x c.1206 issued by Dean Hugh de Mapenore and Hereford Cathedral Chapter, *ibid.*, 213, no.1149. Dean Hugh de Mapenore's predecessor died 30 November 1201 and the charter is witnessed by William Foliot, precentor, who did not die until at least 1206.

254. Hereford cathedral chapter

Confirmation of Bishop William de Vere's grant of Madley church and of the chapel of St Mary Magdalen, Hereford.
[24 September 1200 × 30 November 1201]

A = Hereford D.& C. Muniments, no.1364. 14th-century endorsements: Collatio ecclesie de Maddeleye. Notary's mark. 236 × 118 mm; originally sealed on a tag, but no tag or seal surviving.

Pd, *Hereford charters*, 42.

Universis sancte matris ecclesie filiis. Egidius divina patientia Hereforden' ecclesie minister humilis ? utriusque vite salutem in domino. Iubemur bonum operari ad omnes. maxime autem ad domesticos fidei.[1] inter quos specialissimos habemus sicut tenemur dilectos in Cristo filios nostros ecclesie nostre Herefordensis canonicos. quos sicut videmus et scimus nobis in omnibus obnoxios et devotos. ita eosdem mutuo caritatis affectu devotius amplexamur. considerantes autem clericorum filiorum nostrorum vigilias. labores. et devota obsequia. que beatissime virgini matri domini Iesu. et beato Athelberto

martiri continue inpendunt .' eorum labores consolatione qua possumus et remedio relevare desideramus. domino obedientes.' qui bovi
triteranti precipit os non alligari.[2] Ad supplementum igitur communie que ad sustentationem canonicorum ecclesie nostre deservientium
minus videbatur esse sufficiens .' ecclesiam de Maddeleia in manu
nostra a Ricardo decano Herefordensi qui eam tenuerat resignatam .'
concedimus et conferimus. sicut ante ex felicis memorie predecessoris
nostri venerabilis domini Willelmi de Ver Herefordensis episcopi
donatione eisdem est concessa. Capellam etiam beate Marie Magdalene de Hereford' cum pertinentiis suis sicut prius a prefato domino
Herefordensi est eis collata .' eisdem confirmamus similiter ad communie supplementum. Ut autem priores concessiones duorum beneficiorum que sigillo predecessoris nostri roborantur nullatenus
irritentur .' nostra ergo confirmatio stabilitatis robur optineat .' prefatas donationes vivacis littere munimine. nostrique sigilli testimonio
communimus. Testibus his. Ricardo decano. universoque capitulo
Hereforden'. ceteroque. tam clero quam populo eiusdem civitatis.

[1] Gal. 6[10].
[2] Deut. 25[4].

Dean Richard died 30 November 1201. The church of Madley and the chapel of
St Mary Magdalen belonged to the chapter's common fund at the time of the
earliest cathedral statutes (probably of the 1240s): H.Bradshaw and C.Words-
worth, edd. *Statutes of Lincoln cathedral*, 3 vols. (Cambridge 1892-7), ii.52, 60..

255. Hereford cathedral chapter

*Confirmation to Hereford cathedral chapter of their rights over their
prebends, manors and other lands, and of their powers of jurisdiction.*
[24 September 1200 × 17 November 1215, probably 1202]

A = Hereford D. & C. Muniments, no.1384. 15th-century endorsement: Confirmatio Egidii episcopi super congruentibus spiritualibus prebendarum et maneriorum capituli. 185 × 93 mm; originally sealed on a tag; no seal surviving.

B = Bodl. MS Rawlinson B329 (Hereford cathedral cartulary), fo.161r. s.xiii-xiv.
C = Ibid., fo.3r. s.xv.

Pd, *Hereford charters*, 39.

Universis sancte matris ecclesie filiis. Egidius divina permissione
Herefordensis ecclesie minister. eternam in domino salutem. Vigilan-

tie pastoralis cura nos ammonet dilectorum in Cristo filiorum nostrorum canonicorum Herefordensis ecclesie tranquillitati et paci propensius intendere. et ne cuiusquam malitia perturbentur in posterum ? debita sollicitudine providere. Cupientes igitur redditus et possessiones eorundem filiorum nostrorum debita libertate et integritate gaudere ? iura prebendarum et maneriorum suorum et ceterarum terrarum et reddituum tam in mobilibus quam in inmobilibus consistentia ? nec non et causas ecclesiasticas cum proventibus et emolumentis earum inter homines eorum et de excessibus eorundem hominum emergentes ? sub ea integritate et libertate qua temporibus predecessorum nostrorum gavisi sunt ? eis concedimus. et episcopali autoritate^a confirmamus. districtius inhibentes ? ne cuiquam nostre iurisdictioni supposito ? liceat hanc nostri beneficii confirmationem infringere. vel ei ausu temerario contraire. Si quis vero hoc attemptare presumpserit ? indignationem dei omnipotentis nec non et beate Marie et beati Ethelberti et nostram ? se noverit incursurum.

^{a}sic A.

King John issued a similar confirmation to Hereford Cathedral Chapter on 7 September 1202, *Rot. chart.*, i.256-7.

256. Hereford cathedral chapter

Admission of Walter the clerk on presentation by the dean and chapter to a perpetual vicarage in the church of Upton Bishop.

[24 September 1200 × 17 November 1215]

A = Hereford D. & C. Muniments, no.1380. 14th-century endorsement: Taxatio vicarie de Uptun' per Egidium episcopum et institutio .W. clerici. Ss. 132 × 107 mm; sealed on a tag; seal in natural wax, somewhat damaged, pointed oval with the top broken. Obverse: figure of a bishop holding a staff in his left hand; legend: ....(G)IDII. DEI. G(R)...A. HE(RE)............ .... ; Counterseal: pointed oval with the top broken, 36 × 24 mm. Figure of a clerk holding a book in both hands; legend: .... ECRETUM. EGIDII DE BRAOSE..

B = Bodl. MS Rawlinson B329 (Hereford cathedral cartulary), fo.172r. s.xiii-xiv.

Pd from A, *Hereford charters*, 42.

Omnibus sancte matris ecclesie filiis ad quos presens scriptum pervenerit. Egidius divina permissione Hereford' ecclesie minister ? eternam in domino. salutem. Noverit universitas vestra nos ad presentationem dilectorum in Cristo filiorum. decani et capituli Hereford' Walterum clericum ad ecclesie de Upton' perpetuam vicariam admisisse. et ipsum in eadem ecclesia canonice perpetuum vicarium instituisse. Habebit autem idem .W. in eadem ecclesia nomine perpetue vicarie.' totam terram illius ecclesie. et omnes minutas decimas et obventiones et omnia alia ad ecclesiam de iure spectantia.' exceptis decimis garbarum et reddet capitulo Hereford' annuatim viginti sol(idos). medietatem in festo apostolorum Petri et Pauli et medietatem in festo Sancti Micaelis. et sustinebit omnia onera ecclesie. Ut autem hec nostra institutio perpetue firmitatem stabilitatis optineat.' eam presenti scripto et sigilli nostri testimonio confirmare curavimus. Hiis testibus. Magistris Theob'. Galfrido de Ludel'. Philippo. Map'. Ricardo. Ranulfo. et Ricardo capellanis. Symone et Willelmo clericis. et multis aliis.

All the witnesses to this charter belonged to Giles' household before and after his exile, so it is not possible to date it more closely. See also nos.150 and 202.

257. Hereford cathedral chapter

Grant of the tithes of all the episcopal mills to provide three lamps for the cathedral; in return the dean and chapter have promised to make a distribution of bread for the poor on his anniversary.

[24 September 1200 × 17 November 1215]

B = Bodl. MS Rawlinson B329 (Hereford cathedral cartulary), fo.55r-v. s.xv. C = Hereford, Herefordshire County Record Office , Registers of Bothe, Foxe, and Boner (Register of Bishop Bothe; formerly Hereford, Diocesan Registry), fo.40r. s.xvi in.

Pd from C, *Reg. Bothe*, 62.

Omnibus sancte matris ecclesie filiis ad quos presens scriptum pervenerit Egidius divina permissione Hereford'^{a} ecclesie minister presentis vite prosperitatem et salutis eterne beatitudinem. Ad hoc divina permittente clementia commisse nobis ecclesia presidemus, ut inter cetera caritatis^b opera ad que ex officio pontificali quadam peculiari prerogativa propensius invitamur^c decorem domus dei^{d1} augeamus luminaribus et aliis que ad eius exiguntur^e ornatum perpetua assignando^f alimenta ut igitur solito decentius in ecclesia nostra Hereford'^{a}

domino deserviatur preter luminaria que ex aliorum beneficiis in ea esse consueverunt, vel de cetero fore contigerint,[g] ad inveniendam lucernam trium lampadarum,[h] que nullis temporum intervallibus a sui [i]luminis administratione[i] deficiant, dedimus et assignavimus dilectis in Cristo filiis eiusdem ecclesie decano et capitulo omnes decimas omnium molendinorum nostrorum que ubicumque locorum a nobis vel a predecessoribus nostris iam facta sunt, vel imposterum a nobis vel successoribus nostris fieri contigerint,[j] sive de moneta, sive de fructibus[k] terre debeant decime provenire, cum prius de molendinis illis decime [fo.55v *B*] date non essent et honestius sit ecclesie nostre cathedrali quam aliil ecclesie illas assignare. Predicti siquidem[m] decanus et capitulum solo caritatis[b] qua nos amplectuntur[n] instinctu se nobis promittendo obligaverunt[o] quod quamdiu deo militabit Hereford'[a] ecclesia singulis annis in anniversarii nostri die fiet pauperibus Cristi partitio panis ex septem summis bladi quod ipsi canonici de horreo[p] suo ad hoc ministrabunt pro anime nostre et animarum parentum nostrorum et omnium fidelium defunctorum salute. In cuius rei testimonio presens scriptum sigilli nostri appositione munitum sepedicti canonici suo sigillo communire et corroborare curaverunt. Hiis testibus, Magistris Theob(aldo), Ricardo Rufo,[q] Philippo Map', Hereo de Bukehull', Willelmo de Bukeyngham, Willelmo et Nicholao clericis, Alexandro de Albert,[r] Hugone de Mora laicis et aliis multis.

[1]Ps. 25[8]. [a]Heref' *B*. [b]charitatis *C*. [c]imitamur *B*. [d]domini *B*. [e]eriguntur *B*.
[f]assigando *B*. [g]contigerit *B*.
[h]lampadum *C; this would be better classical Latin but* lampadarum *is used in the Vulgate (Ezech. 1:13)*. [i-i] \administratione / luminis *C* [j]contigerit *B*.
[k]fructubus *B*. [l]*corr. from* aliis *B*. [m]sequidem *B*. [n]amplectimur *B*.
[o]obligaverint *B*. [p]horeo *B*. [q]Ruto *BC*. [r]*sic for* Abitot *BC*.

It is not easy to date this document, but it is likely that Giles issued it 1213 × 1215, after returning from exile in France. This possibility is strengthened slightly by the fact that William has here replaced Simon as Giles' senior clerk and that the new junior clerk is Nicholas, who might be identifiable with Bp Hugh de Mapenore's clerk Nicholas.

258. Hereford cathedral chapter

Inspeximus of charters issued by Bishops Robert Foliot [no.150] and William de Vere [no.202] to the chapter.

[30 November 1201 × 1215, probably before 1208]

A = Hereford D. & C. Muniments, no.741. 14th-century endorsement: Confirmacio Egidii episcopi super collacione R Foliot facta capitulo et super confirmacione W. de Ver de ecclesia de Uptun'. 194 × 197 mm. Sealed on plaited red, yellow, and white silk cord. Seal, in natural wax, broken; two pieces surviving; 68 × ? 45 mm. Head of a bishop and his staff visible on upper fragment while his feet visible on lower one. Legend: .....ILLUM .... HER.............; Counterseal: 42 × 25 mm; pointed oval, head (of a cleric) visible; legend: SEC............. ......RAOSE .
B = Bodl. MS Rawlinson B329 (Hereford cathedral cartulary), fo.171v. s.xiii-xiv.
Pd from A, *Hereford charters*, 40-3.

Universis sancte matris ecclesie filiis ad quos presens scriptum pervenerit Egidius dei gratia Hereforden' ecclesie minister .' eternam in domino salutem. Noverit universitas vestra nos venerablium^a predecessorum nostrorum felicis memorie Roberti Foliot et Willelmi de Ver' Hereforden' episcoporum cartas sub hac forma inspexisse .' Universis sancte matris ecclesie filiis Robertus Foliot dei gratia Hereforden' ecclesie minister humilis .' perpetuam in domino salutem. Universitati vestre notum facimus. quod nos considerantes paucitatem bonorum ad communam dilectorum filiorum nostrorum canonicorum Hereforden' pertinentium deo et beate Marie et Sancto Adelberto ibidem assidue et devote servientium concessimus et dedimus eis ecclesiam manerii nostri de Hupton'. in augmentum communie sue. libere et quiete et honorifice in perpetuum habendam cum terris. decimis. et obventionibus. et omnibus rebus et libertatibus ad eandem ecclesiam pertinentibus. sicut unquam eam aliquis melius. liberius. et quietius tenuit. Volumus etiam et statuimus ut post decessum Reginaldi clerici de Glouc' quem ad presentationem eorundem canonicorum nostrorum perpetuum in eadem ecclesia constituimus vicarium .' liceat eis ad libitum suum de eadem ecclesia de Hupton' libere disponere .' ita videlicet ut eam in proprios usus retineant. vel alii sub certa pensione pro sua voluntate committant. salva in omnibus episcopali dignitate. Ut autem hec nostra donatio in perpetuum rata et illibata permaneat .' ipsam presenti scripto et sigilli nostri testimonio confirmamus. His .t'. Henrico thesaurario London'. Iohanne et Aluredo capellanis nostris. Magistro Edmundo. Waltero de Colewell'. Ernaldo de Stok'. Ranulfo de Salewarp'. Bartholomeo de Eignesham'. Osberto de Ledeb'. Bertramo et Herveio clericis nostris. Willelmo camerario. Petro de parco. Germano coco. Sampsone pistore. Henrico marescallo. Universis sancte matris ecclesie filiis. Willelmus de Ver dei gratia Hereforden' ecclesie minister humilis eternam in domino salutem. Universitati vestre notum esse volumus nos ecclesiam manerii nostri de Hupton' quam Robertus Foliot predecessor noster pie memorie capitulo Hereforden' in augmentum communie sue contulit ? concessisse. et presenti carta nostra confirmasse predicto capitulo. Ut liceat ei omnes fructus predicte ecclesie in proprios usus convertere. vel cui voluerit pro certa concedere pensione. Hiis testibus. Henrico de Ver cancellario et Magistro Willelmo Romano. Magistro Gileberto. et Symone de Langet'. et Reginaldo de Waltham'. et Alexandro. Nos etiam considerantes dilectorum in Cristo filiorum nostrorum canonicorum Hereford' vigilias et labores.' venerabilis predecessoris nostri Willelmi de Ver super eadem donatione confirmationem ratam habemus. et dictis canonicis nominatim ecclesiam de Hupton' in augmentum communie sue divine pietatis intuitu sub presentis instrumenti testimonio episcopali auctoritate in perpetuum confirmamus. Hiis testibus. H. decano Hereford'. Magistro P et W de Kilp' canonicis Herefor'. H. de Braos' et multis aliis.

^asic A.

Hugh de Mapenore became dean of Hereford in 1201 (after 30 November) or 1202. William de Kilpeck became precentor not before 1206. Hugh de Braose does not seem to have witnessed any charters issued by Giles after his exile.

259. Hereford cathedral chapter

Licence to Hereford cathedral chapter to appropriate the chapel of Putley. [1205 × November 1206]

B = Bodl. MS Rawlinson B329 (Hereford cathedral cartulary), fo.170r-v. s.xiii-xiv.

Omnibus sancte matris ecclesie filiis Egidius divina permissione Hereford' ecclesie minister, in illam feliciter introire beatitudinem quam preparavit deus diligentibus se. Ea que venerabiles antecessores nostri super ecclesiastici disposi\ti/one beneficii provida dispensatione et servato per omnia iuris ordine gesserunt dignum est nos grato prosequi favore et commissa nobis auctoritate confirmare. Hinc est quod cognita dilectorum in Cristo filiorum canonicorum Hereford' vita commendabili et honestate religiosa dignum duximus eorum utilitati maxime in hiis que a predecessoribus nostris eis iuste data sunt et concessa providere, ut illorum conditione meliorata fervor devotionis in sublimiora conscendat. Concedimus igitur eis capellam de Putteleg' cum omnibus ad eam de iure spectantibus ad usus proprios retinendam, quam ipsi temporibus antecessorum nostrorum integre et pacifice possederunt. Ut igitur hec nostra concessio inconcusse [fo.170v] firmitatem stabilitatis optineat, eam presenti scripto et sigilli nostri testimonio communire curavimus. Hiis testibus, Magistro Theobaldo, Magistro Galfrido de Ludelowe, Ricardo et Ranulfo capellanis, Simone et Willelmo clericis et multis aliis.

A fine was made in the week after Michaelmas 1207 between Cecily of Evreux and the dean and chapter of Hereford, according to the terms of which Cecily of Evreux renounced her claim to the church of Putley in return for eight marks (Bodl. MS Rawlinson B329, *loc. cit.*). Prior to this, in Michaelmas term 1206 (before 26 November) the canons had brought forward 'an episcopal confirmation' as evidence, which was presumably this document (*CRR*, iv.230). Cecily of Evreux had originally tried to claim the advowson in 1205 (*Curia Regis Rolls*, iv.23), so this charter was probably issued after this point.

260. St Guthlac's priory, Hereford

Partial inspeximus of general confirmation and of the grant of a mill issued by Bishop William de Vere for St Guthlac's priory, Hereford, and confirmation of a grant to St Guthlac's by Geoffrey, Giles' clerk.

[24 September 1200 × 30 November 1201]

B = Oxford, Balliol College MS 271 (cartulary of St Guthlac's, Hereford), fos.99v-100v, no.437. s.xiv in. C = Ibid., fos.99r-v, no.435, in an inspeximus by Archbishop Stephen Langton.

Pd from C, *Acta Stephani Langton*, ed. K.Major, CYS 50 (1950), 146-8.

Universis sancte matris ecclesie filiis E. dei gratia Heref' episcopus*a* eternam in domino salutem. Ad universitatis vestre notitiam volumus pervenire nos autenticum [fo.100r *B*] scriptum venerabilis fratris et predecessoris nostri pie recordationis Willelmi de Ver quondam Heref' episcopi sub huius continentie forma inspexisse. Universis sancte matris ecclesie filiis *b*ad quos presentes litere pervenerint*b* W.*c* dei gratia Hereford' episcopus eternam in domino salutem. Cum multiplici caritatis opere divina gratia animas fidelium salvandas*d* mutaverit, potissimum elemosinarum largitio et Cristi pauperum exhibitio recte credentibus expeditiorem^e ad conspectum domini properant accessum et in perhennitatis sue tabernaculum faciliorem ordinant^f introitum, inde est quod nos dilectorum nobis in Cristo filiorum, videlicet monachorum in monasterio apostolorum Petri et Pauli et Sancti Guthlaci Heref' domino devote famulantium, honestam et regularem conversationem considerantes, et eorum possessiones et facultates secundum affectionis sue fervorem ad bonum hospitalitatis sustinendum et prescripta pietatis opera exequenda secundum ordinis sui institutionem non sufficere manifestius attendentes, possessionum et bonorum suorum quantitatem augere presertim ad perpet(uam) domus^g sue hospitalitatem ordinare sustinendam instinctu publice honestatis et communis utilitatis affectuose studuimus. Nos itaque ecclesiam Sancti Cutberti^h de Hamma ultra Waiam et capellam Sancti Martini intra ambitum castri constructam cum omnibus pertinentiis suis memoratis monachis, sicud ex inspectione instrumentorum suorum ab antiquis temporibus eisdem canonice collatas indubitanter cognovimus, salva Heref' ecclesie dignitate et canonica obedientia nobis et successoribus nostris debita episcopali auctoritate concedimus et confirmamus, et decimas et obventiones earum et subscriptarum ecclesiarum, cum ipsas vacare contigerit, ad honestam ut diximus^i domus sue hospitalitatem iugiter conservandam percipere, et in proprios usus et causas necessarias domus sue liberam habendo inde dispositionem convertere, salva competenti etiam vicariorum sustentatione, pietatis et misericordie intuitu ^{j}eisdem permisimus.^{j} ^{k}Nos vero^k vestigiis predecessorum nostrorum pietate nitentibus inherentes predicto monasterio et monachis ibidem deo servientibus possessiones, ecclesias et alia beneficia in liberam elemosinam concessa inperpetuum quiete possidenda concedimus et confirmamus, ecclesiam^l Sancti Petri que est in foro Heref', cum prebendis, terris, et decimis, et omnibus ad eam^m pertinentibus,^{n} ecclesiam Sancti Audoeni de Hereford' cum omnibus ad eam pertinentibus,^{n} ecclesiam de Acla et de Agneburia, et^o ecclesiam de Mordiford,^{p} et capellam de Bertwaldestreu^q et ecclesiam de maiori Suttona, ^{r}et capellam de minori Suttona,^{r} et ecclesiam de Monitone cum ^{s}omnibus pertinentiis^s et ecclesiam de Mocres^t cum omnibus pertinentiis suis, duas etiam partes totius dominii de Stantona et Russebur' et ^{u}Wethulle, et de Humbra, et Buterleia, et de Streta, Welbleia, et Burhope, et Bodeham, et de Maghene et Stoca, et

Westona, et^u Kempleia, et totam decimam de Godredeshope, et de Oxenhale, tertiam etiam partem decimarum vilanagii^v de Lugwardin'. Ad hec attendentes inopiam predictorum filiorum nostrorum monachorum quam ex aque defectu sustinent, consilio et assensu capituli nostri, eis molendinum nostrum ante portam eorum positum, quod tantum unam marcam argenti solvere consuevit, pro duabus marcis singulis^w annis nobis et successoribus nostris solvendis concessimus imperpetuum, videlicet unam marcam ad Annuntiationem beate Marie et^x unam marcam ad festum Sancti Michaelis. Preterea donationem dilecti [fo.100v B] in Cristo filii nostri Galfridi, clerici nostri,^{y} quam fecit intuitu caritatis prefatis monachis de uno mesuagio, quod de nobis tenuit in directo porte eorundem, ratam ^{z}habentes, salvo^z nobis et successoribus nostris redditu quindecim denariorum annuatim solvendorum. Quia igitur^{aa} utilitati, paci, et securitati virorum religiosorum volumus, quantum secundum deum possumus,^{bb} ^{cc}paterno affectu providere, memoratam concessionem et confirmationem predicti predecessoris nostri W. episcopi^{cc} ratam habentes, episcopali auctoritate concedimus et confirmamus, et^{dd} tam presenti scripto quam sigilli^{ee} nostri et sigilli capituli nostri testimonio communimus. Hiis testibus, Magistris Ricardo Britone, decano Heref',^{ff} Willelmo Foliot, precentore, Willelmo, archidiacono Heref', Hugone, archidiacono Salops',^{gg} Magistro Roberto Folet, Magistro Iohanne Clementis canonicis, ^{hh}Magistro Philippo, Magistro Teobaldo,^{hh} et aliis.

^{a}ecclesie minister C. $^{b-b}$om. B. ^{c}Willelmus C. ^{d}salvandis C.
^{e}expedit'orem B; expeditorem C. ^{f}ordinavit ordinant C. ^{g}d inserted after domus C.
^{h}Gutberti BC. ^{i}duximus BC, in error for diximus. $^{j-j}$transposed C.
$^{k-k}$Preterea nos C. ^{l}C adds scilicet. ^{m}ea B. $^{n-n}$et B. ^{o}om. C. ^{p}Mordford C.
^{q}Bertwaldestre C. $^{r-r}$om. C. $^{s-s}$pertinentiis suis C. ^{t}Mocros C.
$^{u-u}$de Wethulle, et de Humbra, et Buterleia, et de Streta, et de Webbleia, et de Burhope, et de Bodeham, et Magene, et de Stoca, et de Westona, et de C. ^{v}villanagii C.
^{w}C adds marcis and expunges. ^{x}om. C. ^{y}om. C. $^{z-z}$habemus salva B. ^{aa}blurred C.
^{bb}possimus B. $^{cc-cc}$om. B. ^{dd}om. B. ^{ee}siglli B. ^{ff}om. C. ^{gg}de Salopesir' C. $^{hh-hh}$om. B.

Dean Richard Brito died 30 November 1201. William de Vere's charters are nos. 204 and 207 above.

261. St Guthlac's priory, Hereford

Confirmation to St Guthlac's priory, Hereford, of the church of St Peter, Hereford, as they had possessed it before the vicarage was conferred on William de Kilpeck.

[30 November 1201 × 1215, probably before 1208]

B = Oxford, Balliol College MS 271 (cartulary of St Guthlac's, Hereford), fo.102v, no.454. s.xiv in.

Omnibus sancte matris ecclesie filiis ad quos presens scriptum pervenerit Egidius divina permissione Heref' episcopus eternam in domino salutem. Noverit universitas vestra nos concessisse et presenti carta,[a] sigillo nostro roborata, confirmasse priori et monachis Heref' ecclesiam Sancti Petri de Hereford' integre cum omnibus ad eam pertinentibus, sicud eam ante collationem vicarie eiusdem ecclesie domino Willelmo de Kylpeck plenius et melius tenuerint. Hiis testibus, H. decano Heref', Domino Hugone de Brews, Magistro Osberto et Simone presbiteris.

[a] B adds et; possibly a scribal misreading for a punctuation mark.

Hugh de Mapenore became dean after 30 November 1201; William de Kilpeck became precentor after 1206. Hugh de Braose and Master Osbert do not occur in charters known to have been issued after Giles' exile.

262. St Guthlac's priory, Hereford

Confirmation of the charter by which Henry, once prior of St Guthlac's priory, granted the perpetual vicarage of Dormington to Arnold of Gloucester, with the assent of Thomas Carbonel, once abbot of Gloucester.
[30 April 1214 × 18 November 1215]

B = Oxford, Balliol College MS 271 (cartulary of St Guthlac's, Hereford), fo.50r, no.182. s.xiii-xiv in.

Omnibus sancte matris ecclesie filiis ad quos tenor presentium pervenerit Egidius divina permissione Herefordensis episcopus eternam in domino salutem. Noverit universitas vestra nos cartam H. quondam prioris et conventus Hereford' inspexisse, cuius tenoris perpendimus predictos priorem et conventum assensu Thome tunc temporis abbatis Glouc' perpetuam vicariam capelle de Dormiton' concessisse Arnaldo de Glou' capellano. Nos vero predictam concessionem in omnibus iuxta tenorem prenominate carte ratam habentes, eam presenti scripto et sigilli nostri testimonio confirmare curavimus. Hiis testibus, Magistris Theobaldo et Galfrido de Lod', Ricardo et Ranulfo capellanis, Simone et Willelmo clericis, et aliis.

Thomas Carbonel, abbot of Gloucester, died 21 July 1205. Henry, prior of St Guthlac's, last occurs 30 April 1214 (*The Letters of Pope Innocent III: a Calendar*, ed. C.R. and Mary Cheney [Oxford 1967], no.964) and had presumably died or resigned by the time that this confirmation was issued. His grant of the vicarage can be found in Balliol College MS 271, fo.49v, no.179.

263. Pope Innocent III

Joint petition by thirteen bishops of the province of Canterbury (Giles is the fourth last in the list) to Pope Innocent III that the ancient form of election should be adhered to in the coming election of the archbishop of Canterbury: that the bishops of the province and the monks of Canterbury should together elect the archbishop and that the bishop of London, the dean of the province, should publish the election.   [1205]

B = London, St Paul's Cathedral, MS W.D.1 (Liber A sive Pilosus [cartulary of St Paul's cathedral]), fo.18r, no.178.

Pd, *Early charters of the cathedral church of St Paul, London*, ed. M.Gibbs, Camden 3rd ser., lviii, Royal Historical Society (1939), 139-140, no.181.

264. Pope Innocent III

Certificate by Bishops William of London, Giles of Hereford, Reiner of St Asaph, Henry of Llandaff, Robert of Bangor, and Geoffrey of St David's of the canonical election by the prior and convent of Bath and the dean and chapter of Wells of Master Joscelin, canon of Wells, upon the death of Savaric, bishop of Bath, together with a certificate of King John, in the vacancy of the church of Canterbury, and petition to confirm the election.   [23 April × 28 May 1206]

B = Wells, D. & C. Muniments, Liber Albus I (Wells cathedral register, vol. I), fo.54v. s.xiii med.

Cal., *HMCR, Wells*, i.62-3; *Welsh ep. acts*, i, no.390.

Sanctissimo in Cristo patri I. dei gratia summo pontifici humiles et devoti filii sui W. Londoniensis, E. Herefordensis, R.*ª* Sancti Asaph, H. Land', R. Bangorensis, G. Menevensis episcopi salutem et cum omni devotione ac reverentia debitam domino et patri obedientiam.

Noverit sancta paternitas vestra quod cum venerabilis frater noster Savar' bone memorie Bathoniensis episcopus concessisset in fata, et tam Bathoniensis quam Wellensis ecclesia suo fuisset viduata pastore, prior et conventus Bathon' et decanus et capitulum Wellens', ad quos ius eligendi episcopum pertinere dinoscitur, in unum pariter convenerunt, habitoque prout moris est super electione episcopi diligenti tractatu, pari tandem voto, et unanimi assensu in Magistrum Ioscelinum, canonicum Wellensis ecclesie, virum providum, literatum et honestum, consenserunt, ipsumque invocata spiritus sancti gratia in pastorem et episcopum suum canonice ac sollempniter elegerunt. Cui nimirum electioni illustris Rex Anglorum Iohannes suum adhibuit benignus assensum. Quia vero Cantuariensis ecclesia suo noscitur orbata pastore, supplicamus sancte paternitati vestre quatinus nuntios dictarum ecclesiarum benignius admittentes, prenominato electo munus confirmationis conferre dignemini.

a B. *A*.

King John's request to the Curia to confirm the election (ibid., fo.54v), is dated 23 April. Joscelin was elected perhaps on 3 February and was consecrated, by Cardinal John of Ferentino, on 28 May at Reading. See also note to no.265.

265. Cardinal John of Ferentino

Certificate by Bishops William of London, Giles of Hereford, Reiner of St Asaph, Henry of Llandaff, Robert of Bangor and Geoffrey of St David's, in similar terms to no.264, addressed to J(ohn of Ferentino) Cardinal Deacon of Santa Maria in Via Lata and papal legate.

[23 April × 28 May 1206]

B = Wells, D. & C. Muniments, Liber Albus, vol. I (Wells cathedral register, vol. I), fos.54v-55. s.xiii med.

Cal., *HMCR, Wells,* i.63.

Venerabili patri et domino karissimo I., dei gratia sancte Marie in via lata diacono cardinali, apostolice sedis legato, W. de Lond', E. Hereford', R.*a* Sancti Asaph, H. Land', R. Bangorensis, G. Menevensis episcopi salutem, et sincere dilectionis affectum. Noverit paternitas vestra quod cum venerabilis frater noster Savar' bone memorie Bathon' episcopus in fata concessisset et tam Bathoniensis quam

Wellensis ecclesia suo fuisset viduata pastore, prior et conventus [fo.55r] Bathon' et decanus et capitulum Wellens', ad quos ius eligendi episcopum pertinere dinoscitur, in unum pariter convenerunt, habitoque prout moris est super electione episcopi diligenti tractatu, pari tandem voto et unanimi assensu in Magistrum Ioscelinum canonicum Wellensis ecclesie virum providum, literatum et honestum consenserunt, ipsumque invocata spiritus sancti gratia in pastorem et episcopum suum canonice ac sollemniter elegerunt. Cui nimirum electioni illustris rex Anglorum Iohannes suum adhibuit benignus assensum. Quia vero Cantuariensis ecclesia suo noscitur orbata pastore, supplicamus paternitati vestre quatinus nuntios dictarum ecclesiarum benignius admittentes prenominato electo munus confirmationis conferre dignemini.

a B.*A*.

John of Ferentino was sent to England as legate in 1206; he arrived in late April or early May and left in November: C.R.Cheney, 'Cardinal John of Ferentino, Papal Legate in England in 1206', *EHR*, lxxvi (1961), 654-60; *Councils and Synods II*, i.4; W.Maleczek, *Papst und Kardinalskolleg von 1191 bis 1216* Vienna 1984), 146-7. See also no.264 above.

266. Kenilworth priory

Notification by Bishop Giles, Dean Hugh de Mapenore, and William, the precentor of Hereford, acting as papal judges-delegate, of the settlement of the case between Kenilworth priory and Master Hilary concerning the presentation to the vicarage of the church of Brailes in Warwickshire. [30 November 1201 × 1207]

B = BL Add. MS 47677 (Kenilworth Cartulary), fo.227r. s.xvi (after 1514).

Cal., C.R. and Mary Cheney, 'The Letters of Pope Innocent III Concerning England and Wales: Additions and Corrections', *BIHR*, xliv (1971), 110, no.778.

Omnibus etc'*a* E. dei gratia episcopus, H. decanus, et W. precentor Hereford', eternam in domino salutem. Mandatum domini pape suscepimus in hec verba: Innocentius episcopus servus servorum dei, venerabili fratri episcopo dilectis filiis decano et precentori Hereford' salutem et apostolicum benedictionem. Conquerente dilecto filio Hillario clerico, nostris est auribus intimatum quod cum vicariam ecclesie de Brayles canonice fuerit assecutus, salva debita pensione quam priori et canonicis de Kenell' tenetur exsolvere annuatim, idem prior et canonici et quidem alii Coventr' diocesis ipsum, post appellationem ad nos legitime interpositam, super eadem indebita vexatione molestant etc'. Huius igitur auctoritate mandati partibus in presentia nostra constitutis, Hillarius proposuit quod vicariam ecclesie de Brayles, ad presentationem domini regis, canonice erat assecutus. Econtra ex parte prioris et canonicorum de Kennell' fuit responsum quod non canonice.[a] Et in medio reconventionis fuit propositum quod ad ipsos pertinet de iure presentare vicarium ad predictam ecclesiam etc'.

[a] *sic* B.

This case was reheard between 17 April 1208 and 1215 by Mauger, bp of Worcester, Gervase, abbot of Pershore, and Ranulf, prior of Worcester, and their settlement, issued in 1215, upheld Bp Giles'; see *The Letters of Pope Innocent III: a Calendar*, ed. C.R. and Mary Cheney (Oxford 1967), no.787. The previous hearing cannot have taken place much later than the end of 1207 at the latest, since time must be allowed for messages sent to and from the Curia. It is not certain whether the W., precentor, occurring here is William Foliot or William of Kilpeck. Hugh de Mapenore became dean after 30 November 1201.

267. Leominster priory

Confirmation of the settlement made by Bishop Robert Foliot between Roger fitz Maurice and Reading abbey over the tithes of the demesne of Hampton Court and confirmation of a settlement of Bishop Gilbert Foliot concerning tithes from Hampton Court (above, no.109).

[24 September 1200 × 1208]

B = BL Cotton MS Domitian A iii (Leominster priory cartulary), fo.65r-v. s.xiii med.

Omnibus s(ancte) m(atris) e(cclesie) f(iliis) E. Heref' episcopus salutem. Noverit universitas vestra nos venerabilis antecessoris nostri Roberti Foliot Heref' electi cartam inspexisse, in qua continetur quod, cum causa que vertebatur inter Rogerum filium Mauricii et abbatem et monachos de Rading' super decimis [fo.65v] totius dominii de Hamt' ei esset a domino papa commissa, hoc modo sopita est. Predictus R. spontanea voluntate cessit iuri quod se dicebat in illis decimis habere, quas idem electus in manu sua resignatas contulerit abbati et monachis de Rading'. Abbas vero Rading' una cum assensu totius conventus prenominatas decimas eidem Rogero concessit habendas tota vita sua, sub unius aurei pensione annuatim infra octabas Sancti Michaelis domui Rad⟨ing⟩ persolvenda. Inspeximus etiam scriptum autenticum venerabilis antecessoris nostri G. episcopi, in quo continetur quod causa verteretur inter abbatem Rading' et G. de Hant' super decimis de Hamt', quas idem G. ad ecclesiam de Leom' antiquo iure pertinentes tempore gwerre violenter occupatas detinuit. Ecclesia de Leom' super ius suum reclamante, abbas Rading' in eiusdem episcopi presentia per testes omni exceptione maiores sufficienter probavit totum ius parrochiale de Hamt' tam vivorum quam mortuorum ad ecclesiam de Leom' pertinere, et sic ecclesia de Leom' predictarum decimarum possessionum sibi adiudicatam integre recepit. Nos igitur quod a predecessoribus nostris sicut in eorum scriptis autenticis continetur rationabiliter actum est ratum habemus et episcopali auctoritate confirmamus. Noverit etiam universitas vestra Rogerum filium Mauricii predictas decimas de Hamt' in presentia capituli nostri Heref' in manus nostras resignasse, quas nos interventu divine pietatis priori et monachis de Leom' in proprios usus in perpetuum concessimus tenendas. Hanc igitur concessionem perpetue firmitatem stabilitatis optinere desiderantes, eam una cum hiis que in predictis autenticis continentur commissa nobis a deo auctoritate confirmare curavimus, unde presens scriptum tam sigillo nostro quam sigillo capituli nostri Hereford' roboratum confecimus. T' et cetera.

It is likely that Roger fitz Maurice died shortly after 1206 and that therefore this charter predates Giles' going into exile in 1208. On Roger see above no.169.

268. Leominster priory

Inspeximus of confirmation by Bishops Richard de Capella and Gilbert Foliot of grants to Leominster priory.

[24 September 1200 × 17 November 1215]

B = BL Cotton MS Domitian A iii (Leominster priory cartulary), fos.64v-65r. s.xiii med.

Omnibus sancte ma(tris) e(cclesie) f(iliis) Egidius Heref' episcopus salutem. Noverit universitas vestra nos venerabilium antecessorum nostrorum bone memorie Ricardi et G. Heref' episcoporum cartas in hec verba inspexisse. Ego dei gratia Heref' episcopus R. manu mea propria concessi et confirmavi ecclesie Rading' et eius abbati primo domino Hugoni ecclesiam Sancti Petri de Leom' cum omni ad ipsam [fo.65r] pertinente parrochia, scilicet de Bradeford', et de Ach', et de Leena, et de Diliga prima et secunda,[a] que ambe magis proxime sunt Leom', et de Lintheleg', et de Kinardesleg', et de Winet', et de utraque Sarnesfeld, et de Titelleg', de Hopa quoque et de Wavert', de Niwent', et de Gatredehope, de Stok' quoque et de utraque Hethfeld', et de Risebir', et de Humbr', et Gedefenn', et Buterleg', et Bradefeld', et utraque Hamt', et Forda, et Heanoure, et Eatun', et Heent', de Stoct' quoque et Esscet', et Bremesfeld', et Uptun', et Miclat', et Dreit', et Hamenessce, et Wihale, et Putlesd', et Brochamet', et Forda, de Luston quoque et Heia et Crofta. Hec antiqui et autentici viri in presentia mea attestati sunt, et plurima que antiquitus de parrochia Leom' fuerunt pro vetustate nimia se tacuisse dixerunt. Nos vero que supradicta sunt ecclesie Rading' et eius abbati confirmamus, salva iustitia quam unicuique servare debemus. Act' etc'.[b] Gilebertus dei gratia Heref' episcopus dilectis sibi in Cristo[c] universis sancte matris ecclesie Hereford[d] filiis salutem. Predecessoris nostri bone memorie R. Heref' quondam episcopi vestigiis adherentes, que ecclesie Rading' et eius abbati primo domino Hugoni ipse concessit et confirmavit, nos quoque eidem ecclesie et eius abbati domino Rogero concedimus et confirmamus, scilicet ecclesiam Sancti Petri de Leom', cum omni ad ipsam pertinente parrochia, scilicet de Bradeford' et de Ach' et cetera ut supra.[b] Hec antiqui et autentici viri in presentia prefati episcopi sicut in carta ipsius continetur attestati sunt ad parrochiam Leom' pertinere. Que pariter omnia et nos Rading' ecclesie confirmamus, salva iustitia quam unicuique servare debemus. Nos igitur venerabilium antecessorum nostrorum Heref' episcoporum concessionem et confirmationem ratam habentes, eam presentis instrumenti testimonio et sigilli nostri patrocinio roboramus. Hiis testibus et cetera.

[a]i.a et ii.a B.   [b]sic B.   [c]Cristo here; Domino in no.111.   [d]Heford B.

For Richard de Capella's grant and Gilbert Foliot's confirmation see above, nos.11, 111 (pd, *Reading cartularies*, i.287-8, no.354, and *GFL*, no.343); see also nos.300 and 352.

269. Leominster priory

*Mandate to the archdeacons, deans, and priests of the diocese of Hereford
to protect the possessions of Leominster Priory.*
[24 September 1200 × 17 November 1215]

B = BL Cotton MS Domitian A iii (Leominster priory cartulary), fos.65v-66r.
s.xiii med.

E. dei Heref' episcopus omnibus archidiaconis, decanis et presbiteris
in Heref' episcopatu constitutis salutem. Auctoritate qua fungimur
vobis in vi obedientie precipimus quatinus statim ex quo querimonia
monachorum Leom' super eorum ablatis rebus vel possessionibus
suis [fo.66r] turbatis, vel ob iniuriam sibi vel hominibus suis illatam,
delata fuerit, nisi satisfacere voluerint auctoritate nostra omni occasione et dilatione postposita sollempniter omnes illos malefactores,
cum vobis nominati fuerint, candelis accensis, excommunicetis, et
tanquam excommunicatos in quacumque parrochia fuerint ab omnibus usque ad dignam ablatorum satisfactionem cautius vitari precipiatis, et dum moram ibi fecerint divina celebrari ibidem
prohibeatis. Valete.

270. Leominster priory

*Confirmation of the revenue of half a mark from the vicarage of the Holy
Cross and Hope under Dinmore, half a mark from Ford chapel and four
marks from Eye.*
[24 September 1200 × 17 November 1215]

B = BL Cotton MS Domitian A iii (Leominster priory cartulary), fo. 66r. s.xiii
med. Rubric: Idem de dimid. mar' de vicaria Lem' et Hop' et dim' ma de Ford'
et iiij ma de Eya.

Universis et cetera.*a* Sciatis nos caritatis intuitu ecclesie beatorum
apostolorum P(etri) et P(auli) de Leom' confirmasse dimidiam marcam de vicaria que dicitur ad Crucem et de Hop', et de capella de
Forda dimidiam marcam, *b*et de capella de Eya iiii. marcas.*b* Quod ut
perpetua gaudeat firmitate, sigilli nostri appositione communimus.
T' et c'.

*a*sic B.   *b-b*written in a 15th-century hand over an erasure. However the rubric, which
mentions this payment, is contemporary with the text.

Idem in the rubric refers to Bp Giles de Braose, who issued no.269 above, the deed immediately preceding this one in the Leominster cartulary. See also nos.32, 211, 215-6 and 353 below.

*271. Lire abbey

Institution of a vicar in the church of Wilton and regulation of the vicarage.   [24 September 1200 × 17 November 1215]

Mention only, BL Cotton MS Otho B xiv, fo.13v, an inventory from Sheen priory: 'Item carta Egidii Hereford' episcopi super institutione vicarii de Wylton et de taxatione vicarie ibidem.'

*272. Lire abbey

Institution of a vicar in the church of Much Marcle and regulation of the vicarage.   [24 September 1200 × 17 November 1215]

Mention only, BL Cotton MS Otho B xiv (inventory of Sheen priory), fo.20r: 'Item institucio et ordinacio Egidii episcopi Herford' de vicaria de Markely.'

*273. Lire abbey

Confirmation issued by Bishop Giles and Hereford cathedral chapter of the church of Much Marcle.
          [24 September 1200 × 17 November 1215]

Mention only, BL Cotton MS Otho B xiv (inventory of Sheen priory), fo.21r: 'Item confirmacio E. episcopi Herford' et capituli de ecclesia de Markeley.'

274. Little Malvern priory

Confirmation of a grant by Bishop William de Vere of assarts at Deerfold in Worcestershire and of a grant by John of Stanford of land at Horton to Little Malvern priory.
          [24 September 1200 × 17 November 1215, possibly early]

Pd., *Mon. Ang.* iv.449, where it is described as an original coming from the collection of W. Hamper. This may be the same original as a confirmation of Giles' deed, possibly a charter of inspeximus, issued by the dean and chapter of Hereford, which formed part of the Shrewsbury-Talbot Collection (now in the BL), and as such was described in *HMCR*, lv (*Var. Coll.*, ii), 289, but which is now missing.

Universis Cristi fidelibus presens scriptum visuris vel audituris Egidius divina permissione Herefordensis ecclesie minister humilis eternam in domino salutem. Noverit universitas vestra nos pro anima nostra et pro animabus omnium predecessorum et successorum nostrorum concessisse et confirmasse deo et ecclesie Sancti Egidii Minoris Malvernie et monachis eiusdem loci donationem et concessionem quam venerabilis predecessor noster, quondam Herefordensis episcopus, Willelmus, fecit eisdem ecclesie et monachis de assartis de la Dirfaud cum pertinentiis suis, secundum quod plenius continetur in carta eiusdem Willelmi, necnon et concessionem et donationem quam Iohannes de Stanford fecit dictis ecclesie et monachis de tenemento suo et tota terra sua de Horton, cum pertinentiis suis, habend' et tenend' pro nobis et successoribus nostris sibi et successoribus suis, in liberam, puram, et perpetuam elemosinam, quietam et liberam ab omnibus servitiis, ut in homagiis, wardis, releviis, exchaetis, auxiliis, exactionibus, consuetudinibus et demandis, et ab omnibus sectis curiarum nostrarum, hundredorum, halymot, laweday, et omnibus servitiis forinsecis, extrinsecis, et omnibus rebus que ab eisdem pro iam dictis terris et tenementis exigi poterunt in futurum quovismodo. Et ne dictam confirmationem nostram aliquis valeat infirmare, nos eam in premissis omnibus et singulis de consensu et voluntate capituli nostri Hereford autoritate pontificali ratificamus et confirmamus, presertim cum ex tenore carte dicti domini Willelmi manifeste pateat memorati loci conventum in obitu omnium episcoporum Herford de seculo successive migrantium unum annale se celebraturum,[a] pro salute omnium fidelium, in verbo domini fideliter promisisse. Quod quia firmum et stabile in perpetuum volumus permanere, sigillum nostrum presenti scripto apponi facimus. Hiis testibus, Henrico de Stanford, Osberto de Kenecestr', Willelmo de Northinton, Mauricio de Cradel', Radulfo de Hulla, Alano de Walynton, Nicholao Seculari, et multis aliis.

[a]celebratur *sic, Mon. Ang.*

Henry de Stanford was John de Stanford's son, and appears above, nos.179 and 180. Maurice of Cradeley also appears as a witness to episcopal *acta*; see above, nos.179, 180, and 196. Nicholas le Secular occurs as lord of Dinmore in 1223 (*Cal. ch. rolls*, i.37), and Ralph de la Hulle occurs in 1204 (*P.R. 6 John*, 20). The witnesses are episcopal tenants, and this charter was almost certainly issued in the bp's feudal court. Horton was part of the episcopal manor of Edwyn Ralph.

275. Bishop of Llandaff and Gloucester abbey

Settlement by Bishop Giles de Braose, H(ugh de Mapenore), dean of Hereford, and W(illiam Foliot), precentor of Hereford, acting as papal judges-delegate, of the dispute between the bishop of Llandaff and Gloucester Abbey over the church of Newport; the abbey had complained that the bishop had exploited the church of Newport and the judges decided that in future, in accordance with the decrees of the Lateran Council, the bishop should conduct his visitation of the church with only a moderate retinue and that he should obtain only a 'competent' procuration, and also that he should not refuse to admit clerks presented by the abbey to the custody of the church. 11 May 1204

B = PRO C150/1 (Gloucester cartulary), fo.149r new fol, fo.132r old fol., no.520. s.xiv ex.

Pd, *Gloucester cartulary*, ii.58.

Facta est autem hec compositio anno incarnationis dominice m°cc° quarto, quinto idus maii in ecclesia Sancti Ethelberti Hereford'. Quam quia perpetue firmitatem stabilitatis volumus optinere, presenti scripto sigillis nostris appositis confirmare curavimus.

The bp of Llandaff in question was Henry of Abergavenny, 1193-1218.

276. Llanthony priory

Confirmation of grants by his predecessors to Llanthony priory.
[30 November 1201 × 17 November 1215]

B = PRO C115 K1/6679 (Llanthony Cartulary A9), fo.117r-v. s.xiii med. C = Ibid., C115 K2/6683 (Llanthony Cartulary A1), fo.124r, section vi, no.32. s.xiv med.

Universis*a* sancte matris ecclesie filiis ad quos presens scriptum pervenerit E. dei gratia Hereford' ecclesie minister eternam in domino salutem. Quoniam ecclesiastice possessiones a Cristi fidelibus in elemosinam viris religiosis collate exquisitis calumpniantium versutiis non numquam turbari solent, necesse est illas magnorum virorum et fidedignorum testimonio necnon et autenticorum scriptorum*b* patrocinio communiri. Inde est quod Lanthon' ecclesie et venerabilibus et deo dilectis canonicis regularibus ibidem deo servientibus paterna pietate et benignitate prospicere cupientes, inspectis cartis venerabilium patrum predecessorum nostrorum, quorum vestigiis inherere eorumque canonica statuta sequi optamus, omnia beneficia iam percepta seu in futurum canonice percipienda prefate ecclesie Lanthon' et canonicis nostra episcopali auctoritate et presentis scripti patrocinio confirmamus*c* et sigilli nostri appositione roboramus. Confirmamus itaque eis terram extra burgum Hereford' que Mora vocatur liberam et quietam ab omni servitio et consuetudine, excepto quod una hyda terre de Holemera solummodo regis geldum persolvit, mansionem etiam quam Ernaldus presbiter tenuerat extra [fo.117v B] burgum Hereford, cum x. acris terre, liberam et quietam ab omni servitio et consuetudine; similiter etiam*d* acram unam mansioni prefate contiguam de terra Fulconis, ecclesiam quoque de Froma cum omnibus pertinentiis suis, *e*et duas ecclesias de Presteburia,*e* unam sub montibus, alteram super montes, scilicet ecclesiam de Sevenhanton' cum terris et decimis aliisque elemosinis omnibus eisdem ecclesiis pertinentibus aut contingentibus, exceptis duabus portionibus decime de dominio meo, quas habent decanus et cantor Hereford', de blado scilicet tantum et de leguminibus; de parco autem de Prestebiria et de hiis que seminantur vel colliguntur intra designatum ambitum parchi decima remanet ecclesie de Prestebur*f* quia terra fuit villanorum; tria quoque exarta in Presteb' que Leuricus Figulus et Lefwynus Rufus et Erni per ix denariorum redditum per annum tenuerunt, que prefatus episcopus R.[1] per xii. denariorum redditum per annum tenenda et ad ecclesiam de Presteb' pertinenda in perpetuam elemosinam dedit et concessit: unam etiam virgatam terre in eadem villa quam Ernaldus miles dedit eidem ecclesie quando vitam suam in ea mutavit, liberam et quietam ab omni servitio et consuetudine, ita ut heredes eius idem servitium quod pro ea episcopo facere debebant de reliquo feodo suo persolvant; preterea dimidiam virgatam terre in eadem villa cum brachia quadam que eidem appendere solet quam concedente Gilberto episcopo Radulfus predicti Ernaldi filius cum matre sua quando eam in sororem susceperunt in perpetuam elemosinam dedit liberam et quietam ab omni servitio et consuetudine ita ut ipse et heredes eius idem servitium quod pro hac terra episcopo debent de reliquo feodo suo persolvant; ex eiusdem quoque Radulfi donatione x. acras terre quas dedit in perpetuam elemosinam liberas et quietas ab omni servitio et consuetudine. Hec omnia sicut singula in singulis cartis predecessorum nostrorum Roberti, Gilberti, item Roberti et Willelmi de Ver episcoporum Heref' confirmata legimus unum in scriptum redigentes nostri quoque sigilli inpressione in presentia subscriptorum testium confirmamus, Hugonis decani Hereford', Hugonis de Braosa, et aliorum.

*a*Omnibus C. *b*om. B; interlineated C. *c*underlined in a later hand C. *d*et BC. *e-e*underlined in a later hand C. *f*Prestebiria C. [1]Bishop Robert de Béthune.

Hugh became dean of Hereford after 30 November 1201, and the charter is in fact probably datable 1201 × 1208, because Hugh de Braose does not witness any charter of Giles which is definitely datable to the period after his return from exile. In this charter Giles was repeating more or less word for word the confirmation of Robert Foliot (above no.166), though some passages follow the wording of the confirmation issued by Robert de Melun (above no.121). Presumably Llanthony produced both to serve as the basis of Giles' text. See also nos.35-7, 103-4, and 225.

277. Much Wenlock priory

Confirmation of a charter of Bishop William de Vere granting Much Wenlock Priory licence to appropriate the churches of Holy Trinity, Wenlock, and Eaton. [24 September 1200 × 1208]

B = PRO C66/226 (Patent Rolls), 22 Edward III, pt. iii, 1348, membrane 34, contained in an inspeximus issued by Edward III dated 12 October 1348 at Westminster.

C = Ibid., in the same inspeximus, contained in an inspeximus issued by Dean John and Hereford Cathedral Chapter, dated 2 October 1282.

Cal., *Cal. Pat. Rolls, 1348-50*, 187.

Omnibus sancte matris ecclesie filiis ad quos presens scriptum pervenerit Egidius divina permissione Hereford' ecclesie minister eternam in domino salutem. Noverit universitas vestra nos venerabilis antecessoris Willelmi de Ver Hereford' episcopi cartam inspexisse, cuius tenore perpendimus ipsum concessisse fratribus deo et Sancte Milburge in ecclesia de Wenel'[a] deservientibus ut liceat eis ecclesiam de Eaton' et ecclesiam Sancte Trinitatis de Wenel'[a] cum omni sua integritate in usus proprios convertere. Nos vero, attendentes inde predictis fratribus affectuosam karitatem[b] sanctamque[c] devotionem plenius exuberare, illorum beneficia dignum duximus augere, ut illis augmentatis fervor devotionis et amor caritatis, si fieri potest, in sublimiora conscendant.[d] Concedimus igitur et quantum ad nostre pertinet auctoritatis ministerium confirmamus predictis monachis prenominatas ecclesias ad usus proprios in perpetuum cum omnibus ad eas de iure spectantibus optinendas, salvis in omnibus episcopali auctoritate et dignitate et officialium suorum honesta consuetudine. Ut igitur hec nostra concessio et confirmatio perpetue firmitatem stabilitatis optineat, eam presenti scripto et sigilli nostri testimonio confirmare curavimus. Hiis testibus, Magistris Theobaldo, Albino et Galfrido de Ludel',[e] Ricardo et Rauff'[f] capellanis, Symone et Willelmo clericis, Alexandro de Albet', Henrico de Peneb',[g] Iohanne de Camera et multis aliis.

[a]Wenlok' C. [b]caritatem C. [c]sanctam B. [d]conscendat BC.
[e]Lodelawe C. [f]sic for Rannulfo B; Raulph C. [g]Penebrug' C.

For William de Vere's charter see above no.227. Henry (I) of Pembridge, a tenant of William de Braose at Pembridge, died in 1210/11 (Ralph of Pembridge is found paying 100 marks and a horse at Michaelmas 1211 to succeed his father, *PR 13 John*, ed. D.M.Stenton, PRS, n.s., xxviii [1953], 235), and therefore this charter must have been issued before Giles went into exile in 1208.

*277A. Master Philip of Ludlow

Confirmation of Archbishop Hubert Walter's settlement of the dispute between Geoffrey de Lacy, parson of Ludlow, and Master Philip, vicar and schoolmaster of Ludlow, over the vicarage of Ludlow, according to the terms of which Geoffrey had to restore to Philip the half of the church which he claimed in return for an annual pension of 4 marks and five shillings and also full control of the school in Ludlow.

[shortly after late 1203 × April 1204]

Hubert Walter's settlement of the dispute (*EEA* iii, no.536) states that Master Philip should obtain a confirmation from Bp Giles de Braose as soon as possible. There is however no evidence that Philip necessarily did so.

278. Ralph de Wallok'

Grant to Ralph and his heirs of land next to the public street which had been the subject of a dispute between William the treasurer and various other members of the cathedral chapter of Hereford.

[24 September 1200 × 17 November 1215, probably 1213 × 1215]

B = Bodl. MS Rawlinson B329 (Hereford cathedral cartulary), fos.55v-56r. s.xv.

Omnibus sancte matris ecclesie filiis ad quos presens scriptum pervenerit Egidius divina miseratione Herefordensis ecclesie minister eternam in domino salutem. Noverit universitas vestra nos dedisse et concessisse*a* Radulpho de Wallok' et heredibus suis totam terram illam que iacet iuxta stratam publicam de qua contentio fuit inter Willelmum thes(aurarium) ecclesie nostre et Magistrum Alexandrum, M(agistrum) Albinum, Galfridum de Lac' et Helyam de Raden' ut ipse et heredes sui habeant et teneant terram illam de sacristaria libere et quiete ab omni servitio et exactione, reddendo annuatim sacriste ecclesie nostre quinque solidos duobus terminis, ad festum Sancti Michaelis et ad Annuntiationem beate Marie, cum decima illius terre ad emendum oleum quod conburatur in una [fo.56r] lampade in ecclesia nostra imperpetuum. Hoc igitur quia consensu*b* omnium predictorum necnon et consensu*b* totius capituli Hereford' factum est presenti scripto et sigilli nostri testimonio una cum sigillo capituli nostri communire curavimus. Hiis testibus *c*E. thesaurario, Magistro Thoma de Bosebur',*c* Hugone Bukehill clericis et aliis.

*a*conceiss B.   *b*concensu B.   *c-c*Magistro Thoma E thes' de Bosebur' B.

William occurs as treasurer in several charters issued by Giles and others in the early thirteenth century. Elias de Radnor had certainly become treasurer by the end of Giles' episcopate, but may only have obtained the office after Giles' return from exile. He held it until 1230, when he was made bp of Llandaff. It is quite possible that the Master Alexander mentioned as one of the litigants should be identified with the otherwise unidentifiable Master Alexander of Walton, archdn of Hereford and canon, who is commemorated in the cathedral obit book under 16 June (Bodl. MS Rawlinson B328, fo.22v), in which case he may have been archdn briefly after the previous holder of the office, William fitz Walter, was excommunicated in 1215 (Roger of Wendover, *Flores Historiarum*, iii.356). William's first known successor, Master William de Ria, does not occur before 1216 at the earliest (see nos.306, 308-10). Master Thomas of Bosbury was dean from 1216 to 1231. Hugh de Bukehill may be the same person as the Hervey de Bukehill who witnesses no.257 above, in which case Hugh would presumably be a misreading of Hervey. It was the duty of a cathedral treasurer to provide candles and lights, which explains why William the treasurer was involved in a dispute about the revenue from the land in question, and also why it was necessary for Elias of Radnor to appear as a witness. The references to the sacristy and the sacrist in this charter are to be explained by the fact that a cathedral treasurer's duties were equivalent to those of a sacristan in a monastery; indeed the term *sacrista* was sometimes used to describe a treasurer, for example at Rouen cathedral in the first half of the twelfth century: see Diana Greenway, 'The false *Institutio* of St Osmund', 83. Ivo, treasurer of Hereford from the 1150s to the 1180s, is described as *sacrista* in a charter of 1172 (Oxford, Balliol College MS 271, fo.108r).

279. Reading abbey

Admission to the vicarage of the church of Leominster called Ad Crucem *and of Hope under Dinmore of Master S. on presentation by the abbot and monks of Reading.* [24 September 1200 × 17 November 1215]

> B = BL Cotton MS Domitian A iii (Leominster priory cartulary), fo.66r. s.xiii med. Rubric: Idem de presentatione Magistri S. ad vicariam de Lem' et de taxatione eiusdem vicarie.

Universis et cetera.*[a]* Notum vobis fieri volumus quod nos ad presentationem et petitionem venerabilium et in Cristo dilectorum fratrum domini abbatis et conventus Rading' Magistrum S. ad perpetuam vicariam ecclesie de Leom' que dicitur ad Crucem et de Hop' suscepimus, cum omnibus pertinentiis suis habendam et possidendam ea integritate qua W. eiusdem ecclesie vicarius eam habuisse dinoscitur, excepto blado quod dicitur scriftcorn, unde dictus S. nichil percipiet, sed in recompensatione illius bladi habebit panem precipuarum festivitatum, quem W. predecessor suus non percipit, reddendo inde annuatim dimidiam marcam argenti. Predicti monachi omnia onera eiusdem ecclesie tam ad episcopum quam ad archidiaconum pertinentia sustinebunt. Ut autem hec donatio et concessio perpetue robur stabilitatis optineat, eam presentis instrumenti testimonio et sigilli nostri appositione communivimus. T' et cetera.

[a] sic B.

The *idem* in the rubric refers to Giles de Braose, who issued the preceding charters. For *scriftcorn*, see note to no.30 above. See also nos.32, 211, 215-6, 270 and 353.

280. Richard of Kent

Grant in fee to Richard of Kent of half a hide in Colcombe which had been held by William of Colcombe.

[24 September 1200 × 17 November 1215]

B = PRO C115 K2/6683 (Llanthony cartulary A1), fo.127v. s.xiv med.

Sciant omnes tam presentes quam futuri quod ego Egidius dei gratia Hereford' episcopus dedi et concessi Ricardo de Kent, servienti nostro, pro homagio et servitio suo dimidiam hydam terre cum omnibus pertinentiis suis in Calecumbe, videlicet illam quam Willelmus de Calecumbe habuit et tenuit, tenendam et habendam sibi et heredibus suis de nobis et successoribus nostris episcopis in feodo et hereditate, libere et quiete ab omni servitio et exactione quod ad terram pertinet, salvo regali servitio, reddendo inde annuatim nobis et successoribus nostris episcopis ipse et heredes sui septem solidos et unum denarium pro redditu et dono quod ad terram pertinebat quatuor terminis, scilicet ad festum Sancti Andree duos solidos et sex denarios, et ad festum Sancti Iohannis Baptiste decem et octo denarios, et ad Annuntiationem beate Marie decem et octo denarios, et ad festum Sancti Michaelis decem et novem denarios. Quod quia firmum et stabile permanere volumus, id presenti scripto et sigilli nostri appositione confirmavimus. Hiis testibus, Waltero de Braosa, Iohanne fratre suo, Willelmo de Bellocampo et aliis.

Walter and John were two of Giles' younger brothers, according to the family tree in BL Cotton MS Julius D x, fo.30r. The de Beauchamps were tenants of the bp at Upper Sapey.

281. Robert son of Nicholas of London

Confirmation of a grant of a virgate in Prestbury made by Anselm de Mobray to Robert of London as heir of Hingelot and to Hugh Folet; the virgate had been confirmed to Anselm by William de Vere.

[24 September 1200 × 17 November 1215]

B = Bodl. MS Rawlinson B329 (Hereford cathedral cartulary), fos.146v-7r. s.xiii-xiv.

Egidius dei gratia Herefordensis ecclesie minister universis Cristi fidelibus ad quos presens scriptum pervenerit eternam in domino salutem. Ad universitatis vestre notitiam pervenire volumus quod nos donationem unius virgate terre in manerio nostro de Prestebur' quam Anselmus de Mobray' fecit Roberto Londoniensi, filio Nicholai, sicut heredi Hingelot, et Hugoni Folet, quam scilicet idem Anselmus dedit et concessit predicto Hingelot pro homagio et servitio suo, et quam venerabilis predecessor noster Willelmus de Ver prefato Anselmo confirmavit, ratam et acceptam habemus. Et ne processu temporis alicui in dubium venire possit, secundum quod continetur in carta predicti Anselmi prefato Roberto facta de eadem donatione [fo.147r], eam presenti scripto et sigilli nostri attestatione confirmare et corroborare curavimus. Hiis testibus, Roberto de Furches[a] tunc senescallo, Ricardo Foliot, Roberto de Sipton, Reginaldo de Cumton', Willelmo de Aldemonston', Waltero marescallo, Philippo de Suietelo, Willelmo de Perect', Nicholao le Percer, Iordano de Camera, Waltero de Boltesham et multis aliis.

[a]Furthes, B.

Hingelot was still alive 1200 × c.1201; see no.289 below.

282. Shrewsbury abbey

Notification that an inquisition of the clergy of the surrounding countryside held in a general chapter to determine to whom the tithes of the vill of Weston and of the demesne of Henley belonged decided in favour of Shrewsbury abbey.　　[24 September 1200 × 17 November 1215]

B = NLW MS 7851 D (Shrewsbury cartulary), p.310, no. 352. s.xiv.

Pd., *Shrewsbury cartulary*, ii, no.352.

Hiis testibus, Magistris Teobaldo, Galfrido de Ludel', Philippo Map', Ricardo et David capellanis, Simone et Willelmo clericis, et aliis.

283. Tintern abbey

Confirmation to Tintern abbey of a licence to appropriate the church of Woolaston and the chapel of Alvington issued by Bishop William de Vere.
[24 September 1200 × 18 November 1215, probably before 1208]

> B = BL Arundel MS 19 (Tintern abbey cartulary), fo.31v. s.xvi.

Omnibus sancte matris ecclesie filiis ad quos presens scriptum pervenerit Egidius divina permissione Hereford' ecclesie minister presentis vite felicitatem^a et^b eternam beatitudinem. Noverit universitas vestra^c nos venerabilis antecessoris nostri pie memorie Willelmi de Ver Herford' episcopi auctenticum inspexisse instrumentum cuius tenorem perpendimus ipsis abbati et monachis de Tinterna indulsisse ut ipsi ecclesiam de Wolvaston et capellam de Alvynton' cum omnibus ad eas de more spectantibus in usus \suos/ proprios convertant. Nos igitur pium et deo gratum esse considerantes religiosorum portiones augmentare ut crescentibus illorum bonis augeatur et munus deo famulantium ^{d}et in hospitalitate manutenenda caritas^d prenominatas ecclesiam et capellam iuxta prenominati tenorem instrumenti predictis abbati et monachis salvis matricis ecclesie nostre Hereford' iure et dignitate presenti scripto et sigilli nostri appositione confirmamus. Hiis testibus, W. thesaurario Herford', Magistris Theobaldo, Ricardo Rufo, et ceteris.^{e}

^{a}presentis vite fe *written over an erasure B.* ^{b}et *om. B.* ^{c}vestra *om. B.*
$^{d-d}$*om. B; supplied from a confirmation by Bishop Hugh (de Mapenore), because demanded by the sense.* ^{e}eccc' *sic B.*

William the treasurer had probably died or resigned before Giles' return from exile. For Bishop Hugh's confirmation see below, no.315. See also no.237.

284. Tintern abbey

Admission of Adam of Woolaston, clerk, to the church of Woolaston as vicar, on presentation by the abbot and monks of Tintern.
[24 September 1200 × 17 November 1215]

> B = BL Arundel MS 19 (Tintern abbey cartulary), fo.35r. s.xvi.

Omnibus sancte matris ecclesie filiis ad quos presens scriptum pervenerit Egidius divina permissione Herford' ecclesie minister eternam in domino salutem. Noverit universitas vestra nos ad presentationem abbatis et conventus de Tintern' Adam de Wullanston clericum ad ecclesiam de Wullanston admisisse et ipsum in eadem ecclesia cum omnibus ad eam de iure spectantibus sicut eam predecessor eius Abraham plenius tenuit canonice absque omni reclamatione perpetuum vicarium insti\tui/sse sub annua viginti solidorum pensione predictis abbati et conventui persolvenda, medietate ad festum Sancti Michaelis et alia medietate ad Pascha. Ut igitur hec nostra institutio perpetue firmitatem stabilitatis optineat, eam presenti scripto et sigilli nostri testimonio confirmavimus. Hiis testibus, Magistris Theobaldo et Galfrido de Ludesl', Ricardo et Ranulfo capellanis et multis aliis.

285. Walter de Gosebroc

Grant to Walter de Gosebroc of the custody of the wood on the episcopal manor of Ross, and of a virgate at Alton Court in Ross; Walter is to have all the timber and branches in the wood brought down by the storm, crop and lop of all timber, stumps, and bark, but not the cablish and felled timber intended for the bishop. [24 September 1200 × 1214]

B = Hereford, Herefordshire County Record Office, Registrum Ricardi de Swinfield (formerly Hereford, Diocesan Registry), fo.64r old fol., fo.68r new fol.. 1283 × 1317, here *c*.1290.

Pd, *Reg. Swinfield*, 231-2.

Omnibus Cristi fidelibus ad quos presens carta pervenerit Egidius dei gratia Heref' episcopus salutem in domino. Noverit universitas vestra nos dedisse et concessisse et hac nostra presenti carta confirmasse Waltero de Gosebrok' pro homagio et servitio suo custodiam totius bosci nostri in manerio nostro de Ros, et preterea unam virgatam terre cum pertinentiis apud Aleton' in predicto manerio, pro predicto bosco custodiendo. Concessimus etiam eidem Waltero omnia ligna in dicto bosco per tempestatem prostrata, et etiam ramos per tempestatem prostratos, et omnes coperones lignorum prostratorum quocumque modo \prostrata/ sint, excepto cabilicio et exceptis lignis ad opus nostrum prostratis, et omnes ceppos et cortices tempore excoriationis, habend' et tenend' de nobis et successoribus nostris sibi et heredibus suis in perpetuum, bene et in pace, libere et quiete et integre in omnibus libertatibus et omnibus locis et omnibus rebus. Nos vero et successores nostri predictam custodiam totius dicti bosci nostri de Ros, cum omnibus supradictis et cum predicta virgata terre et suis pertinentiis, predicto Waltero et heredibus suis contra omnes gentes in perpetuum warantizabimus, et quia volumus quod hec nostra donatio et concessio rata et stabilis in perpetuum permaneat, hac presenti carta nostra et sigilli nostri impressione illam confirmavimus. Hiis testibus, Iohanne de Say, Waltero, decano de Ros, Radulfo Avenel, Radulfo de Wysham, Iohanne filio Stephani de Heref', Roberto de Aubemar', Roberto de Treges, Willelmo de Hugeleye, Radulfo clerico et multis aliis.

Robert de Tregoz' last occurrence is in 1214 (*Pipe Roll 16 John*, ed. P.M.Barnes, PRS, n.s., xxxv [1962], 137), but he must have died in that year (cf. I.J.Sanders, *English Baronies* [Oxford 1960], 43). Giles' grant was confirmed by Hugh Foliot for Walter's son, Walter; see no.369 below. 'Goosebrook' was a locality in the episcopal manor of Lyde Godfrey. Since the normal meaning of *cabilicium* or cablish is windfallen wood, it is not certain what the drafter of this document intended to mean by using this term.

*286. Walter Walensis

Confirmation of a grant made by William (de Kilpeck) the precentor to his brother Walter Walensis of some land with a grove at Clehonger for a rent of 4s 9d a year. [1206 × 17 November 1215]

Mention only, in an inspeximus and confirmation issued by Dean Thomas (de Bosbury) and the cathedral chapter of Hereford of William's grant (Hereford D. & C. Muniments, no.2866). The William precentor in question must be William de Kilpeck, precentor from a point not earlier than 1206 to -1223, since the inspeximus does not refer to William as being dead and since a brother of William Foliot the precentor would probably have been given the surname Foliot.

287. Wigmore abbey

Composition of a dispute between Wigmore abbey on the one hand and William of Myndtown and Walter the rector of Myndtown, William's

brother, on the other; Walter is to pay twelve pence as a pension to the
church of Lydbury and William and his heirs are to have the advowson.
[24 September 1200 × 17 November 1215]

A = University of London Library, Fuller Collection 19/30. 13th-century endorsement: Carta de Muneda. 15th-century endorsement: Lydbur' Cholton'
Eton' Castrum Episcopi Munede et Brocton'. 180 × 88 mm. Originally sealed
on a tag; seal missing.

Omnibus sancte matris ecclesie filiis. Egidius divina permissione
Herefordensis ecclesie minister ? eternam in domino salutem. Universitati vestre notum facimus. quod controversia que vertebatur
inter abbatem de Wigmora et conventum. et Willelmum de Muneda
et Walterum clericum fratrem predicti Willelmi rectorem ecclesie de
Muned'. super duodecim denariis. quod prefatus abbas et conventus
de Wigem'. a prefato Waltero nomine pensionis de ecclesia de Muneda annuatim ad ecclesiam de Lideburia solvendos exigebant ? hoc
fine coram nobis in forma iuris conquievit sententialiter. Prefatus
Walterus clericus et successores sui ecclesiam de Muned' optinentes ?
de prefata ecclesia de Muned'. tantum xii^{cim}. denarios ecclesie de
Lidebur'. singulis annis nomine pensionis ad annunciationem beate
Marie absque omni reclamatione persolvent. Sepedictus vero Willelmus et heredes sui ius advocationis ecclesie de Muned'. libere quiete
et inconcusse inperpetuum optinebunt. Et ut hec compositio inposterum robur illesum et illibatum optineat.' eam presentis scripti attes-
tatione confirmamus. His testibus. Magistro Philippo. Magistro
Theobaldo. Magistro Osberto. Domino Roberto Corbeth'. Hugone.
Corbeth fratre eius. Philippo de Sai. Widone de Arundel. Rogero de
Esthona. Rogero Porcell'. et multis aliis.

Robert Corbet was baron of Cause from 1176 to 1222 (R.W.Eyton, *Antiquities*,
vii.11-19); Guy of Arundel, who held land at Tetshill and Marlbrook, occurs
c.1202 × 1204, 1209, and before 1215 (*ibid.*, vii.16, vi.106, and xi.188). An
18th-century copy of this charter can be found in Bodl. MS Gough Shropshire 4,
fo.70r, with a note saying that the original was then kept in the parish chest of
Lydbury, Shropshire.

288. William Foliot, precentor of Hereford cathedral

Inspeximus of a grant by Dean Hugh de Mapenore and Hereford cathe-
dral Chapter to William Foliot the precentor of a virgate in Lulham,

together with two bundles of sheaves, an acre and a half of woodland and
an eighth of a stream in Lulham, resigned by Ralph, son of Turebert, to
William, for 8s 3½d per year.

[30 November 1201 × 1215, probably before 1208]

B = Bodl. MS Rawlinson B329 (Hereford cathedral cartulary), fos.26v-27r. s.xv.

Omnibus sancte matris ecclesie filiis ad quos presens scriptum pervenerit Egidius permissione divina Hereforden' ecclesie minister
eternam in domino salutem. Noverit universitas vestra nos dilectorum in Cristo filiorum H. decani et capituli Hereford' in hec verba
cartam inspexisse. Omnibus sancte matris ecclesie filiis ad quos presens carta pervenerit H. Herefordensis ecclesie decanus et eiusdem
loci capitulum eternam in domino salutem. Universitati vestre notum
facimus nos concessisse et dedisse et hac presenti carta nostra confirmasse Willelmo Folyot precentori Hereford' unam virgatam terre in
Lulleham quam Turebertus et Edwynus et Radulfus filii eius
tenuerunt cum duobus urpinis, et omnibus ad predictam virgatam
pertinentibus, item cum una acra *et dimidia* \de bosco in Lynde-
wod/, et cum octava parte gurgitis eiusdem ville, tenendam et habendam sibi et cuicumque eam dare voluit de nobis et successoribus
nostris in feudo et hereditate, libere et integre, honorifice [fo.27r] et
quiete ab omni servitio et exactione que ad predictam terram pertinet,
vel pertinere possit, reddendo inde annuatim nobis et successoribus
nostris pro predicta virgata et duobus urpinis octo solidos, pro acra
vero et dimidia et octava parte gurgitis iii d(enarios) obolum, pro omni
servitio, medietatem scilicet in Annunciatione beate Marie et aliam
medietatem in festo Sancti Michaelis. Sciendum est autem quod
predictus Radulfus predictas terras ad opus predicti precentoris nobis
reddit quietas, licet vero predicto precentori predictam virgatam cum
duobus urpinis et cum acra et dimidia et cum octava parte gurgitis,
salvo predicto servitio nostro cuicumque voluerit dare et quemcum-
que voluerit inde hereditare. Nos etiam predictas terras cum predicta
portione gurgitis prefato precentori et cuicumque eas dederit vel
heredem suum fecerit contra omnes homines warantizabimus. Pro
hac autem concessione et donatione dedit nobis sepedictus precentor
x libras argenti. Et quia hanc donationem et concessionem firmas esse
volumus et illibatas eas presenti pagine attestatione et sigilli nostri
impressione corroboramus. Hiis testibus, W. thesaurario, Hugone

archidiacono, Henrico cancellario, M(agistro) Simone et multis aliis. Nos vero predictam decani et ^{a}capituli donationem^a et concessionem ratam habentes et inconvulsam permanere volentes, eam episcopali auctoritate corroborare et presenti scripto cum sigilli nostri testimonio confirmare curamus. Hiis testibus, M(agistro) Theobaldo, M(agistro) Galfrido, M(agistro) Adam, Alexandro Abetot et aliis.

$^{a-a}$ written over an erasure B.

Hugh de Mapenore became dean after 30 November 1201. The document does not suggest that William Foliot had yet died; he was still alive in 1206, but probably died before Giles went into exile in 1208. William issued a charter bequeathing the land in question to his son John and to John's mother Margaret (pd, Julia Barrow, 'Hereford bishops and married clergy, c.1130-1240', Historical Research, 60 [1987], 7-8). Lulham is to the west of Hereford and to the south of the Wye. The word urpina may possibly be a form of the term urpa, meaning a bundle of sheaves, which occurs in the Customs of the bishopric of Winchester, BL Egerton MS 2418, fo.66v. I am grateful to Richard Sharpe for this information.

289. William the janitor

Confirmation of grants by Bishops Robert Foliot and William de Vere to William the janitor. [24 September 1200 × 1201/1202]

A = Hereford D. & C. Muniments, no. 1358. No medieval endorsements. 206 × 90 mm; originally sealed on a tag, but the seal does not survive.

B = Bodl. MS Rawlinson B329 (Hereford cathedral cartulary), fo.149r. s.xiii-xiv.

Pd from A, *Hereford charters*, 40.

Universis sancte matris ecclesie filiis ad quos presens carta pervenerit ? Egidius .dei. gratia Hereford'. ecclesie minister humilis salutem in vero salutari. Notum vobis facimus quod nos concessimus Willelmo ianitori omnes terras et tenementa cum aisiamentis earum quas idem .W. tenuit in manerio de Presteburi ex donatione venerabilium antecessorum nostrorum. videlicet Roberti Foliot et Willelmi de Ver episcoporum Hereford' quorum cartas inde Willelmo indultas inspeximus. et volumus quod idem Willelmus easdem terras teneat sibi et heredibus suis in perpetuum de nobis et successoribus nostris libere et quiete reddendo singulis annis ad quatuor terminos quatuordecim solidos. videlicet pro una virgata terre et pro duabus essartis octo solidos et pro dimidia virgata terre quatuor solidos et pro uno lundier duos solidos. Quod quia ratum et inconvulsum in perpetuum manere volumus presentis carte serie et sigilli nostri inpressione confirmavimus. et corroboravimus. Hiis testibus. Hugone de Braosa. Magistro Philippo. Magistro Hugone de Map'. Willelmo capellano de Kilpec. Magistro Albino. Magistro Serlone. Roberto de Furches. Willelmo Buteiller. Ricardo. de Kent. Roberto de Schiptun. Philippo camerario. Nicholao de Perers. Radulfo filio eius. Hugone de Kilpec. Ingelot. Rogero Fiillel Waltero Fillel. Iordano. Hereo. et multis aliis.

Master Hugh de Mapenore became dean after 30 November 1201. The word *lundier* may be the same as Old Norse *lundr*, a grove; see *Revised Medieval Latin Word-List from British and Irish Sources*, ed. R.E.Latham, British Academy (London 1965), 283. Hugh de Kilpeck was probably a brother of John, lord of Kilpeck, who died in 1205, rather than John's son Hugh, who only attained his majority 1212 × 1216.

290. Worcester cathedral priory

Inspeximus of a charter by which William de Vere granted a pension from Lindridge Church to the prior and monks of Worcester.   [1205]

B = Worcester Cathedral Library MS A4 (Worcester cathedral cartulary), fo.37v, no.206. s.xiii med.

Pd, *Worcester cartulary*, 109, no.206.

All the names of the witnesses have been omitted by the scribe of the cartulary. For the dating, see *Worcester cartulary, loc. cit..* See also nos.117, 177, 241 and 242.

291. Worcester cathedral priory

Notification of a settlement between Prior Ranulf and the monks of Worcester on the one hand and Archdeacon Osbert of Carmarthen, rector of the church of Lindridge, on the other concerning a pension of three marks from the demesne tithes of Moor Farm and Newnham; in return for an annual pension to Worcester of a hundred shillings the rector of Lindridge may receive all the tithes in question except those of new-born animals belonging to the cathedral priory, tithes of mills belonging to Worcester, of woodland pasture and of the gardens and hay of Munekemedew, Calreham, *and* Menemedew.   Dated *c.*29 June 1206.

B = Worcester Cathedral Library MS A4 (Worcester cathedral cartulary), fo.37v, no.207.

Pd, *Worcester cartulary*, 110, no.207.

Hiis testibus, Ricardo de Sap'.

Sapey was one of the manors of the bishops of Hereford. Osbert occurs as archdn of Carmarthen (diocese of St David's) in 1198 and 1203, when Gerald of Wales excommunicated him (Giraldus, *Opera*, iii.80, 196, 211). He had been succeeded by an archdn C. by 1208 (*Brecon cartulary*, xiv.156).

BISHOP HUGH DE MAPENORE

292. Profession of obedience

Profession of obedience to Archbishop Stephen Langton.
[27 October 1216]

> A = Canterbury D. & C. Ch. Ant. C115, no.84. 13th-century endorsement: Hec professio facta est in ecclesia Cant'. vi° kl. novembris. 154 x 32 mm.
>
> B = Canterbury D. & C. Register A (The Prior's Register), fo.233r. s.xiv med.
>
> Pd, *Canterbury professions*, 64, no.155.

Ego Hugo ecclesie Herefordensis electus. et a te reverende pater Stephane. sancte Cantuariensis ecclesie archiepiscope et tocius Anglie primas consecrandus antistes ⸴ tibi et sancte Cantuariensi ecclesie et successoribus tuis canonice substituendis. debitam et canonicam obedienciam et subieccionem me per omnia exhibiturum profiteor et promitto. et propria manu signo sancte crucis confirmo +*a*

> *a autograph cross A.*

> Hugh made his profession of obedience on 27 October 1216 in Canterbury Cathedral and was consecrated by Bp Silvester of Worcester on 18 December 1216.

293. Brecon Priory

Confirmation to Brecon Priory of the patronage of the church of Byford granted to them by Walter de Traveley.
[1217 × 29 November 1223, probably 1217 × 16 April 1219]

> B = Bodl. MS Carte 108, fos.266v-7r. s.xviii.
>
> Pd, *Brecon cartulary*, xiv.22.

Universis sancte matris ecclesie filiis presens scriptum inspecturis H. divina miseratione Hereford' ecclesie minister eternam in domino salutem. Quoniam iustis postulantium desideriis et precipue virorum religiosorum, qui totam vitam suam in dei laudibus expendunt, paterna provisione duximus annuendum, dilectis filiis priori et conventui de Brecon' ius patronatus ecclesie de Buford', et ultimam presentationem ad dictam ecclesiam nomine eorum factam, secundum tenorem cartarum dilecti filii Walteri de Travel' eiusdem ecclesie patroni, quas diligenter inspeximus, auctoritate pontificali confirmare curavimus. Ut igitur hec nostra confirmatio rata et stabilis in posterum permaneat eam presenti scripto et sigilli nostri appositione duximus roborandum. Hiis testibus, Thoma decano, W. precentore, Elya thesaurario, A. cancellario, Magistris Ricardo et Stephano, canonicis Hereford' ecclesie, Magistro W. [fo.267r] de Gersintun,[a] Magistro El(ia) de Burchull, G. et R. capellanis, Nicholao clerico et multis aliis.

[a]Gersintim' B.

Albinus became chancellor not before 1217, and Master Thomas Foliot had replaced William de Kilpeck as precentor by 29 November 1223. The names of the chaplains and the clerk suggest that this is a charter of Bp Hugh de Mapenore. For Walter de Traveley's charter, see above, no.246. Walter had presented the last vicar, Nicholas, in the name of the priory. Bp Hugh probably issued this confirmation after Nicholas' death or resignation.

*293A. Episcopal tenants at Bromyard

Grant to the episcopal tenants at Bromyard of part of the demesne.
[1216 × 1219]

Mention only, in a grant by Bishop Peter of Aigueblanche, bp of Hereford 1240-1268, to William Labbere of the land in question (BL Add. Charter 13285). Bp Peter's charter merely refers to the land being handed over and says nothing about whether Hugh had issued a written notification.

294. Buildwas Abbey

Composition between the abbey of Buildwas and the church of Wentnor over the tithes and half a virgate of land belonging to the chapel of Kinnerton in Wentnor.   [18 December 1216 × 16 April 1219]

A = Shropshire County Record Office, 259/1. Endorsements: late medieval chestmark in the form of a figure of eight. 16th-century endorsement: Ex his in visitatione mis' extra caus' p'p' (three words illegible) nullum quod (word illegible) xxxvi. 182 × 71 mm. Sealed on a tag, in green wax; impression broken at top and bottom, but probably originally a pointed oval; surviving fragment measures 43 × 43 mm. Obverse: figure in ecclesiastical vestments, holding a staff in his left hand, right hand not visible; legend: ....(G)ONIS ....Counterseal: pointed oval; figure of a bishop, wearing a mitre, kneeling to the right beneath a tripartite pointed arch above which the Virgin sits on a throne with the Child on her knee. Legend: (A)VE MARIA : GRACIA (P).... DOMINUS TECUM.

Omnibus sancte matris ecclesie filiis presens scriptum inspecturis.' H. divina permissione Hereforden' ecclesie minister.' eternam in domino salutem. Cum singulis et universis ad caritatis opera teneamur exhibenda.' ad viros religiosos caritate colendos[a] rationis diligentius respicit intuitus. Unde vestre universitati significamus nos compositionem inter abbatiam de Beldewas et ecclesiam de Wentenour' super decimis et dimidia virgate terre cum eius pertinentiis ad capellam de Kynverton' spectantibus ratam et approbatam habentes.' eam pietatis affectu ad perpetue firmitatis munimen sub presentis scripti et sigilli nostri testimonio auctoritate pontificali confirmasse.

[a] *followed by* nostre *cancelled.*

This is probably a charter of Hugh de Mapenore rather than of Hugh Foliot, because the seal differs from the seal known to have been used by Hugh Foliot in lacking a patterned background. The counterseal, a seal *ad causas*, is likewise different from the seal *ad causas* known to have been used by Hugh Foliot (no.332 below). The scribe of this charter also wrote no.297 below. Kinnerton was granted to Buildwas Abbey 1225 × 1227 by Richard Corbet (*Mon. Ang.* v.358), but he was confirming earlier grants by his tenants.

295. Chirbury priory

Confirmation to Chirbury priory of its prebends and appurtenances, as confirmed by Robert de Bullers, lord of Montgomery, and by Bishops William de Vere and Giles de Braose, Archbishop Hubert Walter, and Pope Innocent III, and grant of a licence to appropriate the prebend that had been held by Alan de Bullers in the parish church of Chirbury.

[18 December 1216 × 1227]

B = PRO E329/370, in an original inspeximus issued by Bishop Richard de Swinfield of Hereford dated 9 October 1289. C = Hereford, Herefordshire County Record Office, Registrum Ricardi de Swinfield (formerly Hereford Diocesan Registry), fo.63v in old fol., fo.67v in new. Contained in an inspeximus issued by Richard de Swinfield, dated 9 October 1289, in turn contained in an inspeximus issued by Hereford Dean and chapter, also dated 9 October 1289.

Pd, *Reg. Swinfield*, 229.

Universis sancte matris ecclesie filiis presens scriptum inspecturis H. divina miseratione Hereford' ecclesie minister eternam in domino salutem. Noverit universitas vestra nos cartam Roberti de Bullers domini de Mungomery et patroni ecclesie de Chyrebyr', et insuper bone memorie W. de Ver et Egidii predecessorum nostrorum, necnon et felicis memorie Innocentii pape tertii et H. Cantuarien' archiepiscopi, autentica instrumenta inspexisse, in quibus ecclesia de Cherebyr' cum prebendis et omnibus pertinentiis suis collata et confirmata dinoscitur dilectis filiis . .[a] priori et canonicis de Sned ad prioratum suum apud Chyrebir', sicut in carta domini fundi continetur, construendum.[b] Nos itaque, dictas concessiones et confirmationes ratas habentes, prebendam que fuit Alani de Bullers in dicta ecclesia tempore nostro vacantem, et prebendas alias cum vacaverint, in usus proprios ad hospitalitatis gratiam commodius exsequendam dictis priori et canonicis concedimus et auctoritate pontificali confirmamus. Ut igitur hec nostra concessio rata et inconcussa futuris temporibus permaneat, eam presenti scripto et sigilli nostri appositione roboravimus. Hiis testibus, Magistris P. et W. de Bergeveny et S. de Thornbir', canonicis Heref', Magistris W. de Gersinton' et Elia de Buckehull', Gregorio et R. capellanis, N. de Bergeven' et Terrico clericis, et multis aliis

[a]*gemipunctus om.* C.   [b]constituendum C.

It is not certain whether this is a charter of Bp Hugh de Mapenore or of Hugh Foliot, though the episcopal clerks in the witness list suggest the former. For William de Vere's confirmation, see above, no.184 (Giles' is missing). Pope Innocent III's confirmation, dated 1 February 1201, is calendared in *The Letters of Pope Innocent III: a Calendar*, ed. C.R. and Mary Cheney (Oxford 1967), no.282. By the early years of Hugh Foliot's episcopate only one prebend was held by a secular priest, a man called Richard, according to a charter of Hugh Foliot (see below, no.319) which was issued well before 1227.

296. Gloucester Abbey

*Composition between Gloucester Abbey and Master Walter of Garsington, rector of the church of Rudford, concerning villein service (*servile obsequium*) and the tithes of assarts, mills, and hay from the parish of Rudford, whereby Walter renounces his claim to all the tithes mentioned except the tithe of the villeins' hay, while Abbot H(enry Blount) and the monks of Gloucester renounce their claim to villein service and to ten marks legal expenses from Walter.* 14 April 1219

B = PRO, C150/1 (Gloucester cartulary), fos.148v-9r (old fol.), fos.165r-6r (new fol.), no.593. s.xiv ex.

Pd, *Gloucester cartulary*, ii.102-3.

This document was originally witnessed but the scribe of the cartulary omitted the witnesses' names. Henry Blount was abbot of Gloucester from 1205 to 23 August 1224. The date of Hugh de Mapenore's death is recorded as 16 April in Hereford Cathedral obit book (Bodl. MS Rawlinson B328, fo.14). If it is 16 April rather than 13 April which has sometimes been offered, it means that Hugh's death must have been very sudden. Hugh Foliot was not elected bp until June.

297. Guala, cardinal and papal legate

Litterae excusatoriae *to the legate Guala.* [December 1217]

A = Canterbury D. & C. Ch. Ant. C110, no.1. 14th-century endorsement: Excusacio Herefordensis episcopi quod pro morbo coepiscopis consecrationi electi Cicestr' non possit interesse. 165 mm wide; 50 mm deep at left-hand side and 39 mm deep at right. Originally sealed on a tongue, traces of which survive; there may perhaps also have been a wrapping tie.

Venerabili patri in Cristo et domino .G. dei gratia tituli Sancti Martini presbitero cardinali et apostolice sedis legato. et dilectis in domino fratribus coepiscopis Anglie .H. divina miseratione Hereford' ecclesie minister ⁒ salutem. et devotam in omnibus reverentiam. Ad vestram petimus pervenire noticiam nos incommoda corporis nostri valitudi-ne*a* detentos ⁒ consecrationi Magistri .R. Cicestr' electi dominica proxima post Epiphaniam domini apud Cantuar' ⁒ nullatenus posse interesse. Unde affectuosius suplicamus.*a* quatinus absentiam nostram dictis die et loco benigne si placet habere velitis excusatam. Nam. vero quicquid super electione dicti electi a vobis domino providente actum fuerit⁒ gratum habebimus et acceptum. Valeat semper in domino sanctitas vestra.

a sic A.

Master Ranulf of Wareham was elected bp of Chichester before 17 December 1217 and was consecrated at Canterbury on 7 January 1218 by the bps of London, Bath and Rochester (*Canterbury professions*, 64, no.156). The scribe of this document also wrote no.294 above. On Guala see H.Tillmann, *Die päpstlichen Legaten in England bis zur Beendigung der Legation Gualas (1218)* (Bonn 1926), 107-20; *Councils and Synods II*, i.49 and H.G.Richardson, 'Letters of the legate Guala', *EHR*, xlviii (1933), 250-9.

298. Haughmond Abbey

Confirmation of a licence of appropriation issued by Giles de Braose, and of the confirmation of Giles' charter issued by Hugh himself as Dean of Hereford and by the Cathedral Chapter to Haughmond Abbey.

[18 December 1216 × 1217/8]

B = Shrewsbury Local Studies Library, Haughmond cartulary, fo.206v. s.xv ex.
C = Shropshire County Record Office, 2922 additional (Dudmaston MS), fo.15r-v. s.xvi ex – xvii in.

Cal., *Haughmond cartulary*, 213, no.1150.

Omnibus sancte matris ecclesie filiis ad quos presens scriptum pervenerit Hugo divina miseratione Hereford' ecclesie humilis minister eternam in domino salutem. Inspeximus cartas bone memorie Egidii quondam Hereford' ecclesie episcopi predecessoris nostri et dilectorum in Cristo filiorum decani et capituli Hereford'[a] in quibus continetur quod ipsi post mortem Magistri Ade qui ecclesiam de Stokes possidet prenominatam ecclesiam de Stokes cum omnibus pertinentiis suis abbati et conventui de Haghmon' in usus proprios confirmaverunt salva debita et competenti vicaria quam ipsi post mortem prenominati Ade viro idoneo et honesto assignabunt. Nos igitur prenominatas cartas quia ad ministerii nostri auctoritatem spectare dinoscuntur confirmamus et corroboramus. Hiis testibus, T. decano Heref', Magistris Albino, Theobaldo, Gaufrido canonicis Hereford', [b]Gregorio et Roberto clericis, Granton et Willelmo Keynel.[b]

[a]Ford' B.   [b-b]etc' B; supplied from C.

For confirmations issued by Giles de Braose and Hugh de Mapenore as dean see *Haughmond cartulary*, nos.1148-9; for a confirmation issued by Bp Hugh Foliot see below, no.335. Although this charter is dated to 1217 × April 1219 in *Haughmond cartulary* it must precede the appointment of Master Albinus as chancellor in 1217 or 1218.

299. John of Hidcote, clerk

Grant in fee to John of Hidcote of half a virgate and twelve acres in the vill of Eign.

[18 December 1216 × 16 April 1219, perhaps 1217 × 1218]

B = Hereford, Herefordshire County Record Office, Registrum Ade de Orleton (formerly Hereford Diocesan Registry), fos.38v-9r. s.xiv in.

Pd, *Reg. Orleton*, 140-1.

Omnibus sancte matris ecclesie filiis ad quos presens scriptum pervenerit Hugo dei gratia Her' episcopus salutem in domino. Noverit universitas vestra nos dedisse et concessisse et presenti carta nostra confirmasse Iohanni clerico de Hudecota pro homagio et servitio suo dimidiam virgatam terre cum omnibus pertinentiis suis in villa de Eyhene illam scilicet quam Ricardus filius Theoderici tenuit, et duodecim acras terre in eadem villa quas Nicholaus Rufus tenuit, tenendas et habendas sibi et heredibus suis, vel cui eas assignare voluerit, de nobis et successoribus nostris in feudo et hereditate, libere et quiete, integre et plenarie, reddendo inde annuatim nobis et successoribus nostris ipse et heredes sui, vel ille cui [fo.39r] eas assignare voluerit, octo solidos ad quatuor terminos, scilicet ad festum Sancti Andree duos solidos et ad Annunciationem beate Marie duos solidos, et ad nativitatem sancti Iohannis Baptiste duos solidos, et ad festum Sancti Michaelis duos solidos, pro omni servitio, et exactione, et consuetudine, et demanda que ad terram illam pertinent vel pertinere possint, salvo servitio domini regis quantum pertinet ad tantam terram in eadem villa. Quod quia ratum et inconcussum debet permanere, presenti id scripto et sigilli nostri munimine dignum duximus corroborare. Hiis testibus, Willelmo le Poer, Iohanne canonico de Bromyard, Waltero de Maurthin, Gregorio capellano, Roberto elemosinario, Rogero de Hompton', Wrennon de Homme, Radulpho de Homtonia, Gilberto de Lutteleya, Nicholao de Hompton', Waltero de Longeford, et multis aliis.

For an inspeximus and confirmation of this charter by Bp Hugh Foliot, see below, no.347. Since the first term-day mentioned in this charter is St Andrew's Day (30 November) it is possible that this charter was issued between Michaelmas and St Andrew's Day in either 1217 or 1218 (since Hugh de Mapenore was consecrated only in December 1216 and died in April 1219).

300. Leominster priory

Inspeximus of charters of Bishops Richard de Capella, Gilbert Foliot and Giles de Braose confirming the possessions of Leominster.

[18 December 1216 × 16 April 1219]

> B = BL Cotton MS Domitian A iii (Leominster priory cartulary), fo.66r-v. s.xiii med.

Omnibus sancte m(atris) e(cclesie) f(iliis) Hugo Heref' episcopus salutem. Noverit universitas vestra nos venerabilium antecessorum nostrorum bone memorie Ricardi [fo.66v], Gileberti, et Egidii Heref' episcoporum cartas et confirmationes in hec verba inspexisse. Ego dei gratia Hereford episcopus Ricardus manu mea propria concessi, et cetera usque in finem, ut supra in precedenti folio.*a* Nos igitur venerabilium antecessorum nostrorum Heref' episcoporum concessionem et confirmationem ratam habentes eam presentis instrumenti testimonio et sigilli nostri patrocinio roboramus, concedentes et auctoritate episcopali confirmantes ecclesie Rading' et domino Symoni eiusdem loci abbati et monachis ibidem deo servientibus totam et integram ecclesiam beati Petri de Leom' cum capellis, cimiteriis, pensionibus, decimis, obventionibus, possessionibus, et omnibus que ad eandem ecclesiam de Leom' pertinent et pertinere debent. Testibus et cetera.

a sic B; for text of Richard's charter see above, no.11; for the text of Gilbert Foliot's charter see GFL, no.343 (cal. above, no.111), and for text of Giles' charter see above, no.268.

Hugh Foliot confirmed this charter; see below, no.352.

301. Leominster priory

Licence issued to Leominster priory to appropriate the chapel of Ford for the salvation of the souls of Giles, Bishop of Hereford, and of Robert and Matilda, the parents of Hugh de Mapenore.

[18 December 1216 × 16 April 1219]

> B = BL Cotton MS Domitian A iii (Leominster priory cartulary), fos.67v-68r. s.xiii med.

Omnibus et cetera.[a] Quoniam religiosorum loca pio semper et benigno favore sunt promovenda, illorum propensius religiosorum volumus provectibus insistere et commodis providere, quos in religione devotiores et circa pauperum exhibitionem assiduos esse novimus et benignos. Nos igitur attendentes domum elemosinarie Leomen' pauperibus oneratam, rebus, redditibus, ac possessionibus fere vacuam [fo.68r], ad pauperes quoque exhibendos cum summa devotione pronam, et si facultatum possibilitas suppeteret, voluntariam, capellam de Ford' cum omnibus pertinentiis suis domui Leom' ad instantiam et petitionem dilecti in Cristo filii W., decani Leom', et ceterorum fratrum suorum ibidem temporibus nostris morantium, pro anima viri venerabilis E. bone memorie predecessoris nostri, et pro animabus Roberti patris nostri et Matildis matris nostre, et aliorum antecessorum et successorum nostrorum, in usus hospitalitatis et pauperum caritative concessimus, salva antiqua et debita pensione dimidie marce annuatim ecclesie Leom' persolvenda. Et ne ea que perpetue firmitatis robur desiderant casu labantur a memoria, hanc nostram concessionem et confirmationem perhenni memorie per scripturam presenti carta sigilli nostri impressione communita dignum duximus commendari. T(estibus) et cetera.

[a]*sic* B.

This charter is confirmed by Bp Hugh Foliot (below, no.350), where the grantor is stated to be Hugh de Mapenore. W., dean of Leominster, is Walter, dean or prior of Leominster Priory (not a rural dean); for the monastic dean of Leominster, see B.R.Kemp, 'The Monastic Dean of Leominster', *EHR*, lxxxiii (1968), 505-515.

302. Leominster priory

Mandate to A(dam), dean of Humber, to induct W(alter), dean of Leominster, in the chapel of Ford.
[18 December 1216 × 16 April 1219]

B = BL Cotton MS Domitian A iii (Leominster priory cartulary), fo.69v. s.xiii med. Rubric: Littere Hugonis primi Heref' episcopi directe decano de Humbr' super capella de Ford' que intrare debent post confirmationem eiusdem in precedenti folio ad tale signum. ∞~

H. dei gratia Hereford episcopus dilecto in Cristo filio A. decano de Humbr' salutem et benedictionem. Noveris nos caritatis intuitu domui Leom' capellam de Ford' cum omnibus pertinentiis in usus hospitalitatis et pauperum concessisse. Quampropter tibi mandamus quod dictam capellam dilecto in Cristo filio W., decano Leom', pacifice habere permittas iterato a nobis super hoc non expectato mandato. Vale.

For Adam, see above, no.245; for Walter, see above, no.301. A similar ∞~ sign to that in the rubric can be found on fo.68r.

303. Leominster priory

Mandate to the archdeacons, rural deans, and priests in the diocese of Hereford to excommunicate those who molest the church of Leominster.
[18 December 1216 × 16 April 1219]

B = BL Cotton MS Domitian A iii (Leominster priory cartulary), fo.68r. s.xiii med.

H. dei gratia Heref' episcopus omnibus archidiaconis, decanis, et presbiteris in Heref' episcopatu constitutis salutem. Auctoritate qua fungimur vobis in vi obedientie precipimus quatinus statim ex quo querimonia monachorum de Leom' super rebus eorum ablatis, vel possessionibus suis turbatis, vel ob iniuriam sibi vel hominibus suis illatam, delata fuerit, nisi satisfacere voluerint, auctoritate nostra, omni occasione et dilatione postposita, sollempniter omnes illos malefactores, cum vobis nominati fuerint, candelis accensis excommunicetis, et tanquam excommunicatos in quacumque parrochia fuerint ab omnibus usque ad condignam ablatorum satisfactionem cautius vitari precipiatis, et dum moram fecerint divina celebrari ibidem perhibeatis.

This is presumably a charter of Hugh de Mapenore rather than of Hugh Foliot because there is a mandate in similar terms issued by Hugh Foliot: see below, no.349.

*304. Lire abbey

Grant or confirmation of the church of Linton to Lire abbey in Normandy.
[18 December 1216 × 16 April 1219]

Mention only, in a summary of a charter of Bp Peter of Aigueblanche, confirming to Lire Abbey 'l'Eglise de l'Intone dans son dioceze, comme elle avoit été donnée a ladite abbaye par Hugues de Mapemore Evêque de Hereford, du consentement de son chapitre, et confirmée par Etienne archevêque de Cantorbery', Evreux, A-D Eure H590, fo.326r, no.xxiii.

*305. Lire abbey

Grant to Lire abbey in Normandy of a licence to appropriate the churches which they possess in the diocese of Hereford (Much Marcle, Fownhope, Linton, Wilton, Lydney, Tidenham, Eardisland, Tenbury Wells and Dewsall), and also of a prebendal stall in Hereford Cathedral.
[18 December 1216 × 16 April 1219]

Summary only, A-D Eure H590, fo.325v (inventory of the cartulary of Lire abbey), no.xviii. s.xviii.

Chartre de H. Evêque de Hereford, par laquelle du consentement de son Chapitre, il ajuge aux Religieux de Lyre, deux portions des Eglises qu'ils possedent dans son dioceze, scavoir de celle de Merkelay, de celle de la Hore, de l'Intone, de Wilton, de l'Idenée, de Thudeham, de Erleslene, de Tamethebe et de fontaine David; l'autre tiers demeurant reservé pour l'Entretien des vicaires desservants lesdites Eglises, dont la presentation appartiendra a l'abbaye: chargeant lesdits vicaires de payer les droits de l'Evêque et de l'archidiacre.
Item cêt Evêque du consentement de son chapitre fait L'Abbé de Lyre chanoine de l'Eglise de Herefort, luy assigne une stale dans le choeur et place au chapitre, avec permission d'y mettre un vicaire a sa place, qui percevra la portion de pain et de cervoise; mais lors que l'abbé ou le procureur general de l'abbaye viendra à Herefort, ils recevront ladite portion de pain et cervoise; et tant que ledit abbé sera a Herefort, il aura sa part, comme chanoine, des oblations du grand autel. Et pour cimenter l'union entre l'Eglise de Herefort et le monastere de Lyre, l'Evêque veut que lors que l'abbé de Lyre, ou quelque Religieux seronts morts, le nom du deffunt sera mis dans le martirologe de ladite Eglise de Herefort, et on fera les mêmes prieres que pour les chanoines; et lors que l'Evêque ou quelque chanoine sera mort, les Religieux de Lyre feront les mêmes prieres ordinaires a la mort de l'abbé ou d'un Religieux. Le chapitre de Herefort promet encore de prendre soin des affaires de l'abbaye de Lyre en Angleterre, lors qu'il en sera requis, aux fraix toutes fois des Religieux.
La dite chartre vidimée et confirmée cy après n°. xxviii. par Pierre Evêque de Herefort; et par l'Archevêque de Cantorbery, suivant la lettre cy après n°. lvi.

This charter was issued by Hugh de Mapenore rather than Hugh Foliot because the latter issued a confirmation of it (no.354) which was in its turn confirmed by an inspeximus of Bp Peter of Aigueblanche (1240-68), which is summarised *ibid.*, fo.326v, no.xxviii. Hugh de Mapenore was following the example of William de Vere, who in 1195 had granted a prebendal stall to the abbot of Cormeilles; see above, no.188. For the regulations concerning the rights of the abbots as canons, see *Lincoln Cathedral Statutes*, ed. H.Bradshaw and C.Wordsworth, 3 vols. (Cambridge 1892-7), ii.59-60. By the mid-thirteenth century the abbots had to maintain two vicars each.

306. Morville priory

Licence to Morville priory to appropriate the chapel of Astley, saving Gerard of Edgmond's possession of the church during his lifetime.

[18 December 1216 × 16 April 1219]

B = NLW MS 7851 D (Shrewsbury cartulary), p.306, no.347. s.xiii ex.

Pd, *Shrewsbury cartulary*, ii, no.347.

Hiis testibus, T. decano, W. archidiacono Hereford', H. archidiacono Salop', et multis aliis.

Morville Priory was a dependency of Shrewsbury Abbey.

307. Ralph de Neville

Letter of recommendation to Ralph de Neville, dean of Lichfield, here styled royal chancellor, on behalf of G(eoffrey) de Longchamp.

[Probably June 1217]

A = PRO SC 1 6/19. No ancient endorsements. 168 mm wide at top, 170 mm wide at base, 52 mm deep. Remains of a tongue; possible remains of a wrapping tie.

Viro venerabili et amico in Cristo·karissimo. Domino .R. de Nevill' decano Lichef(el)d^a et domini regis cancellario .H. divina permissione Hereford' ecclesie minister salutem. et dilectionis semper amplexum. Quanto magis de vobis confidimus tanto securius pro nostris quibus deesse nec possumus nec debemus vobis preces facimus. Sciatis ergo quod dominus G. de Longo Campo tanta familiaritate et dilectione et etiam operum exhibitione nobis est coniunctus et ipsum ita karum habemus et dilectum ? quod mallemus intuitu nostri ipsi multum honoris et commodi impendi. quam nobis ipsis. Quapropter dilectionem vestram quantis possumus precibus exoramus. quatinus intuitu nostri eidem G. in negotiis auxilium et consilium taliter impendatis. ut vobis ad perpetuas teneamur gratiarum actiones et preces nostras sibi senciat efficaces. et certum habeatis quod non est aliquis in diocesi nostra cui magis teneamur vel velimus teneri obnoxii. et utinam vos et alii amici nostri ipsum kariorem reputare velitis. et primicie precum nostrarum erga vos tanto si placet maiorem optineant effectum. Valete semper.

 Document stained.

Document stained.

Geoffrey de Longchamp had been a rebel in 1215 and 1216 (*Rot. lit. claus.*, i.241b, 279b). His lands were restored by Henry III by 27 June 1217 (*ibid.*, 312). It is noteworthy that Bp Hugh places Ralph de Neville's name before his own and that he calls him chancellor, although the title was officially held by Bp Richard Marsh at this time (on this see J. and L.Stones, 'Bishop Ralph de Neville, Chancellor to King Henry III, and his correspondence: a reappraisal', *Archives*, xvi [1984], 231). At one stage Bp Marsh complained to Dean Ralph that Ralph had omitted the title of chancellor in writing to him; see W.W.Shirley, ed. *Royal and Other Historical Letters Illustrative of the Reign of Henry III*, 2 vols., RS (1862-6), i.180, no.157. Ralph de Neville became chancellor eventually in 1226, by which time he had been bp of Chichester for over two years.

308. Reading abbey

Confirmation to the abbey of Reading of the power of appointing monks to Leominster Priory and of removing them. [1217 × December 1218]

B = BL Egerton MS 3031 (Reading abbey cartulary), fo.98r. Here s.xiii in. C = BL Harleian MS 1708 (Reading abbey cartulary), fos.182v-183r. s.xiii med. D = BL Cotton MS Domitian A iii (Leominster priory cartulary), fos.66v-67r. s.xiii med. E = BL Cotton MS Vespasian E xxv (Reading abbey cartulary), fo.108r. s.xiv in. F = Cambridge University Library, MS Dd. ix 38 (Reading abbey cartulary), fo.78r-v. s.xiv.

Pd, *Mon. Ang.* iv.56-57; pd from an inspeximus by Guala, cardinal and papal legate, dated Reading, 18 November, *Reg. Swinfield*, 30; pd *ibid.*, 64, in an inspeximus by Bp Richard de Swinfield; pd, *Reading cartularies*, i.293-4, no.361.

Hiis testibus, Thoma decano, Willelmo precentore, Helia thesaurario, Albino cancellario, Willelmo archidiacono Hereford', Gregorio, Roberto capellanis, Nicholao,^{*a*} Theoderico clericis, et multis aliis.

^{*a*}Richardo E.

This charter is discussed by B.R.Kemp, 'The monastic dean of Leominster', *EHR*, lxxxiii (1968), 508-9, and the dating is that suggested by Z.N. and C.N.L.Brooke, 'Hereford Cathedral Dignitaries', *Cambridge Historical Journal*, viii (1944), 5. Albinus became chancellor not before 1217, and Guala left England in December 1218. Since Guala's inspeximus of 18 November was almost certainly issued in 1218, Hugh's charter is probably datable 1217 × 18 November 1218, and nos.309 and 310 below, which have similar witness lists, were probably issued at the same time. See also no.362 below.

309. Reading abbey

Licence to Reading abbey to appropriate Eye church.
[1217 × 16 April 1219, probably 1217 × 18 November 1218]

B = BL Egerton MS 3031 (Reading abbey cartulary), fo.97v. Here s.xiii in. C = BL Cotton MS Domitian A iii (Leominster priory cartulary), fo.67r-v. s.xiii med.

Pd, B.R.Kemp, 'Hereditary benefices in the medieval English church: a Herefordshire example', *BIHR*, xliii (1970), 13; cal., *Reading cartularies*, i.267, no.333.

Hiis testibus, Th. decano, W. precentore, H. thesaurario, A. cancellario, W. archidiacono Heref', H. archidiacono Salopesire, Gregorio, Roberto capellanis, Nicolao, Turri clericis, Hugone de Fulef' et multis aliis.

For the dating see note to no.308 above.

310. Reading abbey

Notification that Roger, formerly vicar of Eye, has resigned the church into Hugh's hands, and that Hugh has instituted the abbot and monks of Reading abbey in it as parsons, saving a perpetual vicarage.
[1217 × 16 April 1219, probably 1217 × 18 November 1218]

B = BL Egerton MS 3031 (Reading abbey cartulary), fo.100v. Here s.xiii in. C = BL Cotton MS Domitian A iii (Leominster priory cartulary), fo.67v. s.xiii med.

Pd., B.R.Kemp, 'Hereditary benefices in the medieval English church: a Herefordshire example', *BIHR*, xliii (1970), 13-14; cal., *Reading cartularies*, i.267-8, no.334.

Hiis testibus, Thoma decano Hereford', W. archidiacono Heref', H. archidiacono Salopesbir', Magistro Albino cancellario Hereford',

Magistro Nicholao de Wlverehamt', Willelmo le Poher, Domino R. cellerario, et multis aliis.

For the dating, see note to no.308 above. The presence of Hugh Foliot among the witnesses as archdn proves that this is a charter of Hugh de Mapenore. Roger was then re-instituted as vicar by Hugh de Mapenore on presentation by Abbot Simon and the monks of Reading but he was only ordained priest by Bp Hugh Foliot (Kemp, *art. cit.*, 14, quoting a document of 1251).

311. Reginald the clerk

Inspeximus of a charter of Canon William le Poer granting part of the land belonging to his prebend to Reginald the clerk for eight shillings a year.
[18 December 1216 × 29 November 1223, probably 18 December 1216 x 16 April 1219]

B = Bodl. MS Jones 23 (Hereford cathedral cartulary), pp.xvi-xviii. s.xiii ex. C = Bodl. MS Rawlinson B329 (Hereford cathedral cartulary), fos.29v-30r. s.xv. Contemporary marginalia: Vide originale evidenciarum sequenc(ium) in capsula de F.

Pd from B, R.Rawlinson, *The History and Antiquities of the City and Cathedral Church of Hereford* (London 1717), appendix, 45.

Omnibus Cristi fidelibus ad quos presens carta pervenerit Hugo [p.xvii *B*] divina permissione Herefordensis ecclesie minister humilis eternam in domino salutem. Noverit universitas vestra nos cartam dilecti in Cristo filii nostri Willelmi le^a Poer, canonici Hereford', sub hac forma inspexisse. Sciant presentes et futuri quod ego Willelmus le Poer de assensu et voluntate capituli Hereford' ad meliorationem prebende mee dedi et concessi Reginaldo clerico tertiam partem totius terre mee ad prebendam meam pertinentis, que extenditur ex una parte ad vicum iacentem de maiori ecclesia Hereford' ad portam castelli, et ex alia parte extenditur ad terram monachorum^b de Radinges, tenendam et habendam sibi et cuicumque illam^c dare vel assignare voluerit de me et successoribus meis canonicis iure hereditario, libere, integre, et quiete ab omni servitio et exactione que ad terram pertinere possit, reddendo inde annuatim michi et successoribus meis octo solidos, scilicet^d in annunciatione^e beate Marie quatuor solidos et in festo Sancti Michaelis^f quatuor solidos. Quod quia ratum et stabile esse^g volui,^{h} id presenti scripto et sigilli mei impressione confirmavi. Hiis testibus, Thoma decano Herefordensis ecclesie, Willelmo precentore Hereford' et eiusdem loci capitulo, Magistro^i Reginaldo de Radenoure,^{j} Willelmo et Salamone capellanis,^{k} et multis aliis. Nos vero predictam donationem et concessionem ratam et gratam habentes, cum unanimi consensu^l et voluntate capituli Hereford' illam presenti carta et sigilli nostri munimine, auctoritate episcopali confirmavimus. Hiis testibus, Thoma decano Hereford', Willelmo^m precentore [p.xviii B], Helya thesaurario Hereford',^{n} Willelmo^o capellano et canonico, Magistro S. clerico domini^p Herefordensis, ^{q}Gregorio capellano, Magistro Helya de Buckenhull'^{q} et multis aliis.

^{a}om. C. ^{b}monacorum B. ^{c}eam C. ^{d}silicet B. ^{e}anunciatione B. ^{f}Miclaelis B.
^{g}eesse B. ^{h}volumus C. ^{i}Magistris C. ^{j}Radnore C. ^{k}om. C. ^{l}concensu BC.
^{m}W. C. ^{n}om. C. ^{o}W. C. ^{p}om. B. $^{q-q}$om. C.

This inspeximus must have been issued before 29 November 1223, by which time Thomas Foliot had replaced William of Kilpeck as precentor. The Master S., episcopal clerk, is probably identifiable with Master Stephen de Thornbury, who became a canon before 1221. Gregory was a chaplain of Hugh de Mapenore and there is no firm evidence for his being a chaplain of Hugh Foliot, so it is likely that this charter was issued by Hugh de Mapenore.

312. Tintern abbey

Confirmation of the settlement of a dispute, which was heard by the abbot and prior of Gloucester as papal judges-delegate, between Master J(ohn) of Godstow, rector of Tidenham, and the abbey of Tintern, concerning certain tithes in the parish of Tidenham.

[21 September 1218 × 16 April 1219]

B = BL Arundel MS 19 (Tintern cartulary), fo.35v, no. xviii. s.xvi.

Universis sancte matris ecclesie filiis H. dei gratia^a Hereford' episcopus salutem et benedictionem. Cum lis mota inter Magistrum I. Godest', rectorem ecclesie de Thedeh', ex una parte, et abbatem et conventum de Tint' ex altera, coram abbate et priore Glovernie, iudicibus a domino papa delegatis, super quibusdam decimis in parochia de Tedeh' amicabili compositione conquievisset,^{b} nos, dictam compositionem sicut in dictorum iudicum autentico continetur ratam et gratam habentes, eam auctoritate pontificali et sigilli nostri impressione corroboravimus. Hiis testibus, Thoma decano Hereford', Willelmo archidiacono Hereford', H. archidiacono Salopess', W. priore Lant'.

ᵃom. B.   *ᵇconquievissed B.*

The dating of this document poses problems. Although the presence of H(ugh Foliot) as archdn of Shropshire among the witnesses suggests that this is a charter of Hugh de Mapenore, the notification issued by the judges, Abbot Henry (1205-1224) and Prior T. of Gloucester (*ibid.*, fo.35r, continued on fo.36r) is dated St Matthew's day (21 September) 1219. The mandate sent to them by Pope Honorius III, which they quote, is dated 13 December 1217 at the Lateran (Honorius III is known to have been at the Lateran on this date: cf. Potthast, i.496). Abbot R. of Lire issued an inspeximus of the settlement (*ibid.*, fo. 35v), which gives John of Godstow's name in full, and which gives the date of the settlement as St Matthew's day 1209 (*sic*). This was Abbot Robert de l'Isle (1216-1221); see C.Guéry, *Histoire de l'abbaye de Lyre* (Evreux 1917), 657. Lire Abbey owned two thirds of the church of Tidenham (in Gloucestershire), which explains Abbot Robert's interest in the case.

BL Arundel MS 19, a copy of extracts from an earlier Tintern cartulary, now lost, is an unreliable manuscript, and it is probable that the date of the settlement was 21 September 1218. Perhaps the dates, although written in words in this manuscript, had been written in Roman numerals in the earlier cartulary and this led to confusion. The fact that Abbot Robert issued an inspeximus of the settlement would help support this hypothesis: Robert would almost certainly have visited England when Hugh de Mapenore gave Lire Abbey the right to turn its churches in the diocese of Hereford, including Tidenham, into a prebend of Hereford Cathedral (above, no.305). Robert would have come to Hereford to be installed as a prebendary.

BISHOP HUGH

313. Gloucester abbey

Admission of Richard of Monmouth, clerk, to the vicarage of Holme Lacy on presentation by the abbot and monks of Gloucester abbey, and notification of the tithes which he will receive.

[18 December 1216 × 1224]

B = Oxford, Balliol College MS 271 (cartulary of St Guthlac's, Hereford), fo.54v, no.215. s.xiv in. 14th-century marginalia: Hame Lacy. 15th-century marginalia: Taxacio vicarie et quod sustinebit omnia onera. Institutio, li'tatio et ordinatio H. Foliot Heref' episcopi. Notificatio, compositio inter priorem H. et vicarium de Hamme Lacy.

Universis Cristi fidelibus ad quos presens scriptum pervenerit, H. dei gratia Heref' episcopus, salutem in domino. Quia labilis est hominum memoria, volumus quod ea que in presentia nostra canonice acta sunt firmitatis perpetue robur optineant. Quocirca universitati vestre significandum duximus quod nos Ricardum clericum de Monemua ad vicariam ecclesie Sancti Cutberti de Hamma ad presentationem abbatis et conventus Glouc' admisimus et eandem sibi confirmamus auctoritate episcopali, sub articulis et particulis expressis in eorum scripto, quod inspeximus, videlicet totum altalagium et dimidiam virgatam terre cum manso pertinente et aliis pertinentiis et quandam particulam terre^a adiacentem^b predicto manso, et decimam molendini de Hamme, scilicet unam summam^c mextelli dum dominus Walterus de Lacy vixerit, et post dies eius totam decimam eiusdem molendini, dictam summam^c percipiendam^d annuatim in festo Sancti Michaelis, et tres stichas anguillarum pro decima piscium eiusdem molendini; item decimas garbarum et feni de tribus virgatis terre et dimidia in eadem villa, scilicet de una virgata terre quam Gilbertus filius Hugonis tenuit,^{e} et de dimidia virgata terre quam Griffith Petomari tenuit, et^e de duabus virgatis terre quas Agnes vidua tenuit.^{e} Dictus quidem Ricardus omnia onera dictam ecclesiam contingentia sustinebit. In cuius rei testimonio presens scriptum sigilli nostri impressione confirmare curavimus.

[a]B adds cum manso pertinente *but cancels.* [b]adiacente B. [c]sumam B.
[d]percipiendo B. [e]caret sign but no insertion given B.

Walter de Lacy succeeded in 1186 and died in 1241 (W.E.Wightman, *The Lacy Family in England and Normandy* [Oxford 1966], family tree between 260 and 261). The marginal note to this charter saying that it was issued by Hugh Foliot is too late to be necessarily accurate, though the charter was probably issued by Hugh Foliot, because his pontificate was longer than that of Hugh de Mapenore. Prior Joscelin of St Guthlac's presented Richard of Monmouth while Henry Blount (ob. 1224) was still abbot of Gloucester: Balliol College MS 271, fo.54r, no.213.

*314. Lire abbey

Charter concerning the vicarage of Wilton.
[18 December 1216 × 1234]

Mention only, BL MS Cotton Otho B xiv (inventory of Sheen priory cartulary), fo. 13v. s.xv ex.

315. Tintern abbey

Confirmation of a licence of appropriation issued by Bishops William de Vere and Giles de Braose to Tintern abbey.
[18 December 1216 × 1221]

B = BL Arundel MS 19 (Tintern cartulary), fos.31v-2r. s.xvi.

Omnibus sancte matris ecclesie filiis ad quos presens scriptum pervenerit Hugo divina miseratione Hereford'[a] ecclesie minister eternam in domino salutem. Noverit universitas vestra nos venerabilium antecessorum nostrorum pie memorie Willelmi de Ver et Egidii de Breusa episcoporum Herford' auctentica inspexisse instrumenta, quorum tenorem perpendimus ipsos abbati et monachis de Tinterna [fo.32r] indulsisse, ut ipsi ecclesiam \de Wolluaston/ et capellam de Alvynton cum omnibus ad eas de iure spectantibus in usus proprios convertant. Nos igitur, pium et deo gratum esse considerantes religiosorum portiones augmentare,[b] ut crescentibus illorum bonis augeatur et munus deo famulantium et in hospitalitate manutenenda caritas, prenominatas ecclesiam et capellam iuxta prenominatorum tenorem instrumentorum abbati et monachis, salvis matricis ecclesie nostre Herford' iure et dignitate, presenti scripto et^c sigilli nostri appositione \confirmamus/. Huic autem concessioni et confirmationi capitulum Hereford' consentiens sigillum suum huic scripto apposuit. Hiis testibus Thoma decano Hereford', W. priore Leomenister, Magistro Stephano canonico Herefordie, Magistro Almarico, Magistro Helya de Burkehull', cum aliis et cetera.

^{a}Herefford' B. ^{b}aumentare B. ^{c}om. B.

Walter, prior of Leominster, was elected abbot of Shrewsbury in 1221. For William de Vere's and Giles de Braose's charters, see above, nos.237 and 283.

*316. Master Walter de Mouncy, clerk

Confirmation of grant by Chancellor Albinus to Master Walter de Mouncy, clerk.   [1217 × 7 August 1234]

Mention only, BL Cotton MS Otho B xiv (inventory of Sheen priory cartulary), fo.27r. Albinus became chancellor in 1217 or 1218. Master Walter de Mouncy became a canon of Hereford before 1227 (see Appendix I), so the charter was probably issued before 1227.

HUGH FOLIOT

316A. Alberbury priory

Inspeximus of foundation charter issued by Fulk fitz Warin (III) for Alberbury priory as a Grandmontine house, granting it land at Alberbury, Eyton, and Pecknall, fisheries in the Severn in Fulk's own lifetime, the right to set up a mill, pasturage and pannage, the right to take marl from Fulk's land, and freedom from tolls at Fulk's markets.

[1226 × 7 August 1234]

A = Bodl., Deposited Deeds, All Souls College c 1, Alberbury n.ll0. 13th or 14th c. endorsement: Carta confirmationis episcopi Hugonis Foliot. 15th or 16th c. endorsement: Confirmacio prioratus Grand'mont' de Alberbur' super Sabrinam in diocesi Hereford'. 185 × 233 + 34 mm. Sealed on knitted silk cords, originally red; seal a pointed oval in varnished green wax, 64 × 41 mm, showing a bishop in full pontificals, left hand bearing staff turning inwards, right hand raised in benediction; two crescent moons below right hand. Legend: hVG................RATI...RFOR.........PISCOPVS. Counterseal: pointed oval: king standing on corbel, with bird over his head and two crescent moons on each side. Legend: SANCTVS ATHILBERTV. RE... MARTIR.

Omnibus Cristi fidelibus ad quos presens scriptum pervenerit Hugo Foliot dei gratia Hereford' episcopus salutem in domino. Cartam dilecti in Cristo domini Fulconis filii Warini inspeximus in hec verba. Omnibus sancte matris ecclesie filiis ad quos presens scriptum pervenerit Fulco filius Guarini salutem in domino. Noverit universitas vestra me pro salute anime mee et Matildis uxoris mee et Fulconis patris mei et Hawyse matris mee et omnium antecessorum et successorum meorum fundasse et construxisse in honore Dei et gloriose virginis Marie domum quandam fratrum Grandimontensis ordinis in territorio de Alberbur' super Sabrinam. Quibus fratribus ibidem Deo servientibus dedi et concessi et hac presenti carta mea confirmavi de assensu Fulconis filii et heredis mei locum cum pertinenciis suis ubi domus predicta sita est. scilicet a rivulo descendente in terram meam de Alberbur' et terram de Eytun'. quadraginta particatas terre et cum pertinentiis suis in longitudine et totidem in latitudine in bosco meo de Alberbur' super Sabrinam et super prefatum rivulum. et preterea viginti particatas terre cum pertinenciis suis ibidem super Sabrinam in longitudine et decem particatas terre in latitudine et totum pratum meum de Brademed'. et preterea totam terram meam de Pekenhall cum omnibus pertinentiis suis. et preterea viginti quattuor acras terre quas dedi cum corpore uxoris mee. Hec autem omnia vobis ut habeant et teneant in liberam. puram. et perpetuam elemosinam. libere et quiete. et honorifice cum omnibus pertinentiis suis et eysiamentis. in bosco. et plano. cum husbot' et heybot'. et boscum de meo^a ad focum suum licite capiendum. et in pratis et pascuis. in viis et semitis et piscariis in Sabrinam quantum terra mea durat et in molendinis. videlicet ut libere molendinum cum stangnis sibi construere possint ubi sibi magis viderint expedire. In terra sua cum plena redundatione aque super terram meam. et ut liberum habeant conductum aque per totam terram meam usque ad predictum locum absque omni impedimento mei vel heredum meorum. et ut habeant communem pasturam omnimodis animalibus suis per totum boscum meum et totam pasturam meam de Alberbur' et alibi ubicumque propria averia mea habent communem pasturam. et ut habeant centum porcos quietos de pannagio in bosco meo de Alberbur' cum pessonia^b fuerint. et ut marlam libere possint capere et trahere super terram suam ubi^c illam invenerint in terram meam ubi ego vel homines mei illam ceperimus vel rationabiliter capere potuerimus^d cum libero egressu et regressu per totam terram meam sibi et omnibus rebus suis. et ut ipsi et homines sui liberi et quieti sint per omnia mercata mea et nundinas meas de theloneo et omni consuetudine. volo etiam quod prefata domus de Alberbur' nulli alii domui ipsius ordinis subiecta sit nisi soli capitali domui Grandimontis. Hec autem omnia ut supradictum est volo et concedo ut ipsi fratres habeant et teneant in liberam. puram. et perpetuam elemosinam absque omni exactione^e et omni seculari servicio. et ut ego predictus Fulco et heredes mei hec omnia predicta ipsis fratribus warentizabimus contra omnes homines. Ut igitur hec mea donacio futuris temporibus rata et inconcussa permaneat sigilli mei apposicione eam roboravi. Hiis testibus. Willelmo filio Garini. Henrico de Tracy. Radulfo de Hodenet. Willelmo capellano de Dreyton'. Aldulfo de Braci. Matheo Morell'. Hugone de Hoe. Rogero de Prestina. Radulfo clerico. Et multis aliis. Nos igitur hanc donacionem ratam et gratam habentes eam auctoritate episcopali et presenti scripto et sigilli nostri impressione confirmavimus. salvo iure cuiuslibet et salva dignitate Hereford' ecclesie. Hiis testibus. Magistro Willelmo Platun'. Magistro Iohanne Bacun. Ada de Ledebur' persona de Homtun'. Magistro Iohanne de Esteham. Radulfo persona de Linderugge. Rogero capellano.^{f} Godefrido clerico. Willelmo de Geytun' et multis aliis.

^{a}*sic A.* ^{b}pessoria *A.* ^{c}vibi *A.* ^{d}poterimus *A.* ^{e}exaxcione *A.* ^{f}cappellano *A.*

Fulk fitz Warin (III) originally granted his land at Alberbury to Lilleshall abbey in the time of Abbot Alan (d.1226) so that they could set up a dependent house, but Alan's successor, William, rejected the gift, because the endowment was insufficient. Fulk then gave the property to the Grandmontine order, and the new house was founded before 1232 when Henry III confirmed Fulk's grant: see M.Chibnall, 'The priory of Alberbury', *VCH Shropshire*, iii.47.

317. Bockleton church

Institution of John Foliot on the presentation of Robert de Bockleton in the parsonage of Bockleton.
[27 October 1219 × 23 July 1227, probably before 29 November 1223]

B = Bodl. MS Rawlinson B329 (Hereford cathedral cartulary), fo.56r. s.xv. C = *Ibid.*, fo.54r-v.

Universis Cristi fidelibus ad quos presens scriptum pervenerit H. dei gratia Herefordensis ecclesie minister humilis^a eternam in domino salutem. Notum vobis facimus quod nos ad presentationem Roberti de Boclinton' recipimus Iohannem Folyot ad ecclesiam de Boclit'^{b} et ipsum I.^{c} in eadem ecclesia cum omnibus pertinentiis suis in bosco et plano, in pratis et pascuis, in terris et decimis et obventionibus personam canonice et absque omni reclamatione instituimus. Quod ne in posterum deduci possit in irritum presenti carta et sigilli nostri impressione confirmavimus, salva in omnibus tam nostra quam nostrorum successorum episcoporum Heref' canonica iustitia. Hiis testibus, W. archidiacono Hereford', N. archidiacono ^{d}de Salop'ser,^{d} M(agistro) P. de Bergeveney, M(agistro) T. Folyot, ^{e}Iohanne Carbonell', Pagano de Burchehull', R. le Polher, Iohanne Wyard', T. de Yeddefen', Radulfo filio eius, R. Brothant', R. filio eius, Waltero de Wetebeth', Rogero filio eius^e et aliis.

^{a}*om. B.* ^{b}B. *B.* ^{c}*om. B.* $^{d-d}$Salop' *C.* $^{e-e}$*om. C.*

John Foliot, rector of Bockleton, became a canon of Hereford cathedral 1240 × 1268 (Hereford D. & C. Muniments, no.754). He was the son of William Foliot the precentor and held land at Lulham which had been bequeathed to him by his father (see note to no.288 above). He is not to be identified with the John Foliot who was archdn of Shropshire and then chancellor of the cathedral in the 1240s since the two occur together in Hereford D. & C. Muniments no.1872. The *terminus ad quem* of this institution is the death or resignation of Nicholas, archdn of Shropshire, whose successor first occurs before 23 July 1227; however the document is in fact probably earlier than 27 November 1223 by which time Master Thomas Foliot had become precentor.

318. Bockleton church

Institution of John Foliot on the presentation of Robert de Bockleton in the parsonage of Bockleton, saving the vicarage of a certain B. in the church of Bockleton.

[27 October 1219 × -23 July 1227, probably *ante* 29 November 1223]

B = Bodl. MS Rawlinson B329 (Hereford cathedral cartulary), fos.54v-55r. s.xv.

Universis Cristi fidelibus presens scriptum inspecturis H. Folyot divina miseratione Heref' ecclesie minister humilis salutem eternam in domino. Noverit universitas vestra nos ad presentationem dilecti filii Roberti de Boclint' Iohannem Folyot clericum ad ecclesiam de B. recepisse*a* et ipsum in eadem ecclesia personam canonice instituisse, salva B. capellano, vicario eiusdem ecclesie, vicaria sua, videlicet totam ecclesiam, et predicto I. persone unam marcam argenti nomine pensionis annuatim persolvet, et si prefatus B. premori contigerit, liceat predicto I. persone eandem ecclesiam cum omnibus ad eam pertinentibus in usus suos proprios convertere, salvis c. s(olidis) annuatim prestandis ab ipso, vel eo quicumque eandem ecclesiam optinuerit cui assignare volumus. Ipse etiam I., et omnes quicumque pro tempore predictam ecclesiam optinuerint, de predictis c. s(olidis) annuatim fideliter solvendis iuramento prestito, tenebit omnia onera predicte ecclesie et sicut predictus B. vicarius sustinebit. Et, decedentibus personis, prefatus R. de Boclynton, patronus eiusdem ecclesie, ad eandem ecclesiam presentandi liberam habebit [fo.55r] potestatem, et quicumque eum impedierit indignationem Patris et Filii et Spiritus Sancti et beate et gloriose virginis Marie et beati Ethelberti*b* et omnium sanctorum et nostram incurrat. Et ut hec omnia rata et inconvulsa permaneant presenti ea scripto et sigilli nostri appensione confirmare curavimus. Hiis testibus M(agistris) T.Folyot, Symone de Fraxino et W. de Munci^c canonicis Herford' et aliis.

^{a}recipisse *B*. ^{b}Ethilberti *B*. ^{c}Grandi *B*.

For the date see no.317.

319. Chirbury priory

Composition between Chirbury priory and Richard the portionist of Chirbury on the one hand and William the parson of New Montgomery on the other.   [27 October 1219 × -23 July 1227]

> A = PRO E327/52. 14th-century endorsements: Confirmacio bone memorie domini Hugonis Foliot quondam Episcopi Hereford' cuiusdam composicionis habite inter Philippum priorem et canonicos ecclesie de Cherbur' ex parte una et Willelmum rectorem ecclesie de Mungomery ex altera habita super cantaria ecclesie eiusdem de novo constructe. 156 × 135 + 15 mm. Originally sealed on a tag; seal does not survive.
>
> B = PRO C53/19, membr. 6 (Charter Roll, 11 Henry III, pt. ii), contained in an inspeximus of Henry III dated 23 July 1227.
>
> Cal., *Cal. Ch. Rolls*, i.53.

Omnibus Cristi fidelibus ad quos presens scriptum pervenerit.' Hugo Foliot dei gratia Hereford' episcopus.' salutem in domino. Noverit universitas vestra quod hec est compositio facta inter Philippum priorem et canonicos de Chirebir'. et Ricardum personam quarte portionis ecclesie de Chirebir' ex una parte. et Willelmum personam ecclesie de novo Mungomeri ex alia super cantaria ecclesie eiusdem^a de novo constructe. et sepultura mortuorum ibidem habenda in perpetuum. videlicet. quod ecclesia predicta sine contradictione et reclamatione dictorum prioris et conventus qui pro tempore fuerint propriam habeat perpetuo personam. quam dominus rex et heredes sui presentabunt ad eandem. et ipsa ecclesia fontes habeat et sepulturam cum omni alio iure. quo matrices ecclesie utuntur. hoc scilicet modo. persona que pro tempore fuerit instituta singulis annis reddet ecclesie de Chirebir' triginta sol(idos) sterlingorum ad duos terminos. scilicet ad Pascha. quindecim sol(idos). et ad festum Sancti Michaelis quindecim sol(idos) pro composicione oblationum. quas ecclesia de Chyrebir' quondam percipere consuevit de parochianis de Mungomeri. et sub pena dimidie marce prefatis priori et canonicis de

Chirebir' solvenda in quolibet termino. quo dicta persona a solutione ipsorum quindecim solidorum cessabit. Reddet etiam eadem persona ecclesie de Chirbir' medietatem principalis legati de tota parochia de Mungomeri integre. et sine aliqua diminutione qualitercumque fuerit legatum. tam infra castrum quam extra. et hoc tam clerici. et capellani ministrantes in ecclesia de Mungomeri. quam persona eiusdem loci se fideliter servaturos iurabunt coram domino Hereford'. vel eius officiali. Licebit etiam priori et canonicis de Chirbir' libere et sine reclamatione prefate persone et successorum suorum recipere corpora libere tenentium de parochia de Mungomeri. si aliquis eorum corpus suum dare vel reddere voluerit eisdem. salvo in omnibus iure ecclesie de Mungomeri. Hanc igitur composicionem ratam et gratam haben-tes. eam episcopali auctoritate presenti scripto et sigilli nostri munimine. confirmavimus. Hiis testibus Th. decano Hereford'. E. thesaurario Heref'. S. archidiacono Salops'. Th. precentore Heref'. Magistro W. Platun. E. canonico. et Roberto capellanis domini epis-copi. Magistro E. de Buckehull'. God' clerico et aliis.

^a*correction before* eiusdem *A.*

Tied by the seal tags to A is a charter of William de Budlers, parson of Montgom-ery, notifying the composition. Hugh Foliot's charter was issued before 23 July 1227, when Henry III issued his inspeximus, but not long before, since Simon of Edenbridge only succeeded to the archdnry of Shropshire in the mid-1220s, and Thomas Foliot, who occurs as precentor in 1223, may have attained this dignity as late as that year; their predecessors, Nicholas of Wolverhampton and William of Kilpeck, both occur in the early years of Hugh Foliot's episcopate. For the gradual transformation of Chirbury church from a secular minster to an Augustin-ian priory, see no.295 above.

*320. Coddington church

Notification of dedication of three altars in Coddington church.
4 August 1231

Summarised, *Reg. Bothe*, 199.

*321. Coddington church

Mandate concerning the pension payable by the rector of Coddington to two of the rectors of Ledbury. 4 August 1231

Mentioned, *Reg. Bothe*, 199.

322. Conches abbey

Inspeximus of a confirmation issued by Bishop Robert Foliot for Conches abbey of its property in the diocese. [Probably 1233]

A = Evreux, A-D Eure H251. 15th-century endorsements: carta d'Anglia. 18th-century endorsements: A Angleterre collé 4 n6 C de Hugues Foliot evesq' de Herford – fol. 113 R armoire 30e 3e liasse. 175 × 226 + 19 mm. Originally sealed on a tag; tag and seal missing.

B = Ibid., vidimus datable 7 × 21 August 1234, issued by Dean R(alph de Maidstone) and the chapter of Hereford cathedral.

Universis Cristi fidelibus ad quos presens scriptum pervenerit Hugo Folioth dei gratia Hereford' episcopus salutem in domino. Noverit universitas vestra nos cartam bone memorie Roberti Folioth episcopi Hereford' inspexisse in hec verba. Universis sancte matris ecclesie filiis Robertus dei gratia Hereford' ecclesie minister.' eternam in domino salutem. Ex officio iniuncte nobis administrationis tenemur viris religiosis eatenus providere ut beneficia a filiis sancte dei ecclesie in elemosinam perpetuam sibi collata.' pacifice et absque omni vexatione possidere valeant. Inde est quod dilectis fratribus nostris abbati Sancti Petri Castellionis et monachis ibidem deo servientibus paterna pietate prospicere cupientes.' concedimus eis et episcopali auctoritate confirmamus manerium de Munekelen' et ecclesiam eiusdem ville cum universis decimationibus et ceteris obventionibus et omnibus ad eam iure spectantibus salva honesta sustentatione vicarii. Confirmamus etiam eis omnes decimas de dominio de Chabbenour'. cum uno hospite. et decimam illius terre quam idem hospes de eis tenet. et decimam de Hide in omnibus. Confirmamus etiam eis duas partes decimarum de dominio in Bromesberga tam in magnis quam in minutis decimis in omnibus et confirmamus eis duas partes decimarum de dominio de Edithestoc'. in omnibus cum uno hospite. et duas partes decimarum de dominio de la Hide. et duas partes decimarum de dominio Willelmi de Scolle. et duas partes decimarum Hereberti de Espreton'. et unum burgagium in villa Hereford'. et duas partes decimarum de dominio de Alboldelega. et in eadem villa duos hospites et duas partes decimarum de dominio del Bur. et duas partes decimarum de dominio de Worvesleg'. et terram et mansuram que fuit Caure. et duas partes decimarum de feodo Osberti filii Rualdi. et duas partes decimarum de dominio de Linde cum uno hospite. Has elemosinas habent predicti monachi ex donacione Radulfi senioris de Toenio. quas et alia si qua in episcopatu Hereford' habent benefitia canonice adepta.' eis confirmamus. salva dignitate Hereford' ecclesie et successorum nostrorum. canonica iustitia. Quod ne de cetero deduci possit in irritum. presenti carta et sigilli nostri testimonio communimus. Hiis testibus.[a] Willelmo de Stok'. Willelmo Folioth. Waltero de Colewell'. Magistro Nicholao divino. Iohanne canonico. Elur' capellano. Bartholomeo de Eignesham. Osberto de Ledeb'. Nos igitur dictam confirmationem secundum tenorem suprascriptum ratam et gratam habentes eam episcopali auctoritate et sigilli nostri munimine confirmare curavimus. Hiis testibus. Henrico persona de Colewell'. Elya canonico Lanthon'. Magistro Willelmo Platun. Rogero capellano. Ada de Ledebir'. Godef' clerico. Petro clerico. Willelmo de Gaitun'. Waltero de Paris. Waltero camerario. et aliis.

[a]Hiis testibus *partly obscure A*.

Hugh's inspeximus was written by the same scribe as a charter issued by Reginald, abbot of Conches, for Hereford Cathedral in 1233 (Hereford D. & C. Muniments, no.1082), and the two charters were probably issued at the same time. Robert Foliot's charter is no.142. See also no.187.

323. Craswall priory

Confirmation of the grant by Walter de Lacy to the prior of the order of Grandmont and the brothers of Craswall of the ninth sheaf of all corn save oats from all his manors (Weobley, Mansell Gamage, Yarkhill, Holme Lacy, Stanton Lacy, Ludlow, and Rock [Farm] in Ludlow).

[27 October 1219 × 29 November 1223]

B = Bodl. MS Rawlinson B329 (Hereford cathedral cartulary), fo.147v. s.xiii-xiv.

Omnibus Cristi fidelibus presens scriptum inspecturis Hugo Foliot dei gratia Herefordensis episcopus salutem in domino. Noverit universitas vestra quod nos, divine pietatis intuitu, omnia dona que dominus Walterus de Lascy caritative fecit in episcopatu nostro priori

Grandimont' ordinis et fratribus habitantibus in Crassewelle, scilicet nonam garbam frumenti, mistilionis, siliginis et omnis generis bladi preter avenas per omnia maneria predicti domini Walteri de Lascy, videlicet de Wilbel', de Maweshull', de Yarchull', de Hamme, de Stanton', de Ludel', de Akes, sicut in carta eiusdem domini W. de Lascy continetur eisdem priori et fratribus concessimus et auctoritate episcopali confirmavimus, salvo iure cuiuslibet parochialis ecclesie. Et quia volumus quod hec nostra concessio et confirmatio robur perpetue firmitatis optineat presenti scripto sigillum nostrum apponi fecimus. Hiis testibus, Magistro Thoma Foliot, Magistro Willelmo Platun, Elya canonico, Rogero capellano, Ada de Ledebur', Willelmo de Dudelbur', Godefrido, Rogero clericis, Waltero camerario, Waltero Clement et aliis.

> Craswall was founded by Walter de Lacy, probably in the second decade of the thirteenth century (*HRH*, 109). Master Thomas Foliot became precentor before 29 November 1223.

*324. Abbey Dore

Charter for Dore abbey concerning property at or near Bacton.
[27 October 1219 × 7 August 1234]

> Mention only, BL Harleian MS 5804, fo.258r, a 17th-century antiquarian MS containing a list of charters, probably originals (see Davis, *Cartularies*, 37) issued for Dore Abbey. This charter is referred to simply as 'Hugo Foliot Hereford Episcopus' in the section headed *Baketon*. Bacton is about two or three miles north of Dore.

*325. Abbey Dore

Charter of, or charter sealed by, Bishop Hugh Foliot for Dore abbey concerning property at or near Bacton.   October 1220

> Mention only, BL Harleian MS 5804, fo.258r (see note to no.324 above). The reference to the charter, which does not state who issued it, runs 'Anno domini 1220 mense Octobri anno primo post consecrationem Domini H. Folliott Herefordensis episcopi qui huic scripto sigillum suum apposuit.'

326. Abbey Dore

Agreement to a grant by John de Kilpeck to Dore abbey of tithes from forty acres in Treville.   [27 October 1219+ × -7 August 1234]

A = PRO E326/11837. 13th-14th century endorsements: de decimis quadraginta acrarum. 15th-century endorsement: Can. 145 × 90 + 18 mm. Originally sealed on the tag; tag and seal do not survive. Charter has suffered from damp and mould and has been rebacked.

Universis sancte matris ecclesie filiis ad quos presens scriptum pervenerit. Hugo Folyot dei gratia Herefordensis ecclesie episcopus in domino salutem. Quoniam pium et gratum deo esse consideramus portiones religiosorum augmentare. ut crescentibus eorum bonis augeatur et numerus deo famulancium. et in hospitalitate manutenenda caritas sustentetur.' noveritis nos divine pietatis intuitu concessisse et indulsisse dilectis filiis nostris abbati et conventui de Dora. decimas provenientes de quadraginta acris terre in Tr<a>vel^a que fuit foresta regis. quas decimas Iohannes de Kylpec dictis monachis per cartam suam contulit. qui predictas quadraginta acras ab eisdem monachis t<en>et.^{b} quod ne de cetero alicui revocetur in dubium.' illud auctoritate episcopali.' et presenti scripto sigilli nostri appositione munito.' confirmamus. Hiis testibus. Domino Symone archidiacono de Salopeb'. Thoma decano de West'. Waltero de Banneb' tunc senescallo episcopi. Roberto decano de Stratt'. et multis aliis.

^{a}*parchment torn.* ^{b}*surface rubbed.*

Simon of Edenbridge became archdn of Shropshire after 1219 and before 23 July 1227. Walter of Banbury was Hugh Foliot's steward before Adam of Shrewsbury, who occurs as Hugh's steward 1230 × 1234; see below, no.363. This charter is briefly mentioned in BL Harleian MS 5804, fo.258r (see note to no.324).

327. Gloucester abbey

Notification of the arrangements made for the vicarage of Dewchurch with the consent of Richard prior of Kilpeck and Adam vicar of Dewchurch; Adam is to receive the altarage and the mortuary offerings, and tithes of sheaves and hay from the demesne of Ralph de Saucey in the village of Wormton and tithes of hay from the lands of Nicholas le Secular, Cradoc Seisil, Robert of the Mountain, Cradoc son of Abraham,

Simon le Bonde, Abraham the clerk and John Bergavi, and a summa
each of wheat and oats from the grange of the prior of Kilpeck in return for
the third part of the tithes of sheaves from the villeinage of Roger Tyrel of
Wormton; the vicar is to have pasture for his horse and is to find a resident
deacon to serve in the church.   [27 October 1219 × 7 August 1234]

B = PRO C150/1 (now SR 3/38: Gloucester cartulary), fos.211v-212r (fos.194v-
195r old foliation), no.790. s.xiv ex.

Pd, *Gloucester cartulary*, 224, no.789.

The document was originally witnessed but the scribe of the cartulary omitted the
witnesses' names. Hugh's name is given as *Hugo Folioth*. Kilpeck was a dependent
priory of Gloucester Abbey and Wormton, now lost, was a village in the valley of
the Worm Brook in Herefordshire, near Dewchurch.

328. Gloucester abbey

General notification jointly issued by Hugh Foliot, W(alter) de Lacy,
R(ichard) de Samford, and Master H. of Cerne that they had been
ordered to hold inquisitions concerning the forest in Gloucestershire and
that they had decided that the woods of Rodley and Boxline *and the*
covert of Taynton should be put outside the forest laws.   [1225+]

B = Gloucester Cathedral Library, St Peter's Register B, p.25, no.68. s.xiv ex.
Heading: Carta recuperacionis bosci de Sudrugg'.

Universis fidelibus ad quos presentes litere pervenerint H. dei gratia
Hereford' episcopus,[a] W. de Lacy, R. de Samford, et Magister H. de
Cern' salutem in domino. Noverit universitas vestra quod cum de
precepto et de voluntate domini Henrici regis filii regis I. missi
fuissemus per comitatum Glouc' ad [b] deafforestandum boscos qui
positi fuerunt infra regardum vel defensum [c] per voluntatem ipsius
Iohannis [d] regis accepimus per veredictum xxiiii tam militum quam
libere tenentium boscum de Rudele per voluntatem ipsius I. regis et
boscum de Boxline et bruilla de Teynton positos fuisse in regardum
et defensum, quos incontinenti per preceptum domini regis posuimus
extra regardum et defensum; quod ne alicui vertatur in dubium
presenti [e] sigilla nostra apposuimus in testimonium.

[a] episcopo, *sic, B.*   [b] quod ad, *B.*   [c] defensu, *B.*   [d] I. Iohannis, *B.*
[e] scripto *or some other noun om., B.*

Perambulations to decide what land should be taken out of the forest laws were held after the Forest Charter was reissued 11 February 1225. Walter de Lacy died in 1241.

329. Gloucester abbey

Notification to the foresters of the Forest of Dean that the woods of Rodley and Boxline *and the covert of Taynton are to be put outside the forest laws.*   [1225+]

> B = Gloucester Cathedral Library, St Peter's Register B, p.27, no.74. s.xiv ex. Heading: De bosco de Rudele extra regardum per regem H. posito.

H. dei gratia episcopus Hereford', W. de Lacy, Ricardus de Samford, magister H. de Cern' universis forestariis de Dene salutem. Noveritis nos ex precepto domini Regis inquisitionem fecisse de forestis que per dominum Iohannem regem afforestate fuerunt et per veredictum fidelium iuratorum accepimus quod boscus de Rudele et boscus de Boxl' et bruilla de Teyntona positi fuerunt in defensum et in regardum per voluntatem ipsius Iohannis regis, quos incontinenti per preceptum domini regis Henrici posuimus extra regardum. Quare vobis precipimus quatinus vos de predictis boscis contra libertatem a domino rege concessam non intromittatis.

Date as no.328.

330. Gloucester abbey

Inspeximus (issued with Dean Ralph of Hereford and the cathedral chapter) of a charter of Bishop Gerard of Hereford confirming the churches of Churcham (with the chapel of Bulley), Preston, and Taynton, and tithes from Highnam, Churcham, Preston, Brampton Abbotts, Upleadon, Monkhide in Yarkhill, Rodley, Ewias, and Poston in Vowchurch to Gloucester abbey.   [27 October 1231 × 7 August 1234]

> B = Gloucester Cathedral, Seals and Deeds, vol. VIII, no. 1, contained in an original inspeximus issued by Bishop Robert (Burnell) of Bath and Wells and Bishop William of Llandaff, datable 1275 × 1285. C = PRO C150/1 (Gloucester cartulary), fos.65r-66r (fos.48r-49r in old foliation), no.177. s.xiv ex.

Pd from C, *Gloucester cartulary*, i.250-2, no.177.

Universis Cristi fidelibus ad quos presens scriptum pervenerit Hugo
Folyot[a] dei gratia Herefordensis episcopus, R. decanus cum toto
capitulo Hereforden' salutem in eo qui est vera salus. Ad notitiam
vestram volumus pervenire quod nos inspeximus transcriptum cuiusdam carte bone memorie predecessoris nostri Gerardi quondam
Herefordensis episcopi et etiam totius nostri capituli sub sigillo bone
memorie Symonis quondam Wygorn' episcopi mentionem expresse
facientis se cartam predictam inspexisse hanc formam continentem.
Omnibus sancte matris ecclesie filiis hanc cartam nostram inspecturis
vel audituris Gerardus dei gratia Herefordensis episcopus salutem in
eo qui est vera salus animarum. Universitati vestre notum facimus per
presentes quod nos, anno gratie millesimo centesimo, idibus Iulii, una
cum venerabilibus fratribus nostris[b] dominis Sampsone Wygorn',
Gundulfo Roffensi, et Herveo Bangorensi coepiscopis, dedicationi et
consecrationi ecclesie beatorum apostolorum Petri et Pauli, quam
reverendus abbas Serlo in villa Glavorn'[c] construxerat, nostram presentiam simul et ministerium cum omni qua potuimus exhibuisse
devotione, et quia loci prefati conventus quamplures defectus ut in
ornamentis ecclesie et aliis sibi necessariis patiebatur, nos divine
caritatis intuitu predicti conventus necessitatibus compatientes de
consensu totius capituli nostri Herefordensis concessimus predictis
abbati et conventui Glavorn'[c] cenobii[d] et successoribus eorum has[e]
subscriptas ecclesias perpetuis temporibus habendas et in proprios
usus convertendas ad suam et ecclesie sue perpetuam sustentationem,
videlicet ecclesiam de Chircham[f] cum capella de Bolleya[g] et decimis
et aliis pertinentiis suis, ecclesiam de Preston' cum omnibus pertinentiis suis, salva honestis capellanis, qui in dictis ecclesiis ministrabunt,
rationabili sustentatione. Concessimus etiam[h] eisdem religiosis duas
marcas annue pensionis de ecclesia sancti Laurentii de Teynton' et
etiam perceptionem decimarum omnium terrarum suarum quas
propriis laboribus vel sumptibus suis excoluerint in diocesi nostra,
videlicet maneriorum suorum de Hyneham et Chircham,[i] de Preston'
et de Brumpton,[j] [k]de Leden', et etiam duas garbas totius decime
hominum suorum de Leden',[k] de Hyda, salvis rectori ecclesie de
Yarkulle[l] annuatim duobus solidis et una summa frumenti, de
Rodelei,[m] salva rectori ecclesie de Westbury tercia garba decime
provenientis[n] de dominicis terris de Rodele.[o] Concessimus etiam

eisdem omnes decimas de omnibus dominicis terris domini de Ewyas sitis in parochia de Sancta Keyna et decimam cuiusdam culture*b* in Poston'. Preterea omnes ecclesias decimas terras et possessiones quas hactenus in nostra dyocesi sunt adepti eis auctoritate episcopali et unanimi capituli nostri consensu confirmamus perpetuis temporibus possidendas, et ut ea que premissa sunt futuris temporibus inconcussa permaneant, presentem cartam nostram tam sigilli nostri*q* quam sigilli capituli nostri Hereforden' appositione*r* duximus roborandum. Teste tota synodo nostra. Et quia nos cartam predicti predecessoris nostri Gerardi prenotatam prout multorum fidedignorum prestitum nobis sacramentum investigavimus et pro certo comperimus esse combustam una cum ecclesia predicta apostolorum Petri et Pauli in Glouc' anno gratie millesimo centesimo vicesimo secundo, nos predictorum religiosorum et successorum suorum indempnitati in hac parte prospicere volentes, ut tenemur, predictas ecclesias de Chircham*s* et de Preston' et etiam omnes decimas, res et possessiones, easdem*t* per predecessorem nostrum sepedictum et capitulum*u* superius concessas, eisdem religiosis et eorum successoribus iterato concedimus pro nobis et successoribus nostris perpetuo habendas*v* et possidendas et nunc et prius concessas ratas habentes confirmamus et presens scriptum sigilli nostri et capituli nostri appositione roboramus. Omnia premissa concedente et ratificante toto capitulo nostro Herefordensi.

*a*Folioth C.   *b*nostris *om.*, B, *supplied from* C.   *c*Glouc' C.   *d*om. C.   *e*haas C.
*f*Chirchehamme C.   *g*Bulleya C.   *h*etiam *om.*, B, *supplied from* C.
*i*Hynehamm', de Chirchehamme C.   *j*Brompton' C.
*k-k*C *inserts after* de dominicis terris de Rodele.   *l*Harehull' C.   *m*Rodlee C.   *n*proventus C.   *o*Rodleye C.   *p*B *adds* terre.   *q*sigillo nostro C.   *r*om. C.   *s*Chircheham C.
*t*corr. from* eisdem C.   *u*C *adds* nostrum.
*v*habendas perpetuo, *corr. from* habendas perpetuo habendas C.

For a note on Gerard's charter, a forgery, see no. 4 above. Ralph de Maidstone became dean of Hereford in 1231.

331. Gloucester abbey

Confirmation, issued with Dean Ralph de Maidstone and Hereford chapter, of a charter of Gilbert Foliot confirming the grant of Much Cowarne church to Gloucester abbey.

[27 October 1231 × 7 August 1234]

B = Hereford, Herefordshire County Record Office, Registrum Thomae de Cantilupo (formerly Hereford Diocesan Registry), on inserted fo. 17 (a) between fos. 17v and 18. Register 1275 × 1282; hand of inserted fo. probably contemporary. C = Gloucester Cathedral, Seals and Deeds, vol. VIII, no. 1, in original inspeximus, datable 1275 × 1287, issued by Bishop Robert Burnell of Bath and Wells and Bishop William de Breuse of Llandaff. D = PRO C150/1 (Gloucester cartulary), fos.248v-9r, no.918. s.xiv ex.

Pd from B, *Reg. Cantilupe*, 50; from D, *Gloucester cartulary*, iii.7, no.915. B and C are probably contemporaneous; the text here is taken from C.

Universis sancte matris ecclesie filiis Hugo Folyot[a] divina permissione Herforden' episcopus, R. decano cum toto capitulo Hereforden'[b] salutem. Sciatis nos inspexisse cartam bone memorie G. Folyot[c] quondam Hereforden' episcopi cum assensu capituli nostri, in qua continetur ipsos ecclesiam beate Marie de Coura monasterio beati Petri Glouc'[d] concessisse et in proprios usus[e] confirmasse ad luminaria et ornamenta eiusdem monasterii invenienda per manus sacriste eiusdem loci. Et cum nostrum sit rigare quod predecessores nostri plantaverunt, sic enim eadem gratia que plantatori et debetur nutritori, ratam ergo habentes illam donationem, auctoritate qua freti sumus et potestate eandem firmiter concedimus et confirmamus omni eo[f] modo quo carta illa protestatur et[g] in omnibus et cum aliquantulum hesitaremus an ut persona, vel ut vicarius, Magister Willelmus[h] de Glouc' dictam ecclesiam[i] de Coura possideret, idem magister super hiis diligenter a nobis requisitus sub gravi iuramento fatebatur se tantum vicarium existere, et de dicta ecclesia in triginta quinque marcis annuis se obligari sacriste Gloucestrie et illi in tanta pecunia[j] annuatim respondere. Ut igitur nulli posteritati istud vertatur in dubium, dicimus, volumus, et concedimus ut memoratus sacrista ecclesiam suam de Coura ingrediatur et in manu sua retineat quandocumque voluerit, salva sufficienti et honesta sustentatione unius capellani seu vicarii in dicta ecclesia ministrantis, et sint[k] predicti[l] abbas et conventus quieti a synodo nostra sequenda, similiter ab omni procuratione que spectet vel spectare possit ad episcopum Hereforden',[m] visitando ecclesias ad dictum monasterium pertinentes in dyocesi Hereforden'. In cuius rei concessione et confirmatione huic presenti scripto sigilla nostra fecimus apponi, et inhibemus[n] ex parte Dei ne quis contra istam nostram concessionem et confirmationem obviare presumat sub pena illa que expressa est in carta illa quam prediximus a domino G. Folyot,[o] predecessore nostro, sepefato monasterio confecta et collata. Teste toto capitulo nostro.

*a*Folioth *D.*   *b*interlin., *B.*   *c*Foliot *B,* Folioth *D.*   *d*Gloucestr' *BD.*
*e*interlin., ? in later hand, *B.*   *f*over erasure, *B.*   *g*et om., *D.*   *h*Willelmo *C.*
*i*interlin., *B.*   *j*peccunia *C.*   *k*sin *D.*   *l*B adds gemipunctus.   *m*Herefordie *D.*
*n*inhabemus ? *D.*   *o*Foliot *B,* Folioth *D.*

Gilbert Foliot's charter, which confirms a grant made by Bernard of Neufmarché, is printed in *GFL,* 369-70, no.305, and cf. ibid., no.306 on 370; see above, nos.77, 78. For the dating see no.330.

332. Gloucester abbey

Notification that Master Peter of Northampton, vicar of the church of Foy, has agreed to pay 40 shillings pension per year to Gloucester abbey.
Bosbury, 17 October 1233

PRO C150/1 (Gloucester cartulary), fo.70r, no.258. s.xiv ex.

Pd, *Gloucester cartulary,* i.300.

Actum apud Bosebur' in vigilia Sancti Luce, anno gratie mccxxx tertio. In cuius rei etc'.

See also no.333.

333. Gloucester abbey

Notification of arrangements for the payment of a pension from the church of Foy and of the institution of the abbot and convent of Gloucester abbey as parsons of the church.   [probably 17 October 1233]

B = Gloucester Cathedral, Seals and Deeds, vol. VIII, no.1, in an original inspeximus issued by Bishops Robert of Bath and Wells and William of Llandaff, datable 1275 × 1287. C = Ibid., in charter of inspeximus issued by Dean S(tephen Thornberge) of Hereford contained in above inspeximus. D = Ibid., in charter of inspeximus issued by Bishop Ralph de Maidstone of Hereford, dated October 1236, contained in inspeximus of Bishops Robert of Bath and Wells and William of Llandaff. E = PRO C150/1 (Gloucester cartulary), fo.70r, no.259, s.xiv ex. F = Ibid., fo.70r-v, no.260 (in inspeximus by Ralph de Maidstone, see D).

Pd from E, *Gloucester cartulary,* i.300 (F pd. ibid., i.301); Dean Stephen Thornbury's inspeximus is pd. ibid., i.301, but the scribe of the cartulary omitted most of the text of Hugh Foliot's charter.

Universis Cristi fidelibus ad quos presens scriptum pervenerit Hugo
Folyot[a] dei gratia Herefordensis episcopus salutem in domino.
Noverit universitas vestra nos divine pietatis intuitu dedisse et concessisse abbati et conventui sancti Petri Glouc' ibidem deo servientibus tres marcas annuas quas eisdem caritative[b] contulimus nomine
personatus ecclesie de Foya, duobus terminis percipiendas a magistro
Petro de Northampton', vicario eiusdem ecclesie, videlicet in annunciatione[c] beate Marie viginti solidos, et in festo Sancti Michaelis
viginti solidos, salva tota residua portione dicte ecclesie predicto
magistro P., quamdiu vixerit, possidenda, et post decessum eiusdem
P. licebit predictis abbati et conventui totam dictam ecclesiam cum
pertinentiis habere et tenere et in proprios usus iuxta voluntatem
suam convertere. Nos vero dictos abbatem et conventum ad dictam
pensionem nomine personatus admisimus et eosdem in eadem ecclesia canonice instituimus. Quod quia ratum et stabile volumus perpetuo permanere, presenti id scripto[d] et sigilli nostri impressione
confirmavimus.[e] Hiis testibus decano et capitulo Hereford'.[f]

[a]Folioth *EFG*.   [b]carative *F*.   [c]anunciatione *BCD*.   [d]*corr. from* scripto id *F*.
[e]*Text of E ends here.*   [f] Hiis testibus etc' *F*.

This charter was probably issued at the same time as no.332.

334. Haughmond abbey

*Institution of Master John of Worcester in the church of Culmington as
parson on presentation by Abbot Osbert and the canons of Haughmond.*
                              [27 October 1219 × 19 December 1229]

> B = Shrewsbury Local Studies Library, Haughmond abbey cartulary, fo.52r. s.xv
> ex.
>
> Pd, *Haughmond cartulary*, 69, no.271.

Hiis testibus, Magistro Thoma precentore Hereford, Magistro
Roberto Grossoteste, Magistro Ricardo de Hereford' officiali domini
episcopi etc.

Thomas Foliot became precentor before, but not long before, 29 November 1223.
Master Robert Grosseteste became archdn of Leicester before 19 December 1229.

335. Haughmond abbey

Licence to Haughmond abbey to appropriate the church of Stokesay, now that the rector, Master Adam, has died.

[August 1230 × 7 August 1234]

B = Shrewsbury Local Studies Library, Haughmond cartulary, fo.206v. s.xv ex.
C = Shropshire County Record Office, 2922 Additional (Dudmaston MS), fo.15v. s.xvi ex. – xvii in.

Cal., *Haughmond cartulary*, 213, no.1151.

Omnibus sancte matris ecclesie filiis ad quos presens scriptum pervenerit Hugo Foliot divina miseratione Hereford' ecclesie minister humilis eternam in domino salutem. Inspeximus cartas bone memorie Egidii et Hugonis predecessorum nostrorum et dilectorum in Cristo filiorum decani et capituli Hereford', in quibus continetur quod ipsi post mortem Magistri Ade, qui ecclesiam de Stoke possidet, prenominatam ecclesiam, cum omnibus pertinentiis suis, abbati et conventui de Haghmon' in usus proprios confirmaverunt. Nos vero denique*ª* habentes pre oculis post mortem dicti Ade dictam ecclesiam cum pertinentiis suis dictis abbati et conventui inperpetuum possidendam*ᵇ* concessimus, et eosdem in corporalem possessionem eiusdem ecclesie induci fecimus. Hiis testibus, Magistro T. Foliot, Elia canonico Lenthon', Iohanne canonico de Wigemor', *ᶜ*Magistro Willelmo Platun, Adam de Salop canonico Hereford', Rogero capellano, Willelmo de Dudelb', Godefrido clerico.*ᶜ*

*ª*deu B.   *ᵇcrossing out after* possidendam B.   *ᶜ⁻ᶜ*etc B.

In *Haughmond cartulary* this charter is dated 1219 × 1226 because Master Thomas Foliot is not described as precentor or treasurer. But Adam of Shrewsbury became a canon of Hereford only after August 1230, and so Thomas' title (he became treasurer in or just after August 1230) must have been accidentally omitted. See also nos.253 and 298.

336. Hereford cathedral chapter

Inspeximus and ratification of a confirmation by Bishop Gilbert Foliot of a grant by Robert de Chandos to Hereford cathedral of the prebend of Wellington.

[27 October 1219 × 23 July 1227]

A = Hereford Cathedral, D. & C. Muniments, no.2777. 14th-century endorsements: Confirmacio libertatis concesse prebende de Welington'. (Another
hand): script'. (Another hand): Synton (with notarial mark). 173 × 82 + 16 mm.
Originally sealed on a tag; seal does not survive.

B = Hereford, Herefordshire County Record Office, Registrum Ricardi de Swinfield (formerly Hereford Diocesan Registry), fo.21v (fo.17v old foliation).
1283-1317, here 1285 or just after. C = Bodl., MS Rawlinson B329 (Hereford
Cathedral Cartulary), fo.160v. s.xiii-xiv. D = Ibid., fo.10v. s.xv.

Pd, *Reg. Swinfield*, 55-56.

Universis sancte matris ecclesie filiis ad quos presens scriptum pervenerit. Hugo Foliot divina permissione Hereforden' episcopus. eternam in domino salutem. Noverit universitas vestra nos scriptum
auctenticum bone memorie. G. quondam Hereforden' episcopi in hec
verba inspexisse. Gilbertus dei gratia Hereforden' episcopus omnibus
sancte matris ecclesie. filiis ad quos presens scriptum pervenerit
salutem in domino. Notum sit vobis omnibus. Robertum de Chandos
concessisse et dedisse ecclesiam beate Margarete de Welinton' in
prebendam Beate Marie. et Beati Ethelberti de Hereford' in perpetuum. Inde est quod volumus eam esse liberam et quietam ab
omnibus episcopalibus consuetudinibus et auxiliis sicuti ceteras prebendas. Quod quia ratum et inconvulsum manere volumus.' presenti
scripto. et sigilli nostri attestacione confirmavimus. Hiis testibus. N.
episcopo de Land'. Galfrido decano Hereford'. archidiaconis. Petro
et W. Foliot. Reginaldo cantore. Ivone thesaurario cum toto Hereforden' capitulo. Nos igitur predictam cartam ratam habentes.' eam
presenti scripto. et sigilli nostri apposicione roboravimus. Hiis testibus. Th. decano Hereford'. W. archid' Hereford'. N. archid'
Salopesir'. Elya thesaurario. Magistro Petro de Bergeveny. Elya de
Evesham canonicis. et multis aliis.

For Gilbert's confirmation, see *GFL*, no.315 (calendared above, no.84). Hugh
Foliot's inspeximus must be earlier than 23 July 1227, by which date Simon of
Edenbridge had replaced Nicholas as archdn of Shropshire.

337. Hereford cathedral chapter

*Arrangement with Hereford cathedral chapter whereby land at Canon
Pyon is to be separated from Robert Folet's prebend of Woolhope, Robert
Folet renounces two mills in Eign and land at Litley to the bishop, and*

*the bishop confers the land at Canon Pyon on the chapter for their own
uses and grants a tenth of the proceeds of his market at Ledbury and land
at Wellington in Ledbury to whichever prebendary will hold Robert
Folet's prebend.* [27 October 1219 × 29 November 1223]

B = Bodl., MS Rawlinson B329 (Hereford cathedral cartulary), fo.20r-v. s.xv.

Universis sancte matris ecclesie filiis ad quos presens scriptum pervenerit H. Folyot dei gratia Herefordensis episcopus eternam in
domino salutem. Noverit universitas vestra quod terram quandam de
Piona, spectantem ad prebendam domini Roberti Foliot, ad quam
etiam prebendam quedam terra pertinet in villa de Wolvythehope
canonicorum Hereford', ab eadem prebenda separavimus propter
commodum[a] ecclesie nostre Heref' et omnium successorum nostrorum. Predictus enim R. Folyet reddidit nobis et quietumclamavit
totam terram et totum ius quod pater suus W. Folyot vel ipse unquam
tenuerunt vel habuerunt vel dixerunt se habere de predecessoribus
nostris in civitate Heref' vel extra in feodo episcopi Heref'. Remisit
etiam et quietumclamavit predictus R. Folyot totum ius quod habuit
vel dixit se \habere/ de duobus \molendinis/ in Eyene et totum ius
suum in terra de Lutteleg et in terra et in redditu et in omnibus aliis
rebus quod unquam habuit pater suus vel ipse in civitate Heref', vel
in burgo, vel extra, de feodo episcopi, in pratis et pastura, in terra culta
vel inculta, et omnibus locis. Cui etiam donationi vel concessioni
interfuit Reginaldus filius eius et consensum[b] prebuit. Nos vero
considerantes maximum et perpetuum commodum[a] ecclesie nostre
et omnium successorum nostrorum predictam terram de Piona venerabili capitulo nostro Heref' contulimus in puram et perpetuam
elemosinam sicut carta nostra testatur et predictas terras quas predictus Robertus Foliet nobis et successoribus nostris reddidit et quietumclamavit in usus nostros et omnium successorum nostrorum
recipimus et reservamus. Volentes etiam non minus indempnatis
prebende predicte quam commodis[c] nostris vel successorum nostrorum providere, ne predicta prebenda in aliquo dampnificata,
quicumque eam possident, minus sufficiat, eidem prebende et omnibus canonicis eandem pro tempore habituris decimum denarium
omnis proventus nundinarum nostrarum de [fo.20v] Ledebur' in
compensationem terram de Pyona assignavimus et terram de Walynton' in Ledebur' sub Maliverna, illam scilicet quam Samuell' quon-

dam tenuit et postea uxor sua Iuliana, habendam et tenendam omnibus futuris canonicis eiusdem prebende, cum omnibus pertinentiis et libertatibus, de nobis et successoribus libere, quiete, et honorifice, reddendam inde nobis et successoribus nostris duodecim[d] solidos annuatim, scilicet in nativitate Sancti Iohannis Baptiste iii s., et in festo Sancti Michaelis iii s., et in festo Sancti Andree iii s., et in annuntiationem beate Marie iii s., pro omni servitio, exactione, et demanda que ad terram pertineat vel pertinere possit, excepto regali servitio. Preterea assignavimus predicte prebende et omnibus canonicis eandem prebendam habituris terram de Hedel'[1] in parochia de Ledebur', cum omnibus pertinentiis suis et libertatibus, habendam et tenendam de nobis et successoribus nostris libere et quiete reddendo inde nobis et successoribus nostris annuatim xx s. ad quattuor terminos, scilicet ad quemlibet predictorum terminorum v s. pro omnibus servitiis et exactionibus. Nos vero et successores nostri predictum decimum[e] denarium omnium proventuum et exituum nundinarum nostrarum de Ledebur' et predictam terram de Walynton' cum omnibus pertinentiis et libertatibus suis, exceptis regali servitio omnibus futuris, eiusdem prebende canonicis warantizabimus. Eidem si nos et successores nostri non fecerimus, dabimus et assignabimus eidem prebende et omnibus canonicis eam habituris omnes terras et redditus omnes quos predictus R. Folyot nobis reddidit et quietumclamavit vel aliud racionabile excambium secundum iudicium et arbitrium capituli Hereford'. Nos autem hanc concessionem ratam et inconvulsam permanere volentes, huic scripto sigillum nostrum et sigillum capituli nostri apponi fecimus. Hiis testibus, M(agistro) T. Folyot, Roberto le Poher, tunc senescallo, Waltero de Bannebir', Magistro W. de Muney,[f] M(agistro) G. de Bukehull', Waltero de Parys, Bernardo[g] de Ledebur' et Willelmo de Duddeleg et multis aliis.

[a]comodum B.   [b]concensum B.   [c]comodis B.   [d]duodecem B.
[e]predictam decimam B.   [f]sic for Muncy B.   [g]Bernerdo B.
[1]Hazle, near Ledbury.

Thomas Foliot became precentor before 29 November 1223 and Robert le Poher ceased to be steward well before the end of Hugh Foliot's episcopate. Dean Thomas and Hereford chapter leased the land at Pion to Robert Folet's son, Reginald, shortly after this agreement, for a rent of 5s a year. Emma, Reginald's mother, was to hold the land for the same rent for her lifetime if she outlived Reginald (Hereford D. & C. Muniments, no.1361, datable 1219 × 1231). See also no.339. The fifteenth century cartulary copyist assumed that Robert Folet's surname was Foliot: from documents of Robert's own day we know that it was Folet.

*338. Hereford cathedral chapter

Grant to the dean and chapter of Hereford cathedral of a mill and a croft in Eign. [probably 27 October 1219 × 23 July 1227]

Mention only, in a grant by Dean Thomas and the chapter of Hereford Cathedral, datable 1216 × 1231, to William the goldsmith of the same mill and croft, at a rent of 53s a year (Hereford D. & C. Muniments no.1111). The mill was probably one of the ones resigned to Bp Hugh Foliot (above no.337), and so this grant would have been made just after no.337.

339. Hereford cathedral chapter

Grant to the dean and chapter of Hereford cathedral of all the land that Robert Folet had held from him in Canon Pyon to augment their commons. [27 October 1219 × 1231, probably *ante* 29 November 1223]

B = Bodl. MS Rawlinson B329 (Hereford cathedral cartulary), fos.20v-21r. s.xv.

Omnibus Cristi fidelibus ad quos presens scriptum pervenerit H. Folyot ecclesie Herefordensis minister humilis eternam in domino salutem. Ad notitiam omnium volumus pervenire nos, divine caritatis intuitu, dedisse et concessisse et hac presenti carta confirmasse decano et capitulo Heref' ecclesie in puram et perpetuam elemosinam et ad meliorationem commune sue totam terram illam que fuit Roberti*[a]* [fo.21r] Folyot in Pyona tenendam et habendam sibi imperpetuum de nobis et successoribus nostris libere et quiete ab omni servitio et exactione seculari. Nos autem et successores nostri dictam terram cum omnibus pertinentiis suis dictis decano et capitulo contra omnes homines et feminas warantizabimus. Ut autem hec nostra donatio stabilis et firma imposterum perseveret eam presenti scripto et sigilli nostri appositione corroboramus. Hiis testibus, magistris Ricardo Rufo, Iohanne de Wrocestre, W. de Munci, Elya Buckenell', Waltero de Banneburye et multis aliis.

*[a]*Roberti *repeated fo.21r.*

This charter was probably issued at the same time as no.337, and was certainly issued before 1231 (see note to no.337).

340. Hereford cathedral chapter dignitaries

Grant to the dignitaries of Hereford Cathedral and to the other beneficed clergy of the diocese of the right already held by the cathedral canons to a year's revenues from their dignities after their death or their transference to a religious order.   [27 October 1219 × 7 August 1234]

A = Hereford D & C Muniments, no.1165. No medieval endorsements. 175 × 78 + 13 mm. Sealed on a tag; seal: pointed oval, green wax, 73 or 74 × 46 mm. Figure of bishop, standing, left hand bearing staff, right hand raised in benediction. Two crescent moons to left. Legend: + HUGO . FOLIOT . DEI GRATI(A) (H)EREFORDENSIS EPISCOPUS. Counterseal: secretum: an antique gem, oval, 31 × 27 mm., with two figures, possibly Hercules (to right) and a giant. Legend: + SIGLLV' HUGONIS FOLIOT. The first O of Foliot is chipped.

Pd, *Hereford charters*, 47, and *Councils and Synods, II*, i.197-8.

Universis ad quos presens scriptum pervenerit. H. Foliot dei gratia Herefordensis episcopus salutem in domino. Ea que in pias causas conceduntur.' confovere et ampliare pium esse et deo credimus acceptabile. Cum igitur in diocesi nostra obtentum sit et a predecessoribus nostris confirmatum.'*a* ut canonici ecclesie nostre Herefordensis siu*b* decedentes siu*b* in religionem se transferentes ab illo.' tempore fructus prebendarum suarum integre percipiant per annum .' nos consilio virorum prudentum de consensu. capituli nostri Hereford' sacra approbante*c* sinodo idem beneficium in dignitatibus ecclesie nostre esse volumus et auctoritate pontificali confirmamus. Ita quidem quod in dignitatibus constituti post mutationem vite sue suprascriptam integre percipiant per annum exceptis hiis quorum dignitates pocius consistunt in iurisdictione quam in aliis. et exepta*d* sustentatione competenti ministrorum qui*e* officia dictarum dignitatum pro mortuis per annum execuntur. Clericis autem in diocesi nostra beneficiatis. indulgere dignum duximus ut quacumque parte anni siu*b* decedant.' siu*b* in religionem se transferant fructus laborum suorum de propria agricultura ecclesiastica per annum similiter integre percipiant.

*a*con- *of* confirmatum *over correction, A.* *b*sic, A. *c*b *of* approbante *over correction, A.* *d*sic, A. *e*corr. *from* quo *A.*

The arrangement whereby a year's prebendal revenue was granted to the estate of a deceased canon (usually termed the year of grace) seems to have emerged in Europe in the twelfth century, in several cases superseding earlier arrangements by which a year's revenue from a vacant prebend was paid to the fabric of the church or the common fund of the chapter. On this topic see E.Lesne, 'Les origines de la prébende', *Revue historique de droit français et étranger*, 4th ser., viii (1929), 271-2, and J.Barrow, 'Cathedrals, Provosts and Prebends', *Journal of Ecclesiastical History*, xxxvii (1986), 549.

341. Hereford cathedral chapter

Grant to Adam of Shrewsbury, his clerk and a canon of Hereford, and to Hereford cathedral chapter, of land at Gorwell and rents within and without Hereford, saving forty-three shillings and twopence reserved for the support of chaplains in St Catherine's chapel, Hereford, and a meadow to be held by Thomas of Gayton from Adam for three shillings a year, to augment Adam's prebend. [August 1230 × 7 August 1234]

A = Hereford D. & C. Muniments, no.2778. 15th-century endorsements: Episcopi Hugonis Foliot carta confirmationis et ordinationis terre prebendalis de Gorewelle et de xl tribus solidis et duobus denariis debitis annuatim capellanis Sancte Katerine Hereford'. 220 × 120 + 28 mm. Sealed on plaited yellow or green silk cords. Seal: pointed oval, unvarnished natural wax, 64 × 40 mm.; figure of a bishop, standing, holding staff in left hand and raising his right hand in benediction; two crescent moons to left. Legend: ....(O). FOLIOT DEI GRAT.................. EPISCOPUS. Counterseal: a seal *ad causas*: pointed oval, 55 × 35 mm; figure of a king standing on a pedestal, holding a palm in his right hand; two crescent moons on each side. Legend: +SAN(C)TUS ATHILBER.US REX ET MARTIR.

B = Hereford, Herefordshire County Record Office, Registrum Ricardi de Swinfield (formerly Hereford Diocesan Registry), fo.26r (fo.22r in old foliation). 1283-1317, here *c*.1285. C = Bodl. MS Rawlinson B329 (Hereford cathedral cartulary), inserted in bottom margins of fos.20v-21r in a hand different from that of the rest of this half of the MS. s.xv.

Pd from B, *Hereford charters*, 66-67, and *Reg. Swinfield*, 75.

Universis Cristi fidelibus ad quos presens scriptum pervenerit.*a* Hugo Foliot dei gratia Hereford' episcopus. salutem in domino. Noverit universitas vestra. nos dedisse. et concessisse et hac presenti carta nostra confirmasse in perpetuum Ade de Salop' clerico nostro canonico Hereford'. et omnibus successoribus suis canonicis ad emendationem prebende sue. a qua dudum terram Pyone. que ad eandem prebendam pertinebat separavimus. et capitulo nostro Hereford' contulimus totam terram de Gorwelle. et omnes redditus cum omnibus pertinentiis suis. tam in burgo Hereford'. quam extra. que Robertus Folet nobis reddidit. et quieta clamavit pro se et heredibus suis imperpetuum pro predicta terra Pyon'. quam eidem Roberto et heredibus suis dedimus et concessimus. tenendam de capitulo nostro Hereford'. sicut carta nostra eis inde confecta testatur preter quadraginta et tres sol'. et duos denarios quos assignavimus ad sustentationem capellanorum nostrorum deservientium in capella beate Katerine Hereford'. et preter quoddam pratum. quod Thomas de Gaitun' debet tenere de dicto Ada et successoribus suis canonicis pro tribus solidis annuatim persolvendis. tenend' et habend' predictis Ade et omnibus successoribus suis canonicis libere et quiete. integre. pacifice. et honorifice in pratis. pascuis. et pasturis. homagiis. releviis. eschaetis. et omnibus terre profectibus que^a de terra exeunt. vel exire poterunt sine aliquo retenemento ad opus nostrum vel successorum nostrorum. Dictus siquidem Adam pro se et pro omnibus successoribus suis. canonicis terram de Walintun' cum pertinentiis suis. quam dicte prebende sue quondam contulimus in excambium pro predicta terra Pyon'. quietam nobis reddidit. pro predicta terra de Gorwelle. quam predicte prebende cum pertinentiis suis dedimus sicut predictum est. Quod si memoratus Adam. vel aliquis successorum suorum terram prefatam de Walinton' tanquam ad prebendam prefatam pertinentem vendicare voluerit. et eam forte optinuerit.' volumus. quod dicta terra de Gorwelle cum omnibus pertinentiis suis revertatur in usus nostros et successorum nostrorum sicut eam prius habuimus in dominico. Nos vero et successores nostri totam predictam terram de Gorwelle cum omnibus redditibus predictis et omnibus pertinentiis suis sicut predictum est predicto Ade et successoribus suis canonicis contra omnes gentes warantizabimus. Et hanc quidem donationem et concessionem nostram ratam habentes et gratam. et permanere volentes inconcussam.' huic scripto sigillum nostrum et sigillum capituli nostri apponi fecimus. Hiis testibus. Domino Th' Foliot thesaurario Hereford'. Stephano Banastr' eiusdem loci canonico. Magistro. Willelmo Platun. et Iohanne Bacun. Ada de Ledeb'. Iohanne de Ros. Godef' de Merkel' clericis. Waltero de Par'. Waltero camerario. Waltero Clement'. Waltero Muchegros. Iohanne Sprengehos' et aliis.

^{a}*sic for* qui *A.*

Thomas Foliot's predecessor as treasurer, Elias de Radnor, was elected bp of Llandaff shortly before 30 August 1230; cf. *Cal. Pat. Rolls*, ii.394. For the grant to Thomas de Gayton, see no.367 below.

342. Hereford cathedral chapter

Notification that he has granted the hospital which he founded at Ledbury under the Malvern Hills to Hereford cathedral chapter and arrangements for a chantry in it.   Sunday 13 March 1233

> A = Hereford D. & C. Muniments, no.1389. 13th-century endorsement: Ordinacio hospitalis de Ledebur' facta per H. Foliot episcopum. 14th-15th century endorsement: J Perche (with notarial mark). 151 × 145 mm. Originally sealed on tags; seals and tags missing: slits for three seals survive.
>
> B = Hereford, Herefordshire County Record Office, Registrum Ricardi de Swinfield (formerly Hereford Diocesan Registry), fo.20r-v (fos.16r-v in old foliation). 1283-1317, here 1285 or just after. C = Bodl. MS Rawlinson B329 (Hereford cathedral cartulary), fo.153v. s.xiii-xiv. D = Hereford D. & C. Muniments, no.1808. 16th-17th century transcript.
>
> Pd, *Hereford charters*, 70-71.

Omnibus Cristi fidelibus ad quos presens scriptum pervenerit. Hugo Foliot. dei gratia Hereford' episcopus ∴ salutem in domino. Cum tranquillitatis et securitatis acta benigno sint amplexanda favore∴ universitati vestre significamus∴ quod nos pacis et securitatis domus hospitalis Ledebir' sub Malvernia affectantes remedium. dedimus et concessimus dilectis in Cristo filiis decano et capitulo Hereford' liberam dispositionem dicti hospitalis cum pertinentiis sine aliquo retenemento nobis. vel successoribus nostris in dicto hospitali habendo. Idem vero decanus et capitulum percipient in perpetuum quadraginta solidos annuos de dicto hospitali. et omnia bona residua que nunc idem hospitale optinent. vel in futuro optinere poterit∴ cedent in pios usus pauperum. et languidorum in eodem hospitali iacentium. Decedentibus vero fratribus eiusdem hospitalis∴ dicti decanus et capitulum habeant in perpetuum liberam potestatem alios substituere. et secundum voluntatem eorum de omnibus in dicta domo disponere sine contradictione cuiuslibet. Ita quod in nullos alios usus nisi in usus pauperum et languidorum res dicte domus commutabunt. et omnes res. iura et possessiones servabunt. et manutenebunt. et contra omnes viriliter pro posse suo defendent. Si vero tractu temporis deo dante creverint facultatem dicti hospitalis. et suffecerint ad sustentationem duorum capellanorum erunt ibi duo capellani in perpetuum. quorum unus celebrabit divina pro anima nostra et predecessorum et successorum nostrorum et canonicorum Hereford'. et omnium fidelium defunctorum. et alius celebrabit divina pro vivis. et omnibus benefactoribus dicti hospitalis. Decedente vero aliquo canonico Hereford'? uterque capellanus faciet unum tercenale pro anima decedentis. sicut consuevit fieri in maiori ecclesia Hereford'. Nos vero de consensu capituli et de consilio proborum virorum et discretorum publice et sollempniter excommunicavimus omnes illos. qui aliquo tempore in posterum contra predictam ordinationem nostram venerint. vel res. et possessiones diminuerint. vel in aliquo subtrahere. vel commutare presumpserint contra predictam ordinationem nostram. Et hoc fecimus sollempniter convocato clero et populo in maiori ecclesia Hereford' die dominica proxima post festum Sancti Gregorii. Anno gratie millesimo. ducentesimo. tricesimo secundo. Hiis testibus. deo. clero. et populo ad hoc convocato. et capitulo Hereford'. cuius sigillum ad maiorem securitatem presenti scripto est appositum.

Hugh Foliot founded Ledbury Hospital before 1231 (see no.348), probably inspired by the example of Canon Elias de Bristol, who had founded St Ethelbert's hospital in Hereford c.1225; see no.344.

343. Hereford cathedral chapter

Grant of five marks, from the revenue of 100s which he was awarded from the church of Bockleton in the king's court, to endow two chaplains in the chapel of St Catherine's, Hereford, who are to be appointed and supervised by the dean and chapter; out of the remaining two and a half marks two marks are to be distributed to the cathedral canons and half to the clerks of the choir on the anniversary of Hugh's death; Hugh also grants to the chaplains an annual payment of four marks from the church of Presteigne, a rent of 43s. 2d. from Aylestone, and various smaller rents.
                              Sunday 14 March 1232 or 13 March 1233

A = Hereford D. & C. Muniments, no.2098. Late 13th/early 14th century endorsement: Ordinatio capelle Sancte Katerine facta per H. Folioth episcopum. 14th? century notarial sign. 237 × 118 + 22 mm. Sealed with two seals on tags. Left seal: pointed oval, green wax, 56 × 42 mm., badly damaged, with figure of bishop; legend illegible. Counterseal: a seal *ad causas* with figure of a king bearing a palm. Legend: ..ANCTUS ATHILBERTUS REX ET MARTIR. Right seal: much damaged pointed oval, green wax, 60 × 52 mm.; Hereford dean and chapter seal depicting cathedral; legend broken off. Counterseal: pointed oval, 40 × 30 mm., with seated figure, crowned, bearing staff (sceptre?) in left hand, ? orb in right. Legend: +SIGILLUM CAPI.UL' HEREFORDIE.

B = Bodl., MS Rawlinson B329 (Hereford cathedral cartulary), fos.52v-53r. s.xv.

Pd, *Hereford charters*, 71-72.

Universis Cristi fidelibus ad quos presens scriptum pervenerit.' Hugo Foliot dei gratia Hereford' episcopus.' salutem in domino. Noverit universitas vestra. quod nos divina gratia inspirante. quedam de bonis nobis a deo collatis provida consideratione et diligentia nostra mediante adquisitis volentes in pios usus convertere.' disposuimus. concessimus et assignavimus duobus capellanis in perpetuum divina celebrantibus in propriis personis. et non per alios in capella beate Katerine Hereford' pro anima nostra. et predecessorum et successorum nostrorum. et canonicorum Hereford' et omnium fidelium vivorum ac mortuorum quinque marcas de redditu centum solidorum. quem per finalem concordiam in curia domini regis factam adquisivimus de ecclesia de Boclinton' in perpetuum percipiendum iuxta formam cyrographi super hoc confecti in dicta curia et de residuo illius redditus assignavimus capitulo Hereford' duas marcas annuas in perpetuum percipiendas die obitus nostri. et de eodem redditu assignavimus pauperibus clericis de choro*a* Hereford' dimidiam marcam die obitus nostri in perpetuum percipiendam. Preterea. abbas et conventus de Wigemor' divino intuitu concesserunt nobis redditum quatuor marcarum in perpetuum percipiendum de ecclesia sua de Presthemed'. et eundem redditum plene et integre assignavimus dictis capellanis personaliter in dicta capella ministrantibus cum tribus marcis. et tribus solidis. et duobus denariis annuis de redditu quinque marcarum. et quinque solidorum. quem adquisivimus de Roberto Folet. scilicet apud Eilnethestan. De Edrico filio Rogeri.' septem sol'. et tres den'. De Waltero Wardebois.' quatuor sol'. octo denar'. et ob'. De Waltero molendinario. tres sol'. et undecim den'. De Willelmo filio Radulfi. et Rogero fratre eius.' unam marcam. et unum denarium. De Ernaldo piscatore.' duos solidos. decem denarios. et obolum. De Waltero Belle. sexdecim denarios. De Hamone Iudeo.' sexdecim denarios. De Editha Nunna.' octo denarios. De Nicholao cantore.' decem et octo denarios. De Iohanne coco.' sex

solidos. et duos denarios. Decedentibus vero capellanis dicte capelle.ᵃ
dicti decanus et capitulum habeant in perpetuum liberam potestatem
alios substituere. et secundum voluntatem eorum de omnibus in dicta
capella disponere sine contradictione cuiuslibet. Ita quod in nullos
alios usus. nisi in usus capellanorum ibi ministrantium res. vel possessiones dicte capelle commutabunt. et omnes res. iura. et possessiones dicte capelle servabunt. et manutenebunt. et contra omnes
viriliter pro posse suo defendent. Et idem decanus et capitulum
omnes oblationes. et quoscumque proventus dicebant sibi competere
in dicta capella ⸴ ad fabricam dicte capelle remiserunt. et quietos in
perpetuum clamaverunt. Si vero tractu temporis creverint facultates.
et suffecerint ad sustentationem trium capellanorum⸴ erunt ibi tres
capellani in perpetuum. quorum duo celebrabunt divina pro anima
nostra et predecessorum et successorum nostrorum⸴ et canonicorum
Hereford' et omnium fidelium defunctorum. et tertius celebrabit de
die. Decedente vero aliquo canonico Hereford'⸴ tricenale fiet pro
anima decedentis in dicta capella. sicut consuevit fieri in maiori
ecclesia Hereford'. Nos vero de consensu capituli et de consilio proborum virorum et discretorum publice et sollempniter excommunicavimus omnes illos qui aliquo tempore in posterum contra predictam
ordinationem nostram venerint. vel res et possessiones diminuerint.
vel in aliquo subtrahere. vel commutare presumpserint contra predictam ordinationem nostram. Et hoc fecimus sollempniter convocato clero et populo in maiori ecclesia Hereford' die dominica proxima
post festum Sancti Gregorii anno gratie millesimo. ducentesimo tricesimo secundo. Hiis testibus. deo. clero. et populo ad hoc convocato.
et capitulo Hereford'. cuius sigillum ad maiorem securitatem et evi-
dentiam presenti scripto est appositum.

ᵃchoro *repeated and corrected by mark in margin A.*

St Catherine's chapel was one of two episcopal chapels which formed a two-storey
church probably built by Robert of Lotharingia. The other chapel, St Mary
Magdalen's, had been granted to the cathedral chapter by Bp William de Vere (see
no.198). The two chapels stood between the cathedral cloister and the episcopal
palace and were demolished, apart from one wall, in the eighteenth century: on
them, see N.Drinkwater, 'Hereford cathedral: the bishop's chapel of St Katherine
and St Mary Magdalene', *Archaeological Journal*, cxi (1954), 129-137, and
R.Gem, 'The Bishop's Chapel at Hereford: the rôles of patron and craftsman', in
S.Macready and F.H.Thompson, edd. *Art and Patronage in the English Romanesque* (Society of Antiquaries Occasional Papers, N.S. viii (1986), 87-96.

344. Hereford, St Ethelbert's hospital

Grant of an indulgence of twenty days to all benefactors of St Ethelbert's Hospital, Hereford.

Dated 1231 [25 December 1230 × 24 March 1232].

A = Hereford D & C Muniments, no.1388. No medieval endorsements. 289 × 118 + 21 mm. Sealed on loosely plaited green silk cords; seal: green wax, pointed oval, 66 × 43 mm. Figure of bishop, standing, bearing staff in left hand and raising right hand in benediction. Legend: ...UGO..OLIO................OR-DENSIS EPISCOPUS. Counterseal: a seal *ad causas*: pointed oval, 55 × 35 mm., with figure of king (St Ethelbert), standing, bearing palm in right hand; legend: +...ANCTUS ATHIL.........ET MARTIR.

Pd, *Hereford charters*, 67.

Hugo Foliot dei gratia Hereford' episcopus archidiaconis. decanis. personis. vicariis. et universis tam clericis quam laicis in episcopatu Hereford' constitutis.' eternam in domino salutem. Quoniam ut ait apostolus omnes stabimus ante tribunal Cristi.[1] recepturi prout in corpore gessimus sive bonum fuerit.' sive malum. oportet nos diem messionis extreme misericordie operibus prevenire.' ac eternorum intuitu seminare in terris quod reddente Domino cum multiplicato fructu colligere valeamus in celis. Cum igitur ad sustentationem pauperum et egenorum ad elemosinariam Dei et beate Marie et Sancti Ethelberti Hereford' confluentium proprie non suppetant facultates.' universitatem vestram monemus in domino. et in remissione peccatorum vestrorum iniungimus vobis. quatinus de bonis vobis a deo collatis.' pias elemosinas et grata dicte domui karitatis subsidia erogare curetis. ut per subventionem elemosinarum vestrarum pauperum ibidem confluentium inopie consulatur.' Nos autem de misericordia Dei confisi omnibus qui elemosinas aliquas dicte domui karitative erogaverint de iniuncta sibi penitencia pro peccatis de quibus vere fuerint contriti et confessi auctoritate nobis a Deo commissa. viginti dies relaxamus. tanto audacius maiorem indulgentiam dicte domui concedendo. cum constet a dicta domo plures pauperes sustentari. Actum. Incarnationis Domini. Millesimo. Ducentesimo. Tricesimo Primo. anno.

[1] Rom. 14[10].

The hospital of St Ethelbert was founded by Elias de Bristol, a canon of Hereford, in Hereford, *c.*1225, and was put under the supervision of Hereford cathedral chapter from its foundation. D.Whitehead has recently shown that the original site of the hospital lay in a corner of the cathedral graveyard, abutting on to Broad Street: 'St Ethelbert's Hospital, Hereford: its architecture and setting', *Transactions of the Woolhope Naturalists' Field Club*, xlv (1986), 415-25. As shown by C.R.Cheney, *English Bishops' Chanceries* (Manchester 1950), 76-77, the *arenga* is taken from one in an indulgence issued by Archbishop Stephen Langton for the hospital in August 1226 (pd, *Acta Stephani Langton*, ed. K.Major, Canterbury and York Society, 1950, 109, no.90, and *Hereford charters*, 61). Stephen was using the formula laid down for such indulgences by Innocent III at the Fourth Lateran Council (ch.62): see *Extra* V 38.14 (cols.888-889).

345. St Guthlac's priory, Hereford

Notification that Walter de Mucegros, knight, has in his presence quit-claimed all his rights to two mills, one on the Wye beneath Hereford Castle, and the other at Eign, to the prior and monks of St Guthlac's, Hereford. [26 November 1220 × August 1224]

B = Oxford, Balliol College, MS 271 (cartulary of St Guthlac's, Hereford), fo.73v, no.310. s.xiv in.

Universis Cristi fidelibus ad quos presens scriptum pervenerit Hugo Foliot dei gratia Herefordensis episcopus salutem in domino. Noverit universitas vestra quod Walterus de Muchegros, miles, in nostra presentia constitutus pro deo et salute anime sue et Ivete uxoris sue et Milonis filii sui et pro animabus antecessorum et successorum remisit et quietumclamavit pro se et heredibus suis imperpetuum priori et conventui Hereford' totum ius et clamium quod habuit vel habere potuit in duobus molendinis cum pertinentiis suis sitis suburbio Hereford', quorum unum est iuxta ripam Waye sub castro Hereford', alterum vero supra[a] Yene extra portam occidentalem Hereford'. \Cartam/ quam de dictis molendinis habuit coram nobis dicto priori et conventui liberavit. In huius quidem rei testimonium ad instantiam dicti Walteri de Muchegros presenti scripto sigillum nostrum apponere curavimus. Hiis testibus, Magistro Roberto Haket, Ada de Salop', Magistro Willelmo Plat', Ricardo Suk' milite, Rogero de Bartes, Thoma de Gayton, Ada clerico de prioratu et aliis.

[a] *or* citra *(?) B*

For the dating see no.371 below. The two charters have very similar witness lists and must have been issued simultaneously as two parts of a single agreement. Richard Suk' is presumably in error for Richard Fulk'. The mills are Eign Gate

Mill and Castle Mill : see maps in M. Lobel, 'Hereford', in eadem, ed. *Historic Towns*, i.

346. St Guthlac's priory, Hereford

Notification that Prior Jocelin and the monks of St Guthlac's, Hereford, have granted, with the consent of Abbot Thomas of Gloucester, the tithes of the demesne of Sutton St Michael to Bernard the clerk, and grant of a licence to appropriate the tithes after Bernard's death.

[August 1224 × 1228]

B = Oxford, Balliol College, MS 271 (cartulary of St Guthlac's Hereford), fo.87v, no.384. s.xiv in.

Universis Cristi fidelibus presentes literas inspecturis H. dei gratia Herefordensis episcopus salutem et benedictionem. Quoniam dies hominum breves sunt et eorum memoria labilis, volumus ut ea que temporibus nostris et in presentia nostra canonice acta sunt perpetue firmitatis robur optineant. Quocirca discretioni vestre et universitati duximus significandum dilectos filios Iocelinum priorem et conventum Hereford' assensu domini Thome abbatis Glouc' concessisse Bernardo clerico nostro decimas eorum de dominico Maioris*a* Sutton ad ipsorum monasterium Hereford' pertinentes tenendas de eis ad firmam pro xv s. eis annuatim solvendis. Concedimus etiam et episcopali auctoritate confirmamus ut cum de dicto B. humanitus contigerit dicte decime in proprios usus dictorum prioris et conventus pro voluntate eorum libere et sine aliqua contradictione revertantur, non obstante quod Magister Simon de Fraxino predecessor dicti B. dictas decimas de dictis priore et conventu ad firmam tenuit. Quod ne inposterum alicui vertatur in dubium presenti scripto sigilli nostri et capituli nostri attestatione roborare curavimus. Valete.

*a*Moris *B*.

Thomas de Breda was abbot of Gloucester between August 1224 and 1228. Master Simon de Freine was a canon of Hereford. For the dates of Joscelin, prior of St Guthlac's, see no.371.

347. John of Hidcote, clerk

Inspeximus of grant by Hugh de Mapenore to John of Hidcote, clerk.

[27 October 1219 × -1231]

B = Hereford, Herefordshire County Record Office, Registrum Ade de Orleton (formerly Hereford Diocesan Registry), fo.39r. 1317–1327. Heading: Sequitur confirmatio eiusdem facta per dominum Hugonem Foliot quondam episcopum Heref'.

Pd, *Reg. Orleton*, 141-2.

Universis sancte matris ecclesie filiis ad quos presens scriptum pervenerit Hugo Foliot divina miseratione Hereford' ecclesie minister humilis eternam in domino salutem. Cartam bo(ne) me(morie) H. de Mapenobr' predecessoris nostri inspeximus in hec verba. Omnibus sancte matris ecclesie filiis etc ut supra.[a] Nos igitur eandem donationem et concessionem approbantes et ratam habentes eam presenti scripto et sigilli nostri munimine confirmamus. Insuper etiam concessimus et dedimus prefato Iohanni clerico de Hudecote unam acram versus prioratum que vocatur quinque sellionum in eschambium pro quodam mesuagio in Yyene quod idem I. tenuit ex concessione predicti H. predecessoris nostri. Hiis testibus, Roberto le Poher seneschallo, magistris Iohanne de Wrocestr' et W. de Muncy, Ricardo capellano de Prestebur', Waltero de Parys, Waltero de Hop', Ada[b] clerico et aliis.

[a] *text of Hugh de Mapenore's charter om. B.*   [b] Adam B.

Robert le Poher ceased to be Hugh Foliot's steward some time before 1231. Hugh de Mapenore's charter is above, no.299.

348. St Katharine's hospital, Ledbury

Foundation charter of St Katharine's hospital, Ledbury, confirming Walter de Lacy's grant of the churches of Weston Beggard (after the death of Thomas, dean of Weston), and Yarkhill (after the death of Moses, rector of Yarkhill) and Geoffrey de Longchamp's grant of Kempley (after the death of Robert, dean of Kempley).

[27 October 1219 × 1231, late]

B = Hereford D. & C. Muniments, no.2175, in original inspeximus of Dean Thomas and Hereford Chapter, with the same dating limits as Hugh Foliot's charter. C = Hereford, Herefordshire County Record Office, Registrum Ricardi de Swinfield (formerly Hereford Diocesan Registry), fo.20r (fo.16r in old foliation), 1283-1317, here s.xiii ex., in inspeximus of Dean Thomas and Hereford Chapter. D = Bodl. MS Rawlinson B329 (Hereford cathedral cartulary), membrane inserted between fos.153v and 154r, s.xiii ex., contained in inspeximus of Dean Thomas and Hereford Chapter. E = PRO, C66/169, membr. 21 (Patent Roll, 2 Edward III, 1328), in inspeximus of Dean Thomas and Hereford Chapter contained in an inspeximus of Edward III, dated York, 30 February (sic).

Pd from C, *Hereford charters*, 68-70, and *Reg. Swinfield*, 51-52; from E, *Mon. Ang.* vi, pt. ii, 685-6; cal., *Cal. Pat. Rolls, 1327-30*, 245. Since C, D, and E are all direct copies of B, the text below is taken from B, without variants from C, D, or E.

Universis Cristi fidelibus presens scriptum inspecturis Hugo Foliot divina miseratione Hereford' ecclesie minister humilis salutem in domino. Ex commissi nobis officii sollicitudine tenemur ea que divinis locis collatione fidelium mancipantur ut firmam stabilitatem sortiantur episcopalis auctoritatis diligentia roborare. Et quia iuxta est dies perditionis et adesse festinant tempora[1] desiderantibus bona domini in terra viventium[2] necesse est intelligere super egenum et pauperem[3] ut, propter peccata nostra, quibus iram meruimus, positi quasi signum ad sagittam[4] fugere valeamus a facie arcus[5] scelera[a] peregrinationis nostre elemosinarum largitione redimentes. Dum enim per vite presentis lubrica periculose transimus in terris sub securitate per manus egentium pie largita collocamus in celis. Preter elemosinam enim sola[b] nichil ex hac vita portabimus, sed illam per manus pauperum feliciter in celum premittimus. Attendentes igitur inter hec et cetera opera misericordie hospitalitati fere nichil esse preferendum, et tantam eius gratiam quod Loth et Abraham qui homines consueverunt etiam angelos hospitari meruerunt, ipsos etiam tanta mercede remuneratos, quod alter subversionem Sodome evasit et alter ex coniuge sterili filium habere promeruit,[6] hospitale quoddam ad peregrinos et pauperes suscipiendos apud Ledebir' sub Malvernia construximus ad honorem dei et sancte Katerine virginis et omnia pia devotione fidelium eidem hospitali et aliis ibidem deo deservientibus collata vel futuris temporibus conferenda episcopali auctoritate duximus confirmare. Et precipue ex concessione nobis et preclari viri domini Walteri de Lacy ecclesiam de Westun' in usus proprios post decessum Thome decani de Westun' rectoris eiusdem ecclesie convertendam de qua idem Thomas unam libram incensi eidem hospitali annuatim interveniente auctoritate episcopali nomine pensionis persolvit. Et ecclesiam de Kenepeleyh' ex concessione nobilis viri domini Galfridi de Longo Campo post decessum Roberti decani rectoris eiusdem ecclesie qui unam libram incensi nomine pensionis annuatim similiter exsolvit. Et ecclesiam de Yarhull' ex concessione predicti domini Walteri de Lacy post decessum Moysi rectoris eiusdem ecclesie. qui etiam unam libram incensi nomine pensionis annuatim eidem hospitali exsolvit, salvis in predictis ecclesiis debitis consuetudinibus tam episcopalibus quam archidiaconalibus.[c] Preterea dedimus et concessimus ad fundandum idem hospitale duo burgagia in villa de Ledebir', scilicet unum burgagium et dimidium quod emimus de Iohanne filio Gersante, reddendo per annum episcopo decem et octo denarios, et dimidium burgagium quod emimus de Margareta filia Gileberti Franceis, reddendo annuatim sex denarios et unum burgagium in novo vico quod emimus de Roberto de Staninges, reddendo per annum duodecim denarios, nec eadem burgagia umquam magis reddiderunt episcopo. Et quicumque idem hospitale beneficiis et gratia fovere curaverint gratiam divinam et eterne retributionis premia consequantur, et qui contra hoc aliquid attemptare presumpserint, indignatione dei omnipotentis involvantur, nisi celeriter resipiscant. Et ut hec omnia maiori et perpetua gaudeant firmitate invocata gratia et presentia altissimi et precelse genitricis eiusdem et omnium celestium virtutum presenti scripto sigillum nostrum apposuimus. Hiis testibus, Thoma decano Hereford' et eiusdem loci capitulo.

[1]Deut. 32[35].   [2]Ps. 26[13].
[3]Ps. 40[2].   [4]Threni 3[12].
[5]Ps. 59[6].   [6]Gen. 18-19.
[a]celera B.   [b]corr. from solam B.   [c]arch'alibus B.

Dean Thomas de Bosbury died in 1231. Ledbury Hospital was probably founded not long before 1230, in imitation of Canon Elias de Bristol's foundation of St Ethelbert's Hospital in Hereford (see above, no.344); for Ledbury Hospital's subsequent history, see J.G.Hillaby, *The book of Ledbury* (Buckingham 1982), 60-7. Walter de Lacy also granted the advowson of the church of Yarkhill to Ralph de Toeny in marriage with his daughter Petronilla, and it was the subject of a dispute in 1253 (PRO, JUST.I/615 m.46d). I am grateful to David Crouch for this information.

349. Leominster priory

Mandate to the archdeacons, rural deans, and priests in the diocese of Hereford to excommunicate anyone who harms the property of Leominster priory.   [27 October 1219 × 7 August 1234]

B = BL Cotton MS Dom. A iii (Leominster priory cartulary), fo.69r-v (fos.67r-v old foliation). s.xiii med.

H. Foliot Heref' episcopus omnibus archidiaconis, decanis et presbiteris in Heref' episcopatu constitutis salutem. Auctoritate qua
fungimur vobis in vi obedientie precipimus quatinus statim ex quo
querimonia monachorum de Leom' super rebus eorum ablatis et
possessionibus suis turbatis vel ob iniuriam sibi vel hominibus suis
illatam delata fuerit, nisi satisfacere voluerint, auctoritate nostra
[fo.69v] omni occasione et dilatione postposita sollempniter omnes
illos malefactores, cum vobis nominati fuerint, candelis accensis,
excommunicetis et tanquam excommunicatos in quacumque parrochia fuerint ab omnibus usque ad condignam ablatorum satisfactionem cautius vitari precipiatis et dum moram ibi fecerint divina
celebrari ibidem prohibeatis. Valete.

350. Leominster priory

*Inspeximus of a licence issued by Hugh de Mapenore to Leominster priory
(no.301) to appropriate the chapel of Ford.*

[27 October 1219 × 7 August 1234]

B = BL Cotton MS Dom. A iii (Leominster priory cartulary), fos.68v-69r
(fos.66v-67r old foliation). s.xiii med. Rubric: Confirmatio eiusdem[1] de capella
de Ford.

Omnibus et cetera.[a] Noverit universitas vestra nos cartam predecessoris nostri H. bone memorie quondam Heref' episcopi inspexisse sub
hac forma. Omnibus et cetera.[a] Quoniam religiosorum loca et cetera
usque in finem require in ultima pagina precedentis folii.[b] Nos igitur
venerabilis predicti predecessoris nostri vestigiis adherentes dictam
concessionem de capella [fo.69r] de Ford' in usus proprios domui
Leom' perpetuo possidenda cum omnibus pertinentiis suis ratam
habentes, eam presenti scripto et sigilli nostri appositione confirmavimus. Testibus.[c]

[a]*sic B.* [b]*Text of Hugh de Mapenore's charter omitted B.* [c]*Names of witnesses omitted B.*
[1]Reference to Hugh Foliot who issued the two charters immediately preceding this one in
the cartulary.

351. Leominster priory

Inspeximus of the licence to appropriate Eye church granted by Hugh de Mapenore to Leominster priory.   [27 October 1219 × 7 August 1234]

> B = BL Cotton MS Dom. A iii (Leominster priory cartulary), fo.68v (fo.66v old foliation). s.xiii med. Rubric: Confirmatio eiusdem super ecclesia de Eya in proprios usus.

Universis et cetera.*a* Ad universitatis vestre volumus notitiam pervenire nos predecessoris nostri H. bone memorie quondam Heref' episcopi cartam sigillis ipsius et capituli Heref' sigillatam inspexisse sub hac forma. Omnibus et cetera usque in finem. Require in prima pagina precedentis folii.*a* Nos igitur prenominati venerabilis predecessoris nostri vestigiis adherentes suprascriptam ipsius et capituli Hereford' concessionem et confirmationem ratam habentes, eam presenti scripto et sigilli nostri patrocinio confirmare curavimus. T'.*b*

a sic B.   *b Witness list om. B.*

> The *eiusdem* in the rubric refers to Hugh Foliot, who issued the charter immediately preceding it in the cartulary (no.352 below). For Hugh de Mapenore's charter, see no.309; it is printed by B.R.Kemp, 'Hereditary benefices in the medieval English church: a Herefordshire example', *BIHR*, xliii (1970), 13.

352. Leominster priory

Confirmation of acta of Richard de Capella, Gilbert Foliot, Giles de Braose and Hugh de Mapenore confirming that Reading Abbey owns Leominster Priory and its associated chapels.
[27 October 1219 × 7 August 1234]

> B = BL Cotton MS Dom. A iii (Leominster priory cartulary), fo.68r-v (fos.66r-v old foliation). s.xiii med.

Universis sancte matris ecclesie filiis H. Foliot Heref' episcopus in d(omino)*a* salutem. Venerabilium predecessorum nostrorum Ricardi, G., E. et Hugonis quondam Hereford' episcoporum vestigiis adherentes, ea que ecclesie Rading' concesserunt et confirmaverunt nos eorundem concessionem et confirmationem ratam habentes presentis instrumenti testimonio et sigilli nostri patrocinio ecclesie Rad-

ing' confirmamus, scilicet ecclesiam sancti Petri de Lemen' cum omni
ad ipsam [fo.68v] pertinente parrochia, scilicet de Bradeford', et de
Ach', et de Leena, et de Diliga prima et secunda que ambe magis
proxime sunt Leom', et de Lunteleg', et de Kinardel', et de Winnet',
et de utraque Sarnesfeld', et de Titelleg' et de Munkelen', de Hopa
quoque et de Wavert', et de Newet', et de Gatredehop', de Stok'
quoque et de utraque Hethfeld', et de Risebir', et Humbr', et Ged-
defenn, et Butterleg', et Bradefeld, et utraque Hamt', et Forda, et
Henoura, et Eatun', et Heant', et Stoctun' quoque et Estun', et
Brumfeld, et Uptun', et Midlint', et Dreitun', et Hamenesse, et
Whyale, et Putlesd', et Brocmant', et Forde, de Lustun' quoque et
Eya et Crofta, concedentes et auctoritate episcopali confirmantes
ecclesie de Rading' et monachis ibidem deo servientibus totam et
integram dictam ecclesiam beati Petri de Leom', cum capellis, cimiteriis, pensionibus, decimis, obventionibus, possessionibus, et omnibus ad eandem ecclesiam de Leom' pertinentibus, salva Heref'
ecclesie dignitate et canonica iustitia unicuique exhibenda. Testibus.[b]

[a]*sic for* eternam in domino ? B.   [b]*Witnesses' names om. B.*

See nos.11, 111 (*GFL* no.343), 268 and 300.

353. Leominster priory

*Inspeximus of charter of Adam, abbot of Reading, granting the vicarage
of the Holy Cross, Leominster, to Henry of Burton, and arranging the
endowment of the vicarage and the pension (half a mark per annum) which
is to be paid to Reading; Henry may receive one penny and no more for
each mass, reasonable dues for burials, all bread and ale offered by the
faithful of Leominster and Hope-under-Dinmore, fees for trentals and
confession in Lent and pennies for marriages offered on the book at the
priory door. He is also to receive 40s. annually from Reading's income
from Leominster.*   [1226 × 7 August 1234]

B = BL MS Egerton 3031 (Reading abbey cartulary), fo.11v, here s.xiii in. C =
BL Cotton MS Dom. A iii (Leominster priory cartulary), fo.69r (fo.67r old
foliation), s.xiii med.

Pd, *Reading Cartularies*, i. 295-6, no.364.

Adam was elected abbot of Reading in 1226.

*354. Lire abbey

*Confirmation of a charter of Hugh de Mapenore confirming the posses-
sions of the abbey of Lire in the diocese of Hereford; Hugh Foliot excludes
from his confirmation the church of Lydney which Hereford Cathedral
Chapter was claiming.*   [27 October 1219 × 7 August 1234]

Survives only in summarised form, Evreux, A-D Eure, H590 (inventory of Lire
abbey cartulary), fo.326v, no.xxviii (4), s.xviii, within a summary of an inspeximus
issued by Bp Peter of Aigueblanche in the 1260s (the compiler of the cartulary
could not read the end of the date): 'une autre chartre de Hugues Foliot, qui
confirme la precedente, a l'exception de l'Eglise de L'Indenaye, sur laquelle le
Chapitre de L'Indenaye (*sic for* de Hereford) avoit des pretentions; conservant
toutesfois a l'abbaye, dans ladite paroisse et dans celle de St Brevelay, tous ses
revenus en terres et en hommes'.

For Hereford cathedral chapter's claims to Lydney parish church and the chapel
of St Briavel's, see Bodl. MS Rawlinson B329, fos.161r, 165v-168r, and see above,
nos.163, 221. Hugh de Mapenore's confirmation is no.305.

355. Llanthony priory

*Confirmation to Llanthony priory of the right to graze eight oxen in the
episcopal manor of Prestbury.*   [August 1230 × 7 August 1234]

B = PRO C115, K1/6679 (Llanthony cartulary, A9), fo.116v, s.xiii med. C = PRO
C115, K2/6683 (Llanthony cartulary, A1), fo.123v, sect. VI, no.xxx, s.xiv med.
D = Ibid., fo.123v, section vi, no.31, in an inspeximus by Bp Ralph de
Maidstone. E = PRO C115, L1/6689 (Llanthony cartulary, A4), fo.127v,
section no.cii, s.xv. The text is here taken from E.

Universis Cristi fidelibus ad quos presens scriptum pervenerit Hugo
Foliot dei gratia Hereford' episcopus salutem in domino. Noverit
universitas vestra nos divine pietatis intuitu concessisse et hac presenti carta nostra confirmasse dilectis in Cristo priori et conventui
Lanthon' iuxta Gloucestr'^{a} quod habeant imperpetuum^b in parco
nostro et pratis et pasturis in manerio nostro de Presteb' octo boves
euntes cum bobus nostris et successorum nostrorum libere et sine
omni calumpnia, contradictione, et impedimento,^{c} et aliqua vexatione. Quod quia ratum et ^{d}stabile volumus permanere,^{e} presenti id
scripto \et/ sigilli nostri munimine confirmavimus. Hiis^{de} testibus,
Magistro Th. Foliot, thesaurario Hereford', Th. Foliot, persona de

Westbur', *f*Waltero de Banneb',*g* Ada de Salop', canonicis Hereford', Ada de Ledeb', persona de Stanton, Magistro Willelmo Platun, Hugone de Hop', Godefrido clerico, Petro tunc ballivo de Presteb'*fg* et aliis.

*a*Glouc', *BC*.   *b*inperpetuum, *BC*.   *c*impedimen, *C*.   *d-d*cetera, *BC*.
*e-e*om., *D*.   *f-f*om., *BC*.   *g-g*om., *D*.

Adam of Shrewsbury only became a canon after Thomas Foliot became cathedral treasurer (not before August 1230). This charter and the inspeximus issued by Bp Ralph de Maidstone (1234-9) are mentioned in a settlement, dated Hereford, 1 March 1290, between Bp Richard de Swinfield and the prior and convent of Lanthony by Gloucester (*Reg. Swinfield*, 232-3), according to the terms of which the canons of Lanthony quitclaimed their right of pasturage at Prestbury in return for other pasture and handed over Hugh Foliot and Ralph de Maidstone's confirmations to Bp Richard. The original, in a rather garbled form, must have been copied into B before this happened, and C, here as elsewhere, is a direct copy of B. D, a much later witness than B but with a fuller text, must presumably have been copied from another copy of the original kept at Lanthony by Gloucester.

*356. The bishop of London (Roger Niger)

Litterae excusatoriae addressed to the bishop of London and to his fellow bishops on the occasion of the consecration at Canterbury of Master Edmund of Abingdon as archbishop of Canterbury.   [March 1234]

Mention only, in a document issued on 2 April 1234, the day of the consecration, to record the proceedings and the names of those attending: *Early Charters of the Cathedral Church of St Paul, London*, ed. M. Gibbs, Camden 3rd ser., lviii (1939), 140-2, no.182. It states that the bps of Hereford and Lincoln addressed their *litterae excusatoriae* to the bp of London and the other bishops while the other absentees addressed their letters to the archbp-elect and the other bps. All the letters were read aloud by Peter, precentor of St Paul's, and handed over to Master R. de Gloucester, official of the archdn of Canterbury, before the consecration actually took place.

357. Matthew the cook

Grant to Matthew the cook of land at Colcombe which had been granted by Bishop Giles de Braose to Richard de Kent, sold by Richard to Hugh Foliot, granted by Hugh Foliot to Walter of Hope and then resigned by Walter to Hugh Foliot.   [27 October 1219 × August 1230]

B = PRO C115 K2/6683 (Llanthony cartulary A1), fo.128r, section vi, no.52. s.xiv med.

Omnibus sancte matris ecclesie filiis presens scriptum inspecturis H.Foliot divina permissione Hereford' ecclesie minister humilis salutem in domino. Noverit universitas vestra nos dedisse et concessisse Matheo coco pro homagio et servitio suo dimidiam hydam terre cum omnibus pertinentiis in Calecumbe, videlicet illam quam Ricardus de Kent habuit de dono bone memorie Egidii Hereford' episcopi et quam dictus Ricardus nobis vendidit pro tribus marcis, et in curia nostra Hereford' totum ius quod in ea habuit vel habere potuit quietumclamavit, et quam terram Waltero de Hope servienti nostro pro homagio et servitio suo concessimus, et predictus Walterus de Hop' in curia nostra nobis reddidit et totum ius quod in ea habuit vel habere potuit quietumclamavit, tenendam et habendam predicto Matheo coco et heredibus suis de nobis et successoribus nostris episcopis in feodo et hereditate, liberam et quietam ab omni servitio et exactione que ad terram illam pertinet vel pertinere possit, excepto regali servitio, reddendo inde annuatim nobis et successoribus nostris episcopis ipse et heredes sui septem solidos et unum denarium ad quatuor anni terminos, scilicet ad festum Sancti Andree duos solidos et sex denarios, ad annuntiationem beate Marie decem et octo denarios, ad festum Sancti Iohannis Baptiste decem et octo denarios, ad festum Sancti Michaelis decem et novem denarios. Et nos warantizationem quam Ricardus de Kent fecit nobis vel assignato nostro per cartam suam de eadem terra concessimus dicto Matheo et heredibus suis, videlicet quod sicut predictus Ricardus de Kent et heredes sui nobis eandem terram warantizet eodem modo warantizet eam predicto Matheo et heredibus suis tanquam assignatis nostris. Et ut hec nostra donatio et concessio rata et inconcussa permaneat, eam presenti scripto et sigilli nostri appositione confirmavimus. Hiis testibus, Thoma precentore Heref', magistris R. de Hereford', P. de Norhampton', R.Normanno, A. canonico et multis aliis.

See no.280 above. Thomas Foliot became precentor before 29 November 1223 and became treasurer in or shortly after August 1230. The *terminus ad quem* is perhaps even earlier as Master R. de Hereford is almost certainly the Master Richard of Hereford who became episcopal official before 19 December 1229 (see no.334).

358. Much Wenlock priory

Grant of the church of Eaton-under-Heywood in frankalmoign to Much Wenlock priory, with the approval of Hereford cathedral chapter.

[27 October 1219 × 7 August 1234]

B = PRO C66/226, membrane 34 (patent roll for 22 Edward III, 1348); contained within an inspeximus of Edward III, dated 12 October at Westminster.

Cal., *Cal. Pat. Rolls*, 1348-1352, 187.

Universis sancte matris ecclesie filiis ad quos presens scriptum pervenerit H. Foliot divina permissione Hereford' ecclesie minister humilis eternam in domino salutem. Noverit universitas vestra quod cum prior de Weneloc' ad capitulum Hereford' accessisset, coram nobis in pleno capitulo constitutus, iuri quod prius vendicaverat in ecclesia de Etton spontanee pro se et conventu suo renuntians, se gratie nostre et capituli nostri in totum commisit, misericordiam petens et non iudicium. Nos itaque habito tractatu cum capitulo nostro, pensantes dicti prioris et conventus ac fratrum deo et Sancte Milburge deservientium quam religiosa sit conversatio et circa hospites et pauperes, qui Cristi membra reputantur, paupertatem*a* facultatum suarum et providam dispensationem, ad caritatis ipsorum devotionem excitandam et fervorem ampliandum concessimus eis et liberaliter, in puram et perpetuam elemosinam, contulimus dictam ecclesiam de Etton' cum omnibus pertinentiis suis, ita videlicet ut proventus eiusdem in aumentum coquine ipsius conventus plene et integre convertantur, nec liceat alicui proventus ipsos in alios usus transferre, quatinus fratrum in prenominato conventu commorantium in dominicis obsequiis et ministeriis <ut> propensior*b* existat deinceps devotio et quies securior, salva competenti sustentatione vicarii in prefata ecclesia, et salva in omnibus dignitate Hereford' ecclesie. Huic autem concessioni nostre capitulum ecclesie nostre benignum prebuit assensum cum unanimi volunte. In huius rei testimonium nos et capitulum ecclesie nostre presenti scripture sigilla nostra apposuimus. Hiis testibus, Magistro Iohanne de Wrocestr', Magistro Elia de Bukehill', Ada de Wigemore et Ricardo de Prestebir' capellanis, Bernardo et Ricardo de Ledebir' fratribus, Magistro David de Mora, Roberto de Brugia et Willelmo de Dudeleg' clericis, et multis aliis.

*a*pta B. *b*propencior B.

359. Much Wenlock priory

Inspeximus of a licence issued by William de Vere for Much Wenlock priory to appropriate the church of Ditton Priors after the death of its vicar, Master Nicholas of Wolverhampton, archdeacon of Shropshire, and institution of the monks of Much Wenlock in the church now that Nicholas has died.   [27 October 1219 × 7 August 1234]

> B = PRO C66/226, membrane 33 (patent roll for 22 Edward III, 1348), contained within an inspeximus of Edward III, dated 12 October 1348 at Westminster. C = Ibid., membr. 33, in an inspeximus issued by Dean J. and Hereford Cathedral Chapter, dated Friday 2 October 1282, contained in Edward III's inspeximus.
>
> Cal., *Cal. Pat. Rolls, 1348-1352*, 189.

Universis Cristi fidelibus presens scriptum inspecturis H.Foliot divina permissione Hereford' ecclesie minister humilis salutem in domino. Noverit universitas vestra nos cartam bone memorie Willelmi de Ver predecessoris nostri inspexisse sub hac forma. Omnibus sancte matris ecclesie filiis ad quos presens scriptum pervenerit W. dei miseratione Hereford' ecclesie minister humilis eternam in domino salutem. Piarum mentium est viris religiosis in suis necessitatibus tanto propensius^a subvenire^b quanto ipsos obsequiis divinis benignius invigilare,^{c} et in relevandis indigentium necessitatibus propensius credimus laborare. Attendentes igitur hospitalitatis gratiam quam dilecti in Cristo filii monachi Wenlocensis monasterii in communicandis advenientium sarcinis noscuntur impendisse, intuitu pietatis concedimus et presentium auctoritate confirmamus predictis monachis ut licitum sit et liberum^d ecclesiam de Dudintun'^{e} cum omnibus pertinentiis suis post decessum Magistri Nicholai de Hamptun', eiusdem ecclesie vicarii, sibi appropriare et omnia inde provenientia in usus suos convertere. Quod quia et cetera.^{f} Nos igitur predecessoris nostri vestigiis inherentes, et prefatis in Cristo dilectis filiis monachis de Weneloc'^{g} subvenire cupientes, quorum vitam et conversationem deo credimus acceptabilem, eandem ecclesiam de Dudinton' cum omnibus pertinentiis suis post decessum predicti Nicholai, tunc archidiaconi de^h Salopsr', non tantum in usus suos convertere et sibi appropriare concessimus, sed, eodem archidiacono defuncto, ipsos in eadem ecclesia instituimus, et in usus proprios convertendam auctoritate pontificali concessimus et confirmavimus.^{i} Quod ut perpetue stabilitatis robur optineat, presenti scripto sigillum

nostrum apposuimus. Hiis testibus, Simone archidiacono Salopsr',
Magistro Petro de Norhampton', Magistris Philippo de Hayha, Willelmo Platum, Elia de Buchehull',^{j} Philippo de Maddel',^{k} Willelmo
de Duddel',^{l} Godefrido, Ada de Ledeb',^{m} clericis, et aliis.

^{a}propencius B. ^{b}om. c. ^{c}invglare B. ^{d}eis om. from text of William de Vere's actum.
^{e}Dodintone C. ^{f}end of William's actum om. ^{g}Wenlok C. ^{h}om. C. ^{i}confirmamus B.
^{j}Bokehull' C. ^{k}Maddeleye C. ^{l}Duddeleye C. ^{m}Ledebur C.

Master Nicholas of Wolverhampton, vicar of Doddington and after 1219 archdn
of Shropshire, was succeeded as archdn by Simon of Edenbridge before 23 July
1227. This charter probably dates from the mid-1220s, immediately after Nicholas' death. Adam of Ledbury became parson of Staunton between 1230 and 1234
(see no.355).

360. Much Wenlock priory

*Licence to Much Wenlock priory to appropriate the parish church of Clun
and its chapels for the fabric of the priory.*

[August 1230 × 7 August 1234]

B = PRO C66/225, membrane 12 (patent roll for Edward III, 1348, part 2),
   contained in an inspeximus of Edward III, dated 26 July 1348 at Westminster.

Cal., *Cal. Pat. Rolls, 1348-1352*, 135.

Universis Cristi fidelibus ad quos presens scriptum pervenerit Hugo
Foliot dei gratia Hereford' episcopus salutem in domino. Divinis
insudantes obsequiis dignum est ecclesiasticis fovere beneficiis, nec
minus credimus deo acceptum loca sanctorum reverenter visitare et
domum orationis edificare ad invocandum nomen domini et divina
celebranda misteria. Considerantes igitur quod monachi de Weneloc'
nullas habeant facultates nec aliquid beneficii a quocumque mor-
talium ad fabricam vel refectionem ecclesie Sancte Milburge, et quam
pium sit eiusdem ecclesie constructioni vel refectioni subvenire, predictis monachis ibidem deo et Sancte Milburge famulantibus ecclesiam de Clun', cum omnibus pertinentiis suis in capellis, terris,
decimis et obventionibus,^{a} et omnibus aliis rebus, concessimus in
fabricam predicte ecclesie de Wenloc' convertendam, et domnum
Hymbertum, priorem de Wenloc' et eiusdem loci monachos in eadem
ecclesia cum omnibus ad eam pertinentibus personas canonice instituimus, nemine reclamante, ita videlicet quod alicui ex fratribus suis

probate conscie curam fabrice memorate ecclesie de Weneloc committant, qui omnes proventus ecclesie de Clun' et capellarum in fabricam et refectionem ecclesie Sancte Milburge convertat, nec aliquid in alios quoscumque usus distribuat, nisi necessarias expensas faciendas. Nichilominus etiam omnes illos qui contra hoc aliquid attemptare presumpserint, aliter distribuendo vel qualitercumque impediendo quominus omnes fructus et proventus prefate ecclesie de Clun et capellarum in usus cedant memoratos, de voluntate et consensu predictorum monachorum, episcopali auctoritate sollempniter excommunicavimus, salva competenti vicaria capellano in eadem ecclesia deservienti, et salva nobis et successoribus nostris dignitate et auctoritate episcopali. Quod ut perpetue firmitatis robur optineat presenti scripto et sigilli nostri appositione roborare curavimus. Hiis testibus, Magistro Thoma Foliot thesaurario Hereford', magistro Roberto Haket canonico Hereford', Elya canonico Lanthon', Rogero capellano, Magistro Willelmo Platun', Ada de Salop' canonico Hereford', Ada de Ledebir', Willelmo de Dudeleb', Godefrido, clericis, et aliis.

*ª*oventionibus *B*.

Master Thomas Foliot's predecessor as treasurer, Elias of Radnor, was elected bp of Llandaff just before 30 August 1230.

361. Priory of St Leonard's, Pyon

Inspeximus of a charter of the late Stephen of Evreux (Devereux) granting the church of Lyonshall to the priory of St Leonard's, Pyon (or Wormsley). [1228 × 7 August 1234]

B = BL Harleian MS 3586 (Wormsley cartulary), fo.138r. s.xiv med. et ex.

Universis Cristi fidelibus presens scriptum inspecturis H. miseratione divina Heref' ecclesie minister humilis salutem in domino. Noverit universitas vestra nos inspexisse cartam felicis memorie Stephani de Ebroicis sub hac forma. Omnibus Cristi fidelibus presentes literas inspecturis vel audituris Stephanus de Ebroicis salutem in domino. Noverit universitas vestra me divine caritatis intuitu et pro salute anime mee et antecessorum meorum dedisse, concessisse, et hac presenti carta mea confirmasse priori et canonicis Sancti

Leonardi de Pyonia totam ecclesiam de Leonhals, totum scilicet quantum ad me pertinet, nomine prioratus, salva tamen rationabili vicaria, habendam et tenendam dictis priori et canonicis in proprios usus in puram et perpetuam elemosinam absque aliqua contradictione, vexatione, vel calumpnia mei vel heredum meorum. In huius rei testimonium huic scripto sigillum meum apposui. Hiis testibus, Ricardo de Chaundos.[a]

[a]*end of Hugh Foliot's charter om. B.*

Stephen of Evreux died shortly before 31 March 1228: see *Close rolls, 1227-1231,* 31-2. He wrote a letter to Hugh Foliot notifying him of this grant, BL Harleian MS 3586, fo.138r.

362. Reading abbey

Inspeximus of a confirmation by Hugh de Mapenore to Reading abbey (no.308) of the right to move monks to and from Leominster priory.

[27 October 1219 × 7 August 1234]

B = BL Cotton MS Vesp. E xxv (Reading abbey cartulary), fos.120v-121r. s.xiv in.

Cal., *Reading cartularies*, i.295, no.363.

Universis sancte matris ecclesie filiis p(resens) s(criptum) inspecturis H.Folyot dei gratia Heref' episcopus salutem. Ad universitatis vestre notitiam volumus pervenire nos predecessoris nostri H. bone memorie quondam Heref' episcopi cartam sigillo ipsius et capituli Heref' sigillatam inspexisse sub hac forma. Omnibus sancte matris ecclesie filiis p(resens) s(criptum) in(specturis) Hugo dei gratia Herford' episcopus salutem. Cum in fundatione Radyng' monasterii manerium de Leomen' cum omnibus pertinentiis suis et ecclesia eiusdem loci cum omnibus ad eam spectantibus ad sustentationem dicti monasterii de Radyng' essent collata, et abbates Radyng' ab ipsa fundatione monasterii sui liberam habuerunt facultatem ordinandi et disponendi de omnibus que ad ordinem monachicum spectant apud Leomenstr', necnon pro arbitrio suo decanum et monachos quoscumque ad custodiam manerii et ecclesie [fo.121r] deputatos prout eis et monasterio Radyng' visum fuerat expedire constituere et amovere consueverunt. Volentes iura eorum in omnibus illesa conservari, auctoritate pontifi-

cali de consensu totius capituli nostri unanimi ad perpetuam confed-
erationem inter ecclesiam de Hereford' et monasterium Rading' concedimus et confirmamus quod abbas et conventus Radyng' in
perpetuum possessione sua in dictis dispositionibus et consuetudinibus pacifice gaudentes liberam habeant facultatem constituendi et
amovendi monachos quoscumque ad custodiam manerii et ecclesie de
Leom' deputatos et alios, secundum antiquas et usitatas consuetudi-
nes suas substituendi et ordinandi et disponendi de omnibus que ad
ordinem monachicum spectant ibidem, salva in aliis dignitate Hereford' ecclesia. Et ut hec nostra confirmatio perpetuam firmitatem
optineant eam presenti scripto et tam sigilli nostri quam sigilli capituli
nostri appositione communire curavimus. Nos igitur prenominati
venerabilis predecessoris nostri vestigiis adherentes, suprascriptam
ipsius et capituli Herford' concessionem et confirmationem ratam
habentes, eam presenti scripto et sigilli nostri patrocinio confirmare
curavimus.

363. Robert fitz Robert

*Grant to Robert fitz Robert in return for homage and service and 5s 8d
per annum of half a virgate in Cradley, two acres at Cowleigh and one
acre and a fragment of land elsewhere.* [late 1220s × -7 August 1234]

> B = London, Lambeth Palace Library, MS 2214, fo.136r-v. s.xviii med. Copy
> made by Dr A.C.Ducarel on or before 20 June 1751. C = BL Stowe MS 425,
> fo.133r-v. s.xviii med. Copy made 15 January 1754. Both B and C were copied
> from an original inspeximus, issued by Dean Stephen de Thornbury and
> Hereford Cathedral Chapter, of Hugh Foliot's grant. It was apparently sealed
> with the chapter's seal and endorsed 'Carta Stephani decani et capituli Here-
> ford'.

Omnibus Cristi fidelibus ad quos presens scriptum pervenerit Hugo
Foliot dei gratia Hereford' episcopus eternam salutem in domino.
Noverit universitas vestra nos dedisse et concessisse et hac presenti
carta nostra confirmasse Roberto filio Roberti[a] pro homagio et servitio suo unam dimidiam virgate[b] terre cum pertinentiis, illam scilicet
quam Robertus pater eius aliquando tenuit de nobis in villa de
Cradeleg et duas acras terre de asarto super Calilleg Buron circa
fossatas et unam acram terre apud Westburywelle inter terram

Roberti de Cuba^c et terram Rogeri de Hope et quandam particulam terre in veteri gardino inter terram Roberti Palmer et terram Henrici Scissoris tenendam et habendam de nobis et successoribus nostris sibi et heredibus suis in feudo et hereditate libere et quiete plenarie et pacifice in omnibus [fo.136v B] locis et rebus reddendo inde annuatim nobis et successoribus nostris ipse et heredes sui quinque solidos et octo denarios ad quatuor terminos anni, scilicet ad festum Sancti Michaelis septendecim denarios^d et ad festum Sancti Andree apostoli septendecim denarios, et ad annuntiationem beate Marie septen-decim denarios, et ad nativitatem beati Iohannis Baptiste septen-decim denarios, pro omni servitio et consuetudine et exactione et demanda que de terra exiit vel exire poterit, salvo regali servitio ad tantam terram pertinente. Nos vero et successores nostri totam dic-tam terram cum omnibus pertinentiis suis dicto Roberto et heredibus suis contra omnes homines in perpetuum warrentizabimus.^{e} Et ut hec nostra donatio et concessio rata et stabilis permaneat eam presenti scripto et sigilli nostri munimine confirmavimus. Hiis testibus, Ada de Salopbur' tunc seneschallo nostro, Ada de Ledebur tunc se-neschallo de hospitio nostro, Iohanne de Ros, persona de Wyteburne, Philippo de Vinges, Ernaldo^f de Hope, Roberto de Puttevike, Roberto de Hales et aliis.

^{a}*space after* Roberti *BC.* ^{b}virgatam *BC.* ^{c}*sic for* Cumba ? *BC.* ^{d}*om. B.* ^{e}*sic BC.*
^{f}Grualdo *BC.*

Hugh Foliot's hospital was founded shortly before 1231; Adam of Shrewsbury became a canon between August 1230 and 7 August 1234. Dean Stephen Thorn-bury's inspeximus is datable September 1234 × 18 July 1240; it is witnessed by Master H(enry) Boystar (or Bustard) archdn of Hereford, Simon of Edenbridge, archdn of Shropshire, A(dam) of Shrewsbury and G. (*recte* R[oger]) de Calkeberge (or Coldborough), then bailiffs, Philip of Hay, then canon of Hereford, and Lady C. of Eytator (*recte* Escatot). The chapter seal appended to the document is described by Samuel Carte, Lambeth Palace MS 2214, fos.137r-140v, and appears from his description to be the one used by the chapter from the 1170s to the early 13th century.

364. Shrewsbury abbey

Mandate to the archdeacons, deans, and priests in the diocese of Hereford to excommunicate anyone who attempts to disturb the possessions of Shrewsbury abbey.   [27 October 1219 × 7 August 1234]

B = NLW MS 7851 D (Shrewsbury cartulary), p.303, no.339b. s.xiv.

Pd, *Shrewsbury cartulary*, ii.308-9, no.339b.

In *Shrewsbury cartulary* it is suggested that this document was issued *c*.1220 when Shrewsbury abbey was in difficulties after the death or deposition of Abbot Hugh.

365. Shrewsbury abbey

Composition between Shrewsbury abbey and certain clerks and laymen, headed by John, priest of Overton, their procurator, concerning a prebend in the church of Whitchurch, made by H(ugh Foliot), bishop of Hereford, T(homas de Bosbury) dean of Hereford, and S., prior of St Guthlac's Priory, Hereford, acting as papal judges delegate.

Dated 1228, but probably 1220.

B = NLW MS 7851 D (Shrewsbury cartulary), pp.323-4, no.368b. s.xiv.

Pd, *Shrewsbury cartulary*, ii.330-1, no.368b.

In *Shrewsbury cartulary* it is suggested that the date 1228 must be mistaken as the judges cite a mandate addressed to them by Honorius III, dated Viterbo 26 November 1219, and also because S. had been succeeded as prior of St Guthlac's by Joscelin before August 1224. 1219 was the only year in which Honorius was staying at Viterbo in late November (Potthast, i.539-40), so the scribe of the cartulary made no error in copying the mandate.

366. Thomas of Gayton

Grant in fee farm of the whole of the bishop's dwelling-place in Shelwick and of sixty-one acres of arable and of several pieces of meadowland of the episcopal demesne in Shelwick to Thomas of Gayton for fourteen shillings a year.   [27 October 1219 × 7 August 1234]

A = Hereford D & C Muniments, no.1319. Ink faded in places. 15th century endorsements: Concessio Thome de Gayton' de villa de Selwyk et terra et omnibus aliis (?) libertatibus pertinentibus xiiij s pro omnibus servitiis etc et det cet' quater. 225 × 183 + 28 mm. Sealed on a tag; seal: green wax, pointed oval, 70 × 46 mm., with figure of bishop, standing, bearing staff in left hand, and raising right hand in benediction. Legend: .HUGO FOLIOT DEI GRA-TIA HEREFO.DENSIS EPISCOPUS. Counterseal: seal *ad causas*; pointed oval, 57 × 35 mm. Figure of king (St Ethelbert), standing, bearing palm (?). Legend: + ...TUS ATHILBERTUS REX ET MARTIR.

Omnibus sancte matris ecclesie filiis ad quos presens carta pervenerit Hugo Foliot dei gratia Hereford' episcopus salutem in domino.

Noverit universitas vestra quod nos dedimus et concessimus et hac presenti carta nostra confirmavimus. Thome de Gaytun' pro homagio et servitio suo totam manantisam nostram in Selwike sine alicuius retenemento et sexaginta et unam acras terre cum pertinentiis de dominico nostro in campo eiusdem ville. unde viginti acre iacent inter portam curie de Selwike et terram quam Radulfus de Burcot' tenuit de eodem feodo que se extendunt in longum versus orientem et occidentem et in largentem*a* versus orientem super Sciperigfurlong' – et versus occidentem super Middeldich'. et unde una acra iacet ad capud illius terre versus North' in longum. quam Hugo de la Walle tenuit et ex altera parte de Middeldich' viginti acre. unde decem acre extendunt se in longitudine versus orientem inter terram Radulfi de Burc' et unum ad capud predictarum acrarum decem acre iacent inter terram dicti Radulfi. et Th. Walensis. et decem et septem acre et dimidia. que iacent inter villam de Selwike et molendinum de Lude. unde unum capud extendit se versus La Musweye et versus occidentem. et due acre et dimid'. in eodem campo que iacent super viam predictam inter terram Radulfi de Burc' et Th. Walensis et unam acram prati in Walemeye que iacet inter pratum quod fuit Willelmi de Sugwas et Walteri de Burc'. et in prato de La Clive quoddam pratum quod vocatur Refhale. et dimidiam acram prati in eodem prato que iacet inter Refhale et pratum Th. Walensis que se extendit versus Longebuult et aliud capud versus pratum episcopi. et medietatem unius pasture que vocatur Brodeweye scilicet illam medietatem propinquiorem de Selwike que se extendit in longitudine iuxta terram Radulfi de Burc' que vocatur Brokenmers. habendas et tenendas. de nobis et successoribus nostris sibi et heredibus suis vel suis assignatis salvo loco religioso. in feodo et hereditate libere et quiete plenarie et integre bene et in pace. in pratis in pascuis in viis in semitis in aquis in molendinis. et in omnibus locis et in omnibus rebus. cum omnibus libertatibus dictam villam de Selwike contingentibus. reddendo inde annuatim nobis et successoribus nostris ipse et heredes sui vel sui assignati quatuordecim solidos argenti quatuor terminis. scilicet in annuntiatione beate Marie tres solidos. et sex denarios. et in nativitate sancti Iohannis Baptiste tres solidos. et sex denarios. et in festo sancti Michaelis. tres solidos et sex denarios. et in festo sancti Andréé tres solidos. et sex denarios. pro omni servitio. exactione et demanda que de terra exeunt vel exire poterunt. Nos vero et successores nostri predicto Th' et heredibus suis vel suis assignatis totum predictum

tenementum cum omnibus pertinentiis suis contra omnes gentes
warantizabimus. et de sectis curie nostre adquietabimus preter quater
in anno.ᵃ ad rationabiles sumonitiones.ᵇ Nos vero hanc donationem et
concessionem ratam et gratam habentes.ᵃ eam presenti scripto et sigilli
nostri impressione dignumduximusᶜ corroborare. Hiis testibus.
Garino de Grenden' tunc seness'. Domino Hugone de Duddel'. Ada
de Salopesbur'. clerico. Waltero de Paris Waltero camerario. Willelmo de Pipa. Nicholao cantore. Radulfo de Burc'. Gilberto de
Luttel'. Rogero Smalpurs. Roberto Rose. Nicholao de Hampt'.
Roberto clerico. et aliis.

ᵃ*ink faded, A.*   ᵇ*sic, A.*   ᶜ*written as one word, A.*

The bp and church of Hereford held 5 hides at Shelwick (immediately to the north
of Hereford) at Domesday (i, fo.182b). This charter was issued before Adam of
Shrewsbury became a canon (between 1230 and Hugh Foliot's death), and probably before Adam of Shrewsbury's period of office as bp's steward (immediately
before he became a canon).

367. Thomas of Gayton

Grant in fee farm to Thomas of Gayton of all the meadow of Childeshale,
previously held by Robert Folet.   [August 1230 × 7 August 1234]

B = Hereford D & C Muniments, no.1390, contained in an original inspeximus
   issued by Dean Ralph de Maidstone and Hereford Cathedral Chapter, datable
   1231 × 1234. 14 th c. endorsement: Confirmacio decani et capituli de prato de
   Childeshale in Torpesl'. 231 × 196 + 23 mm.. Originally sealed on the tag; seal
   and tag do not survive.
Pd, *Hereford charters*, 67-68.

Universis Cristi fidelibus ad quos presens scriptum pervenerit Hugo
Foliot dei gratia Hereford' episcopus eternam in domino salutem.
Noverit universitas vestra quod nos dedimus et concessimus et hac
presenti carta nostra confirmavimus Thome de Gayton' pro homagio
et servitio suo totum pratum cum omnibus pertinentiis quod vocatur
Childeshale, sine omni retenemento, quod Robertus Folet aliquando
tenuit in dominico, quod extendit in longitudine versus occidentem
ad pratum quod fuit Willelmi de la Rya, versus orientem super la
Dedelak' versus Muchelenesey et quod extendit in latitudine versus
partem australem ad rivum de Lugge. et versus partem aquilonis ad

la Dedelake, habendum et tenendum de nobis et successoribus nostris sibi et heredibus suis, vel suis assignatis, preter quam loco religioso, libere et quiete, integre et pacifice, in omnibus locis et in omnibus rebus, reddendo inde annuatim nobis et successoribus nostris ipse et heredes sui vel sui assignati tres solidos ad quatuor terminos anni, scilicet ad festum Sancti Michaelis novem denarios, ad festum Sancti Andree novem denarios, ad Annuntiationem[a] Beate Marie novem denarios, ad festum Sancti Iohannis Baptiste novem denarios, pro omni seculari servitio, exactione, et demanda que de terra exeunt, vel exire possunt, salvo regali servitio ad tantum pratum pertinente. Nos vero et successores nostri predictum pratum cum omnibus pertinentiis predicto Thome et heredibus suis, vel suis assignatis, contra omnes homines et feminas warantizabimus in perpetuum. Quod quia volumus quod ratum et stabile permaneat in perpetuum, presens scriptum sigilli nostri munimine duximus roborandum. Hiis testibus, Magistro Thoma Foliot thesaurario Hereford', Magistro Roberto Haket, Ada de Salop', canonicis Heref', Willelmo de la Pipa, Nicholao cantore, Radulfo de la Burcot, et multis aliis.

[a]Anunciacionem B.

Thomas Foliot became treasurer after August 1230. The *Torpesl'* mentioned in the endorsement might perhaps be Tupsley, an episcopal manor, now a suburb of Hereford. See also no.341.

368. Walter Clement

Grant to Walter Clement of land in Whitbourne Manor together with the right to take fuel and wood for building and hedging from the episcopal wood at Bringsty which had escheated to the bishop following the hanging of William of Hudynton' for robbery.

[27 October 1219 × 7 August 1234]

B = Hereford, Herefordshire County Record Office, Registrum Thomae de Cantilupo (formerly Hereford Diocesan Registry), fo.16r. 1275 × 1282, here spring of 1276. Heading: Eschaeta felonum / Carta R. de Evesam' / mod' de capris de bosco de Brinhestye de ballia de Bromyard per R. de Evesham. Sunt hec c' feffamentum suum.

Pd, *Reg. Cantilupe*, 43.

Hugo Foliot dei gratia Hereford' episcopus salutem etc'.[a] Noverit
universitas vestra quod nos dedimus et concessimus et hac presenti
carta nostra confirmavimus Waltero Clement pro homagio et servitio
suo totam terram cum pertinentiis suis in manerio nostro de Wyteburne, quam Willelmus de Hudynton' aliquando tenuit, que nostra
ascaeta fuit per latrocinium quod secundum fecit, pro quo suspensus
fuit, tenendam et habendam de nobis et successoribus nostris sibi et
heredibus suis vel assignatis suis in feodo et hereditate libere et quiete,
integre et pacifice ab omnibus servitiis regalibus et omnibus aliis
demandis, sectis, auxiliis, et consuetudinibus que de terra exeunt vel
exire poterunt, et in bosco nostro de Brinkestye \fuayle/ [b] sine vasto
et husbote et heybote per visum ballivi nostri et liberam pasturam
omnimodis locis et rebus, reddendo inde annuatim iii solidos iiii
denarios pro omni servitio, consuetudine, et demanda et exactione
seculari.

[a]sic, B.   [b]interlineated in different hand, B.

369. Walter de Gosebroc

Confirmation of a grant by Bishop Giles de Braose to Walter de Gosebroc
of the custody of the wood of Ross, and of the revenue from a virgate in
Alton which Walter's father had held.
[18 December 1216 × 14 June 1223, probably after 27 October
1219]

A = Herefordshire County Record Office, Episcopal Estates and Revenues Muniments, Box no.16. No ancient endorsements. 209 × 103 mm; sealed originally
on the tag; traces of green wax, but seal does not survive.

Omnibus sancte matris ecclesie filiis ad quos presens scriptum pervenerit. Hugo dei gratia Hereford' episcopus eternam in domino
salutem. Noverit universitas vestra nos concessisse et confirmasse
Waltero de Gosebroch donationem quam Egidius bone memorie
predecessor noster ei fecit scilicet custodiam tocius bosci nostri de Ros
cum omnibus que alii custodes habere solebant. et cum redditu unius
virgate terre in Aleton'. quam Walterus de Gosebroc pater eius tenuit.
que annuatim antecessoribus nostris solebat reddere quinque solidos
quem redditum ipsi Waltero et heredibus suis. sicut predictus Egidius
relaxavit eis relaxamus. pro servitio custodiendi predictum boscum

nostrum. tenendam et habendam sibi et heredibus suis de nobis et successoribus nostris. in feudo et hereditate. libere et quiete. et integre. per predictum servitium faciendum. Quod quia ratum et stabile volumus permanere. presenti id scripto et sigilli nostri testimonio confirmavimus. Hiis testibus. Thoma decano Hereford'. Willelmo eiusdem loci precentore. H. ibidem thesaurario. Roberto Poer tunc senescallo. W. decano de Ros. Thoma persona de Walford. Hugone de Walford. Roberto de Aubermar'. Willelmo de Hugel'. Hugone de Esse. et multis aliis.

Between 1217 and 1223 Walter de Gosebroc gave an annual revenue of twelve pence from his land at Alton to the canons of Hereford Cathedral (Hereford, D. & C. Muniments, no.1099, printed in *Hereford charters*, 45-46). The *terminus ad quem* for both charters is the death of William de Kilpeck, the precentor, which occurred on 14 June, not later than 1223. It is probable that this is a charter of Hugh Foliot and not of Hugh de Mapenore because while Robert le Poher definitely occurs as Hugh Foliot's steward there is no evidence that he was Hugh de Mapenore's. See also no.285 above and *Reg. Swinfield*, 231-2.

*369A. Walter de Hope

Grant of half a hide in Colcombe in fee.   [27 October 1219 × -1234]

Mention only, in no.357 above. No.357 does not specify whether Hugh's grant to Walter took the form of a written document or whether it was merely verbal.

370. Walter of Horlesdone

Grant to Walter de Horlesdone of a mill with land and appurtenances at Upton.   [27 October 1219+ × 1230]

B = Hereford, Herefordshire County Record Office, Registrum Ricardi de Swinfield (formerly Hereford Diocesan Registry), fo.53v (fo.49v old foliation), contained in an inspeximus by Dean Thomas (de Bosbury). 1287 – 1317, here s.xiii ex.

Pd, *Hereford charters*, 60, and *Reg. Swinfield*, 164-5.

Universis Cristi fidelibus ad quos presens carta pervenerit Hugo Folyoth dei gratia Hereford' episcopus salutem in domino. Noverit universitas vestra nos dedisse et concessisse Waltero de Horlesdon' pro homagio et servitio suo molendinum nostrum de Upton' cum tota terra de Upton' et cum omnibus pertinentiis suis et totam terram quam Elfredus molendinarius tenuit cum omnibus pertinentiis suis die qua obiit, et liberum cursum aque ubi melior et utilior illi erit inter terram de Lynton' et terram de Kyngeston', et preterea nos et successores nostri totum meremium ad dictum molendinum necessarium et ad omnia pertinentia sua semper cum opus fuerit inveniemus et auxilium ad illud attrahendum et petras ad idem molendinum necessarias cum opus erit attrahere faciemus, tenendum et habendum sibi et heredibus suis de nobis et successoribus nostris in feodo et hereditate, libere et quiete et integre, in bosco et plano, in pratis et pascuis et stagnis et omnibus libertatibus et locis, reddendo inde annuatim nobis et successoribus nostris triginta quatuor solidos et quatuor denarios ad quatuor terminos anni per episcopatum Hereford' constitutos pro omni servitio, exactione, et demanda. Pro hac donatione et concessione dedit nobis predictus Walterus sex marcas pre manibus et dat annuatim nobis et successoribus nostris dimidiam marcam plus quam aliquis alius dare consuevit pro eodem molendino, et volumus et precipimus quod ballivi nostri de Ros et de Upton' distringant omnes homines et feminas totius ville de Upton' ad sequendum et exercendum^a molendinum nostrum de Upton' cum omnibus molturis suis et ibi morari usque dum possint perficere. Et quia volumus quod hec nostra donatio et concessio rata et stabilis permaneat, eam presenti carta et sigilli nostri munimine confirmavimus. Hiis testibus Thoma precentore Hereford', Waltero de Bannebur' tunc sen(escallo) nostro, Iohanne ballivo de Ros, Thoma persona de Waleford', Henrico fratre eius, Thoma de Caple, Willelmo fratre eius et multis aliis.

^{a}excercendum B.

Thomas Foliot became precentor shortly before 29 November 1223 and became treasurer after August 1230.

371. Walter de Mucegros

Notification that Prior Joscelin and the monks of St Guthlac's, Hereford, have granted to Walter de Mucegros, knight, the advowson of Monnington church in return for half a mark a year, with the proviso that Master

Reginald Foliot is to remain in possession of the church for the rest of his life.   [26 November 1220+ × August 1224]

B = Oxford, Balliol College, MS 271 (cartulary of St Guthlac's), fo.70v, no.293. s.xiv in.

Universis Cristi fidelibus ad quos presens scriptum pervenerit Hugo Foliot dei gratia Hereford episcopus salutem in domino. Universitati vestre dignum duximus significare quod Iocelinus prior et conventus Sancti Guthlaci Hereford', assensu et voluntate domini Henrici abbatis Glouc', in nostra*ᵃ* presentia remiserunt et concesserunt domino Waltero de Muchegros militi et heredibus suis in perpetuum donationem et advocationem ecclesie de Monitona, salva prioratui·*ᵇ* Sancti Guthlaci Hereford' dimidia marca argenti annuatim solvenda ad*ᶜ* festum Sancti Michaelis per personam qui pro tempore affuerat de predicta ecclesia de Monitona, quam ex antiquis temporibus percipere consueverint. Et ne pro hoc aliquid preiudicium magistro Reginaldo Foliot eiusdem ecclesie possit gravare, volumus quod idem magister R. toto tempore vite sue dicte ecclesie pacifica gaudeat possessione. In cuius rei testimonium ad instantiam dicti prioris et conventus presenti*ᵈ* scripto in modum cirographi diviso sigillum nostrum est appensum una cum sigillo partis utriusque. Hiis testibus, Magistro Roberto Haket, Magistro I. de Godstowe, Ada de Salop', Magistro Willelmo Plat', (Ri)c*ᵉ* Fulcone*ᶠ* milite etc.

*ᵃ*vestra B.   *ᵇ*prioratus B.   *ᶜ*a B.   *ᵈ*B *adds* cirographo *and expunges.*   *ᵉ*lacuna B.   *ᶠ*Fukone B.

Prior Joscelin's predecessor, Prior S., died or resigned at least some months after 26 November 1220 (see no.365 above); Abbot Henry Blount of Gloucester died in August 1224. This charter has a similar witness list to no.345, which also records an agreement between Walter de Muchegros and St Guthlac's, and the two documents were probably issued at the same time as parts of a single agreement. Master Reginald Foliot had been one of William de Vere's clerks and was an enemy of Gerald of Wales: see p.lviii above.

APPENDIX I

DATES OF OFFICE OF HEREFORD CATHEDRAL DIGNITARIES AND
CANONS AND OF ARCHDEACONS OF HEREFORD AND SHROPSHIRE

The purpose of this appendix is to explain *termini ad quem* and *a quo* given for certain charters, and so only the dignitaries and canons whose dates of office define Hereford episcopal charters appear here. Complete details of Hereford cathedral dignitaries and canons between the mid-eleventh century and 1300 will be provided in a forthcoming volume of the *Fasti Ecclesiae Anglicanae*.

Deans:

Ralph: first occurs 1131 × 1139 (Oxford, Balliol College, MS 271, fo.55v, no.220), but was probably not made dean until after 1134, since he does not appear in a charter witnessed by the cathedral treasurer, issued in that year (no.17). According to William of Wycombe's Life of Robert de Béthune, he was made dean by Robert de Béthune (Wharton, *Anglia sacra*, ii.312). William, who was clearly hostile to Ralph, describes him as *alienus*, and says that after Robert had appointed him he proved disobedient and Robert had to go to the papal curia to have him deposed. This is presumably a reference to Robert's visit to the pope in Pisa in 1135, when he obtained a papal letter enjoining obedience on his subordinates (*PUE*, ii.152, no.15), but if Ralph was actually deposed he must swiftly have been reinstated, for by the time of the siege of Hereford relations between him and Robert had recovered (*GFL*, nos.1-2). Ralph occurs frequently in charters of the 1140s and 1150s, including two charters dated 1144 (nos.43, 47). Ralph's last occurrence as dean was on 13 December 1157 (*Gloucester Cartulary*, ii.106). His obit was celebrated on 19 October (Bodl. MS Rawlinson B328, fo.41v), and thus he could not have died before 1158.

Geoffrey: last closely datable occurrences are February/March 1179 ('Gloucester register,' 48, where misdated), 1179 × 1181 (no.136: Ralph Foliot archdeacon of Hereford, Miles de Mucegros not yet sheriff of Hereford). He died 31 December (Bodl. MS Rawlinson B328, fo.54), perhaps as early as 1179, but more probably 1180 × 1183 (*terminus ad quem* for nos.136, 147-9, 153, 168). His successor's first dated occurrence as dean is in 1184: see next item.

Jordan: Jordan was made dean before 27 March × 28 May 1184 (*PUE*, ii.418-9); since his predecessor could not have died before 31 December 1179, he could not have succeeded before January 1180 at the earliest (*terminus a quo* for nos.151, 173). He was still in office after 10 August 1186, perhaps as late as June 1187 (no.195 and EEA ii.238), and since his obit was celebrated 30 April (Bodl. MS Rawlinson B328, fo.35r) he cannot have died before 1187. Since he witnessed only one *actum* of William de Vere it is unlikely that he died later than 1187 but it is just possible that he died in 1188 or even 1189: see next item.

Master Richard Brito: Richard occurs as canon of Hereford 10 August 1186 × June 1187 (no.195), and was made dean before 30 January 1189, since he witnessed Hereford D. & C. Muniments no.487 (*Hereford charters*, 33), an undated agreement between the Hospitallers of Dinmore and the chapter of Hereford cathedral which was confirmed by Garin of Nâblus, prior of the Hospitallers in England, in a charter dated 30 January 1189, or 1190 if, though this is less probable, Annunciation dating was used (*Hereford charters*, 34; Hereford D. & C. Muniments no.486); to judge from Balliol College MS 271, fo.89r-v, the Hospitallers preferred Christmas dating. It is therefore most likely that Richard became dean in 1187/8 (*terminus post quem* for 189, 198, 203, 215-6, 225). He died 30 November (Bodl. MS Rawlinson B328, fo.48v) in the year 1201, since he witnesses several of Giles de Braose's early charters (nos.244, 254, 260), but his successor was in office by 29 September 1202: see next item.

Master Hugh de Mapenore: Hugh occurs as episcopal clerk while Richard was still dean (no.244). His first dated occurrence as dean is 29 September 1202 (Hereford D. & C. Muniments, no.595). He therefore became dean between 30 November 1201 × 29 September 1202 (*terminus ad quem* for nos.252 and 289; *terminus a quo* for 258, 261, 266, 276 and 288).

Master Thomas of Bosbury: Thomas became dean on Hugh de Mapenore's election to the see of Hereford in 1216; his earliest occurrence as dean is 1216 × 1217/8 (no.298). His last dated occurrence is 20 December 1230, when he was in London planning a pilgrimage to the Holy Land (*Cal. close rolls, 1227-31*, 463-4); he died

29 September (Bodl. MS Rawlinson B328, fo.38v), and since his successor occurs as dean 28 July 1232 (see next item) he presumably died in 1231 (*terminus ad quem* for nos. 338, 339, and 348).

Master Ralph of Maidstone: First occurs as dean of Hereford 28 July 1232 (*Cal. close rolls*, 1231-4, 91), and was therefore appointed between 29 September 1231 and 28 July 1232 (terminus a quo for nos.330 and 331).

Precentors:

William Foliot: Occurs as canon of Hereford 10 August 1186 × 1187/8 (no.203, Richard Brito not yet dean); became precentor at the same time that Richard was made dean, or only slightly later, since there is no surviving charter witnessed by Richard as dean and William merely as canon (terminus post quem for nos.182, 203, 215-6). He last occurs after 2 October 1205, without surname, but in the company of his successor, William of Kilpeck (Oxford, Balliol College, MS 271, fo.108v, no.482, issued by Prior Henry of St Guthlac's during the abbatiate of Henry abbot of Gloucester). He died 27 March (Bodl. MS Rawlinson B328, fo.11v), not before 1206, but possibly in that year. The William precentor who occurs in 1207 (no.266) could be either William Foliot or William of Kilpeck; so too could the William precentor who was one of the addressees of a letter of Gerald of Wales in 1210-1211 (Giraldus Cambrensis, *Speculum Duorum*, ed. Y.Lefèvre et al. [Cardiff 1974], pp.xl, 160), though William Foliot is more likely, since he was a friend of Gerald's (Gerald of Wales, *Opera omnia*, ed. J.S.Brewer, et al., 8 vols. RS [1861-91], i.268-71). It is possible that William Foliot died as late as 1215. On William's early career see below, under canons.

William of Kilpeck: William probably became precentor before Giles' death (see note to no.286); he also occurs as precentor in three charters datable 27 March 1206 × February 1216 (Hereford D. & C. Muniments, no.799 and Oxford, Balliol College MS 271, fo.15v, nos.1 and 2, all issued while Master Hugh de Mapenore was dean). He died 14 June (Bodl. MS Rawlinson B328, fo.22v), not earlier than 1220, since he occurs as precentor after 27 October 1219 (Bodl. MS Rawlinson B329, fo.135v), and not later than 1223 (see next item). His death provides the *terminus ad quem* for nos.293, 311 and 369.

Master Thomas Foliot: Thomas, the brother of Bishop Hugh Foliot, first occurs as precentor 29 November 1223 (*The great register of Lichfield cathedral*, ed. H.E.Savage, William Salt Archaeological Society Collections for 1924 [1926], no.464), though he occurs without his title of office, but with the *magister* title, in 1224 (*CRR*, xi.316; the use of the *magister* title means that this cannot be a reference to the Thomas Foliot, rector of Westbury, who occurs simultaneously with Master Thomas Foliot, by then treasurer, in no.355). 1223 is thus the *terminus ad quem* for nos.317, 318, 323, 337 and 339.

Treasurers:

William: William witnesses a charter of Giles de Braose (no.283), which was probably issued before Giles' exile 1208-13, since Elias of Radnor occurs as treasurer in a charter almost certainly issued after Giles' return, which mentions a dispute between William the treasurer and the other canons (no.278). William also occurs in Hereford D. & C. Muniments no.724, which was witnessed by William Foliot as precentor, and which is therefore not earlier than 1187 or later than 27 March 1215 at the latest. The obit of a William of Burghill, treasurer, was celebrated on 22 August (Bodl. MS Rawlinson B328, fo.32v); he may be identifiable with this William, although this is not certain. It is possible that William died as late as 1215, but more likely that he died during Giles' years in exile.

Elias of Radnor: Elias of Radnor first occurs as treasurer before 18 November 1215 (no.278). He was elected bishop of Llandaff June × August 1230 and consecrated 1 December 1230 (D.Crouch, ed., *Llandaff episcopal acta* [Cardiff 1989], p.xvi).

Master Thomas Foliot: Thomas succeeded Elias as treasurer, presumably after the latter received royal assent to his election, 30 August 1230 (*Cal. pat. rolls, 1225-32*, 394); this provides a *terminus ad quem* for nos.357 and 370 and a *terminus a quo* for nos.341, 355, 360 and 367.

Chancellors:

Henry de Vere: Henry's last dated occurrence as chancellor was 21 April 1206 (*Rot. litt. pat.*, 21), but he is probably to be identified with the Henry de Vere who received the royal grant of a prebend at Lincoln cathedral 7 September 1208 (D.E.Greenway, ed. *Fasti ecclesiae anglicanae 1066-1300, iii, Lincoln* [London 1977], 127). Henry also occurs in a charter datable 1201 × 20 April 1214 (Hereford D. & C. Muniments, no.159, also witnessed by Master John Clementis, who died at the latest 20 April 1214). His successor, T. (possibly Thomas of Bosbury), occurs once only, in August 1216 (*Cal. papal reg.*, i.40). Henry died on 31 July; it is improbable that he died as late as 1216, since this would have left too little time for the appointment of a successor before the appearance of T., and he is more likely to have died 1209 × 1215.

Master Albinus: Master Albinus was still only a canon when he witnessed no.298, issued after 18 December 1216, but had been made chancellor by the time Hugh de Mapenore issued his three charters for Reading (nos.308-10); the terminus ad quem for no.308 (and by extension for the other two) is 18 November 1218 (see note to no.308). Albinus may have been made chancellor as early as Christmas 1216 but 1217 or 1218 is more likely; this provides the *terminus a quo* for 293, 308, 309, 310 and 316.

Archdeacons of Hereford:

Ralph Foliot: Ralph Foliot was still a canon of Hereford when he occurs in the spring of 1178 (no.141), and also 2 December 1178 (*GFL*, no.410). His predecessor as archdeacon, Peter, last occurs in February or March 1179, at about the time of the Third Lateran Council ('Gloucester register,' 48, where misdated), and died on 15 March (Bodl. MS Rawlinson B328, fo.11v), possibly as early as 1179. Ralph could therefore have succeeded Peter as early as 1179; he occurs as archdeacon of Hereford 15 March 1179 × 1181 (no.136), and 1181 × 1182 (*Recueil des actes de Henri II*, ed. L.Delisle and E.Berger, 3 vols. [Paris 1916-27], ii.215-6). 15 March 1179 is therefore the *terminus a quo* for nos.136, 147-8, 153-4 and 160.

Archdeacons of Shropshire:

Walter Foliot: Walter last occurs shortly after 25 April 1178 (no.141); he had died by Michaelmas 1178 (*P.R. 24 Henry II*, 101).

As his obit was celebrated on 13 August (Bodl. MS Rawlinson B328, fo.31), his death must have occurred on 13 August 1178.

Hugh Foliot: Hugh cannot have succeeded Walter before 13 August 1178, which provides the *terminus a quo* for nos.166, 168 and 171.

Nicholas of Wolverhampton: Nicholas' last dated appearance as archdeacon is in 1222, in the third year of the episcopate of Hugh Foliot, that is, before 27 October 1222 (Oxford, Balliol College MS 271, fo.74v, no.315). He had died or resigned before 23 July 1227, the date of Henry III's inspeximus of a charter of Hugh Foliot witnessed by Nicholas' successor, Simon of Edenbridge (see no.319). This provides the *terminus ad quem* for nos.317, 318 and 336.

Canons:

Adam of Shrewsbury: Adam was episcopal steward, not yet a canon, when he witnessed no.363, issued after the middle of the 1220s; between August 1230 and Hugh Foliot's death he made five appearances as canon (nos.335, 341, 355, 360 and 367; the fact that Thomas Foliot's dignity is omitted in no.341 is probably accidental, for Thomas had become a dignitary before the mid-1220s). It is likely that no.341, a grant by Hugh Foliot enlarging his prebend, was issued when Adam was first collated to a prebend.

Richard Barre: Richard was instituted in the prebend of Moreton and Whaddon by Bishop Baldwin of Worcester, in whose diocese the churches forming the prebend lay, 10 August 1180 × December 1186 (Hereford D. & C. Muniments no.2775). This provides the *terminus a quo* for 168.

Roger fitz Maurice: Roger's last dated occurrence was in 1206, when he was ejected from the deanery of the Vale of Evesham (*Chronicon abbatiae de Evesham*, ed. W.D.Macray, RS [1863], 196); he also occurs 1201 × 1216 in Hereford D. & C. Muniments no.959. Roger is mentioned as dead in a charter issued at the latest in 1228 (Oxford, Balliol College MS 271, fo.70v, no.291), but had probably died long before this point, perhaps while Giles was in exile; his activities as a landlord meant that references to him in the late twelfth and very early thirteenth centuries are plentiful, but they dry up after 1206. No.267 is unlikely to be later than 1208.

Master Walter de Mouncy: was probably not yet a canon when he occurs in or after 1217 (no.316), but had become canon before 29 November 1223 (no.318).

William Foliot: William occurs, as yet not a canon, 1179 × 9 May 1186 (no.163: he attests as William the brother of Archdeacon Ralph after Theobald the almoner), but he had become a canon by the time he witnessed no.142 (issued before 9 May 1186), which he attests in the company of other canons.

William de Stokes: William was only a clerk when he occurs 1163 × 1167 or 6 October 1174 × 13 August 1178 (no.125); this charter is more likely to have been issued by Robert Foliot (1174-86) than by Robert de Melun (1163-7), because it is also attested by Aldred, the dean's chaplain, whose only other appearance in Hereford charters is after 1187, as subdean, a post equivalent to dean's chaplain (Hereford D. & C. Muniments no.233). William de Stokes first occurs as canon in charters datable 6 October 1174 × 10 March 1179 (no.145) and March 1177 (*EEA* ii, no.136). It is likely that William was collated to a prebend between 6 October 1174 and 1176; no.177 was thus probably a charter of Robert Foliot.

APPENDIX II

ITINERARIES OF THE BISHOPS OF HEREFORD 1079-1234

Robert of Lotharingia:

29 December 1079: at Canterbury, where consecrated bishop of Hereford (*Symeonis monachi Dunelmensis opera omnia*, ed. T.Arnold, 2 vols., RS [1882-5], ii.208).

Christmas 1080: at Gloucester (*Councils and Synods I*, ii.631).

29 June 1089: at Gloucester (*Gloucester cartulary*, i.11).

27 January 1091: at Dover (*RRAN*, i, no.315).

May 1092: possibly at Lincoln (*RRAN*, i, no.328, but this has been interpolated).

25 December 1093: at Gloucester (*RRAN*, i, no.338).

March 1095: at Rockingham (Eadmer, *Historia novorum*, 72).

26 June 1095: dies (Florence of Worcester, ii.37; according to the obit book of Liège cathedral, quoted by A.Joris, 'Espagne et Lotharingie vers l'an mil', *Le moyen âge*, xciv [1988], 13, n.29, the date was 27 June, but the Worcester chronicle is more likely to be correct).

Gerard:

9 June 1096: at St Paul's cathedral, London, where consecrated bishop of Hereford (Eadmer, *Historia novorum*, 74).

29 May 1099: at Westminster (*RRAN*, ii, no.412a).

15 July 1100: assists at consecration of Gloucester abbey (*Symeonis monachi Dunelmensis opera omnia*, ed. T.Arnold, 2 vols., RS [1882-5], ii.230).

5 August 1100: at Westminster (*RRAN*, ii, no.488).

14 September 1100: at Westminster (*RRAN*, ii, nos.491-2).

Roger (bishop-elect):

*c.*29 September 1102: at council of Westminster (*Councils and Synods I*, i.673).

c.6 October 1102: dies at London (William of Malmesbury, *De gestis pontificum*, ed. N.E.S.A.Hamilton, RS [1870], 303).

Reinhelm:

18-21 February 1103: likely date of Reinhelm's abortive consecration (*Councils and Synods I*, ii.657n).

11 August 1107: consecrated at Canterbury (Eadmer, *Historia novorum*, 187; Florence of Worcester, ii.56).

c.28 May 1108: at primatial council at London (*Councils and Synods I*, ii.695, 703-4; *RRAN*, ii, no.880).

13 June 1109: at legatine council of London (Eadmer, *Historia novorum*, 208).

17 October 1109: at Nottingham (*RRAN*, ii, no.919).

8 August 1111: at Bishop's Waltham, Hampshire (*RRAN*, ii, no.988).

27 October 1115: dies (Florence of Worcester, ii.68; 28 October according to Bodl. MS Rawlinson B328 [Hereford cathedral obit book], fo.43v). The date given in the obit book may record the date at which the news reached Hereford, assuming Reinhelm to have died outside it, rather than the actual date of death.

Geoffrey de Clive:

26 December 1115: at Canterbury, where consecrated bishop of Hereford (Eadmer, *Historia novorum*, 236; Florence of Worcester, ii.68).

? late summer 1118 (probably after 7 July): at Morville (John of Worcester, 13).

2 February 1119: dies (Symeon of Durham, *Opera omnia*, ed. T.Arnold, 2 vols [RS 1882-5], ii.254; 3 February according to John of Worcester, 14; 4 February according to Bodl. MS Rawlinson B328, fo.4v).

Richard de Capella:

7 January 1121: at Westminster, where elected bishop of Hereford (John of Worcester, 16; *RRAN*, ii, no.1243).

16 January 1121: at Lambeth, where consecrated bishop (John of Worcester, 15-16; Eadmer, *Historia novorum*, ii.290-1).

24 October 1121: at Tewkesbury (John of Worcester, 16-17).

March-April 1123: at Winchester (*RRAN* ii, nos.1391-2, 1400-1).

12 April 1125: at Lambeth (John of Worcester, 19).

24 May 1125: at Canterbury (John of Worcester, 19).

?October 1125: mentioned as a witness to a charter of Henry I probably issued in Rouen, but may not have been present (*RRAN*, ii, no.1428).

13-16 May 1127: at legatine council of Westminster (*Councils and Synods I*, ii.744-5).

15 August 1127: dies at Ledbury, an episcopal manor (John of Worcester, 25).

Robert de Béthune:

28 June 1131: at Rochester, where consecrated bishop of Hereford (Gervas. Cant., ii.381).

8 September 1131: at council of Northampton (*RRAN*, ii, no.1715).

24 April 1132: probably at council of London: see *Councils and Synods I*, ii.758; *RRAN*, ii,no.1736.

c.May 1132: at Windsor (*EEA*, v, no.59n.).

Before 5 August 1133: at Winchester (*RRAN*, ii, no.1765).

Easter 1136 (22 March): at Westminster (*RRAN*, iii, nos.46, 271).

July 1137: at Gloucester, attending burial of Payn fitz John (John of Worcester, 43n).

August 1138: attends Stephen at the siege of Shrewsbury and afterwards at Bridgnorth (D.Cox, 'Two unpublished charters of King Stephen for Wenlock priory', *Transactions of the Shropshire Archaeological and Historical Society*, lxvi [1989], 56-59).

September 1138: visiting Hexham and Carlisle in the company of the legate Cardinal Alberic (*Councils and Synods I*, ii.767-8).

December 1138: at legatine council of Westminster (*Councils and Synods I*, ii.770).

11 June 1139: blesses Gilbert Foliot as abbot of Gloucester at Worcester (Florence of Worcester, ii.115).

December 1139: at Worcester to meet Stephen (John of Worcester, 58).

25 December 1139: at Salisbury in attendance on Stephen (*RRAN*, iii, nos.787, 788).

3 March 1141: at Westminster (R.H.C.Davis, *King Stephen* [London 1967], 56).

*c.*September 1143: at council of Winchester (*Councils and Synods I*, ii.805, 808).

21 March – 16 April 1148: at council of Rheims, where dies 16 April (*Councils and Synods I*, ii.818-9).

Gilbert Foliot

5 September 1148: consecrated at St Omer (A.Morey and C.N.L.Brooke, *Gilbert Foliot and his letters*, 97).

7 December 1152: at legatine council of London (*GFL*, nos.295-7).

spring or summer 1153: summoned to Normandy by Duke Henry; attends Henry at Rouen (*GFL*, nos.104-5 and cf. *RRAN*, iii, no.867 of 1150 x 1154).

? December 1153: at Westminster when treaty made between Stephen and Duke Henry (*RRAN*, iii no.272).

10 October 1154: attends consecration of Roger as archbishop of York, at Westminster (Eyton, *Court, household and itinerary*, 1)

19 December 1154: attends coronation of Henry II (Eyton, *Court, household and itinerary*, 1).

late March 1155: at council of London (Eyton, *Court, household and itinerary*, 7-9).

7 July 1155: at Bridgnorth, Shropshire (Eyton, *Court, household and itinerary*, 11; *GFL*, no.130).

?29 September 1155: at Council of Winchester (Eyton, *Court, household and itinerary*, 13).

28 October 1156: at St Neots (*Councils and Synods I*, ii.835).

17 July 1157: at Council of Northampton (Eyton, *Court, household and itinerary*, 28; *GFL*, no.293).

June 1160: probably at council of London (*Councils and Synods I*, ii.836).

early 1161: at a council at Canterbury (*Councils and Synods I*, ii.841-2).

May 1162: at Council of Westminster (*Councils and Synods I*, ii.845).

3 June 1162: at Canterbury when Thomas Becket consecrated (Eyton, *Court, household and itinerary*, 57).

March 1163: translated to the see of London.

Robert de Melun:

22 December 1163: at Canterbury, where consecrated bishop of Hereford (Gervas. Cant. i.176).

c.25-30 January 1164: at council of Clarendon (*Councils and Synods I*, ii.878; cf. also Eyton, *Court, household and itinerary*, 67).

6-13 October 1164: at council of Northampton (*Councils and Synods I*, ii.912-3; cf. also Eyton, *Court, household and itinerary*, 74-5).

c.31 July 1165: at Oswestry (Eyton, *Court, household and itinerary*, 82).

late January 1167: at Southampton (*MTB*, iii.87; vi.150-4).

26 February 1167: dies (*Ann. mon.* i.50, iv.382: 27 February according to Bodl. MS Rawlinson B328, fo.8).

Robert Foliot

late April 1173: at council of London, where elected bishop of Hereford (*Councils and Synods I*, ii.958, 962).

14 ~~mf141>3df255>~~ 19 July 1174: at Westminster (Eyton, *Court, household and itinerary*, 181).

6 October 1174: at Canterbury, where consecrated bishop of Hereford (Ralph de Diceto, *Opera historica*, ed. W.Stubbs, 2 vols. [RS 1876], i.392).

mid-May 1175: at council of Westminster (*Councils and Synods I*, ii.983).

18 October 1175: at London (*Reading cartularies*, i, nos.277-280 and no.170 above).

late October 1175: at Feckenham (see note to no.179 above).

14-19 March 1176: probably at Westminster (together with many ecclesiastics, the list being headed by Hugo Pierleone, witnesses an undated charter of Henry II given at Westminster and recorded in *Cal. ch. rolls*, iii.350).

6 October 1176: at St Augustine's church, Droitwich (*Cartulary of Daventry priory*, ed. M.Franklin [Northants. Rec. Soc. 35, 1988], no.901, and M.G.Cheney, *Roger, bishop of Worcester, 1164-1179* [Oxford 1981], 247).

13 March 1177: at the Council of London (Roger of Howden, *Chronica*, ed. W.Stubbs, 4 vols. RS 1868-71, ii.121; Eyton, *Court, household and itinerary*, 211).

3 June 1177: possibly at Hereford? for the agreement with Hugh de
Lacy (no.159 above).

16 June 1177: at church of St Peter, Winchcombe (BL Add. Ch.
7013).

14 November 1177: at Leigh near Worcester (M.G.Cheney, *Roger,
bishop of Worcester, 1164-1179* [Oxford 1980], 296).

5-19 March 1179: in Rome for the Third Lateran Council (Roger of
Howden, *Chronica*, ed. W.Stubbs, 4 vols. RS 1868-71, ii.171).

1179, day and month uncertain: at Wigmore to dedicate a new church
for the Augustinian canons moving there from Shobdon (*Mon.
Ang.* vi.344-7).

11 October 1184: St Paul's, London (no.129A).

9 May 1186: dies (*Ann. mon.* i.53, iv.385; Bodl. MS Rawlinson B328,
fo.17v).

William de Vere

25 May-2 June 1186: at council of Eynsham, where elected bishop
(Eyton, *Court, household and itinerary*, 268; cf. Ralph of Diss, *Opera
historica*, ii. 41-2).

10 August 1186: at Lambeth, where consecrated bishop (Ralph of
Diss, *Opera historica*, ii.41).

10 August 1186 ｜mf141>3df255>｜ *c.*1192: possibly visited Ireland at
some point between his consecration in 1186 and *c.*1192, since he
together with Bishops Albinus of Ferns and Macrobius of
Glendalough witnesses a charter of John, archbishop of Dublin
issued between these dates (E.St John Brooks, ed *The Irish
cartularies of Llanthony Prima and Secunda* [Irish Manuscripts
Commission, Dublin 1953], LII, no.64). No place of issue is given
for the charter.

11 February 1188: at Council of Geddington (*Mon Ang.* vi, pt. i, 186,
and Gervas. Cant. i. 409-12); then visits Canterbury with Bishops
Seffrid of Chichester and William of Worcester (Gervas. Cant.,
i.412-3; *Chichester acta*, 143; no.183 below).

? Early March 1188: at Kempsey where Henry II settled a dispute
between William de Vere and Bishop William of Worcester (the
composition is probably later than Jan. 1188 when Ranulf earl of
Chester, who witnesses, was granted the earldom: see J.Barrow, 'A
twelfth-century bishop and literary patron', *Viator*, xviii [1987],

183). It is just possible that, as suggested *ibid.*, William then went to Hereford in company with Archbishop Baldwin, about to start on his tour of Wales to preach the Crusade, but unlikely.

13 March 1188, at the dedication of the infirmary chapel at Waltham abbey (*Waltham charters*, 186-7, no.277, and no.238 above).

3 September 1189: at Westminster (Landon, *The itinerary of King Richard I*, 3).

15 September 1189: at Pipewell (*Gesta regis Henrici II*, ii.85).

16 September 1189: at Geddington (Landon, *The itinerary of King Richard I*, 7).

17 September 1189: at Geddington (Landon, *The itinerary of King Richard I*, 8).

22 October 1191: at London to attend a meeting of bishops held to discuss the forthcoming Canterbury election (*Councils and Synods I*, ii.1037).

27 November 1191: at council of Canterbury (*Councils and Synods I*, ii.1037), and Ralph of Diss, *Opera historica*, ed. W.Stubbs, 2 vols. [RS 1876], ii.103).

4 July 1192: at Gloucester, as royal justice: final concord between abbot of Cirencester and Walter Lohont of Colesborne (*Cirencester cartulary*, i.177, no.182).

6 July 1192: at Gloucester, as royal justice: final concord between Llanthony priory and Gloucester abbey (*Gloucester cartulary*, ii.8). For another case heard by William and his fellow-judges at Gloucester in 1192, probably in early July, see *PR 3 & 4 Richard I* [PRS n.s. 2, 1926], 292): this was a final concord between Robert the younger of Slaughter and Osbert Scot.

27 July 1192: at Worcester, as royal justice: final concord between Evesham abbey and Henry son of Philip (BL Cotton MS Vesp. B xxiv [Evesham cartulary], fo.17v).

10 February 1194: at Westminster (*Councils and Synods I*, ii.1042); Roger of Howden, *Chronica*, ed. W.Stubbs, 4 vols. [RS 1868-71], iii.237).

28 March 1194: at Nottingham (*The charters of Norwich cathedral priory*, ed. B.Dodwell [PRS n.s. 40, 1974], 46, no.81).

30 March 1194: at Nottingham (Landon, *The itinerary of King Richard I*, 86).

17 April 1194: at Winchester (Landon, *The itinerary of King Richard I*, 88-9).

16 September 1194: at Gloucester, as royal justice: final concord
between Richard of Hayford on the one hand and Margaret de
Bohun and Llanthony priory on the other (PRO C115 K1/6681
[Llanthony cartulary A2], fo.174r, section xxi, no.24). From the
same date, as far as can be gathered from the list of judges, one of
whom was William, is probably another final concord, between
Robert of Dinedor and Hereford cathedral chapter, mentioned in
Bodl. MS Rawlinson B329 (Hereford cathedral cartulary), fo.131r.

23 February 1195 (1196 if start of the year is the Annunciation), place
not specified, but possibly Gloucester abbey; witnesses agreement
between Robert of Ewyas and Gloucester abbey (*Gloucester
cartulary*, i.288).

24 December 1198: dies (Gervas. Cant. i.573; Bodl. MS Rawlinson
B328, fo.52v).

Giles de Braose:

24 September 1200: consecrated in the chapel of St Catherine's,
Westminster (no.243).

4 November 1200: at Hereford (*Chartulary of Winchester cathedral*,
ed. A.W.Goodman [Winchester 1927], 192-4, no.452 and *Rot. Ch.*,
78; *Rot. Ch.*, 78-9).

24 August 1203: at Canterbury (*EEA* iii.189, no.532n).

13 – 15 March 1204: at Bridgnorth with John (Eyton, *Antiquities*,
i.265; *Rot. Ch.*, 122).

11 May 1204: in Hereford cathedral; judges dispute between
Gloucester abbey and the bishop of Llandaff (*Gloucester cartulary*,
ii.57-8, and *Letters of Pope Innocent III concerning England: a
calendar*, edd. C.R. and Mary Cheney [Oxford 1967], no.546).

28 June 1204: in Worcester cathedral; judges dispute between Great
Malvern priory and Andrew, vicar of Pershore, on the one hand,
and Pershore abbey on the other (PRO E210/380; Westminster D
& C Muniments 22492; PRO E315/61 [Pershore cartulary],
fo.106v).

August 1204: probably at Woodstock, whither summoned by John
(*Rot. pat.*, 45).

16 February 1207 (1206 if Christmas dating): at Hereford cathedral;
acting as judge in a settlement between the abbeys of Cormeilles

and Flaxley (BL Add. MS 15668 [Newent cartulary], fo.60v; BL Add. MS 18461 [Newent cartulary], fo.86r).

14 June 1207: at Marlborough with John (*Rot. Ch.*, 166)

22 April 1208: at Gloucester with John (*Rot. Ch.*, 177).

6 May 1208: at Lambeth with John (*Rot. Ch.*, 178).

? after 23 May 1208: Giles goes into exile in France (*CRR*, v.152).

1211: probably in Paris when his father was buried; Stephen Langton presided at the funeral (F.M.Powicke, 'Loretta, countess of Leicester', *Historical essays in honour of James Tait*, ed. J.G.Edwards, V.H.Galbraith, and E.F.Jacob [Manchester 1933], 260-1).

16 July 1213: returns to England; arrives at Dover (Wendover, ii.81).

20 July 1213: reaches king at Winchester (Wendover, ii.81).

1 September 1213; at Northampton (B.Dodwell ed. *The charters of Norwich cathedral priory*, pt.1, PRS, n.s. 40 [1974], 25, no.39).

October 1213: ? in London to negotiate with Nicholas of Tusculum (A.Mercati, 'La prima relazione del cardinale Nicolò de Romanis sulla sua legazione in Inghilterra [1213]', in H.W.C.Davis, ed. *Essays in history presented to Reginald Lane Poole* [Oxford 1927], 274-89).

25-6 November 1213: possibly in Hereford to meet John (for John's visit to Hereford see *Rot. ch.*, 195 and *Rot. claus.*, i.140).

10 December 1213: at Reading with John (*Rot. ch.*, 195).

15 December 1213: at Guildford (*Rot. ch.*, 195).

*c.*15 October 1214: accompanying Nicholas of Tusculum on a tour of the Welsh Marches: see no.248 above. A council was held at this time at Wigmore where Nicholas made peace between Giles and Llywelyn on the one hand and Hugh de Mortimer on the other (*Mon. Ang.* vi, pt. i, 350, though Nicholas is mistakenly referred to as Guala).

28 October 1214: at London with John (*Rot. ch.*, 201-2).

1 November 1214: at London (New Temple) (Canterbury D & C MS C.109).

22 November 1214: at London (New Temple) (*Rot. ch.*, 202; cf. *Cal. ch. rolls* i.153-4).

27 December 1214: at Worcester with John (*Rot. ch.*, 206). At some point in 1214 after 7 May Giles blessed Hugh, abbot of Tewkesbury, in Worcester cathedral.

9 January 1215: at London (New Temple) (*Rot. ch.*, 203).

15 January 1215: at London (New Temple) (*Rot. ch.*, 204).

21 January 1215: at London (New Temple) (*Rot. ch.*, 203-4).

late May-June 1215: recapturing Braose lands and castles in Brecon (J.E.Lloyd, *A history of Wales*, 3rd edn., 2 vols. [London 1939], ii.644-5).

21 October 1215: at Rochester to make a fine with John (*Rot. claus.*, i.232.

17 November 1215: Giles dies at Worcester (Bodl. MS Rawlinson B328, fo.46r).

Hugh de Mapenore:

18 December 1216: at Gloucester, where consecrated (*Ann. mon.* ii.287, where dated 6 December).

20 May 1217: at battle of Lincoln (*The chronicle of Melrose*, ed. A.O. and M.O.Anderson [1936], 68).

December 1217: ill; probably in the diocese of Hereford (no.297).

March 1218: at Worcester when Llywelyn made peace with Henry III (*Rot. claus.*, i.378-9).

late April 1218: on 24 April ordered to escort south Welsh to Henry III to do homage (*Cal. pat. rolls 1216-25*, 149-50).

6 June 1218: at the consecration of the new cathedral at Worcester (*Ann. mon.* ii.289 and iv.409-10).

14 April 1219: ? at Hereford or possibly Gloucester (no.296).

16 April 1219: dies (Bodl. MS Rawlinson B328, fo.14r).

Hugh Foliot

27 October 1219: consecrated at Canterbury (*Ann. mon.* i.33, 64; iv.410).

1220: at some point probably visited Shrewsbury, cf. no.365.

October 1220: seals no.325 (probably in Herefordshire).

1221: during this year Hugh is said to have made a pilgrimage to either Compostela or Rome (*Ann. mon.* iii.68).

11 February 1225: at Westminster (*Ann. mon.* i.231).

1225: after 11 February, perambulates forests of Gloucestershire (nos.328, 329).

11 October 1227: at Westminster (*Lincoln reg. ant.*, i.174).

4 August 1231: in Coddington church (nos.320, 321).

13 March 1233: in Hereford cathedral (nos.342, 343).

17 October 1233: at Bosbury (no.332).

March 1234: probably in the diocese of Hereford, perhaps ill; cf. no.356.

7 August 1234: dies (Bodl. MS Rawlinson B328, fo.30r).

INDEX OF PERSONS AND PLACES

Arabic numerals (occasionally with extra items distinguished as A, B, and C) indicate the continuous series of acta and small Roman numerals refer to the pages of the introduction. References to the appendices are by page number prefixed by the abbreviation p. The letter W following a number indicates a witness. English and Welsh place-names are followed by pre-1974 counties, French place-names by departments. Additional abbreviations used for the purposes of the index are ch. for church and abb. for abbey. For further detail in the identification of Herefordshire place-names the reader is advised to refer to B. Coplestone-Crow, *Herefordshire place-names* (British Archaeological Research Reports, British Series 214, 1989).

—cathedral ch. of xxvi, xxx, xxxiii, xxxix, lxiv, ic, cii, 342, pp.317, 320

——burial monopoly of xxxv, xlvii

——dean and chapter of xl, xliii, xlvii, il, liin., lix, lxvii, lxx, lxxxv, lxxxvii, lxxxix, xciv, xcviii, ciii, cviii, 4, 5n., 8n., 17–19, 37, 43n., 46, 50–1, 53, 55W, 82–4, 85W, 108W, 144n., 148n., 149–51, 188, 192n., 196–202, 206W, 244W, 251n., 254–9, 267, 273–4, 278, 286n., 288, 298, 311, 322n., 330–1, 333, 335–43, 344n., 348W, 358–9, 362, 369, pp.304, 317

——barn of 257

——canons of lxxxix, cii, 107, 254, p.306 *and see also* A.; Abergavenny, Master Peter of; Abergavenny, Master William of; Master Albinus; Aqua, David de; Banastre, Henry; Banastre, Stephen; Banbury, Walter of; Barre, Richard; Bosbury, Master Thomas of; Brito, Master Richard; Calco, Hugh de; Clare, Master Robert de; Clementis, Master John; Clifford, Master Geoffrey de; Clifford, Master Hugh de; Colchester, Master John of; Colwall, Walter of; Cumin, William; Master David; Divinus, Master Nicholas; Master Edward; Master Eustace; Evesham, Elias of; Evreux, Gilbert of; Folet, Master Robert; Foliot, Hugh; Foliot, Simon; Foliot, Thomas; Foliot, William; Freine, Master Simon de; Freine, Walter de; Haket, Master Robert; Hay (on Wye), Philip of; Herbert; John; Master Jordan; Kilpeck, William of; Lacy, Geoffrey de; Landa, Robert de; Len', Master Theobald de; Lindsey, Master Philip; Ludlow, Master Geoffrey of; Map, Walter; Mouncy, Master Walter de; Master Nicholas the priest; Northampton, Master Hugh of; Odo, archdeacon of Shropshire; Ordgar; Osbert; Partes, Hugh; Platun, Master William; Poer, William le; Radnor, Elias of; Master Ranulf fitz Erchemar; Reginald, Master; Reginald the chaplain; Master Richard; Richard, son of the chancellor; Rufus, Master Richard; Samson; Shrewsbury, Adam of; Master Simon; Stokes, William de; Thornbury, Master Stephen of; Walton, Master Alexander of; Master William; William the chaplain; Master William medicus; Wolverhampton, Master Nicholas of; Worcester, Master John of

——cantors of *see* precentors

——chancellors of *see* Master Albinus; T.; Vere, Henry de

——commons of 200–1, 329

——deans of lxvii, lxx, 35, 121, 166, 225, 276 *and see also* Aigueblanche, John of; Bosbury, Master Thomas of; Brito, Master Richard; Geoffrey; Gerard; Jordan; Leofwine; Maidstone, Ralph of; Mapenore, Hugh de; Ralph

——dignities of il, 340

——dignitaries of lii, 340 *and see* deans; chancellors; precentors; treasurers

——manuscripts of ciii, 159

——muniments of lxiv, cx

——Obit Book of xxxv, 188, 305

——powers of jurisdiction of 255

——prebends of xxxvi, xliii, xlvii, il, li, 35n., 188, 250, 255, 305, 311; *cf.* xxxiii *and see also* Gorwell; Inkberrow; Moreton and Whaddon; Moreton Parva; Onibury; Wellington; Woolhope

——precentors 35, 121, 166, 225, 276 *and see* Foliot, Master Thomas; Foliot, William; Gilbert; Kilpeck, William of; Reginald; Robert

——scribes associated with cii–ciii

——treasurers of *see* Briennius; Foliot, Master Thomas; Gilbert; Ivo; Radnor, Elias of; William

——graveyard of 151

——rebuilding of xxxv–xxxvi

——Use of, xxxv

——vicars choral of 188, 250, 343

—city of, xxxiii, xxxvi, xlviii, l, lx, 248, pp.311, 315–9

——annual fair of xlviii, 198

——Broad Street in 344n.

——Castle Street in xxxvi

——ditch of 19

——gate of 345

——inhabitants of, *see* Chanteur, Nicholas le; John son of Gersante; Secular, Nicholas le

——Jewish population of xlviii *and see* Hamo the Jew

——King Street in xxxvi

——land inside 121, 166, 173, 225, 276

——land just outside 116, 142, 169n., 187, 322, 337

——marketplace of 21–2, 204, 260

——portreeve of 55

—collegiate ch. of St Guthlac in xxvii, xxix–xxx, xxxix, lxxi, lxxiv, lxxvii, 21, 151n., 155 *and see also* Hereford, priory of St Guthlac's

——graveyard of 151n.

——parish and prebends of 155

—collegiate ch. of St Peter in the marketplace of xxx, xxxv, xxxix, lxiii, lxxi, lxxiv, lxxvii, 7, 17, 21–2, 151n., 155n. *and see also*

—priory (Ben., dependent on Shrewsbury abb.) xxx, 306

Moses, rector of Yarkhill 348

Mouncy, Master Walter de, clerk 316; canon of Hereford lxi, 318W, 337W, 339W, 347W, p.309

Mountain, Robert of the 327

Mucegros, Miles de, lord of Monnington on Wye and sheriff of Hereford (1181–3) 136W, 153W, 218W, p.303

—Miles de, son of Walter 345

—Walter de, grandson of Miles 341W, 345, 371

——wife of, *see* Iveta

Mucel, bp of Hereford xxvin.

Much Cowarne, Herefs., church of 77–8, 144, 193, 331

—parsonage of 251

—vicar of, *see* Adam; Gloucester, Master William of

Muchelenesey, lost, in valley of R.Lugg, Herefs. 367

Much Marcle, church of 101, 162, 218, 272–3, 305

—William of (perhaps priest of) 101W

Much Wenlock, Salop. xxvii, 149n.

—early church at xxix

—parish of 226

—priory of (Cluniac, daughter house of La Charité sur Loire) xxix, lxxxviii, xciii, 226–8, 277, 358–60

——priors of, *see* Humbert; Reginald

Muned', *see* Myndtown

Munemutha, *see* Monmouth

Munekemedew, near Lindridge, Worcs. 291

Munekeslen', *see* Monkland

Musweye, la, lost, in Shelwick, Herefs. 366

Myndtown, Salop (Muned'), church of 287

—Walter of, rector of Myndtown 287

—William of 287

Nâblus, Garnier of, prior of the Hospitallers in England 156, p. 304

Naunton, Glos. 70

Nene, unidentified, rural dean of, *see* Robert

Neufmarché, Bernard of lxxviii, 62n., 77, 331n.

Neville, Ralph de, dean of Lichfield, later bp of Chichester lxxxiv, c, 307

Newent, Glos., church of 188, 255

—cell of (Ben., dependency of Cormeilles abb.),

——prior of, *see* Reginald

Newnham, near Lindridge, Worcs. (Neweham) 291

Newport, Mon., church of 275

Newton, near Leominster, Herefs. (Niwent) 11, 268, 352

—Salop, tithes of 112

Nicholas II, pope xxxii

—abbot of Stoneleigh 161

—archdn of Bedford 39n., 42

—bp of Llandaff 84W, 336

Master Nicholas, canon of Hereford cathedral, *see* Master Nicholas, priest *and* Divinus, Master Nicholas; *post–1190 references may also be to* Wolverhampton, Master Nicholas of

Nicholas, chaplain 208W

—chaplain (another) 208W

—clerk of Bps Giles de Braose and Hugh de Mapenore lx–lxi, 257W; *see also* Abergavenny, Nicholas of, clerk of Bp Hugh de Mapenore

—lay tenant of Roger de Lacy 2W

—priest, canon of Hereford 149W *and possibly also* 183W, 195W, 216

—rector of Byford 246

—representative of the hallmoot of Wellington 83W

—rural dean of Bishop's Frome 27W

—servant of William Foliot the precentor 201W

—steward of Bp Robert de Béthune liin.

Nigel, bp of Ely ci, 14n.

—the usher 55

—fitz Erfast 39–42

Niger, Roger, bp of London 356

Niwent', *see* Newton

Norman, son of Gosbert 47

—R. le 357W

Normandy, p.313

—duke of, *see* Henry II

Northall, William de, bp of Worcester 183, p.315

Northampton pp.312–4, 318

—councils at pp. 312–4

—Master Hugh of, canon of Hereford cathedral 21

—Master Peter of lxii, 357W, 359W; vicar of Foy 332–3

Northinton' (? Norton-by-Bromyard), William of 274W

Norton Canon, Herefs., manor of 201

Norwich, bps of, *see* Everard; William

—Roger of, prior of Llanthony 129A, 172

Nottingham, pp.311, 316

Noyers, Payn de 69

Oakley, lost, Glos., ch. of 105

Ockeridge, in Ledbury, Herefs. (Alkrug'), Alan de 173W

INDEX OF SUBJECTS

Arabic numerals (occasionally with extra items distinguished as A and B) refer to the continuous series of acta and small roman numerals refer to the introduction. The appendices are referred to by page numbers, prefixed by p.